W9-BMJ-629

OFFICIAL STRATEGY GUIDE

HREND

An Introduction to World of Warcraft

World of Warcraft went online six year ago. Players have come to the game in droves, and several expansions (and myriad patches) have changed the way that World of Warcraft (also known as WoW) is played across the world. Some players may find it daunting to enter a Massively Multiplayer Online game, or MMO, because there is so much to learn. With years of content to experience, it may seem as though WoW is too much to handle if you haven't already started playing.

If you're new or are thinking about signing up, this is portion of the guide for you. If you know someone who is hesitant about signing up, this is the portion of the guide for them! If you (or someone you know) is interested in World of Warcraft but has been intimidated by the scope of the game, its large community, or the very nature of MMOs, you've come to the right place. What follows is a step-by-step navigation of signing up, selecting a realm, creating a character, and getting started with your first character.

Who This Is For

New players should use this section of the guide to learn about the game's background, how to manage your account, and all of the game's basics. Players new to WoW and especially to online games in general will get the most from these materials.

Returning players who have been away for a year or more may also want to peruse this section. Changes are a matter of course in online games, and Blizzard has not been resting on its laurels. Even beyond the expansion itself there have been countless improvements to the general game system. If you're coming back but want a reminder or two, this is a good place to get yourself started once again.

General Questions Answered

If you are new to online games, you likely have a few questions about what to expect. What follows are answers to common questions about World of Warcraft.

WHY SHOULD I PLAY WORLD OF WARCRAFT?

World of Warcraft is a high-fantasy world that combines elements of storytelling, task completion, item creation, problem solving, battle, and socializing. Because the game is so vast, you can truly make it your own. Every time you play, your experience is unique.

Some people play because they're hooked on the quests and item upgrades. They're looking to improve their character's weapons and armor. There is always something to do, even after you get to the "end" of the leveling process.

Others play for the people. It's amazing how many people you'll find who are involved in World of Warcraft. World of Warcraft has a large community of players, and they come from many age groups and diverse backgrounds.

Why you should play is actually a trick question (sorry!). The answer is your own, and the fact that you're reading this is all that you need to know. You suspect that there's something fun waiting for you online, and you're right. Don't be nervous. World of Warcraft introduces new players to the game at a comfortable pace, and despite online gaming's reputation you'll find that a surprising number of players are polite and helpful when someone's learning the game and needs to ask questions.

WHAT DOES WORLD OF WARCRAFT HAVE FOR ME?

Major features of World of Warcraft include roleplaying, improving your characters, competing against other people in player versus player combat, upgrading gear, exploring the world, crafting items for yourself and others, and unlocking special achievements.

You're able to try anything in game with just an investment in time. Real world money is only required for the monthly subscription. You won't need to put in any cash beyond that. All equipment is available to all players, assuming that they put in the same time and effort.

Questing centers around thousands of short tasks that are given in game. You can play these for hours on end, but someone with only 20 minutes to spare can still log on, complete a few quests, and get back to the real world. The system makes it that easy!

Roleplaying is about assuming the identity of your character. This is not a mandatory aspect of WoW, even on Roleplaying Servers (where it's encouraged). Instead, this is a game within a game that you create for yourself. You imagine a story for your character and you live through it, revealing that character's background and experiencing their development as you go.

Player versus player (PvP) competition is a big draw for some. You can limit these challenges: most servers only allow players to fight if they specifically request or accept a duel, enter a Battleground, or otherwise set themselves up for PvP combat. Other servers are called PvP servers, and they allow people from different factions to fight openly, whenever and wherever they meet. In a sense, this is a choice as well because no one is forced to play on PvP servers. You choose one because it has sudden, unexpected combat.

Achievements are given for many aspects of WoW play. You might get one for completing a certain quest or by winning in various ways during PvP. Dungeons have quite a few of these, sometimes for fighting in ways that are rather silly.

If you're looking for group activities, join a guild that has fun people. Talk to people in cities or while adventuring, and find out more about their guilds. This is how you discover a guild that's right for you; it's just like making friends in real life. In fact, you might make real life friends out of WoW. Some guilds get so close that they plan activities together, even if they don't live in the same state (or country!).

Q WHO WILL I PLAY WITH?

WoW enables people from all over the world to play with each other in real time. So the simple answer is that you can play with anyone you wish. You can log in and play on your own (called playing solo), you can play with your friends, or you can play with strangers. It's all up to you.

If you're just getting started, ask friends, family members, and coworkers if they play. It's entirely possible that you have experienced gamers in your circle already, even if you didn't realize that they were into WoW. Ask them what server they play on, and consider joining them on that server. This ensures that you're playing in the same "world" as your friends. They'll be able to walk you through the early steps and possibly help you out with starting money, items, or joining a guild.

Coming in alone is harder, but it's still entirely doable. Read through the following pages, then start the game. Click on buttons. Play around, and remember that you cannot be destroyed in WoW. Characters can only be deleted if you choose to delete them. There is no permanent death. There are no substantial ramifications from your mistakes. WoW wants you to play around, try things, and even screw up from time to time. Come in solo if necessary. You won't get into too much trouble, even if you don't know what you're doing at first.

ADDRESSING COMMON CONCERNS

If you, or someone you know, would like to try World of Warcraft, but have some concerns about joining a massive game, the following pages address many of the questions people have about the game.

Q IS WORLD OF WARCRAFT TOO COMPLEX FOR ME?

World of Warcraft has been designed with a gentle learning curve. You begin with basic abilities while the enemies you face initially act more like target dummies, waiting for you to initiate a fight before they respond. You gain additional abilities and options for your characters as you achieve higher levels while taking on increasingly stronger enemies. However, none of this is done in an overwhelming fashion.

The best news is that you are in control of the pace of your advancement. There are no deadlines for earning levels. You don't lose anything you've earned because you take time away from the game. People who had never gamed before have become comfortable in World of Warcraft. Despite what the Gnomes and Goblins tell you, this isn't rocket science. It's a game, and a fun one at that.

The aspect of the game that often takes the most effort to understand is the lingo used by other players. Don't worry. Gamerspeak becomes quite intuitive after you spend time in game. You pick up terms here and there, and soon they are part of your vernacular. To make this easier, a glossary with many of the terms and their definitions has been included in this guide. You do not need to memorize these. They're just here if you need them or have a question.

In the end, World of Warcraft is as complex as you wish to make it. Many players enjoy exploring the vast worlds of Azeroth and Outland on their own, performing quests as they travel. A large percentage of the players join with others to form guilds for their social aspects, to join forces for Player-versus-Player combat, or to come together to take on the challenges designed around 5, 10, or 25 characters working together.

That's the key to enjoying your time in World of Warcraft. Find what you like to do with your time and do it. Don't be afraid to dabble in other activies and test the waters, but you aren't required to do anything with your time. You control the amount of time you spend in the game, so spend it doing the things you enjoy most.

WILL I BECOME ADDICTED?

Millions of people play, and most of them treat the game like any other hobby. You may have read media reports of World of Warcraft players neglecting their real-life responsibilities, with tragic consequences. However, there is nothing uniquely addictive about the World of Warcraft. It offers the same engrossing qualities of any other hobby or pastime.

WHAT ABOUT ALLOWING CHILDREN TO PLAY?

World of Warcraft offers Parental Controls that enable you to restrict your child's playing schedule, even when you're not around. You can also control whether your child can use the in-game voice chat to speak to other players. There are filters to ensure that obscenities aren't shown in the chat windows, and you can avoid the vast majority of goofy or immature players by turning off general chat for your kids. These chat channels allow players communicate with a larger number of players in the game, but you can limit a child's access to random people by cutting off these channels.

With a bit of setup time, you can make it so that kids are playing with you or with people that you've checked out. There are family-oriented guilds that keep the chat clean and go out to have a good time.

Millions of people can't all play in the same place at the same time. As such, World of Warcraft isn't hosted from a single computer. Instead, servers around the world host the many realms where World of Warcraft is played. Each realm is a separate copy of the game where several thousand people play.

Your first act, after you register, patch, and load the game, is to select a realm. If you have friends already playing, contact them and ask which realm to join. Otherwise, you are strongly encouraged to try out one of the realms marked for NEW PLAYERS.

Tuesday Downtime

Blizzard typically uses Tuesdays to perform server maintenance or apply the latest updates (known as patches) to World of Warcraft. The game is often unavailable from early morning until early afternoon, depending on your time zone. Downtimes are often given in Pacific Time since that is the timezone where Blizzard's offices are located.

THE REALM SELECTION SCREEN

Type
Click on this header to sort the list by type.

Your character(s)
The number of characters you have on a given server appears here. It lists the realms on which you have characters at the top of the list.

Realm Name
Click this header to sort the list in alphabetical order. Click on it again to switch between ascending (starting with the letter A) and descending (starting with the letter Z) order.

Population
Click on this header to sort the list by population level.

Geographic Tabs
Click on the tab that's appropriate for where you live.

TYPES OF REALMS

The list of available realms may be daunting the first time you scroll through it, so how do you know which type of realm is for you? Use the following information to help you reach a decision.

Normal	Normal realms are also known as PvE (Player-versus Environment) realms. If you're new to the game, strongly consider a Normal server before trying any other type.
PvP	Player-versus-Player servers. In addition to all the standard aspects of the game, players from opposite factions are free to attack each other in most areas. If you don't know what PvP is, don't choose it.
RP	Roleplaying servers. Environments that encourage players to stay "in character" while playing the game. There are additional rules in place that govern player names, and behavior in public areas. There aren't any mechanical processes that force you to role play your character well (or at all), but it is encouraged in these realms.
RP-PVP	These servers combine the RP crowd with a PvP ruleset.

POPULATION

The last variable to consider is the player population of a server.

Full	New accounts are unable to create characters on Full servers.
High	A large number of players. There's always someone around who might help, but you may be waiting in a queue to log in some nights.
Medium	A robust player base but not too crowded.
Low	Sparse player base. You will always be able to do your task at-hand, but there may not be many people around to help you.
New Players	Newer servers with a lower overall population. If you are trying out World of Warcraft for the first time, choose one of these realms!
Offline	Grayed out servers are briefly unavailable, but will likely be online again soon— save for Tuesday downtimes.

TO MAKE YOUR SELECTION

Click on the realm where you want to play, then click Okay. You are now logged into that server. Since you have no characters, this screen is currently empty. Press Create New Character in the lower-right corner, and turn the page for help in creating your character.

THE CHARACTER CREATION SCREEN

The Character Creation Screen is divided into three sections. The left column has all the options needed to build your avatar (the character you control in the game). You begin with a random character (which appears in the center) that you can customize in multiple ways.

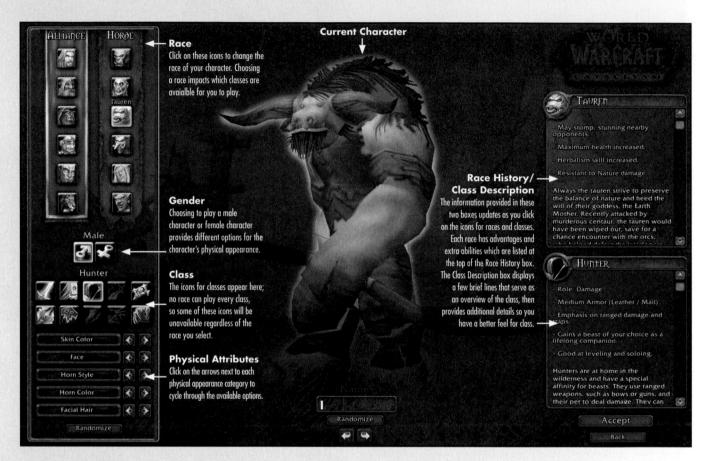

Race
Click on these icons to change the race of your character. Choosing a race impacts which classes are avaialble for you to play.

Gender
Choosing to play a male character or female character provides different options for the character's physical appearance.

Class
The icons for classes appear here; no race can play every class, so some of these icons will be unavailable regardless of the race you select.

Physical Attributes
Click on the arrows next to each physical appearance category to cycle through the available options.

Current Character

Race History/ Class Description
The information provided in these two boxes updates as you click on the icons for races and classes. Each race has advantages and extra abilities which are listed at the top of the Race History box. The Class Description box displays a few brief lines that serve as an overview of the class, then provides additional details so you have a better feel for class.

Current Character

Each time you click on a new option for race, gender, class, or physical appearance, the character displayed here is updated. The gender and the physical appearance choices you make for your character are purely cosmetic; they have no impact on how your character performs in the game. Have fun choosing your hair color and markings. After all, this is your in-game persona; you want to like what you see! You can press Randomize to let the game show you some options.

Some Restrictions

There are restricted races if you don't have certain expansion packs. You cannot play Blood Elves, Draenei, Goblins, or Worgen unless you have the expansion packs associated with those races (Burning Crusade for Blood Elves and Draenei; Cataclysm for Goblins and Worgen).

There is one restricted class: Death Knights. This class requires that you have the Wrath of the Lich King expansion and have a character of at least level 55.

FOR MORE INFORMATION

If you are most interested in playing a specific faction or Race, turn to page **80** for Alliance races, or page **124** for Horde races.

Page 80 Page 86 Page 94 Page 102 Page 108 Page 116   Page 124 Page 130 Page 138 Page 144 Page 150 Page 158

If you are most interested in playing a specific Class, turn to the appropriate page to read about the available classes and their significant characteristics.

Death Knight	Page 175
Druid	Page 166
Hunter	Page 167
Mage	Page 168
Paladin	Page 169
Priest	Page 170
Rogue	Page 171
Shaman	Page 172
Warlock	Page 173
Warrior	Page 174

When you're satisfied with your character's class, race, and appearance, it's time to select a name.

When choosing a name, consider that your character's name is the first impression others have of you in the game. Blizzard has a "Naming Policy" that is designed to discourage players from using character names that are inappropriate to the game. In general, you want to avoid real world names (like celebrities), offensive names, names from other fictional worlds, or trademarked names.

If you really can't think of a name that you want, or if all of your good ones are taken already, try the Randomize button under the bar. It might give you a few suggestions that suit you and are available.

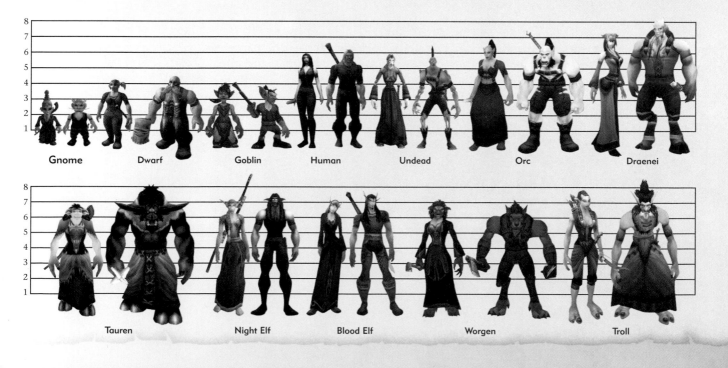

Gnome   Dwarf   Goblin   Human   Undead   Orc   Draenei

Tauren   Night Elf   Blood Elf   Worgen   Troll

TAKING YOUR FIRST STEPS

With your character created, it's time to get into the real game. It seems pretty complex when you first log in to the game, with so many things up on the screen; however, you're free to take as much time as you need to get comfortable before you start adventuring. The following pages introduce you to many aspects of gameplay that you experience during your first time in World of Warcraft. Each of the topics is covered in more detail through this guide, but what you learn in this chapter will get you started in World of Warcraft.

After the opening movie ends you are given control of your character. The first things to do are skim the Beginner Tooltips that appear and take a look at the minimap located at the top right corner of your screen.

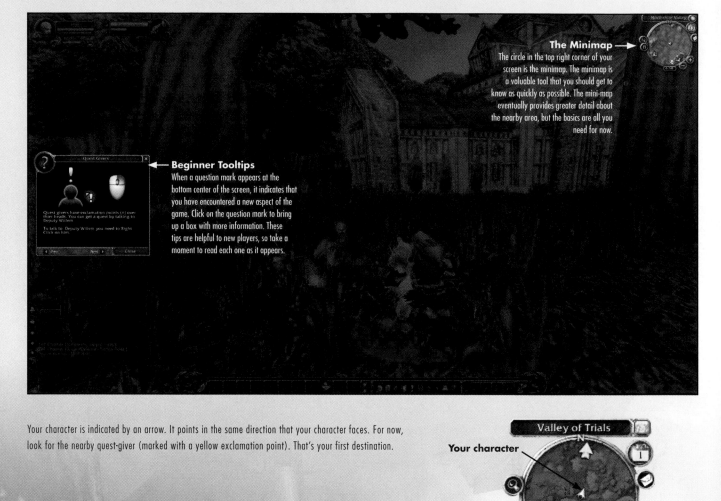

The Minimap
The circle in the top right corner of your screen is the minimap. The minimap is a valuable tool that you should get to know as quickly as possible. The mini-map eventually provides greater detail about the nearby area, but the basics are all you need for now.

Beginner Tooltips
When a question mark appears at the bottom center of the screen, it indicates that you have encountered a new aspect of the game. Click on the question mark to bring up a box with more information. These tips are helpful to new players, so take a moment to read each one as it appears.

Your character is indicated by an arrow. It points in the same direction that your character faces. For now, look for the nearby quest-giver (marked with a yellow exclamation point). That's your first destination.

Your character

Quest giver

MOVE YOUR CHARACTER

There are two ways to control the movement of your character: with your keyboard, or with your mouse. If you prefer to use your keyboard to move your character then use the W, A, S, and D keys. W and S move your character forward and backward, A and D turn your character left and right. To turn, press W to move foward, then press A/D (while still holding down W). Pressing just A or D spins your character in place.

To control your character's movement with the mouse, press the left and right mouse buttons simultaneously to move forward. Your character continues to move forward so long as you hold down both mouse buttons. Slide the mouse to the left or right to turn your character in that direction.

CHAT LOG

In the bottom left corner of your screen is the chat log. Whenever the game or other players want to communicate with you, the text appears here. Two tabs are available ("General" and "Combat Log") but the General tab is all you need to focus on for now.

To say something to anyone nearby, hit enter. If screen doesn't read "Say", then hit enter and type /say. Type in the message you want to share with anyone standing nearby, then press enter.

For a private message, use /whisper to talk with a specific person. Just type in /w along with the name of the person. Type in your private message. If someone whispered you first, you can just press R to respond to that whisper.

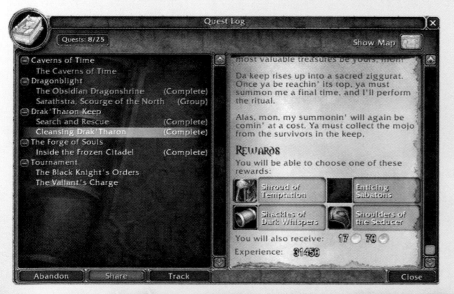

INTERACT WITH A QUEST GIVER

No matter where you start, there's a nearby character with a yellow exclamation point over his or her head. These characters have tasks, for you to perform. These tasks are called Quests in World of Warcraft and they are an integral part of your gaming experience. Right-click on the quest giver to speak with him or her. The quest giver describes a task and offers compensation in the form of money and items. In addition to the listed rewards, you earn Experience Points for completing quests.

COMPLETING QUESTS

After you accept a quest, it is tracked on the screen near the top right corner. To review the quest in greater detail, press the letter L on your keyboard to open your Quest Log. It lists all quests you have accepted but have not yet completed. The quest log also contains a summary of what is expected of you to complete a given quest. The Minimap is updated as well. A thick, golden arrow points in the direction you need to travel for the quest.

ENEMIES

Do some exploring and put your mouse cursor over the different creatures. Look near the bottom right corner of the screen for a small information box to appear. If the enemy is one you need for a quest, target it and start attacking!

Mousing over this enemy brings up an information box here. The game even tells you if you need the creature for a quest.

Mindless Zombie
Level 1 Undead
The Mindless Ones
- Mindless Zombie slain: 0/5

COMBAT

To start fighting a creature, you must first select it by left-clicking while your mouse pointer is on it. Regardless of the character class you chose, for your first fight, move close to your target and attack it with your melee weapon by placing your pointer over it and right-click your mouse one time. If you already selected the enemy with a left-click, press the letter T on your keyboard to start attacking. In the starting area you can defeat any enemy with this basic technique, but in future fights you should start to use your character class abilities to make things go much faster.

If you're at close range, the first attack you make triggers what is known as your auto-attack. This means that your character will continue to strike the enemy again and again with no further action on your part. Every character can do much more than this when you're actively fighting and using abilities, but auto-attacks are good enough to bring down early enemies.

LOOT

Almost all enemies offer some kind of loot. When you have loot waiting, your dead enemy sparkles. Right click to open the enemy loot box, then click on each item to put it into your inventory. If you press Shift and Right-click at the same time, each item is sent directly to your Backpack.

Some quests also award items when you complete them. These items also go directly to your backpack. Any money you collect (just coppers at this point) are also stored in your backpack.

INVENTORY

Everything that your character owns will either be equipped, which means wearing it; or it will be stored in your Backpack. Press the letter B to open your backpack and to see what is inside.

As you collect items (either from killed enemies or collected on quests) they go to your backpack. Every character starts the game with a Hearthstone, which is the blue-and-white item in the first slot.

ACTION BAR

Your Action Bar appears at the bottom of the screen. At low levels, you won't have many abilities here, but that will change as you get further into the game. All characters begin with the number 1 initiating either the starting attack for your class or a simple melee attack. There are other abilities on your Action Bar, but they are different depending on which class and race you chose for your character.

Now that you have taken your first steps, you are ready to handle more of what the game has to offer. Look for more quests in the game and keep playing! Keep this guide handy as there's a great deal more information inside for you. Turn the page to learn more about World of Warcraft!

WHERE TO GO NEXT

If you want to learn more about the User Interface and controlling your character turn to page 16.

If you want to learn more about communicating with other players, turn to page 31.

If you're ready to complete quests, turn to page 27.

If you want learn more about combat and special abilities, turn to page 44.

If you want to learn more about enemies, turn to page 49.

If you're looking for more resources about the game, including setting Parental Controls, turn to page 74.

If you're not sure what a game terms means, use the glossary on page 76.

THE USER INTERFACE

This chapter builds on the concepts introduced in "Taking your First Steps" so some of what follows may be familiar to you if you read that section already.

USING YOUR MOUSE

The mouse pointer is your primary tool for learning about the game world.

Take a moment to move your mouse pointer (which normally appears as a gloved hand) and hover over different people and objects. Your mouse cursor changes dynamically when you pass it over different people, monsters, and objects. Let your mouse do some of the exploration for you. Highlighting things ahead of time lets you avoid fights with monsters that are too powerful to defeat.

CURSOR SYMBOLS

SYMBOL	WHAT THIS MEANS
	Acts as a basic pointer
	Characters who can give you quests
	Characters with whom you can speak
	Trainers who can teach you new skills
	Creatures you can attack

SYMBOL	WHAT THIS MEANS
	Vendors or loot from corpses
	Vendors who can repair your gear
	Guards who can offer directions
	Items or objects that you can open or operate (important for quests)
	Items which act as a Mail Box (you can send or receive in-game mail)

THE GAME INTERFACE

The game interface is everything you use to interact with the game, including your Action Bars, chat windows, and the mini-map. Press Alt and Z together, then wait a second and press them again. Everything that briefly vanished from your screen is considered part of the game interface.

You can also mouse over parts of your game interface. The information you get from these tooltips is invaluable as you gain levels and learn more abilities. Because you can do so many things in the game, the game interface can appear to be complex, so it's broken down here for you.

BUFFS AND DEBUFFS

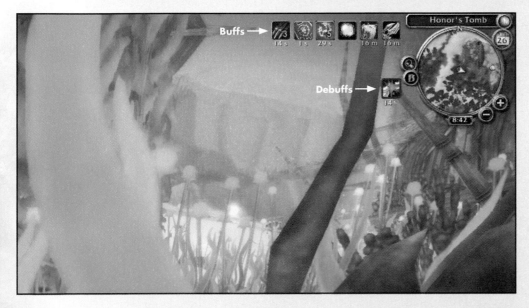

Near your minimap are any positive or negative effects that are currently in place. These effects show up as icons. Buffs (the positive effects) are usually cast by your character or their group members. Debuffs (the negative ones) are usually cast by enemies you are fighting. If you mouse over a buff or debuff, you are given details about its effects and duration. When a buff or debuff is about to expire, the icon that appears here begins to blink.

The most important piece of information to learn about a debuff is what type of debuff it is (the most common are Poison, Disease, Magic, and Curse) because many classes eventually gain abilities that allow you to remove the debuff instantly.

CHARACTER PORTRAIT

The Character Portrait shows your character's face, name, level, life bar, and a second bar which varies with the class you chose.

Life Bar

All character classes have a green health bar. If your health reaches zero, your character dies. When you're out of combat, your health gradually returns to its maximum value. Having an ally use a healing spell on you (using a healing spell on yourself works as well), or eating in-game food replenishes your character's health much faster.

Second Bar

The color of your second bar and what it represents are determined by your class. The same bars are used by all characters, enemies, monsters, and animals in the game.

Target Portrait

When you left-click on an NPC or monster, you target that character. The Target Portrait appears next to your character's portrait and shows the target's face, name, level, and life bars. There is more information about the Target Portait on page 49.

Warriors have a red rage bar, which increases as they take and deal damage. Warriors use accumulated rage to use their special abilities.

Rogues have a yellow energy bar that is consumed as the Rogue uses special combat abilities. Lost Energy regenerates over time.

Mages, Paladins, Priests, and Shamans all have a blue mana bar, which fuels their spells. While mana regenerates slowly over time, the quicker way to replenish your mana is to sit and drink different types of water when you're out of combat.

Leilia
80

Galadra
42

Qwinzy
80

Hunters and their pets have a brown Focus bar that fuels special attacks. Focus regenerates over time.

Warlocks, and Warlock Pets all have a blue mana bar.

Death Knights have a Runic Power bar, which increases and decreases as they use their special abilities.

DRUIDS

Quara
83

Druids start with a mana bar but use different bars as they acquire animal forms starting at level 10. In bear or dire bear form, Druids use a rage bar. In cat form, Druids use an energy bar.

Quara
83

Quara
83

MINIMAP BUTTONS

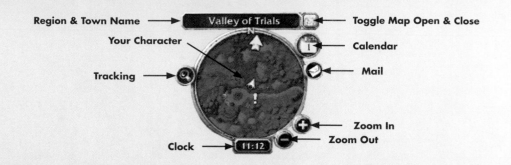

Region & Town Name → **Valley of Trials** ← Toggle Map Open & Close

Your Character

Calendar

Tracking

Mail

Zoom In

Zoom Out

Clock → **11:12**

World Map

This button opens a map of your current region. Locations you have found appear on the map; undiscovered locations remain obscured until you find them. You can also press the letter M to bring this up at any time.

Tracking

The smaller circle on the top left is a menu that allows you to track different things in-game. Click on the circle to get a drop down menu of all things your character can track. If you click on something specific to track, such as Food & Drink, any nearby vendors who sell Food & Drink appear on your minimap.

MORE ON MAPS

One right-click on your region map opens a map of the continent. Clicking the World Map button on the minimap does the same. A second right-click opens the continent-wide map. A third right-click opens the map of the entire world. Left-click on parts of the map to zoom in to that area.

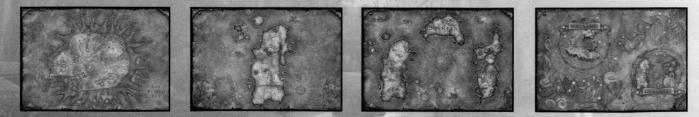

Darnassus is a region of the continent of Kalimdor. Kalimdor is a continent on the world of Azeroth. Azeroth is one of two planets in World of Warcraft.

Under Attack?

The game never pauses, so you can be attacked while staring at the map. If this happens, the map screen is surrounded by a red flashing border to let you know that something is chewing on your leg.

CALENDAR

The calendar shows upcoming in-game events. There are schedules events, such as the Stranglethorn Fishing Extravaganza and the Darkmoon Faire, as well as seasonal feasts and holidays.

If you're in a guild, each guild has it own event tracking. The calendar also tracks battleground holidays and raid lockout resets, but those are for higher level characters. You don't need to worry about those just yet.

CHAT LOGS

If you mouse over the Chat log area, the chat tabs appear. By default, the General log is visible. This displays announcements and the General and LocalDefense channels for your region.

General Log
Your conversations and other non-combat system messages appear under this tab.

Combat Log
The Combat Log offers options for observing what happens to you, other characters nearby, and enemies during combat. You don't need to watch this log while you're fighting since your character portrait and target portrait provide an adequate summary of how any fight is going. Instead, use the combat log to review recently completed fights if you feel something didn't go the way you planned.

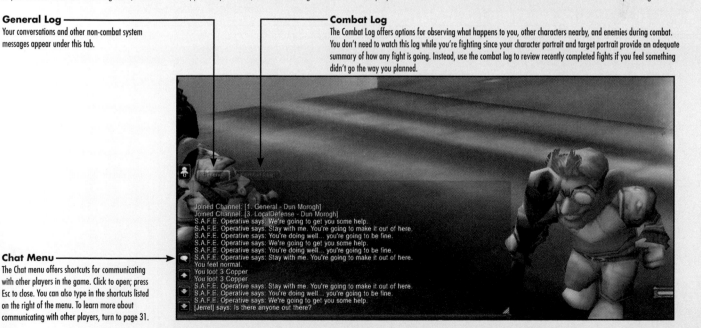

Chat Menu
The Chat menu offers shortcuts for communicating with other players in the game. Click to open; press Esc to close. You can also type in the shortcuts listed on the right of the menu. To learn more about communicating with other players, turn to page 31.

INTERFACE BAR

OPENING AND CLOSING WINDOWS

To open a window, you can either click on the button associated with that window, or use the shortcut key. Hover over a button and look for the letter in parenthesis to find out its shortcut key. Press the same button or key to close a window that was previously opened.

You can have multiple windows open at once, and if you want to close everything at the same time, just hit the Escape key.

Action Bars
Abilities placed in your Action Bar allows quick access to those abilities. The numbers along the top of the buttons on your Action Bar correspond to the number row on your keyboard. If you want to use the ability in the spot marked 1, you can either click on the icon with your mouse or press the number 1 (above the letter Q, not on your number pad) on your keyboard. These bars have 12 slots, using keys 1-0, and then - and = as well.

Reputation
You have the option to track the progress of your Reputation with one group here. To learn more about Reputations, turn to the following page.

Experience Bar
The experience bar is a long strip of 20 bubbles at the bottom of your screen. Highlight this to find out how much experience you need before gaining the next level. This bar fills in real time, so each quest completed, enemy slain, or new area explored causes it to fill. The normal experience color is dark, but the bar turns bright when your character is well rested.

Spellbook

Your Spellbook lists all the spells and abilities that your character has acquired and ones that will be available as your character gains levels. The Spellbook has various tabs that organize your spells by type. When you start the game, all your character's active spells are already in your Action Bar. If you have a pet, a Pet Tab appears here as well. The Pet Tab shows your pet's abilities and commands.

Companions, or vanity pets, are fun to play with. You can summon them and wander around with world with your little buddies. This tab lets you see all of the pets you've discovered.

Mounts are creatures you use as transportation. Each race has specific mounts, but there are ways to acquire other types of mounts as well. You can get your first mount at Level 20.

The **Professions** Tab is empty until you learn a Profession, which are briefly covered in a few pages, with more deatil provided later in the guide.

Rested

All characters start the game in a Normal state. However, if you log out your character "sleeps" and goes into a Rested State. The next time you log in, there will be a notch on your XP bar that indicates how must Rest XP you have accumulated.

Logging out in an Inn or a city adds Rest XP at a much greater rate than logging out in the open. The easiest way to tell if you're in the right place is to look at your character portrait. If your name is flashing yellow, you are in the right spot.

While you are Rested, you earn twice the experience you would normally gain from slaying a monster; the experience earned from turning in completed quests is unchanged. You become less rested as you kill monsters. When your XP bar catches up with your Rest Marker, you feel normal.

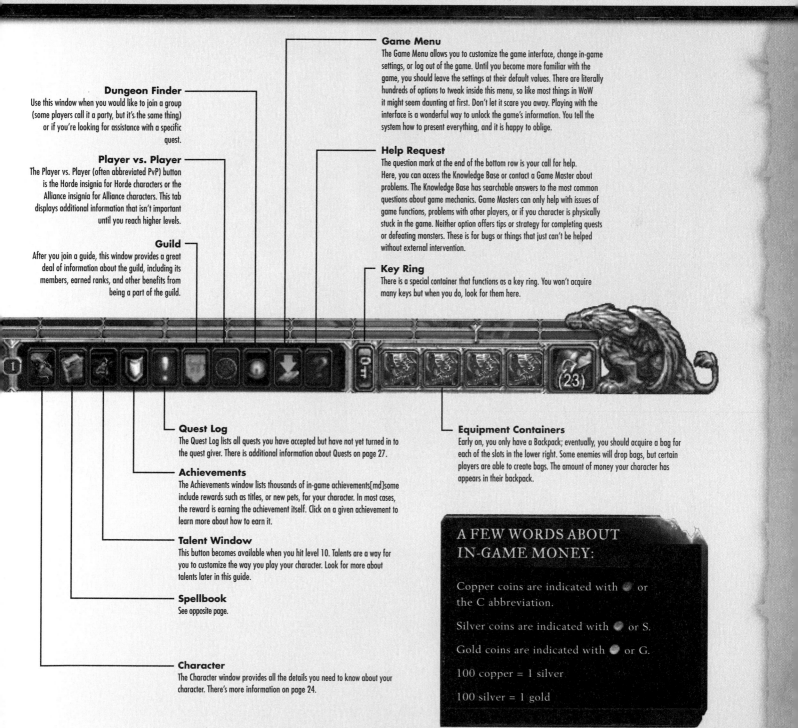

Dungeon Finder
Use this window when you would like to join a group (some players call it a party, but it's the same thing) or if you're looking for assistance with a specific quest.

Player vs. Player
The Player vs. Player (often abbreviated PvP) button is the Horde insignia for Horde characters or the Alliance insignia for Alliance characters. This tab displays additional information that isn't important until you reach higher levels.

Guild
After you join a guide, this window provides a great deal of information about the guild, including its members, earned ranks, and other benefits from being a part of the guild.

Game Menu
The Game Menu allows you to customize the game interface, change in-game settings, or log out of the game. Until you become more familiar with the game, you should leave the settings at their default values. There are literally hundreds of options to tweak inside this menu, so like most things in WoW it might seem daunting at first. Don't let it scare you away. Playing with the interface is a wonderful way to unlock the game's information. You tell the system how to present everything, and it is happy to oblige.

Help Request
The question mark at the end of the bottom row is your call for help. Here, you can access the Knowledge Base or contact a Game Master about problems. The Knowledge Base has searchable answers to the most common questions about game mechanics. Game Masters can only help with issues of game functions, problems with other players, or if you character is physically stuck in the game. Neither option offers tips or strategy for completing quests or defeating monsters. These are for bugs or things that just can't be helped without external intervention.

Key Ring
There is a special container that functions as a key ring. You won't acquire many keys but when you do, look for them here.

Quest Log
The Quest Log lists all quests you have accepted but have not yet turned in to the quest giver. There is additional information about Quests on page 27.

Achievements
The Achievements window lists thousands of in-game achievements[md]some include rewards such as titles, or new pets, for your character. In most cases, the reward is earning the achievement itself. Click on a given achievement to learn more about how to earn it.

Talent Window
This button becomes available when you hit level 10. Talents are a way for you to customize the way you play your character. Look for more about talents later in this guide.

Spellbook
See opposite page.

Character
The Character window provides all the details you need to know about your character. There's more information on page 24.

Equipment Containers
Early on, you only have a Backpack; eventually, you should acquire a bag for each of the slots in the lower right. Some enemies will drop bags, but certain players are able to create bags. The amount of money your character has appears in their backpack.

A FEW WORDS ABOUT IN-GAME MONEY:

Copper coins are indicated with 🔴 or the C abbreviation.

Silver coins are indicated with ⚪ or S.

Gold coins are indicated with 🟡 or G.

100 copper = 1 silver

100 silver = 1 gold

CHARACTER INFORMATION

The Character window has three or four tabs: Character, Reputation, and Currency appear at all times, while some characters also have a Pet tab.

Look at all the combat information on the right side of this window. It's amazing how much there is to take in at first. Luckily, you don't even need to understand all of it yet. Your character has what they need to kick monsters around. What each stat does and what you need to maximize isn't important until you earn more levels.

However, some people are curious right off the bat. If you want to understand more, here's a head's up.

STATISTIC DEFINITIONS

CATEGORY	HOW THIS AFFECTS YOUR CHARACTER
Health	How much damage you can take before dying
Mastery	Improves talent bonuses
Strength	Raises Attack Power (amount varies by class)
Agility	Raises Attack Power (again, the amount varies), Armor, and Critical Hit Rate
Stamina	Increases health
Intellect	Raises mana and spell damage (if applicable)
Spirit	Controls health and mana regeneration
Spell Power	Increases the damage and healing of spells.
Spell Penetration	Reduces enemy resistances.
Mana Regen	The amount of mana restored while out of combat.
Combat Regen	The amount of mana restored while in combat.
Damage	Base damage from your weapon attacks
DPS	Damage over time of your weapon's attacks
Attack Power	Influences physical damage output
Attack Speed	How often you make auto attacks
Haste	Influences Attack and Casting Speed
Hit Chance	Improves your odds of hitting
Crit Chance	Improves your odds of scoring criticals (double damage attacks)
Expertise	Reduces the chance than an enemy will Dodge or Parry your attacks
Armor	Reduces physical damage (highlight to see the % mitigated)
Dodge	Chance to Dodge a physical attack, avoiding 100% damage
Parry	Chance to Parry a physical attack, avoiding 100% damage
Block	Chance to Block with a shield, mitigating additional damage (highlight to see the amount)
Resilience	Reduces the damage from PvP opponents and any pets under their control by a flat percentage
Resistance	Lowers the chance of being affected and reduces the damage from the following sources (Arcane, Fire, Frost, Nature, Shadow)

Currency
Money and points of various types are shown here. These take up no space on your character, and you have access to them at all times.

Reputation
The Reputation window indicates your character's standing with various factions. Factions are groups of associated NPCs found at various points in the game world. Many NPCs are associated with some faction. As you progress through the game, you encounter more factions, and your Reputation page will change. If your Reputation reaches higher levels with some groups, you are able to purchase special gear. If your Reputation reaches lower levels, members of that group become Hostile and eventually attack you on sight.

Character
The Character window shows all the slots for your characters clothing, armor, and weapons. It also shows all the physical and mental statistics that influence your character's performance in the game.

CONTROLLING YOUR CHARACTER

In this section, you learn more about controlling your field of vision in the game and moving your character around the environment. This chapter builds on the concepts introduced in "Taking your First Steps" so some of what follows may be familiar to you if you read that section already.

BASIC MOVEMENT

There are two ways to control the movement of your character: with your keyboard, or with your mouse. By default, your character moves at a run. To switch between running speed and walking speed, press the forward slash key found on your number pad.

JUMP TO IT!

To start out, hit your space bar; it's a big target so it's a natural place to begin. The space bar causes your character to jump. Jumping is often the quickest way to avoid low obstacles, and it won't slow you down if you're running somewhere.

KEYBOARD COMMANDS

If you prefer to use your keyboard to move your character then try to use the W, A, S, and D keys. The arrow keys move your character as well, but using WASD leaves your fingers closer to the number keys used to activate your character's abilities. Of course, there's nothing wrong with using the arrow keys. If you're more comfortable with those keys, then use them while you're playing.

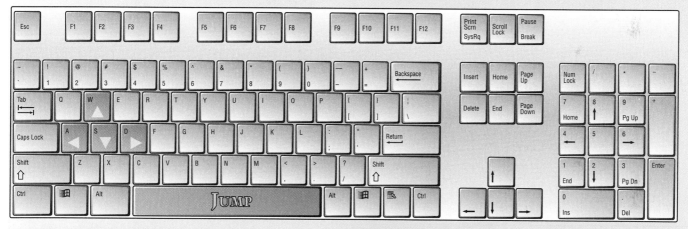

MOUSE CONTROL

To control your character's movement with the mouse, press both mouse buttons simultaneously to move forward. Your character continues to move forward so long as you hold down both mouse buttons. Slide the mouse to the left or right to turn your character in that direction.

STRAFING

Strafing is a way to move left or right while barely changing what you see on screen. If you're not familiar with strafing, take some time now to try it out. Press the Q key to strafe to the left, and press the E key to strafe to the right. Strafing does not cancel Auto-Run.

AUTO-RUN

If you press the Num Lock key, your character starts to run and will continue to run until you cancel it. The following are the quickest ways to cancel Auto-Run:

- press Num Lock again
- press any of the keyboard keys that cause your character to move forward or backward
- press both mouse buttons at the same time.

You retain control of your character when Auto-Run is active. Pressing the keys to turn your character left or right still turn your character and do not cancel Auto-Run. If you want to use your mouse to turn your character, press the right mouse button and slide the mouse left or right.

THE CAMERA

In most games, "camera" refers to your field of view of the gaming world. In World of Warcraft, the default camera view shows a small area, with your character in the middle of the screen. The smoothest way to change what you see is to press the left button on your mouse, and hold it down while you move the mouse. Your character stays in place, but what you see changes. Be careful when moving your mouse forward or back. You may end up staring at the ground or straight upward!

After you get comfortable looking around, do it while your character is in motion. It may be disorienting at first, but try to get the hang of it. It's a big help when you're on the lookout for enemies.

You can also change how far the camera is from your character. Some players like to zoom in tight on their characters; others like to zoom out for a broader view of the game.

To zoom in, press the Home key multiple times or roll your mouse wheel forward. Once you are in first person perspective (meaning you are looking through the eyes of your character) you can't zoom in anymore.

To zoom out, press the End key multiple times or roll your mouse wheel backward. There is a limit to how far you can pull back the view, and it will always center on your character.

QUESTS

Quests tell the stories of the inhabitants of World of Warcraft and sometimes reveal in-game secrets. Questing is also an efficient way to increase your character level, earn money, and acquire improved gear.

WHAT'S WITH ALL THE PUNCTUATION?

(!) Available quest. Talk to the quest-giver now to start the quest.

(?) Incomplete quest. You already have this quest but you have not met all the requirements to complete it yet.

(!) Future quest. You need to gain a few levels to get this quest.

(?) Completed quest. You have completed all the requirements of the quest and you can now speak with the quest-giver to claim your reward.

(!) Repeatable quests. These quests can be done multiple times.

(!) Kill a creature with a red exclamation point over its head to begin a quest.

(!) Not a quest-giver, but a flight master. Speak with these NPCs whenever you find them.

FINDING QUESTS

For most quests, you right-click on the person or item, read the quest, and (if you don't automatically accept the quest) click Accept to add the quest to your log. There are many sources of quests, so keep an eye out for any of the following characters or objects. You may get some quests simply by entering a new zone! Watch for a prompt under your mini-map as you travel to new areas.

QUEST-GIVERS

Quest-givers are identified by the exclamation point floating over their heads. Many quest-givers offer more than one quest. Some quests even come from items!

Items as Quest-Givers

The most common item that gives quests are Wanted Posters. These appear in highly populated areas, frequently offering rewards for local villains who need tracking and killing. There are also items found in the open, or in a camp of creatures that give out quests. All these items have golden exclamation points that appear over them.

Dropped items

Some enemies drop items that initiate a quest. Any item that begins a quest has a gold exclamation point integrated into its icon. Right-click the item to see the quest it offers.

TYPES OF QUESTS

Most quests are designed so you can complete them on your own and do them only once. The are other types of quests, however. Your Quest Log identifies certain quests as one of the following:

Group

A quest with a recommended number of players to complete it. Frequently, the objective is killing a high level monster.

Dungeon

Quests that must be completed inside an instanced dungeon (the earliest you'll see a dungeon is level 15). You must enter the dungeon and complete these quests as part of a group.

Raid

Quests that must be completed with a raid group. Raid groups are essentially multiple groups joined together. You won't need to worry about raid quests until you reach much higher level.

Quest Log

Quests: 17/25   Show Map

- Dragonblight
  - Wanton Warlord   (Group)
- Fishing
  - **Dangerously Delicious**   (Daily)
- Grizzly Hills
  - The Conquest Pit: Bear Wrestling!   (Group)
  - An Intriguing Plan
  - Hour of the Worg   (Group)
  - The Bear God's Offspring
- Icecrown
  - Against the Giants   (Group)
  - Second Chances   (Group)
  - That's Abominable!
- Jewelcrafting
  - Shipment: Blood Jade Amulet   (Daily)
- The Forge of Souls
  - Inside the Frozen Citadel   (Dungeon)
- The Oculus
  - The Struggle Persists   (Dungeon)
- Wintergrasp
  - Bones and Arrows   (PvP)

Abandon   Share   Track   Close

DANGEROUSLY DELICIOUS

Marcia Chase in Dalaran City wants you to bring her 10 Terrorfish.

Terrorfish: 0/10

DESCRIPTION

The best fishing is often the most dangerous. Wintergrasp boasts a bountiful catch for the brazen.

In fact, it's the only place to catch the fabled Terrorfish - a fish both lethal and delicious. Bring me some, and we'll have something to discuss.

REWARDS

You will receive:

Bag of Fishing Treasures

Daily

The quests marked as 'Daily' in your quest log can be completed once each day. These quests come from the quest-givers with blue exclamation points over their heads.

Class

Some quests are available only to a specific class. These quests often lead to learning a new class skill or acquiring a nice piece of gear.

Seasonal

Quests that are available during certain events during the year. Check the in-game calendar for information about events.

MORE QUEST TYPES

While the game doesn't categorize quests in the following ways, most quests fall into one of the following types:

Breadcrumb quests require you to speak with a character in another area, or take an item to another character. They are called breadcrumb because they are designed to lead you to new zone or area with more quests.

There are two types of **collection quests**. The first type does not require you to fight. After accepting the quest, look for objects that sparkle. Put your mouse pointer over the object and right click on it to put it in your backpack. The second type of collection quest involves items that are carried by enemy characters. These enemies must be killed before they surrender their item. Just like the objects in the first type of collection quest, defeated enemies sparkle when they have items for you to pick up.

The object of **kill quests** is to eliminate a number of a specific kind of enemy. These quests are simple and straightforward. Once you find the right type of enemy, it's a matter of taking them down in combat.

In an **escort quest**, you free an in-game victim and lead the character to safety. These quests are usually encountered in out-of-the-way locations while completing other quests.

A **quest chain** is a series of quests that must be completed in certain order. Chained quests aren't marked as such in your quest log, but it's easy to tell when you're in the midst of a quest chain when you speak with the same quest giver many times. Completing a long quest chain can be one of the most satisfying aspects of the game.

QUEST LEVELS

Your Quest Log also indicates the level of difficulty of your quest using corresponding colors. The level of difficulty is a comparison between the level of the quest and your current level. As you gain levels, the quest becomes relatively easier, so the color changes.

QUEST COLOR	DESCRIPTION
Gray	Very easy quest, but not worth much XP.
Green	Easy. Simple to complete solo.
Yellow	Normal. Likely to complete solo.
Orange	Hard. Consider finding help for the quest.
Red	Very Hard. Don't try this quest without some help.

Your Quest Log also indicates the level of difficulty of your quest using corresponding colors. The level of difficulty is a comparison between the level of the quest and your current level. As you gain levels, the quest becomes relatively easier, so the color changes.

If a quest is too difficult for you currently, leave it in your log as long as you can spare the room. The benefit to tackling red and orange quests is that the XP reward is greater; in fact, if you wait until a quest turns Gray to complete it, it's worth only 10% of the XP had you completed it as a Red quest!

COMPLETING QUESTS

 Remember to read the quest text carefully. If you complete several quests simultaneously, you can turn them in at the same point and time. When you complete a quest, the quest tracker points you to where to turn in the quest for your reward. Frequently, you return to the original quest-giver, who is indicated with a gold question mark.

Not all quests requre you to return to a Quest-giver to complete them. When you see this prompt, click on it to complete the quest and get a follow-up quest as well.

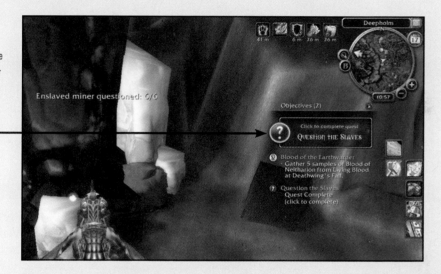

Phasing

While you are questing, or have just completed a quest, you may notice the world around your character undergoes a change. Buildings look different, NPCs might move to different areas, or monsters might be there that weren't before. This sort of change is known as phasing. If you're playing on your own, you may not even notice these changes, or you may consider them just a part of the story being told around you.

If you're in a group, however, it could cause problems. Phasing is individual to each character, meaning two people in the same group could be standing close by and not even see each other! If that happens, look next to the character portraits in the upper left portion of the screen. If you see a swirl next to a party member's portrait, that character is out of phase with you.

There are two ways to get characters back into phase. The first way is to have both players need to complete the same quests. The second way is to move both characters out of the phased area. Phasing isn't worldwide, so you should eventually find a spot where you can see each other again.

Quest Rewards

Sometimes, you have a choice of the rewards you can take, but not all rewards are available to all classes. When you mouse over the available quest rewards, you get a great deal of information.

If you mouse over the item that interests you, the game compares that item with your currently equipped item, so you can see whether it's an improvement.

If an item is shown in red, that means your character/class can't use it. Try to find items that are ideal for your character. For instance, a Warrior can use any type of armor (cloth, leather, mail, or eventually plate). However, quest rewards that are cloth or leather are just trash to them. Don't be hasty when picking a quest reward. See if there is something awesome before you make a final decision.

When there aren't any perfect rewards, compare sale values. It's wise to select the most expensive quest reward if you aren't going to use it.

Soulbound Items

Soulbound items are only usable by your current character. If you have an item that is soulbound, you can use it, sell it, or throw it away. You cannot give it to another player or even another one of your characters. Almost every quest reward is a soulbound item.

Faction Rewards

When you complete some quests, you receive notices in your General Chat Log, indicating that your reputation with certain factions has increased or decreased. This is a way of quantifying which groups in the game have been helped or hindered by your work in the quest.

Failed Quests

It is possible to fail to meet the goals outlined in completing a quest. The quest stays in your log and is marked as Failed. Don't despair! Just abandon the quest (right-click on it) and you can pick it up again from the quest-giver, no questions asked!

A Final Word on Quests

There are thousands of quests in World of Warcraft. You don't have to do them all! In fact, you cannot do them all. Some quests are specific to certain classes, and some are faction specific, so you can't do them without making a character that joins the other side.

You get to decide which quests you want to complete and which you don't. The game leads you through many adventures, but there's nothing stopping you from wandering on your own and finding quests just off the beaten path. You never know when you might just find a message in a bottle that leads to a new quest!

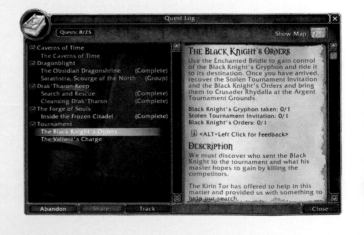

COMMUNICATING WITH OTHER PLAYERS

Like everything else in the game, you can control how much communicating and socializing you want to do with other players. This chapter tells you how to talk to other players, how to ask for help, and make in-game friends.

The most basic way to communicate in the game is to press the Enter key, which opens the Say prompt. You can just type in your comment and press Enter. This message is sent to everyone in your general vicinity.

TRIAL ACCOUNTS

If you're still playing the Trial Version of the game, you have a few communication limitations:

- You cannot trade items with other players or use the Mail system
- You can only use /whisper or /tell with players that have put you on their Friends List
- You can't invite others to join a group.
- You can't speak on the local in-game channels, though you can read what others are talking about

These limitations end as soon as you pay for the account and wait for the game to register that change. A Trial Account that becomes a paying one suffers no long-term penalties or problems of any sort.

WHO CAN HEAR ME?

The different speech commands are in place to let you communicate selectively. You wouldn't want to shout everything to the entire world, right?

Try it out for yourself! Hit Enter, then type "/whisper" followed by your character's name. When you hit space, the prompt changes, and whatever you type next becomes the message you send to yourself after you hit Enter again.

Say:
/say goes to anyone nearby. Speak to players in your vicinity. By default, you see a speech bubble over your head. As long as people nearby are in the same faction as your character, they'll see what you type (players from the opposite faction will see what appears to be gibberish). Because this is public, avoid saying anything awkward or inappropriate.

Whisper:
/whisper (/tell works as well) is a private message for one other player. You must include the character's name after the /whisper. There is no distance limit on these messages.

Reply:
Use /r (or just r) to reply to whomever last whispered to you.

Yell:
/yell is a broadcast message to all players in your region. This is the most awkward communication method in World of Warcraft. It's similar to /say in that it displays your text to anyone within its radius; however, the distance covered is much wider than /say.

Party chat:
/party is a private message that lets you communicate with everyone in your current group at the same time. No one outside of your group can hear this chat even if they're standing in the middle of your party.

Guild Chat:
/guild sends a message to anyone in the same guild as you. No one else can hear you, and members will see what you're typing even if they're half a world away from you.

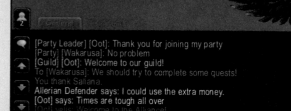

[Party Leader] [Oot]: Thank you for joining my party
[Party] [Wakarusa]: No problem
[Guild] [Oot]: Welcome to our guild!
To [Wakarusa]: We should try to complete some quests!
You thank Saliana.
Allerian Defender says: I could use the extra money.
[Oot] says: Times are tough all over
[Oot] yells: Welcome to the Alliance!

The Chat Menu

All these same commands are available through the Chat menu. Click on the option you want from the Chat menu (it looks like a speech bubble) and select what you want from the list.

All the messages that you send and receive appear in your General chat log. To see older messages, use the up and down arrows. To see the most recent messages, use the end arrow. If you right-click on the General tab, you can customize everything that appears in the chat log, including the background (transparent to solid black) and filters (including text color).

USING VOICE EMOTES

Voice emotes are in-game expressions that your character (not you) can say. Voice emotes have nominal benefit in group situations. You can see a list of them by clicking on the Chat menu (speech bubble) and then mousing over Voice Emote. Click one of the voice emotes to make your character speak.

USING THE CHANNELS

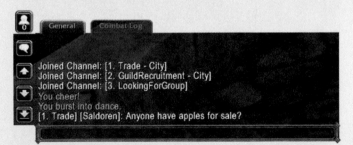

Each time you log into the game or enter a new region, you get a reminder in your General chat log about what channels are available to you. Here is a list of the various common chat channels.

Channels are used to communicate with all players in the same channel. By default, you join the General Chat and LocalDefense channels; you also join the Trade channel, but that only becomes active when you enter one of the big cities found throughout World of Warcraft.

You can leave each of these channels at any time by typing /leave #, where # is the number of the channel.

General
The standard channel for your specific region or major city where your character is currently located. There's a different General channel for every region. This is a good location to ask questions about quests specific to your region.

Trade
This channel links all the major cities in your faction. Players offer goods to be sold and seek goods to purchase. This channel is very busy (and the talk doesn't always stay on topic), so you won't want to stay on indefinitely. Your character must be inside a city to use it.

LocalDefense
This channel informs players when in-game attacks from the opposite faction are being made in your local region. This is primarily of interest to players seeking PvP (or trying to avoid it).

WorldDefense
Similar to LocalDefense, but this channel tells you about opposite faction attacks anywhere in Azeroth.

GuildRecruitment
This channel links all the major cities in your faction. Players use this channel to find guilds or new guild members. You must be inside a city to use this.

LookingForGroup
This channel links all regions in your faction. Player must first specify what she is seeking in the Looking for Group tab (press the i button) in order to gain access to the LookingForGroup channel.

CHANNEL COMMANDS

To see which channels are available, press the letter o for the Social menu and click the Chat tab. In this page, you can see all the channels available in your current location. If you're on a channel, it's white; if you're not on a channel, it's gray. Click on a white channel, and the game shows you all other characters currently on the channel too.

For all the / shortcuts, you press the space bar after the command word, then you type in your message.

	COMMAND	EXAMPLE
Joining a channel	/join <fullnameofchannel>	/join guildrecruitment
Speaking on a channel	/# <Your question or comment goes here>	/5 Seeking guild of mature players to run dungeons
Leaving a channel	/leave <# of channel>	/leave 3

There is absolutely no need for you to stay on any of the in-game channels. If you find them overwhelming, / leave them.

If you enjoy a quiet playing experience, leave the chat channels as soon as possible. The game becomes amazingly calm once you do this. If you like constant banter, look for a guild and/or keep yourself in as many channels as you like.

CUSTOM CHANNELS

EXAMPLE
/join Mikechat

Did you know that you can create your own chat channels? This is a powerful ability for people who are just starting on a server. Maybe you don't have a guild up yet, but you want your friends to be able to speak to you as soon as they arrive. Let them know to /join "Custom Channel Name" as soon as they come on.

This puts you in the Mikechat channel, even if there wasn't one already open. Other people who type that command will be thrown in with you. It's another way to have buddies stay in touch. You can even have a guild within a guild this way, or even a group within a group, and dissolve the temporary chat system when the current task is completed.

ASKING FOR HELP

There are several ways to seek assistance. The most effective way to get a real answer to a specific question is to find another player in your current area who is doing or has done something similar to your current task. You can then use /say if you're in the same area or /whisper if they're too far away to ask a question directly.

A broader way to go about asking for help is sending your query out on the General channel. There are more people on the channel, but they may not be able or willing to help. Sometimes, the General channel is very helpful. Sometimes, it's full of chatting players being silly.

Here's the command for asking a question on the General channel:

> /# <Your question or comment goes here>

By either method, the best way to ensure you get a helpful response is to ask a specific question, and avoid being vague or demanding.

> Bad Example: "I can't find the barrow key!!!"

> Good Example: "Is anyone else looking for the barrow key?"

> Better Example: "I'm having trouble finding the barrow key. Any hints out there?"

An Internet search can be surprisingly powerful for getting a fast response as well. Odds are that if you're having a problem, someone else has bumped into the exact same thing. Searching with "WoW where is the barrow key" would likely get you answers if people in game are just as stumped as you are.

SENDING & RECEIVING MAIL

Use the mail system to send messages, items, or money to other players. Mailboxes are found in all big cities and most towns and villages. They take on various appearances, depending upon their locale.

Any guard in a major area will point you toward a mailbox if you ask them about it. You can also choose to track Mailbox locations on your mini-map.

Receiving Mail

Any time you have mail waiting, the game shows you an icon near your minimap. This looks like a letter, so it's pretty clear what you're expecting.

To get your mail, right-click when you approach and target a mailbox. The first tab that opens is your Inbox. Left-click to open any messages, and click on any items to send them to your Backpack. When an attachment is removed from a piece of mail that doesn't have a message, the mail itself will be deleted.

If you read a piece of mail but leave it in your Inbox, the letter turns gray and can remain in your Inbox for 30 days. When mail expires, it is automatically deleted, including any attachments.

If someone sends you an item by mistake, you can click on Return to immediately send it back to them. You can also Reply to the sender.

Buyer Beware

Sometimes people would scam others through the mail system. They'd send people items through the mail (something small and trivial) but put a Cash on Delivery tag with it. Grabbing the item would cost considerable money.

WoW now has a number of systems in place to reduce or eliminate this type of scam, but it's wise to be careful of mail from strangers. In some ways, real life isn't always that different from WoW.

Should you have any issues, you can always contact Blizzard's in-game support staff, known as GMs. When other players suggest that you "send in a ticket" they mean to send a message through the support system. Click on the big, red "?" to get started.

Sending Mail

The second tab in the mail system is the interface to send mail. Type in the recipient's name very carefully (the game will autocomplete names from your friend list or from people in your guild), and include a subject line if you wish. You cannot send mail to yourself or to players in the opposing faction. You can, however, send mail to other characters that you control that are on the same server.

You decide whether to write a message, send an item, or send money. To attach an item, you can right-click on anything in your Backpack or grab and drag the item over to your letter. To send money, you type in the number of gold, silver, or copper coins you wish to send. Then press Send. The game will ask for your approval.

Each sent message costs 30 copper (plus 30 copper for each attachment), unless you use the C.O.D. option. C.O.D. is for players selling and buying items. By choosing this option, the mail system sends the item, but the transaction only completes when the recipient agrees to pay. Then, one player gets his money and another gets his gear. C.O.D. items expire after only 3 days.

Letters arrive immediately. Items and money can take one hour to arrive unless you're sending messages between members of an older guild. One perk of these guilds is that they can send things through the mail at lightning speed.

USING THE SOCIAL WINDOW

You can use the Social Window to track new friends and find other players in your current region.

Using the Friends List

The first tab of the social window is your Friends List. If you've enjoyed chatting or questing with someone, you should add them to your Friends List so that you can find them again. To add a new name, click Add Friend, type in the name, and click Accept. That player is now added to your Friends List. Any time you open this window, you immediately see whether they are online as well as their current location. From the same window, you can send a message, invite them to a group, or remove their name.

For Private Time

World of Warcraft is a social game, but there are times when you may not want to be disturbed, such as during a tricky fight or while you're in a battleground and you need to concentrate. There are tools built into the game to cover these instances.

If you type /dnd (meaning Do Not Disturb) any player who tries to use a / whisper to contact you gets a message back saying that you're busy. Typing "/ dnd" again turns off the Do Not Disturb notice and people can contact you normally.

You can't like everyone all of the time. If you want to pretend that someone doesn't exist, click the Ignore Tab on the Friends List. Click Ignore Player, type their name, and click Accept. You can always go back and remove players from this list at a later time.

When someone is on your Ignore List, they won't be able to send you messages. Their text is invisible to you, so grouping with someone in this situation is suboptimal. They could be shouting warnings to everyone while you're happily pulling away, ignorant of the trouble. If you're going to /ignore someone, please avoid them entirely!

BATTLE.NET AND REAL ID

Blizzard has been expanding the things you can do between accounts. You can now try to share your Real ID with another player, giving them the ability to contact you even when you're off on another server. This is a nice feature, but you can certainly see why you wouldn't want to give this access to everyone in the game world.

To start a Real ID friend request, type in a person's account name in the friend section and wait for them to accept. Your request appears in the Pending tab of this window, and they can choose to accept or deny the request whenever they see it.

Please consider reserving this power to people that you're close with. Just because someone is in your guild doesn't mean they're your friend in real life. Real ID is certainly for people that you trust.

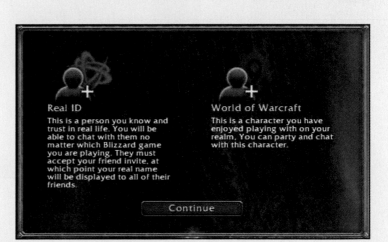

REAL ID FEATURES

- Chat across game servers and even in other Battle.Net games
- Real names are shared between these friends
- See what you friends are doing, not just where they are located
- Broadcast messages to your group of buddies
- All characters from your friend's account are automatically friends of yours, so you won't have to search for each alt and sign them up

If you're in the same place as another player (meaning a character with a blue target portrait), there are several ways you can interact with them directly. Target them and then right-click on their player portrait. You get a short list of ways that you can communicate.

You also see the name of the player's guild in their tooltip. Underneath their name you also see this guild identifier.

INTERACTION METHOD	RESULT
Set Focus	Sets a player portrait in your interface, so that you can keep tabs on their status
Whisper	Another way to whisper to a player
Inspect	Opens the player's Character window, so you can see their armor, PVP status, and Talents
Invite	Invite the player to join a group
Compare Achievements	Used to see who has done more in-game activities
Trade	Opens the Trade window, so two players can buy, sell, trade items, enchant, or unlock items for each other
Follow	Causes your character to follow behind the other person, as long as you can keep up
Duel	Invite another player to fight to the almost-death (no permanent damage is incurred by either party)

TRADING WITH OTHER PLAYERS

Before initiating a trade, you and another player should agree on the item to be sold and the price to be paid. To trade with another player, you must be in the same room. Either party can initiate the trade by right-clicking on the other player's portrait and clicking on Trade. You can also drag an item over a character to open this window.

The left window shows what you wish to trade; the right window what your comrade wishes to trade. There are three different areas for money, items, and items that you do not actually wish to trade. To make a trade, you can type in the amount of money you want to pay or you can right-click on any item in your Backpack to send it to the Trade window. When your side of the transaction is accurate, press Trade; your window turns green. When your comrade does the same, the trade completes.

The "Will not be traded" section is for items that will be modified by another player. This includes equipment that someone will enhance or locked boxes that will be opened. To complete this transaction, place your item in the bottom box, and your comrade goes to work. It is customary to tip a player that performs this service for you.

Be careful about making trades of large sums of money or valuable materials if you don't know the other person. Most players are honest, but you should always be careful about who you do business with.

MORE INFORMATION ABOUT PLAYERS

If you are chatting with someone from afar, or if you see them chatting on a channel, you can find out more about them or initiate a conversation with them by clicking on their name when you see it in the General chat log.

Click on the player name to whisper to them.

Shift+click on the player name, and the game tells you their level, race, class, guild, and current location.

If you're trying to find someone, use the /who command to search for players that match a name, level range, location, or class description. /who is quite useful in this way, but you can only search with it every few seconds. Type too quickly and the server will ignore some of your requests.

Guilds

Most players end up joining a guild at some point, but players join guilds for many different reasons. As long as you're playing with a full version of the game, you can join any guild that invites you. Using multiple characters, you can even be a member of many guilds!

These groups are player-run organizations that form to accomplish some type of goal that is easier through cooperative efforts. They might be involved in PvP events, roleplaying, endgame raiding, leveling, or just about anything else you can consider. There are thousands and thousands of guilds throughout World of Warcraft, some with members that have been adventuring together for longer than World of Warcraft has been released!

Discussing guilds is a lengthy subject better suited to a later section of the guide. If you'd like more information on guilds, turn to page 191.

GROUPS

A group consists of two to five players, with one of them being a leader. When you're in a group, you can use the /p command to chat only with players in your group.

GROUP RULES

These are the automatic group rules in the game:

- Groups divide experience for kills. With enough characters in the group, there is a bonus to the total XP gained, so groups that kill quickly can make more than soloing players. However, this requires an aggressive pace.

- If multiple people are on the same collection quest, each player waits his turn to get a dropped quest item.

- If multiple people are on the same quest to kill a single enemy, all players will be able to loot the associated head, insignia, or other item the quest has requested.

- All members are awarded kill credit for targets as long as they are close enough to the fighting.

To create a group, there are two sets of commands: those you can use if you are in the same room and those you use if the player is in another location.

GROUP COMMAND SUMMARY

COMMAND	EFFECT
Join	If you are asked to join a group, choose Accept or Decline
Create/Invite	If you are creating a group, type: /invite <playername>; You can also right-click on the player portrait, and click Invite. You are now the Leader. Only the Leader can Invite.
Uninvite	To remove a player from your group, type: /kick <playername>. You can also right-click on the player portrait, and click Uninvite. Only the Leader can Uninvite.
Promote	If you are the Leader, you can designate someone else the Leader. Right-click the player portrait, and click Promote.
Leave	To leave your party, right-click your own portrait, and click Leave Party.
Party Chat	/p <Anything you want to say>
F1	Target yourself
F2, F3, F4, F5	Target other party members
F-key	Assist target; this targets anything that the currently selected person is targeting.

Focusing Fire

One of the most fundamental strengths of a group is their ability to kill targets quickly by focusing all attacks on a single target. Five characters attacking five monsters simultaneously are effectively soloing. What's the point? Why would that even help? A few shared buffs would be the only major difference.

However, five people that attack one monster kill it almost immediately. That takes 20% of the damage out of the fight. Always try to /assist the leaders of your group. They should let you know who to /assist. If they don't, actively state that you're going to /assist one of the damage dealers. This encourages others to do the same.

LOOTING OPTIONS

When playing in a group, there are several different options for sharing the loot you find on corpses. The default option is Group Loot, which is the most practical choice at beginning levels and for players who don't know each other. Here is the full list.

Free-For-All	Any player can loot any corpse. This is useful if one player is seeking a specific drop. However, this isn't a good option for strangers on collection quests. Friends get the most out of this because it's fast and easy.
Round Robin	Every player takes his turn in a specified order, just like a hand of cards. You know when it's your turn to loot, because the corpse "sparkles" for you.
Master Looter	The Leader takes all the loot and doles it out at the end. This is primarily used in specific guilds, where point systems are in place to figure out loot distribution.
Group Loot	Has the same rules as Round Robin, with an additional option. When an Uncommon (Green) item appears, the game offers an option for players to roll, as in rolling dice, for the item. This is a good default when dealing with strangers.
Need Before Greed	Similar to Group Loot except that players who cannot equip the valuable items automatically cannot roll for them.

GROUP ETIQUETTE

The following is a short list of guidelines for becoming a reliable group member.

1. Be polite and communicative. Say thanks when someone helps. Apologize if you make a mistake. If someone is new and makes a mistake, be helpful. Don't forget, you were in their place at one point!

2. Confirm what role you need to play in the group: tank, damage dealer, or healer. Try to fill that role as best you can by equipping the best gear for that role and use the abilities that maximize your potential in that style of play.

3. If your class has a buff of some kind, share it with everyone in the group. Do the same with items that your class creates (such as Warlock Healthstones).

4. Share any relevant quests with party members.

5. Tell the group if you must leave at a certain time. Do this as far ahead of time as possible to avoid a sudden, unexpected departure.

6. If multiple players have the same gathering professions (Herbalism, Mining, Skinning), share the resources fairly.

7. Don't loot while others are still fighting. Wait until everyone is safe.

8. Share loot that you can't use. If you get a weapon you can't equip, consider giving it to a player who can.

9. Disband the party only after everyone has completed the quests they started together.

10. Stay close to your group members, so you don't accidentally draw the aggro of extra enemies.

11. State openly if you're going away from keyboard or taking any kind of break.

12. Don't whine if things aren't going your way. Bad groups are out there, and they happen to everyone. Leave (politely) as soon as you can if a group isn't to your liking, but don't make a scene. You never know why someone is having an off day, and hurting their feelings is unnecessary.

These guidelines go both ways. All members in your party should be cooperative and fair. If they aren't, feel free to tell them so and add them to your Ignore List. Occasionally, groups do go poorly. A good rule of thumb is to express your concern and give the group a chance to improve. If members don't cooperate, you can feel justified in leaving mid-group. When you have a great group, say thank you. You can even add your new comrades to your Friends List, or consider joining their guild. If no guild exists, consider starting one.

ADVANCED GROUP PLAY

Grouping changes the nature of World of Warcraft play considerably. Players are no longer focused on doing everything for themselves. Instead of acting as tank, healer, and damage dealer all at once, you get to focus on whatever you do best (while others do the same).

Groups can carry up to five members, and that is what you need to complete most dungeon runs. This is certainly more advanced play, but once you've mastered soloing it shouldn't be too hard a leap to get involved in heavier group play.

This section explains more about roles in a group, and dungeon running.

DUNGEON PREPARATION

Instanced dungeons differ from standard gameplay in other ways:

1. Dungeons are designed for groups—not solo play.

2. Completing a dungeon can be time consuming.

3. The enemies are tougher and more numerous. Expect almost all monsters to be elite.

4. Dungeons are populated with many special monsters, called bosses.

5. Dungeon quests are much harder.

6. The rewards are much richer. You find a much higher percentage of Rare or Epic gear by fighting in dungeons.

WORLD DUNGEONS

You aren't required to take five characters into a dungeon. An overleveled character can solo things to farm for low-level materials. You won't be getting in anyone's way because you'll be in your own copy of the dungeon.

However, taking on any dungeon of appropriate level should be done with all five character slots filled. Everyone should also meet the level requirements of the dungeon and be geared adequately. Even if someone's gear seems a bit low, don't immediately assume they're no good for the dungeon. Give that player a chance before making a snap decision based solely on gear. Poor player skill is far more of a liability than weak gear!

World dungeons are large places designed for more intensive play than standard areas in World of Warcraft. Some world dungeons are bigger than others, but they all have instanced zones. An instance is a specific copy of the dungeon that is for your group only. In the same way that your server is a copy of World of Warcraft, your instance is a copy of a dungeon. You can only enter the same copy of the dungeon if you are in a party with your friends.

GROUP PREPARATION

When you're in a group that is considering a dungeon run, make sure that you know the answers to the following questions.

Who is the main tank? This is the person who will initiate fights, hold aggro, and protect the group. You want to ensure that their job is as easy as possible because your character's life depends on it.

Who is the main healer? Almost any group is going to need one healer, and some are going to need more than one to get through a dungeon. The main healer should be saving all resources for healing. They only try to add damage to a fight when things are going especially well.

Who is dealing damage (DPS)? Everyone who is going to focus on damage is included in the group's DPS (damage per second, but it often is just used as a way to say damage). Damage dealers should assist the most experienced DPS member to ensure that they are all hitting the same targets. To assist a character, click on that character's portrait and press the letter F. You will learn faster ways to assist, but this is the most basic way to assist.

Who will do the pulling? Some main tanks like to have another person bring monsters back to the group. A puller is a character who goes ahead of the group and then lures enemies back to a safer position, where they can be ambushed and killed without the danger of addition targets joining the encounter. If the main tank isn't a puller, this task often falls to a ranged character or someone with stealth.

Who is the group leader? Someone needs to lead, and the others must follow. A tradition is to have the main tank lead, but what if they don't know the dungeon well? A good leader should know an area ahead of time and be a skilled player!

Does everyone have all the dungeon quests? Look in the quest log to make sure that everyone has any pertinent quests. Share everything possible so that everyone gets the most gold and experience from their dungeon run.

How long will it take? Confirm whether anyone has to leave early. Some dungeons are much longer than others, and having someone leave in the middle is a major hassle.

What are the loot rules? Every group must decide on loot rules before starting their fights. You don't want a good item to pop up and get snatched away because you didn't decide on this ahead of time.

Has everyone shared their class buffs? Use class buffs, food, and any other bonus-producing goodies before you start either a challenging quest, or a dungeon run.

Are hunters and warlocks managing their pets? Pets should be set to passive. For specific encounters where precision is key, people may even ask that pets be unsummoned.

LEVEL REQUIREMENTS

Because the content in dungeons is difficult, each dungeon has a recommended level range that all members in your party should meet. Taking someone who is below that level requirement will be problematic because enemies can aggro on that lower-level character from farther away. This makes it much harder to manage fights or sneak through specific areas. It can lead to problems even in cautious groups. Also, higher-level monsters are hard to hit; a character below the minimum isn't going to contribute much toward a group's success.

The best way to find dungeons that are appopriate for your level, use the Dungeon Finder Tool and see what's available to you. Once you hit level 15, there will be at least one instanced dungeon available to you, although you may need to discover its entrance first.

DUNGEON PREPARATION

Here are a few things to take care of before you start a group for a dungeon run.

1. Repair your armor. There's no place to repair in a dungeon. Some characters can use abilities to help out with this, but you shouldn't rely on them (especially considering that most players won't have them until high level).

2. Empty your bags. You often collect a greal deal of loot in a dungeon, so take only essential items in your bags. Having bags full of crummy items is no good when there is expensive dungeon gear to snag. As a last resort, destroy low-quality loot or grey items in your bag to make room for better stuff.

3. Stock up on provisions. Take enough food, water, potions, and reagents.

4. Bring any required quest items. Double-check quest text to see if you need anything while you're in the dungeon to complete the quest.

WIPEOUTS

Wiping occurs when all members of your group die and they have no way to resurrect where they died. If this happens, you must run back from a graveyard and grab your corpse. When this happens inside a dungeon, you must go back into the dungeon's entrance before your body respawns.

Depending on the timing, all the monsters you killed may still be dead or they may have respawned, which means they've reset, and you have to fight them again. This only happens when a group takes a long time to complete a dungeon. This is sometimes a sign that things aren't going well and that people might want to try again another time.

Understandably, groups want to avoid a wipe at all costs, so it's wise to try to save a party member who can resurrect everyone else later. However, if your group does wipe, don't get too upset about it. Wipeouts happen, especially when people are learning new dungeons/encounters.

Your gear suffers a durability hit when your character dies, but the cost isn't that severe. It's easy to make money with questing, selling things on the Auction House, and by general fighting. You aren't going to end up poor because of a few lousy dungeon runs.

PICK UP GROUPS (PUGS)

In this case, PUGs aren't cute little dogs. This refers to groups that are formed by strangers, often using the dungeon finder. These are the hardest groups to win with, but that doesn't mean that they'll always be of low quality. Indeed, you might end up with several people who know a dungeon already or have impressive gear, and the dungeon will be a walk in the park because of it.

The reality of PUGs is that you won't know what to expect. Their quality has such wide variance that you might have a perfect run and follow it up with a nail-biting, hair-pulling attempt that falls flat after an hour.

To limit your time with random groups, remember to /friend people who impress you. Good players make groups a great deal more enjoyable. If you can fill two or three slots with players of known skill, you won't have nearly as much uncertainty in your dungeon delving.

Eventually, you might find a group or guild of people that adventures with you regularly. This leads to considerable advances in tactics and playstyle. It's also a great way to make friends.

DUNGEON FINDER TOOL

Finding a group for larger tasks used to be much harder than it is now. Blizzard implemented a Dungeon Finder system that is quite powerful. You let people know what role you're interested in taking (Tank, Healer, Damage Dealer). Next, you let people know if you have experience in a given dungeon and what you're looking for.

You can set the system to randomly assign you to a dungeon. This gets your character an extra reward (in terms of money, experience, and even items at lower levels).

This system is very fast, especially if you're a tank or healer. Even if not, you can sign up for a dungeon run and wait until the system is ready. No more sitting on your heels, waiting for a dungeon run to begin but needing that one extra person. How cool is that?

TACTICS

Take a look at which abilities you use while soloing. Some of them make perfect sense when you don't have anyone watching your back. However, in a group environment, some of these become a waste of time and resources. If you're not taking aggro from monsters, why use something that raises your survivability by a substantial measure (especially if it takes away from your damage output)?

Figure out how you can best contribute within your role. If you're a tank, learn how to mitigate as much damage as possible. Use abilities that get attention from multiple monsters. Try to keep yourself from going low on health, and learn how to control monsters' positions so that the damage dealers know where to stand in each encounter.

Healers should spend a huge amount of time looking at everyone's health and saving the group from harm. Find ways to do this efficiently during long fights as well as methods to maximize your healing output and mana during tense boss fights. Consider who the most important people are to keep healed (e.g., a tank or another healer). Move as necessary to keep things from pounding on you, and take enemies over to someone else if you do get attention. Being an effective healer isn't only about managing bars, it's also about good communication.

Damage dealers should lay on as much damage as possible without stealing aggro from the main tank. As long as they assist each other to stay on single targets, this is not terribly difficult. They'll rip down individual enemies while the tank holds onto everything else (and preferably the single target as well)!

Don't be afraid to ask questions before a fight. Ask about your role or your abilities. If you don't know a boss encounter, please say so before the pull begins. "I've never fought this guy before. What should I do?"

Some people will be annoyed by this. The majority won't, because they know that you're trying to learn. They also know that your questions might save the group in the pull ahead. If one person didn't know what to do, maybe there were a couple more people who didn't know but were afraid to ask!

Also, use available resources to find out more about your targets. There are people online with writeups to many dungeons. There are also strategy guides (that we've written) that take you through world dungeons and raid encounters. These Dungeon Companions are a great way to have something on hand when you're getting ready for a dungeon run.

HAVE FUN

This section might make dungeons seem awfully intimidating and tough. They can be, but they can also be very satisfying to complete. Dungeons reveal more about the Azeroth storyline, and they hold the most exotic, sometimes amusing, and powerful enemies in the game. For success, enter a dungeon, listen to your leader, and pay close attention, but also have fun!

COMBAT

Explore the area around your character and drag your mouse cursor over the different creatures you see. Look near the bottom right corner of the screen for a small information box to appear. Enemies appear in red text, not green like a friendly NPC or yellow like a neutral one. Some neutral targets can be attacked, but they won't fight until you go after them. Enemies are aggressive; they'll go after you if you get too close! Be ready to defend yourself.

When you chose to fight a creature, you are considered to be in combat. In combat means you are actively targeting, or are the target of, an enemy. It's easy to tell when you're in combat as your character portrait flashes red and your level numbers change to crossed swords. Being in combat means you are unable to perform some actions, such as eating and drinking.

A Different Way to Choose a Target

You can always left-click to select between targets, but there are other ways to find your enemies. Press the Tab key to shift between various monsters that are close to your character. Move near a group of enemies and hit Tab several times to scroll through the various available targets.

The benefits of using Tab include quick target changes with minimal loss of attention to your keyboard and that it targets any nearby enemies—even the ones you can't see. The downside to Tab targeting is that it doesn't reliably target the enemy you want to engage next nor does it always pick the closest target.

Try fighting both ways (manual selection of targets and using Tab) and find what feels more comfortable to you.

ABILITIES AND SPELLS

It's fun to watch a fight unfold, but you must pay attention to more than the action in front of you. During combat, watch for opportunities to use spells or abilities that might trigger at one time or another. Gauge your health and your resources well to know when to unload on a target, when to give up and run, and how it's all going to develop.

Each character begins with a handful of abilities that vary with the class and race you selected for that character. These initial abilities appear on your Action Bar so they are easy to access. Highlight the icons on the Action Bar (or in your spellbook) with your mouse. This brings up a tooltip that provides more information about the ability. Read that panel to find out more about any of your abilities.

Passive Abilities

Some abilities in your spellbook are listed as Passive and don't appear on your Action Bar. These abilities are always active on your character and don't require you to perform an action for them to take effect.

You should get used to your abilities by using them, even if you're unsure of their value at first. Don't be skittish and worry about whether you're doing things perfectly. Just try out things and see how they feel and what they accomplish. The following pages help you understand the information provided in the tooltips and what they mean to you and your character.

ABILITY TERMS

If you're not sure what an ability does or when to use it, the following terms may point you in the right direction. The same terms also apply to abilities that are used during a battle.

COMMON TERM	DEFINITION
Threat	Refers to managing an enemy's attention, either increasing or reducing a monster's attention toward a character. Only applies to groups.
Resist/Resistance	These effects make it harder for certain spells and abilities to "hit" their target and fully damage them
Immune/Immunity	These effects provide full immunity to a given damage type
Fear	These abilities cause a target to run around chaotically; the effect may not break even if the victim takes damage
Daze	These abilities slow their victims
Stun	An ability that prevents the target from taking any action
Root/Snare	Abilities that immobilize the victim; though the target cannot move, they can still fight or use abilities
Interrupt	An ability that stops an enemy spell from completing
Area of Effect (AoE)	Something that has an effect over a wider area, influencing multiple targets within that zone of effect

COMMON TERM	DEFINITION
Curse/Disease/Poison	Debuffs that damage a target in certain ways; these can often be Dispelled or otherwise removed
Damage over Time (DoT)	An ability that inflicts an amount of health damage for a certain number of seconds
Heal	Abilities that restore lost health
Heal over Time (HoT)	These abilities restore health every tick (duration between ticks is defined by the ability)
Auras/Aspects	Buffs that enhance players or groups for an extended period of time
Polymorph	Changes targets into helpless animals for a long time. This effect breaks if the target takes damage.
Sap	Knocks out a target for a long time. This breaks if the target takes damage.
Shield	The ability absorbs damage, preventing the target from losing health as quickly in a fight

Knowing how abilities work can help you put together a plan of action when you face enemies. For example, if you have some sort of stun or interrupt, you can keep an enemy from hitting you with a powerful spell or healing itself.

More About Daze

While there are abilities that daze your character, it's possible to become dazed at almost any time. If an enemy hits you from behind (if, for example, you are running away from a fight) there is a chance for you to become dazed. Being dazed is dangerous as it reduces your running speed, which allows the enemy to get in more attacks while you're trying to get away.

ACTION BARS

Your Action Bar appears at the bottom of the screen. Your Action Bars are the most efficient way to access your character's spells and abilities. At low levels, you won't have many abilities here, but that will change as you get further into the game.

All players have six Action Bars. You can shuffle through your Action Bars in two ways: first, press and hold the Shift key, then press any number between 1 and 6; second, click on the up and down arrows to the right of the button marked with the equals sign (=). The number in the small circle next to the arrows tells you which Action Bar is currently active.

Be logical about the way you set up your Action Bars. It makes a huge difference in your combat effectiveness. It's a bad sign if you find that you must switch Actions Bars often in a regular fight. By the same token, you don't want to shift between numbers too dramatically. This is easier to show with an example or two.

People with a good Action Bar set ups are much faster on the draw. They are using an ability every 1.5 seconds (that's normally the cap on how quickly you can use your abilities). If your character is auto-attacking while you fish around for something to do, that's bad!

It's also normal for a new player. Don't be upset with yourself if this takes time to learn. Instead, attempt to find a setup for yourself that makes sense. As you feel your speed improve, congratulate yourself and think about how much deadlier your character is becoming.

CLICKING VERSUS TYPING

At some point, everyone must click on an ability icon with their mouse pointer. Maybe you've set up five hot bars on your screen and can't get to everything quickly. However, your goal should be to use the keyboard for all possible actions. This is often much faster and lets your character pop through abilities at lightning speed.

Demonstrate this for yourself.

Search for the ability in slot six and left click on it, even if nothing is there.

Press 6 on your keyboard. Which was faster?

Once you're used to the game, teach yourself to use abilities without even looking to see what they are. Memorize where each ability is located and watch your character transform into a killing machine. No one expects you to master this instantly, but it will make your time in the game go much more smoothly.

MORE INFORMATION ABOUT ABILITIES

Casting Time

Every spell or attack has a casting time; this tells you how much time your character needs to make the attack. Instant abilities happen as soon as you press the button with which they're associated. Timed castings can take several seconds, leaving your caster exposed for the entire process. Characters that are casting spells cannot move to defend themselves without halting their current spell cast. They stop making any auto-attacks, and they can't use other spells.

Some enemies (including other characters) have Interrupt abilities to stop spellcasters if used with the proper timing. In addition, damage can set a caster back, forcing them to take more time to get their spell off.

Channeled spells take time as well, but they're a different breed. These start to take affect quickly, but the spellcaster must maintain the magic for its effects to continue. As with timed spells, these effects can be interrupted. Damage doesn't set them back; instead, it sets channeled spells forward, causing them to end prematurely.

Casters often find ways to earn time for themselves to cast spells. They slow enemies, force them to run away, or otherwise make it hard to engage in melee combat while they are busy.

Cooldowns

The Action Bar tooltips also indicate the cooldown times of your various spells and abilities. Cooldown is the amount of time you must wait to use an ability again. Once you use an ability, the Action Bar

shortcut darkens that action until it's ready to be used again. This graphic representation is important because it lets you know what you can do at any given moment.

Cooldowns are represented visually on your Action Bar icons as a clockwise-moving line that moves like a stop watch. When you can't cast a spell due to a cooldown, the game tells you: "That spell isn't ready yet."

There is also a global cooldown that is triggered when most abilities are used. The global cooldown lasts 1.5 seconds. When you use an ability, watch almost every other slot darken as well. Anything that isn't on the global cooldown is able to be used even when you've just finished a different action. These unlinked spells and abilities are often potent, reactive abilities that get you out of trouble without having to wait.

Some abilities have a shared cooldown beyond the global one. For example, a Shaman's Shock spells trigger each other's cooldowns, so you can't blast someone with a different Shock every second and a half.

CATEGORIES OF ABILITIES

All character classes have numerous types of abilities that fall into different categories. It's almost impossible for you to know the exact effect of everything in the game. However, knowing the category of an ability and looking for key words in the text will give you clues as to how best to use that ability.

Schools of Magic

The schools of magic are Arcane, Fire, Frost, Holy, Nature, and Shadow. Some abilities that aren't spells also inflict one of these types of damage. Different enemies are immune or highly resistant to different types of damage. No single school of magic is inherently more powerful than the others.

Most classes who can use spells have access to two or three schools of magic. However, until you gain access to talent trees at level 10, all schools of magic are essentially equal.

Buffs and Debuffs

During combat, buffs and debuffs appear near your minimap. These are also shown underneath your character portrait if you highlight yourself.

Most classes have some sort of buff that they can cast on themselves, a weapon, or their group. You should cast those before combat begins and keep them going whenever possible. The cost of buffs is almost always trivial compared with the benefits they add to your character or others.

During combat, you can be hit with debuffs from your enemies. Most debuffs have a short lifespan, and you may need to wait them out. Other debuffs can be countered by the right spell or item. Many classes inflict their own debuffs on enemies. You might even be able to strip off buffs from enemies too, so these effects go both ways.

If you're buffing group members, realize that you don't need to click on individual people ahead of time. You can use quick keys to do this much faster. F2 - F5 automatically grab people in the positions they take up on your screen. In other words, F2 targets the person just below your character in the group list. F3 grabs the next person. You get the idea.

FIGHTING ADDS

An add is an additional enemy that unexpectedly joins your fight. During the course of battle, there's always a chance for adds to appear and complicate the fight. These additional enemies generally join battle for one of two reasons. First, some enemies try to run away when their health is nearly depleted. This is problematic because the enemy can run out of your attack range and could bring back friends. In other cases, you may be fighting too close to an enemy's patrol path. If the enemy spots you, even if you're already engaged in combat, it will join the fight, and not on your side!

There is a third, and much rarer instance, of adds joining the fight. Some powerful enemies have henchmen that may not join the fight immediately. Instead, the main enemy may wait until some portion of health is gone before calling in reinforcements. That's why it pays to always stay alert in combat!

Pull monsters away from their buddies if you're worried about adds. This is a safer way of fighting, but it takes more time. When you're confident of victory, don't bother doing this.

If you're wondering how to pull monsters, there are many ways to get the job done. For a melee character, hit the monster, step back, hit them again, and repeat. You won't miss auto-attacks by being on the run, and your abilities are often usable on the fly as well.

For ranged characters, this is easier to do in one shot. Cast a spell at long range to start the fight. Next, run like the wind until you're in the place where you'd like to fight them. Turn back around and resume casting.

Keep in mind that if you try to pull a monster too far, they'll "tether" back to their starting point.

RUNNING AWAY

Sometimes you see the writing on the wall, and it says that you're doomed. Perhaps another enemy joined the fight when you were already badly hurt. Maybe a monster was a tad more dangerous than you realized. Whatever the case, you know that you probably won't survive the encounter.

Go ahead and run! If you're by yourself, there is no shame in this. When you're with others, let them know that you're fleeing so that they don't die in your stead.

Some classes are much better at this than others. If you get out of melee range, the monster can't pound on your back during your flight. Also, monsters won't have a chance to daze you! Getting dazed slows your character, giving monsters even more time to attack before they tether and return home.

DYING

This won't be on your list of things to do, but at some point early in your character's life, her health bar will reach zero, and she will die. It might happen because you forgot to refresh your health bar between battles; you

were attacked by multiple enemies simultaneously; or you attacked an enemy who was too tough for you.

Thus, use anything in your repertoire to stun a target or root them in place before you start to flee. Freeze them, hamstring the suckers, use fear effects. Do something. Anything!

Once you're in motion, watch the area ahead of you (don't look back at the thing slavering behind you). Try to avoid other targets during your flight; otherwise, you're just making things worse for yourself.

Finally, avoid running through other people when you're evacuating. Pulling monsters through another person is called "training." Nobody likes getting hit with a train, especially if they get killed or end up fighting creatures that aren't worth experience because you tapped them.

It happens. Everybody dies. Sometimes more than once. Over and over again. The only penalty to dying is that your current armor suffers a 10% durability loss. Durability is essentially the health of your gear. When you take damage, die, or resurrect at the Spirit Healer, your gear slowly loses durability.

When you die, the Release Spirit box appears over your corpse. When you click this button, your character turns into spirit form and is transported to a graveyard with a Spirit Healer.

EATING AND DRINKING

Between battles, you may need to replenish your health or mana. Eating food replenishes your green health bar. Drinking beverages replenishes your mana bar, if you have one. Both health and mana regenerate naturally, but eating and drinking restore your character much faster.

The regeneration rates for both of these resources is tied to your spirit. At low levels, you can move between most fights with little delay.

Right-click on any food or drink that you want to use. Note that these items (and any other usable item) can be dragged onto the bar at the bottom of the screen. This makes the items more available in the future, lowering the time you spend looking through your bags.

To reunite your spirit with your body, you can run back to your corpse; or you can ask the Spirit Healer to resurrect your body at its location. If you Accept resurrection, you receive an additional 25% durability loss in your armor. At later levels, you also suffer resurrection sickness. Resurrection sickness depletes your character's stats, making it nearly impossible to do anything in the game until the sickness disappears. When the debuff icon for Resurrection sickness fades away, your stats return to normal.

Most of the time, you will simply retrieve your corpse by running back to the location where you died. A new arrow appears on your minimap that indicates the exact location of your corpse. The second arrow that appears is to guide you back to the Spirit Healer. Fortunately, ghosts run faster than living characters.

When you reach the general location of your corpse, you get the option to "Resurrect Now?" There is a generous area in which you can resurrect, so that you can avoid any enemies around you. You must retrieve your body from a safe place, because characters resurrect with only 50% of health and mana bars. Eat and drink quickly to restore your health and mana.

ENEMIES

Enemies, monsters, and mobs are all generic terms for anything that you can fight in the game. When you target an enemy, you can get helpful information about it by looking at its portrait and tooltip. The character name might indicate the class of enemy; and a blue mana bar indicates it's some kind of caster who can attack you from afar.

By mousing over the enemy, the tooltip tells you the type of enemy it is. The types of enemy include Humanoid, Beast, Undead, Demon, and Elemental. Some abilities only work against certain types of enemies and will fail if you try to use them against the wrong type of enemy.

TARGET PORTRAIT COLORS

Red

The target is hostile and will attack if you get too close. In PVP situations, players from the other faction also appear with this color.

Yellow

The target is passive and will only fight if you attack first.

Gray

The target has already been attacked by another player. You can still attack this target, but killing it will not give you any experience points and you will not share in any loot. In addition, the kill will not count toward any quests you have.

Green

The target is friendly.

Blue

The target is a player, just like you.

LEVEL NUMBER COLORS ON TARGET PORTRAIT

The color of the target's level number provides important information to you as well.

If the numbers are gray, killing that enemy doesn't provide any benefit other than loot.

Green numbers indicate the enemy is a few levels lower than you, and should be easy for you to kill.

Yellow numbers are for enemies who are close in level to your current level and could be a challenge in a fight.

Red numbers are for enemies that are a few levels higher than you; it's best to avoid combat with them until you are more comfortable playing the game.

If you target an enemy and a skull appears in the place of its level, then that enemy is at least 10 levels higher than you. Avoid enemies like this whenever you encounter them!

Social Monsters

If you see a small group of enemies and aren't sure you could handle them all at the same time, observe them for a moment to see if they move apart from each other. With some patience, you can typically fight each enemy by itself.

However, some creatures are social, and will help their comrades when they are attacked even when they aren't right next to each other. There is no way of identifying which types of monsters are social except through experience.

Murlocs throughout Azeroth are very social and frequently attack in swarms.

Critters

Critters are the non-combat animals you see roaming around, including rabbits, cows, snakes, and prairie dogs. If you attack them, they can't fight back; and you get no XP from killing them. There are, however, achievements attached to interacting with most critters.

Rare Spawns

Creatures with a silver dragon around their portraits are unique mobs with guaranteed drops. Some items they drop are not found on any other creature, while others are guaranteed to drop better than average loot.

If the silver dragon around the creature's portrait has wings, it is an Elite monster. These creatures have the traits of both rare spawns and elite monsters.

Elite Monsters

Elite monsters are powerful enemies, usually the targets of group or dungeon quests. Elites are stronger than their level would indicate. Generally speaking, you can assume that fighting an elite will be as hard as fighting a monster three levels higher. In addition, Elite monsters often have special abilities that make fighting them even trickier.

Elites are identified by the gold dragon around their character portrait and the word Elite in their tooltip.

They Keep Coming Back

The enemies you kill don't stay gone foever. They eventually respawn, meaning an area you cleared of enemies will shortly be filled again.

LOOT

Enemies won't stand against you forever. Every target has a health bar under its name. When this green bar drops to nothing, the creature dies. Almost all enemies offer some kind of loot after they've been defeated. When you have loot waiting, your dead enemy sparkles. Look for this golden shimmering, and rejoice. You've earned something!

Right-click to open the enemy loot box, then click on each item to put it into your inventory. If you press Shift and right-click at the same time, each item is sent directly to your Backpack.

You get loot from looting enemies and from completing quests. Quest rewards go directly to your backpack after you finish the quest. Any money you collect, from any source, goes immediately into your backpack. It can't be lost or unintentionally discarded. Also, money has no weight in World of Warcraft. You can carry half a million gold around if you like.

A loot window is brought up by right-clicking a sparkling, defeated enemy.

 INVENTORY

Click this icon to open your backpack.

For now, all of your possessions are either equipped on your character or are being carried in your backpack. Press the letter b to open your backpack and see what is inside. Another way to do this is to left-click on the brown bag in the lower right.

Eventually, you acquire additional bags to expand your inventory. Characters can each carry up to four bags. More expensive bags can have more slots than your initial backpack, but the starting ones are inexpensive and tiny. They only have a few slots each.

Managing Your Inventory

While doing quests, your Backpack quickly fills with items you loot. When that happens, you can't accept anymore loot, and the game will tell you, "Inventory is full." To make some room, look for a vendor who will buy your useless items. If you aren't near a vendor but still need room, left-click+drag an item to pull it out of your Backpack, and click on the desktop. You get a message asking whether you want to delete the item. Click Yes.

If you get a quest reward, or a loot-drop of a bag of any kind, keep it! It's far more valuable to you for storage than the money you could get from a vendor by selling it. Drag new bags into any of your Equipment Container slots.

Hearthstones

Every character starts the game with a Hearthstone. These special items teleport your character to the last place that they bound. Normally, you bind at inns. These are good locations to log out of the game because you get rested bonus (and thus free experience) by letting your character rest there when you're not playing.

Hearthstones are on a long cooldown timer; this means that you can only use them every 30 minutes, at most. It's best to save these for times when you need to cross a large distance and know where you're teleporting or for times when you're about to log out and want to get someplace safe to rest.

Selling to Vendors

To complement the coppers you've collected from defeating humanoid enemies, you can earn money by selling unneeded items collected from defeated enemies. Since your bag space is limited you should plan to return to your starting area to sell off these items.

Although each vendor sells only a specific type of merchandise, they buy anything that you have. Items that aren't considered gear come in two colors: grey and white.

Grey items are often called "vendor trash" because they have no real purpose other than to be sold to vendors.

White items are useful in some way if you plan to take on a crafting Profession, but there's usually no harm in selling off the items at this point.

I Didn't Mean to Sell That!

If you accidentally sell something you meant to keep, don't worry. At the bottom of each vendor window is a Buyback tab. Click on that tab and purchase the item you sold by mistake.

ITEM NAME TEXT COLOR

COLOR	QUALITY
Gray	Poor
White	Common
Green	Uncommon
Blue	Rare
Purple	Epic
Orange	Legendary

All new characters start out with minimal weaponry, armor, and clothing. In the starting zone, there are three sources of improved gear: looting enemies, completing quests, and armor vendors. For most starting players, the vendors aren't an option because you don't have much money and it's more important for you to save it for training new abilities as you gain levels (more on that soon). If you do have the money and you like to have your character's outfit match, then check out what the vendors have to offer.

You can tell if an item is a new piece of gear because its tooltip includes information about where you wear it (hands, back, chest, etc.). When you find a piece of gear, open your bags and mouse over the item. The color of the first line tells you about the quality of the item. At early levels, you are likely to find only gray, white, and green items.

The next color to look for is red. Red text on an item tells you that you are unable to equip it. It could be that it's a weapon or type of armor you can't use, or that yo u are not high enough level to equip it. If you might be able to use an item after you gain levels, keep it. If you are playing with friends, see if anyone else could use the item. Otherwise, find a vendor and sell off your unusable gear. To equip a piece of gear, right-click it in your bags and it will automatically go into the proper spot in your character sheet. The item should also appear on your character.

COLOR-CODED INFORMATION

This tooltip for Felcloth Hood provides some basic information with colors. The name in green means it is Uncommon quality. The red text tells you why you can't equip it. In this case, the character isn't high enough level.

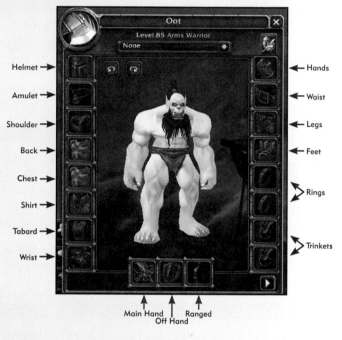

Weapon Skills and Armor Proficiencies

If you're ever wondering which weapons are available to your character, press the letter p and look for an icon that looks like a weapon. This reads "Weapon Skills." Highlight it to see what you character can use in both melee and ranged combat.

The Armor Proficiencies lists the type of armor you can currently use plus whether your character can equip a shield. These limitations are determined entirely by your class. However, some classes get an armor upgrade when they reach higher levels. Warriors and Paladins start the game with only mail, but they eventually learn how to wear plate. Shamans and Hunters start out wearing leather, but can use mail armor when they hit a certain level.

Comparing Equipment

When you mouse over current or new equipment, you can see details about its attributes. At early levels, equipment will have an Armor stat only, so you can choose the piece with the higher level of armor protection. Later in the game, you will begin to find armor that has other stat increases.

Hold down shift while highlighting a potential upgrade. This compares your currently equipped gear with the new item. The game automatically gives you a summary of the stat changes that would occur if you switched.

At early levels, you are likely to find only Poor (gray), Common (white), and Uncommon (green) items. If you cannot use a gray item, sell it. If you find a white or green item, hopefully, you can wear it. If you cannot use a white or green item, you might consider selling it to another player.

After you pass through the earliest game levels, Poor and Common items stop being acceptable for use. You want to switch to Uncommon gear exclusively (i.e., all greens for your weapons, armor, and peripheral equipment).

After level 20, you start seeing more than an occasional blue item. These Rare pieces are quite nice for their time, and you should seek them out. However, it isn't until much later in your career that they become baseline equipment.

Epic gear exists before level 60, but it's not plentiful. Don't even worry about it unless you're doing something very specific. Unless you're stuck at a given level, such as being at the cap, Epic gear isn't necessary. This is equipment that rewards someone for staying a given level and doing an exceptional level of content over time. Thus, you level past the utility of Epic gear throughout most of the game.

Legendary equipment is so rare that most people will never have access to such an item. Even endgame raiders in big guilds can't count on having these items at their disposal.

Heirloom items are usually similar in quality to Rare gear. What is interesting about these items is that they bind to accounts instead of characters. As such, you can hand them down to your alternate characters to help them with their own leveling. In addition, Heirloom gear rises in quality as you level. Think of it as growing with the character.

Armor

When you start the game, most of your armor slots are empty. Eventually you find pieces for your head, shoulders, back, chest, waist, legs, feet, wrist, and hands. If a shield is held in the off hand the character is limited to using weapons that require only one hand to use, but shields provide an amazing amount of armor as well.

Clothing

Clothing pieces fill up your shirt and tabard slot. These don't often have any influence on your character's progression, but they decorate your avatar. Tabards can identify your affiliation with a guild. They can also show an association with certain in-game factions.

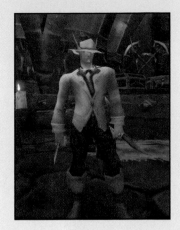

Weapons

All characters have two melee weapon slots. These are taken up by a two-handed weapon, two one-handed weapons, or a weapon and an off-hand item, such as a shield. Class selection determines a great deal of what you end up equipping here.

Your ranged/relic slot is used for a bow, gun, crossbow, wand, or thrown weapon in most cases. Some classes cannot use ranged weapons, so they have magical items, known as relics, to put in the slot instead.

Amulets, Rings and Trinkets

These are higher level item slots. You wear a single amulet around your neck, but get two slots each for rings and trinkets. Some of these items are active. For example, many trinkets grant abilities that you can put on your action bar to give your character a sudden boost in one aspect of play.

Don't worry too much about these until you reach a somewhat higher level.

Repairing Your Equipment

As your gear loses durability, a paperdoll of your armor appears on-screen. Yellow means damaged; red means broken. When your armor is broken, that piece no longer protects you in combat.

To repair your armor, mouse over different vendors until your mouse pointer turns into an anvil. Anvils indicate vendors who are capable of repairing your gear. When you right-click this type of vendor, two icons appear in the vendor window, showing the cost for repair. Click on Repair All Items. At low levels, you don't really need to worry about repairing your gear because you should replace it quickly. As you start gaining levels, repairing your gear becomes more important.

There are other ways that you can give your character an edge. These items don't need to be equipped. Instead, they're used (often permanently) to boost your character or your character's equipment. Some effects are temporary, others are more permanent.

Some of the following suggestions discuss Professions. To learn more about Professions, turn to page **64**.

POTIONS & ELIXIRS

Characters drink potions and elixirs to enhance their performance. Potions, elixirs, and flasks can be made by characters with the Alchemy profession. If you're lucky, potions are sometimes found in treasure chests.

Potions have short-term benefits, only working for the moment after you drink them. These restore health or mana, and they can get you through some nasty times. Potions can be taken during combat, but there is a cooldown timer for their use. You can't bring ten potions into a fight and hope to keep yourself alive indefinitely.

Elixirs buff your character for a somewhat longer period. They can enhance a number of things, including armor, health regeneration, attributes, and so forth.

There are other drinkable items called flasks. These are incredibly expensive because they demand many more reagents during creation. Flasks persist through death and are a common aspect of dungeon runs and raiding.

ARMOR KITS

Armor pieces can be permanently improved by adding armor kits to them. These are usually fairly cheap and can be made with Leatherworking. Early armor kits mainly provide additional armor, but the later ones in the game have much more substantial benefit.

Earthen Leg Armor
Requires Level 80
Item Level 80
Use: Permanently attach earthen armor onto pants to increase resilience rating by 40 and Stamina by 28.

Enchanting the item causes it to become soulbound.
Sell Price: 2

ENCHANTMENTS

Another way to permanently enhance equipment is to have it enchanted. Almost every equippable slot can carry some type of enchantment. Though the temporary cost is quite high, the long-term benefits are substantial if you have most of your gear enchanted. This raises attributes, adds damage to weapons, and is fun to pursue, especially if you have some cash to spare.

Once you reach one of the major cities, search for an Apprentice Enchanter among the players. Because they are trying to boost their enchanting skill, you may be able to get a free enchantment for your gear. It's good form to "tip" your enchanter for this boost to your character's armor.

GLYPHS

As you progress through the levels, Glyphs start coming more into play. Press the letter n to bring up the Talent Screen. From there, select the tab labeled Glyphs to see which ones are open for your character. There are three tiers of Glyphs and you unlock additional slots for Glyphs as you gain levels.

As you kill enemies, complete quests, and discover new aeras, your XP bar fills up with color. When the bar is full, the game congratulates you on rising to a new level. Completing the initial quests you find in your starting village will easily help you go from Level 1 to Level 2.

TRAINING NEW ABILITIES

As you gain levels, the game lets you know when new abilities are available from the trainer. When you train, new abilities automatically go into your spellbook and (for the first few levels) into an open slot on your Action Bar. You're free to move around the skills on your Action Bar in any way that makes sense to you.

LEVEL 5: LEARN A PROFESSION

When you hit level 5, you gain the option of learning a Profession. It isn't necessary for you to learn a Profession, but if you're interested in learning more, turn to page 64.

CHARACTER STATS

Each time your character gains a level, many of their attributes (such as health, mana, Agility, Strength, etc.) are increased. Go into the character window to find out more about these changes.

Discussion of stats is a fairly advanced topic, and stats change at each level, but here are some basics that you should know when you look in this window.

White	By default, your stats should be in white. This is a normal level.
Red	Stats in red are being affected negatively by a debuff, broken armor, or other negative effect.
Green	Stats in green are good and are likely being enhanced by a buff, enhanced armor, or potion.

LEVEL 10: THE BIG CHOICE

At level 10, your character starts to learn talents and must select a specialty. This provides access to abilities that other members of your class won't get unless they too join the same specialty. Talents are yet another advanced topic. In short, they are a way to customize your character, pushing them toward one of three major routes that a class can take.

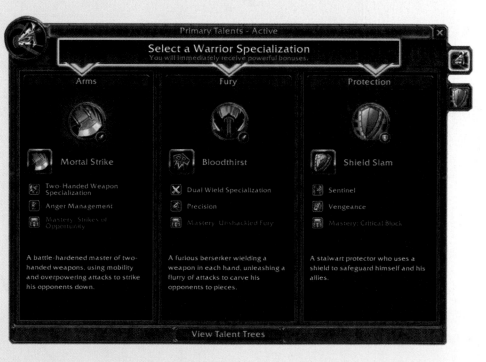

TALENT TREES

Each class has three talent trees. You get your first talent point at level 10, and gain additional points as you level up. The first decision you must make is which tree to select first. If you need a reminder about what each talent tree means, flip to the class information on page 164.

Selecting one of these trees blocks your access to the other two trees until you spend 31 points in your first tree. Each talent tree has a number of tiers from top to bottom. You must spend five talent points in the top tier before you can spend points in the next tier. To get to certain Talents, you must plan in advance where you will spend your talent points.

You must spend five points in tier one before tier two talents become available.

Getting to tier three requires spending ten talent points, but these can be spent in either tier one or tier two. What matters is that you spend five more points in a line to unlock each subsequent tier! This pattern continues with each tier of talents.

If you see an arrow between two talents, that implies that you need to unlock one fully before taking the one next to it (the talent it's pointing toward). You must take all ranks of that talent before you can move on to the next.

Don't try to buy everything, especially when you're first starting off. Many of the best talents in a tree are found farther down, so it's not a great idea to grab 10 or 15 points in the first tier before looking further down the tree.

There are times when you have everything that you want in a tier and still need to invest a bit before moving down. When that happens, look back up through the talent tree and see if there is anything that you didn't get before that you now have time to grab.

Talent Preview

By default, your character won't spend talent points until you click okay and try to move on. The system lets you preview the changes to your talents and read the updated text for them as you prepare to spend your points. This way, you can cancel to back off and try a different selection!

TALENT RANKS

Many talents have several ranks, a range of points that you can apply to them, indicated by X/Y. The first X is the talent points you have spent; Y is the max for that talent. Each additional point in a talent improves its effect by a fair portion. Almost all talents increase in a linear fashion, so you won't get too much more or less from the first point you invest compared with the last one.

RESETTING YOUR TALENTS

If you decide you want to spend your talent points in another way, you can return to your Class Trainer, who will charge a sliding fee for a reset. Occasionally, if a game patch changes talents significantly, Blizzard resets all talent trees, so you need to re-spend your talent points anyway. When that happens there is no associated fee, so you might get a freebie!

At the beginning levels, your only choice is to hoof it when you want to go somewhere. Once you start getting quests that send you to new places, it helps you a great deal to know about all your transportation options.

TRAVELING BY FOOT

It's not glamorous, but everybody starts out running to get to new places. When you're going long distances, use Auto Run (defaults to the NumLock key), so you can focus on controlling your character.

It is possible to walk if you aren't in the mood to run. Though slower, this is fun for roleplaying or setting a tone; it's also good if you're escorting an NPC that is wandering around at a different pace. To walk, tap the / key on the number pad once. Tap it again to resume running.

There is no sprint key, unless you're a Worgen or a Rogue, both of whom have abilities that lets them put on the speed every few minutes.

BUFFS FOR RUNNING

Even on foot, some classes have skills and abilities to increase their speed. They don't start with these abilities at level 1, so keep an eye out with your class trainer to see when the following abilities become available.

Druid

Druids learn a Travel Form that lets them turn into a Cheetah. This gives them considerable speed.

Hunter

Hunters learn an ability called Aspect of the Cheetah, which increases speed indefinitely. You are immediately dazed if you are hit/damaged while using this, so it isn't useful during combat.

Shaman

Shamans learn how to turn into a Ghost Wolf. This form increases speed indefinitely, so its ideal for long journeys.

SWIMMING

At times, you need to swim through bodies of water to get to your location. At other times, you need to dive to find hidden items for quests. Almost every body of water has some sort of aqualife—some of them are hostile.

Controlling your character while swimming differs from controls for running.

SWIMMING CONTROLS

KEY	EFFECT
X	Dive deeper into the water
Spacebar	Swim to the surface
Right-click+mouse movement	Moves the direction your character is swimming
NumLock	Character continues swimming in the same direction

Buffs for Swimming

Swimming is slower than running, unless you have some buffs or abilities. Your character can stay under water for a limited amount time before running out of air and eventually dying, unless you consume the proper potions, or have a Warlock or Shaman around to grant you underwater breathing.

Druids learn how to shift into an Aquatic Form. As a sea lion, these characters can stay underwater as long as they like. They also move faster than other classes. Shaman learn an ability called Water Walking that allows characters to cross water as if it were land. It works for mounted characters as well.

Fatigue

Running out of breath isn't the only danger when you're out in the water. Characters get fatigued if they try to swim for too long in deep water. This prevents people from trying to cross the ocean without a ship. If you see the fatigue bar pop up, return to lighter water as fast as you can. Depth is not an issue in this, so staying at the top of the water won't help.

FLIGHT PATHS

Using flight paths is the most common means of travel in the game. Flight paths are in every city as well as in most regions. Flight Masters are identified by the winged foot icon on your region map.

To access a new flight path, you must discover the two ends of the path on foot. All character start with access to the flight point in their home city. However, you won't be able to use that flight point until you discover another destination attached to it.

Each time you enter a new region or town, look for the flight point using the tracker in your mini-map. Right-clicking on the Flight Master with a green exclamation point gets you the flight point. Right-clicking on him again opens a map that shows you where you can fly. Click on your destination, and you're on your way immediately.

Most flight paths are specific to Alliance or Horde, and each faction flies on different types of beasts. There is a modest fee each time you fly. When you think about it, flying saves you money. The cost of the flight doesn't compare with the money you make questing and killing enemies in the time you've just saved!

Flying is one of the coolest features of the game. You can use your mouse look around you while flying, because you can't fall off a flying mount. This isn't true once you have your own mounts, but that's a different issue.

FACTION-SPECIFIC TRAVEL METHODS

Alliance Ships

Ships are designed for cross-continent travel. Most ship paths are for Alliance destinations, though the path betwen Booty Bay and Ratchet is available to both Horde and Alliance.

Unlike flight paths, there's no need to "discover" a ship path. Simply go to the harbor, find the right dock, and wait for the ship to arrive. Most harbors serve several ships, so you need to speak to the Harbor Master to make sure you're getting on the right one. You may have to wait a few minutes for the ship to arrive, so talk to people nearby, look at talents and achievements, practice your crafting, or just relax.

There is no fee to for a trip on one of these vessels. If you jump or fall off the boat, you must swim for shore.

Zeppelins: Horde Regions

Zeppelins are also designed for cross-continental travel. All zeppelin paths are for Horde destinations.

Unlike flight paths, there's no need to "discover" a zeppelin path. Simply go to the zeppelin tower, find the right platform, and wait for the zeppelin to arrive. Most zeppelin towers serve several ships, so you need to speak to the Zeppelin Master to make sure you're getting on the right flight. You may need to wait a few minutes for the zeppelin to arrive.

There is no fee to for a zeppelin trip. If you jump off the zeppelin, your character will probably die. That said, people can jump off of the Tirisfal Glade zeppelin without dying. Usually. Just don't jump too soon.

Deeprun Tram

The Deeprun Tram is a commuter trip between Stormwind and Ironforge. The trip is as fast as flying, and it's free. The tram stop in Stormwind is located in the Dwarven District. In Ironforge, it's in Tinker Town.

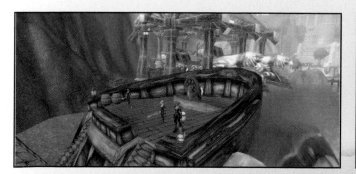

The Silvermoon Portal

A portal connects Silvermoon City and the Undercity. The Undercity portal is located just inside the city walls. The Silvermoon portal is located in Sunfury Spire. This portal is free, but is only for players using the Burning Crusade expansion.

PERSONAL MOUNTS

At Level 20, players earn Apprentice Riding and are eligible to purchase ground mounts. Riding a mount is 60% faster than running. To use a mount after purchasing and learning it, look under your Mounts tab on your character sheet.

You aren't required to use the standard racial mount for your character. By exploring the world, you are likely to find other mounts. Some of these require doing repeated quests to raise your reputation with a given faction, but it's all worthwhile when you want their cool mounts.

Riding is a skill that you only need to train at each tier. Thus, you can have ten mounts and still only need to have trained Riding that first time. The only recurring expense is when you go to buy another type of mount.

There are faster mounts in the game, including epic mounts (that require more intense Riding training) and flying mounts. Flying mounts cost the most, and you won't be able to get involved with those until you're well into expansion content.

RACIAL MOUNT CHOICES

RACE	COMMON MOUNT
Draenei	Elekks
Dwarves	Rams
Gnomes	Mechanostriders
Humans	Horses
Night Elves	Nightsabers
Worgen	None
Blood Elves	Hawkstriders
Goblins	Trikes
Orcs	Wolves
Tauren	Kodos
Trolls	Raptors
Undead	Skeletal Horses

Warlock and Paladin Bonus!

Warlocks and Paladins have special ground mounts that are class specific. Paladin mounts even change depending on your character's race. You get the first mount at level 20, and the second at level 40.

WARLOCK SUMMONS

At Level 42, warlocks learn the Ritual of Summoning. The warlock and two other players can use the spell to summon another player to the warlock from anywhere in the world. This spell is frequently used to bring group members to the same location. Note that the Ritual of Summoning can only be made with everyone being in the same group or raid. This doesn't not work on people outside of your group.

MAGE PORTALS

Mages first learn the ability to Teleport themselves to significant cities. Later, mid-level Mages are able to open Portals that teleport everyone who interacts with them to a specific major city. As Mages level, they learn how to access even more cities (with their race's capital being the first option).

SUMMONING STONES

Dungeons have stones that let people call their groupmates. It only takes two people at the stone to bring everyone else in the group to the proper location. You need to be at an appropriate level for the dungeon at hand; otherwise, this feature will not work.

BANKS AND AUCTION HOUSES

This section discusses your in-game money and how to use banks and auction houses. There's also an introduction to the in-game economy and how to buy and sell items from other players. Making money is not a key focus for new players, but it will become more important to you as you advance in the game.

Trial Limitation

If you are still using the Trial version of the game, you cannot trade items through the Auction House or with other players.

MONEY

You carry your money in your Backpack at all times, and there's an extremely high limit on how much personal gold you can carry. Unless you're approaching a quarter of a million gold, it's not worth worrying about.

At early levels, you won't have much money, so you may be shocked by the cost of many items and what other players are willing to pay. However, the game offers you higher rewards as you complete more difficult quests and as you pursue new ways to earn money.

Here's a quick list of a few ways to earn money:

- Loot the corpses of humanoid enemies.
- Sell off your old Soulbound items or gray items to vendors.
- Sell white & green items directly to other players.
- Sell white & green items through the Auction House.
- Use your profession skills to collect or create items for sale.

You can make the most money using your Professions. Other players may have access to guilds with extensive treasuries, or they might play higher-level characters who are capable of earning hundreds of gold in a single play session. Thus, they're able to pay far more than you for the same amount of work. Use that to your advantage.

BANKS

Each major city has at least one bank. Talk to a city guard for help finding one. Inside are bankers with whom you can interact (right-click). Banks really function as vaults for storing items—not money. Using a bank is a way to free up your bag space and store items that you don't need on a moment-to-moment basis.

When you right-click on a banker, you open your personal vault. The first thing most people notice is that the bank vault is quite large. You have more personal space in there than you would with just your backpack and a few tiny bags. This gets even better!

With a bit of extra money, you can purchase bag slots for your bank vault. These increase in cost dramatically after your first few slots are unlocked, but it's still a wise way to spend money if you're running out of space.

Collect spare bags for the bank vault; taking away ones from your character is foolhardy because it reduces the amount of items you can carry around. Thus, it limits your income from looting and gathering! Always invest in high-quality bags. They pay for themselves better than many alternatives. They also make your life easier.

All banks are linked by their faction. So, even though you deposit your items in one bank, you can access them from any other bank.

GUILD VAULTS

Guilds have their own bank vaults. These groups store money and items to keep them accessible to their guild members. The Guild Master sets a list of permissions that control access to the guild items. Ask members of your guild for details.

AUCTION HOUSES

Auction houses are located in all major cities. Like banks, they are linked by faction. So, you can access the same auctions from any auction house in any city. There are also several neutral auction houses that serve both Horde and Alliance, but you'll need to be around level 40 to reach them.

The Auction Houses in World of Warcraft work very much like real-life online auction sites. You set up a timed auction with a minimum starting price that sells to the highest bidder; you can also set a buyout price that enables players to purchase the item immediately. And, if you find an item you want, you can place a bid or buyout the item immediately.

Right-clicking on any Auctioneer opens the auction interface. It has three tabs: Browse, Bids, and Auctions.

BROWSING

The Browse tab enables you to search through all current auctions. Because there are thousands of available items, you need to use specific criteria to narrow your search.

For example, if you are looking for a low-level healing potion. Type healing potion into the Name box, and hit Enter. The house returns a list of dozens of types of healing potions. If you click on the Lvl arrow, the house orders them by highest level or lowest level first. Hopefully, some Minor Healing Potions are available. If you mouse over the icon for each item, the house tells you exactly what the potion does, so you can confirm it's an item you can use. In addition, the house tells you what you'll be paying per item if you bid or if you buyout the items.

If you don't know the exact name of the item you are looking for, you can use the Filters in the left column to help you search. Insert numbers into the Level Range to control what you're seeing. For instance, a level 12 character looking for new armor might set a level range of 10 to 12. This way that wouldn't have to see anything unequippable or low end.

Clicking the Usable Items option ensures that you only see items that your character can use right now.

Bids

To make a bid, click on the item you want, enter your bid below, and click bid. You won't need to stay online for your bid to remain active. Auctions can last for a very long time, so it's a good idea to go off and do other things. The Auction House mails you your items if you win the bid, so the system is quite simple.

The Bids Tab enables you to keep tabs on the status of these auctions. If you are outbid while you are online, you receive a message in your General chat log. If you've been offline for a while, check the status of these sales by opening the Bids Tab. If someone else is the highest bidder, their name appears in red. This gives you an opportunity to bid again if you wish.

Buyout

Using the buyout option works the same way except that you must meet the buyout price. Like other online options, the benefit is that you get the item right away, but you are likely to pay more when using this option.

Because it's final, the game asks you to confirm payment. Click Accept. As soon as the transaction is complete, you receive a mail flag on your mini-map, indicating that your auction item is already in your mailbox. Retrieve it as you would regular mail.

It's rare not to have a good reason to post items and give a buyout price. Sure, the sky is the limit when people are bidding against each other, but who knows if their bidding war will ever have enough time to meet the maximum value that one of the players would have paid.

Instead, figure out the best prices for your items and go for the throat. People get quite eager for the items they want, and having instant gratification at their fingertips is worth in-game money to them.

When you're uncertain of proper pricing, use the auction house itself or research the item online to see what it's selling for elsewhere. To search locally, act as if you're shopping for the exact item that you're about to sell. Type the item's name into the first page of the auction house and search for it. Undercut your competition by offering the item for a tiny bit less (a single gold, or maybe even a few silver). Either way puts your item above theirs when players search for it!

AUCTIONS

To create an auction of your own, use the Auctions Tab. Start by left-clicking and dragging the designated item into the Auction Item slot. By default, the game enters a common Starting Price for the item. The given starting price may or may not work for your purposes, so feel free to change it. You can also change the duration of the auction and include a Buyout price. Notice the deposit fee. This goes to the auction house, and you cannot get it back. Once you've set up the parameters, click Create Auction.

The item appears as an auction listing for your character. Regardless of whether your item sells, you don't have to do anything more. If the item sells, you receive confirmation and payment through the mail. If your item doesn't sell, the Auction House mails the item back to you, minus their cut.

Neutral Auction Houses take a much higher cut of your final sale price, so they're brutal for high-end sales. The nice thing about them is that they allow for one of the only means of cross-faction exchanges that aren't fueled by violence. You can arrange for specific sales outside the game and then choose a time and place to meet at a neutral Auction House.

USING THE TRADE CHANNEL

Using the Trade channel to buy and sell is a much less structured way to conduct business. Although the Trade channel is designed to discuss trade, bored players frequently discuss other game topics, world events, player issues, and other trivial matters.

If you can get past the din of the crowd, you can get good feedback about the price or availability of an item, and maybe make a decent purchase or sale. In order to show an item on the Trade channel, you can Shift and left-click the item to make a link of it appear in the channel. To do this, you need to use the command to speak on the channel and then Shift and left-click your item:

/Trade Want to sell <Hold down Shift and left-click the item in question>

ABBREVIATION	WHAT IT MEANS
LF	Looking For
WTB	Want To Buy
WTS	Want To Sell
LFW	Looking For Work (Someone is offering their Professional services)
PST	Please Send tell (Please whisper to them privately to get more information or to haggle)

That way, players can click the link for details. Likewise, if someone posts a link in the channel, you can click it to see the item's stats. You can do this for any sort of item, including one that you are seeking for a quest.

Most players use communication shorthand for buying and selling in the Trade channel. Here are a few of the most common abbreviations:

PROFESSIONS

Professions are additional skills for your character, most of which you can learn starting at level 5. Learning Professions is completely optional, but they add additional layers of interaction (and fun!) to your time in World of Warcraft.

There are two categories of Professions: primary and secondary. Each character can choose only two primary Professions. You can as many secondary Professions as you like. There are no class or race restrictions when it comes to choosing a Profession, but some races enjoy advantages for certain Professions.

Some primary Professions involve your character going into the world and looking for specific types of loot. These are called gathering Professions. You might be hunting for metal, animal skins, or herbs. Other Professions use these materials to create items, and they are known as crafting Professions.

Crafting Professions allow characters to produce items for others to use. You might be making permanent items, such as armor or weapons. You might be invested in short-term goodies, like potions. Crafting Professions require a higher investment in money and time than gathering Professions.

Secondary Professions are specific in what they can do. Though more limited in scope than primary Professions, these are easier to pick up, master, and play around with.

PRIMARY PROFESSIONS

There are 11 primary Professions in the game. If you're interested in a certain Profession after reading the brief introductions that follow, there is more detail about each Profession, starting on page 448.

PROFESSION		TYPE	WHAT IT DOES
Alchemy		Crafting	Make potions/elixirs/flasks
Blacksmithing		Crafting	Craft mail and plate armor/melee weapons
Enchanting		Crafting	Improve equipment
Engineering		Crafting	Create gadgets, ranged weapons, bombs and other toys
Inscription		Crafting	Make Glyphs to augment characters
Jewelcrafting		Crafting	Create rings, trinkets, and gems to improve gear
Leatherworking		Crafting	Craft leather and mail armor/armor kits
Tailoring		Crafting	Craft cloth armor and bags
Herbalism		Gathering	Gather herbs
Mining		Gathering	Gather ore
Skinning		Gathering	Gather animal skins

IMPROVING PROFESSIONS

Practicing the Gathering Professions

To increase your skill in Herbalism, Mining, or Skinning, you must simply perform those gathering tasks again and again. Performing the actual task is just like looting: you right-click on the object. Herbs are found on the ground all over the world. Mining veins are usually along ridges or tucked into valleys. They're also plentiful inside caves. Skins are taken from many normal animals or natural monsters.

Each time you gather an item, your skill increases as shown in your General log. Eventually a given type of object "greys out." This means that you can't get points from them anymore (you can still gather them, though). You can tell this because the tag below the object appears in grey instead of green, yellow, orange, or red.

Items shown in red are too high to use. If you try to harvest it, the game lets you know what skill level you need to achieve to harvest the item. Raise your skill in that Profession and they will eventually be accessible.

Practicing the Crafting Professions

To practice the non-gathering Professions, click on the that Profession's icon from your Spellbook or your Action Bar. This opens a window that lists all the recipes you currently know in that Profession. Clicking on the individual recipe shows you all the ingredients required.

If you have all of the required ingredients, the number of times you can use that recipe is indicated beside the name. To make an item, click on the recipe to highlight it, input the number you want, and click Create. Your character automatically cycles through all of the creations in the queue, and you get any points gained in the process.

CRAFTING PROFESSIONS

ALCHEMY

Alchemists use herbs and oils to create potions, elixirs, and flasks with such effects as healing, mana regeneration, invisibility, speed, underwater breathing, and increased strength.

BLACKSMITHING

Blacksmithing uses metal bars to create weaponry and both mail and plate armor. Blacksmiths need a Blacksmithing Hammer and access to an anvil to create items. Many merchants have crafting items, and any of these will sell your character a Blacksmithing Hammer for a trivial amount of money. Anvils are found in most towns and in all cities.

ENCHANTING

Enchanting uses magic recipes to permanently enhance armor and weapons with improvements such as increased stats or resistance to magic. Enchantments require magical ingredients that result from Disenchanting other items. This is a rare case where a crafting Profession is also its own gathering Profession.

Enchanting is a difficult profession for a new player to skill up easily. Guilds often offer the support a person needs to become a higher-level Enchanter without crippling themselves financially.

ENGINEERING

Engineering uses metal and stones to create a variety of useful and fun items, such as goggles, explosives, ranged weapon scopes, bombs, and mechanical animals. Creating different items with Engineering requires a handful of tools, most of which are created by the Engineer. One exception is a Blacksmithing Hammer, which is required for the creation of many Engineering items.

INSCRIPTION

Scribes create glyphs, scrolls, cards, and other paper and book items. Glyphs are class-specific recipes that enhance characters' abilities. At beginning levels, scribes need a Virtuoso Inking Set, herbs, and parchments. To create inks, scribes automatically learn Milling, which turns herbs into inks.

JEWELCRAFTING

Scribes create glyphs, scrolls, cards, and other paper and book items. Glyphs are class-specific recipes that enhance characters' abilities. At beginning levels, scribes need a Virtuoso Inking Set, herbs, and parchments. To create inks, scribes automatically learn Milling, which turns herbs into inks.

At higher levels of Jewelcrafting, you create gems that are slotted into higher-tier equipment. Anything that has red, yellow, blue, or meta slots is letting you know that there are empty spaces for gems there. Jewelcrafters take gems found with metal veins or gained through Prospecting and cut them into finished items that convey various bonuses.

LEATHERWORKING

Leatherworking uses hides and skins to create leather armor, armor kits, and a few other items. Many early Leatherworking items require you to purchase materials from Trade vendors, but you won't need to worry about any required tools for making items.

TAILORING

Tailoring is the weaving and sewing of cloth into armor, shirts, bags, and other items. Cloth is available only as loot drops from humanoid enemies.

GATHERING PROFESSIONS

HERBALISM

Herbalism is the harvesting of herbs from plants. Herbs also occasionally drop from enemies and some enemies can be harvested once they are killed (usually ones that are affiliated with nature).

MINING

Mining is the collection of minerals and ore from natural deposits all over Azeroth. Mining is simple and inexpensive, as the only tool required is a Mining Pick (there are a few weapons that also serve as a mining pick, so read their descriptions carefully). Metal is most often found in hilly or mountainous regions.

SKINNING

Skinning is the act of removing leather and hides from animal corpses. Skinning is simple, inexpensive, and requires only a Skinning Knife. Mousing over an enemy corpse indicates whether it is "skinnable." You can skin your own kills after looting them. In addition, you can skin other people's kills if they loot their targets and leave. It's good to wait a second before doing this in case the other person is also a Skinner and is planning on coming back. You don't want to steal anyone else's work!

SECONDARY PROFESSIONS

There are four secondary Professions in the game, and you can acquire as many of them as you wish. There is no reason not to take all four and to raise them whenever you have the time to spare.

ARCHEOLOGY

Archeology allows players to recover fragments of artifacts from various parts of the world. You turn on artifact tracking (which can be used in concert with tracking for other gathering Professions). Look for special areas within each region and use Surveying to uncover the fragments that are assembled into finished pieces.

COOKING

Cooking uses many of the ingredients you receive as loot to create food for you and your comrades. Certain recipes create food that includes temporary buffs, such as Well Fed, which increases your character's stats.

FIRST AID

First Aid enables you to create bandages for restoring health and antidotes to remove poison. First Aid is most valuable for classes without a healing ability, but everyone benefits from First Aid. Healers can use bandages for times when they're out of mana or are silenced. Bandages are created from cloth drops in the game.

FISHING

With Fishing, you catch fish and you may also catch other marine life, junk, or treasure. To fish, you need a Fishing Pole. Fish are found in any sufficiently deep pool of water (even inside the major cities!) and many types of fish are often found in schools.

CUSTOMIZING THE GAME INTERFACE

After playing the game for a while, you may want to adjust some of the options in the game interface to make certain functions faster or more convenient for you.

The World of Warcraft interface is highly adjustable, so this chapter doesn't try to cover every way in which you can customize the game. Instead, it lists some commonly used options that may be helpful to new players.

Using Auto Loot

Instead of manually clicking on every piece of loot to send it to your Backpack, you can auto-loot your corpses, which is much faster:

1. Press Esc to open the Options menu.

2. Click Interface, and click Controls.

3. Change the Auto Loot options as you see fit.

4. Click Okay when you're done.

In the Auto Loot options, you have several choices. If you check Auto Loot, you only need to right-click to automatically send all loot to your Backpack. The other options are better if you'd like to peruse loot more thoroughly before grabbing any of it.

Open & Close Bags Quickly

Shift+B = Open all bags simultaneously.

Press B = Close all bags simultaneously.

F12 = Open Backpack.

F8, F9, F10, F11 = Use to open other bags individually.

Change the Resolution of Your Monitor

1. Press Esc to open the Options Menu.

2. Click Video, and click Resolution.

3. Under the Resolution options, click the right one for your monitor.

4. Click Okay.

If the game isn't running quickly enough for your tastes, this is the single fastest way to improve the situation. Lower your resolution and see if that helps the situation.

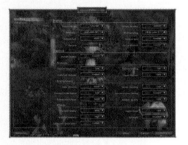

There are also many other graphical options as well. Try changing these to make the game faster or more attractive. There Overall Quality selection is quite strong. If you don't know what everything else does, play around with the Overall Quality specifically until you have speeds that suit your interests.

When in doubt, speed is better than graphical quality. Jitters, poor frame rates, and other problems with speed are insidious. They can ruin your gaming experience without it even being obvious that they are at fault.

Turn Off Beginner Tutorials

1. Press Esc to open the Options menu.

2. Click Interface, and click Help.

3. Unclick Tutorials.

4. Click Okay.

This kills the pop-ups that dominate the early experience with the game. You can turn these off if you feel comfortable with World of Warcraft.

If the pop-ups are something you want and that you'd like to see again, you can reset them here, and the game will act like you're coming back for the first time.

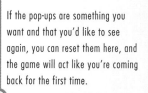

Auto Self Cast

By selecting this, you tell the game to cast positive spells on your character unless you have another, allied character targeted first. Thus, you can heal yourself even during a fight without having to stop, select yourself, and then cast the spell or cast the spell and hit F1. This way is faster than either of those alternatives.

1. Press Esc to open the Options Menu.

2. Click Interface, and click Combat.

3. Check Auto Self Cast.

4. Click Okay.

When grouping, you may want to turn off this option to avoid mistakes, or you can check the Alt key, which enables you to self-cast by pressing Alt while clicking on a spell in your action bar.

Display Action Bars

Instead of accessing other Action Bars by pressing Shift+2, Shift+3, Shift+4, Shift+5, and Shift+6, you can permanently display other Action Bars on your screen:

1. Press Esc to open the Options menu.

2. Click Interface, and click ActionBars.

3. You have the option to display as many as four additional action bars in different places on-screen.

4. Click Okay.

Right Bar corresponds to action bar 3.

Right Bar 2 corresponds to action bar action bar 4.

Bottom Right Bar corresponds to action bar 5.

Bottom Left Bar corresponds to action bar 6.

Though at first your screen seems somewhat more cluttered to have these up all the time, you soon find that it's a gift from the heavens. Having all your abilities onscreen at all times ensures that you know how all of your cooldowns are going! It's also wonderful for crafting; you can set your Profession abilities off to one side, away from your regular combat abilities, but still have access to them when you need them.

Access Action Bars

Shift+1 = Action bar 1 Shift+4 = Action bar 4

Shift+2 = Action bar 2 Shift+5 = Action bar 5

Shift+3 = Action bar 3 Shift+3 = Action bar 3

Once you know where your action are located, this is much faster than switching through multiple Action Bars to get where you need. Jumping from bar one to bar five is just as easy to going from one to two! In addition, keyboard shortcuts are almost always superior to using mouse commands on the interface.

Display Cast Bars for Targets

This option shows the channeling bars for enemy casters. Watching this may help you interrupt their timed spells (although if you see a gray shield on the cast bar, you can't interrupt the spell). It lets you see when to use your interruption abilities. Time those attacks so that the enemies waste effort on a spell only to have it countered at the last possible moment. This is toggled on by default.

1. Press Esc to open the Options Menu.

2. Click Interface, and click Combat.

3. Check Cast Bars On Targets.

4. Click Okay.

Using Key Bindings

The Key Bindings option serves two purposes:
A reminder of shortcut keys already in the game.

You can map your own shortcuts keys, if you wish.

1. Press Esc to open the Options Menu.

2. Click Key Bindings. A scrollable window opens, indicating all the keys that already have shortcuts listed in white. Any key that is not already bound to an action is listed in yellow.

3. To set up a new shortcut, click the Command you want to tie to a specific key. For example, all the bag slots have an F-key shortcut, but the Keyring slot does not. Scroll down to Interface Panel Functions, and click Toggle Keyring.

4. Then choose the key you want to bind it to, such as F7 in this case.

5. Click Okay.

These bindings aren't limited to your keyboard! You can assign functions to your mouse or other input devices as well.

Customize Chat Logs

There are thousands of tiny changes you can make to the way your chat system presents information. Right-click on your chat window's tabs to begin this process. You can change the size of the font. You can define which colors appear from any source of information. You can also change the background color and intensity of the window itself. This is extremely useful for people who have trouble reading the text; darken the window to make it clearer all the time instead of needing to highlight it when you want to read.

Play around with this system as much as you want. You can't really break anything. If the windows end up being too strange, simply "reset" them from the same menu and they're back where they started.

Combat Text Options

You can change the Combat Text options so that you see more on-screen text showing what's happening during combat:

1. Press Esc to open the Options Menu.

2. Click Interface, and click Floating Combat Text.

3. Check Damage to see the damage you deal, and check any other options you wish to see during combat.

Reactive Spells & Abilities is a good reminder for new players of when specific spells are ready.

You may need to experiment to see which items help you and which get in your way.

4. Click Okay.

OTHER SHORTCUTS

COMMAND	EFFECT
Press X	Sit or Stand
Press Z	Unsheathe or Sheathe Your Weapon(s)
Shift+P	Open Window for All Pets
Press V	Show red nameplate and health bar directly over your target in combat
Right-click a buff	Remove any positive buff on self

COMMAND	EFFECT
Shift+I	Open Pet's Spellbook
Esc	Close an open window
Alt+Z	Turn Off Game Interface
PrintScreen	Capture Screenshot (Screenshots are automatically saved in the World of Warcraft/Screenshots directory.)

MACROS

The base game already has a million options to consider, but you might want even more once you understand everything. The Macro system is in place to help you find the perfect WoW experience.

Macros let you trigger abilities in a more complex manner. You have access to any command in the game through this, and you can even chain multiple commands together. This system is found inside your Options menu. Hit the Escape key and select Macros to see what it's all about.

Making a Macro

You can make character-specific Macros or you can make ones that are available to all characters on your account. There are thousands of ideas floating around for good Macros, so one of the best to find these is to hunt around class message boards and see what other people have made.

You can also fool on your own. Click New, select an icon for your Macro and a name for it, and then type in commands. When you're done, drag the Macro onto a valid action bar slot and then you can use the Macro like any normal ability.

Standard slash commands work just fine in Macros. For example: /say /party /dance /flirt

However, you can also use commands that you wouldn't normally type in. /cast is the most common one. This lets you trigger abilities through the Macro system!

Think of the uses for this! Imagine that you're a Rogue that is about to Sap a target. You want everyone in the group to know that you're doing this. Try the following Macro.

> /cast sap

> /p Sapping %t

This Macro uses Sap on the target you currently have selected. It then displays for your group that you are Sapping the monster (and the actual name of that monster will be displayed).

To avoid having to type in ability names, open your Spellbook and shift + left-click the ability while your Macro is open. This automatically fills in the /cast part of the Macro with the ability in question. It's that easy.

You might wonder, "Will this work with items too?"

Try it! Shift-click an item in your backpack or bags while the Macro system is open. The command that appears is /use, but, yes, this works just like the cast system. You can have a Macro trigger your goodies, so long as you have them in your possession when you use the Macro.

This is only the tip of the iceberg with Macros. Now that you know what to look for, you're bound to find a wealth of awesome ideas that are specific to your class or playstyle.

This chapter lists many of the "extras" that you can do in World of Warcraft. Some of these activities will get you in-game rewards, but most are for fun and socializing.

GET A HAIRCUT

Several major cities offer Barbershop services. All races and genders have the option for a makeover for a small fee. Features you can change include hair color, hair style, facial hair, horns, piercings, tattoos, and undead parts.

SOCIALIZE

There are always other players with whom you can chat, exchange items, inspect their gear, or check out their pets and mounts.

USE TRAINING DUMMIES

Training Dummies are mechanical NPCs that you can use for target practice. You can find training dummies of different levels in all major cities.

SEND PEOPLE GIFTS

If you want to remember a friend's birthday or send a player a thank you gift, here are some fun items you can purchase:

Fireworks in Ironforge

Wine & Flowers in Stormwind

Flowers in Thunder Bluff

COLLECT COMPANION PETS

Companion pets, as opposed to hunter pets, are available to all classes in the game. For the most part, companion pets have no effect on gameplay, though you do get Achievements as you collect more and more of them. Pets follow you everywhere you go, but only one can accompany you at a time. You can collect companion pets in a variety of ways—from purchasing them outright to gaining them as quest rewards.

Here are the general locations for some of the most easily obtainable pets.

Engineers are able to craft their own pets, and you can find ever more buddies by completing holiday events, Achivements, or by searching for enemies that drop pets on rare occasions.

COMMON HORDE PETS

PET	LOCATION
Cockroach	Undercity
Snakes	Orgrimmar
Prairie Dog	Thunder Bluff
Dragonhawk Hatchling	Eversong Woods, Fairbreeze Village

COMMON ALLIANCE PETS

PET	LOCATION
Cats	Elwynn Forest, Southeast of Stormwind
Snowshoe Rabbit	Dun Morogh, Amberstill Ranch
Owls	Darnassus
Moths	The Exodar

OTHER PURCHASABLE PETS

PET	LOCATION
Frogs	Darkmoon Faire
Chicken	Shimmering Flats
Birds	Booty Bay, Stranglethorn Vale
Magical Creatures	Stormspire, Netherstorm

CELEBRATE IN-GAME HOLIDAYS

The game offers numerous seasonal holidays with accompanying events, including quests, games, gifts, costumes, and holiday food. Most are week-long holidays that resemble some of our own.

AZEROTH HOLIDAY CALENDAR

JANUARY	NEW YEAR'S DAY
Late Winter	Lunar Festival
February	Love Is in the Air
Spring	Noblegarden
May	Children's Week
June	Midsummer Fire Festival
September	Harvest Festival
September	Pirate's Day
Fall	Brewfest
October	Hallow's End
November	Day of the Dead
November	Pilgrim's Bounty
December	Feast of Winter Veil
December	New Year's Eve

ATTEND IN-GAME EVENTS

Darkmoon Faire is a traveling carnival that appears monthly at a different location in Azeroth. The Faire appears just outside Thunder Bluff in Mulgore and south of Goldshire in Elwynn Forest. The faire offers unique vendors, games, and opportunities for prizes. Players can earn Darkmoon tickets by completing a quest or by bringing requested items to the carnival workers.

The Stranglethorn Fishing Extravaganza is a weekly fishing contest in the Stranglethorn region. This is predominantly a group activity for players who have passed Level 30. When you reach Northrend around level 80, there's another fishing contest run by the Kalu'ak.

The Gurubashi Arena Booty Run is a free-for-all battle experience in Stranglethorn Vale. Go to the arena every three hours when the call goes out throughout the zone. Everyone who attends is flagged for PvP, and the winner gets a prize.

The Call To Arms is a series of weekly Battleground challenges for players interested in PvP combat. The featured Battleground yields more Honor during this period, and there are usually thousands of extra players signing up, meaning that matches are buzzing all day and night.

GO FISHING

You can fish nearly anywhere in the game, depending on your fishing skill. Even the most unlikely bodies of water can yield fish and help increase your skill level. Even fishing in low-level areas will eventually increase your skill.

Bait and lures are available from Trade Supply vendors all over Azeroth. Fishing Trainers will have lures, but they may also have better Fishing Poles that will increase your skill further.

HUNT FOR ACHIEVEMENTS

Darkmoon Faire is a traveling carnival that appears monthly at a different location in Azeroth. The Faire appears just outside Thunder Bluff in Mulgore and south of Goldshire in Elwynn Forest. The faire offers unique vendors, games, and opportunities for prizes. Players can earn Darkmoon tickets by completing a quest or by bringing requested items to the carnival workers.

The Stranglethorn Fishing Extravaganza is a weekly fishing con Achievement hunting is incredibly addictive, especially for a certain type of player. There are people who look through the list each day, pick out a few things to try for, and make it all happen.

And why not? You don't need to wait for the level cap to do this. Sometimes it seems strange to invest time in something that doesn't improve the strength of your character, but is that really important? You can level whenever you want, and it doesn't take that long to hit the cap. Instead, the happiest people seem to be those who set their own goals and have a great time meeting them.

Try this out. You too could become an achievement hunter. test in the Stranglethorn region. This is predominantly a group activity for players who have passed Level 30. When you reach Northrend around level 80, there's another fishing contest run by the Kalu'ak.

The Gurubashi Arena Booty Run is a free-for-all battle experience in Stranglethorn Vale. Go to the arena every three hours when the call goes out throughout the zone. Everyone who attends is flagged for PvP, and the winner gets a prize.

The Call To Arms is a series of weekly Battleground challenges for players interested in PvP combat. The featured Battleground yields more Honor during this period, and there are usually thousands of extra players signing up, meaning that matches are buzzing all day and night.

PLAYER VERSUS PLAYER BATTLES

Up to this point, PVP has been mentioned only in passing. There are two reasons for that. First, PVP generally doesn't get into high gear until you're around level 20. Even on PVP servers, the zones up to level 20 are controlled by one side or the other so you're free to ignore players from the opposite faction as you see fit. Second, PVP is an advanced and incredibly deep topic that is covered later in this guide. However, that doesn't mean PVP is always serious business.

Open World PVP

Sometimes, the most fun in PVP comes from open-world PvP, which offers some of the best and most interesting fights in the game. There isn't a limit on numbers or sides. There isn't a necessity for fairness or timers. Just form a group or raid, and choose somewhere to attack. Fight, laugh, lose, regroup, and watch as more people join both sides of the engagement. These attacks can last for hours.

"What if I'm on a PvE or RP server?" you ask. That's not a big hindrance. Flag yourself for PvP combat and go into an area with players from the enemy faction. One of them will take the bait, and they'll be flagged afterward, whether you win or lose. Encourage more of your own people to join. More of their will too, and soon it'll be just like a PvP server, for a while at least.

If you're looking for more help, or want to know how to restrict certain aspects of the game so your children can play, try the main website for World of Warcraft (www.worldofwarcraft.com). From the home page, you can choose to visit its many community forums, manage your account (including setting Parental Controls), and get news updates relevant to the game in its current state, and what the World of Warcraft team is working on for future patches and expansions.

COMMUNITY FORUMS

Forums are online bulletin boards where players can ask questions, brag, help other players, and read updates from Blizzard staffers. Using forums is like mining for gold: There's a plenty of valuable information in forums, but you must wade through many random topics to find it.

Some of the most helpful forums for new players are Class, Realm, Profession Discussion, and Quest Discussion. With some patience, you should find a great deal of help that should help you

Bug Report Forum
Found a bug in the game? Help us squash it by reporting it here!

Mac Technical Support
If you are experiencing problems installing or patching World of Warcraft, connecting to the realms or are crashing during game play, and you are using a Macintosh computer, post here for assistance.

Blizzard Archive
An archive of official Blizzard responses to various topics related to World of Warcraft.

AUTHENTICATOR

If you're worried about your account being compromised, Blizzard offers another layer of protection from unauthorized access. A Blizzard Authenticator is an additional layer of security for your Battle.net account. There are multiple types of Authenticators, but they all provide the same security.

The Battle.net Authenticator provides you with a unique, one-time code to use in addition to your regular password. For more information, click on Account Security on the main World of Warcraft website.

PARENTAL CONTROLS

Blizzard Entertainment believes that real-world priorities such as homework, chores, and family dinner should take precedence over entertainment. Their Parental Controls provide parents and guardians with easy-to-use tools to set up rules for World of Warcraft play time and manage access to Blizzard Entertainment games in a way that fits your family's situation.

You can set Play-Time Limits, a schedule, and even have weekly reports sent to your e-mail account that provides information about the times your was playing the game, and much more.

REMOTE AUCTION HOUSE

If you have fun "playing the Auction House," you can now access your realm's Auction House from your web browser or mobile device. Anyone can browse the Auction House for free, or subscribe to the premium service which allows you to bid on and buy out auctions with real-time results, create auctions from items in your bags, bank, or mailbox, and collect gold earned in your auctions.

CHARACTER SERVICES

If you want to change something about your character (and a trip to a barber in one of the major cities won't do the trick), Blizzard offers other options to you. Before you decide to use any of the following services, read the helpful FAQs on Blizzard's website for more information.

PAID SERVICES

Each Character Service has a cost associated with it. For more information about fees, visit www.worldofwarcraft.com.

 ## Appearance Change

Apperance Change, or Character Re-Customiation, is an option inherent in Faction and Race Changes, but if you want to change your character model or gender (remember, you can change your character's look with a visit to the barber shop!) without changing your character's race, select Appearance Change. This service lets you change your character's gender, face, hair and skin color, hairstyle, name, and other cosmetic features determined by their race and gender combination.

 ## Character Transfer

There are two types of character transfers. If you start on one realm, but find that you have friends playing on another realm, you have the option to transfer a character to the other realm. In rare instances, usually when a realm's population grows too large, you may be able to transfer a character at no charge. The second type of character transfer involves a move between World of Warcraft accounts. There are many restrictions for this type of transfer.

 ## Faction Change

If you want to see what life is like on the other side, you can change your character's faction from Horde to Alliance, or Alliance to Horde. As a part of the Faction Change, you must select a new race and customize your character's look.

 ## Name Change

Changing your character's name is an option included in some of the other services, but if your character's name is the only thing you wish to change, this service is the one you should choose.

 ## Race Change

If you want to try out a new race which is a part of your current faction, select the Race Change option. The full range of customization options offered by the Character Re-Customization service is included as well.

THE BLIZZARD STORE

The Blizzard Store offers a few items for sale that appear in World of Warcraft. Currently, you can buy a number of vanity pets, and one special mount known as the Celestial Steed.

ARMORY

The World of Warcraft Armory is a great way to learn more about improving your character. You can look up any active characters on the Armory and see what equipment they use, how they spend their talent points, where you can find upgrades for your gear, and so on. Visit the Armory at www.wowarmory.com for more information.

FIND ADDITIONAL RESOURCES

BradyGames strategy guides are a great source for information and fun ideas, but WoW is too big to put into any single book or even a group of books. There are thousands and thousands of sites with WoW information. Beyond the main forums for the game there are guild sites, fan sites, and millions of individual players to talk to.

Don't play this like it's a solo game. It isn't! There are so many knowledgeable people out there, and enjoy sharing their ideas. Talk to people in game. Read the forums. Look up Macros, tactics, questions, and answers as well. If you want to know what to craft or where to find a reagent, entire recipe lists are available. If you have trouble with a quest, don't drop it. Find out if other people have had trouble to. Go online and search with the exact quest name. Pretty much every single quest will pop up something, and usually there is information there that helps you get around problems.

Be eager in your quest for knowledge. None of the best players on your server got there by themselves. It's impossible to know everything about every class and situation. Even people who only play one class are bound to miss a few ideas.

GLOSSARY

The following is a list of important in-game terms and abbreviations. Not all of these are official terms used by Blizzard, but there's a good chance you'll see them used by other players fairly often. You don't need to memorize this list, but it's a handy reference in case you encounter an unfamiliar word or phrase.

A–E

Add — An extra monster that has joined an existing battle.

Alt — A character on your account other than your main character. A secondary character.

AoE or AE — Area of Effect. Often used to talk about abilities that damage enemies in groups.

AFK — Away From Keyboard. Used to show that the player isn't at their computer. When you see a character's name preceded by <Away>, that person is not actively playing the game.

Aggro — A monster's aggressive attention. "That Orc is aggroing on you. Look out!"

Aggro Radius — The radius around the monsters that determines their aggression. You will be attacked if you step within their aggro radius.

AGI — Agility. A character statistic that controls defensive aspects of play and damage for some classes.

AH — Auction House. A place where items are bought and sold between players.

Avatar — Your character and, thus, your representation in the game.

BG — Battleground. This is a place for organized PvP combat.

Buff — A beneficial spell cast on a player or monster.

Caster — A character or monster that uses spells, often at range.

Cheese — To exploit an imbalance in the game.

Combat Pets — A creature controlled by a player that assists during combat.

Creep — An older gaming term for a monster

Critters — Creatures that aren't a threat to a player. These include deer, bunnies, and other fauna that won't aggro on anyone.

Crowd Control (CC) — Any ability that temporarily removes an enemy from a battle. Examples are Sap, Polymorph, and Hex.

DD — Direct Damage. This is a spell that does all of its damage in one hit rather than spreading its damage over time.

Detaunt — Related to aggro. Abilities of this type throw aggro off of a character and force it onto someone/something else.

DMG — Short for damage.

DoT — Damage Over Time. This often refers to an effect that "ticks" every few seconds, applying damage each time there is a tick.

DPS — Damage Per Second. This is a concept that is used to universally evaluate weapons and spells of different speeds.

Debuff — A negative spell cast on a unit that makes it less powerful.

Elite — Monsters with a gold dragon around their icons are elite; they have more health, greater damage output, and sometimes have special abilities.

Experience (XP/EXP) — A stat that rises from exploring, killing monsters, and completing quests. Each tier of experience grants characters a higher level and, thus, more power.

F–L

FH — Full Health.

FM — Full Mana.

FTL — For The Lose or For The Loss. An Internet or sports term that implies that a strategy, concept, or action is weak.

FTW — For The Win. This means that something is powerful or useful.

Gank — To grossly overpower a target and exploit (or decimate) it. "I was fighting a monster and a level 85 Rogue ganked me."

GG — Good Game. Most often used after a battleground or arena match to thank other players for contributing or when someone is about to log off.

GM — Game Master. Someone employed by Blizzard Entertainment to assist and help players.

Griefer — A person who purposely tries to annoy or anger other players.

Grinding — To repeat any activity to achieve a conclusion through sheer investment of time. "I'll keep fighting these Boars to grind out this level." or "I'm grinding reputation with Orgrimmar."

Group — A team of up to five characters that join together to take on a dungeon or a particularly tricky quest.

Hate — See **Threat**.

HP — Hit Points or Health. This is a measure of a character's survivability.

Incoming (INC) — This means an attack is imminent.

Instancing — A copy of an area that is only shared by a specific group. The world is not instanced. Dungeons, raids, and battlegrounds have many copies. These are instances.

INT — Intellect. A character statistic that controls the amount of Mana and efficacy of spells.

Kiting — A style of combat in which a player continually stays out of the combat range of an enemy, usually by running away from it, while simultaneously causing damage to it.

KOS — Kill on Sight. Some NPCs will rush forward and attack players of a different faction the moment they see them. Example: Alliance guards toward Horde players.

KS — Kill Steal. Attempting to hit a monster and thus ensure that you or your group gets to loot it even though another person/group is about to attack the same target.

LFG — Looking For a Group.

LFM — Looking For More. This implies than an existing group has open slots and wants to get more people before starting a quest/dungeon run.

Log — When you log off; disconnect from the game.

LOL — Laughing Out Loud. An Internet term expressing humor.

LOM — Low on Mana. This is a warning from casters that they don't have much healing or damage left to contribute to a fight.

LOS — Line of Sight. Often used as a warning. "Break LOS" means that you should get your character behind cover to avoid a target's attention or attacks.

Loot — To take the treasure from a monster that has been killed or from a chest. The term also refers to the treasure gained in this action.

LVL — Level. A measure of a character's power.

Mez — Short for "Mesmerize." Refers to spells, such as Polymorph, that temporarily incapacitate a target. This is an older gaming term.

MMORPG — Massive Multiplayer Online Role-Playing Game

Mob — An old programming acronym of "Mobile Object Block." Mobs are computer-controlled characters (usually monsters) in the game.

MOG — Massive Online Game

Mount — A summoned, rideable creature. Ground mounts are available early in the game and can be ridden around many areas. Flying mounts are gained at higher level, and they allow players to soar above the world. All of these increase player speed.

MA — Main Assist. A member of a group assigned to select the target for the damage dealers in a group to attack at the same time.

MT — Main Tank. A member of a group that protects the others by holding the monster's attention (their "aggro").

Named — A special monster that is usually stronger than surrounding monsters, with possible special abilities and item drops.

NBG — Need Before Greed. This is a loot system. With this set, only people that need an item as an upgrade will roll dice to see who gets it.

Nerf — To downgrade, to be made softer, or make less effective.

Newbie — A new player.

Newb/Noob — Short for Newbie, but more often used as a pejorative.

Ninja — To try to loot an item without other players knowing or paying attention. Such actions are considered extremely rude.

NP — No Problem.

NPC — An in-game person that is controlled by the server, such as a quest giver.

OOM — Out of Mana. This marks the end of healing or damage output from a caster.

Pat — A patrolling monster. This may be issued as a warning that said creature is coming your way. "PAT!"

PC — Player-controlled Character.

Pet — A creature (NPC) controlled by a player such as a Wolf, Infernal, and so on. Non-combat pets, like kittens or penguins, do not affect combat but are instead summoned to add flavor to a character.

PK — Player Kill or a Player Killer. More of a term for open-world PvP interactions.

POP/Repop — Contraction of "Repopulation." This is a warning that monsters are returning to an area after being slain.

Proc — An effect that is randomly triggered from time to time based on another action taken by a character.

PST — Please Send Tell. Indicates that the person wants to hear back regarding a certain sale or issue.

Puller — A character that pulls monsters for the party, controlling the way a battle initiates.

Pulling — The act of heading out, getting aggro from a monster, and bringing the fight back to a party.

PvE — Player vs. Environment. Combat between players and computer-controlled opponents.

PvP — Player vs. Player. Competition between players that can be as small as a duel or as large as 80 or more players.

Raid — A congregation of player groups that bands together for extremely challenging content or PvP situations.

Res/Rez — Short for "Resurrect." This refers to any spell or ability that can bring a character back to life. "I need a rez. I went AFK and something killed me."

Respawn — The same as "**Pop/Repop.**" A monster can return to the world after being killed. The act of returning is called respawning. The creature itself may also be referred to as a respawn.

Rest — Characters accrue rested bonus while their player is out of the game. This happens when someone logs their character out while inside an inn or within the boundaries of a city. This adds bonus experience during subsequent play.

Roll — This means that you should roll a random number to determine who has the right to get an item. For example: /random 100 generates a number between 1 and 100. The highest roll would win something.

Root — To trap a target in place using a spell or ability.

RP — Role Play. To interact with the game and players as though you are your character, as though you are in a theatre performance.

RPing — Role Playing. See "**RP**."

Shard — Soul Shard. Warlock items that influence their ability to cast certain spells. These are gained by stealing the souls of their victims.

SPI — Spirit. A character statistic that influences mana regeneration.

STA — Stamina. A character statstic that determines the health (HP) of a character.

Stack — A number of identical items placed in a single inventory slot to conserve space. Only certain items can be stacked.

STR — Strength. A character statistic that influences damage for many melee characters.

Tank — A character that takes damage and holds monsters' attention to protect others.

Tap — The first point of damage a monster takes locks its future loot to the character that dealt said damage. This act is called tapping. Creatures that are tapped have their bars go grey so other people know not to mess with them.

Taunt — Related to aggro. Abilities of this type pull aggro off of a target and bring it back to a tank.

Threat — This measures how much a monster wants to kill each member of a group engaged in a fight. The person with the highest threat usually keeps the monster's aggro.

Train — Visiting your class trainer to learn new abilities.

Twink — A low-level character with the best gear, often because of guild assistance or money/gear sent down by a higher-level character played by the same person.

TY — Thank You.

Uber — German slang for "super." This is a common gamer term for something that is impressive.

Vendor Trash — An item that only a vendor/merchant would buy.

WoW — World of Warcraft.

WTB — Want to Buy. Shorthand for saying that someone is looking to purchase something, often listing their intentions afterward.

WTS — Want to Sell. Shorthand for saying that someone has something to sell, often listing their goods afterward.

YW — You're Welcome.

CHOOSING YOUR CHARACTER'S RACE

There are 12 races in the game: six for the Alliance and six for the Horde. Keep in mind that each race has limitations on available classes.

Each race has innate benefits (known as Racial Abilities) that are unique to that race. These are abilities you have in addition to what you get from choosing your class.

FACTIONS

The race you choose determines whether you will be part of the Alliance or the Horde. If you have friends in the game with whom you want to play, you need to choose the same faction if you want to work together in the game. There are no "good" or "bad" sides in this conflict. Both factions have rich storylines and compelling motives.

Horde Races

Though their ways are sometimes brutal and warlike, some of the leaders of the Horde exemplify honor and courage. The various races of the Horde have struggled to free themselves from demonic tyranny, a mindless plague, and countless wars.

Alliance Races

The Alliance gives the appearance of being on the side of righteousness and many of its leaders are good people. However, they are also the source of hypocrisy and considerable lawlessness. The destruction left behind by the Gnomes' scientific mistakes, Dwarven civil wars, and Human misconduct have scarred much of the Eastern Kingdoms.

STARTING OUT WITH FRIENDS

Each race has its own home region, so the race you choose determines where you start in the game. If you and a friend want to start the game together, you must choose the same race so that you start at the same location.

If you and your friend can't agree on the same race, it won't take long to reach the major hubs of the game where you can join up. As a result, it's best to play the exact character you want, even if it means waiting to see your buddies a little bit longer.

The Most Important Factor

It's not uncommon to see that one race might be better suited to the class that you've chosen compared with another, but what if that isn't the race that you had your heart set on? The best thing to do is ignore Racial Abilities if you have any strong preference for a specific race. Bonding with your character is a real thing. Choosing a race that you don't want to play is something that grates on you over time. Don't let that happen. Enjoy your time in the game. In the end, stats aren't a big deal; you won't flounder just because you picked a "weaker" race to go with your class. None of the races are especially overpowered or underpowered. Their bonuses are more of a tiny perk. They help, but they never make or break a class.

DRAENEI

The Draenei are an intelligent and spiritual race who no longer have a homeworld of their own. They fled both their home planet of Argus and then Outland as well. The Legion, a force of horrible evil, has dogged their efforts at every turn. Currently, the Draenei have crash landed on Azeroth in their capital ship (*The Exodar*). Though their ship's engines have been sabotaged, they are ready and willing to continue the battle against evil.

Draenei are dedicated to magic and Holy Light. The Draenei also have a spiritual affinity with the Naaru, energy beings who serve the Holy Light.

Draenei are 7–8 feet tall, with long tails and bipedal hooves. Females have horns of varying shapes and sizes. Males have unique cranial and facial features.

Start location: Ammen Vale in Azuremyst Isle.

Home city: The Exodar.

RACIAL ABILITIES

GEMCUTTING
Jewelcrafting skill (a crafting Profession) increased by 10.

GIFT OF THE NAARU
An ability that restores health to any friendly target.

HEROIC PRESENCE
Draenei are more likely to hit targets with their attacks and spells.

SHADOW RESISTANCE
Shadow spells are less likely to hit a Draenei.

Elekks, the Draenei Racial Mount.

AVAILABLE CLASSES

DEATH KNIGHT | DRUID | HUNTER | MAGE | PALADIN | PRIEST | ROGUE | SHAMAN | WARLOCK | WARRIOR

DRAENEI

Despite being a peaceful race that believes in following the Light, the Draenei had long known little else besides war and hiding when they decided to flee in *The Exodar*, hoping to find new allies to fight beside them against the Burning Legion. With the crash of the great ship, it seemed that all hope was lost. However, the Draenei emerged from the wreckage to find themselves on a remote group of islands off the western coast of Kalimdor. Claiming this mostly unpopulated land as their new home, the Draenei soon explored and established camps over Azuremyst and Bloodmyst Isles. Though you are inexperienced, it is up to you to help your people as best you can. Your path may one day take you across the world, for now your duty begins with securing the safety of your new home.

1	Megelon
2	The Crash Site
3	Ammen Fields
4	Silverline Lake
5	Nestlewood Hills
6	Tolaan
7	Aeun
8	Azure Watch

CRASH SITE

As you come back to consciousness, Megelon is glad to see that **You Survived** the crash while so many did not. He sends you to speak with Proenitus who is waiting for you at the bottom of the hill.

With all the injured from the crash, the Draenei supply of healing crystals is quickly becoming depleted. The only local substitute is the blood of the indigenous vale moths. Proenitus needs your help with **Replenishing the Healing Crystals**. He asks you to bring him vials of this precious blood so the healing can continue. The Vale Moths are found all around the Crash Site, in almost any direction.

Gift of the Naaru

All Draenei have this ability. It heals your target over time and the amount you heal for increases as your attack or spell power increases. While the Gift of the Naaru can't compare with regular healing spells, it is a great boon when you need a bit of extra healing during a fight or to get you ready for the next battle more quickly.

Once you have fulfilled this task, return to the Crash Site. After delivering the vials of blood, Proenitus has an **Urgent Delivery**. He needs you to take the bundle of vials to Zalduun inside the Crash Site. Though they are doing what they can for the injured inside the Crash Site, there are also injured survivors spread throughout Ammen Vale. Zalduun asks you to **Rescue the Survivors** by using your Gift of the Naaru ability on one of the Draenei Survivors.

Before taking care of the survivors, stop by Proentius who asks you to speak with **Botanist Taerix**. Walk around to the side of the Crash Site to find her. Taerix asks you to thin out the nearby **Volatile Mutations** before they overrun the camp. To find the Volatile Mutations, look for the purple crystalline fragments of the power core jutting up from the ground. These weird creatures don't stray far from them. While you're out, use Gift of the Naaru on one of the Draenei Survivors. Once you are finished, return to the botanist.

She appreciated your help in thinning out the mutations, but the problem is much more wide spread. To come up with a solution she needs Lasher Samples from the mutated lashers. For now, you must do **What Must Be Done...**

Before gathering the samples, speak with Apprentice Vishael as she has some **Botanical Legwork** she would like you to do as well. She asks you to gather a few of the corrupted flowers and bring them back to her for study. Once you have finished discussing botany, head into the Crash Site and visit with Zalduun to receive your reward for rescuing the Draenei Survivor.

Your Class Trainer

When you return to the Crash Site your trainer is waiting to speak with you. Take the time to learn the valuable skill they want to teach before moving on with your other quests.

Before heading off to complete your tasks, go out the south side of the Crash Site and speak with Technician Zhanaa and Vindicator Aldar. The technician is doing all she can to make repairs to important devices, but after the crash, the local owlkin carried many of the devices away. She needs you to collect Emitter **Spare Parts** from them so she can complete her task.

Though you can't do anything about the Mutated Owlkin, by performing an **Inoculation** of the others you can at least keep them from becoming infected as well. Vindicator Aldar gives you a special inoculum to stave off the mutation.

After completing all these tasks, head west of the Crash Site and into the Ammen Fields. The Mutated Root Lashers that you need to eliminate are in the area. Don't forget to loot the Lasher Samples off of them. The Corrupted Flowers you need grow among the Mutated Root Lashers.

Even though you still have other tasks to perform in the south, return to Botanist Taerix and Apprentice Vishael first. Taerix has another job for you that leads you in the same direction as the spare parts you are seeking.

Botanist Taerix has developed an agent that may help in **Healing the Lake**. This substance neutralizes the power leaking from the irradiated power core. Disperse the Neutralizing Agent at the Irradiated Power Crystal to bring the energy under control.

Now you are ready to head further south. Dive into Silverline Lake and use the Neutralizing Agent near the crystal. Once you are finished look for the Owlkin you need to inoculate on the far side of the lake. Make you way back to Nestlewood Hills, inoculating any Nestlewood Owlkin you come across on your way. Once you go through the cave passageway there are several spare parts for you to pick up. Once you've finished inoculating the owlkin and gathered the spare parts you need, save yourself some walking and use your Hearthstone to quickly return to the Crash Site and collect your rewards.

There have been several reports of unusual activity up on Shadow Ridge and Vindicator Aldar is worried about **The Missing Scout**. He asks you to head to the other side of Silverline Lake to find his scout, Tolaan. Head southwest, around Silverline Lake until you see Tolaan crouched in the grass. Though he is still alive, you can see that he is badly injured. He was ambushed by **The Blood Elves**! Tolaan sends you to kill the Blood Elves on Shadow Ridge before they can threaten the rest of Ammen Vale.

Head up the path behind him to encounter plenty of Blood Elves. They are a little bit more difficult than the foes you've faced so far, but are not aggressive. Just pick them off one at a time until you have satisfied Tolaan's need for vengeance. When you are finished, return to Tolaan to report your success. Though you've made a good start at slaughtering them, Tolaan believes that if you slay the Blood Elves' leader, they may retreat. Travel to the top of Shadow Ridge and kill Surveyor Candress, the **Blood Elf Spy**.

Look for Surveyor Candress in her tent at the top of the ridge. Take her down as you did her minions and don't worry, the Blood Elves near her are oblivious to your attack. Loot her corpse after you finish the fight for the **Blood Elf Plans**. Right click on them and accept the quest they offer. Next, take them to Vindicator Aldar to examine. He is grateful for the job you did and decides to keep an eye out for this potential new threat. In the meantime Zhanaa has finished **The Emitter** and wishes to speak with you.

Great news! The spare parts you recovered really came in handy. The technician was able to repair the Emitter and get in contact with another group of survivors. Zhanaa asks you to **Travel to Azure Watch** and convince them to send aid and supplies to the Crash Site. Speak with Technician Dyvuun once you arrive.

To reach Azure Watch head west across Ammen Vale. As you move towards the river crossing at Ammen Ford you notice an injured Draenei by the side of the road. Aeun was bringing **Word From Azure Watch** when a few mutated beasts jumped him and injured his leg. He asks that you report to Caregiver Chellan in his stead. Continue down the road and across the river to reach Azure Watch.

With the loss of *The Exodar* your people have no choice but to make this their home. Though the land may seem strange at first, its people fight against the same forces the Draenei have often faced. Despite the fact that the crash ended the lives of many Draenei, you have a chance at forging a new home here. Learn well, heed the teachings of Velen and lend your strength to your new allies. May the light long prevail!

DWARF

Dwarves are a hardy people, due no doubt to living for generations in cold regions, frequently in underground fortresses. Masters of stone and ore, Dwarves are equally skilled at building cities and crafting weaponry. Dwarves are treasure seekers, explorers, and courageous fighters.

Dwarves are 4-5 feet tall, stocky, and muscular. Males prize their elaborate beards; females, their decorative hairstyles and piercings.

Start Location: Coldridge Valley in Dun Morogh

Home city: Ironforge

RACIAL ABILITIES

FROST RESISTANCE

 Frost spells are less likely to hit a Dwarf.

GUN SPECIALIZATION

Dwarves are more likely to get critical hits when firing a gun. This is most beneficial for the Hunter class.

MACE SPECIALIZATION

 Dwarves gain additional Expertise when using Maces in melee combat. Expertise makes it harder for enemies to avoid your attacks.

STONEFORM

Once every two minutes, Dwarves can activate Stoneform. Stoneform removes all poison, disease, and bleed effects and increases armor for 8 seconds.

EXPLORER

Achaeology skill (a secondary Profession) increased by 15. Dwarves also Survey faster than other races.

Rams, the Dwarven Racial Mount

AVAILABLE CLASSES

DEATH KNIGHT · DRUID · HUNTER · MAGE · PALADIN · PRIEST · ROGUE · SHAMAN · WARLOCK · WARRIOR

DWARF

The Dwarves of Dun Morogh are a hardworking, dependable people. Although they greatly enjoy a good pint or a rousing story, they are industrious and highly skilled in working with stone and metal. The great forges and intricate stone buildings of their capital city, Ironforge, attest to this innate talent. The Dwarven passion for digging in the earth has turned from gathering riches to archeological research of late and the recent earthquakes have revealed promising new treasures for study. Unfortunately, that is not all the cataclysm has unearthed. Sheltered by the mountains of Dun Morogh, the effects of the cataclysm are felt even here in secluded Coldridge Valley where your training begins. It is time for you to put aside simple pleasures, pick up your weapons, and join your allies in defending your world.

1   Coldridge Valley
2   Anvilmar
3   Cask of Gnomenbrau
4   Cask of Stormhammer
    Stout
5   Cask of Theramore Pale
    Ale
6   Whitebeard's
    Encampment
7   Soothsayer Shi'kala
    Felix's Bucket of Bolts
8   Soothsayer Rikkari
    Felix's Chest
9   Soothsayer Mirim'koa
    Felix's Box
10 Coldridge Pass

COLDRIDGE VALLEY

While gunning down troggs, Joren Ironstock find time to explain that the big earthquake has shaken the troggs right out of the ground and made them angrier than usual. The mountaineers need help to **Hold the Line**. He asks you to head south and help out his forces by slaying some of the Rockjaw Invaders.

When you return, Joren Ironstock has another job for you. It's time to **Give 'Em What-For!** The troggs value strength above all else and bigger, stronger troggs are the closest things they have to leaders. Joren hopes that if you take out the big Rockjaw Goons the attacks might slow. Before heading out to deal with the Goons, speak with Sten Stoutarm. This all-out trogg invasion has worn down the mountaineers. Sten wants you to take his first aid kit and deliver **Aid for the Wounded**.

Head out into the field where you can see Coldridge Mountaineers doing their best to hold back the Rockjaw Invaders. Help them out by taking down the invaders and bandaging up any wounded you see. When you are finished head back up the hill to report your success.

Joren thinks you can be even more useful elsewhere. Due to the massive trogg attacks, and the earthquake earlier, all civilians have been put on **Lockdown in Anvilmar**. Joren sends you to speak with his wife, Jona Ironstock inside Anvilmar.

ANVILMAR

Jona Ironstock has things well in hand and knows just how to put you to use. She tells you that **First Things First: We're Gonna Need Some Beer**. Luckily, your fellow Dwarves put some beer in storage for just such an emergency as this. Jona gives you the important task of bringing back three casks of the stuff.

Though beer supplies are running low, they haven't yet reached emergency levels so take a moment to speak to Grundel Harkin. It seems the earthquake knocked all sorts of **Dwarven Artifacts** loose from the soil. Grundel asks you to obtain five of these archeological treasures for further study.

Head out of Anvilmar and travel around the east side of the structure to find the Cask of Gnomenbrau. Next, head back west, keeping close to the outer wall of Anvilmar to find the Cask of Stormhammer Stout. To reach the third and final cask follow the road west away from Anvilmar until you see the Cask of Theramore Pale Ale on the right. Along the way keep your eye out for small mounds in the snow. These mark the positions of the recently unearthed artifacts that Grundel Harkin asked you retrieve. After collecting the beer and the artifacts, return to Anvilmar with your prizes.

Grundel's philosophy is that you should **Make Hay While the Sun Shines**. Since you did such a good job of obtaining the Dwarven artifacts, Grundel decides to send you out on another excursion. This time he wants you to retrieve Priceless Rockjaw Artifacts from the Rockjaw Scavengers, though they are unlikely to give them up without a fight. Before doing so, check in with Jona.

Now that the most pressing need has been taken care of, Jona asks for your help in getting **All the Other Stuff**. She sends you out after Boar Haunches for eatin' and Ragged Wolf Hides for blankets.

Meeting Your Trainer

Jona also delivers a letter from your Class Trainer. Before heading out on your other tasks, take the time to speak with your trainer who is in Anvilmar. Learning what they have to teach makes your future endeavors easier to handle.

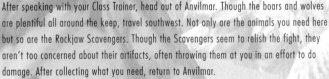

After speaking with your Class Trainer, head out of Anvilmar. Though the boars and wolves are plentiful all around the keep, travel southwest. Not only are the animals you need here but so are the Rockjaw Scavengers. Though the Scavengers seem to relish the fight, they aren't too concerned about their artifacts, often throwing them at you in an effort to do damage. After collecting what you need, return to Anvilmar.

Jona is pleased with your work, but now you are needed elsewhere and **Whietbeard Needs Ye**. Grelin Whitebeard is having trouble with trolls. Report to his camp in Coldridge Valley. To reach the camp head southeast from Anvilmar.

WHITEBEARD'S ENCAMPMENT

Grelin is concerned about **The Troll Menace**. While Anvilmar's attention is focused on the troggs, it's more important than ever that the trolls are kept under control. Grelin tasks you with thinning out their numbers. Before you head out, check with Apprentice Soren and Felix Whindlebolt as well.

Apprentice Soren worries there is more to the trolls than just their usual aggression and wants you to go **Trolling for Information**. He tells you to listen to a soothsayer in each of the three Frostmane camps to try to find out what is going on.

Since you're heading toward the trolls anyway, Felix is hoping you can help him out with **A Refugee's Quandary**. When the earthquake happened he became turned around in all the confusion and the trolls took all of his stuff! He asks you to retrieve his Box, Chest, and Bucket of Bolts from the Frostmane Trolls.

Head southeast out of Whitebeard's camp to reach one of the Frostmane camps. Here you find Soothsayer Shi'kala and Felix's Bucket of Bolts. To eavesdrop on the Soothsayer, stand near each one. After hearing what she has to say, you are ready to pick up Felix's Bucket and move to the next camp. There are plenty of Frostmane Troll Whelps near all three camps, so thin out their numbers as you move from camp to camp.

Head west along the mountains to reach the next troll camp. Listen to Soothsayer Rikkari, grab Felix's Chest, and move on to the third camp. Here you find Soothsayer Mirim'koa and Felix's Box. When you are finished, return to Whitebeard's Encampment.

Though you came back with some good information, it doesn't change the situation much. Grelin knows that the trolls would love to kick the dwarves out of Coldridge Valley and claim it for their own. He sends you on a mission of **Ice and Fire**. Kill the Frostmane's leader, Grik'nir the Cold, Grik'nir's Servants, and the Wayward Fire Elemental.

Head back to the first camp you visited and enter the cave behind it. Make your way deeper inside, taking down the Frostmane Blades you encounter on your way. The passageway in the cavern soon splits, but either way takes you deeper into the cavern to Grik'nir. When you arrive in the large cavern, be careful not to get too close to the Wayward Fire Elemental until you are ready to fight. Unlike the other foes you have faced, the elemental is aggressive and attacks you if you get within range. Deal with the elemental, then prepare to take on Grik'nir the Cold. Though he won't attack you until you make the first move, be prepared for at least one nearby Frostmane Whelp to join the fight. Both the elemental and Grik'nir are tougher opponents than you've faced so far, but neither is anything you can't handle. If you still need to kill Grik'nir's servants, mop up a few more Frostmane Blades on your way out of the cave before returning to Whitebeard.

Stoneform

Being a dwarf has its advantages including Stoneform. When activated this racial ability allows all dwarves to remove Poison, Disease, and Bleed effects and it also increases your armor. The effect doesn't last long, but sometimes a few precious seconds are all you need to turn the tide of battle in your favor.

The appearance of the elemental tells Whitebeard that the earthquake earlier did more than just upset some troggs! He asks you to take **A Trip to Ironforge**. He sends you to speak with Hands Springsprocket in Coldridge Pass. Head east, past Anvilmar, and continue up the road to reach the pass.

COLDRIDGE PASS

Unfortunately, while you're speaking to Hands, an aftershock seals the tunnel you needed to take. Not to fear, **Follow That Gyro-Copter!** Hands sends up a distress signal to the Gnomes. Run back down to Anvilmar to catch a ride on Milo Geartwinge's copter.

Milo is more than happy to give you a ride but first you need to **Pack Your Bags**. Head back into Anvilmar and grab your belongings. You find your Leftover Boar Meat on a small table inside, your Coldridge Beer Flagon is right down the steps in a corner, and your Ragged Wolf-Hide Cloak is in a box upstairs near Teo Hammerstorm, the Shaman Trainer.

Take a moment to say goodbye to Jona Ironstock. She tells you **Don't Forget About Us**. Once you arrive in Kharanos, speak with Tharek Blackstone and let him know what has been happening in Coldridge. Jona is hopeful that he will send some help.

With your personal supplies gathered and your goodbyes said, you are ready to move on to Kharanos. Head back up to Coldridge Valley and let Milo know that you are ready to go.

As the helicopter flies, take a good look at the surrounding lands. Though you may be more comfortable sitting by the fire with a nice pint o' ale than flying over the mountains in a gnomish contraption, you're getting an enviable view of Dwarven territory. While you may be on the inexperienced side right now, no dwarf worth his beard has ever shirked his duty. The world outside is changing and it now falls to you to help protect your home.

GNOME

The eccentric Gnomes once thrived in Gnomeregan, a city deep in the mountains beneath Dun Morogh. When attacked by Troggs, the clever Gnomes released toxic radiation against their attackers—and the gnome citizenry as well. The surviving gnomes fled the city, still sharing their inventions and odd devices with others. They currently use Ironforge, the Dwarven capital, as a place of refuge.

Gnomish and Goblin engineers have a long-standing rivalry. It's uncertain to outsiders which side is more dangerous to their friends and enemies!

Gnomes are approximately 3 feet tall, being the shortest sentient race in Azeroth. They have petite bodies but larger facial features. Gnomes have only 4 fingers per hand. Male and female Gnomes are known for their outrageous hair colors.

Start Location: Gnomeregan in Dun Morogh

RACIAL ABILITIES

ARCANE RESISTANCE

Arcane spells are less likely to hit a Gnome.

ENGINEERING SPECIALIZATION

Engineering skill (a crafting Profession) increased by 15.

ESCAPE ARTIST

Escape the effects of any immobilization or movement speed reduction effect.

EXPANSIVE MIND
Mana pool increased by 5%.

SHORTBLADE SPECIALIZATION
Gnomes gain additional Expertise when using daggers and One-hand swords in melee combat. Expertise makes it harder for enemies to avoid your attacks.

Home city: Ironforge (Tinker Town)

Mechanostriders, the Gnomish Racial Mount

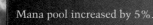
AVAILABLE CLASSES

DEATH KNIGHT · DRUID · HUNTER · MAGE · PALADIN · PRIEST · ROGUE · SHAMAN · WARLOCK · WARRIOR

GNOME

Though the gnomes are grateful for the hospitality of their Dwarven allies in Ironforge. The underground Dwarven city just can't take the place of their own home. After years of exile, the time has finally come to retake Gnomeregan. High Tinker Mekkatorque and his advisors have come up with a plan—Operation: Gnomeregan. The Gnomes plan to boot out Thermaplugg and his cronies and retake their city. You are one of the lucky few to have survived the radiation in Gnomeregan with your wits intact. It's now up to you to help take back your city.

1	Gnomeregan
2	New Tinkertown
3	The Toxic Airfield
4	Jessup McCree
5	Crushcog's Arsenal
6	Brewnall Village
7	Kharanos

GNOMEREGAN

The first thing you see when you wake is Nevin Twistwrench, the commander of the Survivor Assistance Facilitation Expedition, or S.A.F.E. They're here to help the survivors in Gnomeregan but the irradiated leper gnomes are becoming too numerous to hold back and they are **Pinned Down**. Since you now look healthy enough to help out, he asks you to clear out some of the Crazed Leper Gnomes.

Head out of the Old Dormitory and into the Train Depot to see plenty of the Crazed Leper Gnomes. Attack them one at a time and they prove no match for you. You may not like taking out your former comrades, but it has to be done! When you are finished, return to Nevin in the dormitory.

After thinning the numbers of the leper gnomes, it is time to **Report to Carvo Blastbolt**. Look for him in the center of the Train Depot ahead. Though the mission is ending, there are still Gnomes who need rescued. Carvo asks you to **See to the Survivors**. He gives you his emergency teleport beacon so you can get those survivors out of here. The traumatized survivors are scattered throughout the Train Depot. Approach them and use the Teleport Beacon to get them out of harm's way. When you are finished, return to Carvo Blastbolt.

Carvo appreciates your help but now it is time to **Withdraw to the Loading Room!** Follow the ramp south out of the Train Depot and report to Gaffer Coilspring once you reach your destination. You have been down in the radiation a long time, so before you can rejoin the other Gnomes on the surface you must go through **Decontamination**. Gaffer sends you to the Sanitron 500 in the next room to the east. Approach one of the hovering Sanitrons and get in. The Clean Cannons do the rest! When you emerge from the corridor you have been cleansed of radiation!

Speak with Technician Braggle who lets you know that it is time to head **To the Surface**. When you are ready, talk to Torben Zapblast nearby to arrange transport to the surface.

NEW TINKERTOWN

Nevin knows that it's Gnomes like you who will play a big part in **The Future of Gnomeregan**. He sends you to talk with your Class Trainer who oversees your training and adjustment to life back on the surface.

High Tinker Mekkatorque is the leader of all the gnomes and has made a habit of personally meeting every rescued survivor. Head to the war council beneath the tent in the center of New Tinkertown to **Meet the High Tinker**.

The High Tinker is glad to see you made it out. He asks you to watch the holo-table in front of him to learn about Operation: Gnomeregan. It seems Thermaplugg had one last trick up his sleeve and for now, only the S.A.F.E. teams dare to venture into the city. Not content with his minor victory, Thermaplugg has sent his flunky, Razlo Crushcog out to harass the Gnomes on the surface. Mekkatorque knows that what the Gnomes need is **A Triumph of Gnomish Ingenuity**.

Engineer Grindspark has developed a bot that should help clean up the toxic air in the city. High Tinker Mekkatorque sends you to him to offer your help. Head northeast from the High Tinker to reach Engineer Grindspark. He's almost finished with his latest prototype but he can definitely use your help **Scrounging for Parts**. There are all kinds of spare parts just lying around New Tinkertown. Retrieve some for the engineer.

Once you have the spare parts he needs, Engineer Grindspark can finish his prototype and he's got **A Job for the Multi-Bot**. He wants you to use the GS-9x Multi-Bot to clean up Toxic Pools at the Toxic Airfield south of town. Before heading that way, stop to talk to Tock Sprysprocket northeast of Engineer Grindspark. Tock has a task for you in the Airfield as well. As strange as it sounds, he believes that the Toxic Sludges were once Gnomes and the sludge is **What's Left Behind**! He asks you to retrieve the Recovered Possessions of the Gnomes they once were from the Toxic Sludges.

Head south of town to reach the Airfield. Bring your bot close to the toxic pools and it automatically jumps right in and cleans them up. While here, take down some of the Toxic Sludges to retrieve the possessions for Tock.

Your Class Trainer

After reporting back to Grindspark and Tock, take a moment to visit your trainer. You are now ready to learn a useful skill or spell. Follow their instructions before moving on to your next task.

You have been instrumental in clearing up the Toxic Airfield, but there is still more to be done. Corporal Fizzwhistle needs your help in **Dealing with the Fallout**. The Living Contaminations threaten to overrun the town if they aren't thinned out. Destroy a number of them and report back to the corporal.

After accepting your reward, head to the war council in the center of town and speak with Captain Tread Sparknozzle. The cataclysm tore open the caves beneath Frostmane Hold, flooding the troll stronghold with troggs! The troggs drove the trolls out of their home and would surely like to do the same to the Gnomes if they aren't stopped. The demolitions expert, Jessup McCree, was supposed to close the caves but the captain hasn't heard from him. He wants you to go look for him at his camp near Frostmane Hold.

FROSTMANE HOLD

Head south across the Toxic Airfield and you soon see the camps surrounding Frostmane Hold. Jessup has set up camp on the outskirts. He says he can still do the job, but he needs some help from you first. Jessup tells you to **Get Me Explosives Back!** The troggs stole his Powder Kegs and any of them could be carrying the explosives around. Not only did the filthy troggs steal Jessup's powder kegs, his crew is **Missing in Action**. He needs you to rescue his Captured Demolitionists from their cages.

As you move into Frostmane territory, be careful. Unlike the other foes you've faced so far, these Rockjaw Troggs are aggressive and attack you if you get too close. The troggs are scattered all around so try to clear them one at a time as you move towards the makeshift cages holding Jessup's crew. To free the prisoners all you need to do is destroy the flimsy cages. Once you are finished, return to Jessup.

With his recovered crew and powder kegs, Jessup was able to get everything ready to detonate. He now needs your help **Finishin' the Job**. Make your way to the bottom of the cave in the western part of Frostmane Hold. While you're down there, he suggests you take out the head trogg, Boss Bruggor.

To reach the bottom you must battle through a cave full of troggs, often fighting in close quarters. Try to take them one at a time and keep an eye behind you so you don't get unexpected adds! While you can do this on your own, it's a good idea to bring a friend along. When you reach the bottom clear the other troggs out before heading for Boss Bruggor. He's a bit tougher than the other troggs so be ready to use all your abilities to deal with him. With Bruggor out of the way, all you need to do is hit the detonator. Report back to Jessup when you are finished.

Jessup is moving on to other jobs, but before he goes he asks you to do **One More Thing**. Take his report to High Tinker Mekkatorque in New Tinkertown. Head back across the Toxic Airfield to reach the town and deliver the report.

Mekkatorque is happy with the news. With the troggs contained for now, he can turn his attention to other matters. In a bid to stop the Gnomes from retaking Gnomeregan, Razlo Crushcog and his flunkies have set up shop in an old arsenal to the north. The High Tinker wants you to put a stop to **Crushcog's Minions** before they can bring the old mechano-tanks online. Before heading out, check in with Hinkles Fastblast. He asks you to use his Techno-Grenade to destroy the Repaired Mechano-Tanks at the arsenal. He wants to make sure there are **No Tanks!**

Follow the road northeast to reach Crushcog's Arsenal. After thinning out his cronies and taking out the tanks, return to New Tinkertown. After receiving your reward from the High Tinker and Hinkles Fastblast, turn to Kelsey Steelspark to plan your next step.

BREWNALL VILLAGE

While High Tinker Mekkatorque and his military advisors finalize the plans to take down Razlo Crushcog, Kelsey Steelspark asks you to travel to Brewnall Village. Once there speak with Jarvi Shadowstep and offer your help. To reach Brewnall, travel southeast along the road.

When you arrive, Jarvi tells you they are almost ready to move against Crushcog, but his Sentry-Bots need to be handled first. Take the Paintinator down to the lake and use it on Crushcog's Sentry-Bots to **Paint it Black**. Head east down onto Iceflow Lake and use the Paintinator to blind them. When you are finished, return to Jarvi in Brewnall Village.

It is now time to take on Razlo Crushcog himself! The Dwarves of Ironforge have agreed to help the Gnomes deal with this threat. Travel to the small, snow-covered island in Iceflow Lake to lend your aid. Jarvi gives you an orbital targeting device to use during the battle to help guide the High Tinker's special weapons.

High Tinker Mekkatorque does most of the work against Crushcog; your job is just to help him out. When you use the device Jarvi gave you, it produces a target that you can place anywhere on the ground. Place it underneath Crushcog to aim the High Tinker's weapons. While Crushcog is too busy dealing with Mekkatorque to notice your interference, his minions are another matter. Don't get so caught up in using the device that you neglect to take out the flunkies trying to take you down.

After the battle, return to Jarvi Shadowstep. With Crushcog gone it is time for you to move on to help your Dwarven allies who have problems of their own. Follow the road east out of Brewnall Village to reach Kharanos.

Gnomeregan may still lie in Thermaplugg's control, but things are certainly looking up for your people. With Crushcog vanquished and S.A.F.E. rescuing more Gnomes every day, it won't be long before Gnomeregan is under Gnome control and you can once again return to your beloved city. For now, you must leave Operation: Gnomeregan in the hands of other capable Gnomes. Your path lies outward, using the skills you've learned to aid your allies in the wake of the recent cataclysm.

HUMAN

Humans are both proud and ambitious, seeking comfort and glory and to change the world around them. Many humans are laborers, working in the farms, mines, and lumber mills outside of Stormwind, eagerly taking all that nature offers. Humans are also courageous knights, brave on the battlefield and loyal to their comrades.

Humans are 5-6 feet tall, strong and healthy. Human physical traits vary greatly, with a wide palette of skin and hair colors.

Start location: Northshire in Elwynn Forest

Home city: Stormwind

RACIAL ABILITIES

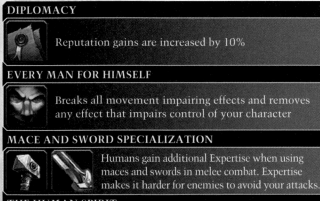

DIPLOMACY

Reputation gains are increased by 10%

EVERY MAN FOR HIMSELF

Breaks all movement impairing effects and removes any effect that impairs control of your character

MACE AND SWORD SPECIALIZATION

Humans gain additional Expertise when using maces and swords in melee combat. Expertise makes it harder for enemies to avoid your attacks.

THE HUMAN SPIRIT

Spirit attribute is increased by 3%

Horses, the Human Racial Mount

AVAILABLE CLASSES

DEATH KNIGHT | DRUID | HUNTER | MAGE | PALADIN | PRIEST | ROGUE | SHAMAN | WARLOCK | WARRIOR

HUMAN

Though they are a younger race, the Humans have carved a place for themselves among the elder races of Azeroth. With the destruction of Lordaeron, the grand city of Stormwind now stands alone as a testament to Human achievement, its forces ever at the ready to deal with any danger. Recent events have scattered the army of Stormwind far and wide to deal with Deathwing and his Twilight forces, leaving the heart of Humanity's empire at risk from lesser threats. Though you yourself are inexperienced, the King has called upon you and every other citizen to rise up to the challenge and defend your home.

1	Northshire
2	Echo Ridge Mine
3	Northshire Vineyards
4	Kurtok the Slayer
5	Falkhaan Isenstrider
6	Goldshire

NORTHSHIRE VALLEY

Northshire has long been a training ground for Humans just beginning to learn their chosen class. Deep within Elwynn Forest its sheltered location provides new recruits ample opportunity to cut their teeth on lesser threats before facing greater challenges. However, with Deathwing and his Twilight armies rampaging over Azeroth, the king has called upon all able bodied citizens to help with the defense of the realm. Speak to Marshal McBride to offer your help. Look for the Marshal standing on the front steps of the abbey.

Marshal McBride is glad to have another new recruit. The Blackrock Orcs have managed to sneak into Northshire and he can use the help **Beating Them Back!**. Head into the nearby forest and kill the attacking Blackrock Worgs! Worgs appear all around the Abbey. After thinning their numbers, report back to the Marshal.

McBride knows that the Orcs won't mistake **Lions for Lambs** and are spying on you right now. Go back into the forest where you killed the Worgs and take out the Blackrock Spies who mostly skulk near the trees. When you are done, return to Marshal McBride.

Meeting Your Trainer

Marshal McBride has a note for you from your Class Trainer. Read the note and take the time to speak with your class trainer before moving on. He or she wants you to learn a valuable skill or spell. Your note indicates exactly where you can find your trainer.

Once you complete the task your trainer set forth it's time for you to **Join the Battle!** Report to Sergeant Willem at the command tent behind Northshire Abbey.

The Blackrock Orcs aren't attacking alone; **They Sent Assassins**! Willem needs a volunteer to go into the field and kill every one of the sneaky little green monsters! Before heading out, speak with Brother Paxton nearby. The priest tells you to **Fear No Evil**. He gives you a prayer book which allows you to cast the Light's healing touch on the injured. The Goblin Assassins and the Injured Stormwind Soldiers are both in the nearby woods. When you are finished, return to Brother Paxton and Sergeant Willem.

Now that you've taken care of the assassins, **The Rear is Clear**. Sergeant Willem sends you back to report to Marshal McBride. Even though the enemy has been cleared out to the north and west, there are still more of them to contend with. They've taken over the vineyard to the east and are burning the nearby forest! It is up to you to stop them. Marshal McBride wants you to thin out the numbers of the **Blackrock Invasion** and collect Blackrock Weapons as proof of their demise.

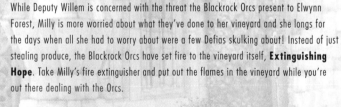

Injured Stormwind Infantry

ANGER ISSUES

Unlike the non-aggressive foes faced up to this point, Blackrock Orcs don't like you and attack if you get too close. Be prepared for a fight before crossing the bridge!

While Deputy Willem is concerned with the threat the Blackrock Orcs present to Elwynn Forest, Milly is more worried about what they've done to her vineyard and she longs for the days when all she had to worry about were a few Defias skulking about! Instead of just stealing produce, the Blackrock Orcs have set fire to the vineyard itself, **Extinguishing Hope**. Take Milly's fire extinguisher and put out the flames in the vineyard while you're out there dealing with the Orcs.

Head east and cross the river to reach the Northshire Vineyards. Fighting aggressive enemies is more challenging than facing their neutral counterparts and requires some caution on your part. If you aren't careful, it can be easy to end up with more enemies than you can handle at once. If your class has ranged abilities, use them to your advantage now by pulling your targets to you into an area already clear of other foes. If you are strictly melee, start with a target on the outskirts that aren't near any other enemy. To use Milly's Fire Extinguisher, face one of the vineyard fires and use the device. This puts out the fire and you can move on to the next. The fire extinguisher only works inside the vineyard, so don't bother trying to put out the flaming trees on either side of it.

After thinning the number of Blackrock Orcs and doing your part in dousing the fires, return to Milly and Deputy Willem. Be careful moving back through the vineyard. Enemies may have reappeared to block your return to the abbey.

Since you've been so successful against the Blackrock Orcs, Marshal McBride has another task to send you back towards the vineyards. With your help there is hope of **Ending the Invasion**. This incursion of Blackrock Orcs is led by Kurok the Slayer, an Orc even more savage than those he leads. The deputy tasks you with ending this threat once and for all!

Follow the river north and cross it near the northern end of the burnt area. The Blackrock's dark-hearted leader is here. Before approaching him, take out any of his nearby followers. You want to face Kurok on his own, and not with his friends joining in unexpectedly. Kurok is a tough foe, so be at full health before the fight begins. After taking him out, return to Marshal McBride with the good news. He's so impressed with the work you've done that he rewards you with a **Commendation**.

Now that you've proven yourself, Marshal McBride wants you to **Report to Goldshire** to continue performing your duty of protecting Elwynn Forest. Follow the road south out of Northshire to the nearby town of Goldshire. On the way you see Falkhaan Isenstrider. He is a firm believer in getting a little **Rest and Relaxation**. His best friend runs the inn in Goldshire and can hook you up with some supplies. Speak to Innkeeper Farley at the Lion's Pride Inn in Goldshire once you arrive.

Even in the best of times, doing your duty is not always easy. Now, with Deathwing and his minions threatening the world at large and other invaders threatening your homeland, it is more important than ever that you rise to the task. Learn your lessons well, grow in your chosen field, and get ready to take your place among the heroes of Stormwind.

NIGHT ELF

Night Elves are perceived as aloof and solitary, preferring nature to conventional cities and the company of their own kind to that of other races. Rather than using nature as a resource, Night Elves seek to be in rhythm with the natural world. Night Elves blend magic and the forces of nature for their protection and strength. This belief places Night Elves in strong opposition to Blood Elves, who have consumed tremendous magic against the flow of nature and who continue to place ambition before reason.

Night Elves are approximately 7 feet tall; they are lithe and athletic. All Night Elves have prominent eyebrows and very long ears. Males have elaborate facial hair. Females have facial tattoos.

Start location: Shadowglen in Teldrassi

Home city: Darnassus

RACIAL ABILITIES

ELUSIVENESS

Night Elf characters move faster while in Stealth, and are harder to detect when using either Stealth or Shadowmeld.

NATURE RESISTANCE
Nature spells are less likely to hit a Night Elf.

QUICKNESS
Melee attacks, and attacks from bows, guns, or thrown weapons, are less likely to hit a Night Elf.

SHADOWMELD
Any Night Elves who remain motionless can blend into shadows, making it difficult for enemies to detect their presence.

WISP SPIRIT
Night Elf spirits are considerably faster than other races. Unfortunately, you only gain this bonus when your character is dead.

Nightsabers, the Night Elf Racial Mount

AVAILABLE CLASSES

DEATH KNIGHT | DRUID | HUNTER | MAGE | PALADIN | PRIEST | ROGUE | SHAMAN | WARLOCK | WARRIOR

NIGHT ELF

The Night Elves, or kaldorei, are an ancient race. After the near destruction of the world tree, Nordrassil, they built the great tree, Teldrassil, where you now stand. This new homeland shelters their people as they commune with the natural world, seeking to preserve nature's balance. They are reclusive and often wary of the younger races, though many Night Elves serve the Alliance in various roles through-

out Azeroth. The recent cataclysm has once again placed the world in jeopardy and has even threatened the slowly healing Nordrassil. With many Night Elves called away to deal with the newly unleashed forces, it is more important than ever that you begin your journey along your chosen path so that you too can lend aid in this time of need.

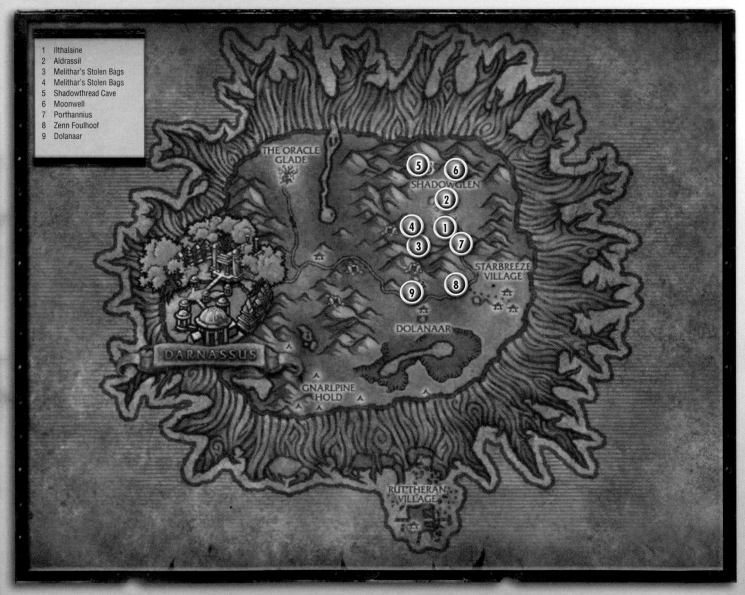

1 Ilthalaine
2 Aldrassil
3 Melithar's Stolen Bags
4 Melithar's Stolen Bags
5 Shadowthread Cave
6 Moonwell
7 Porthannius
8 Zenn Foulhoof
9 Dolanaar

SHADOWGLEN

Like all young Night Elves, you begin your journey in the Shadowglen. This sheltered glade serves as a microcosm of nature's balance in the world. Ilthalaine's job is to maintain **The Balance of Nature** within Shadowglen. The Young Nightsaber population has grown too large for the environment to support. He asks you to thin their numbers so that nature's harmony is preserved. The animals you need are scattered around the immediate area. After culling the population, return to Ilthalaine.

You made a good start with thinning out the younger animal population, but unfortunately, more must be done. Since you seem to know what you're doing, Ilthalaine has another task for you regarding **Fel Moss Corruption**. Grellkin have gathered to the west. Slay them and collect Fel Moss for Ilthalaine's study. Before heading out to take care of the Grellkin, speak with Melithar Staghelm nearby. It seems that the **Demonic Thieves** have stolen his bags! Search for them near the Grellkin while collecting the Fel Moss. They are found all around the Grellkin camp. Since they aren't aggressive you can just wade right in and steal back the bags. Along the way, eliminate the Grellkin to collect the Fel Moss. When you are finished, return to Melithar and Ilthalaine to receive your rewards.

Meeting Your Class Trainer

When you return to Melithar he passes on word from your trainer. Read the message your trainer left for you and take time out from your duties to speak with them in Aldrassil. You are ready to learn a valuable skill from them which helps you in your future endeavors.

After you finish the task your trainer sets forth, they request your aid in pursuing the corruption haunting Shadowglen. Seek out Dentaria Silverglade, **Priestess of the Moon**. you can find her between the two pools just north of Aldrassil.

Dentaria is tending to Iverron who has been poisoned by Webwood Spiders. She needs your help in preparing **Iverron's Antidote**. Collect the Moonpetal Lilies growing around the nearby ponds and return to her.

Worried about the evident corruption in Teldrassil, she asks you to seek out **The Woodland Protector**. The Dryad, Tarindrella, is at the entrance to the Shadowthread Cave. Head north from the Moon Priestess to reach the foreboding entrance.

Corrupted Spiders

The spiders at Shadowthread Cave are different from the other wildlife you have faced so far. They are violently aggressive and attack if you get too close. They can also hit you with Weak Poison, which causes damage over time. Look for Tarindrella at the cave's entrance.

The dryad has returned to deal with the lingering corruption in Teledrassil. The spiders in the Shadowthread Cave suffer more than the other nearby wildlife. She asks you to deal with the **Webwood Corruption** by slaying the affected spiders and she offers you her help with this important task. Make your way deeper into the cave, eliminating the spiders you come across.

After dealing with the Webwood Spiders, Tarindrella sends you to take out their broodmother, Githyiss the Vile. Her **Vile Touch** has infected the whole brood. Head to the northern end of the cave to cut out the corruption at its source. Githyiss is a tougher foe than those you've faced so far. Be sure to clear out any other spiders nearby so you can face her by herself.

Once you defeat Githyiss, Tarindrella finds that the Gnarlpine are somehow involved. These are **Signs of Things to Come.** She tells you to speak with Athridas Bearmantle in Dolanaar if you wish to continue fighting the corruption in Teldrassil later. For now she teleports you back to Dentaria Silverglade.

Though the corruption must be dealt with, Dentaria feels that there is time for you to complete your training in Shadowglen. To learn about the recent history of **Teldrassil: Crown Of Azeroth**, travel to the moonwell and retrieve a phial of its water. Head northeast to reach the sacred pool. Fill your Crystal Phial and listen to the Shade of the Kaldorei. When you are finished, return to Dentaria.

There is one last task you must perform before departing Shadowglen. Take the **Precious Waters** in the Filled Crystal Phial to Tenaron Stormgrip at the top of Aldrassil. Follow the outside ramp at the western base of the tree all the way up to the top to find him.

Though Tenaron could teach you much of your history, he has an important task for you, **Teldrassil: Passing Awareness.** Take the Partially Filled Vessel to Corithras Moonrage in Dolanaar.

Shadowmeld

Night Elves have an innate affinity with nature. One of the ways this manifests is in the racial ability, Shadowmeld. By using this ability you can blend in with the shadows around you, becoming almost invisible. This is useful when you don't want to be noticed or when you bite off a little more than you can chew during a fight. Shadowmeld only lasts as long as you remain completely still.

Follow the road south out of Shadowglen where you encounter Porthannius who asks you to make a **Dolanaar Delivery**. He gives you a package of herbs to deliver to Innkeeper Keldamyr in Dolanaar. Keep following the road and it eventually turns west. Before you reach the town, keep an eye out for Zenn Foulhoof on your right. He also has a task for you.

The strange looking fellow asks you to bring him Nightsaber Fangs, Strigid Owl Feathers and swatches of Webwood Spider Silk. The creatures you need to slay in order to obtain these items are on both sides of the road nearby. Once you have done **Zenn's Bidding**, you are ready to finish your journey to Dolanaar.

Though the boughs of Teldrassil are an ever welcoming home, it will soon be time for you to venture out into the wider world. Your fellow Night Elves and their allies need your help to stem the tide of bloodshed and destruction the recent cataclysm unleashed. Learn well from your elders, remember your honor, and prepare to raise your weapons in defense of your world.

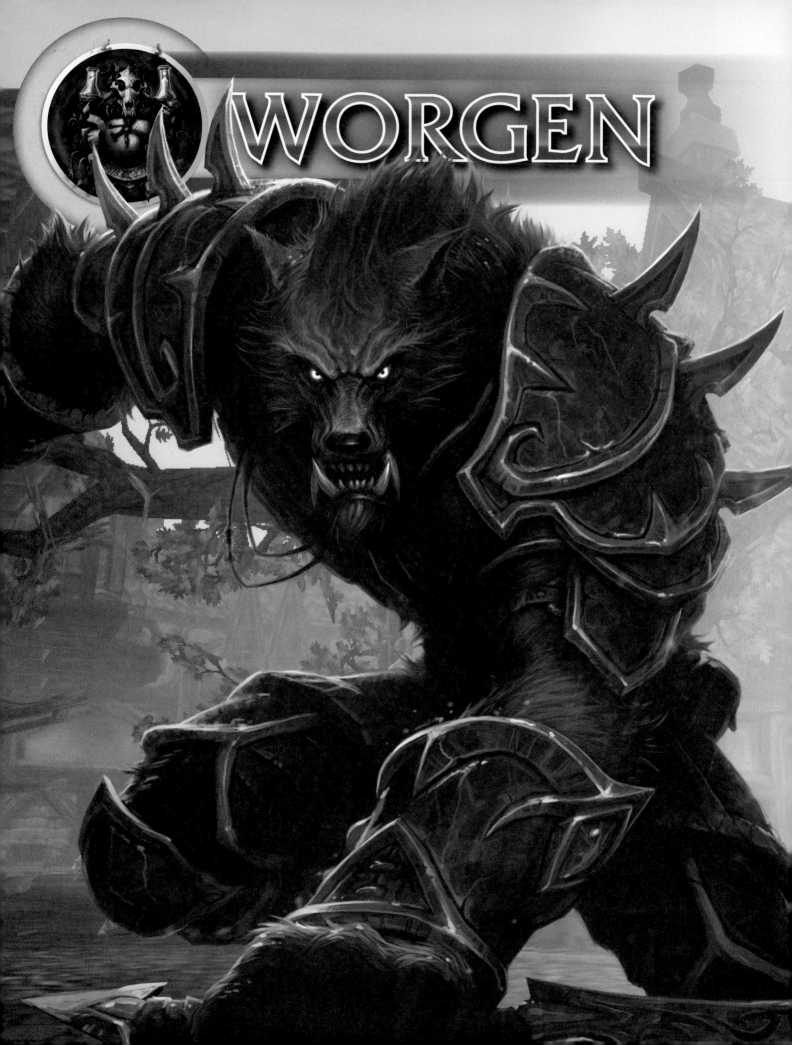

WORGEN

It was once thought that Worgen were evil creatures that came to Azeroth from another dimension. Time has proven this false, as newer knowledge reveals that Worgen are descendants of cursed Night Elven Druids. These Druids worshipped Goldrinn and would take on the form of the wolf. Eventually, this sect lost themselves in madness, and their curse has continued for many generations.

The Greymane Worgen are infected with this curse, but they have fought hard to retain themselves and developed a partial cure to this illness. As such, they are not driven toward uncontrolled violence. These Worgen have reached out to the Alliance, forming the sixth member race of this group.

These Worgen are both human and wolf, able to pass between the two forms. They have full control over themselves, but appear as true Worgen when in such a form, growing thick hair and possessing a canine appearance.

Start Location: Ruins of Gilneas

Home city: Gilneas

RACIAL ABILITIES

ABERRATION
Reduces the duration of all Curses and Diseases used against Worgen

DARKFLIGHT
Activates a Worgen's true form, increasing movement speed for 10 seconds

FLAYER
Skinning skill increased by 15, Worgen do not need to carry a skinning knife and skin faster than other races

TWO FORMS
Turn into your currently inactive form.

VICIOUSNESS
Worgen are more likely to land critical strikes.

Worgen learn the racial ability Running Wild at level 20 instead of using a mount

AVAILABLE CLASSES

DEATH KNIGHT | DRUID | HUNTER | MAGE | PALADIN | PRIEST | ROGUE | SHAMAN | WARLOCK | WARRIOR

WORGEN

The kingdom of Gilneas is one of the oldest human kingdoms in all of Azeroth. Proud and self sufficient, Gilneans have remained aloof from the troubles plaguing the rest of the world, safe behind the towering Greymane Wall. Though they have not shared the same dangers as the rest of Azeroth, their kingdom has its own troubles. Wall or no, Arugal's bestial creations have spread from neighboring Silverpine into Gilneas itself, causing the conflict you now see.

Though the city has known many years of peace, you begin your journey during the its darkest hour. The ferocious Worgen have breached the city's defenses and are pouring into the city itself. King Genn Greymane leads the city's defenders in trying to stop the onslaught. Now it is time for you to do your duty as a loyal citizen of this great city and drive the hideous beasts from the streets!

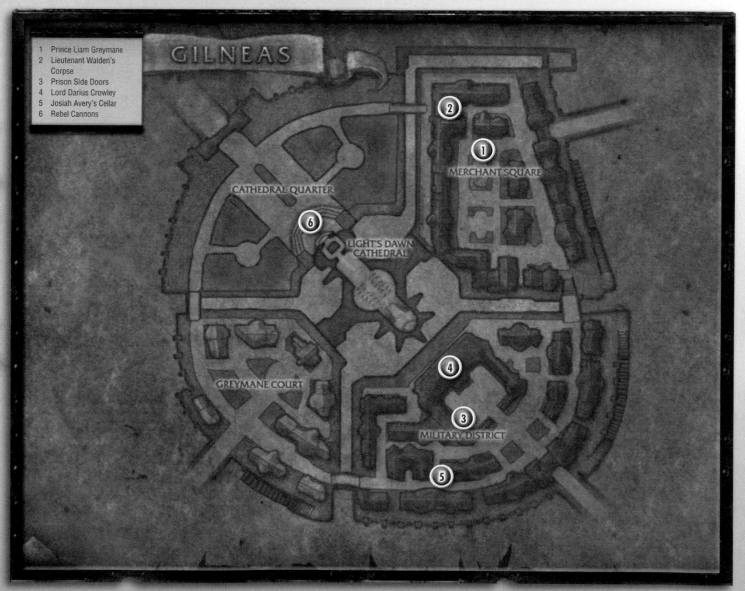

1 Prince Liam Greymane
2 Lieutenant Walden's Corpse
3 Prison Side Doors
4 Lord Darius Crowley
5 Josiah Avery's Cellar
6 Rebel Cannons

GILNEAS

Though many citizens have been evacuated, you begin in Merchant Square. The city is under complete **Lockdown**. Prince Liam Greymane instructs you to find Lieutenant Walden at the northwestern end of the Merchant Square. He can give you further evacuation orders.

Go up the street and follow it to the northwestern corner of Merchant Square, where near the closed gate it's clear that **Something is Amiss**. At your feet you see the mauled corpse of Lieutenant Walden lying on the cobblestones. Deep claw marks gouge his flesh as if a wild beast had torn into him.

Though you hear the sounds of fighting nearby, Prince Liam no doubt needs to know what happened to the Lieutenant. Return to him to deliver the news. As you approach the Prince's position **All Hell Breaks Loose**! Though the Worgen were originally created by Archmage Arugal to fight the Scourge, it is clear that your fellow citizens are now the target of their unbridled aggression! Despite the best efforts of the Prince's men, it seems that the city is in trouble. Lend a hand by slaying a number of these Rampaging Worgen in Merchant Square. These foes aren't aggressive, so don't worry about becoming overwhelmed. Concentrate on one target at a time as you become accustomed to your chosen class.

Before thinning out their numbers, accept the second task the prince offers. As always, his concern is for his people, several of whom have locked themselves up in their homes, trying to remain safe. Prince Liam knows that this won't keep the Worgen at bay for long and he asks you to **Evacuate the Merchant Square** homes before the Worgen do it for you!

Before beginning the evacuation, speak to Gwen Armstead directly south of Prince Liam. Locked behind the Greymane Wall as they are, she knows that the citizens won't make it through the winter without the supplies they have stockpiled. **Salvage the Supplies** as you make your rounds evacuating people.

To evacuate the citizens, open their sparkling doors. You can't enter their homes but as soon as you open their doors they run out. While doing this you also see several supply crates from which to salvage supplies.

BE PATIENT

While nothing stops you from moving out of Merchant Square and into the rest of the city, save yourself some backtracking and wait to explore until after you have finished your tasks in Merchant Square.

After evacuating the citizens and salvaging the necessary supplies, return to Gwen Armstead to receive your payment and then report to Prince Liam. Grateful for your help, he gives you **Royal Orders** commanding you to leave Merchant Square and report to the Military District while he stays behind to guard the retreat. When you arrive report in with Gwen Armstead who has moved to the base of the steps there.

Follow the street east and then turn south. Continue along this road until you reach the stairs leading down into the Military District.

Though most of the citizens made it out of Merchant Square alive, there are Worgen on this side of the city as well. Gwen informs you that **Someone's Looking For You**. Exactly who is looking for you depends on your class. This quest leads you to your class trainer. Follow the road south to find your class specific trainer. They give you a follow up quest to learn an important skill. Learn what they have to offer before moving on to face new challenges.

After you finish your short class-specific quest, your trainer informs you that because there is **Safety in Numbers**, the survivors plan to stick together and make their way to King Greymane to the south. Speak to him to see what else can be done to drive back the Worgen.

Continue following the road and you soon see the king and his royal guards conversing with Lord Godfrey. They are protecting a small group of survivors.

Though Lord Darius Crowley is considered a traitor by many, the King once called him friend. Regardless of what happened in the past, Greymane knows that with the city itself threatened, **Old Divisions** must give way. They need a man like Crowley to help them make it through this attack. Enter the side doors of Stoneward Prison and ask Captain Broderick about Crowley's whereabouts.

Lord Godfrey has a task for you as well. If you're going to head towards the prison anyway, **While You're At It** he wants you to take out Bloodfang Worgen on your way.

Head northwest to enter the prison and enter the side door to the left to find Captain Broderick. He informs you that Crowley is on **The Prison Rooftop**. Climb the stairs to reach the walkway above. The Bloodfang Worgen you encounter here are aggressive and attack if you get too close.

As you approach Lord Crowley and his men, it looks as if they are protecting an injured comrade. One of Crowley's men, Dempsey, has been hit hard and down. So far he is surviving **By The Skin of His Teeth**, but they need a few minutes to stabilize the bleeding before attempting to move him. Help Lord Crowley defend their position against wave after wave of worgen attacks. If you can survive the onslaught you can discuss the situation further with Crowley.

Crowley agrees with King Greymane that they must put aside their quarrel and once again become **Brothers in Arms**. He tells you to send word to Greymane that his men will join the kings' forces to drive back this menace. Make your way back down out of the prison to report your success.

Once Lord Godfrey knows that you finished the task he gave you and has spoken to the king regarding Crowley, King

Greymane has another job for you. Though the King is somewhat unnerved that Crowley managed to sneak such a large amount of weaponry into the city right under his nose, today **The Rebel Lord's Arsenal** might end up saving Gilnean lives. He sends you to find Josiah Avery and requisition the rebel artillery.

Follow the road west while looking for a cellar door to your right. Once you find it open the heavy doors and make your way down into the rebel arsenal. Josiah Avery is cowering in the far corner, just as you approach him he turns with a surprise attack! Luckily for you, Lorna Crowley arrives just in time!

Once Bitten...

As Lorna brings down Avery, you realize that he got in a lucky bite. It looks minor though, surely nothing to be concerned about.

As if run-of-the-mill Worgen weren't dangerous enough, Bloodfang Lurkers have now infiltrated the alleys of Gilneaas. These creatures have the talent of hiding in the darkness and attacking **From the Shadows**. Lorna asks you to use one of her mastiffs to sniff out Worgen hiding in the nearby alleys. You need to clear the way so the defenders can move the cannon out of the cellar to where they can do some good.

Once you accept this job, a faithful mastiff follows at your heels. Head back up out of the cellar and begin moving through the nearby streets. Though they may be good at hiding, the Bloodfang Lurkers can't hide their scent from the keen nose of the trusty mastiff! When you spot a lurker send in the dog to attack and follow it up with attacks of your own. Once you have slain enough of the Bloodfang Lurkers return to Lorna Crowley.

When you return Lorna's dog, she asks you to deliver a **Message to Greymane**. Let King Greymane know that her father's arsenal is at his disposal. You can find the king just around the corner from the building you just left.

The news of the arsenal is most welcome, but Greymane tells you that they can't unleash Crowley's weapons just yet. There is a civilian trapped on the other side of the prison—and not just any civilian. Krennan Aranas is one of the most brilliant alchemists in the world. His knowledge is far too valuable to lose and the king sends you to **Save Krennan Aranas**. King Greymane lends you his own horse for the rescue mission.

You automatically mount the steed and it carries you to where Krennan is stuck in a tree being harried by bloodthirsty Worgen below. Use the horse's ability to rescue the alchemist when you are beneath the tree and return to Lord Godfrey near the cellar.

Lord Godfrey sends you to the king to let him know that you've managed to buy some time. Godfrey believes it is **Time to Regroup** and you must all fall back to Greymane Court.

Follow the road west as it leads into Greymane Court. After you speak with the king, Lord Darius Crowley offers to let you come along for the ride as he makes his way to Light's Dawn Cathedral, where he plans to make a final stand for Gilneas. Sometimes **Sacrifices** are necessary.

When you accept Crowley's offer, you mount up behind him on his horse and travel to the cathedral. Your goal is to round up as many Worgen as you can, getting them to chase you instead of the escaping citizens.

Throw your torch at groups of Worgen to round up as many as you can on the way to the cathedral. When you click on the torch you are given a targeting reticule. Place it on the ground anywhere where Worgen are gathered. When you reach the cathedral steps, speak to Tobias Mistmantle.

NEED MORE WORGEN?

If you don't manage to round up the required amount of Worgen while riding with Crowley, don't worry, you can remount the horse at the cathedral steps and take another turn around the courtyard.

Now that the invading worgen have gathered near the cathedral, it is time to put an end to these creatures **By Blood and Ash**. Tobias Mistmantle instructs you to take control of one of the rebel cannons and use them against the Bloodfang Stalkers gathering before the cathedral.

Aim the cannon at the worgen you see below you and fire. You should be able to amass a decent kill count quickly with such massive firepower at your command. Watch out for Stalkers that try to mount the steps. Your cannon has the ability to fire very close to itself, so keep the steps clear of enemies! Once you have done your part, return to Tobias Mistmantle.

You did a great job decimating the horde of beasts with the cannon but now ammunition is running low. Though the defenders will **Never Surrender, Sometimes Retreat** is necessary. Enter the cathedral and report to Lord Crowley.

Though you fought valiantly, it now comes down to this desperate **Last Stand**. Because of the narrow cathedral door the worgen are forced to filter in a few at a time. Lord Crowley tasks you with killing the Frenzied Stalkers that make it inside the cathedral.

After thinning their numbers considerably, the onslaught stops for a moment, leading Lord Crowley to believe the worst is yet to come. You can take some small comfort in knowing that you've done everything possible to defend your home against these monsters. Trapped like a rat in the cathedral, your future is uncertain. No matter what happens, next, you can be sure that your life is about to change.

BLOOD ELF

The Blood Elves are so named in honor of their high elf ancestors who died during the Scourge invasion of their homeland, Quel'Thalas. Blood Elves seek power through arcane magic, bending it to their will to create warped, beautiful surroundings. Fiercely loyal to their race, Blood Elves will do anything to avenge their ancestors and reclaim their magic power. They are survivors hoping to regain glory once again.

Those of a weak disposition are unable to control their lust for magic and power. This burns away at their wills and turns these Elves into a pathetic, weaker version of what they once were.

Blood Elves are 5-6 feet tall, slim and wiry. Their hair and skin color reflect their affinity to fire and the sun. All Blood Elves have prominent eyebrows and long ears. Males have minimal facial hair. Females have elaborate ear jewelry.

Start location: Sunstrider Isle in Eversong Woods

Home city: Silvermoon City

RACIAL ABILITIES

ARCANE AFFINITY

Enchanting skill (an item-enhancing Profession) is increased by 10.

ARCANE TORRENT

An ability that Silences all enemies within 8 yards for 2 seconds and restores mana, energy, or Runic Power, depending on your class.

MAGIC RESISTANCE

All spells are less likely to hit a Blood Elf.

Hawkstriders, the Blood Elf Racial Mount

AVAILABLE CLASSES

DEATH KNIGHT   DRUID   HUNTER   MAGE   PALADIN   PRIEST   ROGUE   SHAMAN   WARLOCK   WARRIOR

BLOOD ELF

For millennia the High Elves depended on the undiluted magic of the Sunwell. With it they built an enduring society, dedicated to expanding their arcane knowledge and power. This existence came to an end as the then Prince Arthas led the Scourge into Quel'thalas, poisoning the Sunwell. Many elves were lost during this war and the survivors renamed themselves sin'dorei, or Blood Elves, in honor of their fallen kin. Now, Silvermoon City, once the shining center of elven civilization lies partially in ruins, and though the Blood Elves have retaken most of their homeland, the battle scars are still visible and remnants of the Scourge still plague the land. The effects of the Sunwell's poisoning are felt even here, on the relatively peaceful Sunstrider Isle. It is here you begin your journey.

1 The Sunspire
2 Solanian's Journal
3 Solanian's Scrying Orb
4 Solanian's Scroll of
  Scourge Magic
5 Shrine of Dath'Remar
6 Lanthan Perilon
7 Falthrien Academy
8 Outrunner Alarion
9 Falconwing Square

SUNSTRIDER ISLE

As all inexperienced Blood Elves do, you begin your training on Sunstrider Isle. The poisoning of the Sunwell has had an effect on even the wildlife on the isle and Magistrix Erona tasks you with **Reclaiming Sunstrider Isle** from these errant creatures. Though the Mana Wyrms once served the elves as guardians of the Burning Crystals, they have now become a nuisance. You must thin their numbers to bring them under control. Mana Wyrms are plentiful nearby and give you good practice with using your starting spell or skill. Once you have cleared them out a bit, return to Magistrix Erona.

The unchecked power of the Burning Crystals has corrupted more of the isle's wildlife than Erona had originally feared and has affected even the Springpaws. Nothing can restore the felines to their previous uncorrupted state and **Unfortunate Measures** must be taken. She asks you to put down the nearby Springpaw Lynxes and Springpaw Cubs and return their collars to her.

Before heading out to perform this grisly task, there are others in the Sunspire that could use your help. Enter the Sunspire and speak with Well Watcher Solanian standing on a balcony overlooking the bottom floor. He's been so busy with the recent problems at the Sunspire that he hasn't had a chance to collect some of his belongings outside. Retrieve **Solanian's Belongings** for him. They are scattered about Sunstrider Isle. The Well Watcher has another task for you as well. Solanian believes that all Blood Elves should honor the past. He tasks you with visiting **The Shrine of Dath'Remar** Sunstrider to the west. Once there, read the plaque placed there in his honor.

Head out of the Sunspire itself and across to the nearby building. Look for Arcanist Ithanas who can use your help dealing with the creatures threatening to overrun Sunstrider Isle. Bring him **A Fistful of Slivers** and he promises to reward you with a magical boon. Slay mana using creatures on the isle to collect the slivers you need. Mana Wyrms are good targets for this quest as there are plenty of them close together nearby.

After speaking with Ithanas, turn your attention to Arcanist Helion. He cautions you of the dangers of your heritage. Though your innate Arcane Powers are great, they come with a risk of the **Thirst Unending**. Helion warns you against absorbing too much power without releasing it via Arcane Torrent. Failure to expend energy this way can cause you to become one of the Wretched, addicted to arcane energy and hopelessly insane. He asks you to use your Arcane Torrent on a Mana Wyrm for practice.

ARCANE TORRENT

All Blood Elves can perform Arcane Torrent. This racial skill silences nearby enemies, keeps them from casting for a few seconds, and restores a percentage of your own mana. Be ready to use it against casters of all types once they are in range.

Once you have obtained all five quests, you are ready to head out. First, stop by the nearby Mana Wyrms and slay them to collect the Slivers you need. Take the time to use your Arcane Torrent on one to satisfy Arcanist Helion.

Next, head south from the Sunspire to collect Solanian's Journal, and take down any Springpaws in your path. From there continue south to retrieve his Scrying Orb. Now, head northwest to find his Scroll of Scourge Magic. After collecting these belongings, and taking care of any Springpaws you encountered, continue northwest to reach the Shrine of Dath'Remar. Read the plaque dedicated to this elven hero before returning to the Sunspire. If you still need to take down Springpaws, do so on your way back.

Report back to everyone who gave you a task and collect your rewards. When you are finished report to Magistrix Erona. She lets you know that you should visit your trainer but she isn't done with you yet either. Erona has decided that you can be of more use at Falthrien Academy. Follow the path west to find her assistant and **Report to Lanthan Perilon**. Before leaving be sure to finish all other business you have at the Sunspire and take the time to visit your trainer to learn new skills and spells.

FALTHRIEN ACADEMY

To reach Lanthan travel west from the Sunspire. Before he sends you on to the academy he has another task for you. The Tenders, who used to help the elves maintain Sunstrider Isle, have now grown out of control and are showing signs of **Aggression**. They have become dangerous and these walking weeds must be cleared out. Look for them west of Lanthan Perilon. You need both Tenders and the larger Feral Tenders to satisfy the assistant. As with the other creatures you've faced, these are non-aggressive so just take on one at a time to play it safe.

After helping out Lanthan with the Tender problem, he tells you about the task Magistrix Erona originally had in mind for you. Falthrien Academy is home to one of the Wretched, **Felendren the Banished**. He earned this title, and the punishment that goes with it, because he refused to learn to control his desire for more and more arcane energy. Lanthan asks you to slay Felendren's Arcane Wraiths, Tainted Arcane Wraiths and, finally, Felendren himself. Bring his head back as proof of your deed.

Follow the path southwest to reach Falthrien Academy. Once there, work your way up the ramps, eliminating your quota of Wraiths along the way. Don't worry if you don't see many Tainted Arcane Wraiths on the way up; a pair of them share the upper floor with Felendren. Once you reach the top, give the unrepentant Felendren the end he deserves. Don't forget to claim your grisly trophy before returning to Lanthan.

Tainted Arcane Sliver

The Tainted Arcane Wraiths have a chance to drop a Tainted Arcane Sliver which begins a quest. Return it to Arcanist Helion at the Sunspire to receive a reward!

With Falthrien Academy now free of Felendren's taint, Lanthan has another job for you. The messengers that keep information flowing between Silvermoon City and Sunstrider Isle are short handed and can always use help. **Aiding the Outrunners** is a task worthy of your time. Follow the road southeast from Lanthan until you reach Outrunner Alarion along the road.

DAWNING LANE

The Wretched infest the ruins of Silvermoon and attack anyone in the hopes of getting their hands on a few mana crystals. Alarion believes that one of her outrunners has been **Slain by the Wretched**. She asks you to go south into the ruins and look for the Slain Outrunner in Dawning Lane. Unlike the other foes encountered up to this point, the Wretched that haunt the land near Dawning Lane are aggressive and won't hesitate to attack if you veer from the path. If you prefer to avoid unnecessary fights stay on the road. However, if you want to earn some extra experience, take out a few of the wretched on your way. Once you find the unfortunate Outrunner, return back the way you came to Outrunner Alarion.

With another slain outrunner, Alarion is short handed and **Completing the Delivery** is impossible for her to handle on her own. She asks you to deliver the package to the Inn in Falconwing Square. Follow Dawning Lane until you reach the square.

Since the poisoning of the Sunwell, life has greatly changed for your people. There are new paths and new allies that have never been considered before. Learn well from your elders and soon you will be ready to venture outside of your homeland, showing the world that, diminished or not, the power of the Blood Elves is still to be feared.

GOBLIN

Goblins are a creative race that often fails to see the forest for the trees. This might be because of their penchant for cutting down entire swaths of landscape. Many Goblins have a fascination with technology and innovative engineering.

Often found on neutral ground, many Goblins weren't interested in taking sides between the Horde and the Alliance. There isn't much profit in the choice because it closes out a huge market from the other side. However, recent developments in the world have made it impossible for all of the Goblins to sit on the sidelines. As such, some have joined the Horde and are ready to lend their inventions to the cause.

Goblins are tiny creatures, though Gnomes still push them out for the title of smallest fry. These green-skinned people have long ears and equally impressive arms for their size.

Starting Location: Kezan

RACIAL ABILITIES

ROCKET JUMP

Activates a rocket belt to jump forward.

ROCKET BARRAGE
Launches belt rockets at an enemy, dealing fire damage.

BEST DEALS ANYWHERE
Always receive the best discount regardless of faction standing.

BETTER LIVING THROUGH CHEMISTRY

Alchemy (a crafting skill) increased by 15.

TIME IS MONEY
Cash in on an increase to attack and casting speed!

Capital City: Orgrimmar (Goblin Slums)

Motortrike, the Goblin Racial Mount

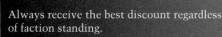

AVAILABLE CLASSES

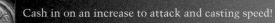

DEATH KNIGHT   DRUID   HUNTER   MAGE   PALADIN   PRIEST   ROGUE   SHAMAN   WARLOCK   WARRIOR

GOBLIN

Under the watchful eye of Trade Prince Gallywix, the Goblins of Kezan are a busy lot. There are always deals to be brokered, goods to be moved, and, most importantly, profits to be made. The entrepreneurial spirit runs strong in every Goblin and you are no exception. As the boss at KTC Headquarters your life is good. You have the best executive assistant money can hire, the respect of your fellow citizens, and a nice stack of macaroons in the bank. There are even rumors that you might one day replace the Trade Prince himself. Yep, the best life a Goblin could ask for. As long as nothing happens to change all that…

1 KTC Headquarters
2 Kaja'Mine
3 Izzy
4 Ace
5 Kajaro Field
6 The Drudge
7 Swindle Street
8 The First Bank of Kezan
9 Gallywix's Villa

KTC HEADQUARTERS

KTC Headquarters is the nerve center of your operation. It sits on the eastern side of Kezan, right next to the Kaja'mine that is the backbone of your business. You begin your day at headquarters by talking to Sassy Hardwrench, your Executive Assistant. There's a problem in the Kaja'mite mine and you need to be **Taking Care of Business**. Head east to find Foreman Dampwick and deliver Sassy's Incentive. Is that ticking you hear?

Head across the yard to find Foreman Dampwick at the top of the road leading down to the mine. After you deliver Sassy's "incentive" Dampwick is ready to tell you what's been going on in the mine. The foreman has a few problems eating into profits—one of them quite literally. First, he has **Trouble in the Mines**. The Tunnel Worms have come back and are eating right through the Kaja'mite. He asks you to enter the mines and exterminate them. As if the worms weren't bad enough, **Good Help is Hard to Find**. The troll slaves seem to think they can just take a break whenever they want and are in need of a serious attitude adjustment. Dampwick suggests you use your Goblin All-In-1-Der Belt to deliver the needed incentive.

Head down into the mine area and look for Defiant Trolls. The lazy good-for-nothings can be found shirking work all over the place. Give 'em a good zap with your belt to get them going again. The Tunnel Worms are found in any of the three mines. Thin them out enough so that maybe Dampwick can do his job.

Once you're done doing the foreman's jobs for him, return to receive your reward. Even though you're his boss, he has the gall to ask for even more help. He's so lucky you don't fire him. He asks you to deliver the Six-Pack of **Kaja'Cola** to Sassy Hardwrench. When you do, she tells you to that Megs in Marketing is looking for you.

Step out of the headquarters and stop to talk with Megs Dreadshredder. She knows that image is second only to profits and suggests you go **Rolling With My Homies**. Take your new Hot Rod around to pick up your friends, Ace, Gobber, and Izzy. Use the key Megs gave you to start up your Hot Rod. Drive south to reach teh other side of the headquarter's pool where you find Izzy lounging. After picking her up, drive north out of KTC Headquarters and stop to pick up Gobber just before you reach the large road running east and west. After he climbs in the car turn left and follow the road to reach Bilgewater Port and Ace. Now that all your friends are in the Hot Rod, return to Megs. She lets you know that Coach Crosscheck, leader of the Bilgewater Buccaneers, is looking for you.

Before you leave, head back into the headquarters to speak with Sassy. Sometimes you have no choice but to **Do It Yourself** and Sassy has just such a job that needs your personal touch. Some deadbeats aren't paying up and you need to get down there and deliver a "collection notice," if ya know what she means. Head down into Drudgetown and deliver a beatdown to Bruno Flameretardant, Frankie Gearslipper, Mack the Hammer, and Sudsy Magee.

Before leaving Headquarters either Candy Cane or Chip Endale has a task for you as well. Which quest giver you get depends on your gender. Males talk with Candy Cane while Females speak to Chip Endale. Your paramour tells you that you must get some new threads before the party which requires you to be **Off to the Bank**. Swing by the First Bank of Kezan and pick up some cash.

Kajaro Field

Start up your Hot Rod again and follow the road into Kajaro Field to find Coach Crosscheck. The coach tells you the Buccaneers are in a heap of trouble! His whole team's on the injured roster and the shredders have had it. The Coach needs you to help him get **The Replacements**. Gather Replacement Parts from all over the nearby area so he can get his Shredders back in the game. Look around the area of the city surrounding the field for the parts you need. Once you have them all, return to the coach.

The Buccaneers are down to their last Shredder, but the Coach gave it a few extra modifications for **Necessary Roughness**. He needs you to climb in that shredder and throw the Footbomb at the Steamwheedle Sharks. Aim at the approaching team and let the Footbombs fly until you have taken them all out. Once you are done, report back to Coach Crosscheck.

Thanks to your efforts, the game is at **Fourth and Goal**. All you have to do now is kick that goal! The coach has made another modification to the Footbomb to give you all the power you need to make a lasting impression on those Sharks. When you're finished return to the coach. Fans will be talking about the goal you kicked for a long time to come. Coach Crosscheck wants you to share your success with Sassy Hardwrench.

Now that you're done playing Footbomb it's time to Now that you're done playing Footbomb it's time to take care of those deadbeats! Drive down into Drudgetown and deliver a beatdown to those fools. When you are finished, hop in your Hot Rod again and head west from Kajaro Field to reach the First Bank of Kezan. Don't let those long lines bother you. Important Goblins like you can go to the head of the queue. Speak with the FBoK Teller to get your Macaroons.

The Teller gives you some advice for putting together **The New You**. Buy some Shiny Bling from Gappy Silvertooth, a Hip New Outfit from Szabo, and some Cool Shades from Missa Spekkies on Swindle Street. Once you've collected your outfit you're ready to head back to headquarters.

Your Class Trainer

Before reporting in, take a moment to speak with your trainer. You are now ready to learn an important skill or spell which helps you out in future endeavors.

After you report in to everyone who gave you a task, it's time to party. Sassy wants you to put on your Awesome Party Ensemble and head on over to the party at the company pool next door to entertain your guests as the **Life of the Party**.

Your new outfit comes with some new responsibilities. You must entertain your guests, but everyone wants something different. Those that are eating could use some more Hor D'oeuvres. Guests carrying sparklers want to see some Fireworks. A few Goblins just want someone to dance with, while others need their glasses refilled with Bubbly. As is to be expected at any good party, a few guests have had a bit too much Bubbly. In these cases, handing them a Bucket is the best option. Once you've entertained your guests, return to Sassy at headquarters.

The party is a success—maybe too much of one. There are **Pirate Party Crashers**! Southsea Pirates are crashing your party! This could be a career-ending catastrophe. Get back to the party and kill those Pirate Party Crashers before they completely ruin your celebration. Unlike the other foes faced up to this point, these pirates are aggressive and attack if you get too close. Try to avoid taking on more Pirate Party Crashers than you can handle at once. When the crashers are dealt with, head back to headquarters and talk to Sassy.

It seems that you have **The Uninvited Guest**. Trade Prince Gallywix himself is waiting for you upstairs. He has a proposition for you. Mount Kajaro is exploding and he has the only way off the island. If you fork over **A Bazillion Macaroons?!** Gallywix promises to save you a spot on his private yacht. Speak with Sassy Handwrench about this proposed deal. She is right outside KTC Headquarters.

Sassy has an idea of where you can get that kind of moolah. You must perform **The Great Bank Heist**. Before heading out to the First Bank of Kezan, speak with Megs Dreadshredder. She has an idea to help collect the money as well; she thinks you should be **Robbing Hoods**. The Trade Prince has already sent hired looters out into the streets of Kezan. Take your Hot Rod and run them down, collecting their already stolen loot in the process!

Before heading out talk to Foreman Dampwick as well. He's willing to do his part to get the macaroons. The Kaja'mite deposits down by the mines are the last known deposits in the world. Use Dampwick's Kablooey Bombs for **Liberating the Kaja'mite** deposits and pick up the chunks. That stuff is priceless! Before you take off, talk to Slinky Sharpshiv. She thinks the best way to get that much money is to steal it from the trade prince himself. She gives you a disguise so you can **Waltz Right In**.

After you talk with everyone, you're ready to go. Head down into the mine first. Look for Kaja'mite deposits all around. Use the bombs to blow them apart and then pick up the chunks. Watch out for the Rebellious Trolls. Now that the Brute Enforcers are gone they are lashing out at anyone who comes near.

When you are finished in the mine, hop in your car and head down the road. The looters are running rampant all over Swindle Street and the surrounding areas. Run them down and collect their ill gotten gains! When you have finished continue on to Gallywix's Villa.

Once you are close to the villa, your disguise activates. The other Mooks will never know you aren't one of them. That is, unless you get too close to Gallywix's Keensnout Potbelly Pigs. These pets can smell you a mile away so steer clear of them. Look for The Ultimate Bomb and The Goblin Lisa in small buildings near the Trade Prince's pool. Maldy's Falcon is upstairs in the villa itself.

After collecting all the priceless art you have no need for stealth anymore. Hop in your Hot Rod and head towards the bank. Once you arrive, go down the stairs to reach the bank vaults. To crack the vault you must use everything from your All-In-1-Der Belt. Once you begin, the correct tool comes up on the screen. You must quickly press this tool to successfully continue. Each time a tool appears, press the corresponding button. Once you do this enough times, the vault opens and you reclaim your personal riches! Now it's time to head back to headquarters.

After you report back to everyone, Sassy counts up your macaroons but you're still coming up short. As usual, she's got a plan. This time she's going to pull a **447**. All you need to do is to collect on the insurance policy on KTC Headquarters. Go inside and Activate the Leaky Stove, Drop a Cigar on the Flammable Bed, Overload the Defective Generator, and use the Gasbot to set it all off.

Once it all goes up in flames the Claims Adjuster appears. Talk to him to turn in your claim. He doesn't have time to inspect the place and pays you the money you're owed. Check with Sassy to see if it's going to be enough. She counts up everything and your **Life Savings** should be enough to pay the Trade Prince. Now all you have to do is hand it over to him. Once you accept the quest, you both hop in the car and she drives you to Gallywix's yacht. In exchange for your Life Savings he offers you passage to Azshara—as a coal scuttling slave! Never trust the Trade Prince.

You aren't sure just what, but something goes wrong on the voyage. You wake up and look around but it sure doesn't look like Azshara to you. Oh well, you worked your way up the corporate ladder before and you can certainly do it again. This is no time to be sitting around half-drowned. Get up and prove you've got what it takes to survive not only the savage boardroom but the savage jungle as well. You've got a financial empire to rebuild. After all, time is money!

ORC

Orcs are large and terrifying to their enemies, but after numerous wars, the Orcs seek peace and a return to their shamanistic heritage. Thrall, their great Warchief, led his people to Durotar, chosen due to its desolate climate and isolated position. Due to their warring heritage, Orcs are courageous on the battlefield. They are also a hardy people, seeking a new path to glory and honor.

Orcs are approximately 6 feet tall, with muscular physiques. Males have very long and unusual facial hair. Females have eclectic hair styles and unusual piercings. All Orcs have some variation of green skin.

Start location: Valley of Trials in Durotar

Home city: Orgrimmar

RACIAL ABILITIES

AXE SPECIALIZATION

Orcs gain additional Expertise when using Axes and Fist Weapons in melee combat. Expertise makes it harder for enemies to avoid your attacks.

BLOOD FURY

Increases attack power or spell power by an amount that increases by level. Lasts 15 seconds.

COMMAND

Damage dealt by Death Knight, Hunter, and Warlock pets increased.

HARDINESS

The duration of Stun effects on Orcs is reduced.

Wolves, the Orc Racial Mount

AVAILABLE CLASSES

DEATH KNIGHT · DRUID · HUNTER · MAGE · PALADIN · PRIEST · ROGUE · SHAMAN · WARLOCK · WARRIOR

ORC

After years of slavery and war, the Orcs founded the nation of Durotar on the shores of eastern Kalimdor. Though they embrace their shamanistic heritage, they also hold the arts of war in high regard. Their capital city Orgrimmar is a city rebuilt for war, teeming with people from all factions of the Horde. Though the new Warchief, Garrosh Hellscream, has his own ideas about how to rule, the Orcs still value strength and honor above all else. The recent events of the cataclysm have made it more vital than ever that young Orcs like you rise to join the ranks of the Horde.

1 The Den
2 Hana'zua
3 Sarkoth
4 Burning Blade Coven
5 Sen'jin Village

VALLEY OF TRIALS

The Valley of Trials provides a relatively safe place for young Orcs to begin their training, though it is not without its own dangers. As Kaltunk notes, you are now of age to battle in the name of the Horde! Though you may yearn for epic battles, that is not yet **Your Place in the World**. Report to Gornek for a task more suitable to one of your inexperience.

Gornek has a job designed for **Cutting Teeth** such as yours. He tells you to slaughter the Mottled Boars found on the nearby farms. When you finish, return to Gornek.

This time he has a more serious job for you. There are **Invaders in Our Home**! Despite that fact that it is in breach of a treaty, humans have infiltrated the valley. Gornek wants you to find them in the south and slay them. Before heading out to rid the valley of humans, speak with Galgar who has a tastier task for you. He wants to make **Galgar's Cactus Apple Surprise**, but he's all out of cactus apples. Collect some for him while you are out taking care of more serious business.

Head south out of the Den area and you almost immediately begin to see the Northwatch Scouts. Their clumsy attempts at stealth can't fool you! Take them down and don't forget to collect the cactus apples while you're out. When you are finished, return to Galgar and Gornek to claim your rewards.

Gornek sends you back out into the field to collect Scorpid Worker Tails. Their venom is used to make antidotes for foolish young Orcs who manage to get themselves inflicted with the **Sting of the Scorpid**.

Meeting Your Class Trainer

Before heading out to take care of those scorpids, take a moment to read the message that Gornek gave you from your Class Trainer. It is time for you to learn a new skill. Take the time out from your duties here to learn what they have to teach you.

After speaking with your trainer, stop by to talk to Foreman Thazz'ril. He has a problem with his **Lazy Peons**. They have a habit of napping on the job. He wants you to take his blackjack and use it on any peons you catch sleeping when they should be working!

Head north, past the farms with the Mottled Boars you slew earlier, to find Scorpid Workers. Take them out, and loot the tails from their corpses. After collecting enough tails, it's time to get those lazy peons back to work! The peons are all around the valley, mostly near the trees they are supposed to be harvesting. If you see one sleeping, walk up to him and smack him with the blackjack. Report back to the foreman when you are through.

Gornek is pleased with your progress and he has taught you all that he can. Speak to Zureetha Fargaze to continue your training. She has made a disturbing discovery. **Vile Familiars** are present in the valley. This can only mean that the Burning Blade has infiltrated the Valley of Trials and are hiding out in a cave to the north. She asks you to go there and defeat the Vile Familiars.

Before taking care of the Burning Blade, speak with Canaga Earthcaller near the Den. He is worried about his friend, **Hana'zua**. He asks you to look for him up near where the Scorpids hunt. Head northeast to find the injured troll. He is pretty bad off but his one concern is that you finish off **Sarkoth**, the large scorpid who attacked him.

Head south along the small path leading up to the plateau. Sarkoth stands out as it is larger than the Scorpid Workers and has a different coloring. When you engage the beast, watch out for its Venom Splash. It spits its venom at you, leaving a pool of it on the ground. When you see it head towards you, move quickly to avoid standing in it. Once you have obtained Sarkoth's Mangled Claw, return to Hana'zua. His injuries are such that he can't make it **Back to the Den** on his own. He wishes you to speak with Gornek to see if there is something that will help him.

Blood Fury

Though mostly civilized these days, when necessary, Orcs can still call on their ferocious side for an edge in battle. Every Orc has the ability to use Blood Fury. This ability increases your attack power or spell power, whichever is more appropriate depending on your class. Put it to use while taking down Sarkoth.

Hana'zua has held on for this long, so he should last a bit longer. Before returning to the Den, head northwest to take care of the Vile Familiars. These vicious little demons are all around outside of the cave. Thin their numbers to lessen the Burning Blade's hold in the valley.

Return to Gornek and let him know about Hana'zua. He promises to help the injured Troll. Afterwards, report to Zureetha. You did a good job with the Familiars, but Zureetha now sends you after something more important—an item of power. She asks you to enter the Burning Blade Coven and retrieve the **Burning Blade Medallion** and slay any Felstalkers in your way.

Before heading out, Thazz'ril has a task for you as well. Since you are entering the Burning Blade Coven anyway, you can retrieve **Thazz'ril's Pick**. He left it behind while surveying the cave and would really appreciate your bringing it back to him.

Head north to reach the Burning Blade Coven. Travel deeper into the cave to find Thazz'ril's Pick near a waterfall. It is a large tool and easy to spot. Clear out the Felstalkers you come across. They can drain your life, so finish them off as quickly as possible.

Continue deeper into the cave until you find Yarog Baneshadow. He is in possession of the Burning Blade Medallion you need. You have no choice but to relieve him of it! Baneshadow is a caster and doesn't hesitate to hit you with Fel Immolate, causing damage over time. Take him out and grab that medallion. If you've already met your quota of Felstalkers, save yourself some walking and use your Hearthstone to make a quick trip back to the Den.

Your time here in the Valley of Trials is at an end, but Zureetha Fargaze needs you to take information on the Burning Blade to Sen'jin village. Once there, speak to Master Gadrin who, no doubt, has more work for you. To reach the village leave the Valley of Trials by the east road and then turn right when the road forks.

Deathwing and his minions are not the only trouble caused by the recent cataclysm. New problems have arisen around the world and now more than ever your Warchief needs strong young Orcs like you. Learn well and strive always to remember the lessons of your elders as you go forth into the world to battle for the glory of the Horde!

TAUREN

The Tauren are a spiritual and nomadic race, wandering the plains for survival and seeking the will of the Earth Mother. Though inherently peaceful, hunting skills are prized as being part of the natural order. Tribal in nature, the Tauren have united under the rule of Baine Bloodhoof in majestic Thunder Bluff.

Tauren are 6-7 feet tall, with very large bulk and weight. Tauren have long tails, bipedal hooves, and only three fingers per hand. Both males and females have horns of varying size and shape.

Start location: Camp Narache in Mulgore

Home city: Thunder Bluff

RACIAL ABILITIES

 CULTIVATION

Herbalism skill (a gathering Profession) increased by 15. Taurens also gather herb nodes faster than other races.

ENDURANCE

Base Health increased by 5%.

NATURE RESISTANCE

Nature spells are less likely to hit a Tauren.

WAR STOMP

Once every two minutes, a Tauren can stun up to 5 enemies within 8 yards for 2 seconds.

Kodos, the Tauren Racial Mount

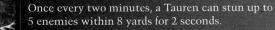

AVAILABLE CLASSES

DEATH KNIGHT · DRUID · HUNTER · MAGE · PALADIN · PRIEST · ROGUE · SHAMAN · WARLOCK · WARRIOR

TAUREN

After centuries of war against their ancestral enemies, the centaur, the Tauren tribes banded together and made this lush land their home. All Tauren are taught to respect the Earthmother and to honor their ancestors. Their capital city, Thunder Bluff, is a center of learning and trade and serves as a shining example of prosperity to all the Horde.

Though the Tauren have managed to mostly keep the peace in Mulgore, recent incursions from the Quillboar and Grimtotem have made the area much more dangerous than it used to be. As it is with all young Tauren, it is now your turn to follow the path you have chosen and learn the skills necessary to defend your homeland.

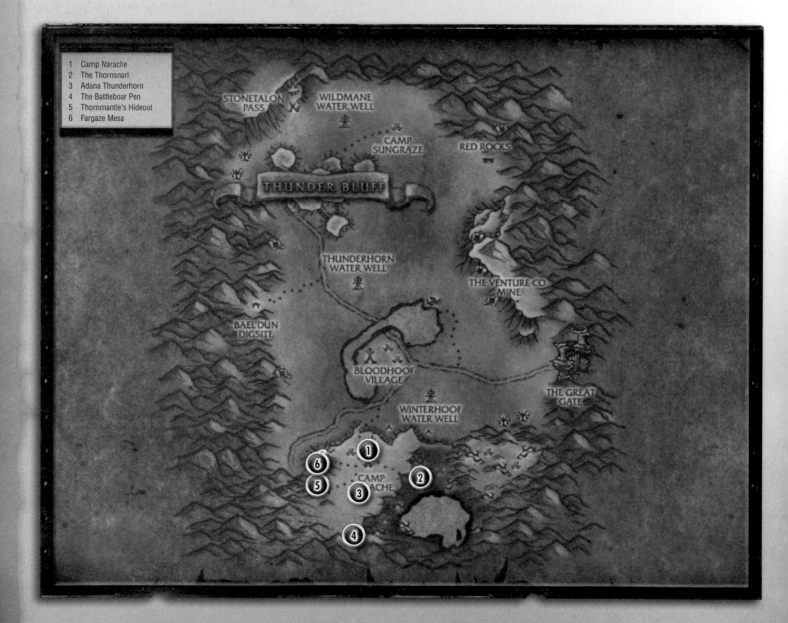

1 Camp Narache
2 The Thornsnarl
3 Adana Thunderhorn
4 The Battleboar Pen
5 Thornmantle's Hideout
6 Fargaze Mesa

CAMP NARACHE

As a fledgling brave you begin your journey in Camp Narache. In the past the small community often happily celebrated the training of young braves but you have arrived at a time of great sorrow. Though the Tauren had managed to keep the Bristleback Quillboar under control for some time, with the recent cataclysm they have begun pouring forth from their thorny homes, expanding their territory and attacking the nearby Tauren. During one such raid, the unthinkable happened and Greatmother Hawkwind was slain. Now, the denizens of Camp Narache have but one thing on their mind—justice.

Chief Hawkwind has a simple task for you. **The First Step** is to speak to his son, Grull Hawkwind, and begin exacting vengeance on the Bristleback! Head east to find Grull. He starts you on the path to become a full fledged brave; your first challenge is the **Rite of Strength**.

To complete this task you must travel into the heart of the Thornsnarl and slay Bristleback Quillboar. Since these foes are occupied with the other Fledgling Braves, it's hard to get yourself into too much trouble. Just attack one at a time and get used to playing the class you have chosen. Once you have slain enough to sate Grull's bloodlust return to him. Thinning out the Bristleback Invaders was helpful, but Grull now has another task for you. New braves like yourself have been captured and it's up to you to rescue them to complete **Our Tribe, Imprisoned**. Venture back into the Thornsnarl to free a number of your comrades. Their cages can be found scattered throughout the Thornsnarl. Once you have freed them, return to Grull.

While there you must also retrieve keys from the Bristleback you fell. Pleased with your work he tells you to **Go to Adana**, south of Camp Narache. She has taken a few braves to that area to root out the rest of the enemy.

LEVEL UP!

Remember once you level up to check your trainer for new skills. You get a quest leading you to your trainer from Rohaku Stonehoof at level 3.

According to Adana, the **Rite of Courage** teaches you never to underestimate your prey. Head to the south and brave the Bristleback's wild gunfire and take back the guns they stole from Camp Narache during the battle. She also sends you to **Stop the Thorncallers** from sowing more seeds to grow their hideous vines. The Bristleback Gun Thieves don't do too much damage to you—they must not have the hang of using the stolen guns! The Thorncallers can be found towards the back of the camp raising their twisting vines. These enemies aren't aggressive so don't be concerned with accidently biting off more than you can chew.

War Stomp

Unlike the soft-footed races, A Tauren's hooves can serve them well in battle. Use your War Stomp to stun nearby enemies for a few precious seconds, giving you an advantage in battle. Try it out while battling the Bristleback.

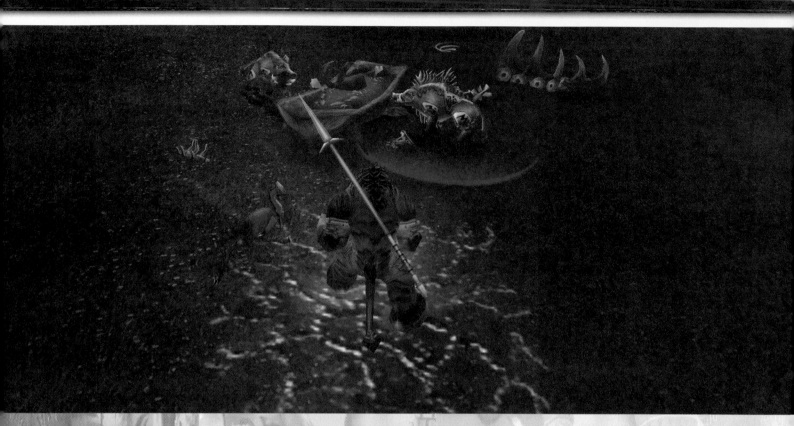

When you return, Adana has other tasks for you. Though it saddens her, Adana knows that the poor, abused Armored Battleboars kept by the Bristleback can never be rehabilitated. She asks you to put a down a number of them, ending their torment. **The Battleboars** don't naturally have a taste for flesh, but the Bristleback feed them a steady diet of gore to make them hungry for the enemy. She asks you to burn this **Feed of Evil** before returning.

Head slightly southwest from Adana to find the Battleboar Pen. Because these creatures are not aggressive, you can walk right up to the feed troughs and toss in the torch by right clicking on it. It ignites the gory food trough and also any nearby Battleboars, giving you easy kills at the same time as you burn the grotesque meals. After burning all three feed troughs, finish off any more Armored Battleboars you need to make Adana's quota and return to her.

Once your grisly task is completed, Adana tells you of the **Rite of Honor**. The Bristleboar you've taken down so far were just a warm up! She asks you to slay Chief Squealer Thornmantle in retribution for his killing of Greatmother Hawkwind.

Though you naturally want to seek vengeance for the Greatmother's death, before heading out speak with Rohaku Stonehoof. He gives you a note from your class trainer. Take the time to read it and return to Camp Narache. Your trainer can teach you skills that will come in handy when facing the Bristleback leader. Once you've learned what your trainer has to teach you, it is time to face the Chief.

Head southwest of Camp Narache to reach Thornmantle's Hideout. He is guarded by two Thornguards near the entrance to his small thornsnarl, so be cautious when you approach. Take them out and move onto the Chief himself to extract vengeance! He is a bit tougher than the rank and file you've been cutting your teeth on, but he isn't anything you can't handle. He likes to toss his torch at you, so be ready for the additional damage this can cause.

When the enemy lies dead at your feet, return to Camp Narache and report to Chief Hawkwind that the deed is done. While nothing can return the Greatmother to your midst, it gives him some comfort to know that you dealt with her murderer. During **Last Rites, First Rites** use the Ceremonial Offering at Greatmother Hawkwind's funeral pyre near the center of Camp Narache.

Though the Greatmother can now be at rest, your journey continues. You must now speak with Dyami Windsoar high atop Fargaze Mesa to the east of Camp Narache. Before heading there take care of any business you may still have in the camp.

You have learned all that Camp Narache has to offer and it is time for you to learn more about your chosen path and the ways of the Earthmother. When you are ready, climb the mesa to find Dyami Windsoar. After speaking to you he begins your **Rite of the Winds**. Drink the Water of Vision he gives you to transform into a vision. This bird form delivers you safely to Bloodhoof Village where your education continues.

TROLL

The Darkspear Trolls fled Stranglethorn Vale after generations of wars with other troll tribes and invaders. The Orcs offered the Trolls a new homeland in Durotar. Sen'jin Village is named in honor of the Trolls' fallen leader. This was the temporary settling point for the Trolls, but they've now pushed out to the Echo Isles, just off the Durotar coastline.

Trolls are wild, from living in the jungle. They are also superstitious, due to their tribe's spiritual practices. They are 7-8 feet tall, the tallest race in Azeroth. Males frequently squat in place, but females do not. Trolls have three fingers per hand and two toes per foot. Both males and females have a variety of tusk styles and wild hair styles.

Start location: Echo Isles in Durotar

Home city: Orgrimmar (Valley of Spirits)

RACIAL ABILITIES

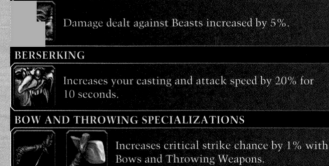

BEAST SLAYING

Damage dealt against Beasts increased by 5%.

BERSERKING

Increases your casting and attack speed by 20% for 10 seconds.

BOW AND THROWING SPECIALIZATIONS

Increases critical strike chance by 1% with Bows and Throwing Weapons.

DA VOODOO SHUFFLE

Reduces the duration of movement impairing effects by 15%.

REGENERATION

Health regeneration rate increased by 10%. 10% of total health regeneration may continue during combat.

Raptors, the Troll Racial Mount

AVAILABLE CLASSES

DEATH KNIGHT — DRUID — HUNTER — MAGE — PALADIN — PRIEST — ROGUE — SHAMAN — WARLOCK — WARRIOR

TROLL

The Darkspear Trolls have long been a race in exile. Chased from their ancestral home, they founded a settlement on the Echo Isles off the southeastern coast of Kalimdor. However, they were forced to abandon it to the mad witch doctor Zalazane. With the witch doctor now destroyed, the Darkspear tribe have moved back to reclaim the Echo Isles as their home. Though they remain a loyal part of the Horde, recent events have made it clear to their leader, Vol'jin, that the Darkspear Trolls must once again become a power in their own right. Though the world is facing the dangers wrought by the recent cataclysm, you have come of age at a proud time for the Darkspear. It is time for you to choose your path and learn what your elders have to teach.

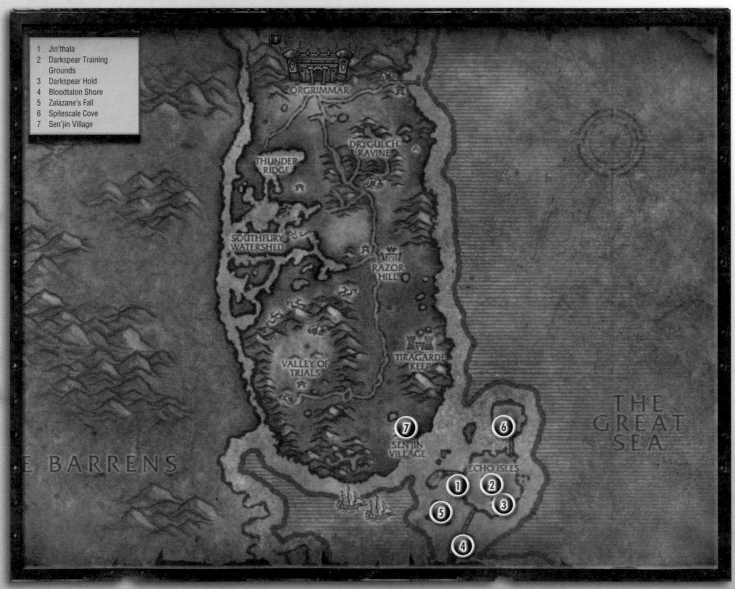

1 Jin'thala
2 Darkspear Training Grounds
3 Darkspear Hold
4 Bloodtalon Shore
5 Zalazane's Fall
6 Spitescale Cove
7 Sen'jin Village

DARKSPEAR ISLE

Your training on Darkspear Isle begins with speaking to Jin'thala. The Darkspear tribe have long been victims and outcasts, fleeing their homes time and time again—but no more. Now is the time for **The Rise of the Darkspear**. It is also time for you to begin your training. He tells you to speak with your Class Trainer to begin. Head up the small hill to enter the grounds.

Who you need to speak with depends on your class, but all the trainers are inside the Darkspear Training Grounds. Though you may be eager to get out into the wide world and help your tribe, before you can move on you must learn **The Basics: Hitting Things**. Your trainer sends you to practice on the nearby Tiki Targets. Once you are finished, return to your trainer.

You may be off to **A Rough Start**, but your next task gives you the chance to put your skills to a more practical use. The local Wildmane Cats are killing all the island boars. Thin their numbers and bring the pelts back to your trainer as proof of the deed. The Wildmane Cats are found all over the island. Leave the center of the training grounds to begin your hunt. Once you have collected enough pelts you are ready to return.

Berserking

No matter how civilized a Troll might be, when battle is joined and the blood starts flowing, more primitive urges must sometimes be heeded. Berserking is an ability available to all Trolls. It significantly increases your attack and casting speed, giving you an advantage during a tough battle. Try it out against Naj'tess!

Once you are finished helping them out, Kijara has another task for you. She wants you to take a promising raptor, one that is **Young and Vicious**, back to Moraya. Kijara needs you to use the Bloodtalon Lasso on Swiftclaw and take him back to the pens near Darkspear Hold. As his name suggests, Swiftclaw is fast and spends his time running quickly around the island. You need to be ready to use your lasso the second you see him. Once you rope hime, you mount up. He isn't stopping for anything so steer him back across the bridge until you reach the pen near the hold. Once you have delivered him safely, speak to Moraya.

After receiving your reward from Moraya, speak with Tortunga. Vol'jin has decided to launch an all out attack on the Naga on the northern part of the isle. Tortunga tells you to speak with Jornun here to get a ride to nearby Spitescale Cove. When you arrive, check in with Morrakki, Captain of the Watch.

SPITESCALE COVE

The raptor deposits you in front of Spitescale Cavern where you find the Captain of the Watch. Morakki has plenty of work for an eager young Troll like you. The Trolls will show **No More Mercy** to the atrocious Naga. He commands you to enter the cavern and kill any Spitescale Naga you see. While you are in there, Morakki also wants you to place a **Territorial Fetish** on every Naga banner you come across to let the Naga know that you mean business. Zuni joins you and gives you a bit of extra help during the fights. Make your way out of the cavern and return to Morakki when you are finished.

The Naga have long plagued the Darkspear but it seems there is a chance to settle this once and for all. The Sea Witch is an **Ancient Enemy**, and the Trolls have been waiting a long time to get a chance at revenge. Head northeast up the hill to speak with Vol'jin. Once there, offer your help in defeating Zar'jira, the Sea Witch.

During the battle, Vol'jin handles the Sea Witch but you have an important part to play. It is up to you to deal with the Manifestations of the Sea Witch. These ethereal foes keep coming throughout the fight and wiping them out deals damage to the Sea Witch herself. Once Vol'jin and Vanira have done some damage to the enemy, she unleashes freezing traps, freezing everyone but you in place. Quickly run behind her and stomp out the braziers she is using to fuel the traps. Once they are out, Vol'jin and Vanira can resume taking her down. Don't let yourself get overwhelmed by the Manifestation. They can be very challenging when not taken on one at a time. Once the witch falls, wait to speak to Vanira who transports you to Darkspear Hold where you can report to Vol'jin to receive your reward.

You've learned everything you could on Darkspear Isle. Now that you helped take down the Sea Witch, it is time for you to leave your home. Cross the shallows to the northwest to reach Sen'jin Village and report to Master Gadrin. He will be able to put a young Troll like yourself to good use.

Though it's been a long time coming, the Darkspear are once again coming into their own. The recent cataclysm has made an already dangerous world much more treacherous and your tribe needs young bloods like you more than ever. Take what you've learned here in your reclaimed homeland and use it to represent your tribe well in the coming challenges. Show your allies and enemies alike that the Darkspear are no longer fugitives, refugees, or exiles, but rather a force to be respected.

UNDEAD

A renegade group of undead broke away from the Scourge army and the rule of the Lich King. Led by Sylvanas Windrunner, this group of undead call themselves the Forsaken. Hated by the living but unwilling to return to the control of the Lich King, the Forsaken wage a continuous battle for their independent survival. They didn't choose undeath, but they see that it has its benefits.

Forsaken are 5-6 feet tall, scrawny, and gaunt. Their skin is deteriorating, and their hair is unkempt. Both males and females have a variety of decomposing features.

Start location: Deathknell in Tirisfal Glades

Home city: The Undercity

Skeletal Horses, the Undead Racial Mount

RACIAL ABILITIES

CANNIBALIZE
Regenerates 7% of total health and mana every 2 seconds for 10 seconds. Only works on Humanoid or Undead corpses within 5 yards.

SHADOW RESISTANCE

Shadow spells are less likely to hit an Undead.

UNDERWATER BREATHING

Underwater Breath lasts 233% longer than normal.

WILL OF THE FORSAKEN

Once every 30 seconds, an Undead can remove any Charm, Fear and Sleep Effect.

AVAILABLE CLASSES

DEATH KNIGHT · DRUID · HUNTER · MAGE · PALADIN · PRIEST · ROGUE · SHAMAN · WARLOCK · WARRIOR

UNDEAD

Bereft of the kingdom, friends, and family that once claimed them, those undead fortunate enough to rise from the ground with their sanity intact have formed a new nation. Pledging allegiance to Lady Sylvanas Windrunner, the Banshee Queen, the Forsaken have claimed Tirisfal Glades as their home. Though the Forsaken Capital, the haunting subterranean Undercity, lies beneath the ruins of Lordaeron in central Tirisfal Glades, there are many who would challenge the Forsaken's claim to this land, seeing in them little more than monsters. Newly joined with the Alliance, the forces of Gilneas mass nearby while the zealots known as the Scarlet Crusade seek to wipe out all undead, making no distinction between Scourge or Forsaken. It is into this world you have risen. Take up your arms, learn well, and prepare to defend not only your new homeland, but your very right to exist.

1 The Shadow Grave
2 Deathknell
3 Night Web's Hollow
4 Rotbrain Encampment
5 Calston Estate

SHADOW GRAVE

You wake to find Agatha, one of the Val'kyr, floating over you as she wakes you up from your dirt nap. Unlike so many **Fresh Out of the Grave** you have awoken with your sanity still intact—one of the Forsaken instead of the mindless Scourge. She tells you to talk to Undertaker Mordo to begin your new life.

No matter what you were in your former life, in this life you start out in a musty grave and you start out working for Mordo. He sends you into The Shadow Grave to fetch his Thick Embalming Fluid and his Corpse-Stitching Twine. He sends along Darnell, who knows the way. Head down into the Shadow Grave and collect the items from a table to the left. Once you have them, return to Mordo.

Not everyone was as lucky as you, rising from the grave with your mind still your own. **Those That Couldn't Be Saved** must be dealt with as well. Mordo sends you to destroy the Mindless Zombies that wander the graveyard. They are pitiful foes, but must be put down. Once you are finished, return to the Undertaker.

Undertaker Mordo has no more use for you, but others might. He sends you to speak with **Caretaker Caice**. Not everyone who rises with their mind intact takes the news of their new circumstance well. Caice asks you to speak with three recently risen, Marshal Redpath, Lilian Voss, and Valdred Moray. All three can be found in the graveyard. After you have spoken to them, return to Caice.

Now that he knows you are ready and willing to make yourself useful, Caretaker Caice sends you **Beyond the Grave**, along with Darnell. Follow the road into the small town of Deathknell and speak with Deathguard Saltain.

161

DEATHKNELL

Deathknell is a small sheltered town perfect for the freshly risen to get used to their new unlives. It has everything a fledgling Forsaken needs, such as class trainers and merchants. There are several townsfolk willing to reward you for performing tasks for them. Since you rose from the grave with little more than the tattered rags on your back, you should accept the jobs they offer you.

Shortly after entering Deathknell you see Deathguard Saltain. He has a **Recruitment** task for you. The buildings to the north and to the east are littered with the corpses of Scarlet Crusade members. Saltain wants you to find them and point at them so that Darnell can pick them up. Once you have filled your Recruitment quota, return to the Deathguard.

Before heading out on corpse duty, go into the chapel and speak with Shadow Priest Sarvis. Though the Lich King is no longer upon the Frozen Throne, his mindless slaves still infest the northern part of Deathknell. Sarvis asks you to deal with **Scourge on Our Perimeter** by killing Rattlecage Skeletons and Wretched Ghouls.

These enemies aren't aggressive, so attack them one at a time and you have no problem taking them out. The Scarlet Crusade corpses can be found all around, inside buildings, sprawled in the street, pretty much anywhere. They are easy to spot. All you need to do is use them to have Darnell pick them up. Don't worry—he's much stronger than he lookds. Once you have gathered the corpses and thinned out the number of Scourge, return to the Forsaken held section of Deathknell to receive your rewards.

When you return to Shadow Priest Sarvis he gives you a scroll from your class trainer. Before leaving the Chapel, Speak with Novice Elreth, who has a task for you. As you saw when you spoke with her earlier, Lillian Voss is having trouble accepting **The Truth of the Grave**. Take Elreth's Hand Mirror to Lillian upstairs in the inn. She needs to see the truth of what she now is.

Before heading to the inn, take the time to read the message from your trainer. At this point your trainer has a class-specific quest for you. It involves learning a key skill from them. Once you complete this you are ready to continue with your other tasks.

Head into the inn and look for Lillian Voss downstairs cowering in the corner. Speak with her to display her reflection in the mirror. Afterwards, return to Novice Elreth with news of Lillian's reaction. Though the news was disappointing, Novice Elreth can see that you, at least, are an asset to the Forsaken. She sends you to speak to **The Executor in the Field**.

Lillan Voss

CANNIBALIZE

While you may not share the Scourge's mindless aggression, you do have one thing in common with them—a taste for flesh! After a battle, use your Cannibalize skill to replenish your health and mana by making a meal out of your fallen undead or humanoid foe.

Follow the road north out of Deathknell. When the road begins to curve to the east, you see Executor Arren. Seeing the state of your armor he offers to help you improve it a bit with pieces of **The Damned**. Bring him Scavenger Paws and 4 Duskbat Wings to get a useful piece of armor. You can find plenty of the creatures to the north and west of Arren's location. Once you've gathered the needed items, return to Executor Arren for your reward!

The Forsaken need gold, but the nearby gold mine in **Night Web's Hollow** is overrun by spiders. Arren tasks you with clearing out both Young Night Web Spiders and the older specimens, Night Web Spiders.

Make Some Room!

Before heading out to deal with the arachnids, visit one of the merchants in Deathknell to clear out your bag. You need as much inventory room as possible to carry any valuable loot you come across.

Head northeast of Deathknell to reach the mine. The Young Night Web Spiders you need skitter around outside of the mine while their larger counterparts make their home inside the mine. These bigger foes can inject you with a weak poison, so watch your health and don't let it get too low. You don't want to be unpleasantly surprised by the extra damage.

After exterminating your quota, return to Executor Arren who has another job for you. Since the Val'kyr arrived, more and more undead are choosing not to join the Forsaken. These troublemakers are **No Better Than the Zombies** and have gathered at a small camp nearby and plan to attack Deathknell! Head east down the road to report to Darnell.

At the request of Shadow Priest Sarvis, Darnell has been keeping an eye on the camp. It's now time for a full out **Assault on the Rotbrain Encampment**. Head southeast to the camp and kill their leader, Marshal Redpath, and 8 Rotbrain Undead. Unlike the other foes you've faced so far, these are aggressive and attack you if you get too close. If you find that you are having trouble, fight next to a Deathguard Protector for some extra help. Once you've thinned out their numbers report back to Shadow Priest Sarvis in Deathknell.

Though you were been helpful in Deathknell, it's time to venture out to offer more assistance to the Forsaken. Deliver the Scarlet Crusade Documents to Sarvis's field agent at the Calston Estate, Deathguard Simmer. He will make good use of this **Vital Intelligence**. Follow the road north from Deathknell to reach the estate.

Few are lucky enough to rise from the grave at all, but you are among those rare fortunate ones to rise with your mind still intact. Though your former ties may be severed you have now found a new home and a new purpose as a member of the Forsaken.

CHOOSING A CLASS

Of all the character-creation decisions, your class choice has the greatest impact on the type of experience you have in World of Warcraft. There are 10 available classes in the game, but not all classes are available to every race. For your first character, you have nine class choices: Druid, Hunter, Mage, Paladin, Priest, Rogue, Shaman, Warrior, and Warlock.

Death Knight

The tenth class is a "hero" class: the Death Knight. This class is available only to players who already have a high-level character. You must wait to create a Death Knight until your first character reaches level 55. Any race can play as a Death Knight.

A QUICK LOOK AT CLASSES

Mage ⚫, Priest ⚫, Rogue ⚫, and Warrior ⚫ are considered the four "basic" classes because they are classic character archetypes from the myths and literature that inspired the creators of World of Warcraft. Warriors and Rogues are primarily melee combat classes, while Mages and Priests prefer to stay at a safe distance in combat.

Druid ⚫, Paladin ⚫, and Shaman ⚫ are the "hybrid" classes because they are versatile characters, equally comfortable fighting up close or using magic spells to harm enemies or heal allies.

Hunter ⚫ and Warlock ⚫ are the "pet" classes, because both rely on a companion pet for a great deal of assistance. Hunters tame wild beasts, while Warlocks summon demonic creatures.

The next thing to consider is how you plan to play the game. The "how" in this case is "How many people will you be playing with?"

Going Solo

If you plan to play solo (which means you'll be playing the game alone for a majority of the time) any class is a viable choice. Because there are already a number of people who play the game alone, large portions of World of Warcraft are designed around people playing solo.

Playing in a Group

If you plan on playing with other people (even if it's just one other person), someone in the group should play a class with access to healing spells, but healing is just one of the roles your character can assume. To keep it simple, imagine that every character falls into one of three categories: tank, healer, and damage dealer.

Tank

Do you enjoy shielding people from harm? Tanks are a good choice for you. They are often the leader of groups, and people respect them when they get the job done. It's not the easiest choice, but it is rewarding. Warriors, Paladins, Druids, and Death Knights may assume the role of tanks.

Healer

Is it okay if someone else does the killing while you support them? Healing may be the way for you. Healers are essential to great groups. They rarely get the glory of a tank, but they are needed, and wise players are quick to thank them for being there. Priests, Shamans, Paladins, and Druids can fill this role.

Damage Dealer

Is self-reliance a big thing for you? Maybe you just want to slaughter when you get the chance, but groups are more of a "take it or leave it" thing. You're a damage dealer. About 60% of a given group is composed of damage dealers. Some may have backup healing (or backup tanking) potential, but their primary role is to disable or kill enemies. Any class can fill this role but Rogue, Mage, Warlock, and Hunter are notable choices because they are dedicated to the task.

Tips for Choosing Your Class

Experienced players debate all day about which classes are the easiest to play, hardest to play, strongest, weakest—you get the idea. As a new player, you should make a choice based on personal preference.

When considering classes, select the role that appeals to you and keep the following things in mind:

- Hunters, Mages, Priests, and Warlocks fight best from a safe distance. You must learn how to control the range of the fight, because you're not built for melee combat. Keep enemies away from you, and you'll be successful.

- Death Knights, Paladins, Rogues, and Warriors fight up-close and personal with their enemies. Melee combat is louder (with the combat noises like clanging weapons) and is generally more chaotic than what ranged classes experience.

- Druids and Shaman can fight at long range or in melee combat, and it's up to you to decide which way you prefer.

WHAT'S NEXT?

Use the following pages as an introduction to the ten classes available in the game. If you aren't sure which class is the one for you, try a few different classes. You may not know what you like until you try it!

MAGE

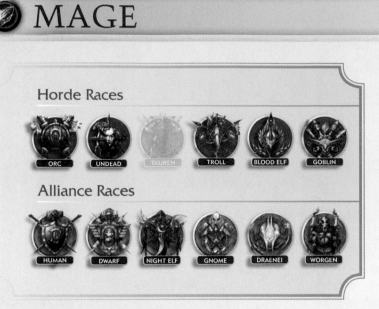

Horde Races

ORC UNDEAD TAUREN TROLL BLOOD ELF GOBLIN

Alliance Races

HUMAN DWARF NIGHT ELF GNOME DRAENEI WORGEN

OVERVIEW

A Mage uses Arcane, Fire, and Frost spells to deal damage to enemies from afar. This class has high damage output, but it's easy for them to die if enemies reach them in melee combat. Mages wear cloth armor, so they have little protection in hand-to-hand fights.

What they do have are abilities that allow them to slow down an enemy's approach, hold enemies in place, or blink away to a safe distance. This is why Mages are an exciting class to play. You aren't always just sitting at long range using the same spell again and again.

PROMINENT CLASS ABILITIES

Polymorph

Polymorph is known as "sheeping", because it turns a targeted enemy into a sheep. While a sheep, the enemy cannot fight or cast spells. Any damage done to the sheep breaks the spell, and you can Polymorph only one target at a time, so be careful when you use it! You aren't limited to turning enemies into sheep. There are items around the world that allow you to turn foes into different animals, such as turtles or cats.

Out of Combat Utility

Mages are excellent damage dealers, but they also have an impressive list of abilities that are a huge help at any time. Mages gain the ability to create food and water to sustain adventuring parties. At higher levels, Mages can Teleport to certain cities around the world, and eventually they create Portals that allow other characters to visit the same places. With a Mage, you are never far from a big city, and your next meal is one spell away!

TALENT TREES

At Level 10, Mages must decide to follow one the following talent trees: Arcane, Fire, or Frost.

 Arcane Mages get to deal more sudden damage, slip out of danger, disable enemies, and so forth. They also offer a good middle of the road point in the Mage talent lines. Fire Mages focus heavily on damage, while Frost Mages get more ways to disable targets. Arcane is in the middle of this path, getting more opportunities to Slow enemies while adding a fair number of damage attacks and instant spells.

Fire Mages are the most predictable, but that doesn't stop them from inflicting frightening amounts of damage. They have a more organized method of attack, and their sustained damage is excellent in groups. However, they aren't great at getting out of trouble. When played solo or in player versus player engagements, they get squished more than their peers.

 Frost Mages are wonderful allies or vile pests, depending on your perspective. They have more ways to save themselves than other Mages, making them hard to kill. They don't deal as much damage as Fire Mages, but there has to be a trade-off somewhere, right?

PROMINENT CLASS ABILITIES

Divine Shield

If things ever get too hot, even for them, they have special toys to get out of trouble. Paladins have several abilities that surround them with divine power. Colloquially, this is called "bubbling," and it protects the Paladin for a brief time, allowing them to catch up on healing or get the heck out of an area.

Blessings

Paladins also aid groups by providing powerful buffs. These can be customized to meet the needs of the people involved, so you don't have to give everyone the same bonus. This makes Paladins fun to have around whether your group is heavy on melee, casters, or whatever else you find.

Horde Races

ORC · UNDEAD · TAUREN · TROLL · BLOOD ELF · GOBLIN

Alliance Races

HUMAN · DWARF · NIGHT ELF · GNOME · DRAENEI · WORGEN

TALENT TREES

At Level 10, Paladins must decide to follow one of the following talent trees: Holy, Protection, or Retribution.

Holy Paladins are dedicated healers. Their best work is done when they can focus on keeping one ally alive, and they're able to remove three types of negative effects with a single spell. No other class can match that!

Protection Paladins are extraordinarily hard to kill, making them great tanks. By consecrating the ground upon which they stand, Protection Paladins do a great job of holding the attention of multiple enemies at the same time, allowing others in the group to perform their tasks unimpeded.

Retribution Paladins use two-handed weapons to deal damage in close quarters. As a Retribution Paladin, you aren't overwhelmed with a large number of abilities, which allows you to become familiar with the class in less time than what other classes may require.

OVERVIEW

Paladins are a hybrid class, making it possible to join a group as a tank, healer, or damage dealer. As a tank or damage dealer, Paladins are able to stay in the thick of battle due to their heavy armor absorbing more damage than many other melee classes can handle.

This flexibility is extremely useful for someone who doesn't have a large guild and the ability to stick to just one role. In addition, this flexibility allows Paladins to tackle difficult tasks on their own since they are able to heal themselves in the midst of battle.

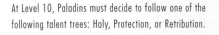

PRIEST

Horde Races

ORC | UNDEAD | TAUREN | TROLL | BLOOD ELF | GOBLIN

Alliance Races

HUMAN | DWARF | NIGHT ELF | GNOME | DRAENEI | WORGEN

OVERVIEW

While traditionally viewed as a healing class, Priests in World of Warcraft are capable of inflicting damage as well. Wearing only cloth armor, Priests are vulnerable to melee attacks at early levels so you must learn to keep enemies at a safe distance.

Priests are highly sought after in group situations. Though you carry a substantial burden (that of keeping the group alive), it's possible to learn the dynamic quickly, especially if you're motivated to be a good healer. It's more challenging to play a Priest solo, but it's far from an impossible task. Priests have everything they need to kill monsters on their own. You may level slower than some other classes, but you don't need a group to have fun.

PROMINENT CLASS ABILITIES

Healing Spells

Priests are in demand for groups because they have a variety of healing spells that work in different ways, but share the same function: keep allies alive. Power Word: Fortitude increases the overall health of allies; Lesser Heal and Greater Heal restore health immediately; Renew restores health to a target over time. You even learn how to encase yourself or an ally in a bubble which absorbs incoming damage!

Shadowform

For the Priests who prefer to specialize in dealing damage rather than restoring health, there is Shadowform. Shadowform literally turns the Priest into a translucent shadow. In Shadowform, Priests deal increased Shadow damage and take a reduced amount of damage. If you enjoy playing a Priest and want to play solo, Shadowform is the way to go.

TALENT TREES

At Level 10, Priests must decide to follow one of the following talent trees: Discipline, Holy, or Shadow.

 Discipline Priests balance their healing and spellcasting. This isn't a damage-dealing line, but it provides a number of effects that mitigate damage, protect Priests and their allies, or aid in casting (whether for damage or healing).

 Holy Priests are the healers' healers. Their goal is to heal well under almost any circumstance. They have almost no offensive strength, but that's the not goal for Holy Priests. Holy Priests are so dedicated to healing, they eventually learn how to continue healing after being killed!

 Shadow Priests violently diverge from the other two Priest trees. Ideal for soloing, Shadow Priests get to have fun tormenting enemies before killing them. Vampiric Embrace funnels a fraction of the health removed from enemies to restore the health of their allies, and Vampiric Touch does the same for mana.

PROMINENT CLASS ABILITIES

Stealth

Stealth is a defining feature of the Rogue class from the earliest period of your leveling. Stealth allows Rogues to move about the world without being seen as easily. Stay behind monsters that are slightly higher level to avoid detection.

Combo Points

Many Rogue abilities stack combo points on a target, exposing them to even nastier attacks. All abilities that use up combo points are more effective as the combo points add up. This makes Rogues especially good at finding single targets and slicing them to ribbons. It's harder for Rogues to take on several enemies at once with equal finesse.

Horde Races

ORC · UNDEAD · TAUREN · TROLL · BLOOD ELF · GOBLIN

Alliance Races

HUMAN · DWARF · NIGHT ELF · GNOME · DRAENEI · WORGEN

TALENT TREES

At Level 10, Rogues must decide to follow one of the following talent trees: Assassination, Combat, or Subtlety.

 Assassination Rogues are the royalty of burst damage. They focus on smaller weaponry, poisons, and sudden attacks. For the biggest sudden numbers, look here! Assassination Rogues gain combo points quickly, and they spend them on pure damage.

 Combat Rogues are more direct. They often use heavier weapons and stand toe to toe with the target, wailing away with an emphasis on outdamaging the enemy. "You die first" is their way of thinking. If you want to have a direct combat character and don't mind light armor, Combat Rogues are a pile of fun.

 Subtlety Rogues are, indeed, the most subtle of the bunch. They rely on more frequent use of special abilities, cooldown improvements, and damage over time abilities. It takes longer to master this talent line compared with the alternatives, but it's always been a rewarding choice for a thinking person's Rogue.

OVERVIEW

Sneaky and sticky-fingered, Rogues are the dirtiest melee fighters around. Rogues use a variety of Stuns and Poisons and can even Blind enemies. Stealth and Distract help Rogues move through areas almost unnoticed, and they can pick up some extra money from enemies by picking their pockets.

If high risk and high reward intrigue you, this is a class that's worth your time and attention. Rogues strike quickly while using weapons in both hands and can often kill anything before it knows what has happened. A Rogue caught flat footed often dies quickly but with all the tricks at their disposal, even wounded Rogues are difficult to finish off before they vanish into thin air.

SHAMAN

Horde Races

ORC UNDEAD TAUREN TROLL BLOOD ELF GOBLIN

Alliance Races

HUMAN DWARF NIGHT ELF GNOME DRAENEI WORGEN

OVERVIEW

Shamans are a hybrid class that can function as melee fighters, ranged casters, or healers. Their elemental powers provide a wide variety of buffs, and you can do a bit of everything in the game while playing one of these heroes.

Shamans draw their strength from the four natural elements (Air, Earth, Fire, Water). This is reflected in the totems they use to improve their performance, and the performance of anyone in a group with them.

PROMINENT CLASS ABILITIES

Shocks

Shocks are a type of spell that a Shaman can use instantly. These spells typically damage your target, and also have a variety of effects including stopping spell casting, or reducing a target's movement speed.

Totems

Totems summon the power of the elements for a variety of effects. Totems are temporary creations, and they can be targeted and destroyed by attacks. There are totems that boost your melee damage, and others that blast nearby enemies with fire. Others are more defensive in nature, and give increased resistance to certain types of magic or restore your health. Shamans can use one totem from each element simultaneously.

TALENT TREES

At Level 10, Shamans must decide to follow one of the following talent trees: Elemental, Enhancement, or Restoration.

 Elemental Shamans use shocks and other spells to take down enemies. They deal damage while standing at a safe distance from melee combat. Elemental Shamans have a few tricks to push away enemies who draw too close, while the Mail armor they wear allows them to stand up to punishment better than most other spell-casting damage dealers.

 Enhancement Shamans thrive in the midst of battle, dealing damage to enemies with a weapon in each hand and a host of spells at their command. Where most classes focus on using either weapons or spells to deal damage, Enhancement Shamans use a balanced mix of spells and weapons in combat.

 Restoration Shamans offer support to the groups they join with healing spells that keep allies alive and fighting. Restoration Shamans are not designed to inflict damage, but their totems boost the abilities of others, making the overall group a more effective fighting force.

PROMINENT CLASS ABILITIES

Demonic Pets

Each Warlock pet is quite different. Imps supplement ranged damage and make the caster harder to kill. Succubi bring more damage to the table. Felhunters are keen anti-casters. Voidwalkers act as a tank. The only downside to these pets is that you can only summon one at a time.

Use of Soul Shards

Warlocks steal the souls of their victims and hold them as Soul Shards, which augment Warlock spells. These items are a resource (not an inventory item), and you can have up to three at once. They are spent to summon pets instantly, improve casting speed for specific spells, or add enhanced effects to others.

Horde Races

ORC · UNDEAD · TAUREN · TROLL · BLOOD ELF · GOBLIN

Alliance Races

HUMAN · DWARF · NIGHT ELF · GNOME · DRAENEI · WORGEN

TALENT TREES

At Level 10, Warlocks must decide to follow one of the following talent trees: Affliction, Demonology, or Destruction.

Affliction Warlocks are the damage over time specialists. They lay down damage over time spells faster than other Warlocks varieties, and they're good at moving from target to target to maximize their ability to keep damage flowing.

Demonology Warlocks are the toughest of the bunch. They're quite hard to kill, and sometimes they even end up tanking specific events. They gain improved pets, more survivability, and can occasionally transform themselves into a Demon (it's as awesome as it sounds).

Destruction Warlocks are the more traditional casters of the three. They improve Shadowbolts and fire spells from the Warlock's repertoire, hitting big-damage numbers and felling single targets quite well.

OVERVIEW

Warlock is the class for anyone who wants to play something sinister. You get to curse people, summon demons, and generally have a malevolent look. Warlocks are ranged casters that employ a combative pet to supplement their already impressive damage total. Though Warlock pets aren't as powerful as Hunter pets, these demonic allies offer a bit more versatility.

Warlocks are masters of inflicting damage over time. When pushed, these casters are able to sacrifice their health to bring even more damage to an engagement. Warlocks scare their healers as much as they do their actual enemies. It's not uncommon to see a Warlock's health dwindle even when nothing is attacking them. You get used to it!

WARRIOR

Horde Races

ORC | UNDEAD | TAUREN | TROLL | BLOOD ELF | GOBLIN

Alliance Races

HUMAN | DWARF | NIGHT ELF | GNOME | DRAENEI | WORGEN

OVERVIEW

Warriors are the quintessential melee class. Wearing heavy armor and wielding many types of weapons, they take on foes with fury and tenacity. A superior tank or a valuable damage dealer, there is always a place for Warriors who know how to play their class well.

Warriors require considerable practical knowledge. They're always doing the most to both gain and spend their Rage (a resource primarily earned through dealing and receiving damage). They must also dance between stances, ensuring that their players need to memorize quite a few keys. The reward is that you get to play a class that always has something new or something that you could do a bit better.

PROMINENT CLASS ABILITIES

Stances

Warriors shift between three stances: Battle, Berserker, and Defensive. Battle Stance is the first you learn, and has a strong mix of deadly abilities. Berserker Stance gives Warriors their best chance for critical hits, and it has access to strong damage abilities. The downside of Berserker Stance is that it causes Warriors to take extra damage. Defensive Stance lowers a Warrior's damage output, but it makes incoming damage easier to handle.

Shouts

Warriors have five different shouts. Battle Shout increases the party's attack power, while Demoralizing Shout reduces the attack power of nearby enemies. Commanding Shout, learned at a much higher level, increases the Stamina of anyone in your group. Only one of these three can be active at a time. The other shouts are more situational. Intimidating Shout causes enemies to flee in terror. Challenging Shout focuses the attention of nearby enemies on the Warrior.

TALENT TREES

At Level 10, Warriors must decide to follow one of the following talent trees: Arms, Fury, or Protection.

Arms Warriors use a two-handed weapon to deal strong burst damage. Their attacks often leave targets bleeding, causing them to suffer additional damage over time.

Fury Warriors equip weapons in both hands which includes the option of using a two-handed weapon in one hand! Few sights instill as much fear as a plate-clad Warrior brandishing two giant weapons.

Protection Warriors are tanks. They have a few options for stunning enemies, but most of all they excel at staying alive. They get additional abilities to extend their lives during tricky battles. They work best in groups, but are capable of tackling quests on their own.

PROMINENT CLASS ABILITIES

Runic Power

Death Knights have six total runes, from Blood, Frost, and Unholy. Use of these builds up Runic Power, a resource that is used for specific combat abilities.

Runeforging

Death Knights get to "enchant" their own weaponry. Runeforging allows a Death Knight to tailor weapons to specific situations with greater flexibility than what is available to other classes.

TALENT TREES

Death Knights must decide to follow one of the following talent trees:

 Blood is the tanking line for Death Knights. Blood Death Knights focus on holding the attention of enemies in combat, and surviving the resulting damage.

 Frost is a melee line that combines damage from direct attacks and Frost-based spells. There are also abilities here to get out of trouble, including slowing down enemies to allow for an easier escape.

 Unholy Death Knights have better overall spellwork, improved damage over time, and superior summonable pets. They even get a special Gargoyle every few minutes.

Horde Races

ORC UNDEAD TAUREN TROLL BLOOD ELF GOBLIN

Alliance Races

HUMAN DWARF NIGHT ELF GNOME DRAENEI WORGEN

OVERVIEW

Death Knights are a Hero class. You can't unlock these characters until you have one character reach level 55. Once there, you can create a Death Knight and have them start at level 55 themselves. There is a specific starting area just for these characters, and they have an awesome backstory that you get to experience.

Death Knights are forced to deal all of their damage at close range, but they wear plate and take hits well. Melee is their natural environment, and they even have abilities that pull enemies into their favorite combat range. Death Knights also get combative pets, which aren't as powerful as Hunter or some Warlock pets, but they add flavor to playing as a Death Knight.

BEYOND THE FALL

With the Horde and Alliance focused on the Lich King and the Scourge in Northrend, an ancient evil stirs essentially undetected in the South Seas. Deathwing, the lord of the Black Dragonflight and one of the five great Dragon Aspects, has finally awoken to confront those who once defeated him. His return sends out waves of devastation that violently reshape the continents of Kalimdor and the Eastern Kingdoms.

The Goblins of the Bilgewater Cartel have long called the South Seas their home, but their islands are devastated in the cataclysm. Forced to leave their village, they seek aid and find a welcome ally in the Horde.

The Greymane Wall, which has long sheltered the people of Gilneas, is destroyed. Unable to hide any longer, the Gilneans rejoin the Alliance and reveal the curse that has kept them in seclusion for so long.

However, both the Goblins and Gilneans are forced to confront a world once again on the brink of open warfare.

The tenuous peace forged by the Horde and Alliance, created to face the threat of the Lich King, is quickly dissolving. Both sides have powerful reasons to view the other with skepticism and scorn, and the voices of the warriors who openly favor the obliteration of their old enemies gain increasing support. Horde and Alliance forces now scramble to claim the land torn asunder in the Cataclysm, resulting in a brutal conflict raging across the land.

Adding to the chaos is a sudden surge in Elementals. Never before seen Elementals of all varieties have claimed lands in Azeroth, attacking anyone who approaches their territory. Not all of these Elementals are violent, while others seem to be under the control of another power. To combat this threat, Thrall has joined the Earthen Ring, a group of shamans dedicated to harmony between the world and the elemental forces. He has named Garrosh Hellscream to succeed him as Warchief, a decision viewed by many with concern due to Garrosh's recklessness and distrust of other races, even those part of the Horde. This belligerence is well matched by Varian Wrynn, King of Stormwind, who would gladly see the Horde destroyed.

Other groups seek to take advantage of this struggle as well. In remote Westfall, the Defias, a group once thought destroyed, is slowly reforming under the leadership of an unknown figure. In Mulgore, the Grimtotem Clan undermines the authority of Thunder Bluff for their own gains. Even the cult of the Twilight Hammer has found another way to further their ultimate goal: to bring about the end of the world.

This is the world you have entered. These are the enemies you must face. Seek out allies, rediscover the world, and uncover Deathwing's plans.

—Welcome to Cataclysm.

OF THE LICH KING

GEOGRAPHIC UPHEAVAL

Deathwing's return changed the geography of many zones (although few were hit as hard as Thousand Needles) and also changed the enemies which appeared in those zones. The level values in the following tables are not exact, but instead provide a general range for each zone. Use the maps on this page for a visual representation of the information provided in the following tables.

OUTLAND

65-68
67-70
60-64
58-63
64-67
62-65
67-70

NORTHREND

77-80
77-80
76-78
77-80
74-77
68-72
71-74
73-75
68-72

70

1-10
10-20
1-10
10-20
40-45
35-40
30-35
1-10
10-20
20-25
25-30
1-12
82-83
20-25
84-85
1-10
10-20
80-82
45-50
45-50
50-55
1-10
15-20
10-15
25-30
50-55
25-30
55-60
30-35

1-10
10-20
10-20
45-50
50-55
78-81
10-20
20-25
25-30
10-20
1-10
30-35
1-10
30-35
35-40
1-6
35-40
40-45
55-60
50-55
45-50
84-85

KALIMDOR

6-12

EASTERN KINGDOMS

HORDE ZONES

STARTING ZONES	LEVEL 6-10	LEVEL 10-20	LEVEL 20-25
Deathknell	Tirisfal Glades	Silverpine Forest	
Sunstrider Isle	Eversong Woods	Ghostlands	
Valley of Trials & Sen'jin Village	Durotar	Azshara	Hillsbrad Foothills
Red Cloud Mesa	Mulgore		
Isle of Kezan	Kezan	Northern Barrens	

ALLIANCE ZONES

STARTING ZONES	LEVEL 6-10	LEVEL 10-20	LEVEL 20-25
Coldridge Vale & Gnomeregan	Dun Morogh	Loch Modan	
Northshire Valley	Elwynn Forest		Wetlands
Shadowglen	Teldrassil	Westfall (10-15) & Redridge Mountains (15-20)	
Gilneas	Gilneas City	Darkshore	
Ammen Vale	Azuremyst Isle	Ruins of Gilneas	Duskwood

NEUTRAL ZONES

LEVEL 20-25	LEVEL 25-30	LEVEL 30-35	LEVEL 35-40	LEVEL 40-45	LEVEL 45-50	LEVEL 50-55	LEVEL 55-60
	Arathi Highlands	Desolace	Dustwallow Marsh		Tanaris	Swamp of Sorrows	Blasted Lands
	Southern Barrens		Eastern Plaguelands	Searing Gorge		
Ashenvale	Northern Stranglethorn		Feralas		Badlands	Burning Steppes	Winterspring
		The Hinterlands		Thousand Needles			
	Stonetalon Mountains	Cape of Stranglethorn	Western Plaguelands		Felwood	Un'Goro Crater	Silithis

OUTLAND ZONES

LEVEL 58-63	LEVEL 60-64	LEVEL 62-65	LEVEL 64-67	LEVEL 65-68	LEVEL 67-70	LEVEL 70
Hellfire Peninsula	Zangarmarsh	Terokkar Forest	Nagrand	Blade's Edge Mountains	Netherstorm	Isle of Quel'Danas
					Shadowmoon Valley	

NORTHREND ZONES

LEVEL 68-72	LEVEL 71-74	LEVEL 73-75	LEVEL 74-77	LEVEL 76-78	LEVEL 77-80
Borean Tundra					Crystalsong Forest
	Dragonblight	Grizzly Hills	Zul'Drka	Sholazar Basin	Icecrown
Howling Fjord					Storm Peaks

CATACLYSM ZONES

LEVEL 78-81	LEVEL 80-82	LEVEL 82-83	LEVEL 84-85
		Deepholm	
		Kelp'thar Forest	Uldum
Mount Hyjal	Vashj'ir	Shimmering Flats	
		Abyssal Depths	Twilight Highlands

PVP

What's waiting for fans of Player versus Player action? Two new Battlegrounds (The Battle for Gilneas, Twin Peaks) for high level characters, an all-new outdoor PVP zone (Tol Barad), and a new system for earning the best PVP gear possible.

If you're not a fan of Arena-style PVP with its relatively small numbers, and the only objective is to kill the other team, but still want a crack at the best PVP gear possible, then Rated Battlegrounds are perfect for you. You earn Conquest Points from either Rated Battlegrounds or Arenas, so you aren't locked into a single way to get the best gear available.

CHANGES TO YOUR CHARACTERS

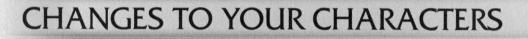

Every character class has undergone big changes in Cataclysm, and there are a number of pages elsewhere in the guide that provides specific help for each class. The information provided here deals with overall changes to the game and how those changes apply to your characters. For example, one change that applies to everyone (although melee classes get the most out of it) is the change to weapon skills. You no longer need to worry about skilling up with a certain type of weapon. If your class can use it, you are immediately proficient with it.

Relics No Longer Class Dependent

The classes that once used specific Relics (Death Knights, Druids, Paladins, and Shaman) no longer need to worry about selecting the correct Sigil, Idol, Libram, or Totem. All these classes now use Relics that now provide benefits that closely resemble the wands and ranged slot items used by other classes.

LEVELING YOUR CHARACTER

The level cap is now 85, but higher levels are only the tip of the iceberg when it comes to the changes to the leveling process. As you reach each higher level, a system message pops up and tells you what's waiting for you at this new level. The benefits include learning a new ability, or having a new talent point to place.

Abilities have undergone extensive changes as well. You may not notice some of these changes if you're starting out at level 80, but many spells and abilities are learned at much earlier or later levels than you remember. Ranks are gone from spells and abilities now. After you train any ability, it automatically improves as you gain levels.

CHARACTER STATS

Many stats are gone. Mana Per 5 Seconds, Defense Rating, Shield Block Rating, and Armor Penetration are essentially gone from the game as individual statistics. Their functionality has been folded into other statistics or built into some talents and abilities. Spell Power appears only on weapons (though characters also get it from their Intellect), and Attack Power is derived entirely from Strength and Agility, depending on your class. All characters, starting at level 50, earn a bonus to a primary stat for using only the correct armor.

Haste Rating affects how quickly your resource (Energy, Focus, Mana, etc.) regenerates. Spirit remains the source for how quickly you regenerate health and mana, and the good news for mana users is the five second rule has been removed. You still regenerate mana faster out of battle, but you no longer need to worry about how long it has been since your last cast while in battle.

For tanks, there is only a Block Rating now, and all blocked attacks have their damage reduced by a flat 30% (although talents can alter this amount). Parry works a bit differently as well. Instead of avoiding 100% of an incoming attack's damage, you instead avoid 50% of the current swing's damage, and 50% of the next swing's damage.

In PVP, Resilience no longer reduces the chance your character suffers a critical strike. Resilience only offers a reduction in damage you take from other characters.

Mastery

Mastery Rating is a new stat found on high level equipment. Your character's Mastery Rating improves your character based on his or her class and talent tree choice.

REFORGING

Reforging allows you to change some secondary stats (and Spirit) on your gear into other stats. Spirit, Critical Strike Rating, Dodge Rating, Expertise Rating, Haste Rating, Hit Rating, Mastery Rating, and Parry Rating are eligible for Reforging. You can change only 40% of the value of one these stats for one of the other stats in the list.

Look for Arcane Reforgers near Enchanting trainers in major cities. They are the NPCs capable of changing your gear. It isn't a free service, but the cost isn't enough that it will break your bank. Gear must have an item level of at least 200 to be eligible for Reforging.

Reforging Example

If a piece of equipment has 100 Hit Rating, and you don't need that much, a trip to the Arcane Reforger can convert up to 40 points of that Hit Rating to, for example, Haste Rating. The modified piece of equipment ends up with 60 Hit Rating and 40 Haste Rating.

TALENT TREES

Talent Trees have become more streamlined. Characters now have fewer talent points (from 71 points to 36 points at level 80) to spend in these smaller talent trees. At level 85, you end up with 41 total talent points to spend, but there's a bit more to the revised system than placing points into certain talents.

You still earn your first talent point at level 10 (unless you're a Death Knight, who still start out at level 55). However, before you spend that talent point you must select one of the three talent trees available to your class as your primary talent tree. This selection provides new abilities immediately, but locks you out of placing talent points into any other tree until after you put your thirty-first point into your primary tree.

CHANGES TO CURRENCY

Before Cataclysm, you earned different types of tokens (such as Emblems and Badges) which you could redeem with certain vendors to obtain improved equipment. This system lead to players holding many types of currency which had no real value as each new raiding tier was opened. In Cataclysm, defeating heroic dungeon and raid bosses awards you either Justice Points or Valor Points. As new raids are made available, each character's Valor Points are converted to Justice Points (up to a certain point limit) and some of the previous equipment available for purchase with Valor Points is available with Justice Points.

The same change happened with PVP points. The Arena Point and Honor Points system has been altered. You still earn Honor Points, but Arena Points were replaced by Conquest Points. It's possible to earn Conquest Points and build your Personal Rating without setting foot in an Arena. Now you have the option to join Rated Battleground teams and enjoy the same rewards as the Arena Teams.

CHANGES TO PROFESSIONS

Professions now have their own tab in the Spellbook, making it easier to see which Professions your character has, and what level of skill they've reached with each. Each Profession window offers more flexibility in displaying what your character can create. You won't need to scroll through pages and pages of recipes any longer.

Gathering materials through Herbalism and Mining now provides experience points! The amount of experience earned from gathering is tied to the type of node you harvest. So a Copper Vein in Elwynn Forest gives the same XP as a Copper Vein in Loch Modan.

Many of the low level items created by the crafting Professions have been updated; in some cases the minimum level to use an item has changed, while other items convey different statistical bonuses. The notable change that impacts most Crafting professions is that crafting some items gives more than one skill up. Look for a special notation in specific crafting menus to see which items this affects.

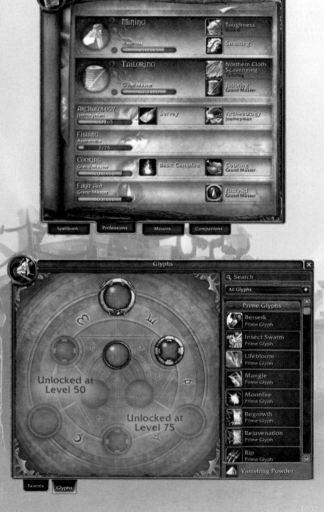

INSCRIPTION

The biggest changes to the existing Professions are to Inscription. Glyphs now come in three varieties (Minor, Major, and Prime) and each character now has three slots for each type, for nine total Glyphs. You unlock one set of slots every 25 levels, meaning your final Glyph slots are opened at level 75. In addition, your characters learn Glyphs upon using them, so you only need to get a Glyph once and you have it forever. Changing Glyphs requires a special reagent which is available from Scribes or for a nominal fee from an Inscription Vendor. Look for the Glyphs tab on the Talent screen to see that character's current Glyphs, and all Glyphs available for that character.

NEW PROFESSION: ARCHAEOLOGY

Archaeology is a secondary Profession, and it is all about exploration and uncovering the past. With Archaeology, you collect fragments from every zone in the game (although you can't dig on Draenor or in Northrend right away) and assemble the pieces into a restored piece.

There are a handful of fun rewards to earn from Archaeology, and you earn some experience points each time you unearth fragments from the past. The best part about Archaeology is that you aren't competing with other players for resources. Each cache of fragments you seek out is tied specifically to your character.

INTERFACE CHANGES

The interface has undergone extensive changes, although you're still able to modify many of these features through the Options Menu. The mini-map has been updated and now provides additional tracking options including a big, yellow arrow to point you in the right direction when you're working on quests. When you're working on a quest to kill a specific, named enemy, look for a skull icon on the mini-map, and a yellow exclamation point to appear in that enemy's portrait.

Changes for Dead Characters

No, not the Forsaken! Should you fall in battle, a big, red arrow appears on the mini-map and points you in the direction of your corpse. There was another, incredibly convenient, addition made to the screen you see as a corpse: a button that allows you to return to the graveyard instantly. If you make a wrong turn and slide off a cliff or find it impossible to return to your body where you died, you now have an easy way to get back to the graveyard.

CHARACTER WINDOW

When you bring up the character window for the first time, you may notice some information missing below the image of your character. Fortunately, that important information is just one click away. Look for an arrow in the bottom right corner of the character screen. Clicking it opens and closes a pane that displays your character's vital statistics. You're free to move the categories of statistics (Attributes, Melee, Ranged, etc.) higher and lower in the listing. Mousing over the values under these categories provides you with more details.

In particular, you should pay attention to the secondary stats such as Hit, Expertise, Haste, and Mastery. By using the information provided in the tooltips, you should gain a greater understanding of how to set up your character's equipment with enchantments and socketed gems

SPELLBOOK WINDOW

The main Spellbook window now shows what abilities you can learn in addition to the abilities you already know. Spells and abilities are still divided into four tabs, so that part should feel familiar.

To see the rest of the changes to the Spellbook, you need to look at the bottom of the Spellbook pane. Your character's Professions, Mounts, and Companions (vanity pets) all now appear as a part of your Spellbook. Drag any of the icons for Professions, Mounts, and Companions to an Action Bar for quick and easy access to them.

PARTY AND RAID OPTIONS

There are a number of new options when it comes to setting up how you view the information of other characters in your parties and raids. Instead of seeing portraits, you can see simple bars that provide a name and current status. Use the options to modify settings such as class-specific coloring, and the size of each frame.

If you plan on participating in many raid groups, spend time getting these settings to your liking before you start your first encounter. Raids are not the best place to tinker with settings!

PHASING

While phasing isn't new for Cataclysm (it was introduced in Wrath of the Lich King), you will see a great deal more of it in Cataclysm. Phasing is a by-product of questing in certain areas. As you complete certain quests, the area may change visually. NPCs might move to different areas, monsters might be there that weren't before, and all of this is fine for other players because they won't see it until they complete the same quests.

The only downside of phasing is that you can't easily help people beat earlier versions of a chained quest if you're on a later phase. They might end up fighting things that you can't see or hurt. If you're in the same area as someone in your group, but can't see them, look for a small circle near their character portrait. Players out of phase with you will have this swirled circle. To become visible to each other again, you must either complete the same quests or move out of the phased area.

NEW REPUTATIONS

Old Alliances have been stirred up by the events of the Cataclysm. Look for new and changed factions in Mount Hyjal, Vashj'ir, Deepholm, Uldum, Twilight Highlands, and Tol Barad.

Most factions offer Championing tabards, which work the same as they did in Wrath of the Lich King. Wear the tabard of a certain faction while you're running heroic dungeons and all reputations gains from killing enemies count toward that faction.

ZONE	ALLIANCE FACTION	HORDE FACTION	NOTABLE ITEMS SOLD
Mount Hyjal	Guardians of Hyjal	Guardians of Hyjal	Intellect/Stamina enchant to helm
Vash'jir	Earthen Ring	Earthen Ring	Stamina/Dodge Rating enchant to helm
Deepholm	Therazane	Therazane	All shoulder enchants
Uldum	Ramkahen	Ramkahen	Agility/Haste Rating enchant to helm
Twilight Highlands	Wildhammer Clan	Dragonmaw Clan	Strength/Mastery Rating enchant to helm
Tol Barad	Tol Barad Wardens	Hellscream's Reach	Mounts and Trinkets

Horde and Alliance Faction Items

Each race has a Quartermaster who sells a Tabard, a 16 slot bag at Revered, and cloaks at Exalted. There are three types of cloaks; each cloak has Stamina while one each has Intellect, Strength, and Agility. Look for these Quartermasters near the flight points in each major city. Some cities have Quartermasters for multiple races, but they're all in the same location.

GUARDIANS OF HYJAL

The Guardians of Hyjal are mainly Druids who work together to protect Nordrassil from the Twilight's Hammer. Much of your reputation gains with the Guardians of Hyjal come from the many quests they have for you in Mount Hyjal. Look for Provisioner Whitecloud, who sells these items, at Nordrassil in Mount Hyjal.

REPUTATION REWARDS

NAME	REQUIREMENT	SLOT	DESCRPTION
Tabard of the Guardians of Hyjal	Friendly	Tabard	Equip: You champion the cause of the Guardians of Hyjal. All reputation gains while in Level 85 Cataclysm dungeons will be applied to your standing with them.
Cloak of the Dryad	Honored, Level 83	Back	572 Armor, +224 Stamina, +149 Intellect, +100 Spirit Equip: Increases your Mastery Rating by 100.
Sly Fox Jerkin	Honored, Level 83	Leather Chest	1527 Armor, +228 Agility, +401 Stamina, Red Socket, Blue Socket, Socket Bonus: +20 Mastery Rating Equip: Improves Critical Strike Rating by 178. Equip: Increases your Mastery Rating by 138.
Galrond's Band	Honored, Level 83	Finger	+149 Strength, +224 Stamina Equip: Increases your Mastery Rating by 100. Equip: Improves your Critical Strike Rating by 100.
Mountain's Mouth	Honored, Level 83	Neck	+149 Strength, +224 Stamina Equip: Increases your Parry Rating by 100. Equip: Increases your Mastery Rating by 100.
Arcanum of Hyjal	Revered, Level 85	Enchant	Use: Permanently adds 60 Intellect and 35 Critical Strike Rating to a head slot item.
Acorn of the Daughter Tree	Revered, Level 85	Neck	+168 Agility, +252 Stamina Equip: Improves Critical Strike Rating by 112. Equip: Improves Haste Rating by 112.
Aessina-Blessed Gloves	Revered, Level 85	Leather Hands	982 Armor, +337 Stamina, +205 Intellect, Yellow Socket, Socket Bonus: +10 Spirit Equip: Increases your Haste Rating by 150. Equip: Increases your Mastery Rating by 130.

NAME	REQUIREMENT	SLOT	DESCRPTION
Waywatcher's Boots	Revered, Level 85	Plate Feet	2268 Armor, +205 Strength, +337 Stamina, Yellow Socket, Socket Bonus: +10 Strength Equip: Improves Critical Strike Rating by 150. Equip: Improves Haste Rating by 130.
Wilderness Legguards	Revered, Level 85	Mail Legs	2032 Armor, +262 Intellect, +454 Stamina, +192 Spirit, Red Socket, Yellow Socket, Socket Bonus: +20 Spirit Equip: Improves Haste Rating by 172.
Treads of Malorne	Exalted, Level 85	Mail Feet	1673 Armor, +233 Agility, +380 Stamina, Yellow Socket, Socket Bonus: +10 Agility Equip: Improves Hit Rating by 149. Equip: Increases your Mastery Rating by 169.
Belt of the Ferocious Wolf	Exalted, Level 85	Plate Waist	1927 Armor, +233 Strength, +380 Stamina, Blue Socket, Socket Bonus: +10 Strength Equip: Improves Critical Strike Rating by 149. Equip: Increases your Master Rating by 169.
Cord of Raven Queen	Exalted, Level 85	Cloth Waist	704 Armor, +233 Intellect, +380 Stamina, +169 Spirit, Blue Socket, Socket Bonus: +10 Intellect Equip: Increases your Mastery Rating by 149.
Wrap of the Great Turtle	Exalted, Level 85	Back	625 Armor, +190 Strength, +286 Stamina Equip: Increases your Dodge Rating by 127. Equip: Increases your Mastery Rating by 127.

RAMKAHEN

The Ramkahen appear exclusively in Uldum. They provide a large portion of the quests you undertake in that zone. To buy the following items, look for Blacksmith Abasi in Ramkahen.

REPUTATION REWARDS

NAME	REQUIREMENT	SLOT	DESCRPTION
Tabard of Ramkahen	Friendly	Tabard	Equip: You champion the cause of Ramkahen. All reputation gains while in Level 85 Cataclysm dungeons will be applied to your standing with them.
Ammunae's Blessing	Honored, Level 83	Finger	+149 Intellect, +224 Stamina, +100 Spirit Equip: Increases your Mastery Rating by 100.
Belt of the Stargazer	Honored, Level 83	Mail Waist	1251 Armor, +179 Agility, +298 Stamina, Blue Socket, Socket Bonus: +10 Critical Strike Rating Equip: Improves Haste Rating by 133. Equip: Improves Critical Strike Rating by 113.
Drystone Greaves	Honored, Level 83	Plate Feet	2151 Armor, +179 Intellect, +298 Stamina, +133 Spirit, Blue Socket, Socket Bonus: +10 Intellect Equip: Improves Haste Rating by 113.
Shroud of the Dead	Honored, Level 83	Back	572 Armor, +149 Strength, +224 Stamina, Equip: Increases your Critical Strike Rating by 100. Equip: Increases your Mastery Rating by 100.
Arcanum of the Ramkahen	Revered, Level 85	Enchant	Use: Permanently adds 60 Agility and 35 Haste Rating to a head slot item.
Quicksand Belt	Revered, Level 85	Leather Waist	884 Armor, +205 Agility, +337 Stamina, Blue Socket, Socket Bonus: +10 Agility Equip: Improves Hit Rating by 150. Equip: Improves Critical Strike Rating by 130.
Red Rock Band	Revered, Level 85	Finger	+120 Strength, +252 Stamina Equip: Increases your Expertise Rating by 98. Equip: Increases your Mastery Rating by 168.

NAME	REQUIREMENT	SLOT	DESCRPTION
Robes of Orsis	Revered, Level 85	Cloth Chest	1160 Armor, +262 Intellect, +454 Stamina, Yellow Socket, Blue Socket, Socket Bonus: +20 Intellect Equip: Improves Hit Rating by 192. Equip: Improves Critical Strike Rating by 172.
Sash of Prophecy	Revered, Level 85	Mail Waist	1306 Armor, +205 Intellect, +337 Stamina, +150 Spirit, Yellow Socket, Socket Bonus: +10 Intellect Equip: Improves Haste Rating by 130.
Desert Walker Sandals	Exalted, Level 85	Cloth Feet	860 Armor, +233 Intellect, +380 Stamina, Yellow Socket, Socket Bonus: +10 Hit Rating Equip: Improves Hit Rating by 169. Equip: Improves Haste Rating by 149.
Gift of Nadun	Exalted, Level 85	Neck	+190 Strength, +286 Stamina Equip: Improves Haste Rating by 127. Equip: Improves Critical Strike Rating by 127.
Sandguard Bracers	Exalted, Level 85	Plate Wrist	1499 Armor, +136 Strength, +286 Stamina Equip: Increases your Dodge Rating by 190. Equip: Increases your Expertise Rating by 111.
Sun King's Girdle	Exalted, Level 85	Plate Waist	1927 Armor, +233 Intellect, +380 Stamina, +169 Spirit, Red Socket, Socket Bonus: +10 Spirit Equip: Improves Haste Rating by 149.
Reins of the Brown Riding Camel	Exalted		Use: Teaches you how to summon this mount. This is a very fast mount.

EARTHEN RING

The Earthen Ring is a gathering of powerful Shamans who strive to repair the damage done during Deathwing's return. Unlike other most factions in Cataclysm, Earthen Ring quests appear in multiple zones. The Quartermaster for the Earthen Ring, Provisioner Arok, resides at the Silver Tide Hollow in Vashj'ir.

REPUTATION REWARDS

NAME	REQUIREMENT	SLOT	DESCRPTION
Tabard of the Earthen Ring	Friendly	Tabard	Equip: You champion the cause of the Earthen Ring. All reputation gains while in Level 85 Cataclysm dungeons will be applied to your standing with them.
Stone-Wrapped Greaves	Honored, Level 83	Plate Legs	2737 Armor, +248 Strength, +401 Stamina, Red Socket, Blue Socket, Socket Bonus: +20 Parry Rating Equip: Increases your Dodge Rating by 138. Equip: Increases your Parry Rating by 158.
Mantle of Moss	Honored, Level 83	Mail Shoulder	1668 Armor, +179 Agility, +298 Stamina, Yellow Socket, Socket Bonus: +10 Agility Equip: Improves Critical Strike Rating by 133. Equip: Improves Haste Rating by 113.
Pendant of Elemental Balance	Honored, Level 83	Neck	+149 Intellect, +224 Stamina, +100 Spirit Equip: Increases your Mastery Rating by 100.
Helm of Temperance	Honored, Level 83	Cloth Head	930 Armor, +208 Intellect, +401 Stamina, Meta Socket, Yellow Socket, Socket Bonus: +30 Intellect Equip: Improves Hit Rating by 138. Equip: Improves Critical Strike Rating by 158.
Arcanum of the Earthen Ring	Revered, Level 85	Enchant	Use: Permanently adds 90 Stamina and 35 Dodge Rating to a head slot item.
Peacemaker's Breastplate	Revered, Level 85	Plate Chest	3298 Armor, +262 Intellect, +454 Stamina, +192 Spirit, Red Socket, Yellow Socket, Socket Bonus: +20 Spirit Equip: Improves Haste Rating by 172.

NAME	REQUIREMENT	SLOT	DESCRPTION
Leggings of Clutching Roots	Revered, Level 85	Leather Legs	1374 Armor, +262 Intellect, +454 Stamina, +202 Spirit, Yellow Socket, Yellow Socket, Socket Bonus: +20 Intellect Equip: Improves Critical Strike Rating by 162.
Cloak of Ancient Wisdom	Revered, Level 85	Back	580 Armor, +168 Intellect, +252 Stamina Equip: Improves Critical Strike Rating by 112. Equip: Improves Haste Rating by 112.
Softwind Cape	Revered, Level 85	Back	580 Armor, +168 Agility, +252 Stamina Equip: Improves Hit Rating by 112. Equip: Improves Haste Rating by 112.
Earthmender's Boots	Exalted, Level 85	Mail Feet	1673 Armor, +233 Intellect, +380 Stamina, +169 Spirit, Yellow Socket, Socket Bonus: +10 Spirit Equip: Improves Critical Strike Rating by 149.
World Keeper's Gauntlets	Exalted, Level 85	Plate Hands	2141 Armor, +233 Intellect, +380 Stamina, +169 Spirit, Red Socket, Socket Bonus: +10 Spirit Equip: Improves Critical Strike Rating by 149.
Flamebloom Gloves	Exalted, Level 85	Cloth Hands	782 Armor, +233 Intellect, +380 Stamina, Blue Socket, Socket Bonus: +10 Intellect Equip: Improves Haste Rating by 149. Equip: Increases your Mastery Rating by 169.
Signet of the Elder Council	Exalted, Level 85	Finger	+190 Agility, +286 Stamina, Requires Level 85 Equip: Improves Haste Rating by 127. Equip: Improves Mastery Rating by 127.

THERAZANE

Therazane is the name of both the faction and its leader. Therazane is a powerful entity who rules over the ground and mountains of Deepholm, and an army of giant elementals. Everyone begins at Hated with Therazane and you must complete most of the other quests in Deepholm before you get the chain that allows you to start improving your Therzane reputation.

REPUTATION REWARDS

NAME	REQUIREMENT	SLOT	DESCRPTION
Lesser Inscription of Charged Lodestone	Honored, Level 85	Enchant	Permanently adds 30 Intellect and 20 Haste Rating to a shoulder slot item.
Lesser Inscription of Jagged Stone	Honored, Level 85	Enchant	Permanently adds 30 Strength and 20 Critical Strike Rating to a shoulder slot item.
Lesser Inscription of Shattered Crystal	Honored, Level 85	Enchant	Permanently adds 30 Agility and 20 Mastery Rating to a shoulder slot item.
Lesser Inscription of Unbreakable Quartz	Honored, Level 85	Enchant	Permanently adds 45 Stamina and 20 Dodge Rating to a shoulder slot item.
Diamant's Ring of Temperance	Revered, Level 85	Finger	+168 Intellect, +252 Stamina Equip: Improves Critical Strike Rating by 112. Equip: Improves Haste Rating by 112.
Felsen's Ring of Resolve	Revered, Level 85	Finger	+168 Strength, +252 Stamina Equip: Increases your Dodge Rating by 112. Equip: Increases your Mastery Rating by 112.

NAME	REQUIREMENT	SLOT	DESCRPTION
Gorsik's Band of Shattering	Revered, Level 85	Finger	+168 Strength, +252 Stamina Equip: Improves Critical Strike Rating by 112. Equip: Improves Haste Rating by 112.
Terrath's Signet of Balance	Revered, Level 85	Finger	+168 Agility, +252 Stamina Equip: Improves Hit Rating by 112. Equip: Increases your Mastery Rating by 112.
Greater Inscription of Charged Lodestone	Exhalted, Level 85	Enchant	Permanently adds 50 Intellect and 25 Haste Rating to a shoulder slot item.
Greater Inscription of Jagged Stone	Exalted, Level 85	Enchant	Permanently adds 50 Strength and 25 Critical Strike Rating to a shoulder slot item.
Greater Inscription of Shattered Crystal	Exalted, Level 85	Enchant	Permanently adds 50 Agility and 25 Mastery Rating to a shoulder slot item.
Greater Inscription of Unbreakable Quartz	Exalted, Level 85	Enchant	Permanently adds 75 Stamina and 25 Dodge Rating to a shoulder slot item.

Tol Barad

Tol Barad Peninsula is an outdoor PVP zone which features Baradin's Wardens and Hellscream's Reach. Unlike other factions, where you purchase items with gold, you must complete daily quests (both in Tol Barad when your faction controls the island and on Tol Barad Peninsula regardless of who owns Tol Barad) to earn Tol Barad Commendations. The Quartermaster for each faction accepts these Commendations as currency when purchasing the following items.

BARADIN'S WARDEN

REPUTATION REWARDS

NAME	REQUIREMENT	SLOT	DESCRPTION
Baradin's Wardens Commendation	Friendly		Use: Increases your Baradin's Wardens reputation by 250.
Baradin's Wardens Healing Potion	Friendly		Use: Restores 6750 to 11250 health Only works in Tol Barad.
Baradin's Wardens Mana Potion	Friendly		Use: Restores 6750 to 11250 mana Only works in Tol Barad.
Baradin's Wardens Bandage	Friendly		Use: Heals 35000 damage over 8 sec Only works in Tol Barad.
Baradin Footman's Tags	Honored, Level 85	Trinket	Equip: Increases your Mastery Rating by 252 Use: Summons a Fallen Footman to your side.
Baradin's Wardens Tabard	Honored		Use: Teleports the caster to Baradin Base Camp on Tol Barad. (4 Hr Cooldown)
Rustberg Gull	Honored		Use: Teaches you how to summon this companion.
Tol Barad Searchlight	Honored		Use: Right Click to set down your Tol Barad Searchlight. (5 Min Cooldown)

NAME	REQUIREMENT	SLOT	DESCRPTION
Baradin's Wardens Battle Standard	Revered, Level 85		Use: Place a Baradin's Wardens Battle Standard with 40000 health that increases the damage of all party members that stay within 45 yards of the Battle Standard by 10%. Lasts 2 min and only works in Tol Barad. (15 Min Cooldown)
Blade of the Fearless	Revered, Level 85	2H Sword	Speed 3.80, 1678 - 2518 Damage, (552.1 damage per second), +302 Strength, +454 Stamina Equip: Improves Critical Strike Rating by 202. Equip: Increases your Expertise Rating by 202.
Dagger of Restless Nights	Revered, Level 85	Dagger	Speed 1.80, 589 - 885 Damage, (409.4 damage per second), +129 Agility, +194 Stamina Equip: Improves Hit Rating by 86. Equip: Improves Critical Strike Rating by 86.
Insidious Staff	Revered, Level 85	Staff	Speed 2.10, 927 - 1392 Damage, (552.1 damage per second), +302 Intellect, +454 Stamina Equip: Improves Haste Rating by 202. Equip: Increases Spell Power by 1732. Equip: Increases your Mastery Rating by 202.

NAME	REQUIREMENT	SLOT	DESCRPTION
Ravening Slicer	Revered, Level 85	1H Axe	Speed 2.60, 745 - 1384 Damage, (409.4 damage per second), +129 Agility, +194 Stamina Equip: Improves Haste Rating by 86. Equip: Increases your Mastery Rating by 86.
Shimmering Morningstar	Revered, Level 85	MH Mace	Speed 2.30, 659 - 1225 Damage, (409.6 damage per second), +129 Intellect, +194 Stamina, +86 Spirit, Equip: Improves Critical Strike Rating by 86. Equip: Increases Spell Power by 1729.
Sky Piercer	Revered, Level 85	Crossbow	Speed 3.00, 1325 - 1988 Damage, (552.2 damage per second), +95 Agility, +143 Stamina Equip: Improves Critical Strike Rating by 63. Equip: Increases your Mastery Rating by 63.
Spear of Trailing Shadows	Revered, Level 85	Polearm	Speed 3.60, 1590 - 2386 Damage, (552.2 damage per second), +302 Agility, +454 Stamina Equip: Improves Hit Rating by 202. Equip: Improves Haste Rating by 202.

NAME	REQUIREMENT	SLOT	DESCRPTION
Impatience of Youth	Exalted, Level 85	Trinket	Equip: Increases your Mastery Rating by 321. Use: Increases your Strength by 1605 for 20 sec. (2 Min Cooldown)
Mandala of Stirring Patterns	Exalted, Level 85	Trinket	+321 Spirit, Equip: Your healing spells have a chance to grant 1926 mastery rating for 10 sec.
Mirror of Broken Images	Exalted, Level 85	Trinket	Equip: Increases your Mastery Rating by 321. Use: Increases Arcane, Fire, Frost, Nature, and Shadow resistances by 400 for 10 sec. (1 Min Cooldown)
Reins of the Spectral Steed	Exalted, Level 85		Use: Teaches you how to summon this mount.
Reins of the Drake of the West Wind	Exalted, Level 85		Use: Teaches you how to summon this mount.
Stump of Time	Exalted, Level 85	Trinket	Equip: Improves Hit Rating by 321. Use: Your harmful spells have a chance to grant 1926 spell power for 15 sec.
Unsolvable Riddle	Exalted, Level 85	Trinket	Equip: Increases your Mastery Rating by 321. Use: Increases your Agility by 1605 for 20 sec. (2 Min Cooldown)

HELLSCREAM'S REACH

REPUTATION REWARDS

NAME	REQUIREMENT	SLOT	DESCRPTION
Hellscream's Reach Commendation	Friendly		Use: Increases your Baradin's Wardens reputation by 250.
Hellscream's Reach Healing Potion	Friendly		Use: Restores 6750 to 11250 health. Only works in Tol Barad.
Hellscream's Reach Mana Potion	Friendly		Use: Restores 6750 to 11250 mana. Only works in Tol Barad.
Hellscream's Reach Bandage	Friendly		Use: Heals 35000 damage over 8 sec. Only works in Tol Barad.
Baradin Grunt's Talisman	Honored, Level 85	Trinket	Equip: Increases your Mastery Rating by 252. Use: Summons a Fallen Grunt to your side.
Hellscream's Reach Tabard	Honored		Use: Teleports the caster to Hellscream's Grasp on Tol Barad. (4 Hr Cooldown)
Rustberg Gull	Honored		Use: Teaches you how to summon this companion.
Tol Barad Searchlight	Honored		Use: Right Click to set down your Tol Barad Searchlight. (5 Min Cooldown)
Hellscream's Reach Battle Standard	Revered, Level 85		Use: Place a Hellscream's Reach Battle Standard with 40000 health that increases the damage of all party members that stay within 45 yards of the Battle Standard by 10%. Lasts 2 min and only works in Tol Barad. (15 Min Cooldown)
Blade of the Fearless	Revered, Level 85	2H Sword	Speed 3.80, 1678 - 2518 Damage, (552.1 damage per second), +302 Strength, +454 Stamina Equip: Improves Critical Strike Rating by 202. Equip: Increases your Expertise Rating by 202.
Dagger of Restless Nights	Revered, Level 85	Dagger	Speed 1.80, 589 - 885 Damage, (409.4 damage per second), +129 Agility, +194 Stamina Equip: Improves Hit Rating by 86. Equip: Improves Critical Strike Rating by 86.
Insidious Staff	Revered, Level 85	Staff	Speed 2.10, 927 - 1392 Damage, (552.1 damage per second), +302 Intellect, +454 Stamina Equip: Improves Haste Rating by 202. Equip: Increases Spell Power by 1732. Equip: Increases your Mastery Rating by 202.

NAME	REQUIREMENT	SLOT	DESCRPTION
Ravening Slicer	Revered, Level 85	1H Axe	Speed 2.60, 745 - 1384 Damage, (409.4 damage per second), +129 Agility, +194 Stamina Equip: Improves Haste Rating by 86. Equip: Increases your Mastery Rating by 86.
Shimmering Morningstar	Revered, Level 85	MH Mace	Speed 2.30, 659 - 1225 Damage, (409.6 damage per second), +129 Intellect, +194 Stamina, +86 Spirit Equip: Improves Critical Strike Rating by 86. Equip: Increases Spell Power by 1729.
Sky Piercer	Revered, Level 85	Crossbow	Speed 3.00, 1325 - 1988 Damage, (552.2 damage per second), +95 Agility, +143 Stamina Equip: Improves Critical Strike Rating by 63. Equip: Increases your Mastery Rating by 63.
Spear of Trailing Shadows	Revered, Level 85	Polearm	Speed 3.60, 1590 - 2386 Damage, (552.2 damage per second), +302 Agility, +454 Stamina Equip: Improves Hit Rating by 202. Equip: Improves Haste Rating by 202.
Impatience of Youth	Exalted, Level 85	Trinket	Equip: Increases your Mastery Rating by 321. Use: Increases your Strength by 1605 for 20 sec. (2 Min Cooldown)
Mandala of Stirring Patterns	Exalted, Level 85	Trinket	+321 Spirit Equip: Your healing spells have a chance to grant 1926 mastery rating for 10 sec.
Mirror of Broken Images	Exalted, Level 85	Trinket	Equip: Increases your Mastery Rating by 321. Use: Increases Arcane, Fire, Frost, Nature, and Shadow resistances by 400 for 10 sec. (1 Min Cooldown)
Reins of the Spectral Wolf	Exalted, Level 85		Use: Teaches you how to summon this mount.
Reins of the Drake of the West Wind	Exalted, Level 85		Use: Teaches you how to summon this mount.
Stump of Time	Exalted, Level 85	Trinket	Equip: Improves Hit Rating by 321. Use: Your harmful spells have a chance to grant 1926 spell power for 15 sec.
Unsolvable Riddle	Exalted, Level 85	Trinket	Equip: Increases your Mastery Rating by 321. Use: Increases your Agility by 1605 for 20 sec. (2 Min Cooldown)

WILDHAMMER CLAN

This Alliance-only faction appears in other places, but it's in the Twilight Highlands that these dwarves begin to offer more to their allies. Look for Craw MacGraw, the Wildhammer Clan Quartermaster in Twilight Highlands.

REPUTATION REWARDS

NAME	REQUIREMENT	SLOT	DESCRPTION
Tabard of the Wildhammer Clan	Friendly	Tabard	Equip: You champion the cause of the Wildhammer Clan. All reputation gains while in Level 85 Cataclysm dungeons will be applied to your standing with them.
Gloves of Aetherial Rumors	Honored, Level 83	Cloth Hands	715 Armor, +179 Intellect, +298 Stamina, +133 Spirit, Yellow Socket, Socket Bonus: +10 Intellect Equip: Increases your Hit Rating by 133. Equip: Increases your Mastery Rating by 113.
Helm of the Skyborne	Honored, Level 83	Mail Head	1807 Armor, +208 Intellect, +401 Stamina, +171 Spirit, Meta Socket, Red Socket, Socket Bonus: +30 Critical Strike Rating Equip: Improves Critical Strike Rating by 117.
Mantle of Wild Feathers	Honored, Level 83	Leather Shoulder	1145 Armor, +159 Intellect, +298 Stamina, +123 Spirit, Yellow Socket, Socket Bonus: +10 Spirit Equip: Improves Haste Rating by 103.
Swiftflight Leggings	Honored, Level 83	Leather Legs	1336 Armor, +228 Agility, +401 Stamina, Red Socket, Yellow Socket, Socket Bonus: +20 Critical Strike Rating Equip: Improves Critical Strike Rating by 168. Equip: Improves Haste Rating by 148.
Arcanum of the Wildhammer	Revered, Level 85	Enchant	Use: Permanently adds 60 Strength and 35 Mastery Rating to a head slot item.
Band of Singing Grass	Revered, Level 85	Finger	+168 Intellect, +252 Stamina Equip: Improves Hit Rating by 112. Equip: Increases your Mastery Rating by 112.

NAME	REQUIREMENT	SLOT	DESCRPTION
Crown of Wings	Revered, Level 85	Plate Head	2680 Armor, +196 Strength, +454 Stamina, Meta Socket, Red Socket, Socket Bonus: +30 Dodge Rating Equip: Increases your Dodge Rating by 242. Equip: Increases your Expertise Rating by 137.
Gryphon Talon Gauntlets	Revered, Level 85	Plate Hands	2061 Armor, +205 Strength, +337 Stamina, Yellow Socket, Socket Bonus: +10 Critical Strike Rating Equip: Improves Critical Strike Rating by 150. Equip: Improves Haste Rating by 130.
Windhome Helm	Revered, Level 85	Mail Head	1887 Armor, +242 Agility, +454 Stamina, Meta Socket, Yellow Socket, Socket Bonus: +30 Agility Equip: Improves Critical Strike Rating by 182. Equip: Improves Haste Rating by 162.
Belt of the Untamed	Exalted, Level 85	Leather Waist	939 Armor, +233 Intellect, +380 Stamina, +169 Spirit, Yellow Socket, Socket Bonus: +10 Spirit Equip: Improves Haste Rating by 149.
Gryphon Rider's Boots	Exalted, Level 85	Plate Feet	2355 Armor, +253 Strength, +380 Stamina, Yellow Socket, Socket Bonus: +10 Parry Rating Equip: Increases your Parry Rating by 139. Equip: Increases your Mastery Rating by 159.
Lightning Flash Pendant	Exalted, Level 85	Neck	+190 Intellect, +286 Stamina Equip: Improves Critical Strike Rating by 127. Equip: Increases your Mastery Rating by 127.
Stormbolt Gloves	Exalted, Level 85	Leather Hands	1043 Armor, +233 Agility, +380 Stamina, Yellow Socket, Socket Bonus: +10 Haste Rating, Equip: Improves Haste Rating by 169. Equip: Improves Critical Strike Rating by 149.

DRAGONMAW CLAN

The Dragonmaw Clan has been a thorn in the side of adventurers in the Wetlands for many years, but now they've carved out a piece of the Twilight Highlands. While your initial interactions with these orcs are less than cordial, you can eventually earn their respect and gain access to their powerful items. Grot Deathblow, the Dragonmaw Clan Quartermaster found in Twilight Highlands, offers these items for sale.

REPUTATION REWARDS

NAME	REQUIREMENT	SLOT	DESCRPTION
Tabard of the Dragonmaw Clan	Friendly	Tabard	Equip: You champion the cause of the Dragonmaw Clan. All reputation gains while in Level 85 Cataclysm dungeons will be applied to your standing with them.
Bone Fever Gloves	Honored, Level 83	Cloth Hands	715 Armor, +179 Intellect, +298 Stamina, +133 Spirit, Yellow Socket, Socket Bonus: +10 Intellect Equip: Increases your Hit Rating by 133. Equip: Increases your Mastery Rating by 113.
Helm of the Brown Lands	Honored, Level 83	Mail Head	1807 Armor, +208 Intellect, +401 Stamina, +171 Spirit, Meta Socket, Red Socket, Socket Bonus: +30 Critical Strike Rating Equip: Improves Critical Strike Rating by 117.
Leggings of the Impenitent	Honored, Level 83	Leather Legs	1336 Armor, +228 Agility, +401 Stamina, Red Socket, Yellow Socket, Socket Bonus: +20 Critical Strike Rating Equip: Improves Critical Strike Rating by 168. Equip: Improves Haste Rating by 148.
Spaulders of the Endless Plains	Honored, Level 83	Leather Shoulder	1145 Armor, +159 Intellect, +298 Stamina, +123 Spirit, Yellow Socket, Socket Bonus: +10 Spirit Equip: Improves Haste Rating by 103.
Arcanum of the Dragonmaw	Revered, Level 85	Enchant	Use: Permanently adds 60 Strength and 35 Mastery Rating to a head slot item.
Band of Lamentation	Revered, Level 85	Finger	+168 Intellect, +252 Stamina Equip: Improves Hit Rating by 112. Equip: Increases your Mastery Rating by 112.

NAME	REQUIREMENT	SLOT	DESCRPTION
Gauntlets of Rattling Bones	Revered, Level 85	Plate Hands	2061 Armor, +205 Strength, +337 Stamina, Yellow Socket, Socket Bonus: +10 Critical Strike Rating Equip: Improves Critical Strike Rating by 150. Equip: Improves Haste Rating by 130.
Grinning Fang Helm	Revered, Level 85	Plate Head	2680 Armor, +196 Strength, +454 Stamina, Meta Socket, Red Socket, Socket Bonus: +30 Dodge Rating Equip: Increases your Dodge Rating by 242. Equip: Increases your Expertise Rating by 137.
Snarling Helm	Revered, Level 85	Mail Head	1887 Armor, +242 Agility, +454 Stamina, Meta Socket, Yellow Socket, Socket Bonus: +30 Agility Equip: Improves Critical Strike Rating by 182. Equip: Improves Haste Rating by 162.
Boots of Sullen Rock	Exalted, Level 85	Plate Feet	2355 Armor, +253 Strength, +380 Stamina, Yellow Socket, Socket Bonus: +10 Parry Rating Equip: Increases your Parry Rating by 139. Equip: Increases your Mastery Rating by 159.
Liar's Handwraps	Exalted, Level 85	Leather Hands	1043 Armor, +233 Agility, +380 Stamina, Yellow Socket, Socket Bonus: +10 Haste Rating, Equip: Improves Haste Rating by 169. Equip: Improves Critical Strike Rating by 149.
Withered Dream Belt	Exalted, Level 85	Leather Waist	939 Armor, +233 Intellect, +380 Stamina, +169 Spirit, Yellow Socket, Socket Bonus: +10 Spirit Equip: Improves Haste Rating by 149.
Yellow Smoke Pendant	Exalted, Level 85	Neck	+190 Intellect, +286 Stamina Equip: Improves Critical Strike Rating by 127. Equip: Increases your Mastery Rating by 127.

GUILDS

The Guild system received an extensive overhaul for Catacslym, and the benefits of guild membership have been increased exponentially. The system rewards stable guilds, so it pays both to be a good guild member and a good guild leader.

TYPES OF GUILDS

When recruiting, guilds usually indicate what kind of guild they are, which helps them attract the appropriate players:

Leveling guilds emphasize working with new or low-level players to increase their character level. They often focus on questing and basic dungeon runs.

Social guilds work on friendship and socializing (or even roleplaying) in addition to standard gameplay. These have a slight advantage in staying together, and they often have extremely simple rules!

PvP guilds focus on player-versus-player gaming in the battlegrounds or elsewhere in the world. Due to the competative nature of PVP, many PVP guilds aren't prone to accept new players without a trial period.

Raiding guilds try to complete endgame content with much larger groups. They often hit Heroic Dungeons and 10- or 25-character raids on a frequent basis. They're likely to have more specific rules on playtimes and character readiness than many other guilds. They're also the best way to see the hardest content in the game.

FINDING A GUILD

You can turn on the GuildRecruitment channel from any major city to see who's looking for new members or to post your own message about seeking a guild.

Joining the channel: /join guildrecruitment

Speaking on a channel: /3 Seeking guild of mature players to run dungeons.

It's easy to find a guild. In fact, you may be asked to join guilds by total strangers. The trick is finding an active and stable guild that suits your purposes. If you meet a player that you enjoy playing with, it's completely appropriate for you to inquire about their guild. Keep in mind that there are no rules for monitoring of guilds, so guild behavior varies widely. The following are some criteria you should consider if you're looking for a guild.

GUILD SIZE AND MEMBERSHIP

Guilds can be large or small, and neither is better than the other. A small guilds are usually more intimate and friendly, but you have fewer players to game with. A large guild will feel less personal, but there are more players on whom you can rely.

Most people feel more comfortable in a guild with members with some similar interests. If you're new to the game, you may not be comfortable in a guild of aggressive players. On the other hand, if you want to improve your combat skills, being around more experienced players may benefit you. You can find guilds of varying age, gender, and life experiences. In addition, you should inquire about the playing hours of other guild members. That way, you'll get a sense of whether this is a place where you'll fit in.

STRUCTURE

Like any group, each guild has different rules and leadership. Some guilds establish regular gaming nights where guild members meet to complete certain tasks. Other guilds set up regular social events.

Much of the success of a guild relies on the key officers who provide direction for the other members. The Guild Leader sets up access to the guild vault for sharing money and equipment. The leadership also determines how to deal with the inevitable conflicts that arise within any group.

COOPERATION

A strong guild encourages cooperation among its members. This means that players will help you complete quests—even if they don't have the same quest, and you will be expected to reciprocate. Guilds are also good opportunities for improving your Professions. Guild members are often willing to provide the raw materials for your Profession if you supply them, or the guild in general, with improved gear.

JOINING A GUILD

To join a guild, you need to get an invite from a guild officer. You might get an invitation right away, or you may have to wait until a particular member is online. Once you accept the guild invitation, you'll be added to the guild channel, and you'll start seeing the ongoing guild chat.

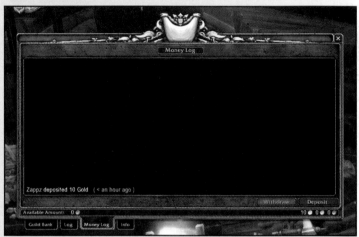

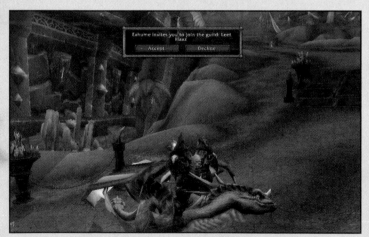

LEAVING A GUILD

To leave, type /gquit.

Joining a guild is not like getting married. It is, however, like dating: you may need to join successive guilds before you find one that really suits you. If you decide to leave your guild, it's good form to tell the Guild Leader that you're leaving and why.

THE DOWNSIDE OF GUILDS

Really, there is only one big downside to play with guilds. They expose you to drama. Any large group of people has its politicking and foolishness. Don't expect gaming to change that at all!

Guilds can break apart in the span of hours, even after they've been together for years. It's essential to find a guild with calm, friendly, and still firm leadership if you want to stay in one place for as long as possible. Larger isn't necessarily better for this. Age helps (both of the guild and of its player base), but that is no proof against drama either.

Instead, the actions of a guild's players speak the loudest. Observe multiple members of a guild in various circumstances. How are they in groups? Are they polite? Serious? Do they cause any trouble? How do they handle troublemakers?

For the best results, try out for a guild and let them work just as hard to impress you. Find people who like doing the same things that you enjoy. It pays for itself in the long run, even if you spend a good while on your own, looking for the right fit.

CREATING A GUILD

If you'd prefer to lead rather than follow, find four other people and make your own guild. This starts when you go to a major city and purchase a Guild Charter. They cost 10 silver, and you can find the Guild Master NPC that sells them with the help of the local guards.

This is the only upfront money that is needed for a guild to be put together. You use the charter to get another people to sign, and once you have all the signatures you are ready to go. Bring the charter back to the Guild Master and turn it in.

Different characters from the same account cannot log in to sign the charter once one character from that account has already signed it. Thus, you need five different players to work together when forming a guild.

People who sign your charter don't need to remain in the guild after it forms. They can leave instantly if they like, so even a single person can be in a guild (by themselves). If you pay others to help you put things together, this is quite doable. It's lonely, but some people prefer things that way.

Once you have a guild, go about naming your ranks, accruing 10 gold to create a guild symbol for your tabards, and have some fun. You should determine major rules for your guild as early as possible. Don't wait for problems to arise before thinking of solutions.

This about the following issues at length. Are there any requirements for membership? What are your rules of conduct? How is loot distributed in guild groups? Who is eligible to handle disputes? What roles do the ranks of guild officers play? Next, figure out other aspects of the guild. Are there rules about guild chat? Language issues? Donations to the guild fund?

There aren't many right or wrong answers here. Pick the people who are right for you and play the way you like. If other people aren't comfortable with that, they can leave (just try not to let there be any rancor about it). Set a good table and the people you like are bound to stay to enjoy it.

GUILD RANKS

Guilds have the following ranks for their members: Initiate, Member, Veteran, Officer, and Leader. What the ranks actually indicate varies from guild to guild. Each guild has only one Leader, but Officers can do many guild management tasks.

If you want to be involved in guild management, ask the existing officers what you can do to help and what is expected for someone to advance. In some guilds, raising your hand might be enough. In others, that rookie period where you feel like the new blood may take over a year. Make sure you know what you're getting into.

GUILD VAULT

Each guild can buy a Guild Bank tabs at the Guild Vault. Some guilds are wealthy, and some are poor. The vault is always managed by the Guild Leader, who decides what kind of access each member gets. Vaults can hold anything, including gold, weapons, armor, recipes, and other shared items.

GUILD TABARD

A tabard is a tunic bearing the colors and insignia of your guild. It indicates your allegiance to your guild, but there is no in-game benefit to wearing a guild tabard. Purchasing a tabard costs 1 gold. If you leave one guild and join another, you can use the same tabard; the insignia updates as you change guilds.

GUILD BENEFITS

The primary benefit of joining a guild is that you are never alone in the game. Being part of a guild is like being part of a club or team. Your guild mates are there when you have questions or problems in the game or when you just want to play with a group.

Playing with the same people also builds tremendous rapport. It's easier to complete dungeons and raids when you can communicate well with other people, and getting to know everyone in a guild aids that process.

Guilds have their own vaults to exchange materials, and they often have far more advanced crafters than people who are soloing. Because members of these Professions have multiple gatherers on their side, they raise their skills quickly and then provide their work to others on the team at a trivial rate (or free of charge).

GUILD PERKS

Guilds are now leveling creatures. The more its members gain experience, the more the guild is able to provide for them. Guild bonuses include increased experience gain for its members, faster mount speeds, instant item sending between guild members (through the mail), and much more.

Nearly everything the members of the guild do in the game works to increase the guild's level. There is a cap on just how much experience a guild can earn each day, but don't let that stop you from having fun! In addition to the experience the guild needs to reach higher levels, members of the much build their own standing within the guild.

GUILD PERKS

Level	Spell	Description
2	Fast Track (Rank 1)	Experience gained from killing monsters and completing quests increased by 5%.
3	Mount Up	Increases speed while mounted by 5%. Not active in Battlegrounds or Arenas.
4	Mr. Popularity (Rank 1)	Reputation gained from killing monsters and completing quests increased by 5%.
5	Cash Flow (Rank 1)	Each time you loot money from an enemy, an extra 5% money is generated and deposited directly into your guild bank.
6	Fast Track (Rank 2)	Experience gained from killing monsters and completing quests increased by 10%.
7	Reinforce (Rank 1)	Items take 5% less durability loss when you die.
8	Hasty Hearth	Reduces the cooldown on your Hearthstone by 15 minutes.
9	Reinforce (Rank 2)	Items take 10% less durability loss when you die.
10	Chug-A-Lug (Rank 1)	The duration of buffs from all guild cauldrons and feasts is increased by 50%.
11	Mobile Banking	Summons your guild bank. Instant, 1 hour cooldown
12	Mr. Popularity (Rank 2)	Reputation gained from killing monsters and completing quests increased by 10%.
13	Honorable Mention (Rank 1)	Increases Honor points gained by 5%.

GUILD PERKS

Level	Spell	Description
14	Working Overtime	Increases the chance to gain a skill increase on tradeskills by 10%.
15	The Quick and the Dead	Increases health and mana gained when resurrected by a guild member by 50% and increases movement speed while dead by 100%. Does not function in combat or while in a Battleground or Arena.
16	Cash Flow (Rank 2)	Each time you loot money from an enemy, an extra 10% money is generated and deposited directly into your guild bank.
17	G-Mail	In-game mail sent between guild members now arrives instantly.
18	For Great Justice	Increases Justice points gained by 5%.
19	Honorable Mention (Rank 2)	Increases Honor points gained by 10%.
20	Happy Hour	Increases the number of flasks gained from using a flask cauldron by 100%.
21	Have Group, Will Travel	Summons all raid or party members to the caster's current location.
22	Chug-A-Lug (Rank 2)	The duration of buffs from all guild cauldrons and feasts is increased by 100%.
23	Bountiful Bags	Increases the quantity of materials gained from Mining, Skinning, Herbalism, and Disenchanting.
24	Bartering	Reduces the price of items from all vendors by 5%.
25	Mass Resurrection	Brings all dead party and raid members back to life with 35% health and 35% mana. Cannot be cast when in combat.

GUILD ACHIEVEMENTS

Guild Achievements are new for Cataclysm. These achievements appear in your Achievement pane under the Guild tab. Most of these achievements mirror your standard achievements with the added stipulation of accomplishing many of them in a group made up primarily of members of your guild. Eighty percent of your group (4/5, 8/10, or 20/25 depending on the achievement) needs to be from the same guild in order to trigger most of these achievements.

These achievements span every facet of the game. Completion of dungeons, and participating in PVP battles are examples of achievements that must be done in a guild-heavy group. Other achievements keep track of the combined efforts of the individuals in the guild. Getting at least one of every class from each possible race to level 85 is an example of such an achievement, as is having Illustrious Grand Masters in every Profession. The slaughter of tens of thousands of Critters by the members of the guild is even an achievement!

GUILD REPUTATION AND REWARDS

Guilds can't simply add players with high level characters or maxed out Professions. Each character must achieve a certain standing with the guild in order for their accomplishments to count. This also applies to players. You can't join a guild and instantly gain access to everything the guild has unlocked. You must put in time and effort before you benefit from the work the guild as a whole has completed. Gaining Guild Reputation happens as you're accomplishing the tasks that boost your guild's level, so it's a win/win situation!

GUILD REWARDS

Item	Achievement Required	Cost (in gold)	Use/Description
Shroud of Cooperation	A Class Act	150	Teleports the caster to Orgrimmar/Stormwind City. (8 Hr Cooldown)
Wrap of Unity	Guild Level 15	300	Teleports the caster to Ogrimmar/Stormwind City. (4 Hr Cooldown)
Cloak of Coordination	Master Crafter	500	Teleports the caster to Ogrimmar/Stormwind City. (2 Hr Cooldown)
Guild Page	Alliance Slayer/Horde Slayer	300	Teaches you how to summon this companion.
Guild Herald	Profit Sharing	500	Teaches you how to summon this companion.
Dark Phoenix Hatchling	United Nations	300	Teaches you how to summon this companion.
Armadillo Pup	Critter Kill Squad	300	Teaches you how to summon this companion.
Banner of Cooperation	Working as a Team	100	Place a Guild Battle Battle Standard that increases the experience and honor gain of all guild members that stay within 45 yards of the Battle Standard by 2%. Lasts 2 min. (15 Min Cooldown)
Standard of Unity	Guild Cataclysm Dungeon Hero	200	Place a Guild Battle Battle Standard that increases the experience and honor gain of all guild members that stay within 45 yards of the Battle Standard by 4%. Lasts 2 min. (15 Min Cooldown)
Battle Standard of Coordination	A Daily Routine	300	Place a Guild Battle Battle Standard that increases the experience and honor gain of all party members that stay within 45 yards of the Battle Standard by 6%. Lasts 2 min. (15 Min Cooldown)
Recipe: Seafood Magnifique Feast	That's A Lot of Bait	150	Requires Cooking (525). Teaches you how to cook a Seafood Magnifique Feast.
Recipe: Broiled Dragon Feast	Set the Oven to "Cataclysmic"	150	Requires Cooking (500). Teaches you how to cook a Broiled Dragon Feast.
Recipe: Cauldron of Battle	Mix Master	150	Requires Alchemy (525). Teaches you how to make a Cauldron of Battle.
Recipe: Big Cauldron of Battle	Better Leveling Through Chemistry	150	Requires Alchemy (525). Teaches you how to make a Big Cauldron of Battle.
Guild Vault Voucher (7th Slot)	Guild Level 5	10000	Right-click to unlock a 7th guild vault tab and allow purchase.
Guild Vault Voucher (8th Slot)	Stay Classy	20000	Right-click to unlock an 8th guild vault tab and allow purchase.
Worn Stoneskin Gargoyle Cape	Guild Level 10	1200	Strength DPS Heirloom Cloak (level 1-85) that increases experience gained from killing monsters and completing quests. Increased by 5%
Inherited Cape of the Black Baron	Guild Level 10	1200	Agility DPS Heirloom Cloak (level 1-85) that increases experience gained from killing monsters and completing quests. Increased by 5%
Ancient Bloodmoon Cloak	Guild Level 10	1200	Spellcaster Heirloom Cloak (level 1-85) that increases experience gained from killing monsters and completing quests. Increased by 5%
Tattered Dreadmist Mask	Guild Level 20	1500	Spellcaster Cloth Heirloom Helm (level 1-85) that increases experience gained from killing monsters and completing quests. Increased by 10%.
Preened Tribal Warfeathers	Guild Level 20	1500	Spellcaster Leather Heirloom Helm (level 1-85) that increases experience gained from killing monsters and completing quests. Increased by 10%.
Stained Shadowcraft Cap	Guild Level 20	1500	Leather DPS Heirloom Helm (level 1-85) that increases experience gained from killing monsters and completing quests. Increased by 10%.
Mystical Coif of Elements	Guild Level 20	1500	Spellcaster Mail Heirloom Helm (level 1-85) that increases experience gained from killing monsters and completing quests. Increased by 10%.
Tarnished Raging Bersker's Helm	Guild Level 20	1500	Agility Mail DPS Helm (level 1-85) that increases experience gained from killing monsters and completing quests. Increased by 10%.
Polished Helm of Valor	Guild Level 20	1500	Plate DPS Heirloom Helm (level 1-85) that increases experience gained from killing monsters and completing quests. Increased by 10%.
Reins of the Kro'Kar Annihiliator	Guild Level 25	1500	Teaches you how to summon this mount.
Reins of the Dark Phoenix	Guild Glory of the Cataclysm Raider	3000	Teaches you how to summon this mount.

THE WORLD OF AZEROTH
POST CATACLYSM

The following pages show the maps for the cities and regions of Eastern Kingdoms, Kalimdor, and the Maelstrom, in alphabetical order by continent. Each region includes information on fishing, mining, herbalism, and skinning as well as reputation information. In addition, the note on all non-city pages tells you where to start if you wish to quest in that zone. Happy hunting!

⬤ Alliance Area   ⬤ Horde Area   ⬤ Neutral Area   ☠ World Dungeon Entrance

REPUTATION INFORMATION Ravenholdt, Booty Bay, Everlook, Ratchet, Gadgetzan, Undercity

ABYSSAL DEPTHS

The westernmost region of Vashj'ir, the Abyssal Depths, is separated from the Shimmering Expanse by the deep fissure known as the Abyssal Breach. On the other side, in the southern portion of the area, both Horde and Alliance members have a place to catch their breath in Tenebrous Cavern and Darkbreak Cove, respectively. The dying ancient, L'Ghorek, fills a great deal of the western part of the region and the same poisons affecting it have likewise affected the surrounding aquatic flora.

REPUTATION INFORMATION Bilgewater Cartel, Earthen Ring

RESOURCE LEGEND

FISHING - SURFACE

Freshwater	Ocean
	Murglesnout
	Fathom Eel
	Deepsea Sagefish
	Algaefin Rockfish
	Giant Sunfish
	Bonescale Snapper
	Deep Sea Monsterbelly

FISHING - CAVES

Freshwater	Ocean
	Murglesnout
	Algaefin Rockfish

MINING

Metal	Min Skill Level
Obsidium Deposit	425

HERBALISM

Herb	Min Skill Level
Stormvine	425

SKINNING

Creature	Level
Bloodcrazed Thresher	82
Chasm Stalker	82
Crushing Eel	82
Pyreshell Scuttler	81
Scourgut Remora	81
Seabrush Terrapin	81
Spinescale Hammerhead	81

Questing in Abyssal Depths

Before you travel to the Abyssal Depths, visit any major city controlled by your faction to obtain the quest Warchief's Command: Vashj'ir!, or Hero's Call: Vash'jir!. Completion of the quests which begin there leads to Abyssal Depths and the major questlines found within the zone.

ABYSSAL DEPTHS LEGEND

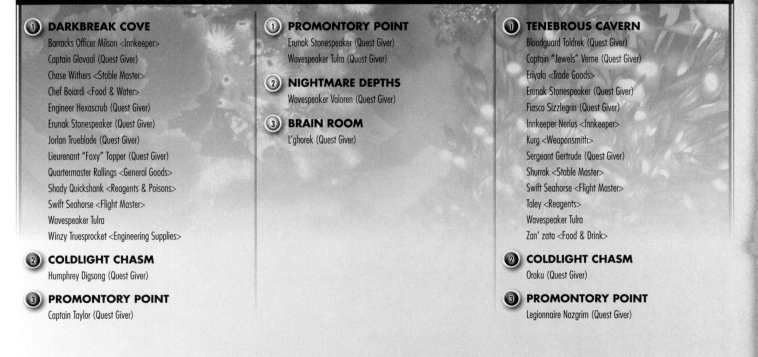

① DARKBREAK COVE

Barracks Officer Milson <Innkeeper>
Captain Glovaal (Quest Giver)
Chase Withers <Stable Master>
Chef Boiardi <Food & Water>
Engineer Hexascrub (Quest Giver)
Erunak Stonespeaker (Quest Giver)
Jorlan Trueblade (Quest Giver)
Lieurenant "Foxy" Topper (Quest Giver)
Quartermaster Rallings <General Goods>
Shady Quickshank <Reagents & Poisons>
Swift Seahorse <Flight Master>
Wavespeaker Tulra
Winzy Truesprocket <Engineering Supplies>

② COLDLIGHT CHASM

Humphrey Digsong (Quest Giver)

③ PROMONTORY POINT

Captain Taylor (Quest Giver)

① PROMONTORY POINT

Erunak Stonespeaker (Quest Giver)
Wavespeaker Tulra (Quest Giver)

② NIGHTMARE DEPTHS

Wavespeaker Valoren (Quest Giver)

③ BRAIN ROOM

L'ghorek (Quest Giver)

① TENEBROUS CAVERN

Bloodguard Toldrek (Quest Giver)
Captain "Jewels" Verne (Quest Giver)
Eriyala <Trade Goods>
Erunak Stonespeaker (Quest Giver)
Fiasco Sizzlegrin (Quest Giver)
Innkeeper Nerius <Innkeeper>
Kurg <Weaponsmith>
Sergeant Gertrude (Quest Giver)
Shurrak <Stable Master>
Swift Seahorse <Flight Master>
Taley <Reagents>
Wavespeaker Tulra
Zan' zata <Food & Drink>

② COLDLIGHT CHASM

Oraku (Quest Giver)

③ PROMONTORY POINT

Legionnaire Nazgrim (Quest Giver)

ARATHI HIGHLANDS

The Arathi Highlands' gentle rolling hills are home to robust wildlife such as the aggressive raptors and spiders that overrun much of the area. Both Trolls and Ogres have established small camps in the region and defend their territory zealously, making caution necessary when traveling. The devious Syndicate holds the former Alliance outpost of Stromgarde Keep in the southwest and doesn't take well to visitors. Both the Alliance and the Horde have well-established bases in the region at Refuge Point and Hammerfall, respectively, though they are spaced far enough apart that altercations are rare, but this status quo may not last. The Forsaken have recently built a camp of their own near Thoradin's Wall to the northwest, threatening to tip the balance of power in the region.

REPUTATION INFORMATION   Ravenholdt, Booty Bay, Everlook, Ratchet, Gadgetzan, Undercity

RESOURCE LEGEND

NODE FISHING

Freshwater	Ocean
Raw Greater Sagefish	Oily Blackmouth
	Firefin Snapper

OPEN WATER FISHING

Freshwater	Ocean
Raw Longjaw Mud Snapper	Raw Rainbow Fin Albacore
Raw Bristle Whisker Catfish	Firefin Snapper
	Oily Blackmouth

MINING

Metal	Min Skill Level
Tin Vein	65
Silver Vein	75
Iron Vein	125
Gold Vein	155

HERBALISM

Herb	Min Skill Level
Bruiseweed	100
Wild Steelbloom	115
Grave Moss	120
Kingsblood	125
Liferoot	150
Fadeleaf	160
Goldthorn	170
Khadgar's Whisker	185

SKINNING

Creature	Level
Highland Fleshstalker	28-29
Highland Strider	25-26
Highland Thrasher	27-28

Questing in Arathi Highlands

The Arathi Highlands quest for both factions start with Warchief's Command: Arathi Highlands!, or Hero's Call: Arathi Highlands!. If you're already in Arathi Highlands and don't want to return to a city, find Captain Nials at Refuge Pointe (Alliance), or Dark Ranger Alina at Galen's Fall (Horde).

ARATHI HIGHLANDS LEGEND

① REFUGE POINT

Androd Fadran <Leatherworking Supplies>
Captain Nials (Quest Giver)
Cedrik Prose <Gryphon Master>
Commander Amaren (Quest Giver)
Drovnar Strongbrew <Alchemy Supplies>
Emily Jackson <Stable Master>
Field Marshal Oslight (Quest Giver)
Hammon Karwn <Superior Tradesman>
Jannos Ironwill <Superior Macecrafter>
Narj Deepslice <Butcher>
Radulf Leder
Samuel Hawke <League of Arathor Supply Officer>
Sergeant Maclear
Skuerto (Quest Giver)
Targot Jinglepocket <Smokywood Pastures>
Vikki Lonsav <Innkeeper>
Wanted Board (Quest Giver)

② GO'SHEK FARM

Kinelory (Quest Giver)
Quae (Quest Giver)

③ STROMGARDE KEEP

Apprentice Kryten (Quest Giver)

① ARATHI HIGHLANDS

Shards of Myzrael (Quest Giver)

② FALDIR'S COVE

Captain Steelgut (Quest Giver)
Deckhand Moishe
Doctor Draxlegauge (Quest Giver)
First Mate Nilzlix
Lolo the Lookout
Professor Phizzlethorpe (Quest Giver)
Shakes O' Breen (Quest Giver)

③ DRYWHISKER GORGE

Iridescent Shards (Quest Giver)

④ CIRCLE OF INNER BINDING

Stone of Inner Binding (Quest Giver)

⑤ ARATHI HIGHLANDS

Dark Iron Entrepreneur <Specialty Goods>

① GALEN'S FALL

Audrid Grenich <Poison & Supplies>
Bat Handler Rhoda <Bat Handler>
Dark Ranger Alina (Quest Giver)
Deathstalker Maudria (Quest Giver)
Galen Trollbane (Quest Giver)
Genavie Callow (Quest Giver)
Goutgut (Quest Giver)

② HAMMERFALL

Deathmaster Dwire (Quest Giver)
Deathstalker Mortis
Doctor Gregory Victor (Quest Giver)
Drum Fel (Quest Giver)
Gor' mul (Quest Giver)
Graud <General Good>
Innkeeper Adegwa <Innkeeper>
Jun' ha <Tailoring Supplies>
Keena <Trade Goods>
Korin Fel
Kosco Copperpinch <Smokywood Pastures>
Mu' uta <Bowyer>
Rutherford Twing <Defilers Supply Officer>
Slagg <Superior Butcher>
Tharlidun <Stable Master>
The Black Bride
Tunkk <Leatherworking Supplies>
Urda <Wind Rider Master>
Uttnar <Butcher>
Zaruk (Quest Giver)

③ ARATHI HIGHLANDS

Brumm Winterhoof <Elemental Leatherworking Trainer>

BADLANDS

Never a hospitable place, the Badlands are dry, dusty, and dangerous. The craggy peaks and desolate flatlands have been altered by the cataclysm, most notably by the long black fissure known as the Scar of the Worldbreaker. The Horde town of Kargath was buried in an avalanche, its ruins now home to the dragon Nyxondra and her brood. New Kargath is more heavily fortified than its namesake, befitting the threats to the area. The Alliance now has more of a presence here with Dragon's Mouth, not far from New Kargath, being an important stop. The region is still filled with aggressive wildlife and Ogres, among other things, making traveling dangerous.

REPUTATION INFORMATION Booty Bay, Gadgetzan, Everlook, Ratchet

RESOURCE LEGEND

NODE FISHING

Freshwater	Ocean
	Oily Blackmouth
	Firefin Snapper

OPEN WATER FISHING

Freshwater	Ocean
	Stonescale Eel
	Raw Rockscale Cod
	Raw Spotted Yellowtail
	Raw Glossy Mightfish
	Raw Summer Bass
	Firefin Snapper
	Big-Mouth Clam
	Winter Squid

MINING

Metal	Min Skill Level
Gold Vein	155
Mithril Deposit	175
Truesilver Deposit	205

HERBALISM

Herb	Min Skill Level
Wild Steelbloom	115
Grave Moss	120
Kingsblood	125
Fadeleaf	160
Goldthorn	170
Khadgar's Whisker	185
Dragon's Teeth	195
Sungrass	230
Golden Sansam	260

SKINNING

Creature	Level
Billy Goat	44-45
Darkflight Flameblade	46-47
Darkflight Shadowspeaker	46-47
Darkflight Soldier	46-47
Elder Crag Coyote	45-46
Feral Crag Coyote	44-45
Nyxondra's Broodling	46-47
Rabid Crag Coyote	46-47
Raging Whelp	46-47
Ridge Huntress	45-46
Ridge Stalker	44-45
Ridge Stalker Patriarch	46-47
Scalding Whelp	44-45
Scorched Guardian	44-45

Questing in Badlands

An Eastern Plaguelands quest, Fuselight, Ho!, sends you to quest in the Badlands. If you arrive from a zone other than the Eastern Plaguelands, go to Fuselight-by-the-Sea and speak to Eddie Flofizzle.

BADLANDS LEGEND

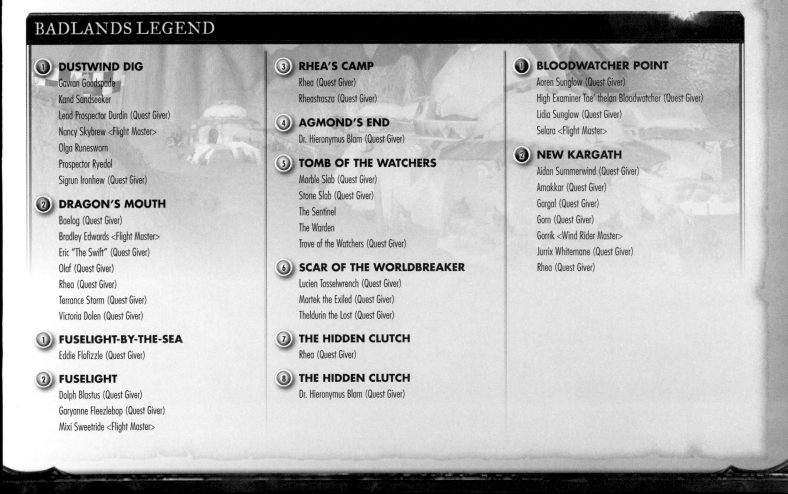

① DUSTWIND DIG
Gavran Goodspade
Kand Sandseeker
Lead Prospector Durdin (Quest Giver)
Nancy Skybrew <Flight Master>
Olga Runesworn
Prospector Ryedol
Sigrun Ironhew (Quest Giver)

② DRAGON'S MOUTH
Baelog (Quest Giver)
Bradley Edwards <Flight Master>
Eric "The Swift" (Quest Giver)
Olaf (Quest Giver)
Rhea (Quest Giver)
Terrance Storm (Quest Giver)
Victoria Dolen (Quest Giver)

① FUSELIGHT-BY-THE-SEA
Eddie Flofizzle (Quest Giver)

② FUSELIGHT
Dolph Blastus (Quest Giver)
Garyanne Fleezlebop (Quest Giver)
Mixi Sweetride <Flight Master>

③ RHEA'S CAMP
Rhea (Quest Giver)
Rheastrasza (Quest Giver)

④ AGMOND'S END
Dr. Hieronymus Blam (Quest Giver)

⑤ TOMB OF THE WATCHERS
Marble Slab (Quest Giver)
Stone Slab (Quest Giver)
The Sentinel
The Warden
Trove of the Watchers (Quest Giver)

⑥ SCAR OF THE WORLDBREAKER
Lucien Tosselwrench (Quest Giver)
Martek the Exiled (Quest Giver)
Theldurin the Lost (Quest Giver)

⑦ THE HIDDEN CLUTCH
Rhea (Quest Giver)

⑧ THE HIDDEN CLUTCH
Dr. Hieronymus Blam (Quest Giver)

① BLOODWATCHER POINT
Aoren Sunglow (Quest Giver)
High Examiner Tae' thelan Bloodwatcher (Quest Giver)
Lidia Sunglow (Quest Giver)
Selara <Flight Master>

② NEW KARGATH
Aidan Summerwind (Quest Giver)
Amakkar (Quest Giver)
Gargal (Quest Giver)
Gorn (Quest Giver)
Gorrik <Wind Rider Master>
Jurrix Whitemane (Quest Giver)
Rhea (Quest Giver)

BLASTED LANDS

As the name illustrates, the Blasted Lands have been damaged and warped by the presence of the Dark Portal. In the center of the region, the portal gives intrepid adventurers access to Outland. In the north, Nethergarde Keep, long a bastion of Alliance power in the area, is now under Horde control. To the southwest the recently revealed Red Reaches are home to the vicious Naga. At the southern tip of the wooded Tainted Scar lies the Worgen town of Surwich, giving the Alliance a convenient access point to the region.

REPUTATION INFORMATION   Bilgewater Cartel, Gilneas

RESOURCE LEGEND

NODE FISHING

Freshwater	Ocean
Raw Greater Sagefish	Oily Blackmouth
	Firefin Snapper
	Stonescale Eel
	Floating Wreckage

OPEN WATER FISHING

Freshwater	Ocean
Lightning Eel	Stonescale Eel
Raw Redgill	Raw Spotted Yellowtail
Raw Whitescale Salmon	Darkclaw Lobster
Plated Armorfish	Large Raw Mightfish
Raw Nightfin Snapper	Raw Summer Bass
Raw Sunscale Salmon	Big-Mouth Clam

MINING

Metal	Min Skill Level
Gold Vein	155
Mithril Deposit	175
Truesilver Deposit	205
Small Thorium Vein	230
Rich Thorium Vein	255

HERBALISM

Herb	Min Skill Level
Firebloom	205
Sungrass	230
Gromsblood	250
Golden Sansam	260
Dreamfoil	270
Mountain Silversage	280

SKINNING

Creature	Level
Ashmane Boar	57-57
Felbeast	50-51
Felhound	56-57
Helboar	52-53
Manahound	58-59
Manahound	60-60
Rabid Snickerfang	53-54
Redstone Basilisk	55-56
Redstone Crystalhide	51-52
Scorpok Lasher	52-53
Scorpok Snapper	46-47
Scorpok Stinger	46-47
Snickerfang Hyena	55-56
Starving Snickerfang	45-46
Tainted Black Bear	57-58
Tainted Screecher	57-58

Questing in Blasted Lands

Horde characters can visit a major city and get the quest, Warchiefs Command: Blasted Lands! or report directly to Okrilla at Dreadmaul Hold. Alliance players could start with Hero's Call: Blasted Lands!, or go to Nethergarde Keep and seek out Quartermaster Lungertz.

BLASTED LANDS LEGEND

① NETHERGARDE KEEP
Alexandra Constantine <Gryphon Master>
Bernie Heisten <Food & Drink>
Buttonwillow McKittrick (Quest Giver)
Commander Vines
Corporal Nobsy
Enohar Thunderbrew (Quest Giver)
Gina Gellar <Stable Master>
Keri Thunderbrew <Alcohol>
Leyan Steelson (Quest Giver)
Mama Morton <Innkeeper>
Marcy Lewis <Poisons & Reagents>
Nina Lightbrew <Alchemy Supplies>
Quartermaster Lungertz (Quest Giver)
Sarah Lightbrew <Enchanting Supplies>
Sergeant Krolan
Strumner Flintheel <Armorer>
Thadius Grimshade
Tonya Lightbrew <Inscripting Supplies>
Watcher Mahar Ba (Quest Giver)

② SERPENT'S COIL
Kasim Sharim (Quest Giver)
Loramus Thalipedes (Quest Giver)

③ THE DARK PORTAL
Advisor Sevel
Quartermaster Apone <General Goods>
Watch Commander Relthorn Netherwane (Quest Giver)
Watcher Grimeo (Quest Giver)

④ SURWICH
Cenarion Observer Shayana (Quest Giver)
Donna Berrymore <Innkeeper>
Garrod Pubhammer
Graham McAllister <Hippogryph Master>
Maurice Essman <Blacksmithing Supplies>
Mayor Charlton Connisport (Quest Giver)
Stephan Kebbel <Fishing Supplies>
Willard C. Bennington <Stable Master>

① BLASTED LANDS
Salt-Flop (Quest Giver)

② THE RED REACHES
Neptool (Quest Giver)

① DREADMAUL HOLD
Chef Braf <Food & Drink>
Innkeeper Grak <Innkeeper>
Kroff <Stable Master>
Master Aitokk (Quest Giver)

Neka <Reagents & Poisons>
Okrilla (Quest Giver)
Overseer Struk <Blacksmithing Supplies>
Preda <Wind Rider Master>

② NETHERGARDE MINES
Rofilian Dane (Quest Giver)
Tak' arili (Quest Giver)

③ DREADMAUL FURNACE
Bloodmage Drazial
Bloodmage Lynnore (Quest Giver)
Loramus Thalipedes (Quest Giver)

④ THE DARK PORTAL
Quartermaster Dekrok <General Goods>
Warlord Dar' toon (Quest Giver)
Watcher Wazzik (Quest Giver)

⑤ SUNVEIL EXCURSION
Aeilara <Trade Goods>
Clarya Sunveil
Janella <Food & Drink>
Rohan Sunveil (Quest Giver)
Salaran <Weaponsmith>
Salena <Dragonhawk Master>

⑥ BLASTED LANDS
Elijah Dawnflight (Quest Giver)

DEADWIND PASS

The road that winds through the mountains of Deadwind Pass is the only way to travel from Duskwood to the Swamp of Sorrows on foot. Travelers that stick to the road can make the passage pretty safely, as long as they can avoid the predatory Sky Shadows. In the southeast, Deadwind Ogres make their home, ready to waylay anyone foolish enough to travel into the Vice. Nestled among the southern mountains of the pass lies Karazhan. Once the dark wizard Medivh's seat of power, it is still a dangerous place. Its arcane energies have leaked across the region, warping trees and unsettling the dead. Whether using the pass as a shortcut or bravely heading to the dark tower, adventurers are advised to be wary while traveling through the pass.

REPUTATION INFORMATION The Violet Eye

RESOURCE LEGEND

NODE FISHING

None

OPEN WATER FISHING

Freshwater	Ocean
Barbed Gill Trout	
Bloodfin Catfish	
Crescent-Tail Skullfish	
Lightning Eel	
Raw Whitescale Salmon	
Raw Sunscale Salmon	
Plated Armorfish	
Raw Nightfin Snapper	
Raw Redgill	

MINING

Metal	Min Skill Level
None	

HERBLISM

Herb	Min Skill Level
None	

SKINNING

Creature	Level
Doomhound Mastiff	59-60
Doomhound Ravager	57-58

Questing in Deadwind Pass

Quests for Deadwind Pass are tied to Karazan, the level 70 instanced raid dungeon in the southern end of the zone.

DEADWIND PASS LEGEND

① KARAZHAN

Apprentice Darius

Archmage Leryda (Quest Giver)

Archmage Alturus (Quest Giver)

DUN MOROGH

The snowy peaks of Dun Morogh are home to both the Dwarves and the Gnomes. For years the great Dwarven capital of Ironforge has lent shelter to the exiled Gnomes. Now, the Gnomes have mobilized to take back their city, Gnomeregan. While this is an ambitious undertaking itself, the recent cataclysm has caused unexpected trouble for both groups. The cataclysm pushed the aggressive Troggs out of their holes in greater numbers, displacing the Frostmane Trolls. The Dwarves and their allies find themselves fighting both these hostile groups at once. In the northeast, at the Ironforge Airfield, the traitorous Dark Iron Dwarves have taken advantage of the distraction to launch an all-out attack. With their forces spread so thin, the Dwarves and Gnomes are hard pressed to defend their homeland.

REPUTATION INFORMATION
Ironforge, Gnomeregan Exiles

RESOURCE LEGEND

NODE FISHING

None

OPEN WATER FISHING

Freshwater	Ocean
Raw Brilliant Smallfish	
Raw Longjaw Mud Snapper	

MINING

Metal	Min Skill Level
Copper Vein	1

HERBALISM

Herb	Min Skill Level
Peacebloom	1
Silverleaf	1
Earthroot	15

SKINNING

Creature	Level
Black Bear	6-7
Crag Boar	5-6
Elder Crag Boar	7-8
Ice Claw Bear	7-8
Juvenile Snow Leopard	5-6
Large Crag Boar	6-7
Scarred Crag Boar	9-10
Snow Leopard	7-10
Snow Leopard Cub	9
Snow Tracker Wolf	5-7
Starving Winter Wolf	8-9
Winter Wolf	7-8
Young Black Bear	5-6

Questing in Dun Morogh

Dun Morogh is the beginning zone for both Dwarves and Gnomes. Low level characters from other Alliance races visiting the zone should check out Kharanos for quests.

DUN MOROGH LEGEND

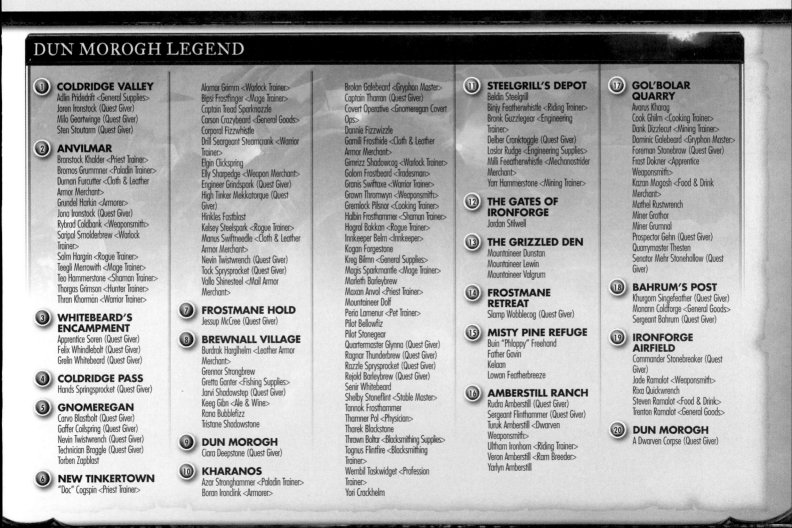

1 COLDRIDGE VALLEY
Adlin Pridedrift <General Supplies>
Joren Ironstock (Quest Giver)
Milo Geartwinge (Quest Giver)
Sten Stoutarm (Quest Giver)

2 ANVILMAR
Branstock Khalder <Priest Trainer>
Bromos Grummner <Paladin Trainer>
Durnan Furcutter <Cloth & Leather Armor Merchant>
Grundel Harkin <Armorer>
Jona Ironstock (Quest Giver)
Rybrad Coldbank <Weaponsmith>
Saripal Smolderbrew <Warlock Trainer>
Solm Hargrin <Rogue Trainer>
Teegli Merrowith <Mage Trainer>
Teo Hammerstone <Shaman Trainer>
Thorgas Grimson <Hunter Trainer>
Thran Khorman <Warrior Trainer>

3 WHITEBEARD'S ENCAMPMENT
Apprentice Soren (Quest Giver)
Felix Whindlebolt (Quest Giver)
Grelin Whitebeard (Quest Giver)

4 COLDRIDGE PASS
Hands Springsprocket (Quest Giver)

5 GNOMEREGAN
Carvo Blastbolt (Quest Giver)
Gaffer Coilspring (Quest Giver)
Nevin Twistwrench (Quest Giver)
Technician Braggle (Quest Giver)
Torben Zapblast

6 NEW TINKERTOWN
"Doc" Cogspin <Priest Trainer>

Alamar Grimm <Warlock Trainer>
Bipsi Frostfinger <Mage Trainer>
Captain Tread Sparknozzle
Carson Crazybeard <General Goods>
Corporal Fizzwhistle
Drill Seargeant Steamcrank <Warrior Trainer>
Elgin Clickspring
Elly Sharpedge <Weapon Merchant>
Engineer Grindspark (Quest Giver)
High Tinker Mekkatorque (Quest Giver)
Hinkles Fastblast
Kelsey Steelspark <Rogue Trainer>
Manus Swiftneedle <Cloth & Leather Armor Merchant>
Nevin Twistwrench (Quest Giver)
Tock Sprysprocket (Quest Giver)
Vallo Shinesteel <Mail Armor Merchant>

7 FROSTMANE HOLD
Jessup McCree (Quest Giver)

8 BREWNALL VILLAGE
Burdrak Harglhelm <Leather Armor Merchant>
Grennor Strongbrew
Gretta Ganter <Fishing Supplies>
Jarvi Shadowstep (Quest Giver)
Keeg Gibn <Ale & Wine>
Rana Bubblefizz
Tristane Shadowstone

9 DUN MOROGH
Ciara Deepstone (Quest Giver)

10 KHARANOS
Azar Stronghammer <Paladin Trainer>
Boran Ironclink <Armorer>

Brolan Galebeard <Gryphon Master>
Captain Tharran (Quest Giver)
Covert Operative <Gnomeregan Covert Ops>
Dannie Fizzwizzle
Garnili Frosthide <Cloth & Leather Armor Merchant>
Gimrizz Shadowcog <Warlock Trainer>
Golorn Frostbeard <Tradesman>
Granis Swiftaxe <Warrior Trainer>
Grawn Thromwyn <Weaponsmith>
Gremlock Pilsnor <Cooking Trainer>
Halbin Frosthammer <Shaman Trainer>
Hogral Bakkan <Rogue Trainer>
Innkeeper Belm <Innkeeper>
Kogan Forgestone
Kreg Bilmn <General Supplies>
Magis Sparkmantle <Mage Trainer>
Marleth Barleybrew
Maxan Anvol <Priest Trainer>
Mountaineer Dolf
Peria Lamenur <Pet Trainer>
Pilot Bellowfiz
Pilot Stonegear
Quartermaster Glynna (Quest Giver)
Ragnar Thunderbrew (Quest Giver)
Razzle Sprysprocket (Quest Giver)
Rejold Barleybrew (Quest Giver)
Senir Whitebeard
Shelby Stoneflint <Stable Master>
Tannok Frosthammer
Thamner Pol <Physician>
Tharek Blackstone
Thrawn Boltar <Blacksmithing Supplies>
Tognus Flintfire <Blacksmithing Trainer>
Wembil Taskwidget <Profession Trainer>
Yori Crackhelm

11 STEELGRILL'S DEPOT
Beldin Steelgrill
Binjy Featherwhistle <Riding Trainer>
Bronk Guzzlegear <Engineering Trainer>
Delber Cranktoggle (Quest Giver)
Loslor Rudge <Engineering Supplies>
Milli Feeatherwhistle <Mechanostrider Merchant>
Yarr Hammerstone <Mining Trainer>

12 THE GATES OF IRONFORGE
Jordan Stilwell

13 THE GRIZZLED DEN
Mountaineer Dunstan
Mountaineer Lewin
Mountaineer Valgrum

14 FROSTMANE RETREAT
Slamp Wobblecog (Quest Giver)

15 MISTY PINE REFUGE
Buin "Phloppy" Freehand
Father Gavin
Kelaan
Lowan Featherbreeze

16 AMBERSTILL RANCH
Rudra Amberstill (Quest Giver)
Sergeant Flinthammer (Quest Giver)
Turuk Amberstill <Dwarven Weaponsmith>
Ultham Ironhorn <Riding Trainer>
Veron Amberstill <Ram Breeder>
Yarlyn Amberstill

17 GOL'BOLAR QUARRY
Avarus Kharag
Cook Ghilm <Cooking Trainer>
Dank Dizzlecut <Mining Trainer>
Dominic Galebeard <Gryphon Master>
Foreman Stonebrow (Quest Giver)
Frast Dokner <Apprentice Weaponsmith>
Kazan Mogosh <Food & Drink Merchant>
Mathel Rustwrench
Miner Grothor
Miner Grumnal
Prospector Gehn (Quest Giver)
Quarrymaster Thesten
Senator Mehr Stonehallow (Quest Giver)

18 BAHRUM'S POST
Khurgorn Singefeather (Quest Giver)
Monann Coldforge <General Goods>
Sergeant Bahrum (Quest Giver)

19 IRONFORGE AIRFIELD
Commander Stonebreaker (Quest Giver)
Jade Ramalot <Weaponsmith>
Rixa Quickwrench
Steven Ramalot <Food & Drink>
Trenton Ramalot <General Goods>

20 DUN MOROGH
A Dwarven Corpse (Quest Giver)

DUSKWOOD

The cursed land of Duskwood is covered by a pall of darkness, making the malevolent creatures that inhabit the place feel right at home. Though many of the region's human inhabitants have long since fled or fallen victim to the dangers, the town of Darkshire remains as the largest hold-out of civilization in the area. The strong, stubborn people who claim the town as their home have learned to survive surrounded by lurking dangers on all sides.

REPUTATION INFORMATION Stormwind

RESOURCE LEGEND

NODE FISHING

Freshwater	Ocean
Raw Sagefish	

OPEN WATER FISHING

Freshwater	Ocean
Raw Longjaw Mud Snapper	Raw Rainbow Fin Albacore
Raw Bristle Whisker Catfish	Firefin Snapper
	Oily Blackmouth

MINING

Metal	Min Skill Level
Copper Vein	1
Tin Vein	65
Silver Vein	75
Iron Vein	125
Gold Vein	155

HERBLISM

Herb	Min Skill Level
Briarthorn	70
Bruiseweed	100
Wild Steelbloom	115
Grave Moss	120
Kingsblood	125

SKINNING

Creature	Level
Black Ravager	22-23
Black Ravager Mastiff	25-26
Blackbelly Forager	22-22
Coalpelt Bear	23-24
Dire Wolf	20-21
Prowling Darkhound	23-24
Rabid Dire Wolf	20-21
Starving Dire Wolf	19-20
Young Black Ravager	23-24

Questing in Duskwood

To start you journey in Duskwood, visit a major Alliance city for the quest, Hero's Call: Duskwood! or report to Commander Althea Ebonlocke at Darkshire.

DUSKWOOD LEGEND

1 DARKSHIRE

Alyssa Eva <Reagents>
Ambassador Berrybuck
Anchorite Delan
Barkeep Hann <Bartender>
Benjamin Carevin
Calor (Quest Giver)
Chef Grual (Quest Giver)
Clarise Gnarltree <Blacksmithing Trainer>
Clerk Daltry (Quest Giver)
Cog Glitzspinner
Commander Althea Ebonlocke (Quest Giver)
Councilman Millstipe
Danielle Zipstitch <Tailoring Supplies>
Elaine Carevin
Farrin Daris
Felicia Maline <Gryphon Master>
Finbus Geargrind <Engineering Trainer>
Frank Carlson <Blacksmithing Supplies>
Gavin Gnarltree <Weaponsmith>
Gunder Thornbush <Tradesman>
Herble Baubletump <Engineering & Mining Supplies>
Hogan Ference
Innkeeper Trelayne <Innkeeper>

Jonathan Carevin
Lohgan Eva <Tailoring Supplies>
Lord Ello Ebonlocke (Quest Giver)
Mabel Solaj <General Goods>
Madame Eva (Quest Giver)
Malissa <Poison Supplies>
Matt Johnson <Mining Trainer>
Morg Gnarltree <Armorer>
Role Dreuger
Scott Carevin <Mushroom Seller>
Sheri Zipstitch <Tailoring Supplies>
Sirra Von' Indi
Stevern Black <Stable Master>
Tavernkeep Smitts (Quest Giver)
Tobias Mistmantle (Quest Giver)
Town Crier
Viktori Prism' Antras (Quest Giver)
Watcher Backus
Watcher Brownell
Watcher Bukouris
Watcher Fraizer
Watcher Hartin
Watcher Jan
Watcher Jordan

Watcher Keefer
Watcher Keller
Watcher Ladimore
Watcher Mocarski
Watcher Royce
Watcher Wollpert
Watchmaster Sorigal

2 BEGGAR'S HAUNT

Abercrombie (Quest Giver)

3 DUSKWOOD

Blind Mary (Quest Giver)

4 DUSKWOOD

Apprentice Fess (Quest Giver)
Watcher Dodds
Watcher Paige

5 RAVEN HILL

Sister Elsington (Quest Giver)
Wilkinson <General Goods>
John Shelby <Gryphon Master>
Jitters (Quest Giver)
Ella <Reagents>
Oliver Harris (Quest Giver)
Sven Yorgen (Quest Giver)

EASTERN PLAGUELANDS

The Eastern Plaguelands were once part of the kingdom of Lordaeron with the great city of Stratholme lying in the northwest. After the Scourge ravaged the land, little was left but diseased ground, plagued wildlife, and monstrous flora. The Argent Crusade has long had a presence at Light's Hope Chapel. Now, with this base newly fortified, they have created outposts throughout the region. The Scarlet Crusade still works to oust the undead from Stratholme, and are quick to make enemies of anyone who doesn't share their calling. The Pestilent Scar that once gouged the land now houses a small lake and the appearance of normal grass and other plants seems to signal the land is at last beginning to heal. Despite these changes this is still a land besieged by the Scourge, as well as other serious threats.

REPUTATION INFORMATION Argent Crusade

RESOURCE LEGEND

NODE FISHING

Freshwater	Ocean
Raw Greater Sagefish	
Floating Wreckage	

OPEN WATER FISHING

Freshwater	Ocean
Raw Mithril Head Trout	Stonescale Eel
Raw Redgill	Raw Rockscale Cod
Oily Blackmouth	Raw Spotted Yellowtail
Raw Nightfin Snapper	Raw Glossy Mightfish
Raw Sunscale Salmon	Raw Summer Bass
Lightning Eel	Firefin Snapper
	Big-Mouth Clam
	Winter Squid

MINING

Metal	Min Skill Level
Iron Vein	125
Gold Vein	155
Mithril Deposit	175
Truesilver Deposit	205
Small Thorium Vein	230
Rich Thorium Vein	255

HERBALISM

Herb	Min Skill Level
Stranglekelp	85
Grave Moss	120
Liferoot	150
Khadgar's Whisker	185
Arthas' Tears	220
Sungrass	230
Golden Sansam	260
Dreamfoil	270
Mountain Silversage	280
Sorrowmoss	285
Black Lotus	300

SKINNING

Creature	Level
Blighthound	40-41
Frenzied Plaguehound	41-42
Greater Plaguehound	43-44
Landlocked Grouper	41-42
Monstrous Plaguebat	43-44
Noxious Plaguebat	41-42
Plaguebat	40-41
Plagued Swine	43-44
Plaguehound	41
Plaguehound Runt	40-41

Questing in Eastern Plaguelands

Grab either Warchief's Command: Eastern Plaguelands!, or Hero's Call: Eastern Plaguelands before venturing to this zone for the first time.

EASTERN PLAGUELANDS LEGEND

1 LIGHT'S HOPE CHAPEL
Khaelyn Steelwing <Gryphon Master>

1 THONDORIL RIVER
Fiona (Quest Giver)
Frax Bucketdrop <Flight Master>

2 DEATH'S STEP
Tarenar Sunstrike (Quest Giver)

3 THONDORIL RIVER
Gidwin Goldbraids (Quest Giver)

4 CROWN GUARD TOWER
Argus Highbeacon (Quest Giver)
Carlin Redpath (Quest Giver)
Chromie (Quest Giver)
Fiona
Gidwin Goldbraids
Janice Myers <Flight Master>
Tarenar Sunstrike (Quest Giver)
Urk Gagbaz (Quest Giver)

5 DARROWSHIRE
Pamela Redpath (Quest Giver)

6 EASTERN PLAGUELANDS
Rayne (Quest Giver)

7 LIGHT'S SHIELD TOWER
Argus Highbeacon
Betina Bigglezink (Quest Giver)
Devon Manning <Flight Master>
Fiona
Frederick Calston (Quest Giver)
Vex' tul (Quest Giver)

8 LIGHT'S HOPE CHAPEL
Argus Highbeacon
Beezil Linkspanner
Caretaker Alen
Craftsman Wilhelm
Dispatch Commander Metz
Duke Nicholas Zverenhoff
Emissary Gormok
Emissary Whitebeard
Fiona
Gidwin Goldbraids (Quest Giver)
Jase Farlane <Trade Supplies>
Jessica Chambers <Innkeeper>
Leonid Barthalomew the Revered (Quest Giver)
Lord Maxwell Tyrosus (Quest Giver)
Master Craftsman Omarion (Quest Giver)
Packmaster Stonebruiser
Quartermaster Miranda Breechlock

Rimblat Earthshatter (Quest Giver)
Smokey LaRue (Quest Giver)
Tarenar Sunstrike (Quest Giver)

9 TYR'S HAND
Archmage Angela Dosantos (Quest Giver)
Crusade Commander Korfax
Crusade Commander Eligor Dawnbringer

10 TYR'S HAND
Crusade Commander Korfax (Quest Giver)

11 TYR'S HAND
Crusade Commander Eligor Dawnbringer
(Quest Giver)

12 TYR'S HAND
Archmage Angela Dosantos (Quest Giver)

13 EASTWALL TOWER
Argus Highbeacon
Deacon Andaal (Quest Giver)
Fiona (Quest Giver)
Gamella Cracklefizz (Quest Giver)
Gidwin Goldbraids
Richard Trueflight <Flight Master>
Rimblat Earthshatter
Tarenar Sunstrike (Quest Giver)
Vex' tul (Quest Giver)

14 NORTHPASS TOWER
Argent Officer Irizarry (Quest Giver)
Argus Highbeacon (Quest Giver)
Fiona (Quest Giver)
Grayson Ironwing <Flight Master>
Kirkian Dawnshield (Quest Giver)
Rimblat Earthshatter
Tarenar Sunstrike (Quest Giver)

15 EASTERN PLAGUELANDS
Corpseburner Tim (Quest Giver)

16 PLAGUEWOOD
Crusader Kevin Frost (Quest Giver)
Tarenar Sunstrike (Quest Giver)

17 PLAGUEWOOD
Gidwin Goldbraids (Quest Giver)

18 PLAGUEWOOD TOWER
Argent Apothecary Judkins (Quest Giver)
William Kielar Jr. <Flight Master>

19 TERRORDALE
Augustus the Touched (Quest Giver)
Egan

1 LIGHT'S HOPE CHAPEL
Georgia <Bat Handler>

ELWYNN FOREST

Home to the Alliance capital of Stormwind, the fields and woods of Elwynn Forest have remained mostly untouched by the cataclysm. The exception to this is the Northshire Vineyards which have been taken over by Blackrock Orcs who are attempting to burn them to the ground. Elsewhere, in places like Goldshire, the Eastvale Logging Camp, and the Westbrook Garrison, Stormwind troops deal with more mundane threats like bandits, Gnolls, and Murlocs.

REPUTATION INFORMATION   Stormwind

RESOURCE LEGEND

NODE FISHING

None

OPEN WATER FISHING

Freshwater	Ocean
Raw Brilliant Smallfish	Raw Slitherskin Mackerel
Raw Longjaw Mud Snapper	

MINING

Metal	Min Skill Level
Copper Vein	1

HERBALISM

Herb	Min Skill Level
Peacebloom	1
Silverleaf	1
Earthroot	15

SKINNING

Creature	Level
Gray Forest Wolf	7-8
Longsnout	10-11
Mangy Wolf	5-6
Porcine Entourage	7
Prowler	9-10
Rockhide Boar	7-8
Stonetusk Boar	5-6
Young Forest Bear	8-9

Questing in Elwynn Forest

As the starting zone for Humans, questing ultimately begins at Northshire. Other Alliance characters of slightly higher level in the area should visit Goldshire for quests.

ELWYNN FOREST LEGEND

1 NORTHSHIRE VALLEY
Ashley Blank <Hunter Trainer>
Brother Paxton (Quest Giver)
Brother Danil <General Supplies>
Dane Winslow
Sergeant Willem (Quest Giver)
Dermot Johns <Cloth & Leather Armor Merchant>
Drusilla La Salle <Warlock Trainer>
Eagan Peltskinner
Godric Rothgar <Armorer & Shieldcrafter>
Jorik Kerridan <Rogue Trainer>
Marshal McBride (Quest Giver)
Milly Osworth (Quest Giver)

2 NORTHSHIRE ABBEY
Brother Sammuel <Paladin Trainer>
Khelden Bremen <Mage Trainer>
Llane Beshere <Warrior Trainer>
Priestess Anetta <Priest Trainer>

3 NORTHSHIRE VALLEY
Falkhaan Isenstrider

4 ELWYNN FOREST
Alchemist Mallory <Alchemy Trainer>
Herbalist Pomeroy <Herbalism Trainer>

5 ELWYNN FOREST
Donni Anthania <Crazy Cat Lady>

6 GOLDSHIRE
Aaron
Adele Fielder <Leatherworking Trainer>
Cameron
Dana
Helene Peltskinner <Skinning Trainer>

John
Jose
Lisa

7 CRYSTAL LAKE
Jason Mathers <Fishmonger>
Lee Brown <Fishing Trainer>
Matt

8 GOLDSHIRE
Andrew Krighton <Armorer & Shieldcrafter>
Barkeep Dobbins <Bartender>
Bartlett the Brave <Gryphon Master>
Benjamin Foxworthy <Hunter Trainer>
Bo
Brog Hamfist <General Supplies>
Brother Wilhelm <Paladin Trainer>
Corina Steele <Weaponsmith>
Cylina Darkheart
Erma <Stable Master>
Innkeeper Farley <Innkeeper>
Joshua
Keryn Sylvius <Rogue Trainer>
Kurran Steele <Cloth & Leather Armor Merchant>
Lien Farner <Profession Trainer>
Lyria Du Lac <Warrior Trainer>
Mark
Marshal Dughan (Quest Giver)
Maximillian Crowe <Warlock Trainer>
Melika Isenstrider
Merissa Stilwell
Michelle Belle <First Aid Trainer>
Priestess Josetta <Priest Trainer>
Remen Marcot
Remy "Two Times" (Quest Giver)

Smith Argus (Quest Giver)
Tharynn Bouden <Trade Supplies>
Toddrick <Butcher>
Tomas <Cooking Trainer>
William Pestle (Quest Giver)
Zaldimar Wefhellt <Mage Trainer>

9 GOLDSHIRE
Kira Songshine <Traveling Baker>

10 MACLURE VINEYARDS
Billy Maclure (Quest Giver)
Gerard Tiller (Quest Giver)
Joshua Maclure <Vintner>
Maybell Maclure (Quest Giver)
Pa Maclure

11 THE STONEFIELD FARM
"Auntie" Bernice Stonefield (Quest Giver)
Gramma Stonefield
Homer Stonefield <Fruit Seller>
Ma Stonefield (Quest Giver)

12 THE STONEFIELD FARM
Tommy Joe Stonefield (Quest Giver)

13 CRYSTAL LAKE
Guard Roberts

14 TOWER OF AZORA
Dawn Brightstar <Arcane Goods>
Kitta Firewind <Enchanting Trainer>
Morley Eberlein <Clothier>
Theocritus

15 ELWYNN FOREST
Bounty Board (Quest Giver)
Guard Thomas (Quest Giver)

16 EASTVALE LOGGING CAMP
Eldrin <Tailoring Trainer>
James Clark
Sara Timberlain (Quest Giver)

17 EASTVALE LOGGING CAMP
Drake Lindgren <General & Trade Supplies>
Eric
Goss the Swift <Gryphon Master>
Jay
Katie Hunter <Horse Breeder>
Kevin
Kyle
Marshal Haggard
Marshal McCree (Quest Giver)
Rallic Finn <Bowyer>
Randal Hunter <Riding Trainer>
Solomon
Supervisor Raelen (Quest Giver)
Terry Palin <Lumberjack>

18 WESTBROOK GARRISON
Deputy Rainer (Quest Giver)
Quartermaster Hicks <Master Weaponsmith>
Quartermaster Hudson <Armorer & Shieldcrafter>
Sergeant De Vries <Morale Officer>
Veldan Lightfoot <Leather Armor Merchant>
Wanted Poster

19 HOGGER HILL
Westfall Deed (Quest Giver)

EVERSONG WOODS

Eversong Woods, the homeland of the Blood Elves, is a beautiful land with clear lakes, green hills, and forests full of colorful trees. Sprinkled among these natural beauties, the Blood Elves built tall gracefull structures which sit in harmony with their surroundings. Even this idyllic setting is not without dangers. The Dead Scar, an ugly, barren strip of diseased land, bisects the woods, a constant reminder of the Scourge invasion. The Wretched, pitiful husks of the Blood Elves they once were, haunt the areas near the capital, making travel dangerous. Many creatures native to the island have become feral and aggressive as well. It is a lucky thing that Eversong Woods has remained untouched by the recent cataclysm. The Blood Elves have enough work to do still recovering from the Scourge.

REPUTATION INFORMATION   Silvermoon City, Tranquillien

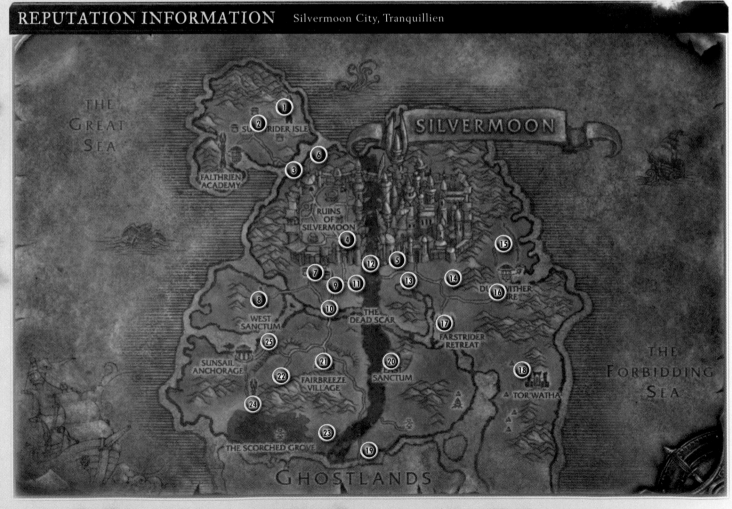

RESOURCE LEGEND

NODE FISHING
None

OPEN WATER FISHING

Freshwater	Ocean
Raw Brilliant Smallfish	Raw Slitherskin Mackerel
Raw Longjaw Mud Snapper	

MINING

Metal	Min Skill Level
Copper Vein	1

HERBLISM

Herb	Min Skill Level
Peacebloom	1
Bloodthistle	1
Silverleaf	1
Earthroot	15

SKINNING

Creature	Level
Crazed Dragonhawk	7-8
Elder Springpaw	8-9
Feral Dragonhawk Hatchling	5-6
Lake Snapper	7-8
Springpaw Matriarch	9-10
Springpaw Stalker	6-7

Questing in Eversong Woods

Eversong Woods is the starting zone for the Blood Elf race. Non-Blood Elf members of the Horde who travel to Eversong Woods for quests should stop at Stillwhisper Pond just outside of Silvermoon City.

EVERSONG WOODS LEGEND

1 THE SUNSPIRE
Arcanist Helion (Quest Giver)
Arcanist Ithanas (Quest Giver)
Delios Silverblade <Warrior Trainer>
Faraden Thelryn <Armorsmith>
Jainthess Thelryn <Cloth & Leather Merchant>
Jesthenis Sunstriker <Paladin Trainer>
Julia Sunstriker <Mage Trainer>
Magistrix Erona (Quest Giver)
Matron Arena <Priest Trainer>
Pathstalker Kariel <Rogue Trainer>
Raelis Dawnstar <Weaponsmith>
Ranger Salina <Hunter Trainer>
Shara Sunwing <General Supplies>
Summoner Teli'Larien <Warlock Trainer>
Well Watcher Solanian (Quest Giver)
Yasmine Teli'Larien

2 SUNSTRIDER ISLE
Lanthan Perilon (Quest Giver)

3 DAWNING LANE
Outrunner Alarion (Quest Giver)

4 FALCONWING SQUARE
Aeldon Sunbrand (Quest Giver)
Aleinia <Jewelcrafting Trainer>
Anathos <Stable Master>
Celoenus <Warlock Trainer>
Daestra
Duelist Larenis <Weapon Master>
Farsil <Armor & Shield Merchant>
Garridel <Mage Trainer>
Geron <Weapon Merchant>
Hannovia <Hunter Trainer>

Innkeeper Delaniel <Innkeeper>
Kanaria <First Aid Trainer>
Kyrenna <Cheese Vendor>
Landraelanis <Tradesman>
Saren <Profession Trainer>
Magister Jaronis (Quest Giver)
Noellene <Paladin Trainer>
Ponaris <Priest Trainer>
Quarelestra <Cooking Trainer>
Sergeant Kan'ren
Sheri <General Goods>
Sleyin <Weapon Vendor>
Tannaria <Rogue Trainer>
Telenus <Pet Trainer>
Vara <Cloth & Leather Merchant>
Wanted Poster <Quest Giver>
Skymaster Skyles <Dragonhawk Master>
Marsilla Dawnstar
Lothan Silverblade <Warrior Trainer>

5 EVERSONG WOODS
Skymistress Gloaming <Dragonhawk Master>
Kinamisa <Leatherworking Supplies>
Mathreyn <Skinning Trainer>
Sathein <Leatherworking Trainer>

6 EVERSONG WOODS
Master Kelerun Bloodmourn (Quest Giver)

7 NORTH SANCTUM
Apprentice Veya
Prospector Anvilward
Ley-Keeper Caidanis (Quest Giver)
Solanin <Bag Vendor>
Silanna

8 WEST SANCTUM
Ley-Keeper Velania (Quest Giver)

9 EVERSONG WOODS
Apprentice Ralen (Quest Giver)

10 EVERSONG WOODS
Apprentice Meledor (Quest Giver)

11 EVERSONG WOODS
Ranger Selron

12 THE DEAD SCAR
Ranger Jaela (Quest Giver)

13 STILLWHISPER POND
Erilia <Enchanting Vendor>
Instructor Antheol (Quest Giver)

14 THURON'S LIVERY
Winaestra <Hawkstrider Breeder>
Perascamin <Riding Trainer>

15 DUSKWITHER GROUNDS
Groundskeeper Wyllithen (Quest Giver)

16 EVERSONG WOODS
Apprentice Loralthalis (Quest Giver)

17 FARSTRIDER RETREAT
Zalene Firstlight <Food & Drink>
Lieutenant Dawnrunner (Quest Giver)
Paelarin <Bowyer>
Arathel Sunforge <Blacksmithing Trainer>
Areyn <General Goods>
Magister Duskwither (Quest Giver)

18 TOR'WATHA
Ven'jashi (Quest Giver)

19 EVERSONG WOODS
Apothecary Thedra (Quest Giver)
Courier Dawnstrider (Quest Giver)

20 EAST SANCTUM
Apprentice Mirveda (Quest Giver)

21 FAIRBREEZE VILLAGE
Skymaster Brightdawn <Dragonhawk Master>
Halis Dawnstrider <General Goods>
Magistrix Landra Dawnstrider (Quest Giver)
Ranger Degolien (Quest Giver)
Marniel Amberlight (Quest Giver)
Ardeyn Riverwind (Quest Giver)
Sathiel <Trade Supplies>
Velan Brightoak (Quest Giver)
Jilanne

22 SALTHERIL'S HAVEN
Botanist Tyniarrel <Herbalism Trainer>
Sempstress Ambershine <Tailoring Trainer>
Arcanist Sheynathren <Alchemy Trainer>
Magistrix Eredania <Enchanting Trainer>
Lord Saltheril (Quest Giver)
Elisara Sunstriker

23 RUNESTONE FALITHAS
Runewarden Deryan (Quest Giver)

24 GOLDENBOUGH PASS
Larianna Riverwind (Quest Giver)

25 EVERSONG WOODS
Captain Kelisendra (Quest Giver)
Velendris Whitemorn (Quest Giver)
Sailor Melinan <Drink Vendor>

GHOSTLANDS

Ghostlands is a region shrouded in darkness. The plants seem twisted and sickly while the local fauna are well suited to the environment—quick and deadly. The Dead Scar runs through the area, emanating from the undead stronghold of Deatholme in the south. The Blood Elves and their allies in Tranquillien must constantly work to keep the Scourge in check. To the east lies Zul'Aman, home to bands of vicious forest trolls. The Farstriders stationed at Farstrider Enclave do their best to battle the Amani Trolls who are constantly making trouble on the eastern side of the Ghostlands. Though for now, the Blood Elves and their allies have everything well in hand, they can always use the help of stalwart members of the Horde in their constant struggle to maintain control of the region.

REPUTATION INFORMATION Silvermoon City, Tranquillien, Undercity

RESOURCE LEGEND

NODE FISHING

None

OPEN WATER FISHING

Freshwater	Ocean
Raw Brilliant Smallfish	Ocean Blackmouth
Raw Longjaw Mud Snapper	Raw Rainbow Fin Albacore
Raw Bristle Whisker Catfish	Raw Slitherskin Mackerel

MINING

Metal	Min Skill Level
Copper Vein	1
Tin Vein	65
Silver Vein	75

HERBALISM

Herb	Min Skill Level
Peacebloom	1
Silverleaf	1
Earthroot	15
Mageroyal	50
Briarthorn	70
Bruiseweed	100

SKINNING

Creature	Level
Ghostclaw Lynx	13-14
Ghostclaw Ravager	16-17
Lesser Scourgebat	16-18
Mistbat	9-10
Plagued Snapper	12-13
Starving Ghostclaw	9-10
Vampiric Mistbat	13-15

Questing in Ghostlands

If you're heading into the Ghostlands after questing in Eversong Woods, you should have a quest that guides you to your first quest giver in Ghostlands. If you're not coming from Eversong Woods, start out at Tranquillien.

GHOSTLANDS LEGEND

1 ELRENDAR RIVER
Keltus Darkleaf (Quest Giver)

2 UNDERLIGHT MINES
Apprentice Shatharia (Quest Giver)

3 TRANQUILLIEN
Advisor Valwyn (Quest Giver)
Apothecary Renzithen (Quest Giver)
Arcanist Vandril (Quest Giver)
Blacksmith Frances <Blacksmithing Supplies>
Dame Auriferous (Quest Giver)
Deathstalker Maltendis (Quest Giver)
Deathstalker Rathiel (Quest Giver)
Eralan <Poison Supplies>
High Executor Mavren (Quest Giver)
Innkeeper Kalarin <Innkeeper>
Magister Darenis (Quest Giver)
Magistrix Aminel (Quest Giver)
Master Chef Mouldier (Quest Giver)
Paniar <Stable Master>
Provisioner Vredigar
Quartermaster Lymel (Quest Giver)
Ranger Lethvalin (Quest Giver)
Rathis Tomber (Quest Giver)
Skymaster Sunwing <Dragonhawk Master>
Terellia <Trade Supplies>
Wanted Poster (Quest Giver)

4 SANCTUM OF THE SUN
Arcanist Janeda (Quest Giver)
Magister Idonis (Quest Giver)
Magister Kaendris (Quest Giver)
Magister Quallestis

5 ANDILIEN ESTATE
Apprentice Vor'el (Quest Giver)

6 AN'TELAS
Magister Sylastor (Quest Giver)

7 DEATHOLME
Apothecary Enith

8 DEATHOLME
Ranger Vedoran

9 DEATHOLME
Apprentice Varnis

10 AMANI CATACOMBS RANGER
Lilatha (Quest Giver)

11 FARSTRIDER ENCLAVE
Apothecary Venustus (Quest Giver)
Captain Helios (Quest Giver)
Farstrider Dusking
Farstrider Sedina (Quest Giver)
Farstrider Solanna (Quest Giver)
Heron Skygaze <Food & Drink>
Narina <Bowyer>
Ranger Krenn'an (Quest Giver)
Ranger Vynna (Quest Giver)
Wanted Poster (Quest Giver)

12 GHOSTLANDS
Geranis Whitemorn (Quest Giver)

13 LAKE ELRENDAR
Lieutenant Tomathren
Ranger Valanna (Quest Giver)

14 GHOSTLANDS
Dying Blood Elf (Quest Giver)

HILLSBRAD FOOTHILLS

Though the land itself has not undergone changes due to the Cataclysm, there have been many changes of ownership in the region. The region now encompasses the Alterac Mountains where Ogres still roam. Though there are pockets of resistance, the Horde has a firm control on this region. The former Alliance town of Southshore is no more and its ruins are occupied by the Horde. The Syndicate, which once had a strong presence in the region, has been ousted from Durnholde Keep and from their smaller holdings as well. Though the Horde has a tight hold of the verdant region for now it is a safe bet that the Alliance won't permanently relinquish this valuable piece of land without a fight.

REPUTATION INFORMATION Undercity

RESOURCE LEGEND

NODE FISHING

Freshwater	Ocean
Raw Sagefish	Oily Blackmouth
	Firefin Snapper
	Schooner Wreckage

OPEN WATER FISHING

Freshwater	Ocean
Raw Longjaw Mud Snapper	Raw Rainbow Fin Albacore
Raw Bristle Whisker Catfish	Firefin Snapper
	Oily Blackmouth

MINING

Metal	Min Skill Level
Tin Vein	65
Gold Vein	155

HERBALISM

Herb	Min Skill Level
Mageroyal	50
Briarthorn	70
Stranglekelp	85
Bruiseweed	100

SKINNING

Creature	Level
Blighted Bear	20-21
Cave Yeti	22-23
Elder Gray Bear	19-20
Ferocious Yeti	23
Foothill Stalker	22-23
Giant Yeti	25-26
Hill Stag	22-23
Infested Bear	19-20
Mountain Yeti	24-25
Snapjaw	22-23
Starving Mountain Lion	23-24
Vicious Black Bear	23-24
Vicious Gray Bear	22-23
Wild Gryphon	40
Wild Horse	25

Questing in Hillsbrad Foothills

Horde characters should get the quest Warchief's Command: Hillsbrad Foothills! from any major city before venturing to Hillsbrad Foothills. The only quests for Alliance characters found in Hillsbrad are tied to the Alterac Valley battleground. All characters should check out the Brazzie Farmstead for an entertaining line of quests.

HILLSBRAD FOOTHILLS LEGEND

1. ALTERAC MOUNTAINS
Captain Armando Ossex
Grumbol Grimhammer
Lieutenant Haggerdin (Quest Giver)
Prospector Stonehewer (Quest Giver)
Sergeant Durgen Stormpike (Quest Giver)
Thanthaldis Snowgleam <Stormpike Supply Officer>

1. BRAZIE FARMSTEAD
Brazie the Botanist (Quest Giver)

1. SOUTHPOINT GATE
Apothecary Underhill (Quest Giver)
Harland Waldek <Weaponsmith>
High Executor Darthalia (Quest Giver)
Marsha Duchamp <Food &Drink>
Pamela Stutzka <Bat Handler>

2. AZURELODE MINE
Baby
Captain Keyton (Quest Giver)
Spider-Handler Sarus (Quest Giver)

3. AZURELODE MINE
Dumass (Quest Giver)

4. THE SLUDGE FIELDS
Beauxbeaux
Flesh-Shaper Arnauld (Quest Giver)

Gordon Finley <Poisons & Reagents>
Innkeeper Hershberg <Innkeeper>
Karren Dresner <Alchemy>
Kenneth Lamb <General Goods>
Marcus Hagnod <Leatherworking Supplies>
Shannon Lamb <Stable Master>
Warden Stillwater (Quest Giver)

5. THE SLUDGE FIELDS
Shovel (Quest Giver)

6. THE SLUDGE FIELDS
Johnny Awesome (Quest Giver)
Master Apothecary Lydon (Quest Giver)

7. RUINS OF SOUTHSHORE
Darla Harris <Bat Handler>
Helcular (Quest Giver)
Serge Hinott (Quest Giver)

8. RUINS OF SOUTHSHORE
Kingslayer Orkus (Quest Giver)
Kasha

9. PURGATION ISLE
Kasha
Kingslayer Orkus (Quest Giver)

10. TARREN MILL
Advisor Duskingdawn (Quest Giver)
Aranae Venomblood <Herbalism Trainer>

Christoph Jeffcoat <Tradesman>
Craig Hewitt
Daryl Stack <Tailoring Trainer>
Deathguard Humbert (Quest Giver)
Deathguard Samsa (Quest Giver)
Delia Verana
Derek Nightfall (Quest Giver)
Hans Zandin
High Warlord Cromush (Quest Giver)
Innkeeper Shay <Innkeeper>
Jason Lemieux <Mushroom Seller>
Kayren Soothallow <General Goods>
Keeper Bel'varil (Quest Giver)
Krusk (Quest Giver)
Magus Wordeen Voidglare
Mallen Swain <Tailoring Supplies>
Melisara (Quest Giver)
Monika Sengutz
Novice Thaivand
Ott <Weaponsmith>
Overwatch Mark I
Shara Blazen
Tallow
Tara Coldgaze
Theodore Mont Claire <Stable Master>
Vinna Wayne
Zarise <Bat Handler>
Zixil <Merchant Supreme>

11. ALTERAC MOUNTAINS
Corporal Teeka Bloodsnarl (Quest Giver)
Dillord Copperpinch <Smokywood Pastures>
Jorek Ironside <Frostwolf Supply Officer>
Usha Eyegouge
Voggah Deathgrip (Quest Giver)
Warmaster Laggrond (Quest Giver)

12. EASTPOINT TOWER
Ansel Tunsleworth <Stable Master>
Captain Jekyll (Quest Giver)
Chesterfield Cobbles <General Goods>
Darren Longfellow <Bat Handler>
Dreadguard Molina
Dreadguard Spiering
Drull
Evan Banlip <Engineering Supplies>
Innkeeper Durgens <Innkeeper>
Nils Beerot (Quest Giver)
Patricia Eyesley <Herbalism Supplies>
Tog'thar

13. DUN GAROK
Captain Ironhill's Ghost (Quest Giver)

14. STAHNBRAD
Gol'dir
Phillip Harding <Bat Handler>

IRONFORGE

Built deep into the heart of the Khaz Modan Mountains, Ironforge is a uniquely Dwarven capital. Despite being completely underground, its immense caverns and broad roads make it feel as open as any above ground city. At the heart of the city lies the Great Forge. Here Dwarven craftsmen use the immense heat of the molten rock continuously pouring through the city to forge the masterful items for which the Dwarves are known.

REPUTATION INFORMATION   Ironforge, Gnomeregan Exiles

RESOURCE LEGEND

NODE FISHING
None

OPEN WATER FISHING	
Freshwater	Ocean
Raw Brilliant Smallfish	
Raw Longjaw Mud Snapper	

IRONFORGE LEGEND

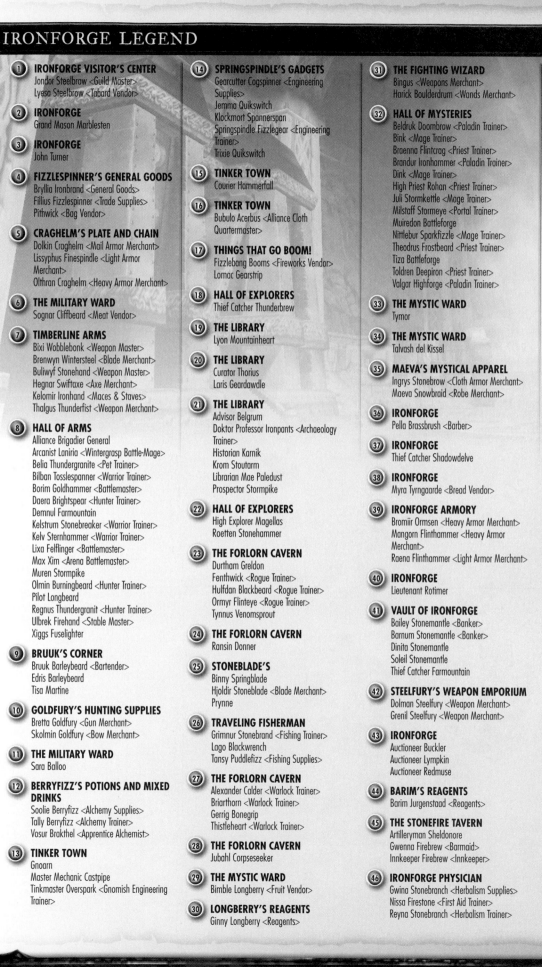

(1) IRONFORGE VISITOR'S CENTER
Jondor Steelbrow <Guild Master>
Lyesa Steelbrow <Tabard Vendor>

(2) IRONFORGE
Grand Mason Marblesten

(3) IRONFORGE
John Turner

(4) FIZZLESPINNER'S GENERAL GOODS
Bryllia Ironbrand <General Goods>
Fillius Fizzlespinner <Trade Supplies>
Pithwick <Bag Vendor>

(5) CRAGHELM'S PLATE AND CHAIN
Dolkin Craghelm <Mail Armor Merchant>
Lissyphus Finespindle <Light Armor Merchant>
Olthran Craghelm <Heavy Armor Merchant>

(6) THE MILITARY WARD
Sognar Cliffbeard <Meat Vendor>

(7) TIMBERLINE ARMS
Bixi Wobblebonk <Weapon Master>
Brenwyn Wintersteel <Blade Merchant>
Buliwyf Stonehand <Weapon Master>
Hegnar Swiftaxe <Axe Merchant>
Kelomir Ironhand <Maces & Staves>
Thalgus Thunderfist <Weapon Merchant>

(8) HALL OF ARMS
Alliance Brigadier General
Arcanist Laniria <Wintergrasp Battle-Mage>
Belia Thundergranite <Pet Trainer>
Bilban Tosslespanner <Warrior Trainer>
Borim Goldhammer <Battlemaster>
Daera Brightspear <Hunter Trainer>
Demnul Farmountain
Kelstrum Stonebreaker <Warrior Trainer>
Kelv Sternhammer <Warrior Trainer>
Lixa Felflinger <Battlemaster>
Max Xim <Arena Battlemaster>
Muren Stormpike
Olmin Burningbeard <Hunter Trainer>
Pilot Longbeard
Regnus Thundergranit <Hunter Trainer>
Ulbrek Firehand <Stable Master>
Xiggs Fuselighter

(9) BRUUK'S CORNER
Bruuk Barleybeard <Bartender>
Edris Barleybeard
Tisa Martine

(10) GOLDFURY'S HUNTING SUPPLIES
Bretta Goldfury <Gun Merchant>
Skolmin Goldfury <Bow Merchant>

(11) THE MILITARY WARD
Sara Balloo

(12) BERRYFIZZ'S POTIONS AND MIXED DRINKS
Soolie Berryfizz <Alchemy Supplies>
Tally Berryfizz <Alchemy Trainer>
Vosur Brakthel <Apprentice Alchemist>

(13) TINKER TOWN
Gnoarn
Master Mechanic Castpipe
Tinkmaster Overspark <Gnomish Engineering Trainer>

(14) SPRINGSPINDLE'S GADGETS
Gearcutter Cogspinner <Engineering Supplies>
Jemma Quikswitch
Klockmort Spannerspan
Springspindle Fizzlegear <Engineering Trainer>
Trixie Quikswitch

(15) TINKER TOWN
Courier Hammerfall

(16) TINKER TOWN
Bubulo Acerbus <Alliance Cloth Quartermaster>

(17) THINGS THAT GO BOOM!
Fizzlebang Booms <Fireworks Vendor>
Lomac Gearstrip

(18) HALL OF EXPLORERS
Thief Catcher Thunderbrew

(19) THE LIBRARY
Lyon Mountainheart

(20) THE LIBRARY
Curator Thorius
Laris Geardawdle

(21) THE LIBRARY
Advisor Belgrum
Doktor Professor Ironpants <Archaeology Trainer>
Historian Karnik
Krom Stoutarm
Librarian Mae Paledust
Prospector Stormpike

(22) HALL OF EXPLORERS
High Explorer Magellas
Roetten Stonehammer

(23) THE FORLORN CAVERN
Durtham Greldon
Fenthwick <Rogue Trainer>
Hulfdan Blackbeard <Rogue Trainer>
Ormyr Flinteye <Rogue Trainer>
Tynnus Venomsprout

(24) THE FORLORN CAVERN
Ransin Donner

(25) STONEBLADE'S
Binny Springblade
Hjoldir Stoneblade <Blade Merchant>
Prynne

(26) TRAVELING FISHERMAN
Grimnur Stonebrand <Fishing Trainer>
Lago Blackwrench
Tansy Puddlefizz <Fishing Supplies>

(27) THE FORLORN CAVERN
Alexander Calder <Warlock Trainer>
Briarthorn <Warlock Trainer>
Gerrig Bonegrip
Thistleheart <Warlock Trainer>

(28) THE FORLORN CAVERN
Jubahl Corpseseeker

(29) THE MYSTIC WARD
Bimble Longberry <Fruit Vendor>

(30) LONGBERRY'S REAGENTS
Ginny Longberry <Reagents>

(31) THE FIGHTING WIZARD
Bingus <Weapons Merchant>
Harick Boulderdrum <Wands Merchant>

(32) HALL OF MYSTERIES
Beldruk Doombrow <Paladin Trainer>
Bink <Mage Trainer>
Braenna Flintcrag <Priest Trainer>
Brandur Ironhammer <Paladin Trainer>
Dink <Mage Trainer>
High Priest Rohan <Priest Trainer>
Juli Stormkettle <Mage Trainer>
Milstaff Stormeye <Portal Trainer>
Muiredon Battleforge
Nittlebur Sparkfizzle <Mage Trainer>
Theodrus Frostbeard <Priest Trainer>
Tiza Battleforge
Toldren Deepiron <Priest Trainer>
Valgar Highforge <Paladin Trainer>

(33) THE MYSTIC WARD
Tymor

(34) THE MYSTIC WARD
Talvash del Kissel

(35) MAEVA'S MYSTICAL APPAREL
Ingrys Stonebrow <Cloth Armor Merchant>
Maeva Snowbraid <Robe Merchant>

(36) IRONFORGE
Pella Brassbrush <Barber>

(37) IRONFORGE
Thief Catcher Shadowdelve

(38) IRONFORGE
Myra Tyrngaarde <Bread Vendor>

(39) IRONFORGE ARMORY
Bromiir Ormsen <Heavy Armor Merchant>
Mangorn Flinthammer <Heavy Armor Merchant>
Raena Flinthammer <Light Armor Merchant>

(40) IRONFORGE
Lieutenant Rotimer

(41) VAULT OF IRONFORGE
Bailey Stonemantle <Banker>
Barnum Stonemantle <Banker>
Dinita Stonemantle
Soleil Stonemantle
Thief Catcher Farmountain

(42) STEELFURY'S WEAPON EMPORIUM
Dolman Steelfury <Weapon Merchant>
Grenil Steelfury <Weapon Merchant>

(43) IRONFORGE
Auctioneer Buckler
Auctioneer Lympkin
Auctioneer Redmuse

(44) BARIM'S REAGENTS
Barim Jurgenstaad <Reagents>

(45) THE STONEFIRE TAVERN
Artilleryman Sheldonore
Gwenna Firebrew <Barmaid>
Innkeeper Firebrew <Innkeeper>

(46) IRONFORGE PHYSICIAN
Gwina Stonebranch <Herbalism Supplies>
Nissa Firestone <First Aid Trainer>
Reyna Stonebranch <Herbalism Trainer>

(47) THE GREAT FORGE
Gryth Thurden <Gryphon Master>

(48) THISTLEFUZZ ARCANERY
Elise Brightletter <Inscription Trainer>
Erdunor Whitespire <Arcane Reforger>
Gimble Thistlefuzz <Enchanting Trainer>
Thargen Heavyquill <Inscription Supplies>
Thonys Pillarstone
Tilli Thistlefuzz <Enchanting Supplies>

(49) THE BRONZE KETTLE
Daryl Riknussun <Cooking Trainer>
Emrul Riknussun <Cooking Supplies>

(50) THE GREAT FORGE
Brombar Higgleby

(51) THE GREAT FORGE
Bengus Deepforge <Blacksmithing Trainer>
Groum Stonebeard
Grumnus Steelshaper <Armorsmith Trainer>
Ironus Coldsteel <Weaponsmith Trainer>
Myolor Sunderfury
Rorgath Stonebeard
Thurgrum Deepforge <Blacksmithing Supplies>
Tormus Deepforge

(52) THE GREAT FORGE
Farseer Eannu
Farseer Javad <Shaman Trainer>

(53) DEEP MOUNTAIN MINING GUILD
Geofram Bouldertoe <Mining Trainer>
Golnir Bouldertoe <Mining Supplies>

(54) BURBIK'S SUPPLIES
Burbik Gearspanner <Trade Supplies>

(55) THE GREAT FORGE
Sraaz <Pie Vendor>

(56) STONEBROW'S CLOTHIER
Jormund Stonebrow <Tailoring Trainer>
Mistina Steelshield <Alliance Cloth Quartermaster>
Outfitter Eric <Specialty Tailoring Supplies>
Poranna Snowbraid <Tailoring Supplies>
Uthrar Threx

(57) FINESPINDLE'S LEATHER GOODS
Balthus Stoneflayer <Skinning Trainer>
Bombus Finespindle <Leatherworking Supplies>
Fimble Finespindle <Leatherworking Trainer>
Gretta Finespindle

(58) THE GREAT FORGE
Ambassador Slaghammer

(59) THE HIGH SEAT
Deliana
Kurdran Wildhammer
Moira Thaurissan
Mountaineer Barleybrew
Muradin Bronzebeard
Royal Historian Archesonus
Senator Barin Redstone

(60) DEEPRUN TRAM
Haggle
Monty

ISLE OF QUEL'DANAS

Located off the northern coast of the Eastern Kingdoms, the Isle of Quel'Danas is home to the ancient Sunwell. Once the main source of Elven power, it was befouled by the Scourge invasion which left behind remnants still seen to this day on the island. Naga and Murlocs infest the eastern coast while the Wretched populate the land around Dawnstar Village. Dawnblade forces occupy the center of the island as well. The Aldor and Scryers have put aside their differences to form the Shattered Sun Offensive. They hold Dawnstar Village and are ever vigilant against the encroaching threats.

REPUTATION INFORMATION Shattered Sun Offensive

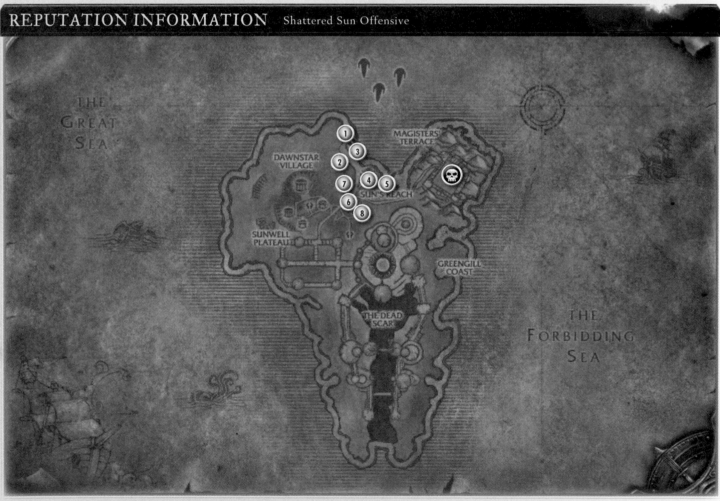

RESOURCE LEGEND

NODE FISHING

None

OPEN WATER FISHING

Freshwater	Ocean
Giant Sunfish	Jaggal Clam
	Lightning Eel
	Luminous Bluetail

MINING

Metal	Min Skill Level
Adamantite Vein	325
Rich Adamantite Vein	350
Khorium Vein	375

HERBLISM

Herb	Min Skill Level
Nightmare Vine	365
Mana Thistle	375

SKINNING

None

Questing in Isle of Quel'Danas

The quests for Isle of Quel'Danas are all tied to the Shattered Sun Offensive. Visit Shattrath City when you reach level 70 for more information.

ISLE OF QUEL'DANAS LEGEND

(1) SUN'S REACH HARBOR

Ayren Cloudbreaker

Ohura <Dragonhawk Master>

(2) SHATTERED SUN STAGING AREA

Captain Theris Dawnhearth (Quest Giver)

Drill Sergeant Bahduum

Eldara Dawnrunner (Quest Giver)

Exarch Larethor (Quest Giver)

Vindicator Xayann (Quest Giver)

(3) SUN'S REACH HARBOR

Anchorite Kairthos (Quest Giver)

Archmage Ne' thul

Caregiver Inaara <Innkeeper>

Kaalif <Reagent Vendor>

K'iru

Mar' nah (Quest Giver)

Sentinel

(4) SUN'S REACH HARBOR

Seraphina Bloodheart <Stable Master>

Sereth Duskbringer <Poison Supplier>

Shaani <Jewelcrafting Supplies>

Theremis <Keeper of Lost Artifacts>

Yrma <Transmuter of Sin' dorei Relics>

(5) SILVERMOON'S PRIDE

Captain Valindria (Quest Giver)

(6) SUN'S REACH SANCTUM

Anchorite Ayuri (Quest Giver)

(7) SUN'S REACH SANCTUM

Astromancer Darnarian (Quest Giver)

Battlemage Arynna (Quest Giver)

Harbinger Inuuro (Quest Giver)

Tradesman Portanuus (Quest Giver)

(8) SUN'S REACH ARMORY

Karynna <Exotic Gear Purveyor>

Kayri <Exotic Gear Purveyor>

Magister Ilastar (Quest Giver)

Olus <Exotic Gear Purveyor>

Smith Hauthaa (Quest Giver)

Soryn <Exotic Gear Purveyor>

Tyrael Flamekissed <General Goods>

Vindicator Kaalan (Quest Giver)

KELP'THAR FOREST

The northeastern area of Vashj'ir is known as the Kelp'thar Forest. The serene beauty of the underwater area belies the dangers lurking around every corner. Much of the aquatic wildlife found here isn't happy with intrusion into their territory and finds that travelers make good snacks. The Naga here are no less vicious than their more familiar counterparts. Gilbins, aquatic cousins to Goblins, are interested in picking up treasure and don't particularly care whether it comes from a wrecked ship or your bloated corpse, so use caution when approaching Gurboggle's Ledge or the many shipwrecks lying on the sea floor.

REPUTATION INFORMATION Earthen Ring

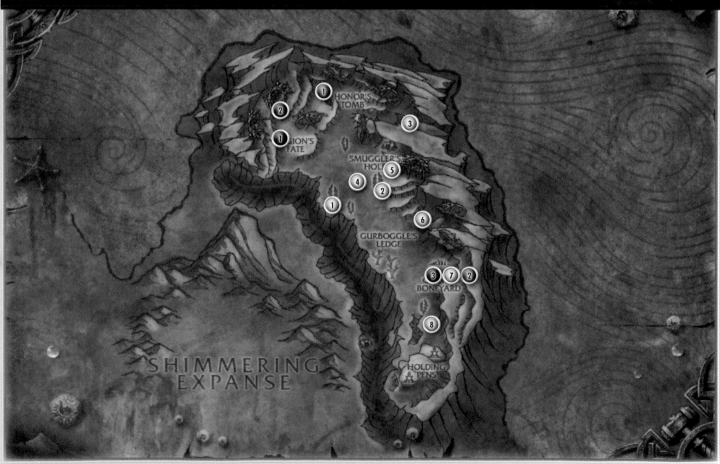

RESOURCE LEGEND

FISHING - SURFACE

Freshwater	Ocean
	Murglesnout
	Fathom Eel
	Deepsea Sagefish
	Algaefin Rockfish
	Giant Sunfish
	Bonescale Snapper
	Deep Sea Monsterbelly

FISHING - CAVES

Freshwater	Ocean
	Murglesnout
	Algaefin Rockfish

MINING

Metal	Min Skill Level
Obsidium Deposit	425
Elementium Vein	475
Rich Elementium Vein	500

HERBALISM

Herb	Min Skill Level
Stormvine	425
Azshara's Veil	450

SKINNING

Creature	Level
Blackfin	80
Brinescale Serpent	80
Famished Great Shark	80
Ravenous Thresher	80
Sabreclaw Skitterer	80
Slickskin Eel	80
Slitherfin Eel	80

Questing in Kelp'thar Forest

Before you travel to Kelp'thar Forest, visit any major city controlled by your faction to obtain the quest Warchief's Command: Vashj'ir!, or Hero's Call: Vashj'ir!. Completion of the quests which begin there leads to the major questlines found within this zone.

KELP'THAR FOREST LEGEND

1 THE BRINY CUTTER
Captain Taylor (Quest Giver)
Erunak Stonespeaker (Quest Giver)

2 DEEPMIST GROTTO
Private Pollard (Quest Giver)

1 SHALLOW'S END
Erunak Stonespeaker (Quest Giver)
Moanah Stormhoof (Quest Giver)
Rendel Firetongue

2 KELP FOREST
Adarrah (Quest Giver)

3 SMUGGLER'S HOLE
Adarrah (Quest Giver)
Broken Bottle (Quest Giver)
Captain Samir (Quest Giver)
Mack Fearsen (Quuest Giver)
Swift Seahorse <Flight Master>

4 KELP FOREST
Sunken Crate (Quest Giver)

5 BUDD'S DIG
Budd (Quest Giver)

6 ACCURSED REEF
Budd (Quest Giver)

7 DEEPMIST GROTTO
Erunak Stonespeaker (Quest Giver)
Moanah Stormhoof (Quest Giver)
Rendel Firetongue (Quest Giver)

8 HOLDING PENS
Naga Tridents (Quest Giver)

1 THE IMMORTAL COIL
Erunak Stonespeaker (Quest Giver)
Legionnaire Nazgrim (Quest Giver)

2 LEGION'S FATE
Alliance S.E.A.L Equipment (Quest Giver)

3 DEEPMIST GROTTO
Gurrok (Quest Giver)

LOCH MODAN

Loch Modan is a pleasant looking, wooded area tucked into the mountains of Khaz Modan. It takes its name from the large lake that used to make up the central part of the region. With the recent destruction of the great Stonewrought Dam, the Loch has now been drained, leaving behind only small pools to mark its former location. The Mo'grosh Ogres are as active as ever in the region and visitors to Ironband's Excavation Site should watch out for new dangers near the dig. The Troggs are still a problem in Loch Modan and Twilight Cultists have established a camp as well.

REPUTATION INFORMATION   Ironforge

RESOURCE LEGEND

NODE FISHING

Freshwater	Ocean
Raw Sagefish	

OPEN WATER FISHING

Freshwater	Ocean
Raw Brilliant Smallfish	Raw Slitherskin Mackerel
Raw Longjaw Mud Snapper	Oily Blackmouth
Raw Bristle Whisker Catfish	Raw Rainbow Fin Albacore

MINING

Metal	Min Skill Level
Copper Vein	1
Tin Vein	65
Silver Vein	75

HERBALISM

Herb	Min Skill Level
Peacebloom	1
Silverleaf	1
Earthroot	15
Mageroyal	50
Briarthorn	70

SKINNING

Creature	Level
Black Bear	11-12
Black Bear Patriarch	16-17
Bobcat	16-17
Elder Mountain Boar	16-17
Grizzled Black Bear	13-14
Hill Fox	16
Hill Grizzly	15-16
Lakebed Snapper	16-17
Loch Crocolisk	14-15
Loch Frenzy	12-13
Mangy Mountain Boar	14-15
Mountain Boar	10-11
Mudbelly Boar	16-16
Young Threshadon	19-20

Questing in Loch Modan

Ideally, you should pick up Hero's Call: Loch Modan! from any major city before heading to the zone. If you're already on the way to Loch Modan without the quest, start out in Thelsamar.

LOCH MODAN LEGEND

1 SOUTH GATE OUTPOST
Pilot Hammerfoot (Quest Giver)

2 VALLEY OF KINGS
Captain Rugelfuss (Quest Giver)
Mountaineer Cobbleflint (Quest Giver)
Mountaineer Naarh
Mountaineer Tyraw
Mountaineer Wallbang (Quest Giver)
Thorvald Deepforge

3 VALLEY OF KINGS
Mountaineer Kalmir
Mountaineer Zaren

4 THELSAMAR
Bailor Stonehand
Brock Stoneseeker <Mining Trainer>
Cannary Caskshot (Quest Giver)
Dakk Blunderblast (Quest Giver)
Drac Roughcut <Tradesman>
Ghak Healtouch <Alchemy Trainer>
Greishan Ironstove <Traveling Merchant>
Honey Goldenoat <Baker>
Innkeeper Hearthstove <Innkeeper>
Jern Hornhelm (Quest Giver)
Kali Healtouch <Herbalism Trainer>
Karm Ironquill <Mining Supplies>
Lina Hearthstove <Stable Master>
Magistrate Bluntnose
Morhan Coppertongue <Metalsmith>
Mountaineer Bludd
Mountaineer Cragg

Mountaineer Dalk
Mountaineer Droken
Mountaineer Fazgard
Mountaineer Gwarth
Mountaineer Harn
Mountaineer Janha
Mountaineer Kadrell (Quest Giver)
Mountaineer Kamdar
Mountaineer Langarr
Mountaineer Modax
Mountaineer Ozmok
Mountaineer Roghan
Mountaineer Stenn
Mountaineer Swarth
Mountaineer Uthan
Mountaineer Wuar
Rann Flamespinner <Tailoring Supplies>
Thorgrum Borrelson <Gryphon Master>
Torren Squarejaw (Quest Giver)
Vidra Hearthstove (Quest Giver)
Vrok Blunderblast <Gunsmith>
Wanted! (Quest Giver)
Yanni Stoutheart <General Supplies>

5 GRIZZLEPAW RIDGE
Stolen Explorer's League Document (Quest Giver)

6 THE LOCH
Khara Deepwater <Fishing Supplies>
Stolen Explorers' League Document (Quest Giver)
Warg Deepwater <Fishing Trainer>

7 ALGAZ STATION
Gathor Brumn <Armorer>
Mountaineer Brokk
Mountaineer Ganin
Mountaineer Hammerfall
Mountaineer Luxst
Mountaineer Morran
Mountaineer Stormpike (Quest Giver)
Mountaineer Yuttha
Mountaineer Zwarn
Scout Dorli (Quest Giver)

8 DUN ALGAZ
Mountaineer Dokkin
Mountaineer Rockgar

9 LOCH MODAN
Huldar (Quest Giver)
Miran

10 IRONBAND'S EXCAVATION SITE
Aldren Cordon <Clothier>
Magmar Fellhew (Quest Giver)
Prospector Ironband (Quest Giver)

11 LOCH MODAN
Stolen Explorer's League Document (Quest Giver)

12 IRONBAND'S EXCAVATION SITE
Stolen Explorer's League Document (Quest Giver)

13 THE FARSTRIDER LODGE
Bingles Blastenheimer (Quest Giver)
Claude Erksine <Pet Trainer>
Cliff Hadin <Bowyer>
Dargh Trueaim <Hunter Trainer>
Daryl the Youngling (Quest Giver)
Eeryven Grayer <Gryphon Master>
Gravin Steelbeard <Stable Master>
Irene Sureshot <Gunsmith>
Kat Sampson <Leather Armor Merchant>
Marek Ironheart (Quest Giver)
Safety Warden Pipsy (Quest Giver)
Vyrin Swiftwind <Innkeeper>
Xandar Goodbeard <General Supplies>

14 LOCH MODAN
Stolen Explorers' League Document (Quest Giver)

15 LOCH MODAN
Stolen Explorers' League Document (Quest Giver)

16 THE LOCH
Ando Blastenheimer (Quest Giver)

17 MO'GROSH STRONGHOLD
Ashlan Stonesmirk (Quest Giver)
Kelt Thomasin

18 STONEWROUGHT DAM
Deek Fizzlebizz <Engineering Trainer>

NORTHERN STRANGLETHORN

During the cataclysm, the violent whirlpool known as the Sundering ripped the land almost in two, forever changing the landscape of the former Stranglethorn Vale. Grom'gol Base Camp escaped plunging into the vortex with the nearby coast. It has been joined by an Alliance camp, Fort Livingston, to the south and a new Horde encampment, Bambala, to the east. After years of hunting the surrounding jungles, Nessingwary's Expedition has expanded into a more permanent base for taking on the various jungle creatures.

REPUTATION INFORMATION   Stormwind, Orgrimmar

REBEL CAMP ①

RUINS OF ZUL'KUNDA

NESINGWARY'S EXPEDITION ①

KURZEN'S COMPOUND

VENTURE CO BASE CAMP

BAMBALA ③

③

ZUL'GURUB

②

GROM'GOL BASE CAMP ①

THE VILE REEF

MOSH'OGG OGRE MOUND

②

FORT LIVINGSTON ②

THE CAPE OF STRANGLETHORN

RESOURCE LEGEND

NODE FISHING

Freshwater	Ocean
Raw Sagefish	Oily Blackmouth
	Firefin Snapper
	Schooner Wreckage

OPEN WATER FISHING

Freshwater	Ocean
Raw Longjaw Mud Snapper	Raw Rainbow Fin Albacore
Raw Bristle Whisker Catfish	Firefin Snapper
	Oily Blackmouth

MINING

Metal	Min Skill Level
Tin Vein	65
Silver Vein	75
Iron Vein	125
Gold Vein	155

HERBALISM

Herb	Min Skill Level
Stranglekelp	85
Bruiseweed	100
Kingsblood	125
Wild Steelbloom	115
Liferoot	150

SKINNING

Creature	Level	Creature	Level
Bloodscalp Panther	25-26	Saltwater Crocolisk	26-27
Bloodscalp Tiger	25-26	Shadowmaw Panther	26-27
Cold Eye Basilisk	29-30	Skullsplitter Panther	28-28
Crystal Spine Basilisk	25-26	Skullsplitter Tiger	28-28
Elder Shadowmaw Panther	29-30	Snapjaw Crocolisk	26-27
Elder Snapjaw Crocolisk	27-28	Stone Maw Basilisk	24-25
Elder Stranglethorn Tiger	26-27	Stranglethorn Raptor	24-25
Ironjaw Basilisk	29-30	Stranglethorn Tiger	25-26
Jungle Stalker	26-27	Stranglethorn Tigress	29-30
Kurzen War Panther	24-25	Thrashtail Basilisk	29-30
Kurzen War Tiger	24-25	Vale Howler	26-27
Lashtail Raptor	25-26	Young Lashtail Raptor	23-24
Panther	25-26	Young Panther	24-25
River Crocolisk	25-26	Young Stranglethorn Raptor	23-24
		Young Stranglethorn Tiger	24-25

Questing in Northern Stranglethorn

Horde players bound for Northern Stranglethorn should begin their journey with the Warchief's Command: Northern Stranglethorn! quest, or head directly to Grom'gol Base Camp. Alliance players begin with Hero's Call: Northern Stranglethorn Vale! or report to Lieutenant Doren at the Rebel Camp.

NORTHERN STRANGLETHORN LEGEND

(1) REBEL CAMP

Berrin Burnquill (Quest Giver)
Bloodlord Mandokir (Quest Giver)
Brother Nimetz (Quest Giver)
Corporal Bluth <Camp Trader>
Corporal Kaleb (Quest Giver)
Corporal Sethman (Quest Giver)
Emerine Junis (Quest Giver)
James Stillair <Gryphon Master>
Lieutenant Doren (Quest Giver)
Osborn Obnoticus (Quest Giver)
Sergeant Yohwa (Quest Giver)

(2) FORT LIVINGSTON

Robert Rhodes <Gryphon Master>
Wulfred Harrys (Quest Giver)
Priestess Thaalia (Quest Giver)
Livingston Marshal (Quest Giver)
Daniel Roberts <Blacksmithing Supplies>
Ghaliri (Quest Giver)
Kinnel (Quest Giver)

(1) NESINGWARY'S EXPEDITION

Ajeck Rouack (Quest Giver)
Barnil Stonepot (Quest Giver)
Drizzlik (Quest Giver)
Hemet Nesingway Jr. (Quest Giver)
Jaquilina Dramet <Superior Axecrafter>
Krazek (Quest Giver)
Sergeant S.J. Erlgadin (Quest Giver)

(2) BAL'LAL RUINS

Lashtail Hatchling (Quest Giver)

(3) NORTHERN STRANGLETHORN

Galvan the Ancient

(1) GROM'GOL BASE CAMP

Angrun <Herbalism Trainer>
Bloodlord Mandokir (Quest Giver)
Brawn <Leatherworking Trainer>
Bubbling Cauldron (Quest Giver)
Commander Aggro' gosh (Quest Giver)
Durik <Stable Master>
Far Seer Mok' thardin (Quest Giver)
Hragran <Cloth & Leather Armor Merchant>
Innkeeper Thulbek <Innkeeper>
Kragg <Hunter Trainer>

Krakk <Superior Armorer>
Mudduk <Cooking Trainer>
Nargatt <Food & Drink>
Nemeth Hawkeye (Quest Giver)
Nerrist <Trade Goods>
Nez' raz
Nimboya (Quest Giver)
Squibby Overspeck
Thysta <Wind Rider Master>
Uthok <General Supplies>
Vharr <Superior Weaponsmith>
Zudd <Pet Trainer>

(2) NORTHERN STRANGLETHORN

Se'jib <Tribal Leatherworking Trainer>

(3) BAMBALA

Durango <General Goods>
Kil' karil (Quest Giver)
Kin' weelay (Quest Giver)
Morango <Trade Goods>
Pechanga <Reagents & Poisons>
Priestess Hu' rala (Quest Giver)
Raskha <Gryphon Masterr>
Skeezy Whillzap (Quest Giver)
Surkhan (Quest Giver)

REDRIDGE MOUNTAINS

The Redridge Mountains seem an idyllic, peaceful place. The town of Lakeshire is on the shores of Lake Everstill where fishing is a main industry. However, outside the town there are many threats to the unwary. Small camps of Gnolls dot the landscape, harassing travelers. The more serious threat comes from the Blackrock Orcs. They have moved into the region in earnest, pressing outward from Stonewatch in attempt to lay claim to the territory. The denizens of Lakeshire watch hopefully as their forces fight to keep the Orcs off of their very doorsteps.

REPUTATION INFORMATION Stormwind

RESOURCE LEGEND

NODE FISHING

Freshwater	Ocean
Raw Sagefish	
Floating Debris	

OPEN WATER FISHING

Freshwater	Ocean
Raw Brilliant Smallfish	Raw Slitherskin Mackerel
Raw Longjaw Mud Snapper	Oily Blackmouth
Raw Bristle Whisker Catfish	Raw Rainbow Fin Albacore

MINING

Metal	Min Skill Level
Copper Vein	1
Tin Vein	65

HERBALISM

Herb	Min Skill Level
Earthroot	15
Mageroyal	60
Briarthorn	70
Bruiseweed	100

SKINNING

Creature	Level
Black Dragon Whelp	17-18
Forest Stalker	18-19
Great Goretusk	14-15
Lake Thresher	25
Redridge Fox	15-16
Redridge Fox Cub	8-9
Servant of Ilgalar	18

Questing in Redridge Mountains

Get the quest Hero's Call: Redridge Mountains! from a major Alliance city, or report directly to Watch Captain Parker at Tower Watch.

REDRIDGE MOUNTAINS LEGEND

(1) TOWER WATCH

Darcy Parker (Quest Giver)
Guard Bateman
Guard Flippit
Libby Parker
Wanted! (Quest Giver)
Watch Captain Parker (Quest Giver)

(2) REDRIDGE MOUNTAINS

Ariena Stormfeather <Gryphon Master>
Deputy Feldon
Guard Ashlock
Guard Hiett
Guard Howe
Guard Pearce

(3) LAKESHIRE

Alma Jainrose <Herbalism Trainer>
Amy Davenport <Tradeswoman>
Antonio Perelli <Traveling Salesman>
Arantir
Bailiff Conacher (Quest Giver)
Barkeep Daniels
Bartender Wental <Food & Drink>
Big Earl
Bridge Dmitri
Bridge Worker Alex
Bridge Worker Daniel
Bridge Worker Jess
Bridge Worker Matthew
Bridge Worker Trent

Chef Breanna
Colonel Troteman (Quest Giver)
Crystal Boughman <Cooking Trainer>
Danforth
Dockmaster Baren
Dorin Songblade <Armorer>
Dumpy
Effsee
Erin
Foreman Oslow (Quest Giver)
Franklin Hamar <Tailoring Supplies>
Gerald Crawley <Poison Supplies>
Gloria Femmel <Cooking Supplies>
Gretchen Vogel <Waitress>
Guard Adams
Guard Berton
Guard Clarke
Hannah
Henry Chapal <Gunsmith>
Innkeeper Brianna <Innkeeper>
Jamin
John J. Keeshan (Quest Giver)
Jorgensen
Kara Adams <Shield Crafter>
Karen Taylor <Blacksmithing & Mining Supplies>
Kimberly Hiett <Bowyer>
Krakauer
Lamar Veisilli <Fruit Seller>
Lindsay Ashlock <General Supplies>
Lucius

Madison
Magistrate Solomon (Quest Giver)
Marshal Marris (Quest Giver)
Martie Jainrose (Quest Giver)
Matthew Hooper <Fishing Trainer>
Messner
Narnie
Nathan
Nida
Penny <Stable Master>
Rachel
Roger
Shawn (Quest Giver)
Sherman Femmel <Butcher>
Verner Osgood
Vernon Hale <Fishing Supplies>
Wiley the Black
Yorus Barleybrew
Zem Leeward

(4) RETHBAN CAVERNS

Ettin Control Orb (Quest Giver)

(5) ALTHER'S MILL

Messner (Quest Giver)

(6) RENDER'S CAMP

Jorgensen (Quest Giver)
Ticky the Alchemist <Alchemical Goods>

(6) RENDER'S ROCK

Krakauer (Quest Giver)

(8) RENDER'S ROCK

Danforth (Quest Giver)

(9) CAMP EVERSTILL

John J. Keeshan (Quest Giver)
Messner (Quest Giver)
Danforth (Quest Giver)
Krakauer (Quest Giver)
Jorgensen
Arlen Marsters <Gryphon Master>

(10) REDRIDGE MOUNTAINS

Brubaker (Quest Giver)

(11) SHALEWIND CANYON

John J. Keeshan (Quest Giver)
Messner
Danforth (Quest Giver)
Krakauer
Jorgensen
Nora Baldwin <Gryphon Master>
Wilma Ranthal <Skinning Trainer>
Clyde Ranthal <Leatherworking Supplies>
Colonel Troteman (Quest Giver)

(12) KEESHAN'S POST

John J. Keeshan
Messner
Danforth (Quest Giver)
Krakauer
Jorgensen
Colonel Troteman (Quest Giver)

RUINS OF GILNEAS

The Greymane Wall once separated the lands of Gilneas from the rest of the Eastern Kingdoms. Though this protected the Gilneans from many outside threats, they have had their own troubles to deal with, leaving the center of the kingdom, Gilneas City, in ruins. Earthquakes brought on by the cataclysm not only wrecked the stout gates of the Greymane Wall but also ripped through Gilneas, causing major flooding and damage. With the destruction of the Greymane Wall and the new threats brought on by the cataclysm, it is time for the Gilneans to join the Alliance to face the dangers before them.

GILNEAS CITY

If you want to see the map of Gilneas (the Worgen starting zone), turn to the section titled "Your First Day as a Worgen" on page 118.

REPUTATION INFORMATION Gilneas, Darnassus

RESOURCE LEGEND

NODE FISHING
None

OPEN WATER FISHING

Freshwater	Ocean
Raw Brilliant Smallfish	Raw Slitherskin Mackerel
Raw Longjaw Mud Snapper	

MINING

Metal	Min Skill Level
Copper Vein	1

HERBALISM

Herb	Min Skill Level
Peacebloom	1
Silverleaf	1
Earthroot	15

SKINNING

Creature	Level
Attack Mastiff	6
Blackwald Fox	8-9
Brown Stag	100
Fox	6-7
Gilnean Mastiff	12-13
Marsh Snapper	6-7
Mist Fox	5-6
Mountain Mastiff	7
Swamp Adder	7-8
Swamp Crocolisk	7-9
Tracking Wolf	2-3

Questing in Ruins of Gilneas

Worgen characters end up in the Ruins of Gilneas as a part of their starting quests, but there's no reason for other Alliance characters to visit the zones for quests. Horde characters are sent here briefly as a part of a questline that originates in Silverpine Forest.

RUINS OF GILNEAS LEGEND

1 DUSKHAVEN
Amelia Atherton <First Aid Trainer>
Celestine of the Harvest <Druid Trainer>
Chris Moller <Pie Vendor>
Gerard Walthorn <Weapons Vendor>
Gwen Armstead (Quest Giver)
Huntsman Blake <Hunter Trainer>
Jack "All-Trades" Derrington <Profession Trainer>
Krennan Aranas <Royal Chemist>
Lord Godfrey (Quest Giver)
Loren the Fence <Rogue Trainer>
Mary Oxworth <Banker>
Myriam Spellwaker <Mage Trainer>
Prince Liam Greymane (Quest Giver)
Samantha Buckley <General Goods Vendor>
Sergeant Cleese <Warrior Trainer>
Sister Almyra <Priest Trainer>
Vitus Darkwalker <Warlock Trainer>
Willa Arnes <Innkeeper>

2 ALLEN FARMSTEAD
Lord Godfrey (Quest Giver)
Marie Allen <General Goods Vendor>
Melinda Hammond (Quest Giver)
Prince Liam Greymane (Quest Giver)

3 CROWLEY ORCHARD
Lorna Crowley (Quest Giver)
Son of Goldrin (Quest Giver)

4 WAHL COTTAGE
Grandma Wahl (Quest Giver)

5 HAYWARD FISHERY
Ron Hayward
Sebastian Hayward (Quest Giver)
Tim Hayward
Trent Hayward
Walt Hayward

6 GREYMANE MANOR
King Genn Greymane (Quest Giver)
Princess Tess Greymane
Queen Mia Greymane (Quest Giver)

7 STAGECOACH CRASH SITE
Prince Liam Greymane (Quest Giver)dw

8 STORMGLEN VILLAGE
Celestine of the Harvest <Druid Trainer>
Gwen Armstead (Quest Giver)
Huntsman Blake <Hunter Trainer>
Jack "All-Trades" Derrington <Profession Trainer>
Loren the Fence <Rogue Trainer>
Lorna Crowley (Quest Giver)
Marie Allen <General Goods Vendor>
Mary Oxworth <Banker>
Myriam Spellwaker <Mage Trainer>
Sergeant Cleese <Warrior Trainer>
Sister Almyra <Priest Trainer>
Vitus Darkwalker <Warlock Trainer>
Willa Arnes <Innkeeper>

9 THE BRADSHAW MILL
Belrysa Starbreeze (Quest Giver)

10 TAL'DOREN
Lord Darius Crowley (Quest Giver)
Lyros Swiftwind
Talran of the Wild
Vassandra Stormclaw (Quest Giver)

11 ROAD TO TEMPEST REACH
Krennan Aranas (Quest Giver)

12 TEMPEST'S REACH
King Genn Greymane (Quest Giver)
Lord Godfrey
Lord Hewell

13 LIVERY OUTPOST
Celestine of the Harvest <Druid Trainer>
Huntsman Blake <Hunter Trainer>

Karen Murray <General Goods Vendor>
Krennan Aranas (Quest Giver)
Loren the Fence <Rogue Trainer>
Lorna Crowley (Quest Giver)
Magda Whitewall (Quest Giver)
Marcus (Quest Giver)
Myriam Spellwaker <Mage Trainer>
Sergeant Cleese <Warrior Trainer>
Sister Almyra <Priest Trainer>
Vitus Darkwalker <Warlock Trainer>

14 GILNEAS CITY
King Genn Greymane (Quest Giver)
Lorna Crowley (Quest Giver)

15 ADERIC'S REPOSE
Krennan Aranas (Quest Giver)

16 KEEL HARBOR
Admiral Nightwind (Quest Giver)
Jack "All-Trades" Derrington <Profession Trainer>
Lord Darius Crowley (Quest Giver)
Lorna Crowley (Quest Giver)
Marie Allen <General Goods Vendor>
Tobias Mistmantle

1 FORSAKEN FORWARD COMMAND
Deathstalker Commander Belmont (Quest Giver)
Forward Commander Onslaught (Quest Giver)
Arthura
Bat Handler Doomair <Flight Master>
Provisioner Angelus <General Goods>

2 RUTSAK'S GUARD
Captain Rutsak (Quest Giver)

3 EMBERSTONE VILLAGE
Arthura
Deathstalker Commander Belmont (Quest Giver)

4 TEMPEST'S REACH
Deathstalker Commander Belmont (Quest Giver)
Arthura

SEARING GORGE

The dark, desolate, mountainous Searing Gorge lives up to its name. The ground is burnt and blackened, with little plant life and plenty of aggressive wildlife. At the center of the region lies the Cauldron, a deep gouge in the earth rich with precious metals. This land has long been the haunt of Dark Iron Dwarves and they can still be found here, along with an influx of Fire Elementals. The Thorium Brotherhood still struggles to maintain control of the region.

REPUTATION INFORMATION   Thorium Brotherhood, Therazane

RESOURCE LEGEND

NODE FISHING

None

OPEN WATER FISHING

None

MINING

Metal	Min Skill Level
Gold Vein	155
Mithril Deposit	175
Truesilver Deposit	205
Dark Iron Vein	230
Small Thorium Vein	230

HERBALISM

Herb	Min Skill Level
Firebloom	205
Sungrass	230

SKINNING

Creature	Level
Incendosaur	48-49

Questing in Searing Gorge

Whether you have the faction-based starter quests (Warchief's Command or Hero's Call) or not, all characters start at the same place with the same NPC: Jack Rockleg at Thorium Advance.

SEARING GORGE LEGEND

1 THORIUM POINT
Lanie Reed <Gryphon Master>

1 THORIUM ADVANCE
Lunk (Quest Giver)
Prisanne Dustcropper (Quest Giver)
Jack Rockleg (Quest Giver)
Burrian Coalpart (Quest Giver)

2 SEARING GORGE
Lunk (Quest Giver)

3 THORIUM POINT
Master Smith Burninate
Hansel Heavyhands (Quest Giver)
Evonice Sootsmoker
Taskmaster Scrange (Quest Giver)
Lookout Captain Lolo Longstriker (Quest Giver)
Overseer Oilfist (Quest Giver)
Lunk

4 PYROX FLATS
Lunk (Quest Giver)

5 FIREWATCH RIDGE
Zamael Lunthistle (Quest Giver)

6 IRON SUMMIT
Fergus Gravelsmasher <Blacksmithing Supplies>
Ernest Slabstuff <General Goods>
Gaven Crunchore <Trade Goods>
Doug Deepdown <Flight Master>
Karn Cragcare <Stable Master>
Agnes Flimshale (Quest Giver)
Velma Rockslide <Innkeeper>
Mountain-Lord Rendan (Quest Giver)
Lunk (Quest Giver)

7 THE SLAG PIT
Mountain-Lord Rendan (Quest Giver)

8 THE SLAG PIT
Evonice Sootsmoker (Quest Giver)

9 THE SLAG PIT
Taskmaster Scrange (Quest Giver)
Hansel Heavyhands

10 THE SLAG PIT
Overseer Oilfist (Quest Giver)

1 THORIUM POINT
Grisha <Wind Rider Master>

SHIMMERING EXPANSE

The central region of Vashj'ir, the Shimmering Expanse, holds many points of interest for any explorer. The beauty of the Shimmering Grotto pulls in many—just watch out for the native sea life. The great ancient Nespirah lies near the center of the region, under attack from Twilight cultists. The stunning Ruins of Vashj'ir to the southwest, along with those on Beth'mora Ridge, give you the opportunity for a closer look at the civilizations that once flourished here.

REPUTATION INFORMATION   Argent Dawn

RESOURCE LEGEND

FISHING - SURFACE

Freshwater	Ocean
	Murglesnout
	Fathom Eel
	Deepsea Sagefish
	Algaefin Rockfish
	Giant Sunfish
	Bonescale Snapper
	Deep Sea Monsterbelly

FISHING - CAVES

Freshwater	Ocean
	Murglesnout
	Algaefin Rockfish

MINING

Metal	Min Skill Level
Elementium Vein	475
Rich Elementium Vein	500

HERBALISM

Herb	Min Skill Level
Stormvine	425
Azshara's Veil	425

SKINNING

Creature	Level	Creature	Level
Anemone Frenzy	80	Silversand Burrower	80
Barbfin Skimmer	80	Silverscale Snapper	80
Deepseeker Crab	80-81	Slickback Remora	81
Giant Driftray	81	Snapjaw Grouper	81
Glittergill Grouper	80	Softshell Sea Turtle	80
Green Sand Crab	80	Speckled Sea Turtle	80
Luxscale Grouper	81	Spikeshell Skitterer	80
Oceanic Broadhead	80	Spiketooth Eel	80
Ravenous Oceanic Broadhead	80	Spineshell Pincer	80
		Splitclaw Skitterer	80
Sand Ray	81	Spotted Swellfish	81
Sandskin Pincer	80	Swarming Serpent	80
Sea Snake	80	Vashj'ir Sea Snake	80

Questing in Shimmering Expanse

Before you travel to the Shimmering Expanse, visit any major city controlled by your faction to obtain the quest Warchief's Command: Vashj'ir!, or Hero's Call: Vash'jir!. Completion of the quests which begin there leads to Shimmering Expanse and the major questlines found within the zone.

SHIMMERING EXPANSE LEGEND

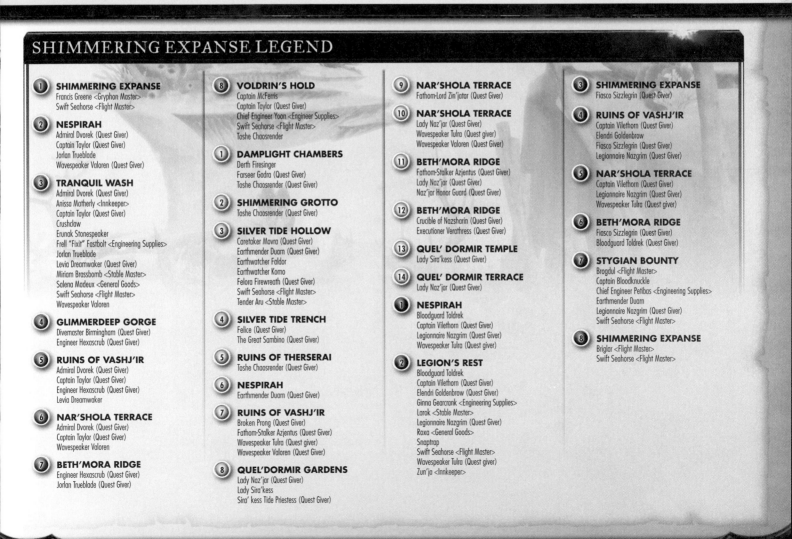

1 SHIMMERING EXPANSE
Francis Greene <Gryphon Master>
Swift Seahorse <Flight Master>

2 NESPIRAH
Admiral Dvorek (Quest Giver)
Captain Taylor (Quest Giver)
Jorlan Trueblade
Wavespeaker Valoren (Quest Giver)

3 TRANQUIL WASH
Admiral Dvorek (Quest Giver)
Anissa Matherly <Innkeeper>
Captain Taylor (Quest Giver)
Crushclaw
Erunak Stonespeaker
Frell "Fixit" Fastbolt <Engineering Supplies>
Jorlan Trueblade
Levia Dreamwaker (Quest Giver)
Miriam Brassbomb <Stable Master>
Salena Madeux <General Goods>
Swift Seahorse <Flight Master>
Wavespeaker Valoren

4 GLIMMERDEEP GORGE
Divemaster Birmingham (Quest Giver)
Engineer Hexascrub (Quest Giver)

5 RUINS OF VASHJ'IR
Admiral Dvorek (Quest Giver)
Captain Taylor (Quest Giver)
Engineer Hexascrub (Quest Giver)
Levia Dreamwaker

6 NAR'SHOLA TERRACE
Admiral Dvorek (Quest Giver)
Captain Taylor (Quest Giver)
Wavespeaker Valoren

7 BETH'MORA RIDGE
Engineer Hexascrub (Quest Giver)
Jorlan Trueblade (Quest Giver)

8 VOLDRIN'S HOLD
Captain McFerris
Captain Taylor (Quest Giver)
Chief Engineer Yoon <Engineer Supplies>
Swift Seahorse <Flight Master>
Toshe Chaosrender

1 DAMPLIGHT CHAMBERS
Derth Firesinger
Farseer Gadra (Quest Giver)
Toshe Chaosrender (Quest Giver)

2 SHIMMERING GROTTO
Toshe Chaosrender (Quest Giver)

3 SILVER TIDE HOLLOW
Caretaker Movra (Quest Giver)
Earthmender Duarn (Quest Giver)
Earthwatcher Faldor
Earthwatcher Komo
Felora Firewreath (Quest Giver)
Swift Seahorse <Flight Master>
Tender Aru <Stable Master>

4 SILVER TIDE TRENCH
Felice (Quest Giver)
The Great Sambino (Quest Giver)

5 RUINS OF THERSERAI
Toshe Chaosrender (Quest Giver)

6 NESPIRAH
Earthmender Duarn (Quest Giver)

7 RUINS OF VASHJ'IR
Broken Prong (Quest Giver)
Fathom-Stalker Azjentus (Quest Giver)
Wavespeaker Tulra (Quest giver)
Wavespeaker Valoren (Quest Giver)

8 QUEL'DORMIR GARDENS
Lady Naz'jar (Quest Giver)
Lady Sira'kess
Sira' kess Tide Priestess (Quest Giver)

9 NAR'SHOLA TERRACE
Fathom-Lord Zin'jatar (Quest Giver)

10 NAR'SHOLA TERRACE
Lady Naz'jar (Quest Giver)
Wavespeaker Tulra (Quest giver)
Wavespeaker Valoren (Quest Giver)

11 BETH'MORA RIDGE
Fathom-Stalker Azjentus (Quest Giver)
Lady Naz'jar (Quest Giver)
Naz'jar Honor Guard (Quest Giver)

12 BETH'MORA RIDGE
Crucible of Nazsharin (Quest Giver)
Executioner Verathress (Quest Giver)

13 QUEL' DORMIR TEMPLE
Lady Sira'kess (Quest Giver)

14 QUEL' DORMIR TERRACE
Lady Naz'jar (Quest Giver)

1 NESPIRAH
Bloodguard Toldrek
Captain Vilethorn (Quest Giver)
Legionnaire Nazgrim (Quest Giver)
Wavespeaker Tulra (Quest giver)

2 LEGION'S REST
Bloodguard Toldrek
Captain Vilethorn (Quest Giver)
Elendri Goldenbrow (Quest Giver)
Ginna Gearcrank <Engineering Supplies>
Larok <Stable Master>
Legionnaire Nazgrim (Quest Giver)
Roxo <General Goods>
Snaptrap
Swift Seahorse <Flight Master>
Wavespeaker Tulra (Quest giver)
Zun'ja <Innkeeper>

3 SHIMMERING EXPANSE
Fiasco Sizzlegrin (Quest Giver)

4 RUINS OF VASHJ'IR
Captain Vilethorn (Quest Giver)
Elendri Goldenbrow
Fiasco Sizzlegrin (Quest Giver)
Legionnaire Nazgrim (Quest Giver)

5 NAR'SHOLA TERRACE
Captain Vilethorn (Quest Giver)
Legionnaire Nazgrim (Quest Giver)
Wavespeaker Tulra (Quest giver)

6 BETH'MORA RIDGE
Fiasco Sizzlegrin (Quest Giver)
Bloodguard Toldrek (Quest Giver)

7 STYGIAN BOUNTY
Brogdul <Flight Master>
Captain Bloodknuckle
Chief Engineer Petibas <Engineering Supplies>
Earthmender Duarn
Legionnaire Nazgrim (Quest Giver)
Swift Seahorse <Flight Master>

8 SHIMMERING EXPANSE
Briglar <Flight Master>
Swift Seahorse <Flight Master>

SILVERMOON CITY

Situated in the northern part of Eversong Woods, the Blood Elf capital, Silvermoon City, is filled with beautiful buildings and wide, open walkways. Though the western half of the city remains in ruins, the eastern half holds all the amenities one would expect from a major city. Shops of every variety can be found in the Bazaar and inside the Royal Exchange. Farstriders' Square holds many trainers and other useful services while Sunfury Spire in the northern part of the city is the seat of Lor'themar Theron, Regent Lord of Quel'Thalas.

REPUTATION INFORMATION Silvermoon City

RESOURCE LEGEND

NODE FISHING	
None	

OPEN WATER FISHING	
Freshwater	Ocean
Raw Brilliant Smallfish	Raw Slitherskin Mackerel
Raw Longjaw Mud Snapper	

SILVERMOON CITY LEGEND

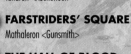

① WALK OF ELDERS
Conjurer Tyren
Gatewatcher Aendor

② WAYFARER'S REST
Innkeeper Jovia <Innkeeper>
Quelis <Cooking Supplies>
Sylann <Cook>

③ VELAANI'S ARCANE GOODS
Velanni <Alchemy Supplies & Reagents>
Zathanna <Wand Vendor>

④ WALK OF ELDERS
Harene Plainwalker <Druid Trainer>

⑤ THE BAZAAR
Bithrus <Fireworks Vendor>

⑥ SILVERMOON FINERY
Andra <Clothier>
Rathin <Bag Vendor>
Zyandrel <Cloth Armor Merchant>

⑦ KEELEN'S TRUSTWORTHY TAILORING
Deynna <Tailoring Supplies>
Galana <Apprentice Tailor>
Keelen Sheets <Tailoring Trainer>
Sirigna'no
Sorim Lightsong <Horde Cloth Quartermaster>

⑧ THE BAZAAR
Parnis <Tradesman>

⑨ THE BAZAAR
Darise <Auctioneer>
Feynna <Auctioneer>
Jenath <Auctioneer>
Vynna <Auctioneer>

⑩ THE BAZAAR
Noraelath <Leather Armor Merchant>
Welethelon <Blunt Weapon Merchant>

⑪ BLADES & AXES
Feledis <Axe Vendor>
Rahein <Blade Vendor>

⑫ GENERAL GOODS
Sathren Azuredawn <General Goods>
Zalle <Reagents>

⑬ THE BAZAAR
Lyria Skystrider
Melaya Tassier
Priest Ennas
Rarthein
Terric Brightwind
Vaeron Kormar

⑭ SHIELDS OF SILVER
Keeli <Mail Armor Merchant>
Tynna <Plate Armor Merchant>
Winthren <Shield Merchant>

⑮ THE BANK OF SILVERMOON
Ceera <Banker>
Elana <Banker>
Hatheon <Banker>

⑯ WALK OF ELDERS
Arcanist Myndimendez
Michael Schweitzer <Minstrel Manager>
Roitau
Steven Thomas

⑰ SILVERMOON REGISTRY
Kredis <Tabard Vendor>
Tandrine <Guild Master>
Bergrisst <The Tauren Chieftains>
Chief Thunder-Skins <The Tauren Chieftains>
Mai'Kyl <The Tauren Chieftains>
Samuro <The Tauren Chieftains>
Sig Nicious <The Tauren Chieftains>

⑱ WALK OF ELDERS
Lynalis <Leatherworking Trainer>
Talmar <Apprentice Leatherworker>
Tyn <Skinning Trainer>
Zaralda <Leatherworking Supplies>

⑲ SILVERMOON CITY
Worker Mo'rrisroe

⑳ SILVERMOON JEWELRY
Anim <Apprentice Jewelcrafter>
Gelanthis <Jewelcrafting Supplies>
Kalinda <Jewelcrafting Trainer>

㉑ WALK OF ELDERS
Alestus <First Aid Trainer>
Drathen <Fishing Trainer>
Olirea <Fishing Supplies>

㉒ THE RELIQUARY
Aelnara
Doranir
Elynara <Archaeology Trainer>

㉓ SILVERMOON CITY INN
Blood Knight Adept
Blood Knight Stillblade
Innkeeper Velandra <Innkeeper>
Vinemaster Suntouched <Wine & Spirits Merchant>

㉔ ROYAL EXCHANGE BANK
Daenice <Banker>
Novia <Banker>
Periel <Banker>

㉕ ROYAL EXCHANGE AUCTION HOUSE
Caidori <Auctioneer>
Ithillan <Auctioneer>
Tandron <Auctioneer>

㉖ FARSTRIDERS' SQUARE
Mathaleron <Gunsmith>

㉗ THE HALL OF BLOOD
Alenjon Sunblade <Battlemaster>
Bipp Glizzitor <Arena Battlemaster>
Champion Bachi <Paladin Trainer>
Champion Vranesh
Horde Warbringer
Ileda <Weapon Master>
Initiate Colin
Initiate Emeline
Irissa Bloodstar <Battlemaster>
Ithelis <Paladin Trainer>
Knight-Lord Bloodvalor
Magistrix Caradess <Wintergrasp Battle-Mage>
Osselan <Paladin Trainer>

㉘ FARSTRIDERS' SQUARE
Celana <Bowyer>

㉙ SILVERMOON CITY
Lord Solanar Bloodwrath
Magister Astalor Bloodsworn

㉚ THE RANGERS' LODGE
Halthenis <Pet Trainer>
Kieupid <Pet Trainer>
Oninath <Hunter Trainer>
Shalenn <Stable Master>
Tana <Hunter Trainer>
Zandine <Hunter Trainer>

㉛ FARSTRIDERS' SQUARE
Belil <Mining Trainer>
Zelan <Mining Supplies>

㉜ FARSTRIDERS' SQUARE
Alsudar the Bastion <Warrior Trainer>
Beldis <Warrior Trainer>
Bemarrin <Blacksmithing Trainer>
Eriden <Blacksmithing Supplies>
Mirvedon <Apprentice Blacksmith>
Sarithra <Warrior Trainer>

㉝ SILVERMOON CITY
Danwe <Engineering Trainer>
Gloresse <Apprentice Engineer>
Yatheon <Engineering Supplies>

㉞ COURT OF THE SUN
Trayanise

㉟ COURT OF THE SUN
Dolothos <Apprentice Enchanter>
Lelorian <Inscription Supplies>
Lyna <Enchanting Supplies>
Sedana <Enchanting Trainer>
Zantasia <Inscription Trainer>

㊱ COURT OF THE SUN
Botanist Nathera <Herbalism Trainer>
Camberon <Alchemy Trainer>
Melaris <Alchemy Supplies>
Razia <Apprentice Alchemist>

㊲ SUNFURY SPIRE
Aldrae <Priest Trainer>
Aurosalia
Belestra <Priest Trainer>
Elrodan
Grand Magister Rommath
Halduron Brightwing
Inethven <Mage Trainer>
Lor'themar Theron
Lotheolan <Priest Trainer>
Narinth <Portal Trainer>
Quithas <Mage Trainer>
Zaedana <Mage Trainer>

㊳ THE SANCTUM
Alamma <Warlock Trainer>
Keyanomir
Talionia
Torian
Zanien <Warlock Trainer>

㊴ MURDER ROW
Darlia <Poison Supplies>
Elara <Rogue Trainer>
Instructor Cel
Nerisen <Rogue Trainer>
Trainee Alcor
Trainee Firea
Trainee Sinthar
Zelanis <Rogue Trainer>

㊵ COURT OF THE SUN
Ambassador Kelemar
Cheneta
Dela Runetotem
Kristine Denny
Tatai

SILVERPINE FOREST

Though it was once a beautiful forest filled with life, Silverpine Forest long ago succumbed to the disease left by the Scourge, warping its trees into sickly caricatures of their former selves and twisting the wildlife to suit the environment. Once bordered on the south by the great Greymane Wall, Silverpine now stands open to Gilneas and the Forsaken forces are locked in bitter battle to stop the Worgen from invading. The Forsaken have long had a presence here, centered in the Sepulcher. What was little more than a crypt is now the site of an entrenched Horde settlement. The Gnolls have been cleared out of Fenris Isle as Hillsbrad Refugees seek to create a safe haven at the keep there. Shadowfang Keep is still home to Arugal's creations who care not for the political changes taking place outside their refuge. Even though it has undergone several changes since the cataclysm, one thing has not changed—Silverpine Forest is still a dangerous place.

REPUTATION INFORMATION Undercity

RESOURCE LEGEND

NODE FISHING

Freshwater	Ocean
Raw Sagefish	Oily Blackmouth
	Firefin Snapper

OPEN WATER FISHING

Freshwater	Ocean
Raw Brilliant Smallfish	Raw Slitherskin Mackerel
Raw Longjaw Mud Snapper	Oily Blackmouth
Raw Bristle Whisker Catfish	Raw Rainbow Fin Albacore

MINING

Metal	Min Skill Level
Copper Vein	1
Tin Vein	65
Silver Vein	75

HERBALISM

Herb	Min Skill Level
Silverleaf	1
Earthroot	15
Mageroyal	50
Briarthorn	70
Stranglekelp	85

SKINNING

Creature	Level
Bloodsnout Worg	16-17
Darktusk Boar	13
Ferocious Grizzled Bear	10-11
Giant Rabid Bear	11-12
Gilnean Hound	13-14
Gilnean Warhound	14-15
Highlands Fox	13-14
Inconspicuous Bear	17-18
Marsh Crocolisk	18-19
Rabid Worg	11-11
Worg	9-10

Questing in Silverpine Forest

If you didn't get Warchief's Command: Silverpine Forest! prior to your trip to the zone, go to Forsaken High Command and look for Grand Executor Mortuus.

SILVERPINE FOREST LEGEND

1 FORSAKEN HIGH COMMAND
Agatha
Apothecary Chase <Alchemy Supplies>
Apothecary Harrington <General Goods>
Apothecary Marry <Trade Supplies>
Apothecary Witherbloom (Quest Giver)
Arthura
Bat Handler Maggotbreath <Flight Master>
Daschla
Deathstalker Commander Belmont (Quest Giver)
Grand Executor Mortuus (Quest Giver)
High Apothecary Shana T'veen (Quest Giver)
High Warlord Cromush
Lady Sylvanas Windrunner (Quest Giver)

2 THE IVAR PATCH
Deathstalker Rane Yorick (Quest Giver)

3 FORSAKEN REAR GUARD
Apothecary Wormcrud (Quest Giver)
"Salty" Rocka <Stable Master>
"Salty" Gorgar <General Goods>
Warlord Torok (Quest Giver)
Admiral Hatchet (Quest Giver)
Commander Hickley <Innkeeper>

4 THE SEPULCHER
Admiral Hatchet (Quest Giver)
Advisor Sorrelon
Agatha
Alexandre Lefevre <Leather Armor Merchant>
Andrea Boynton <Clothier>
Andrew Hilbert <Trade Supplies>
Apothecary Renferrel
Arthura
Astor Hadren
Dalar Dawnweaver (Quest Giver)
Daschla
Deathguard Podrig
Edwin Harly <General Supplies>
Guillaume Sorouy <Blacksmithing Trainer>
Gwyn Farrow <Mushroom Merchant>
High Executor Hadrec
High Warlord Cromush
Innkeeper Bates <Innkeeper>
Johan Focht <Mining Trainer>
Karos Razok <Bat Handler>
Lady Sylvanas Windrunner (Quest Giver)
Lilly <Enchanting Supplies>
Mura Runetotem
Nadia Vernon <Bowyer>
Patrice Dwyer <Poison Supplies>

Sarah Goode <Stable Master>
Sebastian Meloche <Armorer>
Shadow Priest Allister
Warlord Torok (Quest Giver)

5 LORDAMERE LAKE
Horde Communication Panel (Quest Giver)
Killian Sanatha <Fisherman>

6 DEEP ELEM MINE
Master Forteski (Quest Giver)

7 THE FORSAKEN FRONT
Admiral Hatchet
Agatha
Arthura
Baron Ashbury (Quest Giver)
Daschla (Quest Giver)
High Warlord Cromush (Quest Giver)
Lady Sylvanas Windrunner (Quest Giver)
Lord Godfrey (Quest Giver)
Lord Walden (Quest Giver)
Steven Stutzka <Bat Handler>
Warlord Torok

8 THE GREYMANE WALL
High Warlord Cromush
Lady Sylvanas Windrunner (Quest Giver)

STORMWIND

The Alliance capital of Stormwind is perhaps the largest and most densely populated of all the great cities of Azeroth. Its sturdy walls hold everything a traveler needs to feel at home. Flooding caused by the recent cataclysm has completely submerged the former Park District, as well as flooded other areas of the city. Despite this, its citizens still carry on their daily business.

REPUTATION INFORMATION Stormwind

RESOURCE LEGEND

NODE FISHING

Freshwater	Ocean
None	

OPEN WATER FISHING

Freshwater	Ocean
Raw Brilliant Smallfish	Raw Slitherskin Mackerel
Raw Longjaw Mud Snapper	

STORMWIND LEGEND

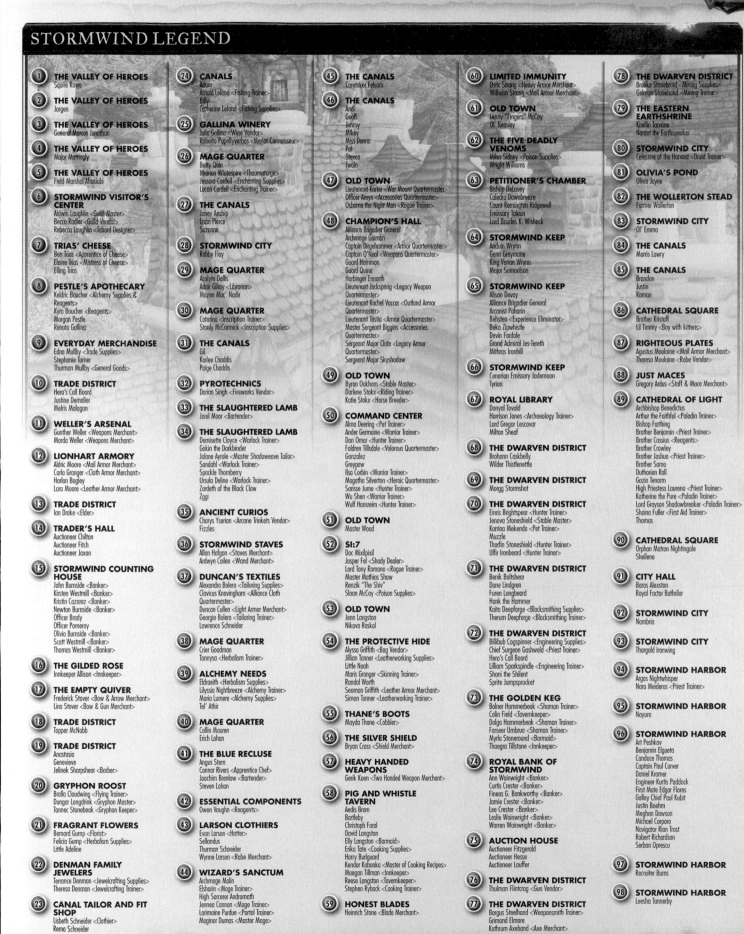

1 THE VALLEY OF HEROES
Squire Rowe

2 THE VALLEY OF HEROES
Jorgen

3 THE VALLEY OF HEROES
General Marcus Jonathan

4 THE VALLEY OF HEROES
Major Mattingly

5 THE VALLEY OF HEROES
Field Marshal Afrasiabi

6 STORMWIND VISITOR'S CENTER
Aldwin Laughlin <Guild Master>
Becca Radler <Guild Vendor>
Rebecca Loughlin <Tabard Designer>

7 TRIAS' CHEESE
Ben Trias <Apprentice of Cheese>
Elaine Trias <Mistress of Cheese>
Elling Trias

8 PESTLE'S APOTHECARY
Keldric Boucher <Alchemy Supplies & Reagents>
Kyra Boucher <Reagents>
Morgan Pestle
Renato Gallina

9 EVERYDAY MERCHANDISE
Edna Mullby <Trade Supplies>
Stephanie Turner
Thurman Mullby <General Goods>

10 TRADE DISTRICT
Hero's Call Board
Justine Demalier
Melris Malagan

11 WELLER'S ARSENAL
Gunther Weller <Weapons Merchant>
Marda Weller <Weapons Merchant>

12 LIONHART ARMORY
Aldric Moore <Mail Armor Merchant>
Carla Granger <Cloth Armor Merchant>
Harlan Bagley
Lara Moore <Leather Armor Merchant>

13 TRADE DISTRICT
Ian Drake <Elder>

14 TRADER'S HALL
Auctioneer Chilton
Auctioneer Fitch
Auctioneer Jaxon

15 STORMWIND COUNTING HOUSE
John Burnside <Banker>
Kirsten Westmill <Banker>
Kristin Cazarez <Banker>
Newton Burnside <Banker>
Officer Brady
Officer Pomeroy
Olivia Burnside <Banker>
Scott Westmill <Banker>
Thomas Westmill <Banker>

16 THE GILDED ROSE
Innkeeper Allison <Innkeeper>

17 THE EMPTY QUIVER
Frederick Stover <Bow & Arrow Merchant>
Lina Stover <Bow & Gun Merchant>

18 TRADE DISTRICT
Topper McNabb

19 TRADE DISTRICT
Anastasia
Genevieve
Jelinek Sharpshear <Barber>

20 GRYPHON ROOST
Bralla Cloudwing <Flying Trainer>
Dungar Longdrink <Gryphon Master>
Tannec Stonebeak <Gryphon Keeper>

21 FRAGRANT FLOWERS
Bernard Gump <Florist>
Felicia Gump <Herbalism Supplies>
Little Adeline

22 DENMAN FAMILY JEWELERS
Terrance Denman <Jewelcrafting Supplies>
Theresa Denman <Jewelcrafting Trainer>

23 CANAL TAILOR AND FIT SHOP
Lisbeth Schneider <Clothier>
Rema Schneider

24 CANALS
Adam
Arnold Leland <Fishing Trainer>
Billy
Catherine Leland <Fishing Supplies>

25 GALLINA WINERY
Julia Gallina <Wine Vendor>
Roberto Pupellyverbos <Merlot Connoisseur>

26 MAGE QUARTER
Betty Quin
Ithulian Whitespire <Thaumaturge>
Jessora Cordell <Enchanting Supplies>
Lucan Cordell <Enchanting Trainer>

27 THE CANALS
Janey Anship
Lisan Pierce
Suzanne

28 STORMWIND CITY
Robby Flay

29 MAGE QUARTER
Acolyte Dellis
Adair Gilray <Librarian>
Mazen Mac' Nadir

30 MAGE QUARTER
Catarina <Inscription Trainer>
Stanly McCormick <Inscription Supplies>

31 THE CANALS
Gil
Karlee Chaddis
Paige Chaddis

32 PYROTECHNICS
Darian Singh <Fireworks Vendor>

33 THE SLAUGHTERED LAMB
Jarel Moor <Bartender>

34 THE SLAUGHTERED LAMB
Demisette Cloyce <Warlock Trainer>
Gakin the Darkbinder
Jalane Ayrole <Master Shadoweave Tailor>
Sandahl <Warlock Trainer>
Spackle Thornberry
Ursula Deline <Warlock Trainer>
Zardeth of the Black Claw
Zggi

35 ANCIENT CURIOS
Charys Yserian <Arcane Trinkets Vendor>
Fizzles

36 STORMWIND STAVES
Allan Hafgan <Staves Merchant>
Ardwyn Cailen <Wand Merchant>

37 DUNCAN'S TEXTILES
Alexandra Bolero <Tailoring Supplies>
Clavicus Knavingham <Alliance Cloth Quartermaster>
Duncan Cullen <Light Armor Merchant>
Georgio Bolero <Tailoring Trainer>
Lawrence Schneider

38 MAGE QUARTER
Crier Goodman
Tannysa <Herbalism Trainer>

39 ALCHEMY NEEDS
Eldraeith <Herbalism Supplies>
Lilyssia Nightbreeze <Alchemy Trainer>
Maria Lumere <Alchemy Supplies>
Tel' Athir

40 MAGE QUARTER
Collin Mauren
Erich Lohan

41 THE BLUE RECLUSE
Angus Stern
Connor Rivers <Apprentice Chef>
Joachim Brenlow <Bartender>
Steven Lohan

42 ESSENTIAL COMPONENTS
Owen Vaughn <Reagents>

43 LARSON CLOTHIERS
Evan Larson <Hatter>
Sellandus
Thurman Schneider
Wynne Larson <Robe Merchant>

44 WIZARD'S SANCTUM
Archmage Malin
Elsharin <Mage Trainer>
High Sorcerer Andromath
Jennea Cannon <Mage Trainer>
Larimaine Purdue <Portal Trainer>
Maginor Dumas <Master Mage>

45 THE CANALS
Caretaker Folsom

46 THE CANALS
Andi
Geoff
Jimmy
Mikey
Miss Danna
Pat
Steven
Twain

47 OLD TOWN
Lieutenant Karter <War Mount Quartermaster>
Officer Areyn <Accessories Quartermaster>
Osborne the Night Man <Rogue Trainer>

48 CHAMPION'S HALL
Alliance Brigadier General
Archmage Gaiman
Captain Dirgehammer <Armor Quartermaster>
Captain O'Neal <Weapons Quartermaster>
Guard Hammon
Guard Quine
Harbinger Ennarth
Lieutenant Jackspring <Legacy Weapon Quartermaster>
Lieutenant Rachel Vaccar <Outland Armor Quartermaster>
Lieutenant Tristia <Armor Quartermaster>
Master Sergeant Biggins <Accessories Quartermaster>
Sergeant Major Clate <Legacy Armor Quartermaster>
Sergeant Major Skyshadow

49 OLD TOWN
Byron Oakhorn <Stable Master>
Darlene Stokx <Riding Trainer>
Katie Stokx <Horse Breeder>

50 COMMAND CENTER
Alma Deering <Pet Trainer>
Ander Germaine <Warrior Trainer>
Don Omar <Hunter Trainer>
Faldren Tillsdale <Valorous Quartermaster>
Gonzalez
Greypaw
Ilsa Corbin <Warrior Trainer>
Magatha Silverton <Heroic Quartermaster>
Sarisse Jume <Hunter Trainer>
Wu Shen <Warrior Trainer>
Wulf Hansreim <Hunter Trainer>

51 OLD TOWN
Master Wood

52 SI:7
Doc Mixilpixil
Jasper Fel <Shady Dealer>
Lord Tony Romano <Rogue Trainer>
Master Mathias Shaw
Renzik "The Shiv"
Sloan McCoy <Poison Supplies>

53 OLD TOWN
Jenn Langston
Nikova Raskol

54 THE PROTECTIVE HIDE
Alyssa Griffith <Bag Vendor>
Jillian Tanner <Leatherworking Supplies>
Little Noah
Maris Granger <Skinning Trainer>
Randal Worth
Seoman Griffith <Leather Armor Merchant>
Simon Tanner <Leatherworking Trainer>

55 THANE'S BOOTS
Mayda Thane <Cobbler>

56 THE SILVER SHIELD
Bryan Cross <Shield Merchant>

57 HEAVY HANDED WEAPONS
Gerik Koen <Two Handed Weapon Merchant>

58 PIG AND WHISTLE TAVERN
Aedis Brom
Bartleby
Christoph Faral
David Langston
Elly Langston <Barmaid>
Erika Tate <Cooking Supplies>
Harry Burlguard
Kendor Kabonka <Master of Cooking Recipes>
Maegan Tillman <Innkeeper>
Reese Langston <Tavernkeeper>
Stephen Ryback <Cooking Trainer>

59 HONEST BLADES
Heinrich Stone <Blade Merchant>

60 LIMITED IMMUNITY
Osric Strang <Heavy Armor Merchant>
Wilhelm Strang <Mail Armor Merchant>

61 OLD TOWN
Lenny "Fingers" McCoy
Ol' Beasley

62 THE FIVE DEADLY VENOMS
Miles Sidney <Poison Supplies>
Wright Williams

63 PETITIONER'S CHAMBER
Bishop DeLavey
Caledra Dawnbreeze
Count Remington Ridgewell
Emissary Taluun
Lord Baurles K. Wishock

64 STORMWIND KEEP
Anduin Wrynn
Genn Greymane
King Varian Wrynn
Major Samuelson

65 STORMWIND KEEP
Alison Devay
Alliance Brigadier General
Arcanist Paharin
Behsten <Experience Eliminator>
Beka Zipwhistle
Devin Fardale
Grand Admiral Jes-Tereth
Mithras Ironhill

66 STORMWIND KEEP
Cenarion Emissary Jademoon
Tyrion

67 ROYAL LIBRARY
Donyal Tovald
Harrison Jones <Archaeology Trainer>
Lord Gregor Lescovar
Milton Sheaf

68 THE DWARVEN DISTRICT
Brohann Caskbelly
Wilder Thistlenettle

69 THE DWARVEN DISTRICT
Morgg Stormshot

70 THE DWARVEN DISTRICT
Einris Brightspear <Hunter Trainer>
Jenova Stoneshield <Stable Master>
Karrina Mekenda <Pet Trainer>
Muzzle
Thorfin Stoneshield <Hunter Trainer>
Ulfir Ironbeard <Hunter Trainer>

71 THE DWARVEN DISTRICT
Benik Boltshear
Dane Lindgren
Furen Longbeard
Hank the Hammer
Kaita Deepforge <Blacksmithing Supplies>
Therum Deepforge <Blacksmithing Trainer>

72 THE DWARVEN DISTRICT
Billibub Cogspinner <Engineering Supplies>
Chief Surgeon Gashweld <Priest Trainer>
Hero's Call Board
Lilliam Sparkspindle <Engineering Trainer>
Shoni the Shilent
Sprite Jumpsprocket

73 THE GOLDEN KEG
Bolner Hammerbeak <Shaman Trainer>
Colin Field <Tavernkeeper>
Dalga Hammerbeak <Shaman Trainer>
Farseer Umbrua <Shaman Trainer>
Myrla Stoneround <Barmaid>
Thoegra Tillstone <Innkeeper>

74 ROYAL BANK OF STORMWIND
Ann Wainwright <Banker>
Curtis Crester <Banker>
Fineas G. Bankworthy <Banker>
Jamie Crester <Banker>
Lee Crester <Banker>
Leslie Wainwright <Banker>
Warren Wainwright <Banker>

75 AUCTION HOUSE
Auctioneer Fitzgerald
Auctioneer Hesse
Auctioneer Lauffer

76 THE DWARVEN DISTRICT
Thulman Flintcrag <Gun Vendor>

77 THE DWARVEN DISTRICT
Borgus Steelhand <Weaponsmith Trainer>
Grimand Elmore
Kathrum Axehand <Axe Merchant>

78 THE DWARVEN DISTRICT
Brooke Stonebraid <Mining Supplies>
Gelman Stonehand <Mining Trainer>

79 THE EASTERN EARTHSHRINE
Koellin Tarvane
Narat the Earthspeaker

80 STORMWIND CITY
Celestine of the Harvest <Druid Trainer>

81 OLIVIA'S POND
Olivia Jayne

82 THE WOLLERTON STEAD
Farmer Wollerton

83 STORMWIND CITY
Ol' Emma

84 THE CANALS
Morris Lawry

85 THE CANALS
Brandon
Justin
Roman

86 CATHEDRAL SQUARE
Brother Kristoff
Lil Timmy <Boy with kittens>

87 RIGHTEOUS PLATES
Agustus Moulaine <Mail Armor Merchant>
Theresa Moulaine <Robe Vendor>

88 JUST MACES
Gregory Ardus <Staff & Mace Merchant>

89 CATHEDRAL OF LIGHT
Archbishop Benedictus
Arthur the Faithful <Paladin Trainer>
Bishop Farthing
Brother Benjamin <Priest Trainer>
Brother Cassius <Reagents>
Brother Crowley
Brother Joshua <Priest Trainer>
Brother Sarno
Duthorian Rall
Gazin Tenorm
High Priestess Laurena <Priest Trainer>
Katherine the Pure <Paladin Trainer>
Lord Grayson Shadowbreaker <Paladin Trainer>
Shaina Fuller <First Aid Trainer>
Thomas

90 CATHEDRAL SQUARE
Orphan Matron Nightingale
Shellene

91 CITY HALL
Baros Alexston
Royal Factor Bathrilor

92 STORMWIND CITY
Nambria

93 STORMWIND CITY
Thargold Ironwing

94 STORMWIND HARBOR
Argos Nightwhisper
Nara Meideros <Priest Trainer>

95 STORMWIND HARBOR
Nayura

96 STORMWIND HARBOR
Art Peshkov
Benjamin Elgueta
Candace Thomas
Captain Paul Carver
Daniel Kramer
Engineer Kurtis Paddock
First Mate Edgar Flores
Galley Chief Paul Kubit
Justin Boehm
Meghan Dawson
Michael Corpora
Navigator Rian Trost
Robert Richardson
Serban Oprescu

97 STORMWIND HARBOR
Recruiter Burns

98 STORMWIND HARBOR
Leesha Tannerby

SWAMP OF SORROWS

The most significant change to the low-lying Swamp of Sorrows is in the lake along its eastern edge. The sea water has risen, making this lake into a bay, though the Temple of Atal'Hakkar, also known as the Sunken Temple, is still found in the center. North of the temple, the Alliance has founded a fortified town, Marshtide Watch, while Stonard, a long standing Horde oupost, still lies in the south. In the northeast corner the neutral town of Bogpaddle stands ready to host adventurers. The Harborage, which formerly dealt with both factions, has become a haven for the Alliance.

REPUTATION INFORMATION   Orgrimmar, Stormwind

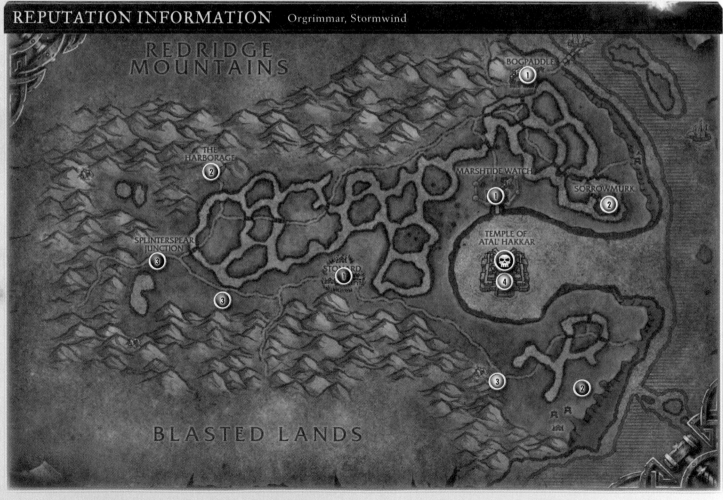

RESOURCE LEGEND

NODE FISHING

Freshwater	Ocean
	Oily Blackmouth
	Firefin Snapper
	Stonescale Eel
	Floating Wreckage

OPEN WATER FISHING

Freshwater	Ocean
Lightning Eel	Stonescale Eel
Raw Redgill	Raw Spotted Yellowtail
Raw Whitescale Salmon	Darkclaw Lobster
Plated Armorfish	Large Raw Mightfish
Raw Nightfin Snapper	Raw Summer Bass
Raw Sunscale Salmon	Big-Mouth Clam

MINING

Metal	Min Skill Level
Truesilver Deposit	205
Small Thorium Vein	230
Rich Thorium Vein	255

HERBALISM

Herb	Min Skill Level
Stranglekelp	85
Golden Sansam	260
Sorrowmoss	285

SKINNING

Creature	Level	Creature	Level
Adolescent Whelp	34-35	Sawtooth Snapper	41-42
Corrupted Guardian	52-53	Scalebane Captain	43-44
Dreaming Whelp	35-36	Shadow Panther	39-40
Elder Dragonkin	45	Sorrow Screecher	52-53
Green Scalebane	42-43	Sorrowmurk Snapjaw	50
Green Wyrmkin	41-42	Stagalbog Serpent	52-53
Marshtide Steed	53-54	Stonard Kodo Beast	53-54
Sawtooth Crocolisk	38-39	Swamp Jaguar	36-37
Sawtooth Crocolisk	52	Wyrmkin Dreamwalker	42-43
		Young Sawtooth Crocolisk	35-36

Questing in Swamp of Sorrows

Hero's Call: Swamp of Sorrows! and Warchief's Command: Swamp of Sorrows both send you to Trade Baron Silversnap at Bogpaddle. If you skipped these introductory quests, start with him anyway.

SWAMP OF SORROWS LEGEND

1 MARSHTIDE WATCH
Holaaru (Quest Giver)
Hull Forgehammer <Blacksmithing Supplies>
Joanna Blueheart (Quest Giver)
Paola Baldwin <Gryphon Master>
Rebecca Blackman <Food & Drink>

2 THE HARBORAGE
Anchorite Avuun (Quest Giver)
Joran <Stable Master>
Magtoor
Masat T' andr <Superior Leatherworker>
Verad <Innkeeper>
Yedrin <Flight Master>

3 SWAMP OF SORROWS
Watcher Biggs

1 BOGPADDLE
Brono Goodgrove (Quest Giver)
Bullets Bigblast <Engineering Supplies>
Cap' n Greech
Dronk Drophammer <Blacksmithing Supplies>
Frankie Goodtimes <Food & Drink>
Mitch Yostpaddle <Trade Goods>
Pierre Fishflay (Quest Giver)
Shecky Shrimpshoot <Stable Master>

Skeezie <Gryphon Master>
Skinner Selma <Leatherworking Supplies>
Spike Coilee <Herbalism Supplies>
Trade Baron Silversnap (Quest Giver)
Zipper Sizzlesnap <Fishing Supplies>

2 SORROWMURK
Crazy Larry (Quest Giver)
Darbo Stableflux <Blacksmithing Supplies>
Kizter Kahboom <Engineering Supplies>
Lil' Crazy Daisy
Lil' Crazy Jerry

3 STAGALBOG
Baba Bogbrew (Quest Giver)
Brita Bramblebrush <Alchemy Supplies>
Sid Shillcopper <Food & Drink>

4 THE TEMPLE OF ATAL'HAKKAR
Lord Itharius (Quest Giver)

1 STONARD
Banalash <Trade Supplies>
Breyk <Wind Rider Master>
Cersei Dusksinger
Dar
Dispatch Commander Ruag (Quest Giver)
Gharash <Blacksmithing Supplies>

Greshka
Grimnal <Mail & Plate Merchant>
Grokar <Pet Trainer>
Grunt Tharlak
Grunt Zuul
Haromm <Shaman Trainer>
Hartash <Weapon Merchant>
Hekkru <Stable Master>
Infiltrator Marksen
Innkeeper Karakul <Innkeeper>
Kartosh <Warlock Trainer>
Lorrin Foxfire <Portal Trainer>
Malosh <Warrior Trainer>
Ogromm <Hunter Trainer>
Rartar <Alchemy Supplies>
Rogvar <Alchemy Trainer>
Thralosh <Cloth & Leather Armor Merchant>
Thultash <Food & Drink Vendor>
Thultazor <Alchemy Supplies & Reagents>

2 MISTY REED POST
Katar
Tok' Kar

3 SPLINTERSPEAR JUNCTION
Helgrum the Swift
Neeka Bloodscar

THE CAPE OF STRANGLETHORN

Deathwing's return tore the former Stranglethorn Vale in two. The southern half of the former Stranglethorn Vale has become known as the Cape of Stranglethorn. Sprawling Booty Bay on the southern tip of the region has been joined by two more camps in the north—the Explorers' League Digsite for the Alliance and Hardwrench Hideaway for the Horde. Harsh metal rigs rise out of the Crystal Shore while the Naga have fortified their presence in the south. Even with these changes the Cape of Stranglethorn remains a familiar place with both new and old threats lurking among the jungle foliage.

REPUTATION INFORMATION Bilgewater Cartel, Booty Bay, Everlook, Gadgetzan, Ratchet, Explorers' League

RESOURCE LEGEND

NODE FISHING

Freshwater	Ocean
Raw Greater Sagefish	Oily Blackmouth
	Firefin Snapper
	Bloodsail Wreckage

OPEN WATER FISHING

Freshwater	Ocean
Raw Bristle Whisker Catfish	Firefin Snapper
Raw Mithril Head Trout	Raw Rockscale Cod
	Oily Blackmouth
	Raw Spotted Yellowtail

MINING

Metal	Min Skill Level
Tin Vein	65
Silver Vein	75
Iron Vein	125
Gold Vein	155

HERBALISM

Herb	Min Skill Level
Stranglekelp	85
Liferoot	150
Fadeleaf	160
Goldthorn	170

SKINNING

Creature	Level	Creature	Level
Elder Mistvale Gorilla	31-32	Mistvale Gorilla	32-33
Ironjaw Behemoth	30	Mokk the Savage	32
Jaguero Stalker	31-32	Silverback Patriarch	32-33
Jungle Panther	32-33	Skymane Bonobo	31-32
Jungle Thunderer	37-38	Skymane Gorilla	32
King Mukla	33	Southsea Mako	32-33
		Young Jungle Stalker	36-37

Questing in The Cape of Stranglethorn

Hero's Call: The Cape of Stranglethorn! instructs you to report to Bronwyn Hewstrike at the Explorer's League Digsite. Warchief's Command: The Cape of Stranglethorn! orders you to Sassy Hardwrench at Hardwrench Hideaway.

THE CAPE OF STRANGLETHORN LEGEND

1 EXPLORERS' LEAGUE DIGSITE
Bronwyn Hewstrike (Quest Giver)
Colin Swifthammer <Gryphon Master>
Dask "The Flask" Gobfizzle (Quest Giver)
Goris (Quest Giver)
Hambone
Linzi Hewstrike (Quest Giver)
Maywiki (Quest Giver)

2 BOOTY BAY
Airwyn Bantamflax
Gyll <Gryphon Master>

1 THE GREAT ARENA
Stone Guard Towhide (Quest Giver)
Short John Mithril

2 RUINS OF ABORAZ
Message in a Bottle (Quest Giver)

3 BOOTY BAY
Auctioneer Graves
Auctioneer Kresky
Auctioneer O'reely
Baron Revilgaz (Quest Giver)
Barrel of Doublerum (Quest Giver)
Blixrez Goodstitch <Leatherworking Supplies>
Bossy
Brikk Keencraft <Blacksmithing Trainer>
Captain Hecklebury Smotts (Quest Giver)
Caravaneer Ruzzgot
Catelyn the Blade
Crank Fizzlebub
Crazk Sparks <Fireworks Merchant>

Deeg (Quest Giver)
Dizzy One-Eye (Quest Giver)
Fargon Mortalak <Superior Armorer>
Fin Fizracket (Quest Giver)
First Mate Crazz (Quest Giver)
Fleet Master Seahorn (Quest Giver)
Flora Silverwind <Herbalism Trainer>
Glyx Brewright <Alchemy Supplies>
Grarnik Goodstitch <Tailoring Trainer>
Grimestack <Stable Master>
Grizzlowe
Haren Kanmae <Superior Bowyer>
Hurklor <Blacksmithing Supplies>
Ian Strom <Rogue Trainer>
Innkeeper Skindle <Innkeeper>
Jansen Underwood <Blacksmithing Supplies>
Jaxin Chong <Alchemy Trainer>
Jutak <Blade Trainer>
Kebok
Kelsey Yance <Cook>
Kizz Bluntstrike <Macecrafter>
Landro Longshot
Markel Smythe
Mazk Snipeshot <Engineering Supplies>
McGavan
Myizz Luckycatch <Fishing Trainer>
Narkk <Pirate Supplies>
Nixxrax Fillamug <Food & Drink>
Oglethorpe Obnoticus <Gnomish Engineering Trainer>
Old Man Heming <Fishing Supplies>
Privateer Bloads
Qixdi Goodstitch <Cloth Armor & Accessories>
Rickle Goldgrubber <Banker>

Rizgiz <Leatherworking Supplies>
Scooty
"Sea Wolf" MacKinley (Quest Giver)
"Shaky" Phillipe (Quest Giver)
Sly Garrett <Shady Goods>
Sprogger
Viznik Goldgrubber <Banker>
Wharfmaster Lozgil
Whiskey Slim
Wigcik <Superior Fisherman>
Xizk Goodstitch <Tailoring Supplies>
Zarena Cromwind <Superior Weaponsmith>

4 SPIRIT DEN
Witch Doctor Unbagwa

5 JAGUERO ISLE
Princess Poobah (Quest Giver)

6 WILD SHORE
Cowardly Crosby <Tailoring Supplies>

7 THE CAPE OF STRANGLETHORN
Yancey Grillsen (Quest Giver)

8 THE RIPTIDE
Captain Keelhaul (Quest Giver)
Garr Salthoof (Quest Giver)
"Pretty Boy" Duncan (Quest Giver)
Sweet Gary Guns <Gun Vendor>
Wailing Mary Smitts

9 THE CRIMSON VEIL
"Dead-Eye" Drederick McGumm (Quest Giver)

Enormous Shawn Stooker
Fleet Master Firallon (Quest Giver)
Harry No-Hooks <Birds and Rum>
Ironpatch (Quest Giver)
Squawky Jr.

10 THE DAMSEL'S LUCK
Brutus
Captain Stillwater's Charts (Quest Giver)
Gurlgrl <Sword Vendor>
Long John Copper

1 HANDWRENCH HIDEAWAY
Bobber Spazzspark <Fishing Supplies>
Captain Bartholomew Softbeard
Chabal (Quest Giver)
Finzy Watchwoozle <Stable Master>
Flem Gizzix (Quest Giver)
Gmurgl
Gruzz Thinxlotz <Engineering Supplies>
Hizzle <Gryphon Master>
Innkeeper Draxle <Innkeeper>
Marpi Greenwrench <Herbalism Supplies>
Mixmaster Jasper (Quest Giver)
Orgus
Pop Sodaslam <Food & Drink>
Sassy Handwrench (Quest Giver)
Smity Hammerhead <Blacksmithing Supplies>

2 BOOTY BAY
Garley Lightrider
Gringer <Wind Rider Master>

THE HINTERLANDS

The wooded hills and rising cliffs of the Hinterlands have remained mostly unaffected by the recent cataclysm. Though there have been few physical changes on the land, like elsewhere, both the Horde and the Alliance have increased their presence in the area. Raventusk Village to the east and Aerie Peak to the west are joined by new smaller encampments across the region. Among the other wildlife, Wolves and Owlbeasts roam the forests, making overland travel dangerous for unprepared travelers. The Vilebranch Trolls still hold the temple of Jintha'Alor, but the Horde and the Wildhammer Dwarves have small camps at its base, striving to keep the Vilebranch in check.

REPUTATION INFORMATION Exodar, Undercity

RESOURCE LEGEND

NODE FISHING

Freshwater	Ocean
Raw Greater Sagefish	Oily Blackmouth
	Firefin Snapper

OPEN WATER FISHING

Freshwater	Ocean
Raw Bristle Whisker Catfish	Firefin Snapper
Raw Mithril Head Trout	Raw Rockscale Cod
	Oily Blackmouth
	Raw Spotted Yellowtail

MINING

Metal	Min Skill Level
Tin Vein	65
Silver Vein	75
Iron Vein	125
Gold Vein	155
Mithril Deposit	175
Truesilver Deposit	205

HERBALISM

Herb	Min Skill Level
Stranglekelp	85
Bruiseweed	100
Wild Steelbloom	115
Kingsblood	125
Liferoot	150
Fadeleaf	160
Goldthorn	170
Khadgar's Whisker	185
Purple Lotus	210
Sungrass	230
Ghost Mushroom	245
Golden Sansam	260
Mountain Silversage	280

SKINNING

Creature	Level
Cobaltine Dragonspawn	48-49
Cobaltine Wyrmkin	49-50
Mangy Silvermane	30
Saltwater Snapjaw	30-31
Silvermane Howler	32-33
Silvermane Stalker	31-32
Silvermane Wolf	34-35
Verdantine Boughguard	62
Verdantine Oracle	61
Verdantine Tree Warder	60
Vilebranch Raiding Wolf	32-33
Vilebranch Wolf	46-47
Vilebranch Wolf Pup	32

Questing in The Hinterlands

Warchief's Command: The Hinterlands! sends you to Revantusk Village to talk to Elder Torntusk. Hero's Call: The Hinterlands! Instructs you to visit Aerie Peak and speak with Gryphon Master Talonaxe.

THE HINTERLANDS LEGEND

1 AERIE PEAK
Agnar Beastamer
Ambassador Rualeth
Claira Kindfeather
Drakk Stonehand <Leatherworking Trainer>
Gryphon Master Talonaxe (Quest Giver)
Gunthrum Thunderfist <Flight Master>
Harggan <Blacksmithing Supplies>
Howin Kindfeather
Innkeeper Thulfram <Innkeeper>
Killium Bouldertoe <Stable Master>
Nioma <Leatherworking Supplies>
Truk Wildbeard <Bartender>

2 STORMFEATHER OUTPOST
Brannik Ironbelly <Armorsmith>
Brock Rockbeard <Gryphon Master>
Dron Blastbrew (Quest Giver)
Grella Stonefist <General Goods>
Innkeeper Keirnan <Innkeeper>
Kerr Ironsight (Quest Giver)
Tathan Thunderstone <Stable Master>

3 THE HINTERLANDS
Doran Steelwing (Quest Giver)
Fraggar Thundermantle (Quest Giver)
Tracker Yoro (Quest Giver)

4 QUEL'DANIL LODGE
Anchorite Traska (Quest Giver)
Gilda Cloudcaller (Quest Giver)

5 SHADRA'ALOR
Wildhammer Lookout (Quest Giver)

1 THE HINTERLANDS
Gigget Zipcoil <Trade Supplies>
Ruppo Zipcoil <Engineering Supplies>

2 THE HINTERLANDS
Homing Robot OOX-09/HL (Quest Giver)

3 SHINDIGGER'S CAMP
Gilveradin Sunchaser
Rhapsody Shindigger

1 REVANTUSK VILLAGE
Elder Torntusk (Quest Giver)
Gorkas <Wind Rider Master>

Grognard (Quest Giver)
Huntsman Markhor (Quest Giver)
Katoom the Angler (Quest Giver)
Lard (Quest Giver)
Malcom Fendelson (Quest Giver)
Mystic Yayo' jin (Quest Giver)
Oran Snakewrithe (Quest Giver)
Otho Moji' ko (Quest Giver)
Renn' az
Smith Slagtree <Blacksmithing Supplies>

2 JINTHA'ALOR
Eliza Darkgrin (Quest Giver)
Kotonga (Quest Giver)
Primal Torntusk (Quest Giver)

3 HIRI'WATHA RESEARCH STATION
Apothecary Surlis (Quest Giver)
Bitsy <Innkeeper>
Darkcleric Marnal (Quest Giver)
Janice Winters <General Goods>
Kellen Kuhn <Bat Handler>
Marvin Winters <Mail Armor>
Roslyn Paxton <Stable Master>

4 SHADRA'ALOR
Deathstalker Lookout (Quest Giver)

TIRISFAL GLADES

Home to the Forsaken capital, the Undercity, Tirisfal Glades is a richly wooded region dotted with smaller towns and farms. In the southwest, the Shadow Grave welcomes newly risen Forsaken back to the world before sending them on to the small towns of Deathknell and Brill. Though firmly under Forsaken control, Tirisfal Glades is not without danger. The Scarlet Monastery, a stronghold for the zealous Scarlet Crusade, is in the northeast. To the southeast the newly fortified Bulwark defends against the rampant Scourge infesting the neighboring Plaguelands. Their unwavering defense serves as a reminder that even in the Forsaken homeland, constant vigilance is required to keep the peace.

REPUTATION INFORMATION   Argent Dawn, Undercity

RESOURCE LEGEND

NODE FISHING

None

OPEN WATER FISHING

Freshwater	Ocean
Raw Brilliant Smallfish	Raw Slitherskin Mackerel
Raw Longjaw Mud Snapper	
Sickly Looking Fish	

MINING

Metal	Min Skill Level
Copper Vein	1

HERBLISM

Herb	Min Skill Level
Peacebloom	1
Silverleaf	1
Earthroot	15

SKINNING

Creature	Level
Cursed Darkhound	7-8
Decrepit Darkhound	5-6
Greater Duskbat	6-7
Plagued Bruin	8-9
Ravenous Darkhound	9-10
Vampiric Duskbat	8-9

Questing in Tirisfal Glades

Tirisfal Glades is the starting zone for Undead characters. Other Horde players who want to check out the quests in this Undead-themed zone should start at Brill.

TIRISFAL GLADES LEGEND

1 THE BULWARK
Argent Quartermaster Hasana
Argent Officer Garush

1 THE DEATHKNELL GRAVES
Aradne
Arthura
Agatha
Daschla
Undertaker Mordo (Quest Giver)
Caretaker Caice (Quest Giver)
Deathguard Balteus
Deathguard Hansel

2 DEATHKNELL
Deathguard Saltain (Quest Giver)
Xavier the Huntsman <Hunter Trainer>
Maximillion <Warlock Trainer>
Dark Cleric Duesten <Priest Trainer>
Isabella <Mage Trainer>
Novice Elreth (Quest Giver)
Shadow Priest Sarvis (Quest Giver)
Blacksmith Rand <Apprentice Armorer>
Harold Raims <Apprentice Weaponsmith>
Kayla Smithe
Venya Marthand
Deathguard Oliver
Executor Arren (Quest Giver)
Deathguard Phillip
Maquell Ebonwood
Joshua Kien <General Supplies>
Archibald Kava <Cloth & Leather Armor Merchant>
David Trias <Rogue Trainer>
Dannal Stern <Warrior Trainer>
Lilian Voss
Deathguard Bartrand
Deathguard Randolph

3 OUTSIDE DEATHKNELL
Calvin Montague

4 CALSTON ESTATE
Deathguard Swallon
Franklin Brinklestein <General Goods>
Therisa Sallow <Profession Trainer>
Deathguard Simmer (Quest Giver)
Apothecary Johaan (Quest Giver)
Sedrick Calston (Quest Giver)
Dark Cleric Claressa <Priest Trainer>
Maressa Milner <Warlock Trainer>
Larah Firesong <Mage Trainer>
Karla Fain <Warrior Trainer>
Darna Wood <Hunter Trainer>
Shernon the Footpad <Rogue Trainer>

5 SCARLET PALISADE
Lilian Voss

6 COLD HEARTH MANOR
Bowen Brisboise <Tailoring Trainer>
Constance Brisboise <Apprentice Clothier>
Deathguard Dillinger (Quest Giver)

7 TIRISFAL GLADES
Deathguard Abraham

8 BRILL
Hamlin Atkins (Mushroom Vendor)
Deathguard Lawrence
Anette Williams <Bat Handler>
Faruza <Herbalism Trainer>
Carolai Anise <Alchemy Trainer>
Selina Weston <Alchemy & Herbalism Supplies>
Nurse Neela <First Aid Trainer>
Audrid Grenich <Poison & Reagent Supplies>
Austil de Mon <Warrior Trainer>
Executor Zygand (Quest Giver)
Deathguard Cyrus

Deathguard Morris (Quest Giver)
Cain Firesong <Mage Trainer>
Vance Undergloom <Enchanting Trainer>
Deathguard Mort
Junior Apothecary Holland (Quest Giver)
Deathguard Burgess
Eliza Callen <Leather Armor Merchant>
Nedric Sallow <Profession Trainer>
Oliver Dwor <Apprentice Weaponsmith>
Abe Winters <Apprentice Armorer>
Doreen Beltis
Abigail Shiel <Trade Supplies>
William Saldean <Grain & Feed Vendor>
Innkeeper Renee <Innkeeper>
Mrs. Winters <General Supplies>
Marion Call <Rogue Trainer>
Magistrate Sevren (Quest Giver)
Rupert Boch <Warlock Trainer>
Gina Lang
Dedlow Wormwood <Hunter Trainer>
Yvette Farthing
Ageron Kargal
Deathguard Terrence
Dark Cleric Beryl <Priest Trainer>
Shadow Priestess Malia
Sahvan Bloodshadow
Ratslin Maime
Claire Willower
Morganus <Stable Master>
Velma Warnam <Riding Trainer>
Zachariah Post <Undead Horse Merchant>
Thomas Arlento
Deathguard Gavin
Deathguard Royann
Deathguard Kel
Deathguard Bartholomew
The Chef <Cooking Trainer>
Jamie Nore

9 DEATH'S WATCH WAYSTATION
Shelene Rhobart <Leatherworking Trainer>
Rand Rhobart <Skinning Trainer>
Deathguard Linnea (Quest Giver)
Gretchen Dedmar
Martine Tramblay <Fishing Supplies>

10 TIRISFAL GLADES
Zapetta <Durotar Zeppelin Master>
Hin Denburg <Stranglethorn Vale Zeppelin Master>
Meefi Farthrottle <Howling Fjord Zeppelin Master>

11 BRIGHTWATER LAKE
Clyde Kellen <Fishing Trainer>

12 GUNTHER'S RETREAT
Gunther Arcanus (Quest Giver)

13 GARREN'S HAUNT
Apothecary Jerrod (Quest Giver)
Apprentice Crispin (Quest Giver)

14 AGAMAND MILLS
Coleman Farthing (Quest Giver)

15 THE BULWARK
High Executor Derrington (Quest Giver)
Apothecary Dithers (Quest Giver)
Werg Thickblade <Leatherworking Supplies>
Kramlod Farsight <Bowyer & Gunsmith>
Shadow Priestess Vandis (Quest Giver)
Timothy Cunningham <Bat Handler>
Mehlar Dawnblade
Bardu Sharpeye
Provisioner Elda <Innkeeper>
Mickey Levine

16 SCARLET ENCAMPMENT
Lieutenant Sanders (Quest Giver)

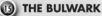

TOL BARAD PENINSULA

Tol Barad Peninsula is a desolate place. Both the Horde and the Alliance have tentative holds on the southern and eastern shores, respectively, which provide the only safe areas in the region. The center of the peninsula, known as The Darkwood, is home to massive arachnids and their brood of young. Spirits haunt The Restless Front, forever locked in endless battle while hungry undead roam the Forgotten Hill. In the north, Crazed Soldiers try to hold down the fort at Farson Hold, no longer recognizing friend from foe. In the northeast, Rustberg Village appears to be an oasis from the destruction and chaos infecting the rest of the region. However, even this tidy village is populated by Suspicious Villagers and Bandits who don't like intruding outsiders. Travelers surviving the dangers of the peninsula can travel south along the Blackstone Span to reach the nearby battlefield of Tol Barad.

REPUTATION INFORMATION Baradin's Wardens, Hellscream's Reach

RESOURCE LEGEND

NODE FISHING

Freshwater	Ocean
	Sealed Crate
	Azshara's Veil
	Volatile Water

OPEN WATER FISHING

Freshwater	Ocean
	Murglesnout
	Algaefin Rockfish
	Deepsea Sagefish

MINING

Metal	Min Skill Level
Elementium	475

HERBALISM

Herb	Min Skill Level

SKINNING

Creature	Level
Baradin Crocolisk	85
Putrid Worg	83

Questing in Tol Barad Peninsula

The daily quests on Tol Barad Peninsula open up at level 85, and are tied to your faction. Horde players work with Hellscream's Reach, while Alliance players get their orders from the Baradin's Wardens.

TOL BARAD PENINSULA LEGEND

1 BARADIN BASE CAMP

Kevin Geissler <Armorsmith>

Brazie <Baradin's Wardens Quartermaster>

Sergeant Gray (Quest Giver)

Commander Marcus Johnson

Lieutenant Farnsworth (Quest Giver)

Dar Rummond

Camp Coordinator Brack (Quest Giver)

1 HELLSCREAM'S GRASP

Captain Prug (Quest Giver)

Private Sarlosk (Quest Giver)

Tulgar Flamefist

Karosh <Armorsmith>

3rd Officer Kronkar (Quest Giver)

Pogg <Hellscream's Reach Quartermaster>

Commander Larmash

TWILIGHT HIGHLANDS

The Twilight Highlands is a region encompassing a wide range of geographical features. In the northwest the verdant grasses of the Vermillion Redoubt provide an incongruous setting for the conflict there. The fortress of Grim Batol looms in the mountains on the western edge, while the eerie Bastion of Twilight towers above the darkened ground in the southwest. The Twilight Highlands are bordered by the sea on the east, where both the Horde and Alliance have made ingress onto its inhospitable shores. The Twilight Cult has a strong presence here, causing trouble for both the other inhabitants and newcomers alike.

REPUTATION INFORMATION
The Earthen Ring, Bilgewater Cartel, Wildhammer Clan

Questing in Twilight Highlands

Before you travel to the Twilight Highlands, visit any major city controlled by your faction to obtain the quest Warchief's Command: Twilight Highlands!, or Hero's Call: Twilight Highlands!.

RESOURCE LEGEND

NODE FISHING

Freshwater	Ocean
Highland Guppy School	Algaefin Rockfish

OPEN WATER FISHING

Freshwater	Ocean
Sharptooth	Murglesnout
Highland Guppy	Algaefin Rockfish
Striped Lurker	Deepsea Sagefish
	Volatile Water

MINING

Metal	Min Skill Level
Elementium Vein	475
Rich Elementium Vein	500
Pyrite Deposit	525

HERBALISM

Herb	Min Skill Level
Cinderbloom	425
Twilight Jasmine	525

SKINNING

Creature	Level	Creature	Level
Crazed Mountain Lion	85	Mountain Eagle	85
Delta Crocolisk	84	Obsidian Charscale	85
Faceless Nightmare	84	Obsidian Pyrewing	85
Frenzied Thresher	84	Obsidian Venomwing	85
Gaunt Mountain Lion	84	Obsidian Viletongue	85
Glopgut Warhound	84		
Highland Black Drake	85	Rivergorge Crocolisk	85
Highland Elk	84	Tawny Owl	84
Highland Ram	84	Twilight Wyrmkiller	85
Highland Worg	84	Untamed Gryphon	84

TWILIGHT HIGHLANDS LEGEND

① HIGHBANK
Fargo Flintlocke (Quest Giver)
Lieutenant Fawkes (Quest Giver)
"Doc" Schweitzer
Deorim <Enchanting Supplies>
Senthii <Shard Trainer>
Leah Drewry <Tailoring Supplies>
Sal Ferraga <Cloth Trader>
Oslow Pliny <Jewelcrafting Supplies>
Evan <Cook>
Ashley Downs <Reagents>
Casandra Downs <Alchemy & Inscription Supplies>
Misty Merriweather <Hide & Leather Trader>
Alexandra Merriweather <Leatherworking Supplies>
Frank Natale <Engineering & Mining Supplies>
Lynn Baxter <Morale Officer>
Philip O' Tool <Weapons Vendor>
Brundall Chiselgut <Metal Trader>
Dorgan Slagfist <Blacksmith>
Richard Maschner <Blacksmithing Supplies>
Frederick Zyda <Furnace Master>
Glenn Arbuckle <Gryphon Master>
Bonnie Hennigan <Stable Master>
Talaa
Innkeeper Francis <Innkeeper>
Simon Chandler <Quest Giver>
Kurdran Wildhammer (Quest Giver)
Innkeeper Teresa <Innkeeper>
Thordun Hammerblow (Quest Giver)

② TWILIGHT SHORE
Lieutenant Emry (Quest Giver)
Fargo Flintlocke (Quest Giver)

③ TWILIGHT SHORE
Thordun Hammerblow (Quest Giver)

④ OBSIDIAN BREAKERS
Ephram Hardstone (Quest Giver)

⑤ FIREBEARD'S PATROL
Keegan Firebeard (Quest Giver)
Farstad Stonegrip <Gryphon Master>
Cailin Longfellow (Quest Giver)
Meara
Parlan
Aprika
Bren Stoneforge <Blacksmith>
Mackay Firebeard
Innkeeper Corlin <Innkeeper>
Hurley Hoppleham <Food & Drink>
Dierdre <Trade Goods>

⑥ FIREBEARD'S CEMETERY
Ian Firebeard (Quest Giver)

⑦ THE BONEYARD
Duglas Mullan (Quest Giver)
Edana Mullan (Quest Giver)
Sully Kneecapper

⑧ OBSIDIAN FOREST
Keeland Doyle

⑨ GORSHAK WAR CAMP
Mackay Firebeard (Quest Giver)
Ella Forgehammer (Quest Giver)
Brom Forgehammer (Quest Giver)
Bahrum Forgehammer (Quest Giver)

⑩ DUNWALD HOLDOUT
Keely Dunwald (Quest Giver)
Flynn Dunwald (Quest Giver)

⑪ DUNWALD HOVEL
Donnelly Dunwald (Quest Giver)

⑫ DUNWALD RUINS
Eoin Dunwald (Quest Giver)

⑬ DUNWALD MARKET ROW
Cayden Dunwald (Quest Giver)

⑭ THUNDERMAR
Berkan Thunderfist <Reagents>
Naveen Tendernose <Innkeeper>
Colin Thundermar (Quest Giver)
Craw MacGraw <Wildhammer Clan Quartermaster>
Tarm Deepgale <Stable Master>
Nivvet Channelock (Quest Giver)
Winifred Earlywind <Trade Goods>
Caelyb Coppercrag <Blacksmith>
Low Shaman Blundy (Quest Giver)
Fanny Thundermar (Quest Giver)
Sloan Simmersquall <Food & Drink>
Doran Talonheart <Gryphon Master>

⑮ KIRTHAVEN
Shaina Talonheart <Gryphon Master>
Baird Darkfeather <Stable Master>
Kurdran Wildhammer (Quest Giver)
Russell Brower (Quest Giver)
Fanny Thundermar
Vaughn Blusterbeard <Innkeeper>
Glenda Breezeboot <Reagents>
Carrick Irongrin <Blacksmith>
Logan Breezeboot <Trade Goods>
Cecily Stormbrow <Food & Drink>
Keegan Firebeard (Quest Giver)
Grundy MacGraff (Quest Giver)
Lachlan MacGraff (Quest Giver)

⑯ GLOPGUT'S HOLLOW
Colin Thundermar (Quest Giver)

⑰ VICTOR'S POINT
Nicole Gillet <General Goods>
Ben Mora <Innkeeper>
Garon Grey
Matthew Churchill <Stable Master>
Angus Stillmountain <Gryphon Master>
Desmond Chadsworth <Gryphon Master>
Daniel Lanchester <Reagents>
Brian Terrel <Bowyer>

① THE BLACK BREACH
Eye of Twilight (Quest Giver)

② RING OF THE ELEMENTS
Earthmender Duarn (Quest Giver)
Initiate Goldmine (Quest Giver)
Tharm Wildfire
Earthcaller Torunscar (Quest Giver)
Toshe Chaosrender
Earthcaller Yevaa (Quest Giver)
Golluck Rockfist (Quest Giver)

③ RUINS OF DRAKGOR
Earthcaller Yevaa (Quest Giver)

④ ISO'RATH
Earthcaller Yevaa (Quest Giver)
Initiate Goldmine

⑤ VERMILLION REDOUBT
Calen (Quest Giver)
Lirastrasza (Quest Giver)
Aquinastrasz <Vermillion Redoubt Flight Master>

⑥ VERMILLION REDOUBT
Velastrasza (Quest Giver)
Baleflame (Quest Giver)

⑦ GRIM BATOL
Calen (Quest Giver)
Lirastrasza
Alexstrasza the Life-Bender

⑧ HIGHLAND FOREST
Lirastrasza (Quest Giver)
Velastrasza (Quest Giver)
Baleflame

⑨ OBSIDIAN LAIR
Baleflame (Quest Giver)

⑩ CRUCIBLE OF CARNAGE
Wodin the Troll-Servant
Gurgthock (Quest Giver)

⑪ LOCH VERRALL
Countess Verrall (Quest Giver)

⑫ ELEMENTIUM DEPTHS
Initiate Goldmine (Quest Giver)
Twilight Rune of Earth (Quest Giver)

⑬ ALTAR OF TWILIGHT
The Hammer of Twilight (Quest Giver)

① REMAINS OF THE FLEET
Admiral Stonefist (Quest Giver)
Warlord Krogg (Quest Giver)
Juice Gnugat (Quest Giver)
Horzog

② DRAGONMAW PORT
Ornak (Quest Giver)
Gregor (Quest Giver)
Zaela (Quest Giver)
Gorthul <Dragonmaw Flight Master>
Garrosh Hellscream (Quest Giver)
Artesh (Quest Giver)
Kanath <Stable Master>
Innkeeper Lutz <Innkeeper>
Lizzy "Lemons" <Food & Drink>
Marlow Harston
Cerie Bowden
Frenk <General Goods>
Brot <Leatherworking Supplies>
Threm Blackscalp <Hide & Leather Trader>
Aristaleon Sunweaver <Cloth Trader>
Hortak Kenzo <Tailoring Supplies>
Digel East Nickens <Reagents>
Gregory Kauffman <Jewelcrafting Supplies>
Una Kobuna <Alchemy and Inscription Supplies>
Victor Quivias Enchanting Supplies>
Agatian Fallanos <Shard Trader>
Zim Bamzabble <Engineering Supplies>
Jodan <Dragonmaw Armorsmith>
Kuldar Steeltooth <Metal Trader>
Grizz
Dakam

③ SLITHERING COVE
Fergus Gearchum (Quest Giver)
Gralok (Quest Giver)

④ TWILIGHT SHORE
Rok' tar (Quest Giver)
Juice Gnugat (Quest Giver)

⑤ BLOODGULCH
Harkkan (Quest Giver)
Torth
Narkrall Rakeclaw (Quest Giver)
Griff (Quest Giver)
Mallia (Quest Giver)
Garona Halforcen (Quest Giver)
Bramok Gorewing <Wind Rider Master>
Zaela (Quest Giver)
Naka Scaleblade <Blacksmith>
Garm Bonehew <Food & Drink>
Rukh Zumtarg <Stable Master>
Innkeeper Turk <Innkeeper>
Laka Scaleblade <Reagents>
Grot Deathblow (Quest Giver)
Malkar (Quest Giver)

⑥ THE GULLET
Zaela (Quest Giver)
San'shigo <Wind Rider Master>
Rotgrum (Quest Giver)
Buunu (Quest Giver)
Uchek

⑦ DRAGONMAW PASS
Patch (Quest Giver)
Newt
Ticker
Grit
Warlord Krogg
Volt

⑧ WYRM'S BEND
Warlord Krogg (Quest Giver)
Patch (Quest Giver)
Newt
Ticker
Grit
Volt

⑨ CRUSHBLOW
Tokrog <Wind Rider Master>
Jon-Jon Jellyneck <Wind Rider Master>
Warlord Zaela (Quest Giver)
Lady Cozwynn (Quest Giver)
Zay' hana <Stable Master>
Innkeeper Krum <Innkeeper>
Malo' wo <Food & Drink>
Hama Brightleaf <Reagents>
Zoklaw Irtak <Blacksmith>
Rek Moshfang <Trade Goods>

⑩ THE TWILIGHT CITADEL
Garona Halforcen (Quest Giver)

⑪ ELEMENTIUM DEPTHS
Earthcaller Yevaa
Initiate Goldmine

⑫ THE KRAZZWORKS
Captain Krazz (Quest Giver)
Flashbang Rothman (Quest Giver)
Brett the Bomber (Quest Giver)
Victor Vaporizer
Warlord Krogg
Harpo Boltknuckle <Flight Master>
Meks Megaflux <Engineering Supplies>
Kazz Fetchum <Stable Master>
Innkeeper Gene <Innkeeper>
Jr. Chef Kracket
Newt
Commander Molotov
Chef Sizzlebang <Food & Drink>

UNDERCITY

Located deep beneath the ruins of Lordaeron in Tirisfal Glades, the Undercity has grown greatly from the warren of dungeons and catacombs it once was. The city is laid out in concentric rings, making it easy to navigate. The upper ring, known as the Trade Quarter, holds important shops and services like the Bank, the Inn, the Barber, and many more. Below you can find more specialized shops and profession trainers, as well as class trainers in each of the four quadrants of the outer ring.

REPUTATION INFORMATION Undercity

RESOURCE LEGEND

NODE FISHING		
Freshwater	Ocean	
None		

OPEN WATER FISHING	
Freshwater	Ocean
Raw Brilliant Smallfish	
Raw Longjaw Mud Snapper	
Sickly Looking Fish	

UNDERCITY LEGEND

1 TRADE QUARTER
Mortimer Montague <Banker>
Ophelia Montague <Banker>
Randolph Montague <Banker>
William Montague <Banker>

2 TRADE QUARTER
Anya Maulray <Stable Master>
Innkeeper Norman <Innkeeper>

3 TRADE QUARTER
Thomas Mordan <Reagents>

4 TRADE QUARTER
Tawny Grisette <Mushroom Vendor

5 TRADE QUARTER
Edward Cairn <Elder>
Naznik Sureshave <Barber>

6 TRADE QUARTER
Apothecary Vallia
Kraxx

7 TRADE QUARTER
Eleanor Rusk <General Goods>

8 TRADE QUARTER
Felicia Doan <Trade Supplies>

9 TRADE QUARTER
Michael Garrett <Bat Handler>
Patrick Garrett

10 TRADE QUARTER
Gordon Wendham <Weapons Merchant>
Louis Warren <Weapons Merchant>

11 TRADE QUARTER
Timothy Weldon <Heavy Armor Merchant>
Velora Nitely
Walter Ellingson <Heavy Armor Merchant>

12 TRADE QUARTER
Daniel Bartlett <Trade Supplies>
Lauren Newcomb <Light Armor Merchant>

13 TRADE QUARTER
Eunice Burch <Cooking Trainer>
Raleigh Andrean
Ronald Burch <Cooking Supplies>

14 TRADE QUARTER
Christopher Drakul <Guild Master>
Edward Remington <Guild Tabard Designer>
Merill Pleasance <Tabard Vendor>
Royal Overseer Bauhaus

15 TRADE QUARTER
Jeremiah Payson <Cockroach Vendor>

16 TRADE QUARTER
Harbinger Balthazad

17 UNDERCITY
Auctioneer Tricket

18 CANALS
Auctioneer Naxxremis

19 CANALS
Auctioneer Cain
Dark Ranger Cyndia

20 UNDERCITY
Auctioneer Yarly

21 UNDERCITY
Auctioneer Stockton

22 UNDERCITY
Auctioneer Leeka

23 CANALS
Hepzibah Sedgewick

24 UNDERCITY
Auctioneer Epitwee

25 UNDERCITY
Auctioneer Rhyker

26 CANALS
Apothecary Katrina

27 CANALS
Edrick Killian
Mattie Alred

28 TAILOR
Josef Gregorian <Tailoring Trainer>
Lucille Castelton <Robe Vendor>
Millie Gregorian <Tailoring Supplies>
Ralston Farnsley <Horde Cloth Quartermaster>
Rhiannon Davis
Sheldon Von Croy <Cloth Armor Merchant>
Sydney Upton <Staff Merchant>
Victor Ward
Zane Bradford <Wand Vendor>

29 MAGIC QUARTER
Davitt Hickson
Reginald Grimsford
Selina Pickman

30 MAGIC QUARTER
Andrew Brownell
Samantha Shackleton

31 ARCHAEOLOGY
Adam Hossack <Archaeology Trainer>
Jorah Annison
Salazar Bloch <Book Dealer>

32 MAGIC QUARTER
Adrian Bartlett
Jezelle Pruitt
Victor Bartholomew
Winifred Kerwin

33 MAGIC QUARTER
Anastasia Hartwell <Mage Trainer>
Bethor Iceshard
Godrick Farsan
Hannah Akeley <Reagents>
Josephine Lister <Master Shadoweave Tailor>
Kaal Soulreaper <Warlock Trainer>
Kaelystia Hatebringer <Mage Trainer>
Lexington Mortaim <Portal Trainer>
Luther Pickman <Warlock Trainer>
Martha Strain
Pierce Shackleton <Mage Trainer>
Richard Kerwin <Warlock Trainer>
Silas Zimmer

34 MAGIC QUARTER
Carendin Halgar
Morley Bates <Fungus Vendor>

35 MAGIC QUARTER
Armand Cromwell <Fishing Trainer>
Lizbeth Cromwell <Fishing Supplies>

36 ROGUE'S QUARTER
Charles Seaton <Blade Merchant>
Ezekiel Graves <Poison Supplies>
Nathaniel Steenwick <Thrown Weapons Merchant>

37 ROGUES' QUARTER
Mary Edras <First Aid Trainer>

38 ROGUES' QUARTER
Arthur Moore <Leatherworking Trainer>
Dan Golthas <Apprentice Leatherworker>
Gillian Moore <Leather Armor Merchant>
Jonathan Chambers <Bag Vendor>
Joseph Moore <Leatherworking Supplies>
Killian Hagey <Skinning Trainer>

39 ROGUES' QUARTER
Dark Ranger Anya

40 ROGUES' QUARTER
Cedric Stumpel

41 ROGUES' QUARTER
Walter Soref <Locksmith>

42 ROGUES QUARTER
Gothard Winslow

43 ROGUES' QUARTER
Carolyn Ward <rogue Trainer>
Gregory Charles <Rogue Trainer>
Mennet Carkad
Miles Dexter <Rogue Trainer>
Susan Tillinghast

44 ROGUES' QUARTER
Elizabeth Van Talen <Engineering Supplies>
Estelle Gendry
Franklin Lloyd <Engineering Trainer>
Graham Van Talen
Lucian Fenner

45 THE APOTHECARIUM
Ickabod Pimlen <Inscription Supplies>
Lavinia Crowe <Enchanting Trainer>
Malcomb Wynn
Margaux Parchley <Inscription Trainer>
Thaddeus Webb <Enchanting Supplies>

46 THE APOTHECARIUM
Alessandro Luca <Blue Moon Odds & Ends>

47 THE APOTHECARIUM
Katrina Alliestar <Herbalism Supplies>
Martha Alliestar <Herbalism Trainer>

48 THE APOTHECARIUM
KEEPER BEL'DUGUR

49 THE APOTHECARIUM
Apothecary Lycanus
Parqual Fintallas

50 THE APOTHECARIUM
Andron Gant

51 THE APOTHECARIUM
Algernon <Alchemy Supplies>
Doctor Marsh

52 THE APOTHECARIUM
Apothecary Keever
Apothecary Lycanus
Apothecary Zinge
Chemist Cuely
Chemist Fuely
Doctor Herbert Halsey <Alchemy Trainer>
Doctor Martin Felben
Master Apothecary Faranell
Overseer Kraggosh
Theodore Griffs
Thersa Windsong

53 THE APOTHECARIUM
Ganoosh

54 THE APOTHECARIUM
Boyle

55 ROYAL QUARTER
Deathstalker Fane <Battlemaster>
Horde Warbringer

56 ROYAL QUARTER
Magistrix Erembria <Wintergrasp Battle-Mage>
Misery <Battlemaster>
Rex Pixem <Arena Battlemaster>

57 ROYAL QUARTER
Aleric Hawkins
Ambassador Sunsorrow
Bragor Bloodfist
Champion Cyssa Dawnrose <Paladin Trainer>
Lady Sylvanas Windrunner
Sharlindra

58 WAR QUARTER
Dark Ranger Clea
Gerard Abernathy
Joanna Whitehall
Leona Tharpe
Theresa

59 WAR QUARTER
Abigail Sawyer <Bow Merchant>
Brom Killian <Mining Trainer>
Sarah Killian <Mining Supplies>

60 WAR QUARTER
Archibald <Weapon Master>
Benijah Fenner <Weapon Merchant>
Francis Eliot <Weapon Merchant>
Geoffrey Hartwell <Weapon Merchant>

61 WAR QUARTER
Basil Frye
Helena Atwood
James Van Brunt <Blacksmithing Trainer>
Mirelle Tremayne <Heavy Armor Merchant>
Nicholas Atwood <Gun Merchant>
Samuel Van Brunt <Blacksmithing Supplies>

62 WAR QUARTER
Alyssa Blaye
Eldin Partridge
Sergeant Houser
Sergeant Rutger
Travist Bosk

63 WAR QUARTER
Andrew Hartwell
Apolos <Hunter Trainer>
Brother Malach
Chloe Curthas
Edward
Lysta Bancroft
Marla Fowler
Richard Van Brunt
Riley Walker
Riley Walker
Robert Gossom
Tyler

64 WAR QUARTER
Derek the Undying <Mage Trainer>

65 WAR QUARTER
Aelthalyste <Priest Trainer>
Angela Curthas <Warrior Trainer>
Baltus Fowler <Warrior Trainer>
Christoph Walker <Warrior Trainer>
Father Lankester <Priest Trainer>
Father Lazarus <Priest Trainer>

WESTERN PLAGUELANDS

The Western Plaguelands have at long last begun recovering from the damage done by the Scourge plague. Fields that have long lay fallow have been reclaimed, farms are being rebuilt, and abandoned strongholds hold life once again. The Argent Crusade has expanded its influence, pushing the overly zealous Scarlet Crusade out of Haerthglen and making it their seat of operations in the region. The Cenarion Circle set up a camp at the Menders' Stead and is lending its aid to heal the land. Though the Western Plaguelands is recovering, it is still full of dangers. Much of the wildlife is still feral and Redpine Gnolls have moved into the area in great numbers. Along with smaller infested pockets of undead, the ruined city of Andorhal is still teeming with Scourge. Both the Alliance and the Horde have stationed troops there to try to eradicate the undead threat.

REPUTATION INFORMATION   Argent Crusade, Undercity, Stormwind

TIRISFAL GLADES

HAERTHGLEN ③

②

DALSON'S FARM

THE MENDERS STEAD

FELSTONE FIELD ②

①

④ GAHRRON'S WITHERING

THE BULWARK

①

THE WRITHING HAUNT

① ANDORHAL

③

⑤ SCHOLOMANCE

⑥

② CHILLWIND CAMP

③ UTHER'S TOMB

RESOURCE LEGEND

NODE FISHING

Freshwater	Ocean
Raw Greater Sagefish	
Waterlogged Wreckage	

OPEN WATER FISHING

Freshwater	Ocean
Raw Bristle Whisker Catfish	
Raw Mithril Head Trout	

MINING

Metal	Min Skill Level
Iron Vein	125
Gold Vein	155

HERBALISM

Herb	Min Skill Level
Stranglekelp	85
Kingsblood	125
Liferoot	150
Fadeleaf	160
Khadgar's Whisker	185
Blindweed	235

SKINNING

Creature	Level
Bullmastiff	35-36
Diseased Black Bear	35-36
Diseased Grizzly	55-56
Diseased Wolf	36-37
Elder Foulmaw Hydra	55-57
Foulmaw Hydra	52-54
Hulking Plaguebear	36-37
Rabid Fox	36-37
Shaggy Black Bear	35-36
Whitetail Fox	35-36

Questing in Western Plaguelands

Warchief's Command: Western Plaguelands! sends Horde players to Koltira Deathweaver at Andorhal, while Hero's Call: Western Plaguelands! Orders Alliance players to report to Thassarian at Andorhal.

WESTERN PLAGUELANDS LEGEND

1 ANDORHAL
Lurid (Quest Giver)
Thassarian (Quest Giver)
Lang Loosegrip (Quest Giver)

2 CHILLWIND CAMP
Alchemist Arbington
Alexia Ironknife
Anchorite Truuen
Argent Officer Pureheart (Quest Giver)
Argent Quartermaster Lightspark
Bibilfaz Featherwhistle <Gryphon Master>
Commander Ashlam Valorfist (Quest Giver)
Flint Shadowmore
High Priestess MacDonnell (Quest Giver)
Leonard Porter <Leatherworking Supplies>
Mother Matterly <Innkeeper>
Thurman Grant (Quest Giver)

3 UTHER'S TOMB
High Priest Thel'danis (Quest Giver)

1 THE MENDER'S STEAD
Adrine Towhide (Quest Giver)
Damion Steel
Durnt Brightfalcon
Field Agent Kaartish (Quest Giver)
Marge Heffman <Gryphon Master>
Selyria Groenveld (Quest Giver)
Zen' Kiki

2 NORTHRIDGE LUMBER CAMP
Kelly Dumah (Quest Giver)
Nathaniel Dumah (Quest Giver)

3 HEARTHGLEN
Bree Ironstock
Daria L' Rayne (Quest Giver)
High Cleric Alphus
Highlord Tirion Fordring
Lieutenant Myner (Quest Giver)
Magus Bisp
Morris Vant <Argent Blacksmith>
Outfitter Mendelev <Cloth Armor>

4 GAHRRON'S WITHERING
Scourge Cauldron (Quest Giver)

5 CAER DARROW
Artist Renfray

6 SORROW HILL
Marlene Redpath
Myranda the Hag

1 ANDORHAL
Agatha
Arthura
Daschla
Jearl Donald (Quest Giver)

2 CHARRED OUTPOST
Lindsay Ravensun (Quest Giver)

3 ANDORHAL
Lurid (Quest Giver)

WESTFALL

Despite the problems caused by the cataclysm, Stormwind has finally decided to tend to its own back yard. Sentinel Hill has been fortified and expanded and Alliance forces are in the process of retaking the town of Moonbrook. The Defias Brotherhood has seemingly retreated into the Deadmines, abandoning the land they once held. Unfortunately, the changes in Westfall are not all for the better. In the west, the Raging Chasm, a large gaping hole in the ground with a swirling vortex of energy at the center, has formed. Gnoll camps dot the landscape, Murlocs still swarm the Gold Cost, and vicious mercenaries have claimed Mortwake's Tower. Desperate refugees, fleeing from the destruction wrought by the cataclysm, have poured into Westfall, willing to do whatever it takes to survive.

REPUTATION INFORMATION Stormwind

RESOURCE LEGEND

NODE FISHING

Freshwater	Ocean
Raw Sagefish	Oily Blackmouth
	Firefin Snapper
	Floating Debris

OPEN WATER FISHING

Freshwater	Ocean
Raw Brilliant Smallfish	Raw Slitherskin Mackerel
Raw Longjaw Mud Snapper	Oily Blackmouth
Raw Bristle Whisker Catfish	Raw Rainbow Fin Albacore

MINING

Metal	Min Skill Level
Copper Vein	1
Tin Vein	65

HERBALISM

Herb	Min Skill Level
Peacebloom	1
Silverleaf	1
Earthroot	15
Mageroyal	50
Briarthorn	70
Stranglekelp	85
Bruiseweed	100

SKINNING

Creature	Level
Coyote	10-11
Coyote Packleader	11-12
Goretusk	12-13
Hulking Goretusk	14-15
Young Goretusk	10-11

Questing in Westfall

The target of the Hero's Call: Westfall! Quest, Lieutenant Horatio Laine at the Jansen Stead, kicks off the mystery-filled quests that take place in Westfall.

WESTFALL LEGEND

1 THE JANSEN STEAD
Lieutenant Horation Laine (Quest Giver)

2 FURLBROW'S PUMPKIN FARM
Hoboair <Gryphon Master>
Jimb "Candles" McHannigan (Quest Giver)
Lieutenant Horation Laine (Quest Giver)
Mama Celeste (Quest Giver)
Two-Shoed Lou (Quest Giver)

3 SALDEAN'S FARM
Farmer Saldean (Quest Giver)
Salma Saldean (Quest Giver)

4 SENTINEL HILL
Captain Danuvin (Quest Giver)
Christopher Hewen <Trade Supplies>
Gina MacGregor <Trade Supplies>
Hope Saldean (Quest Giver)
Innkeeper Heather <Innkeeper>
Kirk Maxwell <Stable Master>
Lieutenant Horation Laine
Marshal Gryan Stoutmantle (Quest Giver)
Mike Miller <Bread Merchant>
Protector Bialon
Protector Deni
Protector Dorana
Protector Dutfield
Protector Gariel
Protector Leick
Protector Weaver
Quartermaster Lewis <Quartermaster>
Scout Galiaan (Quest Giver)
Scout Riell
William MacGregor <Bowyer>

5 WESTFALL LIGHTHOUSE
Captain Grayson (Quest Giver)

6 LONGSHORE
Kriggon Talsone <Fisherman>

7 THE DUST PLAINS
Agent Kearnen (Quest Giver)

8 MOONBROOK
Captain Alpert (Quest Giver)
Private Jackson <Provisioner>
Thoralius the Wise (Quest Giver)
Tina Skyden <Gryphon Master>

9 THE DAGGER HILLS
Grimbooze Thunderbrew

WETLANDS

As the name suggests, the Wetlands have always been a damp, marshy region, home to many creatures, like Murlocs and Crocolisks, who thrive in just such an environment. With the cataclysm, the water levels have risen, creating a large lake in the east and almost sinking Menethil Harbor. The port town was heavily damaged and most of it remains flooded, though the townsfolk strive to keep their businesses running. The docks were damaged as well, but ships are once again up and running and you can still find transport to Theramore and Northrend from there.

Questing in Wetlands

Visit any Alliance city to get the quest Hero's Call: Wetlands!. If you didn't get the quest, report to Mountaineer Rharen at Dun Algaz.

REPUTATION INFORMATION   Ironforge, Stormwind

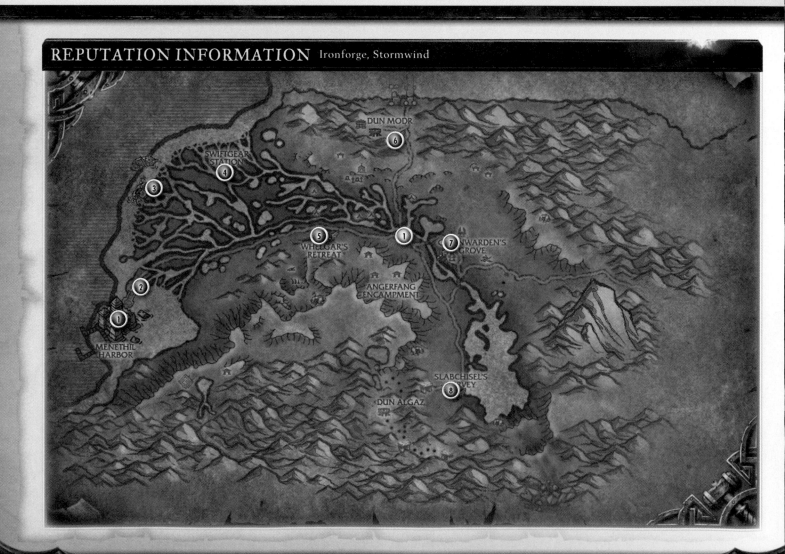

RESOURCE LEGEND

NODE FISHING

Freshwater	Ocean
Raw Sagefish	Oily Blackmouth
Schooner Wreckage	Firefin Snapper
	Schooner Wreckage

OPEN WATER FISHING

Freshwater	Ocean
Raw Longjaw Mud Snapper	Raw Rainbow Fin Albacore
Raw Bristle Whisker Catfish	Firefin Snapper
	Oily Blackmouth

MINING

Metal	Min Skill Level
Copper Vein	1
Tin Vein	65
Silver Vein	75
Iron Vein	125
Gold Vein	155

HERBALISM

Herb	Min Skill Level
Mageroyal	50
Briarthorn	70
Stranglekelp	85
Bruiseweed	100
Wild Steelbloom	115
Grave Moss	120
Kingsblood	125
Liferoot	150

SKINNING

Creature	Level	Creature	Level
Crimson Whelp	25-26	Highland Scytheclaw	22-23
Displaced Threshadon	20	Lost Whelp	24-25
Ebon Slavehunter	24-25	Mottled Raptor	22-23
Ebon Whelp	24	Mottled Razormaw	26-27
Elder Razormaw	25	Mottled Riptooth	28-28
Flamescale Drake	39	Mottled Screecher	22
Flamesnorting Whelp	26-27	Mottled Scytheclaw	25-26
Giant Wetlands Crocolisk	25-26	Ocean Shredfin	22-23
Harbor Shredfin	21-22	Red Whelp	23-24
Highland Lashtail	24-25	Wetlands Crocolisk	22-24
Highland Raptor	23-24	Young Wetlands Crocolisk	21-22
Highland Razormaw	22-23		

WETLANDS LEGEND

1 **MENETHIL HARBOR**
Adam Lind
Andrea Halloran
Archaeologist Flagongut
Bart Tidewater
Bethaine Flinthammer <Stable Master>
Brahnmar <Armorer>
Brak Durnad <Weaponsmith>
Caitlin Grassman
Camerick Jongleur
Captain Stoutfist (Quest Giver)
Derina Rumdnul (Quest Giver)
Dewin Shimmerdawn <Alchemy Supplies>
Edwina Monzor <Bowyer>
Falkan Armonis <Reagents>
First Mate Fitzsimmons (Quest Giver)
Fremal Doohickey <First Aid Trainer>
Gimlok Rumdnul
Glorin Steelbrow
Gruham Rumdnul <General Supplies>
Hargin Mundar
Harold Riggs <Fishing Trainer>
Innkeeper Helbrek <Innkeeper>
Jennabink Powerseam <Tailoring Supplies & Specialty Goods>
Jesse Halloran
Junder Brokk
Karl Boran (Quest Giver)
Kersok Prond <Tradesman>
Lieutenant Timothy Clark
Ludin Farrow <Dockmaster>
Mikhail <Bartender>
Murndan Derth <Gunsmith>
Murphy West

Naela Trance <Bowyer>
Neal Allen <Engineering Supplies & General Goods>
Red Jack Flint
Regina Halloran
Samor Festivus <Shady Dealer>
Shellei Brondir <Gryphon Master>
Stuart Fleming <Fishing Supplies>
Tapoke "Slim" Jahn
Telurinon Moonshadow <Herbalism Trainer>
Unger Statforth <Horse Breeder>
Valstag Ironjaw
Vincent Hyal

2 **WETLANDS**
Tarrel Rockweaver
Thomas Booker

3 **THE LOST FLEET**
First Mate Snellig (Quest Giver)

4 **SWIFTGEAR STATION**
Fradd Swiftgear (Quest Giver)
Innkeeper Daughny <Innkeeper>
James Halloran (Quest Giver)
Shep Goldtend <Stable Master>
Shilah Slabchisel (Quest Giver)
Teep Topup <Engineering & Mining Supplies>
Wenna Silkbeard <Special Goods Dealer>

5 **WHELGAR'S RETREAT**
Cedric Bronzeflint <General Goods>
Damon Baelor <Gryphon Master>
Merrin Rockweaver (Quest Giver)
Ormer Ironbraid (Quest Giver)
Prospector Whelgar (Quest Giver)

6 **DUN MODR**
Breg Fullbeard <Provisioner>
Caleb Baelor <Gryphon Master>
Longbraid the Grim (Quest Giver)
Motley Garmason
Rhag Garmason
Roggo Harlbarrow
Thargas Anvilmar (Quest Giver)

7 **GREENWARDEN'S GROVE**
Aluril <Reagents>
Ferilon Leafborn (Quest Giver)
Halana <Hippogryph Master>
Huntress Iczelia (Quest Giver)
Innkeeper Larisal <Innkeeper>
Jeffrey Gregarius
Rethiel the Greenwarder (Quest Giver)
Salustred <Stable Master>
Vasuuvata
Victorina <Weaponsmith>

8 **SLABCHISEL'S SURVEY**
Brisket
Darvish Quickhammer <Blacksmithing Supplies>
Dunlor Marblebeard (Quest Giver)
Elgin Baelor <Gryphon Master>
Forba Slabchisel (Quest Giver)
Surveyor Thurdan (Quest Giver)

9 **DUN ALGAZ**
Mountaineer Grugelm (Quest Giver)
Mountaineer Rharen (Quest Giver)

1 **WETLANDS**
Kixxle <Potions & Herbs>

ASHENVALE

Ashenvale, the ancestral home of the Night Elves, is filled with lush trees, abundant wildlife, and several Night Elf settlements. The rich lumber found in the forest is a desirable resource, and the Horde long ago established a small foothold in the region for the purpose of harvesting the numerous trees. However, the Night Elves zealously guarded the natural beauty of Ashenvale and even with the Warsong Lumber Camp the Horde never made many inroads into the area. Since the recent cataclysm, this has changed. The Horde has a much stronger military presence and is besieging key Alliance settlements like Astranaar. The Alliance has answered in turn and managed to wrest control of a portion of the Warsong Lumber Camp away from their foes. Zoram'gar Outpost has been fortified and the Alliance has established a small camp along the Zoram Strand as well, unwilling to let their enemies control the coast.

REPUTATION INFORMATION   Orgrimmar, Darnassus

Questing in Ashenvale

The Alliance introduction to Ashenvale is Hero's Call: Ashenvale! which sends you to Sentinel Shyela at Ordanil's Retreat. The Horde's Warchief's Command: Ashenvale! sends characters to Kadrak at the Mor'shan Rampart on the border between the Northern Barrens and Ashenvale.

RESOURCE LEGEND

NODE FISHING

Freshwater	Ocean
Raw Sagefish	Oily Blackmouth
	Firefin Snapper

OPEN WATER FISHING

Freshwater	Ocean
Raw Longjaw Mud Snapper	Firefin Snapper
Raw Bristle Whisker Catfish	Oily Blackmouth

MINING

Metal	Min Skill Level
Copper Vein	1
Tin Vein	65
Silver Vein	75
Iron Vein	125
Gold Vein	155

HERBALISM

Herb	Min Skill Level
Mageroyal	50
Briarthorn	70
Stranglekelp	85
Bruiseweed	100
Wild Steelbloom	115
Kingsblood	125
Liferoot	150

SKINNING

Creature	Level
Ashenvale Bear	20
Blink Dragon	22
Elder Ashenvale Bear	21-22
Elder Shadowhorn Stag	23-24
Emeraldom Boughguard	25
Emeraldon Oracle	25
Emeraldon Tree Warder	25
Felslayer	24-25
Ghostpaw Alpha	23-24
Ghostpaw Runner	19-20
Shadowhorn Stag	21-22
Wild Buck	19-20

ASHENVALE LEGEND

(1) ORENDIL'S RETREAT
Evenar Stillwhisper (Quest Giver)
Sentinel Shyela (Quest Giver)
Visera Softloam <Food & Drink>

(2) BATHRAN'S HAUNT
Bathran (Quest Giver)

(3) BLACKFATHOM CAMP
Shindrell Swiftfire (Quest Giver)
Solais <Flight Master>
Talen (Quest Giver)
Varas <Weapon Vendor>

(4) MAESTRA'S POST
Liladris Moonriver (Quest Giver)
Moon Priestess Maestra (Quest Giver)
Orendil Broadleaf (Quest Giver)
Sentinel Avana (Quest Giver)
Sentinel Onaeya (Quest Giver)

(5) LAKE FALATHIM
Keeper Heartwise (Quest Giver)
Teronis' Corpse (Quest Giver)

(6) ASTRANAAR
Ayyndia Floralwind <Leatherworking Trainer>
Aeolynn <Clothier>
Daelyshia <Hippogryph Master>
Dagri
Dalria <Trade Goods>
Fahran Silentblade <Poison Vendor>
Faldreas Goeth' Shael (Quest Giver)
Haljan Oakheart <General Goods>
Hephaestus Pilgrim (Quest Giver)
Innkeeper Kimlya <Innkeeper>
Korra
Lardan <Leatherworking Supplies>
Llana <Reagent Supplies>
Maliynn <Food & Drink Vendor>
Maluressian <Stable Master>
Nantar <Baker>
Pelturas Whitemoon (Quest Giver)
Raene Wolfrunner (Quest Giver)
Relara Whitemoon
Sentinel Luara
Sentinel Thenysil (Quest Giver)
Tandaan Lightmane <Leather Armor Merchant>
Vindicator Palanaar (Quest Giver)
Xai' ander <Weaponsmith>

(7) THISTLEFUR HOLD
Vear Darksnout (Quest Giver)

(8) FOREST SONG
Anchorite Buurg (Quest Giver)
Apprentice Boulian
Architect Nemos (Quest Giver)
Auhula
Illiyana (Quest Giver)
Kayneth Stillwind (Quest Giver)
Phaedra <Weapon Master>
Suralais Farwind <Hippogryph Master>

(9) XAVIAN
Anilia (Quest Giver)

(10) WARSONG LUMBER CAMP
Gnarl (Quest Giver)
Sentinel Luciel Starwhisper (Quest Giver)
Vindicator Vedaar (Quest Giver)

(11) THE DOR'DANIL BARROW DEN
Gaivan Shadewalker (Quest Giver)

(12) RAYNEWOOD TOWER
Avrus Illwhisper (Quest Giver)
Elestren <Heavy Armor Merchant>
Sentinel Melyria Frostshadow (Quest Giver)
Shael' dryn (Quest Giver)

(13) RAYNEWOOD RETREAT
Halannia (Quest Giver)

(14) THE SKUNKWORKS
The Bomb (Quest Giver)

(15) THUNDER PEAK
Sabina Pilgrim

(16) KROLG'S HUT
Krolg (Quest Giver)

(17) HOUSE OF EDUNE
Aleanna Edune
Becanna Edune
Benjari Edune (Quest Giver)
Elenna Edune
Goodie
Sulan Dunadaire
William Dunadaire

(18) BOLYUN'S CAMP
Alenndaar Lapidar <Hunter Trainer>
Bolyun (Quest Giver)
Harlown Darkweave <Leatherworking Supplies>

(19) THE SHRINE OF AESSINA
Big Baobob (Quest Giver)

(20) SILVERWING GROVE
Gapp Jinglepocket <Smokywood Pastures>
Hutihu
Illiyana Moonblaze <Silverwing Supply Officer>
Sentinel Farsong
Su' ura Swiftarrow

(21) STARDUST SPIRE
Bhaldaran Ravenshade <Bowyer>
Gnombus the X-Terminator (Quest Giver)
Huntress Jalin
Myre Moonglide <Flight Master>
Professor Kakxok Gyromate (Quest Giver)
Sentinel Velene Starstrike (Quest Giver)

(1) THUNDER PEAK
Arcantus (Quest Giver)
Core (Quest Giver)
The Vortex (Quest Giver)

(1) FALLEN SKY LAKE
Gorat (Quest Giver)

(2) WARSONG LUMBER CAMP
Gorka (Quest Giver)

(3) SPLINTERTREE POST
Advisor Sunsworn
Burkrum <Heavy Armor Merchant>
Durak (Quest Giver)
Ertog Ragetusk
Fahrak
Framnali
Har' alen
Innkeeper Kaylisk <Innkeeper>
Kadrak (Quest Giver)
Kuray' bin (Quest Giver)
Locke Okarr (Quest Giver)
Mastok Wrilehiss (Quest Giver)
Pixel (Quest Giver)
Qeeju <Stable Master>
Splintertree Demolisher (Quest Giver)
Valusha (Quest Giver)
Vera Nightshade
Vhulgra <Wind Rider Master>
Yama Snowhoof

(4) SATYRNAAR
Krokk (Quest Giver)

(5) KARGATHIA KEEP
Guardian Menerin (Quest Giver)
Overseer Gorthak (Quest Giver)

(6) NIGHTSONG WOODS
Guardian Gurtar (Quest Giver)

(7) SILVERWIND REFUGE
Blood Guard Aldo Rockrain (Quest Giver)
Captain Tarkan (Quest Giver)
Chief Blastgineer Bombgutz
Cromula (Quest Giver)
Dro Shadowfree <Leatherworking Supplies>
Flooz (Quest Giver)
Innkeeper Chin' toka <Innkeeper>
Kitanga <Poisons & Reagents>
Scout Utvoch
Senani Thunderheart (Quest Giver)
Sergeant Dontrag
Vorcha <Stable Master>
Wind Tamer Shoshok <Flight Master>

(8) HELLSCREAM'S WATCH
Broyk (Quest Giver)
Captain Goggath (Quest Giver)
Drek <Stable Master>
Innkeeper Linkasa <Innkeeper>
Karang Amakkar (Quest Giver)
Mitsuwa (Quest Giver)
Shenara <Blacksmithing Supplies>
Thraka <Wind Rider Master>
Tweedle (Quest Giver)

(9) THISTLEFUR HOLD
Ruul Snowhoof (Quest Giver)

(10) THE SKUNKWORKS
Chief Bombgineer Sloder
Foreman Jinx (Quest Giver)

(11) THUNDER PEAK
Stikwad

(12) RAYNEWOOD RETREAT
Thagg (Quest Giver)

(13) ZORAM'GAR OUTPOST
Andruk <Wind Rider Master>
Beh' tor <Poisons & Reagents>
Commander Grimfang (Quest Giver)
Dagrun Ragehammer (Quest Giver)
Innkeeper Duras <Innkeeper>
Kil' Hiwana <Fishing Trainer>
Lursa <Stable Master>
Marukai (Quest Giver)
Muglash (Quest Giver)
Targol
Toral <Blacksmithing Supplies>
Wik' Tar <Fish Merchant & Supplies>

AZSHARA

Located north of Durotar, the land of Azshara has undergone many changes. Orgrimmar built a set of rear gates leading directly into the region, facilitating travel from Durotar. After losing their home on Kezan, the Goblins of the Bilgewater Cartel have made Azshara their home. Their skilled engineers have even reshaped the land into a semblance of the Horde symbol, to demonstrate their new allegiance. These same engineers built a Rocketway system that spans the region, making it easier for the Goblins and their Horde allies to travel throughout the area. Bilgewater Harbor, an impressive Goblin city, sits in the center of the bay. The Alliance, no longer content to share this region, is launching almost constant attacks against their foes, though this altercation isn't the only danger in the area. The Naga still have a strong presence, as do the Legash Demons. The northeast is ruled by dragonkin, hostile to any who trespass. To the west, the Trade Prince built the Gallywix Pleasure Palace, proving that even in the wilds of Azshara you can still find the finer things in life.

REPUTATION INFORMATION Bilgewater Cartel

Questing in Azshara

Warchief's Command: Azshara! sends you to Labor Captain Grabbit at the Orgrimmar Rear Gate, who sends you on your initial quests in the zone.

RESOURCE LEGEND

NODE FISHING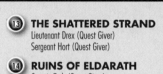

Freshwater	Ocean
Raw Sagefish	Oily Blackmouth
	Firefin Snapper

OPEN WATER FISHING

Freshwater	Ocean
Raw Brilliant Smallfish	Raw Slitherskin Mackerel
Raw Longjaw Mud Snapper	Oily Blackmouth
Raw Bristle Whisker Catfish	Raw Rainbow Fin Albacore

MINING

Metal	Min Skill Level
Copper Vein	1
Tin Vein	65
Silver Vein	75

HERBALISM

Herb	Min Skill Level
Peacebloom	1
Silverleaf	1
Earthroot	15
Mageroyal	50
Briarthorn	70

SKINNING

Creature	Level
Bilgewater Seal	15-16
Cenarion Hippogryph	32
Coralshell Lurker	15-16
Greystone Basilisk	11-12
Mistwing Cliffdweller	12-13
Mistwing Ravager	17-19
Mosshoof Courser	16-17
Sable Drake	19
Sable Drakonid	19
Static-Charged Hippogryph	12-13
Thunderhead Hippogryph	17-18
Thunderhead Stagwing	18-19
Weakened Mosshoof Stag	9-10
Yellowfin Shark	15-16

AZSHARA LEGEND

1. **ORGRIMMAR REAR GATE**
   Ag' tor Bloodfist (Quest Giver)
   Labor Captain Grabbit (Quest Giver)

2. **ORGRIMMAR ROCKETWAY EXCHANGE**
   Beezle Spinspark <Engineering Supplies>
   Custer Clubnik (Quest Giver)
   Foreman Fisk (Quest Giver)
   Horzak Zignibble (Quest Giver)
   Malynea Skyreaver (Quest Giver)
   Private Worcester (Quest Giver)

3. **MOUNTAINFOOT STRIP MINE**
   Headquarters Radio (Quest Giver)
   Weapons Cabinet (Quest Giver)

4. **FORLORN RIDGE**
   Captain Grektar
   Commander Molotov (Quest Giver)
   Glix Grinlock (Quest Giver)
   Xiz "The Eye" Salvoblast (Quest Giver)

5. **SOUTHERN ROCKETWAY TERMINUS**
   Assistant Greely (Quest Giver)
   Bombardier Captain Smooks (Quest Giver)
   Friz Groundspin (Flight Master)
   Geezle Spinspark <Engineering Supplies>
   Hobart Grapplehammer (Quest Giver)
   Jr. Bombardier Hackel
   Torg Twocrush (Quest Giver)

6. **AZSHARA**
   Gormungan

7. **THE SECRET LAB**
   Twistex Happytongs (Quest Giver)

8. **THE SECRET LAB**
   Subject Nine (Quest Giver)

9. **THE SECRET LAB**
   Secret Lab Squawkbox (Quest Giver)

10. **STORM CLIFFS**
    Naga Power Stone (Quest Giver)

11. **BILGEWATER HARBOR**
    Bleenik Fizzlefuse
    Captain Desoto (Quest Giver)
    Captain Krazz
    Commander Molotov (Quest Giver)
    Devon Rackled
    Feena Simplesap <Poisons & Reagents>
    Fleep
    Gurlorn (Quest Giver)
    Heron Tuns
    Kalec (Quest Giver)
    Kroum <Wind Rider Master>
    Mixi <Innkeeper>
    Newt
    Patch
    Private Permudo
    Smoot
    Sorata Firespinner
    Stek Orespazz <Blacksmithing Supplies>
    Stella Boomboom <Stable Master>
    Teemo (Quest Giver)
    Ticker
    Uncle Bedlam
    Volt
    Warlord Krogg
    Wrenchmen Recruitment Poster (Quest Giver)
    Zizo Seasizzle <Fishing Supplies>

12. **THE SHATTERED STRAND**
    Ruckus (Quest Giver)

13. **THE SHATTERED STRAND**
    Lieutenant Drex (Quest Giver)
    Sergeant Hort (Quest Giver)

14. **RUINS OF ELDARATH**
    Captain Tork (Quest Giver)
    Sergeant Zelks (Quest Giver)
    Tora Halotrix (Quest Giver)

15. **RUINS OF ARKKORAN**
    Ergil (Quest Giver)

16. **NORTHERN ROCKETWAY EXCHANGE**
    Andorel Sunsworn (Quest Giver)
    Feezle Spinspark <Engineering Supplies>
    Haggrum Bloodfist (Quest Giver)
    Sorata Firespinner (Quest Giver)

17. **DARNASSIAN BASE CAMP**
    Upper Scrying Stone (Quest Giver)

18. **DARNASSIAN BASE CAMP**
    Lower Scrying Stone (Quest Giver)

19. **RUINS OF NORDRESSA**
    Image of Archmage Xylem (Quest Giver)
    Quarla Whistlebreak (Quest Giver)
    Teresa Spireleaf (Quest Giver)
    Tharkul Ironskull (Quest Giver)
    Will Robotronic (Quest Giver)

20. **ARCANE PINNACLE**
    Image of Archmage Xylem (Quest Giver)
    Lobos
    Phloem
    Raethas Dawnseer
    Zoey Wizzlespark

21. **BEAR'S HEAD**
    Coral Moongale
    Fib Gyrojolt
    Image of Archmage Xylem
    Joanna (Quest Giver)
    Lux
    Morta the Wretch
    Tex Vortacoil <Reagents>

22. **BEAR'S HEAD**
    Anara
    Spirit of Azuregos (Quest Giver)

23. **NORTHERN ROCKETWAY TERMINUS**
    Azuregos (Quest Giver)
    Blitz Blastospazz <Flight Master>
    Feno Blastnoggin (Quest Giver)
    Jellix Fuselighter (Quest Giver)
    Kalec (Quest Giver)
    Meezle Spinspark <Engineering Supplies>

24. **GALLYWIX ROCKET EXCHANGE**
    Leezle Spinspark <Engineering Supplies>

25. **VALORMOK**
    Andorel Sunsworn (Quest Giver)
    Chawg (Quest Giver)
    Jr. Bombardier Hackel (Quest Giver)
    Kroum (Quest Giver)
    Wind Rider Gorsch

26. **TALRENDIS POINT**
    Slinky Sharpshiv (Quest Giver)

27. **TALRENDIS POINT**
    Bombardier Captain Smooks
    Gorek

AZUREMYST ISLE

The wooded grasslands and hills of Azuremyst Isle are the adopted home of the Draenei. The eastern section of the isle is known as Ammen Vale, here young Draenei first set out after recovering from the crash. The remains of their crashed ship, the *Exodar*, serve as their capital city along the western coast of the island and a smaller settlement, Azure Watch, lies near the center. The friendly Stillpine Furbolgs can be found to the north, while the south is populated by less hospitable creatures. Luckily unaffected by the recent cataclysm, Azuremyst Isle is the perfect training ground for inexperienced Draenei.

REPUTATION INFORMATION Exodar

Questing in Azuremyst Isle

Azuremyst Isle is the starting zone for Draenei. Low level Alliance characters from other races who wish to quest in this zone should start at Azure Watch.

RESOURCE LEGEND

NODE FISHING

Freshwater	Ocean
Raw Brilliant Smallfish	Oily Blackmouth

OPEN WATER FISHING

Freshwater	Ocean
Raw Brilliant Smallfish	Raw Slitherskin Mackerel
Raw Longjaw Mud Snapper	Oily Blackmouth
Raw Bristle Whisker Catfish	Raw Rainbow Fin Albacore

MINING

Metal	Min Skill Level
Copper Vein	1

HERBALISM

Herb	Min Skill Level
Peacebloom	1
Silverleaf	1
Earthroot	15

SKINNING

Creature	Level
Death Ravager	10
Greater Timberstrider	7-9
Infected Nightstalker Runt	7-8
Moongraze Buck	7-8
Moongraze Stag	5-6
Nightstalker	8-9
Ravager Ambusher	8-9
Ravager Hatchling	7-8
Ravager Specimen	9-10
Timberstrider	6-8
Timberstrider Fledgling	5-6

AZUREMYST ISLE LEGEND

1 AMMEN VALE
Megelon (Quest Giver)

2 THE CRASH SITE
Proenitus (Quest Giver)
Botanist Taerix (Quest Giver)
Apprentice Vishael (Quest Giver)
Apprentice Tedon
Aurok <Armorsmith>
Jel <Cloth & Leather Merchant>
Aurelon <Paladin Trainer>
Valaatu <Mage Trainer>
Firmanvaar <Shaman Trainer>
Kore <Warrior Trainer>
Keilnei <Hunter Trainer>
Zalduun <Priest Trainer>
Ryosh <General Supplies>
Mura <Weaponsmith>
Technician Zhanaa (Quest Giver)
Vindicator Aldar (Quest Giver)

3 AMMEN VALE
Tolaan (Quest Giver)

4 AZUREMYST ISLE
Aeun (Quest Giver)

5 AMMEN FORD
Diktynna (Quest Giver)

6 AZURE WATCH
Acteon <Hunter Trainer>
Anchorite Fateema <First Aid Trainer>
Artificer Daelo <Engineering Trainer>
Arugoo of the Stillpine
Buruk <Pet Trainer>
Caregiver Chellan <Innkeeper>
Cryptographer Aurren (Quest Giver)
Daedal <Alchemy Trainer>
Dulvi (Quest Giver)
Esbina <Stable Master>
Exarch Menelaous (Quest Giver)
Guvan <Priest Trainer>
Heur <Herbalism Trainer>
Jaeleil
Kioni <Cloth & Leather Merchant>
Nabek <Weapons & Armor Merchant>
Otonambusi <General Goods>
Ruada <Warrior Trainer>
Semid <Mage Trainer>
Technician Dyvuun
Tullas <Paladin Trainer>
Tuluun <Shaman Trainer>
Valn <Profession Trainer>
Zaldaan <Flight Master>
Ziz <Tradesman>

7 AZUREMYST ISLE
Totem of Yor (Quest Giver)

8 AZUREMYST ISLE
Totem of Tikti (Quest Giver)

9 MOONGRAZE WOODS
Totem of Coo (Quest Giver)

10 EMBERGLADE
Temper (Quest Giver)

11 STILLPINE HOLD
Ergh of the Stillpine <Trade Supplies>
Gurf <Skinning Trainer>
High Chief Stillpine (Quest Giver)
Kurz the Revelator (Quest Giver)
Moordo <Leatherworking Trainer>
Parkat Steelfur <General Goods>
Stillpine the Younger (Quest Giver)

12 ODESYUS' LANDING
"Cookie" McWeaksauce <Cooking Trainer & Supplies>
Admiral Odesyus (Quest Giver)
Archaeologist Adamant Ironheart (Quest Giver)
Blacksmith Calypso <Blacksmithing Trainer & Supplies>
Erin Kelly <Tailoring Trainer>
Logan Daniel <General Goods>
Priestess Kyleen Il'dinare (Quest Giver)

13 AZUREMYST ISLE
Engineer "Spark" Overgrind

14 BRISTLELIMB VILLAGE
Totem of Vark (Quest Giver)

15 VALAAR'S BERTH
Huntress Kella Nightbow (Quest Giver)
Shalannius <Druid Trainer>

16 AZUREMYST ISLE
Magwin (Quest Giver)

17 THE VEILED SEA
Cowlen (Quest Giver)

BLOODMYST ISLE

As the crashing Exodar came to rest on nearby Azuremyst Isle, many of its more poisonous components landed on Bloodmyst Isle to the south. Large red crystals dot the landscape, their toxic radiation seeping into the ground and giving everything the blood red tinge that is the source of the island's name. The contamination has not only affected the land and the local plant life, but has also made many of the native creatures more aggressive. The Draenei established a large outpost, Blood Watch, in the eastern part of the isle in order to help repair the damage done by their ship. Outside of this safe haven, the island abounds with danger and young Draenei and their allies do well to be cautious here.

REPUTATION INFORMATION Exodar, Stormwind, Gnomeregan Exiles

WYRMSCAR ISLAND

⑤

THE WARP PISTON

④

AMBERWEB PASS

③

AXXARIEN

②

⑥

BLOOD WATCH

BLOODCURSE ISLE

THE CRYO-CORE

①

THE VECTOR COIL

⑦

WRATHSCALE LAIR

NAZZIVIAN

⑧

BLACKSILT SHORE

KESSEL'S CROSSING

⑨

RESOURCE LEGEND

NODE FISHING

Freshwater	Ocean
Raw Brilliant Smallfish	Oily Blackmouth

OPEN WATER FISHING

Freshwater	Ocean
Raw Brilliant Smallfish	Raw Slitherskin Mackerel
Raw Longjaw Mud Snapper	Oily Blackmouth
Raw Bristle Whisker Catfish	Raw Rainbow Fin Albacore

MINING

Metal	Min Skill Level
Copper Vein	1
Tin Vein	65
Silver Vein	75

HERBALISM

Herb	Min Skill Level
Peacebloom	1
Silverleaf	1
Earthroot	15
Mageroyal	50
Briarthorn	70
Bruiseweed	100

SKINNING

Creature	Level
Bloodmyst Hatchling	10-11
Bloodmyst Ravager	13-14
Brown Bear	9-10
Elder Brown Bear	15-16
Enraged Ravager	16-17
Grizzled Brown Bear	12-13
Saurian Slayer	17-19
Veridian Broodling	17-18
Veridian Whelp	16-17

Questing in Bloodmyst Isle

Players who complete the quests in Azuremyst Isle are sent to Bloodmyst Isle. Other players may start with Hero's Call: Bloodmyst Isle!, which sends you to Vorkhan the Elekk Herder at Kessel's Crossing.

BLOODMYST ISLE LEGEND

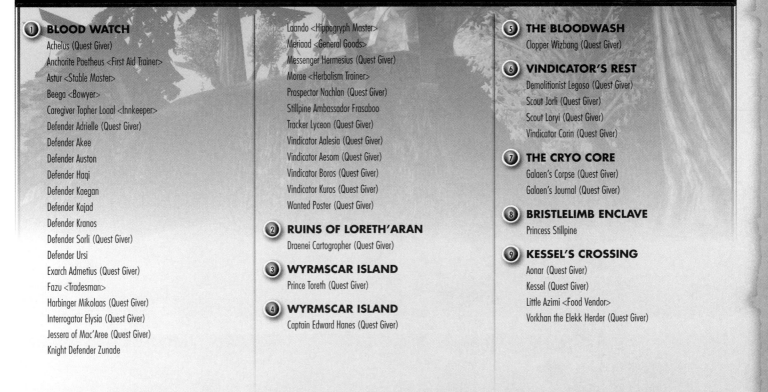

1 BLOOD WATCH
Achelus (Quest Giver)
Anchorite Paetheus <First Aid Trainer>
Astur <Stable Master>
Beega <Bowyer>
Caregiver Topher Loaal <Innkeeper>
Defender Adrielle (Quest Giver)
Defender Akee
Defender Auston
Defender Haqi
Defender Kaegan
Defender Kajad
Defender Kranos
Defender Sorli (Quest Giver)
Defender Ursi
Exarch Admetius (Quest Giver)
Fazu <Tradesman>
Harbinger Mikolaas (Quest Giver)
Interrogator Elysia (Quest Giver)
Jessera of Mac'Aree (Quest Giver)
Knight Defender Zunade

Laando <Hippogryph Master>
Meriaad <General Goods>
Messenger Hermesius (Quest Giver)
Morae <Herbalism Trainer>
Prospector Nachlan (Quest Giver)
Stillpine Ambassador Frasaboo
Tracker Lyceon (Quest Giver)
Vindicator Aalesia (Quest Giver)
Vindicator Aesom (Quest Giver)
Vindicator Boros (Quest Giver)
Vindicator Kuros (Quest Giver)
Wanted Poster (Quest Giver)

2 RUINS OF LORETH'ARAN
Draenei Cartographer (Quest Giver)

3 WYRMSCAR ISLAND
Prince Toreth (Quest Giver)

4 WYRMSCAR ISLAND
Captain Edward Hanes (Quest Giver)

5 THE BLOODWASH
Clopper Wizbang (Quest Giver)

6 VINDICATOR'S REST
Demolitionist Legoso (Quest Giver)
Scout Jorli (Quest Giver)
Scout Loryi (Quest Giver)
Vindicator Corin (Quest Giver)

7 THE CRYO CORE
Galaen's Corpse (Quest Giver)
Galaen's Journal (Quest Giver)

8 BRISTLELIMB ENCLAVE
Princess Stillpine

9 KESSEL'S CROSSING
Aonar (Quest Giver)
Kessel (Quest Giver)
Little Azimi <Food Vendor>
Vorkhan the Elekk Herder (Quest Giver)

DARKSHORE

Once peaceful Darkshore has been hit hard by the recent cataclysm. Where gently rolling wooded hills once lay, jagged and sundered wrecks of land comprise the region. The elements have become unbalanced and a great storm rages in the heart of the region, held in check only by the power of Malfurion Stormrage at its vortex. Much of the wildlife has been destroyed, and those specimens that remain regard any intrusion as hostile. Twilight Cultists have unearthed something from the cracked landscape and work around the clock to free their treasure. Perhaps most chilling is the loss of Auberdine. This Night Elf port has been completely destroyed and the refugees have founded a new settlement, Lor'danel north of the Ruins of Auberdine from which they intend to protect their land.

REPUTATION INFORMATION Darnassus

Questing in Darkshore

While Worgen and Night Elf characters are directed to Darkshore after wrapping up quests in their respective starting zones, Hero's Call: Darkshore! guides any Alliance character to Priestess Dentaria at Lor'danel.

RESOURCE LEGEND

NODE FISHING

Freshwater	Ocean
Raw Sagefish	Oily Blackmouth
	Firefin Snapper

OPEN WATER FISHING

Freshwater	Ocean
Raw Brilliant Smallfish	Raw Slitherskin Mackerel
Raw Longjaw Mud Snapper	Oily Blackmouth
Raw Bristle Whisker Catfish	Raw Rainbow Fin Albacore

MINING

Metal	Min Skill Level
Copper Vein	1
Tin Vein	65
Silver Vein	75

HERBALISM

Herb	Min Skill Level
Peacebloom	1
Silverleaf	1
Earthroot	15
Mageroyal	50
Briarthorn	70
Stranglekelp	85
Bruiseweed	100

SKINNING

Creature	Level	Creature	Level
Captured Rabid Thistle Bear	13-14	Ghost Saber	19-20
Coastal Frenzy	14-16	Grizzled Thistle Bear	17-18
Consumed Thistle Bear	18-19	Hungry Thistle Bear	12-13
Corrupted Thistle Bear	10-11	Moonstalker	12-15
Corrupted Thistle Bear Matriarch	11	Moonstalker Matriarch	18-19
Dangerfish	17-18	Moonstalker Runt	10-11
Darkshore Stag	12-13	Moonstalker Sire	17-18
Darkshore Thresher	12-14	Rabid Thistle Bear	13-14
Deep Sea Threshadon	23-25	Thistle Bear	11-12
Den Mother	18-19	Thistle Cub	9-10
Elder Darkshore Thresher	16-18	Whitetail Stag	17-19
Fiendishfish	16-17	Young Grizzled Thistle Bear	15-16

DARKSHORE LEGEND

1 LOR'DANEL
Ayriala <General Goods>
Caylais Moonfeather <Hippogryph Master>
Cerellean Whiteclaw (Quest Giver)
Ceriale Duskwhisper <Clothier>
Faeyrin Willowmoon <Tailoring Trainer>
Gershala Nightwhisper
Gorbold Steelhand (Gorbold Steelhand)
Grimclaw
Harlon Thornguard <Armorer & Shieldsmith>
Innkeeper Kyteran <Innkeeper>
Jaelysia <Stable Master>
Jenna Lemkenilli <Engineering Trainer>
Johnathan Staats
Nyrisse <Leather Armor>
Periale <Mining Trainer>
Priestess Dentaria (Quest Giver)
Priestess Serendia (Quest Giver)
Ranger Glynda Nal' Shea (Quest Giver)
Sentinel Lendra
Shaldyn
Taryel Firestrike <Blacksmithing Trainer>
Tharnariun Treetender
Volcor (Quest Giver)
Wizbang Cranktoggle (Quest Giver)

2 MIST'S EDGE
Buzz Box 413 (Quest Giver)

3 DARKSHORE
Buzz Box 723 (Quest Giver)

4 CLIFFSPRING FALLS
Tharnariun Treetender (Quest Giver)

5 CLIFFSPRING HOLLOW
Disgusting Workbench (Quest Giver)

6 MIST'S EDGE
Moon Priestess Tharill (Quest Giver)

7 BASHA'ARAN
Arya Autumnlight (Quest Giver)

8 WITHERING THICKET
Grimclaw
Seraphine (Quest Giver)
Keeper Karithus (Quest Giver)

9 WRECKAGE OF THE SILVER DAWNING
Gary
Foolhardy Adventurer

10 RUINS OF MATHYSTRA
Balthule Shadowstrike (Quest Giver)
Lieutenant Morra Starbreeze (Quest Giver)
Mathas Wildwood (Quest Giver)
Rembar Bellanne <Provisioner>
Sentinel Tysha Moonblade (Quest Giver)

11 SHATTERSPEAR WAR CAMP
Alanndarian Nightsong (Quest Giver)
Sentinel Aynasha (Quest Giver)

12 AUBERDINE REFUGEE CAMP
Sentinel Selarin (Quest Giver)
Priestess Alinya
Elisa Steelhand <Blacksmithing Supplies>
Corvine Moonrise (Quest Giver)
Kyndri <Baker>
Ullanna <Trade Supplies>

13 RUINS OF AUBERDINE
Yalda (Quest Giver)
Archaeologist Hollee (Quest Giver)

14 THE EYE OF THE VORTEX
Malfurion Stormrage (Quest Giver)
Thessera
Aroom
Selenn
Elder Brownpaw

15 MOONTOUCHED DEN
Aroom (Quest Giver)

16 AMETH'ARAN
Selenn (Quest Giver)

17 BLACKWOOD CAMP
Elder Brownpaw (Quest Giver)

18 EARTHSHATTER CAVERN
Thessera (Quest Giver)

19 GROVE OF THE ANCIENTS
Balren of the Claw (Quest Giver)
Delanea <Flight Master>
Felros (Quest Giver)
Foriel Broadleaf (Quest Giver)
Kathrena Winterwisp (Quest Giver)
Larien (Quest Giver)
Onu (Quest Giver)
Orseus
Syleath Fairglade <General Goods>

20 TWILIGHT VALE
Elder Brolg (Quest Giver)
Gren Tornfur (Quest Giver)

21 THE MASTER'S GLAIVE
Cultist Altar (Quest Giver)

22 REMTRAVEL'S EXCAVATION
Archaeologist Groff (Quest Giver)
Jr. Archaeologist Ferd (Quest Giver)
Prospector Remtravel (Quest Giver)

23 WILDBEND RIVER
Darkscale Assassin (Quest Giver)

24 NAZJ'VEL
Malfurion Stormrage (Quest Giver)
Warlord Wrathspine (Quest Giver)

DARNASSUS

The Night Elf capital Darnassus is built upon the branches of the great tree, Teldrassil. Demonstrating the Night Elves reverence for nature, the city's airy stone structures rise up between massive trees and carefully tended foliage. The beautiful Temple Gardens form the heart of the city, while craftsmen, traders, and trainers of all types are found to the east.

REPUTATION INFORMATION Darnassus

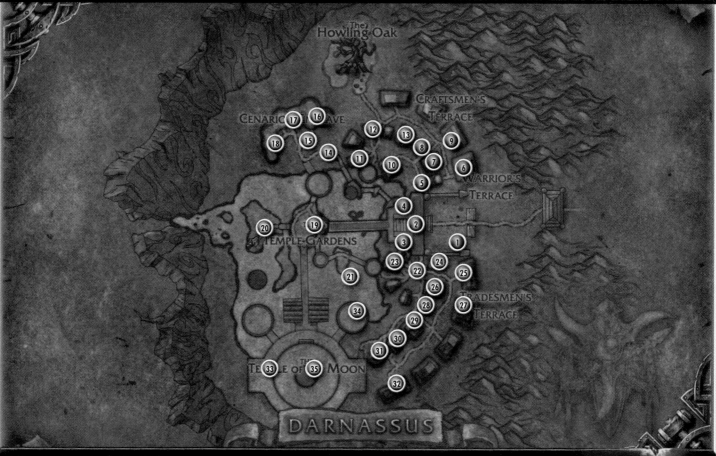

RESOURCE LEGEND

NODE FISHING
None

OPEN WATER FISHING	
Freshwater	Ocean
Raw Brilliant Smallfish	Raw Slitherskin Mackerel
Raw Longjaw Mud Snapper	

DARNASSUS LEGEND

① DARNASSUS
Fyrenna <Food & Drink Vendor>
Mydrannul <General Goods>
Shylenai <Owl Trainer>

② WARRIOR'S TERRACE
Huntress Skymane
Sildanair <Warrior Trainer>
Thyn' tel Bladeweaver

③ WARRIOR'S TERRACE
Ariyell Skyshadow <Weapon Merchant>
Cylania <Night Elf Armorer>
Ilyenia Moonfire <Weapon Master>
Mathiel

④ WARRIOR'S TERRACE
Alliance Brigadier General
Arcanist Dulial
Arias' ta Bladesinger <Warrior Trainer>
Darnath Bladesinger <Warrior Trainer>
Elanaria
Fima Five-Fingers
Landuen Moonclaw
Rissa Shadeleaf

⑤ CRAFTSMAN'S TERRACE
Herald Moonstalker

⑥ CRAFTSMAN'S TERRACE
Ellaercia <Guild Tabard Designer>
Lysheana <Guild Master>
Shalumon <Tabard Vendor>

⑦ TAILORING
Elynna <Tailoring Supplies>
Me' lynn <Tailoring Trainer>
Raedon Duskstriker <Alliance Cloth
Quartermaster>
Trianna

⑦ LEATHERWORKING
Darianna
Eladriel <Skinning Trainer>
Faldron
Lotherias
Saenorion <Leatherworking Supplies>
Telonis <Leatherworking Trainer>

⑧ GENERAL TRADE
Mythrin' dir <Trade Supplies>

⑨ CRAFTSMEN'S TERRACE
Innkeeper Saelienne <Innkeeper>

⑩ ARGENT DAWN
Argent Guard Manados
Dawnwatcher Selgorm
Dawnwatcher Shaedlass

⑩ ALCHEMY
Ainethil <Alchemy Trainer>
Milla Fairancora
Sylvanna Forestmoon
Ulthir <Alchemy Supplies>

⑪ COOKING
Alegorn <Cooking Trainer>
Fyldan <Cooking Supplies>

⑫ FIRST AID
Dannelor <First Aid Trainer>

⑬ ENCHANTING
Aladrel Whitespire <Arcane Reforger>
Feyden Darkin <Inscription Trainer>
Illianna Moonscribe <Inscription Supplies>
Lalina Summermoon
Taladan <Enchanting Trainer>
Vaean <Enchanting Supplies>

⑭ DARNASSUS
Dendrythis <Food & Drink Vendor>
Huntress Ravenoak

⑮ DARNASSUS
Jartsam <Riding Trainer>
Lelanai <Saber Handler>

⑯ DARNASSUS
Alassin <Stable Master>
Corand
Dorion <Hunter Trainer>
Jeen' ra Nightrunner <Hunter Trainer>
Jocaste <Hunter Trainer>
Nightshade
Shadow
Silvaria <Pet Trainer>

⑰ DARNASSUS
Cyroen <Reagents>
Denatharion <Druid Trainer>
Fylerian Nightwing <Druid Trainer>
Mathrengyl Bearwalker <Druid Trainer>

⑱ DARNASSUS
Faelyssa
Kyrai <Poison Supplies>

⑱ CENARION ENCLAVE
Anishar <Rogue Trainer>
Erion Shadewhisper <Rogue Trainer>
Syurna <Rogue Trainer>

⑲ DARNASSUS
Garryeth <Banker>
Idriana <Banker>
Lairn <Banker>

⑳ DARNASSUS
Crildor
Leora <Hippogryph Master>
Sarin Starlight
Sister Starlight

㉑ TRADESMEN'S TERRACE
Astaia <Fishing Trainer>
Talaelar <Fish Vendor>
Voloren <Fishing Supplies>

㉒ TRADESMEN'S TERRACE
Huntress Leafrunner
Jaeana <Meat Vendor>

㉓ TRADESMEN'S TERRACE
Auctioneer Cazarez
Auctioneer Golothas
Auctioneer Silva'las
Auctioneer Tolon

㉔ GENERAL GOODS
Ellandrieth <General Goods>

㉔ BAGS
Yldan <Bag Merchant>

㉕ TRADESMEN'S TERRACE
Jareth Wildwoods

㉖ WEAPONS
Glorandiir <Axe Merchant>
Kieran <Weapon Merchant>
Merelyssa <Blade Merchant>
Mythidan <Mace & Staff Merchant>

㉗ TRADESMEN'S TERRACE
Treshala Fallowbrook

㉘ FLETCHER
Landria <Bow Merchant>

㉘ THROWN WEAPONS
Turian <Thrown Weapons Merchant>

㉙ CLOTH ARMOR
Vinasia <Cloth Armor Merchant>

㉙ TWO HANDED WEAPONS
Ealyshia Dewwhisper <Two Handed Weapon
Merchant>

㉚ MAIL ARMOR
Melea <Mail Armor Merchant>

㉚ SHIELDS
Caynrus <Shield Merchant>

㉛ LEATHER ARMOR
Cyridan <Leather Armor Merchant>

㉜ STAFF
Andrus <Staff Merchant>

㉜ ROBE
Anadyia <Robe Vendor>

㉝ DARNASSUS
Chief Archaeologist Greywhisker

㉞ THE TEMPLE GARDENS
Chardryn <Herbalism Supplies>
Firodren Mooncaller <Herbalism Trainer>

㉟ THE TEMPLE OF THE MOON
Archmage Mordent Evenshade
Astarii Starseeker <Priest Trainer>
Daros Moonlance
Elissa Dumas <Portal Trainer>
Emissary Valustraa <Mage Trainer>
Gracina Spiritmight
Jandria <Priest Trainer>
Lariia <Priest Trainer>
Malfurion Stormrage
Priestess Alathea <Priest Trainer>
Rukua <Paladin Trainer>
Scholar Arunel <Archaeology Trainer>
Sentinel Cordressa Briarbow
Sentinel Dalia Sunblade
Sentinel Stillbough
Tyrande Whisperwind

DESOLACE

The dry, dusty lands of windswept Desolace have greatly changed since the cataclysm. A surplus of fresh water has replaced the small, fetid pools which were once the only sources of water in the area. At the center of Desolace, once dominated by the sorrow-filled Kodo Graveyard, is the Cenarion Wildlands. This lush paradise is an oasis of abundant plant life in the former rocky desert. While this is a positive change, not everything has improved in the region. The Magram centaur have conquered Kolkar territory and abandoned their former village to the Burning Blade who continue to be a problem thoughout the region. The Mauradine still guard the path to Mauradon, making travel through the Valley of Spears difficult. Both the Horde and Alliance have established new bases in the area and can use all the help they can get to tame the dangers of this land.

REPUTATION INFORMATION Darkspear Trolls, Explorers' League

Questing in Desolace

Even though the target of Warchief's Command: Desolace! is Furien, and the target of Hero's Call: Desolace is Officer Jankie, they're both located at the same place: Tethris Aran. Even if you skip these initial quests, Tethris Aran should be your first stop in Desolace.

RESOURCE LEGEND

NODE FISHING

Freshwater	Ocean
Raw Greater Sagefish	Oily Blackmouth
	Firefin Snapper

OPEN WATER FISHING

Freshwater	Ocean
Raw Bristle Whisker Catfish	Firefin Snapper
Raw Mithril Head Trout	Raw Rockscale Cod
	Oily Blackmouth
	Raw Spotted Yellowtail

MINING

Metal	Min Skill Level
Iron Vein	125
Gold Vein	155

HERBALISM

Herb	Min Skill Level
Wild Steelbloom	115
Kingsblood	125
Liferoot	150
Goldthorn	170
Khadgar's Whisker	185
Gromsblood	250

SKINNING

Creature	Level	Creature	Level
Aged Kodo	31-32	Murderous Bonepaw	32-33
Ancient Kodo	32-33	Rabid Bonepaw	32-33
Bonepaw Hyena	31-32	Raging Kodo	37-39
Burning Blade Nightmare	40	Raging Thunder Lizard	31-32
Captured Stallion	40	Rejuvenated Thunder Lizard	32
Crazed Sandstrider	37-39	Revitalized Basilisk	32
Dying Kodo	32-33	Roving Kodo	36-37
Elder Thunder Lizard	32-33	Sandstrider	30-31
Enraged Kodo	33	Sar'theris Hammerhead	31-32
Gritjaw Basilisk	30-31	Scorpashi Lasher	32-33
Hulking Gritjaw Basilisk	32-33	Scorpashi Snapper	30-31
Ley Hunter	39-40	Scorpashi Venomlash	34-35
Mage Hunter	34-35	Shadowprey Orca	33-34
Magram Bonepaw	37-38	Snapjaw Basilisk	31-32
Mana Eater	37-38	Starving Bonepaw	30-31
Maraudine Bonepaw	33-34		

DESOLACE LEGEND

1 TETHRIS ARAN
Officer Jankie (Quest Giver)

2 NIJEL'S POINT
Baritanas Skyriver <Hippogryph Master>
Captain Pentigast (Quest Giver)
Christi Galvanis <General Goods>
Corporal Melkins (Quest Giver)
Innkeeper Lyshaerya <Innkeeper>
Janet Hommers <Food & Drink>
Keeper Marandis
Kreldig Ungor (Quest Giver)
Maxton Strang <Mail Armor Merchant>
Shelgrayn <Stable Master>
Talendria
Vahlarriel Demonslayer (Quest Giver)

3 ETHEL RETHOR
Karnitol's Chest (Quest Giver)

4 THARGAD'S CAMP
Moira Steelwing <Gryphon Master>
Thargad (Quest Giver)
Dumti (Quest Giver)

1 SARGERON
Cup of Elune (Quest Giver)

2 SARGERON
Elune's Brazier (Quest Giver)

3 SARGERON
Elune's Handmaiden (Quest Giver)

4 DESOLACE
Bizby (Quest Giver)

5 KORMEK'S HUT
Bibbly F'utzbuckle (Quest Giver)
Willow

6 ETHEL RETHOR
Cenarion Researcher Korrah (Quest Giver)
Korra's Hippogryph <Flight Master>

7 SLITHERBLADE SHORE
Valishj (Quest Giver)

8 RANAZJAR ISLE
Lord Hydronis (Quest Giver)

9 KARNUM'S GLADE
Botanist Ferrah (Quest Giver)
Brell Farglenn <Reagents>
Fina Stillgrove <Stable Master>
Garren Darkwind (Quest Giver)
Howah Deeptan <Leatherworking Supplies>
Innkeeper Dessina <Innkeeper>
Karnum Marshweaver (Quest Giver)
Khan Leh' prah (Quest Giver)
Lastrea Greengale <Flight Master>
Stronghoof Gentlebend <Blacksmithng Supplies>
Thressa Amberglen (Quest Giver)

10 THUNK'S ABODE
Cenarion Embassador Thunk (Quest Giver)
Thunk's Wyvern <Flight Master>

11 DESOLACE
Smoldering Stone (Quest Giver)

12 MAGRAM TERRITORY
Khan Kammah (Quest Giver)

13 SCRABBLESCREW'S CAMP
Smeed Scrabblescrew (Quest Giver)

14 KODO GRAVEYARD
Hornizz Brimbuzzle (Quest Giver)

15 BOLGAN'S HOLE
Khan Shodo (Quest Giver)

16 MARAUDON
Broken Relic (Quest Giver)
Kherrah (Quest Giver)

17 VALLEY OF SPEARS
Melizza Brimbuzzle

18 SAR'THERIS STRAND
Selendra

19 SHOK'THOKAR
Khan Leh' prah (Quest Giver)

20 SHOK'THOKAR
Khan Kammah
Khan Leh' prah
Khan Shodo (Quest Giver)

1 TETHRIS ARAN
Furien (Quest Giver)

2 FURIEN'S POST
Cerelia (Quest Giver)
Drumion <Food & Drink>
Narimar <Flight Master>
Sorrem (Quest Giver)

3 DESOLACE
Ancient Tablets

4 GHOST WALKER POST
Felgur Twocuts (Quest Giver)
Gurda Wildmane
Harnor <Food & Drink>
Kireena <Trade Goods>
Maurin Bonesplitter (Quest Giver)
Muuran <Superior Macecrafter>
Narv Hidecrafter <Leatherworking Trainer>
Nataka Longhorn (Quest Giver)
Takata Steelblade

5 SHADOWPREY VILLAGE
Aboda <Stable Master>
Drulzegar Skraghook
Hae' Wilani <Axecrafter>
Innkeeper Sikewa <Innkeeper>
Jinar' Zillen (Quest Giver)
Lah' Mawhani <Trade Supplies>
Mai' Lahii (Quest Giver)
Malux <Skinning Trainer>
Rokaro
Roon Wildmane (Quest Giver)
Taiga Wisemane (Quest Giver)
Tukk <General Goods>
Vark Battlescar
Wulan <Cooking Supplies>

DUROTAR

Home to both the Orcs and Trolls, the rocky land of Durotar has seen many changes since the cataclysm. The Southfury River flooded the central portion of the western side of the region, filling the deep valley there and creating the Southfury Watershed. To the east, Bladefist Bay sports a dock providing transport to the sunken lands of Vashj'ir. The capital city of Orgrimmar has been heavily fortified and the Dranosh'ar Blockade stands before it, providing an extra line of defense. In the south, the Trolls have reclaimed the Echo Isles and young Trolls begin their training there.

REPUTATION INFORMATION Orgrimmar, Darkspear Trolls

Questing in Durotar

Durotar is the home of the starting zones for both the Trolls (Echo Isles) and Orcs (Valley of Trials). Other Horde characters who wish to quest in Durotar should begin at Razor Hill.

RESOURCE LEGEND

NODE FISHING
None

OPEN WATER FISHING

Freshwater	Ocean
Raw Brilliant Smallfish	Raw Slitherskin Mackerel
Raw Longjaw Mud Snapper	

MINING

Metal	Min Skill Level
Copper Vein	1

HERBALISM

Herb	Min Skill Level
Peacebloom	1
Silverleaf	1
Earthroot	15

SKINNING

Creature	Level	Creature	Level
Armored Scorpid	7-8	Drowned Thunder Lizard	9-10
Bloodtalon Scythemaw	8-9	Durotar Tiger	7-8
Bloodtalon Taillasher	6-7	Elder Mottled Boar	8-9
Clattering Scorpid	5-6	Felstalker	3-4
Corrupted Bloodtalon Scythemaw	10-11	Lightning Hide	10-11
Corrupted Dreadmaw Crocolisk	11-12	Mature Swine	9-11
Corrupted Mottled Boar	10-11	Mottled Boar	1
Corrupted Scorpid	10-11	Scorpid Worker	3
Dire Mottled Boar	6-7	Thunder Lizard	9-10
Dreadmaw Crocolisk	10	Venomtail Scorpid	9
Dreadmaw Toothgnasher	8-9	Wild Mature Swine	9-11

DUROTAR LEGEND

① THE VALLEY OF TRIALS
Acrypha <Mage Trainer>
Canaga Earthcaller
Duokna <General Goods>
Foreman Thazz'ril (Quest Giver)
Frang <Warrior Trainer>
Galgar
Gornek (Quest Giver)
Hraug
Huklah <Cloth & Leather Armor Merchant>
Kaltunk (Quest Giver)
Karranisha <Hunter Trainer>
Kzan Thornslash <Weaponsmith>
Magga
Nartok <Warlock Trainer>
Rarc <Armorer & Shieldcrafter>
Rwag <Rogue Trainer>
Shikrik <Shaman Trainer>
Zlagk <Butcher>
Zureetha Fargaze

② THE VALLEY OF TRIALS
Farmer Krella
Farmer Lok'lub

③ THE VALLEY OF TRIALS
Hana'zua

④ DARKSPEAR ISLE
Jin'thala

⑤ DARKSPEAR TRAINING GROUNDS
Legati <Rogue Trainer>
Nekali <Shaman Trainer>
Nortet <Warrior Trainer>
Ortezza <Hunter Trainer>
Soratha <Mage Trainer>
Tunari <Priest Trainer>
Voldreka <Warlock Trainer>
Zen'Tabra <Druid Trainer>

⑥ DARKSPEAR HOLD
Gora'tin <General Goods>
Hira'jin

Jornun
Morakki
Moraya (Quest Giver)
Sortura <Cloth & Leather Armor Merchant>
Tora'jin (Quest Giver)
Torenda <Food & Drink>
Tortunga (Quest Giver)
Vanira
Vol'jin (Quest Giver)

⑦ DARKSPEAR ISLE
Notera

⑧ BLOODTALON SHORE
Kijara (Quest Giver)
Tegashi (Quest Giver)

⑨ SPITESCALE CAVERN
Morrakki

⑩ SEN'JIN VILLAGE
Bom'bay (Quest Giver)
Hai'zan <Butcher>
Handler Marnlek <Bat Handler>
Kali Remik
K'waii <General Goods>
Lar Prowltusk (Quest Giver)
Lau'Tiki <Fishing Trainer>
Master Gadrin (Quest Giver)
Master Vornal
Miao'zan <Alchemy Trainer>
Mishiki <Herbalism Trainer>
Raider Jhash
Tai'tasi <Trade Supplies>
Trayexir <Weapon Merchant>
Ula'elek
Vel'rin Fang
Xar'Ti <Riding Trainer>
Zansoa <Fishing Supplies>
Zjolnir <Raptor Handler>
Cona <Shaman Trainer>
Den'chulu <Druid Trainer>
Yeniss <Warior Trainer>
Parata <Priest Trainer>

Bomsanchu <Mage Trainer>
Gusini <Warlock Trainer>
Munalti <Rogue Trainer>
Jamai <Hunter Trainer>

⑪ RAZOR HILL
Burok <Flight Master>
Cook Torka
Cutac <Cloth & Leather Armor Merchant>
Dhugru Gorelust <Warlock Trainer>
Dwukk <Blacksmithing Trainer>
Flakk <Trade Supplies>
Gail Nozzywig (Quest Giver)
Gar'Thok (Quest Giver)
Ghrawt <Bowyer>
Grimtak <Butcher>
Harruk <Pet Trainer>
Innkeeper Grosk <Innkeeper>
Jabul <Druid Trainer>
Jark <General Goods>
Kitha
Krunn <Mining Trainer>
Mukdrak <Engineering Trainer>
Ophek
Orgnil Soulscar (Quest Giver)
Rawrk <First Aid Trainer>
Runda <Profession Trainer>
Shoja'my <Stable Master>
Swart <Shaman Trainer>
Tai'jin <Priest Trainer>
Takrin Pathseeker
Takrin Pathseeker (Quest Giver)
Tarshaw Jaggedscar <Warrior Trainer>
Thotar <Hunter Trainer>
Uhgar <Weaponsmith>
Un'Thuwa <Mage Trainer>
Wuark <Armorer & Shieldcrafter>
Yelnagi Blackarm

⑫ DUROTAR
Harroc
Rokar Bladeshadow

⑬ DUROTAR
Injured Razor Hill Grunt (Quest Giver)

⑭ RAZOR HILL
Thonk (Quest Giver)

⑮ RAZORMANE GROUNDS
Raggaran (Quest Giver)

⑯ SOUTHFURY WATERSHED
Zen'Taji (Quest Giver)

⑰ TOR'KREN FARM
Misha Tor'kren (Quest Giver)

⑱ SOUTHFURY WATERSHED
Grandmatron Tekla (Quest Giver)

⑲ DEADEYE SHORE
Gaur Icehorn
Ghislania
Griswold Hanniston
Spiketooth (Quest Giver)

⑳ DUROTAR
Margoz
Vek'nag (Quest Giver)

㉑ BLADEFIST BAY
Commander Thorak (Quest Giver)
Legionnaire Nazgrim

㉒ DUROTAR
Rezlak (Quest Giver)

㉓ THE DRANOSH'AR BLOCKADE
Gor the Enforcer (Quest Giver)
High Overseer Bloodmane
Shin Stonepillar (Quest Giver)

㉔ ROCKTUSK FARM
Krakka

㉕ SHRINE OF THE DORMANT FLAME
Telf Joolam

DUSTWALLOW MARSH

The marshy jungles of Dustwallow Marsh are home to many dangerous creatures waiting to make a meal out of unwary travelers. The Alliance town of Theramore sits at the eastern edge of the region, an island connected only by the well-guarded highway leading out of it. This road now extends west through the entire region, making overland travel to the Southern Barrens much easier. To the northwest sits Brackenwall Village, providing members of the Horde a home base in the marsh. The Goblin run town of Mudsprocket in the south welcomes travelers from both factions. The zone still hosts many familiar dangers, but the Grimtotem have recently become more active, causing problems in both the central and northern areas.

REPUTATION INFORMATION

Questing in Dustwallow Marsh

Horde quests begin at Brackenwall Village. If you have Warchief's Command: Dustwallow Marsh!, look for Krog in the village. Hero's Call: Dustwallow Marsh! for Alliance characters ends with Calia Hastings on Theramore Isle.

RESOURCE LEGEND

NODE FISHING

Freshwater	Ocean
Raw Greater Sagefish	Oily Blackmouth
Waterlogged Wreckage	Firefin Snapper

OPEN WATER FISHING

Freshwater	Ocean
Raw Bristle Whisker Catfish	Firefin Snapper
Raw Mithril Head Trout	Raw Rockscale Cod
	Oily Blackmouth
	Raw Spotted Yellowtail

MINING

Metal	Min Skill Level
Tin Vein	65
Silver Vein	75
Iron Vein	125
Gold Vein	155
Mithril Deposit	175
Truesilver Deposit	205

HERBALISM

Herb	Min Skill Level
Stranglekelp	85
Kingsblood	125
Liferoot	150
Fadeleaf	160
Goldthorn	170
Khadgar's Whisker	185

SKINNING

Creature	Level	Creature	Level
Bloodfen Lashtail	37-38	Grimtotem Spirit Wolf	30
Bloodfen Raptor	36-37	Mottled Drywallow Crocolisk	36-37
Bloodfen Razormaw	38-39	Mudrock Borer	40
Bloodfen Screecher	36-37	Mudrock Burrower	39-40
Bloodfen Scytheclaw	37-38	Mudrock Snapjaw	36-37
Drywallow Crocolisk	35-36	Mudrock Spikeshell	35-36
Drywallow Daggermaw	38-39	Mudrock Tortoise	36-37
Drywallow Snapper	35-36	Murk Thresher	36-37
Drywallow Vicejaw	36-37	Noxious Flayer	35-36
Elder Murk Thresher	37-38	Noxious Reaver	37-38
Firemane Ash Tail	37-38	Noxious Shredder	36-37
Firemane Devourer	38-39	Scorchscale Drake	40-41
Firemane Flamecaller	38-39	Searing Hatchling	39-40
Firemane Scalebane	37-38	Searing Whelp	38-39
Firemane Scout	37-38	Young Murk Thresher	35-36

DUSTWALLOW MARSH LEGEND

1 THERAMORE ISLE
Adjutant Tesoran (Quest Giver)
Alchemist Narett <Alchemy Trainer>
Amie Pierce
Archmage Tervosh
Baldruc <Gryphon Master>
Bartender Lillian <Bartender>
Brant Jasperbloom <Herbalism Trainer>
Brother Karman <Paladin Trainer>
Calia Hastings (Quest Giver)
Captain Andrews
Captain Evencane <Warrior Trainer>
Captain Garran Vimes (Quest Giver)
Captain Thomas
Cassa Crimsonwing
Caz Twosprocket (Quest Giver)
Charity Mipsy <General Goods>
Clerk Lendry
Combat Master Criton
Combat Master Szigeti
Commander Samaul
Craig Nollward <Cook>
Dahne Pierce
Decedra Willham
"Dirty" Michael Crowe (Quest Giver)
Doctor Gustaf VanHowzen (Quest Giver)
Dwane Wertle <Chef>
Gregor MacVince <Horse Breeder>
Guard Byron (Quest Giver)
Guard Edward
Guard Jarad
Guard Kahil
Guard Lana
Guard Lasiter
Guard Narrisha
Guard Tark
Hans Weston <Armorer & Shieldsmith>

Helenia Olden <Trade Supplies>
Horace Alder <Mage Trainer>
Ingo Woolybush
Innkeeper Janene <Innkeeper>
Jensen Farran <Bowyer>
Lady Jaina Proudmoore (Quest Giver)
Lieutenant Aden (Quest Giver)
Lieutenant Khand
Lieutenant Nath
Major Mills
Marie Holdston <Weaponsmith>
Medic Helaina
Medic Tamberlyn
Michael <Stable Master>
Mikal Pierce
Morgan Stern (Quest Giver)
Pained
Piter Verance <Weaponsmith & Armorer>
Privateer Groy
Sara Pierce
Sergeant Amelyn (Quest Giver)
Smiling Jim (Quest Giver)
Spot
Timothy Worthington <Tailoring Trainer>
Torq Ironblast <Gunsmith>
Uma Bartulm <Herbalism & Alchemy Supplies>
Ysuria <Portal Trainer>

2 THERAMORE ISLE
Babs Fizzletorque (Quest Giver)

3 SENTRY POINT
Captain Wymor (Quest Giver)

4 DREADMURK SHORE
Renn McGill (Quest Giver)

5 NORTH POINT TOWER
Captain Darill (Quest Giver)
Sergeant Lukas (Quest Giver)

6 DUSTWALLOW MARSH
Private Hendel

7 DUSTWALLOW MARSH
"Stinky" Ignatz (Quest Giver)

8 LOST POINT
Balos Jacken (Quest Giver)

9 MUDSPROCKET
Thyssiana

1 SHADY REST INN
Black Shield (Quest Giver)
Inspector Tarem
Suspicious Hoofprint (Quest Giver)
Theramore Guard Badge (Quest Giver)

2 SWAMPLIGHT MANOR
"Swamp Eye" Jarl (Quest Giver)
Loose Dirt (Quest Giver)
Mordant Grimsby (Quest Giver)

3 TABETHA'S FARM
Andello Porter
Apprentice Garion (Quest Giver)
Apprentice Morlann (Quest Giver)
Regina Salister <Trade Goods>
Tabetha (Quest Giver)

4 BEEZIL'S WRECK
Moxie Steelgrille (Quest Giver)

5 MUDSPROCKET
Axle <Innkeeper>
Brogg (Quest Giver)
Drazzit Dripvalve (Quest Giver)

Dyslix Silvergrub <Flight Master>
Gizzix Grimegurgle (Quest Giver)
Krixil Slogswitch <Food & Drink>
Razbo Rustgear <Weapon & Armor Merchant>
Wanted Poster (Quest Giver)

6 NAT'S LANDING
Nat Pagle (Quest Giver)

7 DUSTWALLOW MARSH
Paval Reethe

1 DUSTWALLOW MARSH
Mudcrush Durtfeet

2 BRACKENWALL VILLAGE
Alto Stonespire <Reagents & Poisons>
Balandar Brightstar (Quest Giver)
Do' gol (Quest Giver)
Draz' Zilb (Quest Giver)
Ghok' kah <Tailoring Supplies>
Krak <Armorer>
Krog (Quest Giver)
"Little" Logok (Quest Giver)
Nazeer Bloodpike (Quest Giver)
Ogg' marr <Butcher>
Overlord Mok' Morokk (Quest Giver)
Shardi <Wind Rider Master>
Tharg (Quest Giver)
Wanted Poster (Quest Giver)
Zanara <Bowyer>
Zulrg <Weaponsmith>

3 DUSTWALLOW MARSH
Ogron (Quest Giver)

4 MUDSPROCKET
Nyse

FELWOOD

Twisted trees and diseased wildlife populate the dark forests of Felwood. The Cenarion Circle still works to heal the land of the corruption left behind by the Burning Legion. Blood Venom Post, the Horde's main holding in the area, has been overrun by sinister slime. The Goblins built an encampment to the north, while the Deadwood Furbolgs have expanded and fortified their own village. The demons of Jadefire Run have done some work to the surrounding architecture and Felpaw Village has undergone an expansion as well.

REPUTATION INFORMATION   Timbermaw Hold

RESOURCE LEGEND

NODE FISHING
None

OPEN WATER FISHING

Freshwater	Ocean
Raw Mithril Head Trout	
Raw Redgill	
Oily Blackmouth	
Raw Nightfin Snapper	
Raw Sunscale Salmon	
Lightning Eel	

MINING

Metal	Min Skill Level
Gold Vein	155
Mithril Deposit	175
Truesilver Deposit	205

HERBALISM

Herb	Min Skill Level
Purple Lotus	210
Arthas' Tears	220
Sungrass	230
Gromsblood	250
Golden Sansam	260
Dreamfoil	270
Mountain Silversage	280
Sorrowmoss	285

SKINNING

Creature	Level
Angerclaw Bear	44-45
Angerclaw Grizzly	51-52
Angerclaw Mauler	46-47
Corrupt Courser	1
Crazed Stag	1
Felpaw Ravager	51-52
Felpaw Scavenger	46-47
Felpaw Wolf	44-45
Felrot Courser	47-48
Jaedenar Hound	45-46
Jaedenar Hunter	45-46
Jaedenar Mana Leech	1
Jaedenar Stalker	1
Maddened Stag	1
Rabid Screecher	47-48

Questing in Felwood

Speak with Tenell Leafrunner at the Emerald Sanctuary to begin your adventures in Felwood. He is the target of both the Warchief's Command: Felwood! and Hero's Call: Felwood quests, as well.

FELWOOD LEGEND

1 TALONBRANCH GLADE
Mishellena <Hippogryph Master>
Kaerbrus <Hunter Trainer>
Shi'alune
Nalesette Wildbringer <Stable Master>
Willard Harrington <Blacksmithing Supplies>
Malygen <General Goods>
Mylini Frostmoon <Weapon Merchant>
Denmother Ulrica (Quest Giver)
Lyros Swiftwind (Quest Giver)
James Trussel <Food & Drink>

2 IRONTREE CAVERN
Alton Redding (Quest Giver)

1 EMERALD SANCTUARY
Gorrim <Emerald Circle Flight Master>
Ivy Leafrunner
Grazle (Quest Giver)
Kelek Skykeeper
Tenell Leafrunner (Quest Giver)
Taronn Redfeather (Quest Giver)

2 FELWOOD
Totem of Ruumbo (Quest Giver)

3 FELWOOD
Maybess Riverbreeze (Quest Giver)

4 RUINS OF CONSTELLAS
Arcanist Delaris (Quest Giver)
Eridan Bluewind (Quest Giver)
Impsy (Quest Giver)

5 WILDHEART POINT
Chyella Hushglade <Hippogryph Master>
Jessir Moonbow (Quest Giver)
Farlus Wildheart (Quest Giver)
Greta Mosshoof (Quest Giver)

6 SHADOW HOLD
Captured Arko'narin (Quest Giver)

7 BLOODVENOM FALLS
Kelnir Leafsong (Quest Giver)
Altsoba Ragetotem (Quest Giver)

8 WHISPERWIND GROVE
Hanah Southsong <Hippogryph Master>
Huntress Selura (Quest Giver)
Isural Forestsworn (Quest Giver)
Hurah <Stable Master>
Innkeeper Wylaria <Innkeeper>
Arch Druid Navarax

9 IRONTREE WOODS
Seedling Protector (Quest Giver)

10 JADEFIRE RUN
Feronas Sindweller (Quest Giver)

11 TIMBERMAW HOLD
Nafien (Quest Giver)
Ferli (Quest Giver)

12 FELPAW VILLAGE
Drizle (Quest Giver)

1 IRONTREE CLEARING
Darla Drilldozer (Quest Giver)
Dirzak Pryocrank <Flight Master>
Deputy Clunky (Quest Giver)
Buzz Chopsaw <Trade Supplies>
Spinz Shredbark <Engineering Supplies>
Muzz Flimspan <General Goods>
Kester Killbomb <Blacksmithing Supplies>

2 IRONTREE CAVERN
Master Control Pump (Quest Giver)

FERALAS

The rich, verdant jungle of Feralas has seen some recent changes. Floodwaters consumed the island outpost Feathermoon Stronghold, forcing the Alliance to rebuild on the coast. New Thalanaar was affected by the flooding in nearby Thousand Needles, and is under constant attack by the opportunistic Grimtotem. West of New Thalanaar, the Woodpaw Gnolls have become bold, attacking Camp Mojache in constant waves. The jungle has become even more dangerous as Corrupted Dryads roam the Lower Wilds. The Gordunni Ogres still hold Dire Maul and the surrounding areas, despite the best efforts of both the Horde and the Alliance. The two factions may need to put their differences aside if either is to survive the dangers in this region.

REPUTATION INFORMATION Thunder Bluff, Orgrimmar, Darnassus, Steamwheedle Cartel

Questing in Feralas

Hero's Call: Feralas! sends Alliance characters to Telaron Windflight at Dreamer's Rest, and that remains your first stop even if you skipped that initial quest. The Horde begins at Camp Ataya, with Warchief's Command: Feralas! ordering you to find Konu Runetotem.

RESOURCE LEGEND

NODE FISHING

Freshwater	Ocean
Raw Greater Sagefish	Oily Blackmouth
	Firefin Snapper
	Waterlogged Wreckage

OPEN WATER FISHING

Freshwater	Ocean
Raw Bristle Whisker Catfish	Firefin Snapper
Raw Mithril Head Trout	Raw Rockscale Cod
	Oily Blackmouth
	Raw Spotted Yellowtail

MINING

Metal	Min Skill Level
Silver Vein	75
Iron Vein	125
Gold Vein	155

HERBALISM

Herb	Min Skill Level
Purple Lotus	210
Arthas' Tears	220
Sungrass	230
Gromsblood	250
Golden Sansam	260
Dreamfoil	270
Mountain Silversage	280
Sorrowmoss	285

SKINNING

Creature	Level
Feathermoon Nightsaber	36
Feral Scar Yeti	37
Frayfeather Hippogryph	37
Frayfeather Patriarch	38
Frayfeather Skystormer	37
Frayfeather Stagwing	37
Groddoc Ape	36-37
Ironfur Bear	36-37
Jademir Echospawn	36
Longtooth Howler	43-44
Longtooth Runner	36
Noxious Whelp	35-35
Rage Scar Yeti	36
Sharphorn Stag	35
Sprite Darter	37
Sprite Dragon	38
Vale Screecher	36-37
Zukk'ash Stinger	38-39
Zukk'ash Tunneler	38-39
Zukk'ash Wasp	38-39
Zukk'ash Worker	38-39

FERALAS LEGEND

1. DREAMER'S REST
Afran <Bowyer>
Andoril <Innkeeper>
Erina Willowborn (Quest Giver)
Selor <Flight Master>
Telaron Windflight (Quest Giver)
Veir <Stable Master>

2. FEATHERMOON STRONGHOLD
Antarius <Stable Master>
Brannock <Fishing Trainer>
Faralorn <General Supplies>
Harklane <Fish Supplies>
Innkeeper Shyria <Innkeeper>
Irela Moonfeather <Hippogryph Master>
Jadenvis Seawatcher <Reagents>
Karonas
Kylanna Windwhisper <Alchemy Trainer>
Logannas <Alchemy Supplies>
Mardrack Greenwell <Food & Drink>
Pratt McGrubben 4.x (Quest Giver)
Quantas Jonesprye
Savanne <Fishing Supplies>
Shandris Feathermoon (Quest Giver)
Vivianna <Trade Supplies>
Xylinnia Starshine <Enchanting Trainer>

3. RUINS OF FEATHERMOON
Tambre (Quest Giver)

4. TOWER OF ESTULAN
Apprentice of Estulan <Enchanting Supplies>
Arcosin
Aryenda <Flight Master>
Estulan (Quest Giver)
Handler Tessina (Quest Giver)
Silvia (Quest Giver)
Vestia Moonspear (Quest Giver)

5. SHADEBOUGH
Adella (Quest Giver)
Cymerdi <Weapon Vendor>
Falfindel Waywarder (Quest Giver)
Handler Jesana (Quest Giver)
Provisioner Tria <General Goods Vendor>
Seyala Nightwisp <Hippogryph Master>

6. NEW THALANAAR
Caryssia Moonhunter (Quest Giver)
Rendow (Quest Giver)

1. THE TWIN COLOSSALS
Gregan Brewspewer

2. THE FORGOTTEN COAST
Zorbin Fandazzle (Quest Giver)

3. FERAL SCAR VALE
Homing Robot OOX-22/FE

4. DARKMIST RUINS
Empty Pedestal (Quest Giver)
Sensiria (Quest Giver)

5. LARISS PAVILION
Azj' Tordin

6. THE EMERALD SUMMIT
Ysondre

1. CAMP ATAYA
Adene Treetotem <Innkeeper>
Cohanae <Leatherworking Supplies>
Konu Runetotem (Quest Giver)
Sora <Stable Master>
Talo Thornhoof (Quest Giver)
Tono <Wind Rider Master>

2. STONEMAUL HOLD
Ajaye <Stable Master>
Chonk
Gombana (Quest Giver)
Jangdor Swiftstrider (Quest Giver)
Kerthunk <Blacksmithing Supplies>
Lucretia <Food & Drink>
Mergek <Wind Rider Master>
Orhan Ogreblade (Quest Giver)
Swar'jan (Quest Giver)
Wuu

3. CAMP MOJACHE
Blaise Montgomery
Bronk <Alchemy Supplies>
Cawind Trueaim <Gunsmith & Bowyer>
Chief Spirithorn (Quest Giver)
Hadoken Swiftstrider (Quest Giver)
Hahrana Ironhide <Leatherworking Trainer>
Innkeeper Greul <Innkeeper>
Jannos Lighthoof <Druid Trainer>
Jawn Highmesa (Quest Giver)
Krueg Skullsplitter (Quest Giver)
Kulleg Stonehorn <Skinning Trainer>
Loorana <Food & Drink>
Orik'ando
Ruw <Herbalism Trainer>
Sage Korolusk
Sage Palerunner (Quest Giver)
Sheendra Tallgrass <Trade Supplies>
Shyn <Wind Rider Master>
Shyrka Wolfrunner <Stable Master>
Tarhus <Reagents>
Witch Doctor Uzer'i
Worb Strongstitch <Light Armor Merchant>

4. WOODPAW HILLS
Woodpaw Battle Map (Quest Giver)

5. LARISS PAVILION
Xerash Fireblade

MOONGLADE

The small region of Moonglade is home to the Cenarion Circle. This group of druids and their allies have come together to study and protect nature, regardless of their faction. The single town of Nighthaven serves as a hub of most activity in the region and flight masters are found in the southern part of the zone.

REPUTATION INFORMATION Cenarion Circle

RESOURCE LEGEND

NODE FISHING

Freshwater	Ocean
Raw Greater Sagefish	

MINING

Metal	Min Skill Level
None	

HERBALISM

Herb	Min Skill Level
None	

SKINNING

Creature	Level
None	

OPEN WATER FISHING

Freshwater	Ocean
Raw Mithril Head Trout	
Raw Redgill	
Oily Blackmouth	
Raw Nightfin Snapper	
Raw Sunscale Salmon	
Lightning Eel	

Questing in Moonglade

There are many errands—including a handful of quests originating in other zones—that send you to visit the Druids of Moonglade; however, Moonglade is not a questing zone. Unless you're a Druid, your trips to Moonglade are often brief.

MOONGLADE LEGEND

(1) MOONGLADE
Sindrayl <Hippogryph Master>

(1) STORMRAGE BARROW DENS
Clintar Dreamwalker
Dreamwarden Lurosa

(2) SHRINE OF REMULOS
Keeper Remulos
Tajarri

(3) MOONGLADE
Great Bear Spirit

(4) NIGHTHAVEN
Daeolyn Summerleaf <General Goods>
My' lanna <Food & Drink Merchant>
Umber

(5) NIGHTHAVEN
Bessany Plainswind
Zen' Balai <Druid Trainer>

(6) NIGHTHAVEN
Dargon <Food & Drink Merchant>
Lorelae Wintersong <Trade Supplies>

(7) NIGHTHAVEN
Aronus
Bunthen Plainswind <Thunder Bluff Flight Master>
Emissary Windsong (Quest Giver)
Malvor <Herbalism Trainer>
Silva Fil' naveth <Darnassus Flight Master>

(8) NIGHTHAVEN
Loganaar <Druid Trainer>
Meliri <Weaponsmith>
Moren Riverbend
Narianna <Bowyer>
Rabine Saturna

(9) NIGHTHAVEN
Darnall <Tailoring Supplies>
Geenia Sunshadow <Speciality Dress Maker>
Mylentha Riverbend

(10) NIGHTHAVEN
Celes Earthborne

(11) NIGHTHAVEN
Dendrite Starblaze
Kharedon <Light Armor Merchant>

(1) MOONGLADE
Faustron <Wind Rider Master>

MOUNT HYJAL

Home to the wounded world tree, Nordrassil, Mount Hyjal has been sealed off from the outside world giving the tree time to heal. With the cataclysm, Nordrassil is in danger once again. Ragnaros and his minions have set up their base of operations in the south at Sulfuron Spire. In addition, The Twilight Hammer has infiltrated the area, moving out from Darkwhisper Gorge to do their own destructive work. The Guardians of Hyjal need help in cleansing the region of these trespassers and care not for political allegiances. Those wishing to help should waste no time in traveling to Nordrassil in the north. The fate of the world rests here.

REPUTATION INFORMATION Guardians of Hyjal

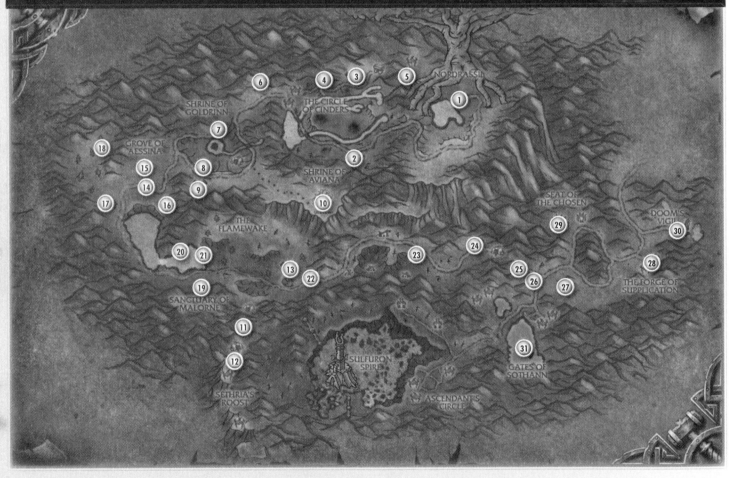

Questing in Mount Hyjal

Horde players begin their trek through Mount Hyjal in Orgrimmar with Warchief's Command: Mount Hyjal! Cenarion Emissary Blackhoof sends you to Moonglade before your trip to Mount Hyjal. The same thing goes for the Alliance and Hero's Call: Mount Hyjal! Look for Cenarion Emissary Jademoon in Stormwind for a quick trip to Moonglade.

RESOURCE LEGEND

NODE FISHING

Freshwater	Ocean
Mountain Trout	
Volatile Water	

OPEN WATER FISHING

Freshwater	Ocean
Sharptooth	
Mountain Trout	
Striped Lurker	
Volatile Water	

MINING

Metal	Min Skill Level
Obsidium Deposit	425

HERBALISM

Herb	Min Skill Level
Azshara's Veil	425
Cinderbloom	425
Stormvine	425

SKINNING

Creature	Level
Ashbearer	80
Charbringer	80
Core Hound	80
Deeprock Incendosaur	80
Emissary of Flame	81
Faerie Dragon	80
Fleeing Stag	80
Hyjal Grizzleclaw	80
Hyjal Stag	80
Sethria's Hatchling	81
Spinescale Basilisk	80-81
Spinescale Matriarch	82
Twilight Dragonkin	81
Twilight Dragonkin Armorer	81
Twilight Juggernaut	81
Young Twilight Drake	82

MOUNT HYJAL LEGEND

(1) NORDRASSIL
Aili Greenwillow <Stable Master>
Anren Shadowseeker (Quest Giver)
Fayran Elthas <Flight Master>
Lenedil Moonwing <General Goods>
Sebelia <Innkeeper>
Tholo Whitehoof (Quest Giver)
Tiala Whitemane
Toron Rockhoof <Blacksmithing Supplies>
Ysera (Quest Giver)

(2) MOUNT HYJAL
Malfurion Stormrage (Quest Giver)
Windspeaker Tamila (Quest Giver)

(3) RUINS OF LAR'DONIR
Alysra (Quest Giver)

(4) TWILIGHT COMMAND POST
Scout Larandia (Quest Giver)

(5) BARROW DENS
Arch Druid Fandral Staghelm
Captain Saynna Stormrunner (Quest Giver)

(6) WOLF'S RUN
Jadi Falaryn (Quest Giver)
Oomla Whitehorn (Quest Giver)

(7) SHRINE OF GOLDRINN
Berin Connad <Blacksmithing Supplies>
Ian Duran
Mirala Fawnsinger <General Goods>
Rio Duran (Quest Giver)
Royce Duskwhisper (Quest Giver)
Spirit of Lo' Gosh (Quest Giver)
Takrik Ragehowl (Quest Giver)
Vision of Ysera (Quest Giver)

(8) GAR'GOL'S HOVEL
Eye of Twilight (Quest Giver)
Kristoff Manheim (Quest Giver)
The Twilight Apocrypha (Quest Giver)
Twilight Cauldron (Quest Giver)

(9) FIRELANDS FORGEWORKS
Jordan Olafson (Quest Giver)
Yargra Blackscar (Quest Giver)

(10) SHRINE OF AVIANA
Aviana (Quest Giver)
Borun Thundersky
Choluna (Quest Giver)
Dinorae Swiftfeather <Flight Master>
Isara Riverstride <Innkeeper>
Jandunel Reedwind <General Goods>
Morthis Whisperwing
Mysterious Winged Spirit (Quest Giver)
Nunaha Grasshoof <Leatherworking Supplies>
Oltarin Graycloud <Stable Master>
Skylord Omnuron (Quest Giver)
Thisalee Crow (Quest Giver)

(11) SETHRIA'S ROOST
Thisalee Crow (Quest Giver)

(12) SETHRIA'S ROOST
Codex of Shadows (Quest Giver)

(13) FIRELANDS HATCHERY
Farden Talonshrike (Quest Giver)
Numa Skyclaw

(14) RIM OF THE WORLD
Laina Nightsky (Quest Giver)

(15) GROVE OF AESSINA
Avrilla
Elizil Wintermoth <Flight Master>
Jalin Lakedeep <Leatherworking Supplies>
Limiah Whitebranch <Stable Master>
Matoclaw (Quest Giver)
Mylune (Quest Giver)
Salirn Moonbear <Innkeeper>
Tomo <General Goods>

(16) BLACKHORN'S PENANCE
Tyrus Blackhorn (Quest Giver)

(17) THE INFERNO
Subjugated Inferno Lord (Quest Giver)

(18) WHISTLING GROVE
Keeper Taldros (Quest Giver)

(19) SANCTUARY OF MALORNE
Arch Druid Hamuul Runetotem (Quest Giver)
Inoho Stronghide <Leatherworking Supplies>
Nenduil Meadowshade <General Goods>
Rayne Feathersong (Quest Giver)
Vision of Ysera (Quest Giver)

(20) ASHEN LAKE
Tortolla (Quest Giver)

(21) THE FLAMEWAKE
Nordu (Quest Giver)

(22) THE REGROWTH
Niden (Quest Giver)
Tortolla (Quest Giver)

(23) THE SCORCHED PLAINS
Captain Irontree (Quest Giver)
Logram (Quest Giver)

(24) THE CRUCIBLE OF FLAME
Garunda Mountainpeak (Quest Giver)

(25) DARKWHISPER PASS
Elementalist Ortell (Quest Giver)
Aeolos

(26) DARKWHISPER GORGE
Twilight Recruiter Maruk

(27) THE TWILIGHT GAUNTLET
Condenna the Pitiless (Quest Giver)
Instructor Cargall (Quest Giver)

(28) THE FORGE OF SUPPLICATION
Edric Downing <Butcher>
Grunka <General Goods>
Instructor Devoran (Quest Giver)
Instructor Mordenn
Instructor Mylva (Quest Giver)
Mahaega Grimforge <Blacksmithing Supplies>
Outhouse Hideout (Quest Giver)

(29) SEAT OF THE CHOSEN
Butcher
Gromm' ko
High Cultist Azennios
Karr' gonn

(30) DOOM'S VIGIL
Commander Jarod Shadowsong (Quest Giver)
Maurice (Quest Giver)

(31) GATES OF SOTHANN
Althera <Flight Master>
Aronus (Quest Giver)
Cenarius (Quest Giver)
Commander Jarod Shadowsong (Quest Giver)
Ildrin Farglad <Leatherworking Supplies>
Motah Tallhorn <General Goods>

MULGORE

At first glance Mulgore seems to be a peaceful land filled with rolling green hills, clear lakes, and towering bluffs. Thunder Bluff, the Tauren capital, rises from the grassy plains to tower over northern Mulgore. In the far south of the region, young braves learn the ways of their chosen class and how to follow the path of the Earthmother as they spend time in Camp Narache. Though the land itself is as vibrant as ever, danger lurks in areas long thought safe. To the east, the Great Gate stands between Mulgore and the war-torn Barrens while enemies that were barely a threat before, like the Bristleback and the Grimtotem, have begun threatening the peaceful way of life the Tauren fought so hard to obtain.

REPUTATION INFORMATION   Thunder Bluff

RESOURCE LEGEND

NODE FISHING

None

OPEN WATER FISHING

Freshwater	Ocean
Raw Brilliant Smallfish	
Raw Longjaw Mud Snapper	

MINING

Metal	Min Skill Level
Copper Vein	1

HERBLISM

Herb	Min Skill Level
Peacebloom	1
Silverleaf	1
Earthroot	15

SKINNING

Creature	Level
Adult Plainstrider	1-10
Armored Battleboar	1-10
Elder Plainstrider	1-10
Flatland Cougar	1-10
Flatland Prowler	1-10
Kodo Bull	1-10
Kodo Calf	1-10
Kodo Matriarch	1-10
Prairie Stalker	1-10
Prairie Wolf	1-10
Prairie Wolf Alpha	1-10
Swoop	1-10
Taloned Swoop	1-10
Wiry Swoop	1-10
Young Battleboar	1-10

Questing in Mulgore

As the starting zone for all Tauren, Mulgore's quest begin in Camp Narache. Other Horde characters who decide to visit the Tauren lands at low levels should begin at Bloodhoof Village.

MULGORE LEGEND

1 CAMP NARACHE

Chief Hawkwind (Quest Giver)
Gart Mistrunner <Druid Trainer>
Lanka Farshot <Hunter Trainer>
Harutt Thunderhorn <Warrior Trainer>
Sunwalker Helaku <Paladin Trainer>
Seer Ravenfeather <Priest Trainer>
Meela Dawnstrider <Shaman Trainer>
Kawnie Softbreeze <General Goods>
Varia Hardhide <Leather Armor Merchant>
Marjak Keenblade <Weaponsmith>
Bronk Steelrage <Armorer & Shieldcrafter>
Moodan Sungrain <Baker>
Brave Running Wolf
Brave Windfeather
Brave Lightning Horn
Brave Proudsnout
Brave Greathoof

2 RED CLOUD MESA

Rohaku Stonehoof (Quest Giver)
Adana Thunderhorn (Quest Giver)

3 OUTSIDE OF CAMP NARACHE

Grull Hawkwind (Quest Giver)

4 FARGAZE MESA

Dyami Windsoar (Quest Giver)

5 BLOODHOOF VILLAGE

Ahmo Thunderhorn (Quest Giver)
Brave Cloudmane
Brave Dawneagle
Brave Ironhorn
Brave Leaping Deer
Brave Rainchaser
Brave Rockhorn
Brave Strongbash
Brave Swiftwind
Brave Wildrunner
Chaw Stronghide <Leatherworking Trainer>
Gennia Runetotem <Druid Trainer>
Harant Ironbrace <Armorcrafter & Shieldcrafter>
Harb Clawhoof <Kodo Mounts>
Harken Windtotem <Quest Giver>
Harn Longcast <Fishing Supplies>
Hulfnar Stonetotem
Innkeeper Kauth <Innkeeper>
Jhawna Oatwind <Baker>
Kar Stormsinger <Riding Trainer>
Kennah Hawkseye <Gunsmith>
Krang Stonehoof <Warrior Trainer>

Kyle the Frenzied
Lalum Darkmane <Profession Trainer>
Magrin Rivermane
Mahnott Roughwound <Weaponsmith>
Maur Raincaller (Quest Giver)
Moorat Longstride <General Goods>
Mull Thunderhorn (Quest Giver)
Narm Skychaser <Shaman Trainer>
Pyall Silentstride <Cooking Trainer>
Reban Freerunner <Pet Trainer>
Ruul Eagletalon <Quest Giver>
Seer Alsoomse <Priest Trainer>
Seikwa <Stable Master>
Sunwalker Iopi <Paladin Trainer>
Tak <Wind Rider Master>
Thontek Rumblehoof
Varg Windwhisper (Quest Giver)
Var'jun
Vira Younghoof <First Aid Trainer>
Vorn Skyseer
Wunna Darkmane <Trade Goods>
Yaw Sharpmane <Hunter Trainer>
Yonn Deepcut <Skinning Trainer>
Zarlman Two-Moons

6 STONEBULL LAKE

Uthan Stillwater <Fishing Trainer>

7 STONEBULL LAKE NEAR BRIDGE

Ahab Wheathoof <The Old Rancher> (Quest Giver)
Brave Darksky

8 MULGORE

Morin Cloudstalker

9 CAMP SUNGRAZE

Una Wildmane (Quest Giver)
Lorekeeper Raintotem (Quest Giver)
Skorn Whitecloud (Quest Giver)
Eyahn Eagletalon (Quest Giver)

NORTHERN BARRENS

The recent cataclysm ripped the Barrens in two, creating the chasm known as the Great Divide. The Northern Barrens retained much of its familiar flora and fauna and return visitors see many familiar sights. Still firmly under Horde control, the Crossroads sits at the heart of the region with Nozzlepot's Outpost and the Mor'shan Rampart providing travel points in the north. The Wailing Caverns to the southwest are still an important stop for fledgling adventurers to cut their teeth. The neutral town of Ratchet continues to trade with members of both the Horde and the Alliance, while the Southsea Pirates hold onto Fray Island to the southeast.

REPUTATION INFORMATION Orgrimmar, Ratchet

Questing in Northern Barrens

There are only Horde quests in Northern Barrens, and they begin with Kargal Battlescar at Far Watch Post. Finishing quests at Razor Hill in Durotar and Warchief's Command: Northern Barrens! both send you to him.

RESOURCE LEGEND

NODE FISHING

Freshwater	Ocean
Deviate Fish	Oily Blackmouth
Raw Sagefish	Firefin Snapper

OPEN WATER FISHING

Freshwater	Ocean
Raw Brilliant Smallfish	Raw Slitherskin Mackerel
Raw Longjaw Mud Snapper	Oily Blackmouth
Raw Bristle Whisker Catfish	Raw Rainbow Fin Albacore

MINING

Metal	Min Skill Level
Copper Vein	1
Tin Vein	65
Silver Vein	75
Iron Vein	125

HERBALISM

Herb	Min Skill Level
Peacebloom	1
Silverleaf	1
Earthroot	15
Mageroyal	50
Briarthorn	70
Bruiseweed	100
Kingsblood	125

SKINNING

Creature	Level	Creature	Level
Barrens Giraffe	15-16	Savannah Patriarch	15-16
Barrens Kodo	19-20	Savannah Prowler	14-15
Grazing Zhevra	11-12	Silithid Protector	18-19
Hecklefang Hyena	15-16	Sunscale Consort	16
Hecklefang Snarler	18-19	Sunscale Lashtail	11-13
Kolkar Packhound	13	Sunscale Raptor	11-12
Lost Barrens Kodo	14-15	Sunscale Ravager	15
Muck Frenzy	14-15	Sunscale Screecher	13-14
Oasis Snapjaw	14-15	Sunscale Scytheclaw	16
Razormane Wolf	11-12	Thunderhawk Hatchling	18-20
Savannah Highmane	12-13	Wandering Barrens Giraffe	18-19
Savannah Huntress	11-12	Zhevra Charger	17-18
Savannah Matriarch	17-18	Zhevra Runner	13

NORTHERN BARRENS LEGEND

1 RATCHET
Acolyte Fenrick
Acolyte Magaz
Acolyte Wytula
Babagaya Shadowcleft <Warlock Trainer>
Bragok <Flight Master>
Captain Thalo' thas Brightsun (Quest Giver)
Chief Engineer Foote
Crane Operator Bigglefuzz
Fuzruckle <Banker>
Gagsprocket <Engineering Supplies>
Gazlowe (Quest Giver)
Gazrog (Quest Giver)
Grazlix <Armorer & Shieldcrafter>
Grimble
Hargash
Innkeeper Wiley <Innkeeper>
Ironzar <Weaponsmith>
Jazzik <General Supplies>
Kilxx <Fisherman>
Liv Rizzlefix
Matero Zeshuwal
Mebok Mizzyrix (Quest Giver)
Menara Voidrender
Mupsi Shacklefridd
Nagulon
Ranik <Trade Supplies>
Reggifuz <Stable Master>
Sashya
Strahad Farsan
Tinkerwiz <Engineering Trainer>
Vazario Linkgrease <Goblin Engineering Trainer>
Vexspindle <Cloth & Leather Armor Merchant>
WANTED (Quest Giver)
Wharfmaster Dizzywig (Quest Giver)
Wrenix the Wretched
Zikkel <Banker>
Zizzek <Fishing Supplies>

2 THE TIDUS STAIR
Islen Waterseer
Mahren Skyseer

3 THE MERCHANT COAST
Baron Longshore (Quest Giver)
Charlie

4 SOUTHFURY RIVER
Horton Hornblower

1 FAR WATCH POST
Ak' Zeloth
Halga Bloodeye (Quest Giver)
Kargal Battlescar (Quest Giver)
Martang <Cloth & Leather Armor Merchant>

2 NORTHERN BARRENS
Dorak (Quest Giver)

3 NORTHERN BARRENS
Uzzek
Lokarbo <Butcher>

4 GROL'DOM FARM
Carthok <Stable Master>
Durnok <Leather Armor Merchant>
Innkeeper Kerntis <Innkeeper>
Karu
Kranal Fiss (Quest Giver)
Mankrik (Quest Giver)
Rocco Whipshank (Quest Giver)
Togrik (Quest Giver)
Una Wolfclaw (Quest Giver)

5 THORN HILL
Grol'Dom Kodo (Quest Giver)

6 THE CROSSROADS
Apothecary Helbrim (Quest Giver)
Barg <General Supplies>
Devrak <Wind Rider Master>
Grenthar
Halija Whitestrider <Clothier>
Hraq <Blacksmithing Supplies>
Hula' mahi <Reagents, Herbs & Poison Supplies>
Innkeeper Boorand Plainswind <Innkeeper>
Jahan Hawkwing <Leather & Mail Armor Merchant>
Kalyimah Stormcloud <Bags & Sacks>
Kil' hala <Tailoring Trainer>

Korran
Larhka <Beverage Merchant>
Moorane Hearthgrain <Baker>
Nargal Deatheye <Weaponsmith>
Serga Darkthorn (Quest Giver)
Sikwa <Stable Master>
Tari' qa <Trade Supplies>
Thork (Quest Giver)
Tonga Runetotem (Quest Giver)
Traugh <Blacksmithing Trainer>
Uthrok <Bowyer & Gunsmith>
Wrahk <Tailoring Supplies>
Zargh <Butcher>

7 THE FORGOTTEN POOLS
Ta' jari (Quest Giver)
Telar Highstrider (Quest Giver)

8 NORTHERN BARRENS
Jerrik Highmountain (Quest Giver)

9 THE STAGNANT OASIS
Gorgal Angerscar (Quest Giver)
Shoe (Quest Giver)

10 NORTHERN BARRENS
Duhng <Cooking Trainer>
Grub
Gruk
Guard Taruc
Tarban Hearthgrain <Baker>

11 NORTHERN BARRENS
Thun'grim Firegaze

12 RATCHET
Brewmaster Drohn

13 NORTHERN BARRENS
Kala'ma (Quest Giver)

14 FRAY ISLAND
Tony Two-Tusks (Quest Giver)

15 Nozzlepot's Outpost
Brak Blusterpipe (Quest Giver)
Frazzik <Armorer & Shieldcrafter>
Gazrix <Flight Master>
Innkeeper Kritzle <Innkeeper>
Niriap <General Goods>
Nozzlepot
Sputtervalve (Quest Giver)
Vernon Soursprye <Stable Master>

16 NORTHERN BARRENS
Control Console (Quest Giver)

17 NORTHERN BARRENS
Wenikee Boltbucket (Quest Giver)

18 THE SLUDGE FEN
Wizzlecrank's Shredder (Quest Giver)

19 NORTHERN BARRENS
Falla Sagewind

20 NORTHERN BARRENS
Lanti' gah
Regthar Deathgate (Quest Giver)

21 NORTHERN BARRENS
Darsok Swiftdagger (Quest Giver)

22 MOR'SHAN BASE CAMP
Captain Shatterskull
Gargok
Hecht Copperpinch <Smokywood Pastures>
Kelm Hargunth <Warsong Supply Officer>

23 NORTHERN BARRENS
Mogg
Pooka

24 MOR'SHAN RAMPARTS
Brutusk
Dinah Halfmoon (Quest Giver)
Gort Goreflight <Flight Master>
Kadrak (Quest Giver)
Marrok <General Goods>
Ornag <Weapon Merchant>
Truun (Quest Giver)

ORGRIMMAR

Located in northern Durotar, Orgrimmar has long served as the capital of the Horde. The changes wrought by the cataclysm have deeply affected the city. The new Warchief, Garrosh Hellscream, has strengthened the city's defenses which has greatly altered the interior of the city as well. Though many business and services have moved, Orgrimmar still offers everything a visitor needs.

REPUTATION INFORMATION   Orgrimmar

ORGRIMMAR

THE CLEFT OF SHADOW

RAGEFIRE CHASM

RESOURCE LEGEND

NODE FISHING
None

OPEN WATER FISHING	
Freshwater	Ocean
Raw Brilliant Smallfish	Raw Slitherskin Mackerel
Raw Longjaw Mud Snapper	

ORGRIMMAR LEGEND

① THE VALLEY OF STRENGTH
Overlord Runthak

② ORGRIMMAR GENERAL STORE
Shimra <Trade Supplies>
Trak' gen <General Goods>

③ THE BROKEN TUSK
Barkeep Morag
Doyo' da
Gamon
Goma
Grunt Komak
Grunt Mojka
Innkeeper Gryshka <Innkeeper>
Kozish
Sarok
Zazo

④ THE VALLEY OF STRENGTH
Scout Stronghand
Scout Tharr
Warcaller Gorlach

⑤ THE AUCTION HOUSE
Auctioneer Drezmit
Auctioneer Fazdran
Auctioneer Ralinza
Auctioneer Xifa
Grunt Grimful
Grunt Thathung
Grunt Wabang

⑥ BANK OF ORGRIMMAR
Branzlit <Banker>
Grunt Karus
Grunt Koma
Grunt Soran
Kixa <Banker>
Perixa <Banker>
Rilgiz <Banker>

⑦ NAROS' ARMORY
Gonto <Mining Trainer>
Lutah <Mining Supplies>
Naros <Plate Armor Merchant>
Punra <Blacksmithing Supplies>
Rogg <Blacksmithing Trainer>
Sana <Mail Armor Merchant>

⑧ GROMMASH HOLD
Ambassador Dawnsinger
Dark Cleric Cecille <Priest Trainer>
Drok' var <Valorous Quartermaster>
Eitrigg
Garrosh Hellscream
Gotura Fourwinds
Gunra <Heroic Quartermaster>
Master Pyreanor <Paladin Trainer>
Mokvar
Sauranok the Mystic
Tyelis <Priest Trainer>
Zor Lonetree

⑨ THE VALLEY OF STRENGTH
Garyl <Tabard Vendor>
Goram <Guild Vendor>
Urtharo <Weapon Merchant>
Urtrun Clanbringer <Guild Master>
Warchief's Command Board

⑩ THE VALLEY OF STRENGTH
Horthus <Reagents>
Olvia <Meat Vendor>
Shan' ti <Fruit Vendor>

⑪ HALL OF LEGENDS
Advisor Willington
Blood Guard Hini'wana
Brave Stonehide <Accessories Quartermaster>
Chieftain Earthbind
Councilor Arial D'Anastasis
Doris Chiltonius <Armor Quartermaster>
First Sergeant Hola'mahi <Legacy Armor Quartermaster>
Grunt Bek' rah
Grunt Korf
Horde Warbringer
Lady Palanseer <Armor Quartermaster>
Raider Bork <War Mount Quartermaster>
Sergeant Thunderhorn <Weapons Quartermaster>
Stone Guard Zarg <Legacy Weapon Quartermaster>

⑫ GOBLIN SLUMS
Auctioneer Fenk
Bezzil <Stable Master>
Boss Mida
Brother Silverhallow <Priest Trainer>
Bruiser Janx <Warrior Trainer>
Conjurer Mixli <Mage Trainer>
Crablegs
Dankin Farsnipe <Hunter Trainer>
Denk Hordewell <General Goods>
Engineer Niff
Environmental Engineer Linza <Shaman Trainer>
"Jack" Pisarek Slamfix <Engineering Trainer>
Karizi Porkpatty <Cooking Supplies>
Kark Helmbreaker <Blacksmithing Trainer>
Kazit
Kazrali the Witch <Warlock Trainer>
Krenk Choplimb <First Aid Trainer>
Lizna Goldweaver <Tailoring Supplies>
Nipnuk
Nivi Weavewell <Tailoring Trainer>
Nuzo <Banker>
Pezik Lockfast <Trade Supplies>
Sanzi <Barmaid>
Tanzi <Barmaid>
Tinza Silvermug <Innkeeper>
Vish the Sneak <Rogue Trainer>
Vizna Bangwrench <Engineering Supplies>
Zarbo Porkpatty <Cooking Trainer>
Zerit <Banker>
Zido Helmbreaker <Blacksmithing Supplies>
Zik Mixmaster <Bartender>

⑬ THE VALLEY OF SPIRITS
Berserker Zanga <Warrior Trainer>
Huntress Kuzari <Hunter Trainer>
Mimbubu

⑭ THE VALLEY OF SPIRITS
Fiznak
Shadow-Walker Zuru <Priest Trainer>
Unjari Feltongue <Warlock Trainer>
Uthel'nay <Mage Trainer>
Zirazi the Star-Gazer <Portal Trainer>

⑮ THE VALLEY OF SPIRITS
Auctioneer Ziji
Batamsi <Food & Drink>
Huju <Trade Supplies>
Jandi <Herbalism Trainer>
Jin'diza <General Goods>
Makavu <Banker>
Night-Stalker Ku'nanji <Rogue Trainer>
Old Umbehto <Fishing Trainer & Supplies>
Scout Manslayer
Sesebi <Druid Trainer>
Sijambi <Innkeeper>
Vehena <Horde Cloth Quartermaster>
Witch Doctor Umbu <Shaman Trainer>
Xan'tish <Snake Vendor>
Xen'to <Cooking Supplies>
Xon'cha <Stable Master>
Zamja <Cooking Trainer>
Zeal'aya <Reagents & Poisons>

⑯ THE VALLEY OF SPIRITS
Keldran

⑰ ORGRIMMAR
Zankaja

⑱ ORGRIMMAR
Bebri Coifcurl <Barber>

⑲ ORGRIMMAR
Doras <Wind Rider Master>
Drakma <Wind Rider Keeper>
Maztha <Flying Trainer>

⑳ ORGRIMMAR
Bort

㉑ THE VALLEY OF WISDOM
Zugra Flamefist

㉒ THE VALLEY OF WISDOM
Farseer Krogar

㉓ THE VALLEY OF WISDOM
Nahu Ragehoof <Warrior Trainer>
Nohi Plainswalker <Hunter Trainer>
Sahi Cloudsinger <Shaman Trainer>
Scout Obrok
Seer Liwatha <Priest Trainer>
Shalla Whiteleaf <Druid Trainer>
Sunwalker Atohmo <Paladin Trainer>

㉔ AUCTION HOUSE
Auctioneer Sowata

ORGRIMMAR LEGEND

(24) THE VALLEY OF WISDOM
Cenarion Emissary Blackhoof
Hiwahi Three-Feathers <Tailoring Trainer>
Kaja <Bow & Rifle Vendor>
Kardris Dreamseeker <Shaman Trainer>
Lonto <Stable Master>
Miwana <Innkeeper>
Opuno Ironhorn <Blacksmithing Trainer>
Rento <Skinning Trainer>
Sagorne Creststrider <Shaman Trainer>
Searn Firewarder
Sian'tsu <Shaman Trainer>
Tatepi <Banker>

(24) GENERAL GOODS & TRADE SUPPLIES
Isashi <Trade Supplies>
Owato <General Goods>

(25) BORSTAN'S FIREPIT
Arugi <Cooking Trainer>
Borstan <Meat Vendor>
Marogg
Suja <Cooking Supplies>

(26) THE MIGHTY PEN
Moraka <Inscription Supplies>
Nerog <Inscription Trainer>
Sarlek
Tamaro
Zilzibin Drumlore

(27) THE ARBORETUM
Brunda <Herbalism Supplies>
Muraga <Herbalism Trainer>

(28) GODAN'S RUNEWORKS
Enchanter Farendin <Thaumaturge>
Godan <Enchanting Trainer>
Jhag
Kithas <Enchanting Supplies>

(29) YELMAK'S ALCHEMY AND POTIONS
Jes' rimon
Kor' geld <Alchemy Supplies>
Whuut
Yelmak <Alchemy Trainer>

(30) THE DRAG
Asoran <General Goods>
Magenius <Reagents>

(31) DROFFERS AND SON SALVAGE
Dran Droffers
Malton Droffers

(32) NOGG'S MACHINE SHOP
Nogg
Rilli Greasygob
Roxxik <Engineering Trainer>
Sovik <Engineering Supplies>
Thund

(33) ORGRIMMAR ORPHANAGE
Orphan Matron Battlewail
Tosamina

(34) GOTRI'S TRAVELING GEAR
Gotri <Bag Vendor>

(35) MAGAR'S CLOTH GOODS
Borya <Tailoring Supplies>
Magar <Tailoring Trainer>
Ollanus <Cloth Armor Merchant>
Rashona Straglash <Horde Cloth Quartermaster>
Snang
Tor'phan <Cloth & Leather Armor Merchant>

(36) KODOHIDE LEATHERWORKERS
Handor <Cloth & Leather Armor Merchant>
Kamari
Karolek <Leatherworking Trainer>
Morgum <Leather Armor Merchant>
Tamar <Leatherworking Supplies>
Thuwd <Skinning Trainer>

(37) THE DRAG
Felika <Trade Supplies>

(38) ORGRIMMAR COUNTING HOUSE
Binzella <Banker>
Fibi <Banker>
Pank <Banker>
Vink <Banker>

(39) THE WYVERN'S TAIL
Gravy <Bartender>
Herezegor Flametusk
Innkeeper Nufa <Innkeeper>

(40) THE VALLEY OF HONOR
Belgrom Rockmaul
Blademaster Ronakada <Warrior Trainer>
Frostwolf Ambassador Rokhstrom
Grezz Ragefist <Warrior Trainer>
Horde Warbringer
Karg Skullgore
Magister Savarin
Sawemba
Slahtz <Experience Eliminator>
Sorek <Warrior Trainer>
Zeggon Botsnap

(41) LUMAK'S FISHING
Lumak <Fishing Trainer>
Murky
Razgar
Shankys <Fishing Supplies>
Zas' Tysh

(42) TRADER'S HALL
Auctioneer Drezbit
Auctioneer Kuvi
Auctioneer Vizput
Auctioneer Zilbeena

(43) HUNTER'S HALL
Kildar <Riding Trainer>
Ogunaro Wolfrunner
Ormak Grimshot <Hunter Trainer>
Shim' la
Sian'dur <Hunter Trainer>
Xao'tsu <Pet Trainer>
Xon'cha <Stable Master>

(44) THE VALLEY OF HONOR
Greela "The Grunt" Crankchain
War-Hunter Molog

(45) RED CANYON MINING
Gorina <Mining & Jewelcrafting Supplies>
Lugrah <Jewelcrafting Trainer>
Makaru <Mining Trainer>

(46) THE BURNING ANVIL
Aturk the Anvil
Borgosh Corebender <Weaponsmith>
Galthuk <Two-Handed Weapons Merchant>
Kelgruk Bloodaxe <Weaponsmith Trainer>
Koru <Mace & Staves Vendor>
Krathok Moltenfist
Okothos Ironrager <Armorsmith>
Orokk Omosh
Ox
Saru Steelfury <Blacksmithing Trainer>
Shayis Steelfury <Armorsmith Trainer>
Shorna <Weapon Vendor>
Snarl
Sumi <Blacksmithing Supplies>
Tumi <Heavy Armor Merchant>
Ug' thok
Zendo'jian <Weapon Vendor>

(47) THE CLEFT OF SHADOW
Craven Drok

(48) DARKFIRE ENCLAVE
Gan' rul Bloodeye
Gizput
Grol' dar <Warlock Trainer>
Kurgul
Mirket <Warlock Trainer>
Zevrost <Warlock Trainer>

(49) THE CLEFT OF SHADOW
Cazul

(50) SHADOWDEEP REAGENTS
Hagrus <Reagents>

(51) IRONWOOD STAVES AND WANDS
Katis <Wand Merchant>
Muragus <Staff Merchant>

(52) REKKUL'S POISONS
Kor' ghan
Rekkul <Poison Supplies>

(53) SHADOWSWIFT BROTHERHOOD
Gest <Rogue Trainer>
Gordul <Rogue Trainer>
Ormok <Rogue Trainer>

(54) THE SLOW BLADE
Kareth <Blade Merchant>

(55) ARCANE ENCLAVE
Gija <Mage Trainer>
Marud <Mage Trainer>
Rundok <Portal Trainer>
Ureda <Mage Trainer>

(56) DARK EARTH
Kor'jus <Mushroom Vendor>

(57) THE CLEFT OF SHADOW
Neeru Fireblade

SILITHUS

Located in southern Kalimdor, the desert sands of Silithus have been largely untouched by the cataclysm. The Cenarion Hold lies near the center of the region, giving the druids of the Cenarion Circle a good vantage point from which to monitor the incursion of the Twilight Cultists as well as the intimidating silithids that populate their various Hives. Though it may have remained unchanged, the familiar dangers of the desert are more than enough to threaten travelers who stray from the roads.

REPUTATION INFORMATION   Cenarion Circle

THE CRYSTAL VALE

HIVE'ASHI

TWILIGHT POST

TWILIGHT BASE CAMP

HIVE'ZORA

TWILIGHT OUTPOST

STAGHELM POINT

VALOR'S REST

CENARION HOLD

BONES OF GRAKKAROND

SOUTHWIND VILLAGE

UN'GORO CRATER

HIVE'REGAL

TEMPLE OF AHN'QIRAJ

RUINS OF AHN'QIRAJ

Questing in Silithus

The majority of the quests in Silithus come from the Cenarion Circle, and they begin with Windcaller Proudhorn at Cenarion Hold. Both Hero's Call: Silithus! and Warchief's Command: Silithus! order you to speak with him as well.

RESOURCE LEGEND

MINING

Metal	Min Skill Level
Truesilver Deposit	205
Small Thorium Vein	230
Rich Thorium Vein	255

HERBALISM

Herb	Min Skill Level
Sungrass	230
Golden Sansam	260
Dreamfoil	270
Mountain Silversage	280

SKINNING

Creature	Level
Dredge Crusher	54-55
Dredge Striker	54-55
Hive'Ashi Ambusher	54-55
Hive'Ashi Defender	55-56
Hive'Ashi Drone	55-56
Hive'Ashi Sandstalker	55-56
Hive'Ashi Stinger	55-56
Hive'Ashi Swarmer	55-56
Hive'Ashi Worker	55-56
Hive'Regal Ambusher	55-56
Hive'Regal Burrower	55-56
Hive'Regal Hive Lord	55-56
Hive'Regal Slavemaker	55-56
Hive'Regal Spitfire	55-56
Hive'Zora Hive Sister	55-56
Hive'Zora Reaver	55-56
Hive'Zora Tunneler	55-56
Hive'Zora Wasp	55-56
Hive'Zora Waywatcher	55-56
Stonelash Flayer	54-55
Stonelash Pincer	54-55
Stonelash Scorpid	54-55

SILITHIS LEGEND

1 CENARION HOLD
Cloud Skydancer <Hippogryph Master>
Rifleman Torrig (Quest Giver)

2 ALLIANCE ENCAMPMENT
Chief Expeditionary Requisitioner Enkles
Janela Stouthammer
Sergeant Carnes
Arcanist Nozzlespring
Marshal Bluewall

1 VALOR'S REST
Jarund Stoutstrider
Layo Starstrike
Zannok Hidepiercer <Leatherworking Supplies>

2 CENARION HOLD
Aurel Goldleaf
Baristolth of the Burning Sands
Beetix Ficklespragg (Quest Giver)
Bor Wildmane (Quest Giver)
Calandrath <Innkeeper>
Commander Mar'alith (Quest Giver)
Garon Hutchins
Geologist Larksbane (Quest Giver)
Huum Wildmane (Quest Giver)
J.D. Shadesong
Kania <Enchanting Supplies>
Khur Hornstriker <Reagents>
Mishta <Trade Supplies>
Noggle Ficklespragg
Squire Leoren Mal'derath <Stable Master>
Vargus <Blacksmith>
Vish Kozus
Wanted Poster: Deathclasp (Quest Giver)
Windcaller Kaldon
Windcaller Proudhorn (Quest Giver)

3 BRONZEBEARD ENCAMPMENT
Frankal Stonebridge (Quest Giver)
Glibb
Rutgar Glyphshaper (Quest Giver)

4 ORTELL'S HIDEOUT
Hermit Ortell (Quest Giver)

5 STAGHELM POINT
Ralo'shan the Eternal Watcher

6 THE SCARAB DIAS
Jonathan the Revelator

1 CENARION HOLD
Runk Windtamer <Wind Rider Master>
Scout Bloodfist (Quest Giver)

2 HORDE ENCAMPMENT
Apothecary Quinard
General Kirika (Quest Giver)
Krug Skullsplit
Merok Longstride
Shadow Priestess Shai

SOUTHERN BARRENS

The Southern Barrens are covered by sparse dry grasses and few trees. The exception to this is the new Overgrowth in the north. This area has become a lush oasis under the watch of the druid, Naralex, though it holds its own dangers. At the far southern edge of the land, the Great Lift has been destroyed, making overland travel to Thousand Needles much more difficult. Unlike its northern counterpart, the Southern Barrens are in a constant state of conflict. Alliance forces have aggressively moved into the territory from the east coast, attempting to create a supply route from Northwatch Hold to their stronghold Theramore. The Alliance-held Northwatch Hold is under constant attack by Horde forces. The two factions strive fiercely with each other in the Battlescar, neither one holding clear dominance. The Tauren, fearing an incursion by the Alliance, have erected the Great Gate to block the way into Mulgore. Camp Taurajo lies in ruins—a burnt husk to remind onlookers of the cost of war.

REPUTATION INFORMATION — Orgrimmar, Thunderbluff, Stormwind

Questing in Southern Barrens

Horde characters who complete the quest in Northern Barrens are sent to Nara Pathfinder at the High Road. Warchief's Command: Southern Barrens! does the same. For Alliance characters, Hero's Call: Southern Barrens! sends you to Commander Walpole at Stonetalon Pass.

RESOURCE LEGEND

NODE FISHING

Freshwater	Ocean
	Oily Blackmouth
	Firefin Snapper

OPEN WATER FISHING

Freshwater	Ocean
Raw Bristle Whisker Catfish	Firefin Snapper
Raw Mithril Head Trout	Raw Rockscale Cod
	Oily Blackmouth
	Raw Spotted Yellowtail

MINING

Metal	Min Skill Level
Iron Vein	125

HERBALISM

Herb	Min Skill Level
Kingsblood	125
Liferoot	150
Goldthorn	170
Khadgar's Whisker	185

SKINNING

Creature	Level	Creature	Level
Deviate Terrortooth	31-32	Silithid Creeper	20-21
Dusthoof Giraffe	29-30	Silithid Harvester	24
Elder Barrens Giraffe	22-23	Silithid Swarmer	31-32
Elder Zhevra	31-32	Stormhide	22-23
Greater Barrens Kodo	24-25	Stormsnout	30-31
Greater Thunderhawk	23-24	Swift Zhevra	20-21
Hecklefang Scavenger	30-31	Terrortooth Runner	29-30
Hecklefang Stalker	22-23	Terrortooth Scytheclaw	30-31
Landquaker Bull	35	Thunderhawk Cloudscraper	20-22
Landquaker Kodo	34-35	Thunderhead	20-21
Plains Pridemane	33	Thunderstomp	24
Plains Prowler	32-33	Wooly Kodo	25-26
Savannah Boar	34	Zhevra Courser	20-21

SOUTHERN BARRENS LEGEND

(1) STONETALON PASS
Commander Walpole (Quest Giver)

(2) STONETALON PASS
Janice Mattingly (Quest Giver)

(3) HONOR'S STAND
Beathan Firebrew <Alcohol Vendor>
Brandon Merriweather <Stable Master>
Commander Singleton
Gary Henton <Weapon Vendor>
John Johnson <Flight Master>
Lieutenant Worley
Logistics Officer Renaldo <Innkeeper>
Nibb Spindlegear (Quest Giver)
Quartermaster Lawson <General Goods>

(4) NORTHWATCH HOLD
Admiral Aubrey (Quest Giver)
Bill Williamson <Flight Master>
Camran <Mail Armor>
Cannoneer Smythe (Quest Giver)
Carey Willis <Stable Master>
Cranston Fizzlespit <Alchemy Supplies>
Horton Gimbleheart (Quest Giver)
Jeffrey Long (Quest Giver)
Killick
Nathan Blaine
Norbin
Quartermaster Rutherford <General Goods>
Thomas Paxton (Quest Giver)
Tolliver Houndstooth (Quest Giver)

(5) THE MERCHANT COAST
Captain Fisher

(6) SOUTHERN BARRENS
Dockmaster Lewis

(7) SOUTHERN BARRENS
Mangled Body

(8) TEEGAN'S EXPEDITION
Corporal Teegan (Quest Giver)
Goucho (Quest Giver)
Hannah Bridgewater (Quest Giver)
Ol' Durty Pete

(9) FORWARD COMMAND
Ambassador Gaines (Quest Giver)
Donnach <Blacksmithing Supplies>
General Hawthorne (Quest Giver)
Karl
Quartermaster Winfred <General Goods>
Sam Trawley (Quest Giver)
Shaina

(10) FORT TRIUMPH
Quartermaster Higgins <General Goods>
Serena Arclight <Engineering Supplies>
Barton Trask
Commander Roberts (Quest Giver)
Roger Sternbach <Trade Goods>
Mizzy Pistonhammer (Quest Giver)
Steve Stevenson <Flight Master>
Logan Talonstrike (Quest Giver)
Werner Eastbrook <Stable Master>
Logistics Officer Salista <Innkeeper>

(11) TWINBRAID'S PATROL
General Twinbraid (Quest Giver)
Hurlston Stonesthrow (Quest Giver)

(12) BAEL MODAN EXCAVATION
Marley Twinbraid (Quest Giver)

(13) BAEL MODAN
Bael' dun Survivor (Quest Giver)
Marley Twinbraid (Quest Giver)
Weezil Slipshadow (Quest Giver)
Wounded Bael' dun Officer (Quest Giver)

(14) FRAZZLECRAZ MOTHERLODE
Big Nasty Plunger (Quest Giver)

(1) OVERGROWN CAMP
Naralex (Quest Giver)
Muyoh (Quest Giver)

(2) THE NIGHTMARE SCAR
Naralex (Quest Giver)

(3) FIRESTONE POINT
Dorn Redearth (Quest Giver)
Larhasha
Mahka (Quest Giver)
Tauna Skychaser (Quest Giver)
Zang' do

(1) THE HIGH ROAD
Nura Pathfinder (Quest Giver)

(2) THE HIGH ROAD
Holgom (Quest Giver)
Tunawa Stillwind (Quest Giver)

(3) HUNTER'S HILL
Innkeeper Hurnahet <Innkeeper>
Kilrok Gorehammer (Quest Giver)
Kurinika Spiritseeker <General Goods>
Munada <Stable Master>
Onatay (Quest Giver)
Ramja Skyspinner <Clothier>
Seereth Stonebreak
Unega <Flight Master>

(4) CAMP UNA'FE
Byula
Gahroot <Butcher>
Kelsuwa
Lane Tallgrass (Quest Giver)
Makaba Flathoof (Quest Giver)
Murhane <Leather Armor>
Tawane (Quest Giver)
Turrana <General Goods>

(5) VENDETTA POINT
Jorn Skyseer (Quest Giver)
Kirge Sternhorn (Quest Giver)
Mahani <Tailoring Trainer>
Sanuye Runetotem <Leather Armor Merchant>
Tatternack Steelforge (Quest Giver)
Warlord Bloodhilt
Winnoa Pineforest (Quest Giver)

(6) DESOLATION HOLD
Calder Gray (Quest Giver)
Crador <Flight Master>
Crawgol (Quest Giver)
Grantor <Stable Master>
Innkeeper Lhakadd <Innkeeper>
Quartermaster Dernhak <General Goods>
Terndak <Weapon Vendor>
Tomusa (Quest Giver)
Warlord Bloodhilt (Quest Giver)
Warlord Gar' dul (Quest Giver)

(7) FIELDS OF BLOOD
Karthog

(8) SOUTHERN BARRENS
Brine

(9) SPEARHEAD
Nato Raintree (Quest Giver)
Gann Stonespire (Quest Giver)

(10) BAEL MODAN
Weezil Slipshadow (Quest Giver)

(11) SOUTHERN BARRENS
Mankrik (Quest Giver)

(12) FIRESTONE POINT
Mankrik

STONETALON MOUNTAINS

The rocky peaks of the Stonetalon Mountains have seen many changes since the cataclysm. What was once mostly wilderness with only a few scattered camps now has an increased Horde and Alliance presence throughout. The Venture Co., once a major player in the region, has consolidated its assets at Cragpool Lake and the Horde has engaged the vicious Grimtotem in battle. Streams of lava now run through the Charred Vale where dragonkin and elementals roam. Perhaps the most stunning change is to Stonetalon Peak itself. A Harbinger has taken up residence at the sacred site and Invading Tendrils rise up from the ground to protect their master.

REPUTATION INFORMATION Thunderbluff

Questing in Stonetalon Mountains

The first stop for Horde players who pick up Warchief's Command: Stonetalon Mountains! is Silverwind Refuge in Ashenvale. Speak with Blood Guard Aldo Rockrain to get started on questing in Stonetalon Mountains. Hero's Call: Stonetalon Mountains! sends Alliance characters to Huntress Jalin at Stardust Spire on the border between Ashenvale and Stonetalon Mountains.

RESOURCE LEGEND

NODE FISHING

Freshwater	Ocean
Raw Greater Sagefish	

OPEN WATER FISHING

Freshwater	Ocean
Raw Longjaw Mud Snapper	Raw Rainbow Fin Albacore
Raw Bristle Whisker Catfish	Firefin Snapper
	Oily Blackmouth

MINING

Metal	Min Skill Level
Copper Vein	1
Tin Vein	65
Silver Vein	75

HERBALISM

Herb	Min Skill Level
Mageroyal	50
Briarthorn	70
Bruiseweed	100
Wild Steelbloom	115

SKINNING

Creature	Level
Antlered Courser	22-23
Black Dragon Whelp	28-29
Black Drake	29-29
Blackened Basilisk	23-24
Chimaera Matriarch	28
Cliff Stormer	29-29
Fey Dragon	24-25
Fledgling Chimaera	25-27
Great Courser	24-25
Pridewing Consort	28-29
Pridewing Skyhunter	23-24
Pridewing Wyvern	28-29
Raging Cliff Stormer	18-19
Scorched Basilisk	27-28
Singed Basilisk	25-26
Stonetalon Ram	27-28
Twilight Runner	23-24
Wily Fey Dragon	26-27
Young Chimaera	23-25
Young Pridewing	19-20

STONETALON MOUNTAINS LEGEND

(1) TRUSHOT POINT
Kalen Trueshot (Quest Giver)

(2) WINDSHEAR MINE
Boog the "Gear Whisperer" (Quest Giver)
Minx (Quest Giver)
Sentinel Heliana (Quest Giver)

(3) WINDSHEAR HOLD
Adrius <Stable Master>
Alice (Quest Giver)
Alithia Fallowmere (Quest Giver)
Allana Swiftglide <Flight Master>
Anderov Ryon
Arcanist Valdurian (Quest Giver)
Big Papa
Lord Fallowmere (Quest Giver)
Neophyte Starcrest (Quest Giver)
Northwatch Captain Kosak (Quest Giver)
Ol' Irongoat <Blacksmith>
Ryan Mills <Trader>

(4) WINDSHEAR CRAG
Huntress Illiona (Quest Giver)

(5) MIRKFALLON POST
Fiora Moonsoar <Flight Master>
Scout Commander Barus (Quest Giver)
Scout Mistress Yvonia (Quest Giver)

(6) THE SLUDGEWERKS
"Goblin" Pump Controller (Quest Giver)

(7) THAL'DARAH OVERLOOK
Donald Dealright <Trader>
Elder Sareth' na (Quest Giver)
Fahlestad <Stable Master>
Master Thal' darah (Quest Giver)
Mirin
Poppy <Engineer>
Sentinel Mistress Geleneth (Quest Giver)
Teloren <Hippogryph Master>
Valos Shadowrest <Innkeeper>

(8) FARWATCHER'S GLEN
Ceyora <Flight Master>
Hierophant Malyk (Quest Giver)
Houndmaster Jonathan (Quest Giver)
Innkeeper Bernice <Innkeeper>
Iolo
Salsbury the "Help" (Quest Giver)
Teldorae <Stable Master>
Vera

(9) NORTHWATCH EXPEDITION BASE CAMP
"Cookie" McWeaksauce (Quest Giver)
Chief Explorer Jansun <Blacksmith>
Explorer Tabby Triloc <Trader>
Force Commander Valen (Quest Giver)
Kaluna Songflight <Flight Master>
Lyanath <Innkeeper>

(10) THE DEEP REACHES
Corporal Wocard (Quest Giver)
Lieutenant Paulson (Quest Giver)
Steeltoe McGee (Quest Giver)

(11) GRIMTOTEM POST
Ton Windbow (Quest Giver)
Grundig Darkcloud (Quest Giver)

(1) CRAGPOOL LAKE
STAY OUT! (Quest Giver)

(1) THE FOLD
Bastia
Kilag Gorefang (Quest Giver)
Saurboz (Quest Giver)
Taluka the Hunter <Food and Drink>
Vernal the Fixer <Engineer>
Ya' mon <Trader>

(2) WINDSHEAR CRAG
Blastgineer Fuzzwhistle (Quest Giver)

(3) KROM'GAR FORTRESS
Barshuk Heavyhammer <Blacksmith>
Chief Blastgineer Bombgutz (Quest Giver)
Clarissa (Quest Giver)
Felonius Stark <Innkeeper>
Gelbin <Stable Master>
Kormal the Swift <Flight Master>
Krom' gar Quartermaster <Quartermaster>
Large Daddy
Mirkin <Trader>
Overlord Krom' gar (Quest Giver)
Spy-Mistress Anara (Quest Giver)

(4) THE DEEP REACHES
Blastgineer Igore (Quest Giver)
Scout Utvoch (Quest Giver)
Sergeant Dontrag (Quest Giver)

(5) MALAKA'JIN
Zillane <Flight Master>
Subjugator Devo (Quest Giver)
Witch Doctor Jin' Zil (Quest Giver)
Xen' Zilla
Ken' zigla
Denni' ka (Quest Giver)

(6) WEBWINDER PATH
Darn Talongrip (Quest Giver)

(7) THE SLUDGEWERKS
Flok <Flight Master>
Jibbly Rakit (Quest Giver)

(8) CLIFFWALKER POST
Garrosh Hellscream
General Grebo (Quest Giver)
High Chieftain Cliffwalker (Quest Giver)
Masha Cliffwalker (Quest Giver)
Orna Skywatcher <Flight Master>
Overlord Krom' gar (Quest Giver)

(9) THAL'DARAH GROVE
Orthus Cliffwalker (Quest Giver)

(10) SUN ROCK RETREAT
Gereck <Stable Master>
Innkeeper Jayka <Innkeeper>
Hgarth <Enchanting Trainer>
Krond <Butcher>
Grawnal <General Goods>
Borand <Bowyer>
Kulwia <Trade Supplies>
Tharm <Wind Rider Master>

TANARIS

While the dusty desert sands of Tanaris still bake under the sun, the region has developed a new coastline. Steamwheedle Port has been swallowed by the sea and the formerly landlocked Gadgetzan is now a port. The sea swell stopped just short of washing into the Caverns of Time, leaving it unaffected. In addition to creating a new coastline, the cataclysm also unblocked the way into neighboring Uldum to the southwest, giving access to this mysterious land.

REPUTATION INFORMATION   Bilgewater Cartel, Gadgetzan, Booty Bay, Ratchet, Everlook, Keepers of Time

Questing in Tanaris

Gadgetzan is the central hub for questing in Tanaris, and it should be your first stop. Both Warchief's Command: Tanaris! and Hero's Call: Tanaris! send you there, but Horde players report to Megs Dreadshredder, while Alliance characters are sent to Kelsey Steelspark.

RESOURCE LEGEND

NODE FISHING

Freshwater	Ocean
	Stonescale Eel
	Firefin Snapper
	Oily Blackmouth
	Floating Wreckage

OPEN WATER FISHING

Freshwater	Ocean
	Stonescale Eel
	Raw Rockscale Cod
	Raw Spotted Yellowtail
	Raw Glossy Mightfish
	Raw Summer Bass
	Firefin Snapper
	Big-Mouth Clam
	Winter Squid

MINING

Metal	Min Skill Level
Mithril Deposit	175

HERBALISM

Herb	Min Skill Level
Firebloom	205
Sungrass	230

SKINNING

Creature	Level	Creature	Level
Basking Cobra	46	Creature	Level
Blisterpaw Hyena	44-45	Hazzali Sandreaver	46-47
Centipaar Sandreaver	47-48	Hazzali Stinger	46-47
Centipaar Stinger	48-49	Hazzali Swarmer	46-47
Centipaar Swarmer	49-50	Hazzali Tunneler	48-49
Centipaar Tunneler	47-48	Hazzali Wasp	47-48
Centipaar Wasp	47-48	Hazzali Worker	46-47
Centipaar Worker	47-48	Noxious Tunneler	49
Dune Rattler	45-46	Rabid Blisterpaw	46-47
Dune Worm	47	Sand Slitherer	47-48
Duneclaw Broodlord	47-48	Scorpid Duneburrower	46-47
Duneclaw Burrower	44-45	Scorpid Dunestalker	46-47
Duneclaw Lasher	44-45	Scorpid Hunter	40-41
Duneclaw Matriarch	45-45	Scorpid Tail Lasher	44-45
Duneclaw Stalker	46-47	Starving Blisterpaw	41-42
Giant Surf Glider	48-50	Steeljaw Snapper	45-46
Glasshide Basilisk	44-45	Sunburst Adder	47-48
Glasshide Gazer	46-47	Surf Glider	47-48
Glasshide Petrifier	48-49	Unearthed Fossil	47-48

TANARIS LEGEND

① GADGETZAN
Bera Stonehammer <Gryphon Master>
Kelsey Steelspark (Quest Giver)

② LOST RIGGER COVE
Kelsey Steelspark (Quest Giver)

③ STEELSPARK STATION
Kelsey Steelspark (Quest Giver)
Rations Officer Flexgear <Food & Drink>

④ SOUTHMOON RUINS
Brod Anvilbeard <General Goods>
Fedli Caskcheer <Food & Drink Vendor>
Flinn (Quest Giver)
Hilda Runesworn
Prospector Gunstan (Quest Giver)
Thurda <Flight Master>

① GADGETZAN
Alchemist Pestlequgg <Alchemy Supplies>
Auctioneer Beardo
Bip Nigstrom
Blizrik Buckshot <Gunsmith>
Buzzek Bracketswing <Engineering Trainer>
Derotain Mudsipper
Dirge Quikcleave <Butcher>
Don Carlos (Quest Giver)
Dr. Dealwell (Quest Giver)
Driz Plunkbow (Quest Giver)
Ecton Brasstumbler <Arena Vendor>

Evee Copperspring <Arena Vendor>
Gimblethorn <Banker>
Grux Sparklesnap <Reagents>
Innkeeper Fizzgrimble <Innkeeper>
Jhordy Lapforge <Engineer>
Katrina Turner
Krinkle Goodsteel <Blacksmithing Supplies>
Laziphus <Stable Master>
Marin Noggenfogger
Max Luna
Mux Manascrambler
Nixx Sprocketspring <Goblin Engineering
Trainer>
Pikkle <Mining Trainer>
Qizzik <Banker>
Quinn
Rumsen Fizzlebrack
Shreev
Sprinkle Noggenfogger <Noggenfogger
Elixir>
Vixton Pinchwhistle <Brutal Arena Vendor>
Vizzklick <Tailoring Supplies>
Wrinkle Goodsteel <Superior Armorer>

② CAVERNS OF TIME
Alexton Chrome <Tavern of Time>
Alurmi <Keepers of Time Quartermaster>
Anachronos
Andormu (Quest Giver)

Bortega <Reagents & Poison Supplies>
Galgrom <Provisioner>
Nozari
Steward of Time (Quest Giver)
Yarley <Armorer>
Zaladormu

③ BOOTLEGGER'S OUTPOST
Carmen Ibanozzle <Innkeeper>
Narain Soothfancy (Quest Giver)
Slick Dropdip <Flight Master>
Zeke Bootscuff (Quest Giver)

④ TANARIS
Homing Robot OOX-17/TN

⑤ BROKEN PILLAR
Marvon Rivetseeker

⑥ SANDSORROW WATCH
Chelsea Rustflutter
Gus Rustflutter (Quest Giver)
Mazoga (Quest Giver)
Snart Razzlegrin <General Goods>
Trenton Lighthammer

⑦ ULDUM
Antediluvean Chest (Quest Giver)

⑧ TANARIS
Lamba Ginwhistle
Lixi Greasenozzle
Porsha Brassbearing

⑨ THISTLESHRUB VALLEY
Adarrah (Quest Giver)
Budd
Kurzel
Mack
Samir
Tanzar
Turgore

① GADGETZAN
Bulkrek Ragefist <Wind Rider Master>
Megs Dreadshredder (Quest Giver)

② LOST RIGGER COVE
Megs Dreadshredder (Quest Giver)

**③ DUNEMAUL
RECRUITMENT CAMP**
Dunemaul "Emissary"
Grohk <General Goods>
Megs Dreadshredder (Quest Giver)

④ DAWNRISE EXPEDITION
Chase Everseek <Trade Goods>
Cordelia Everseek <Food & Drink>
Examiner Andoren Dawnrise (Quest Giver)
Raina Sunglide <Flight Master>
Selia Sunglow
Sherm (Quest Giver)

TELDRASSIL

Teldrassil, home of the Night Elves, lies off the northern coast of Kalimdor. The great tree rises out of the ocean with the lands of this region resting in its boughs. The Night Elf capital, Darnassus, is located on the western side, while the Shadowglen, a training ground for young Night Elves, is to the east. The town of Dolanaar is in the center while Rut'theran Village is off the southern coast of Teldrassil, at the base of the massive tree. While most of Teldrassil felt no effect of the cataclysm, Rut'theran Village suffered flooding, like so many areas. However, ships still dock at the small village and the portal leading directly to Darnassus still functions, making Rut'theran an important travel hub.

REPUTATION INFORMATION   Darnassus

RESOURCE LEGEND

NODE FISHING

None	

OPEN WATER FISHING

Freshwater	Ocean
Raw Brilliant Smallfish	Raw Slitherskin Mackerel
Raw Longjaw Mud Snapper	

MINING

Metal	Min Skill Level
Copper Vein	1

HERBALISM

Herb	Min Skill Level
Peacebloom	1
Silverleaf	1
Earthroot	15
Mageroyal	50

SKINNING

Creature	Level
Elder Nightsaber	8-9
Feral Nightsaber	10-11
Mangy Nightsaber	2
Nightsaber Stalker	7-8
Sentinel Nightsaber	10
Thistle Boar	2-3
Young Thistle Boar	1-2

Questing in Teldrassil

All Night Elf characters begin in Shadowglen, which is part of Teldrassil. Any other Alliance characters who want to experience the Night Elf starting zone should stop at Dolanaar.

TELDRASSIL LEGEND

(1) SHADOWGLEN
Ilthalaine (Quest Giver)
Melithar Staghelm (Quest Giver)
Dirania Silvershine

(2) ALDRASSIL
Alyissia <Warrior Trainer>
Andiss <Armorer & Shieldcrafter>
Ayanna Everstride <Hunter Trainer>
Dellylah <Food & Drink Vendor>
Doranel Amberleaf
Frahun Shadewhisper <Rogue Trainer>
Freja Nightwing <Leather Armor Merchant>
Gilshalan Windwalker
Janna Brightmoon <Clothier>
Keina <Bowyer>
Khardan Proudblade <Weaponsmith>
Lyrai <General Supplies>
Mardant Strongoak <Druid Trainer>
Moriana Dawnlight
Rhyanda <Mage Trainer>
Shanda <Priest Trainer>
Tenaron Stormgrip (Quest Giver)

(3) SHADOWGLEN
Dentaria Silverglade (Quest Giver)
Iverron

(4) SHADOWTHREAD CAVE
Tarindrella (Quest Giver)

(5) SHADOWGLEN
Porthannius (Quest Giver)

(6) TELDRASSIL
Zenn Foulhoof (Quest Giver)

(7) DOLANAAR
Aldia <General Supplies>
Arthridas Bearmantle (Quest Giver)
Brannol Eaglemoon <Clothier>
Byancie <First Aid Trainer>
Citarrre Mapleheart
Corithras Moonrage
Cyndra Kindwhisper <Alchemy Trainer>
Danlyia <Food & Drink Vendor>
Dazalar <Hunter Trainer>
Fidelio <Hippogryph Master>
Innkeeper Keldamyr <Innkeeper>
Iranis Shadebloom <Profession Trainer>
Irriende <Mage Trainer>
Jannok Breezesong <Rogue Trainer>
Jeena Featherbow <Bowyer>
Kal <Druid Trainer>
Keldas <Pet Trainer>
Kyra Windblade <Warrior Trainer>
Laurna Morninglight <Priest Trainer>
Malorne Bladeleaf <Herbalism Trainer>
Melarith
Meri Ironweave <Armorer & Shieldcrafter>
Narret Shadowgrove <Trade Supplies>
Nyoma <Cooking Supplies>

Orenthil Whisperwind
Sentinel Kyra Starsong (Quest Giver)
Sentinel Shaya
Seriadne <Stable Master>
Shalamon <Weaponsmith>
Sinda <Leather Armor Merchant>
Syral Bladeleaf (Quest Giver)
Tallonkai Swiftroot (Quest Giver)
Zarrin <Cook>

(8) STARBREEZE VILLAGE
Gaerolas Talvethren (Quest Giver)

(9) BAN'ETHIL BARROW DEN
Oben Rageclaw (Quest Giver)

(10) TELDRASSIL
Huntress Nhemai
Huntress Yaeliura
Moon Priestess Amara (Quest Giver)

(11) LAKE AL'AMETH
Denalan (Quest Giver)

(12) LAKE AL'AMETH
Strange Fruited Plant (Quest Giver)

(13) WELLSPRING HOVEL
Ardan Softmoon <Leatherworking Supplies>
Denalan (Quest Giver)
Nadyia Maneweaver <Leatherworking Trainer>
Radnaal Maneweaver <Skinning Trainer>
Rellian Greenspyre (Quest Giver)

(14) THE ORACLE GLADE
Strange Fronded Plant (Quest Giver)

(15) THE ORACLE GLADE
Alanna Raveneye <Enchanting Trainer>
Draelan <Enchanting Supplies>
Priestess A'moora (Quest Giver)
Sentinel Arynia Cloudsbreak (Quest Giver)

(16) TELDRASSIL
Corithras Moonrage (Quest Giver)

(17) POOLS OF ARLITHRIEN
Tarindrella (Quest Giver)

(18) RUT'THERAN VILLAGE
Androl Oakhand <Fishing Trainer>
Daryn Lightwind (Quest Giver)
Eralas Ambersky (Quest Giver)
Krennan Aranas
Nessa Shadowsong <Fishing Supplies>
Sentinel Morsel Mistdancer
Vesprystus <Hippogryph Master>

THE EXODAR

Once part of Tempest Keep, the great ship, *Exodar*, was used by the Draenei to escape their enemies. It came crashing down on remote Azuremyst Isle off the western coast of Kalimdor. Now, the ship's wreckage serves as the Draenei capital. Though the sheer size of the ship can seem daunting to first time visitors, all necessary goods and services can be easily located in one of the three wings leading out of the central section, the Seat of the Naaru.

REPUTATION INFORMATION The Exodar

THE EXODAR

The Crystal Hall

Seat of the Naaru

The Vault of Lights

Traders' Tier

RESOURCE LEGEND

NODE FISHING	
None	

OPEN WATER FISHING	
Freshwater	Ocean
Raw Brilliant Smallfish	Raw Slitherskin Mackerel
Raw Longjaw Mud Snapper	Oily Blackmouth
Raw Bristle Whisker Catfish	Raw Rainbow Fin Albacore

THE EXODAR LEGEND

1 **THE EXODAR**
Aalun <Riding Trainer>
Torallius the Pack Handler <Elekk Breeder>

2 **SEAT OF THE NAARU**
Stephanos <Hippogryph Master>

3 **INN**
Arthaid <Stable Master>

4 **INN**
Caregiver Breel <Innkeeper>
Miglik Blotstrom <Arena Battlemaster>

5 **COOKING**
Mumman <Cook>
Phea <Cooking Supplies>

6 **SEAT OF THE NAARU**
Cuzi <Bag Vendor>
Onnis <General Goods>

7 **SEAT OF THE NAARU**
Herald Bran'daan

8 **SEAT OF THE NAARU**
Nurguni <Tradesman>

9 **SEAT OF THE NAARU**
O'ros

10 **JEWELCRAFTING**
Arred <Jewelcrafting Supplies>
Farli <Jewelcrafting Trainer>
Padaar

11 **THE CRYSTAL HALL**
Duumehi
Ereuso
Nus <First Aid Trainer>

12 **THE CRYSTAL HALL**
Seer Skaltesh

13 **THE CRYSTAL HALL**
Chakaa
Drysc
Sayari

14 **THE CRYSTAL HALL**
Sulaa <Shaman Trainer>

15 **THE CRYSTAL HALL**
Dekin <Fishing Supplies>

16 **FISHING**
Erett <Fishing Trainer>

17 **THE CRYSTAL HALL**
Sixx <Moth Keeper>

18 **THE CRYSTAL HALL**
Gurrag <Shaman Trainer>

19 **THE CRYSTAL HALL**
Farseer Nobundo <Shaman Trainer>
Foreman Dunaer
Valon

20 **ENCHANTING**
Egomis <Enchanting Supplies>
Kudrii
Nahogg <Enchanting Trainer>
Sessoh <Inscription Supplies>
Thoth <Inscription Trainer>

21 **BANK**
Jaela <Banker>
Kellag <Banker>
Ossco <Banker>

22 **ANCHORITES' SANCTUM**
Caedmos <Priest Trainer>
Fallat <Priest Trainer>
Izmir <Priest Trainer>

23 **THE VAULTS OF LIGHTS**
Prophet Velen

24 **THE VAULT OF LIGHTS**
Liedel the Just <Battlemaster>

25 **THE VAULT OF LIGHTS**
Alliance Brigadier General
Arcanist Nazalia <Wintergrasp Battle-Mage>

26 **THE VAULT OF LIGHTS**
Hunara <Battlemaster>

27 **ALCHEMY & HERBALISM**
Altaa <Alchemy Supplies>
Cemmorhan <Herbalism Trainer>
Deriz
Lucc <Alchemy Trainer>

28 **VINDICATOR'S SANCTUM**
Baatun <Paladin Trainer>
Jol <Paladin Trainer>
Kavaan <Paladin Trainer>

29 **THE VAULT OF LIGHTS**
Audrid
Curzon
Emony
Tobin
Torias

30 **HALL OF THE MYSTICS**
Bati <Mage Trainer>
Edirah <Mage Trainer>
Harnan <Mage Trainer>
Lunaraa <Portal Trainer>
Musal <Alchemy Supplies & Reagents>
Oss <Wand Vendor>

31 **TRADER'S TIER**
Funaam <Guild Master>
Issca <Tabard Vendor>

32 **TAILORING**
Dugiru <Alliance Chief Quartermaster>
Kayaart
Neii <Tailoring Supplies>
Refik <Tailoring Trainer>

33 **LEATHERWORKING & SKINNING**
Akham <Leatherworking Trainer>
Feruul
Haferet <Leatherworking Supplies>
Remere <Skinning Trainer>

34 **MINING & SMITHING**
Arras <Blacksmithing Supplies>
Edrem
Merran <Mining Supplies>
Miall <Blacksmithing Trainer>
Muaat <Mining Trainer>

35 **ENGINEERING**
Feera <Engineering Supplies>
Ghermas
Ockil <Engineering Trainer>

36 **HUNTERS' SANCTUM**
Avelii <Bowyer>
Deremiis <Hunter Trainer>
Ganaar <Pet Trainer>
Killac <Hunter Trainer>
Muhaa <Gunsmith>
Vord <Hunter Trainer>

37 **TRADER'S TIER**
Ahonan <Warrior Trainer>
Behomat <Warrior Trainer>
Kazi <Warrior Trainer>

38 **RING OF ARMS**
Fingin <Poison Supplies>
Handiir <Weapon Master>

39 **PLATE ARMOR & SHIELDS**
Gotaan <Plate Armor Merchant>
Treall <Shield Merchant>

40 **BLADED WEAPONS**
Ven <Blade Vendor>

41 **BLUNT WEAPONS**
Ellormin <Blunt Weapon Merchant>

42 **TRADER'S TIER**
Gornii <Cloth Armor Merchant>
Mahri <Leather Armor Merchant>

43 **TRADER'S TIER**
Yil <Mail Armor Merchant>

44 **AUCTION HOUSE**
Eoch <Auctioneer>
Fanin <Auctioneer>
Iressa <Auctioneer>

45 **THE EXODAR**
Artificer Andren
Artificer Drenin

46 **REAGENTS**
Bildine <Reagents>

47 **THE CRYSTAL HALL**
Hobahken <Shaman Trainer>

THOUSAND NEEDLES

The region known as Thousand Needles is a deep canyon filled with many towering rock pillars which give the area its name. The recent cataclysm filled the canyon with water, flooding all but the highest peaks and creating a great lake where the Shimmering Flats once were. In the center of the lake floats Fizzle and Pozzik's Speedbarge, open to all. Adventurers wishing to enter Razorfen Downs can now access the dungeon at the northern side of the canyon. Taking advantage of the chaos the flooding caused, the Grimtotem are making a concentrated effort to take over key areas like Freewind Post while the Twilight Hammer controls most of the southern ridge of the canyon.

REPUTATION INFORMATION Bilgewater Cartel

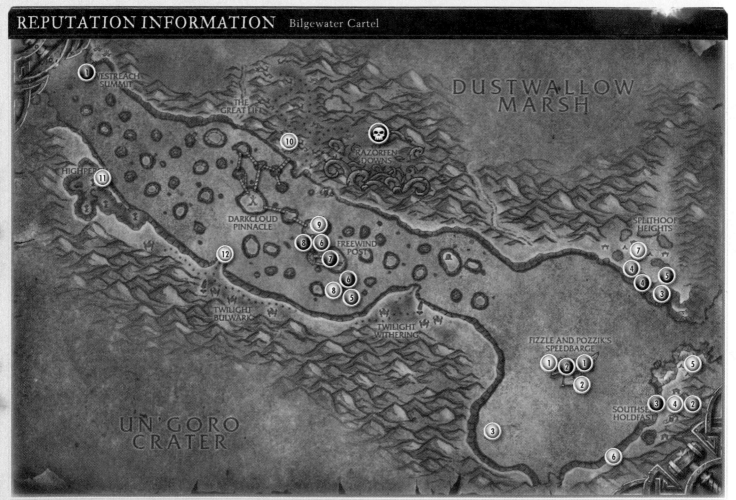

Questing in Thousand Needles

Considering the amount of damage done to Thousand Needles, you may not be surprised that questing in the area actually begins in neighboring zones. Hero's Call: Thousand Needles! sends you to Caryssia Moonhunter at New Thalanaar on the border between Feralas and Thousand Needles, while Warchief's Command: Thousand Needles! results in a trip to Mudsprocket in Dustwallow Marsh to speak with Nyse.

RESOURCE LEGEND

NODE FISHING

Freshwater	Ocean
Raw Greater Sagefish	Stonescale Eel
	Firefin Snapper
	Oily Blackmouth
	Floating Wreckage

OPEN WATER FISHING

Freshwater	Ocean
	Stonescale Eel
	Raw Rockscale Cod
	Raw Spotted Yellowtail
	Raw Glossy Mightfish
	Raw Summer Bass
	Firefin Snapper
	Big-Mouth Clam
	Winter Squid

MINING

Metal	Min Skill Level
Silver Vein	75
Iron Vein	125
Gold Vein	155
Mithril Deposit	175
Truesilver Deposit	205

HERBALISM

Herb	Min Skill Level
Stranglekelp	85
Liferoot	150
Sungrass	230

SKINNING

Creature	Level
Highperch Wind Rider	43-44
Silithid Ravager	40-41
Silithid Wasp	40-41
Silithid Defender	40-41
Barbed Gasgill	42-43
Remora Scrounger	40-41
Needlespine Cobra	40-41
Needlespine Shimmerback	40-41
Scorpid Cliffcrawler	40-41
Siltwash Terrapin	43-44
Stranded Sparkleshell	43-44
Venomous Cloud Serpent	40
Cloud Serpent	40

THOUSAND NEEDLES LEGEND

1 FIZZLE & POZZIK'S SPEEDBARGE
Drag Master Miglen (Quest Giver)
Jinky Twizzlefixxit (Quest Giver)
Mazzer Stripscrew (Quest Giver)
Rizzle Brassbolts (Quest Giver)
Tilly Topspin <Flight Master>

2 SOUTHSEA HOLDFAST
Wizzle Brassbolts (Quest Giver)

3 SPLITHOOF HEIGHTS
Crazzle Sprysprocket (Quest Giver)

4 SPLITHOOF HEIGHTS
Kravel Koalbeard

5 FREEWIND POST
Brienna Starglow (Quest Giver)
Quentin (Quest Giver)

6 DARKCLOUD PINNACLE
Feralas Sentinel (Quest Giver)

1 FIZZLE & POZZIK'S SPEEDBARGE
Daisy <Bartender>

2 RACEWAY RUINS
Submerged Outhouse

3 SUNKEN DIG SITE
Brivelthwerp (Quest Giver)

4 SOUTHSEA HOLDFAST
Spirit of Tony Two-Tusk (Quest Giver)

5 SOUTHSEA HOLDFAST
Ajamon Ghostcaller (Quest Giver)

6 TIRTH'S HAUNT
"Plucky" Johnson

7 SPLITHOOF HEIGHTS
Khan Ablinh (Quest Giver)
Khan Blizh (Quest Giver)
Skycaller Vrakthris (Quest Giver)

8 FREEWIND POST
Starn <Gunsmith & Bowyer>

9 DARKCLOUD PINNACLE
The Rattle of Bones (Quest Giver)

10 DARKCLOUD PINNACLE
Lakota Windsong (Quest Giver)

11 HIGHPERCH
Pao' ka Swiftmountain (Quest Giver)

12 TWILIGHT BULWARK
Lakota Windsong (Quest Giver)

1 WESTREACH SUMMIT
Kanati Greycloud (Quest Giver
Motega Firemane (Quest Giver)
Nah' te <Wind Rider Master>

2 FIZZLE & POZZIK'S SPEEDBARGE
Griznak (Quest Giver)
Pozzik (Quest Giver)
Razzeric (Quest Giver)
Rugfizzle (Quest Giver)
Zamek (Quest Giver)
Zazzix Boomride <Flight Master>

3 SOUTHSEA HOLDFAST
Synge (Quest Giver)

4 SPLITHOOF HEIGHTS
Riznek (Quest Giver)

5 SPLITHOOF HEIGHTS
Trackmaster Zherin

6 FREEWIND POST
Bor' zehn
Nag' zehn
Rau Cliffrunner (Quest Giver)
Thalia Amberhide

7 FREEWIND POST
Montarr (Quest Giver)

8 DARKCLOUD PINNACLE
Freewind Brave

THUNDER BLUFF

The Tauren capital of Thunder Bluff is an impressive sight. Built on top of towering mesas, the city has a large central region containing many profession trainers, shops, and services, as well as three smaller rises, housing class trainers and other important persons, all connected by sturdy bridges swaying high above the plains of Mulgore.

REPUTATION INFORMATION Thunder Bluff

RESOURCE LEGEND

NODE FISHING	
None	

OPEN WATER FISHING	
Freshwater	Ocean
Raw Brilliant Smallfish	
Raw Longjaw Mud Snapper	

THUNDER BLUFF LEGEND

1 THUNDER BLUFF
Tal <Wind Rider Master>

2 HEWA'S ARMORY
Ahanu <leather Armor Merchant>
Elki <Mail Armor Merchant>
Hewa <Cloth Armor Merchant>

3 THUNDER BLUFF BANK
Atepa <Banker>
Bulrug <Stable Master>
Chesmu <Banker>
Torn <Banker>

4 BRIDGE TO HUNTER RISE
Innkeeper Pala <Innkeeper>

5 THUNDER BLUFF WEAPONS
Ansekhwa <Weapon Master>
Jyn Stonehoof <Weapons Merchant>

6 TRADE GOODS AND SUPPLIES
Shadi Mistrunner <Trade Supplies>

7 THUNDER BLUFF
Chepi <Reagents>

8 KURUK'S GOODS
Kuruk <General Goods>
Pakwa <Bag Vendor>

9 THUNDER BLUFF CIVIC INFORMATION
Krumn <Guild Master>
Thrumn <Tabard Vendor>

10 STONEHOOF GEOLOGY
Brek Stonehoof <Mining Trainer>
Kurm Stonehoof <Mining Supplies>

11 BRIDGE TO SPIRIT RISE
Sage Truthseeker

12 THUNDER BLUFF
Auctioneer Gullem
Auctioneer Stampi

13 BREADS AND GRAINS
Fyr Mistrunner <Bread Vendor>

14 KARN'S SMITHY
Karn Stonehoof <Blacksmithing Trainer>
Orm Stonehoof
Taur Stonehoof <Blacksmithing Supplies>
Thrag Stonehoof

15 THUNDER BLUFF
Eyahn Eagletalon
Hunter Sagewind

16 THUNDER BLUFF ARMORERS
Fela <heavy Armor Merchant>
Grod <Leather Armor Merchant>
Mahu <Leatherworking & Tailoring Supplies>
Mak
Mooranta <Skinning Trainer>
Rumstag Proudstrider <Horde Cloth Quartermaster>
Tagain <Cloth Armor Merchant>
Tarn
Tepa <Tailoring Trainer>
Una <Leatherworking Trainer>
Varen Tallstrider
Vhan

17 DAWNSTRIDER ENCHANTERS
Mot Dawnstrider
Nata Dawnstrider <Enchanting Supplies>
Teg Dawnstrider <Enchanting Trainer>

18 BENA'S ALCHEMY
Bena Winterhoof <Alchemy Trainer>
Kray
Mani Winterhoof <Alchemy Supplies>

19 CLOUDWEAVER'S BASKETS
Tand <Basket Weaver>

20 HOLISTIC HERBALISM
Kormin Winterhoof <Herbalism Trainer>
Nida Winterhoof <Herbalism Supplies>

21 FRUITS AND VEGETABLES
Nan Mistrunner

22 THUNDERHORN'S ARCHERY
Kuna Thunderhorn <Bowyer & Fletching Goods>

23 RAINSTICKS
Sunn Ragetotem <Staff Merchant>

24 KODO STEAK AND RIBS
Kaga Mistrunner <Meat Vendor>

25 WINTERHOOF TOTEMS
Tah Winterhoof

26 MOUNTAINTOP BAIT & TACKLE
Kah Mistrunner <Fishing Trainer>
Sewa Mistrunner <Fishing Supplies>

27 THUNDER BLUFF
Baine Bloodhoof

28 THUNDERHOOF'S FIREARMS
Hogor Thunderhoof <Guns Merchant>

29 RAGETOTEM ARMS
Delgo Ragetotem <Axe Merchant>
Etu Ragetotem <Mace & Staff Merchant>
Kard Ragetotem <Sword & Dagger Merchant>
Ohanko <Two Handed Weapon Merchant>

30 THUNDER BLUFF
Sura Wildmane <War Harness Vendor>

31 ASKA'S KITCHEN
Aska Mistrunner <Cooking Trainer>
Naal Mistrunner <Cooking Supplies>

32 THUNDER BLUFF
Zangen Stonehoof

33 THUNDER BLUFF
Hunter Ragetotem

34 THE POOLS OF VISION
Apothecary Zamah
Archmage Shymm <Mage Trainer>
Birgitte Cranston <Portal Trainer>
Clarice Foster
Delano Morisett <Warlock Trainer>
Father Cobb <Priest Trainer>
Jensen Thomasson <Warlock Trainer>
Malakai Cross <Priest Trainer>
Mertle Murkpen <Inscription Supplies>
Miles Welsh <Priest Trainer>
Morairania Horton <Warlock Trainer>
Poshken Hardbinder <Inscription Trainer>
Thurston Xane <Mage Trainer>
Ursyn Ghull <Mage Trainer>

35 SPIRIT RISE
Krendle Bigpockets <Orgrimmar Zeppelin Master>

36 SPIRIT RISE
Pawe Mistrunner

37 HALL OF SPIRITS
Beram Skychaser <Shaman Trainer>
Siln Skychaser <Shaman Trainer>
Tigor Skychaser <Shaman Trainer>
Xanis Flameweaver

38 SPIRITUAL HEALING
Pand Stonebinder <First Aid Trainer>

39 ELDER RISE DRUMS
Sheza Wildmane

40 ELDER RISE
Ghede

41 HALL OF ELDERS
Arch Druid Hamuul Runetotem
Kym Wildmane <Druid Trainer>
Nara Wildmane
Seer Beryl <Priest Trainer>
Seer Kaya <Priest Trainer>
Sheal Runetotem <Druid Trainer>
Tahu Sagewind <Priest Trainer>
Turak Runetotem <Druid Trainer>

42 ELDER RISE
Bashana Runetotem

43 THUNDER BLUFF
Hunter Sagewind

44 HUNTER RISE
Kon Yelloweyes

45 HUNTER RISE
Aponi Brightmane <Paladin Trainer>
Melor Stonehoof
Sunwalker Reha <Paladin Trainer>
Sunwalker Saern <Paladin Trainer>

46 HUNTER'S HALL
Henen Ragetotem
Holt Thunderhorn <Hunter Trainer>
Kary Thunderhorn <Hunter Trainer>
Ker Ragetotem <Warrior Trainer>
Sark Ragetotem <Warrior Trainer>
Torm Ragetotem <Warrior Trainer>
Urek Thunderhorn <Hunter Trainer>

47 HUNTER RISE
Hesuwa Thunderhorn <Pet Trainer>

48 HUNTER RISE
Mosarn

49 HUNTER RISE
Fizim Blastwrench <Arena Battlemaster>
Ruk Warstomper <Battlemaster>

50 HUNTER RISE
Horde Warbringer
Magister Dalhyr <Wintergrasp Battle-Mage>
Mosha Starhorn <Battlemaster>

51 THUNDER BLUFF
Halpa <Prairie Dog Vendor>

ULDUM

Many explorers spent their lives searching in vain for the fabled land of Uldum. Lying hidden from the rest of Azeroth for millennia, this region has only now been rediscovered when the cataclysm damaged the Titan machinery that had kept it hidden for so long. Like its neighbors, Tanaris and Silithus, Uldum is primarily a desert land. A great river flows through its center creating a green fertile band along its banks. It is the homeland of the Tol'vir, an ancient race who once served the great Titans. Some of their descendents, the Neferset, have sided with Deathwing and have a strong presence in their ancient home city in the south. Other descendants of the Tol'vir, the more amiable Ramkahen, work against them. In addition to this rivalry the newly opened land lures those that would come searching for powerful Titan relics, both for study and for more nefarious purposes.

REPUTATION INFORMATION Ramkahen

Questing in Uldum

Your first quest in Uldum begins with either Hero's Call: Uldum! or Warchief's Command: Uldum! but both send you to western Tanaris to help Adarrah and her caravan as it travels into Uldum.

RESOURCE LEGEND

NODE FISHING

Freshwater	Ocean
Blackbelly Mudfish	Fathom Eel
Volatile Water	Volatile Water

OPEN WATER FISHING

Freshwater	Ocean
Sharptooth	Murglesnout
Blackbelly Mudfish	Fathom Eel
Lavascale Catfish	Deepsea Sagefish
Volatile Water	Volatile Water

MINING

Metal	Min Skill Level
Elementium Vein	475
Rich Elementium Vein	500
Pyrite Deposit	525

HERBALISM

Herb	Min Skill Level
Cinderbloom	425
Whiptail	500

SKINNING

Creature	Level
Armadillo	83
Armagedillo	84
Bloodsnarl Hyena	82-83
Deathsting Scorpid	83
Desert Lion	83
Majestic Duneprawler	83
Mangy Hyena	83
Neferset Crocolisk	82-83
Riverbed Crocolisk	82-83
Sand Scorpid	84
Sand Serpent	83
Scalemother Hevna	83
Shaggy Desert Coyote	83
Stillwater Slitherer	82-83
Tiger	85
Venomblood Scorpid	83
Venomscale Scorpid	85
Wild Camel	84
Young Crocolisk	83

ULDUM LEGEND

1. LOST CITY OF THE TOL'VIR
Adarrah
Budd (Quest Giver)
Harkor
Mack
Prince Nadun (Quest Giver)
Samir
Tanzar

2. RAMKAHEN
Adarrah (Quest Giver)
Advisor Kathem
Akhet
Blacksmith Abasi <Ramkahen Quartermaster>
Darwishi <Stable Master>
Gyasi <Reagents>
Harrison Jones (Quest Giver)
Jahi <General Goods>
Kazemde <Innkeeper>
King Phaoris
Kurzel <Flight Master>
Prince Nadun (Quest Giver)
Samir

3. SEAL OF THE SUN KING
Sun Priest Asaris (Quest Giver)
Sun Priest Iset

4. MAR'AT
Asaq
Budd
Chuma <Trade Supplies>
Hanbal <Inks>
Husani <Butcher>
Ishaq <Bags>
Mack (Quest Giver)
Mosegi <Tailoring Supplies>
Samaki <Fishing Supplies>
Tanzar
Umi <Produce>

5. TAHRET GROUNDS
Nomarch Teneth (Quest Giver)

6. KHARTUT'S TOMB
Harrison Jones (Quest Giver)

7. OBELISK OF THE STARS
Elaborate Disc (Quest Giver)
Harrison Jones
Sand Pygmy Corpse (Quest Giver)
Schnottz Scout (Quest Giver)

8. ARSAD TRADE POST
General Ammantep (Quest Giver)
Prince Nadun (Quest Giver)

9. ORSIS
Prophet Hadassi (Quest Giver)

10. ORSIS
Sand-Covered Hieroglyphs (Quest Giver)

11. VIR'NAAL DAM
High Priest Amet (Quest Giver)

12. RAMKAHEN LEGION OUTPOST
High Commander Kamses (Quest Giver)
Salhet (Quest Giver)
Sergeant Mehat (Quest Giver)

13. SUNWATCHER'S RIDGE
Salhet (Quest Giver)

14. AKHENET FIELDS
Vizier Tanotep (Quest Giver)

15. OBELISK OF THE SUN
Harrison Jones (Quest Giver)

16. SCHNOTTZ'S LANDING
Belloc Brightblade (Quest Giver)
Commander Schnottz (Quest Giver)
Evax Oilspark <Flight Master>
Harrison Jones (Quest Giver)
Prolific Writer (Quest Giver)

17. NAHOM
Salhet (Quest Giver)
Sun Prophet Tumet (Quest Giver)

18. SURVEYOR'S OUTPOST
A.I.D.A Terminal (Quest Giver)

19. M.A.C. DRIVER
Fusion Core (Quest Giver)

20. NEFERSET CITY OUTSKIRTS
King Phaoris (Quest Giver)
Salhet (Quest Giver)

21. OASIS OF VIR'SAR
Aaron "Sandy Toes" Williamson <Reagents>
"Chesty" Jake Excavation Supplies & Repairs>
Farah Tamina <Stable Master>
Harrison Jones (Quest Giver)
Jock Lindsey <Flight Master>
Sullah (Quest Giver)
Yasmin <Innkeeper>

22. SULLAH'S SIDESHOW
Sullah (Quest Giver)

23. CHAMBER OF THE MOON
Harrison Jones (Quest Giver)

24. CHAMBER OF THE MOON
Harrison Jones
Sullah (Quest Giver)

25. PILGRIM'S PRECIPICE
Harrison Jones (Quest Giver)

UN'GORO CRATER

The jungle lands of Un'Goro Crater have been undamaged by the cataclysm, though there have been some changes to the region. Marshal's Refuge, the neutral outpost along the northern ridge of the crater, has been overrun by Stone Guardians. The residents have set up camp at Marshal's Stand, south of Fire Plume Ridge. Northwest of the ridge is the Mossy Pile, a smaller camp also open to everyone. Because of its remote location, the crater is teeming with all types of primitive wildlife.

REPUTATION INFORMATION   Cenarion Cirlce

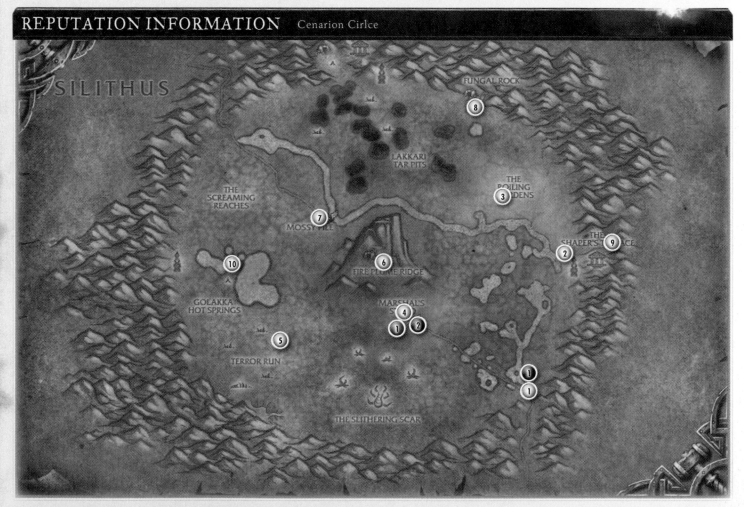

Questing in Un'Goro Crater

Make Williden Marshal at Marshal's Stand your first stop in Un'Goro Crater. Both Hero's Call: Un'Goro Crater! and Warcchief's Command: Un'Goro Crater! send you to him there.

RESOURCE LEGEND

NODE FISHING

Freshwater	Ocean
Raw Greater Sagefish	

OPEN WATER FISHING

Freshwater	Ocean
Lightning Eel	
Raw Redgill	
Raw Whitescale Salmon	
Plated Armorfish	
Raw Nightfin Snapper	
Raw Sunscale Salmon	

MINING

Metal	Min Skill Level
Gold Vein	155
Mithril Deposit	175
Truesilver Deposit	205
Dark Iron Vein	230
Small Thorium Vein	230
Rich Thorium Vein	255

HERBALISM

Herb	Min Skill Level
Stranglekelp	85
Liferoot	150
Sungrass	230

SKINNING

Creature	Level	Creature	Level
Devilsaur	54-55	Plated Stegodon	52-54
Diemetradon	51-52	Pterrordax	50-52
Elder Diemetradon	54-55	Ravasaur	48-49
Fledgling Pterrordax	48-50	Ravasaur Hunter	49-50
Frenzied Pterrordax	52-54	Ravasaur Runner	49-50
Gorishi Hive Guard	54	Spiked Stegodon	53-54
Gorishi Hive Queen	56	Stegodon	52-53
Gorishi Reaver	51-53	Thunderstomp Stegodon	54-55
Gorishi Stinger	52-53	Tyrant Devilsaur	54-55
Gorishi Tunneler	52-53	Un'Goro Gorilla	52-53
Gorishi Wasp	51-52	Un'Goro Stomper	52-53
Gorishi Worker	51-52	Un'Goro Thunderer	52-53
Ironhide Devilsaur	54-56	Venomhide Ravasaur	50-51
		Young Diemetradon	49-50

UN'GORO CRATER LEGEND

1 MARSHAL'S STAND
Mulgin

1 UN'GORO CRATER
Garl Stormclaw (Quest Giver)
Torwa Pathfinder (Quest Giver)

2 THE MARSHLANDS
Ithis Moonwarden (Quest Giver)

3 THE ROILING GARDENS
Crate of Foodstuffs (Quest Giver)

4 MARSHAL'S STAND
Gibbert <Weapon Merchant>
Gryfe <Flight Master>
Hol' anyee Marshal (Quest Giver)
Innkeeper Dreedle
J.D. Collie (Quest Giver)
Krakle (Quest Giver)
Nergal <General Goods>
Nolen Tacker (Quest Giver)
Quixxil (Quest Giver)
Spraggle Frock (Quest Giver)
Un' Goro Examinant (Quest Giver)
Williden Marshal (Quest Giver)
Zen' Aliri

5 TERROR RUN
Research Equipment (Quest Giver)

6 FIRE PLUME RIDGE
Ringo (Quest Giver)

7 MOSSY PILE
Doreen (Quest Giver)
Dramm Riverhorn <Light Armor Merchant>
Flizzy Coilspanner <Flight Master>
Gremix
Karna Remtravel (Quest Giver)
Shizzle (Quest Giver)
Tara (Quest Giver)

8 FUNGAL ROCK
A-Me 01 (Quest Giver)

9 THE SHAPER'S TERRACE
Nablya (Quest Giver)

10 GOLAKKA HOT SPRINGS
Maximillian of Northshire (Quest Giver)
Pimento
Spark Nilminer (Quest Giver)

1 UN'GORO CRATER
Mor'vek (Quest Giver)

2 MARSHAL'S STAND
Larion

WINTERSPRING

The snowy hills and mountains of Winterspring have remained mostly untouched by the recent cataclysm. The small town of Everlook serves as the region's center, offering goods and services—as well as a few townsfolk willing to reward adventurers for some help. Frostwhisper Gorge, to the south, has been taken over by water elementals, ousting the giants that once called it home. Frostsabers still hunt in the north, willing to make a meal out of any unwary travelers. Other aggressive wildlife haunt the snowy hills, requiring travelers either to stick to the roads or prepare to fight. The Timbermaw Furbolgs strive against their vicious cousins, the Winterfall, while near Mazthoril, the Blue Dragonflight must deal with a threat from within.

REPUTATION INFORMATION Timbermaw Hold, Ironforge

Questing in Winterspring

Look for Donova Snowden at Frostfire Hot Springs, just off the road that runs between Timbermaw Hold and Lake Kel'theril. She's the starting point for the quests in the zone and the target of both Hero's Call: Wintersrping! and Warchief's Command: Winterspring!.

RESOURCE LEGEND

NODE FISHING

None

OPEN WATER FISHING

Freshwater	Ocean
Lightning Eel	
Raw Redgill	
Raw Whitescale Salmon	
Plated Armorfish	
Raw Nightfin Snapper	
Raw Sunscale Salmon	

MINING

Metal	Min Skill Level
Truesilver Deposit	205
Small Thorium Vein	230
Rich Thorium Vein	255

HERBALISM

Herb	Min Skill Level
Mountain Silversage	280
Icecap	290

SKINNING

Creature	Level	Creature	Level
Altered Beast	51-54	Frostsaber Pride Watcher	52-53
Chillwind Chimaera	52-53	Frostsaber Stalker	52-53
Chillwind Ravager	57-59	Hederine Manastalker	59-60
Cobalt Broodling	55-56	Ice Thistle Matriarch	51-52
Cobalt Mageweaver	57-58	Ice Thistle Patriarch	51-52
Cobalt Scalebane	56-57	Ice Thistle Yeti	51-52
Cobalt Whelp	54-55	Lost Ravager	54-55
Cobalt Wyrmkin	55-56	Rabid Shardtooth	59-60
Coldlurk Burrower	51-52	Rogue Ice Thistle	53-55
Displaced Warp Stalker	54-55	Shagpelt Ram	51-52
Elder Shardtooth	57-58	Shardtooth Bear	49-50
Fledgling Chillwind	53-55	Shardtooth Mauler	52-53
Frostsaber	52-53	Snowy Wolf	51-52
Frostsaber Cub	55-56	Spell Eater	54-56
Frostsaber Huntress	52-53	Winterhorn Stag	51-52

WINTERSPRING LEGEND

1 EVERLOOK
Maethrya <Hippogryph Master>

2 FROSTSABER ROCK
Rivern Frostwind (Quest Giver)

1 EVERLOOK
Auctioneer Grizzlin
Azzleby <Stable Master>
Blixxrak <Light Armor Merchant>
Deez Rocksnitch (Quest Giver)
Evie Whirlbrew <Alchemy Supplies>
Felnok Steelspring
Gogo
Harlo Wigglesworth
Himmik <Food & Drink>
Innkeeper Vizzie <Innkeeper>
Izzy Coppergrab <Banker>
Jack Sterling
Kilram (Quest Giver)
Legacki
Lilith the Lithe (Quest Giver)
Lunnix Sprocketslip <Mining Supplies>
Malyfous Darkhammer
Meggi Peppinrocker
Nixxrak <Heavy Armor Merchant>
Nymn
Qia <Trade Supplies>
Seril Scourgebane (Quest Giver)

Umaron Stragarelm
Umi Rumplesnicker
Wixxrak <Weaponsmith & Gunsmith>
Xizzer Fizzbolt <Engineering Supplies>
Zap Farflinger

2 TIMBERMAW HOLD
Salfa (Quest Giver)

3 SNOWDEN CHALET
Donova Snowden (Quest Giver)
Witch Doctor Mau'ari (Quest Giver)

4 WINTERFALL VILLAGE
Burndl (Quest Giver)
Tanrir (Quest Giver)

5 LAKE KEL'THERIL
Kelek Skykeeper (Quest Giver)

6 LAKE KEL'THERIL
Kaldorei Spirit (Quest Giver)
Quel'dorei Spirit (Quest Giver)
Sin'dorei Spirit (Quest Giver)

7 STARFALL VILLAGE
Gormir Stoneshaper
Lyranne Feathersong <Food & Drink>
Natheril Raincaller <General Goods>
Syurana <Trade Supplies>
Wynd Nightchaser (Quest Giver)

8 BAN'THALLOW BARROW DEN
Marcy Curtainfire
Remma Curtainfire
Rinno Curtainfire (Quest Giver)
Sana Curtainfire

9 GOODGRUB SMOKING PIT
Barbie Cutesazz <Food & Drink>
Francis Morcott (Quest Giver)
Jeb Guthrie (Quest Giver)
Jez Goodgrub (Quest Giver)
Trapper Kiefer <Leatherworking Supplies>

10 WINTERSPRING
Jadrag the Slicer (Quest Giver)

11 BERYL EGRESS
Daleohm <Blacksmithing Supplies>
Haleh (Quest Giver)
Jaron Stoneshaper
Maseel <General Goods>
Zakk Sinon

1 EVERLOOK
Yugrek <Wind Rider Master>

DEEPHOLM

The dark underworld of Deepholm has a unique beauty. Towering crystalline structures dot the landscape; strange creatures call it home, ruled by Therazane, the Stonemother. She doesn't like intruders in her realm, and only begrudgingly accepts those outsiders who prove their worth in the battle against the invading Twilight Hammer. When Deathwing emerged from the confines of Deepholm, the World Pillar was shattered. Now, the Earthen Ring has arrived in Deepholm to do battle with the Twilight Hammer and attempt to repair the fractured pillar before it spells the doom of all of Azeroth.

REPUTATION INFORMATION Earthen Ring

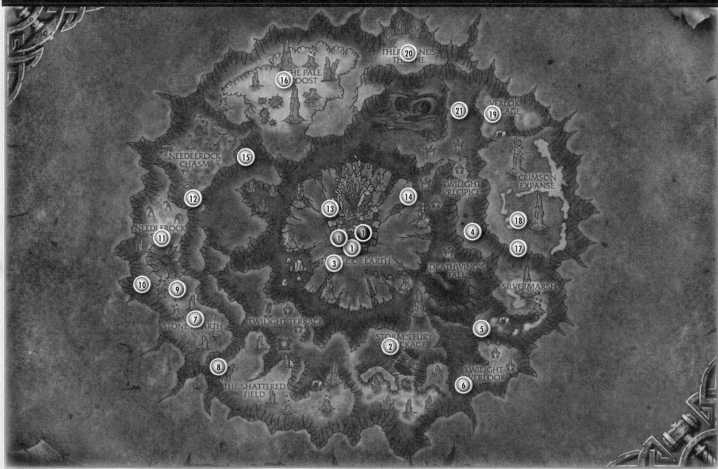

RESOURCE LEGEND

NODE FISHING

Freshwater	Ocean
Albino Cavefish	
Volatile Water	

OPEN WATER FISHING

Freshwater	Ocean
Sharptooth	
Albino Cavefish	
Lavascale Catfish	
Volatile Water	

MINING

Metal	Min Skill Level
Obsidian Deposit	425
Elementium Vein	475
Rich Elementium Vein	500

HERBALISM

Herb	Min Skill Level
Heartblossom	475

SKINNING

Creature	Level
Crystal Gorged Basilisk	83
Crystalspawn Giant	83
Deadly Crystalgazer	80
Elder Twilight Pyremaw	83
Gorgonite	83
Jadecrest Basilisk	81-82
Rock Borer	82
Shalehide Basilisk	83
Stone Bat	83
Stone Drake	83
Stonecore Flayer	82
Stonescale Drake	81-82
Twilight Dragonspawn	81-82
Twilight Pyremaw	83
Twilight Scalesister	81-82
Unbound Earth Rager	82

Questing in Deepholm

To reach Deepholm and begin questing there, you should first travel to Orgrimmar or Stormwind and complete the quest, The Maelstrom. When you have completed that quest, pick up either Hero's Call: Deepholm! or Warchief's Command: Deepholm! to start your journey to the Maelstrom.

DEEPHOLM LEGEND

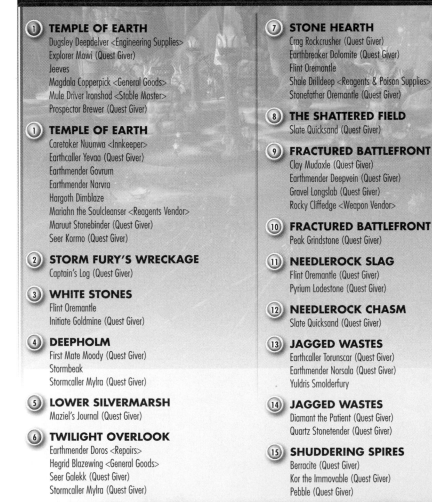

(1) TEMPLE OF EARTH
Dugsley Deepdelver <Engineering Supplies>
Explorer Mowi (Quest Giver)
Jeeves
Magdala Copperpick <General Goods>
Mule Driver Ironshod <Stable Master>
Prospector Brewer (Quest Giver)

(1) TEMPLE OF EARTH
Caretaker Nuunwa <Innkeeper>
Earthcaller Yevaa (Quest Giver)
Earthmender Govrum
Earthmender Narvra
Hargoth Dimblaze
Mariahn the Soulcleanser <Reagents Vendor>
Maruut Stonebinder (Quest Giver)
Seer Kormo (Quest Giver)

(2) STORM FURY'S WRECKAGE
Captain's Log (Quest Giver)

(3) WHITE STONES
Flint Oremantle
Initiate Goldmine (Quest Giver)

(4) DEEPHOLM
First Mate Moody (Quest Giver)
Stormbeak
Stormcaller Mylra (Quest Giver)

(5) LOWER SILVERMARSH
Maziel's Journal (Quest Giver)

(6) TWILIGHT OVERLOOK
Earthmender Doros <Repairs>
Hegrid Blazewing <General Goods>
Seer Galekk (Quest Giver)
Stormcaller Mylra (Quest Giver)

(7) STONE HEARTH
Crag Rockcrusher (Quest Giver)
Earthbreaker Dolomite (Quest Giver)
Flint Oremantle
Shale Drilldeep <Reagents & Poison Supplies>
Stonefather Oremantle (Quest Giver)

(8) THE SHATTERED FIELD
Slate Quicksand (Quest Giver)

(9) FRACTURED BATTLEFRONT
Clay Mudaxle (Quest Giver)
Earthmender Deepvein (Quest Giver)
Gravel Longslab (Quest Giver)
Rocky Cliffedge <Weapon Vendor>

(10) FRACTURED BATTLEFRONT
Peak Grindstone (Quest Giver)

(11) NEEDLEROCK SLAG
Flint Oremantle (Quest Giver)
Pyrium Lodestone (Quest Giver)

(12) NEEDLEROCK CHASM
Slate Quicksand (Quest Giver)

(13) JAGGED WASTES
Earthcaller Torunscar (Quest Giver)
Earthmender Norsala (Quest Giver)
Yuldris Smolderfury

(14) JAGGED WASTES
Diamant the Patient (Quest Giver)
Quartz Stonetender (Quest Giver)

(15) SHUDDERING SPIRES
Berracite (Quest Giver)
Kor the Immovable (Quest Giver)
Pebble (Quest Giver)

(16) THE PALE ROOST
Terrath the Steady (Quest Giver)

(17) CRIMSON EXPANSE
Gorsik the Tumultuous (Quest Giver)

(18) CRIMSON EXPANSE
Earthmender Norsala
Windspeaker Lorvarius (Quest Giver)

(19) VERLOK STAND
Ruberick (Quest Giver)

(20) THERAZANE'S THRONE
Boden the Imposing
D' lom the Collector <General Goods>
Diamant the Patient
Earthcaller Torunscar (Quest Giver)
Felsen the Enduring (Quest Giver)
Gorsik the Tumultuous (Quest Giver)
Ibdil the Mender <Repairs>
Ma' haat the Indomitable
Ruberick (Quest Giver)
Terrath the Steady
Therazane (Quest Giver)

(21) HALCYON EGRESS
Boden the Imposing (Quest Giver)
Therazane (Quest Giver)

(1) TEMPLE OF EARTH
Beast-Handler Rustclamp <Stable Master>
Examiner Rowe (Quest Giver)
Reliquary Jes' ca Darksun (Quest Giver)
Rixi "The Driller" Bombdigger <Engineering Supplies>
Varx Hagglemore <General Goods>

THE LOST ISLES

The Lost Isles are a pair of islands previously unknown to either the Horde or Alliance. The surviving members of the Bilgewater Cartel were shipwrecked on the southwestern coast of the smaller island, on Shipwreck Shore. Exploration leads to the discovery of valuable Kaja'mite, but the island holds dangers as well as riches. The Alliance has downed a Horde vessel and has established a beachhead on the northwestern part of the small island. The surviving Horde members have established a base camp in the east and are willing to accept new allies from the cartel.

Both islands have a rich wildlife, some of which are very aggressive. While the islands may have been unknown to the familiar denizens of Azeroth, the larger of the two is not uninhabited. The vicious tribe of Oostan calls the center of the island home. They build their settlements around the caldera of a not quite dormant volcano where they worship the great turtle, Volcanoth—and they don't take kindly to visitors. The northwestern side of the large island has been claimed by Trade Prince Gallywix who is always eager to turn a profit, even in these trying circumstances.

THE MAP FOR KEZAN

If you're looking for the map for Kezan, the Goblin starting zone, it's included on page 132 in the beginner section of the guide.

REPUTATION INFORMATION Bilgewater Cartel, Orgrimmar

RESOURCE LEGEND

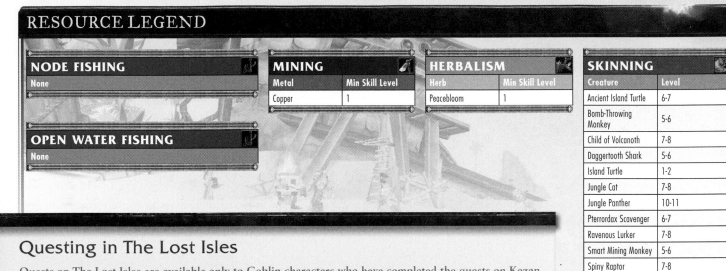

NODE FISHING
None

OPEN WATER FISHING
None

MINING

Metal	Min Skill Level
Copper	1

HERBALISM

Herb	Min Skill Level
Peacebloom	1

SKINNING

Creature	Level
Ancient Island Turtle	6-7
Bomb-Throwing Monkey	5-6
Child of Volcanoth	7-8
Daggertooth Shark	5-6
Island Turtle	1-2
Jungle Cat	7-8
Jungle Panther	10-11
Pterrordax Scavenger	6-7
Ravenous Lurker	7-8
Smart Mining Monkey	5-6
Spiny Raptor	7-8
Teraptor Hatchling	5-6

Questing in The Lost Isles

Quests on The Lost Isles are available only to Goblin characters who have completed the quests on Kezan.

LOST ISLES LEGEND

(1) SHIPWRECK SHORE
Doc Zapnozzle (Quest Giver)
Geargrinder Gizmo (Quest Giver)

(2) SHIPWRECK SHORE
Ace
Bamm Megabomb <Hunter Trainer> (Quest Giver)
Brett "Coins" McQuid <Recovered Supplies>
Candy Cane
Chip Endale
Coach Crosscheck
Doc Zapnozzle <First Aid Trainer>
Evol Fingers <Warlock Trainer>
Fizz Lighter <Mage Trainer>
Gobber
Grimy Greasefingers <Innkeeper>
Izzy
Maxx Avalanche <Shaman Trainer> (Quest Giver)
Megs Dreadshredder
Sally "Salvager" Sandscrew <Slightly Damp Salvage>
Sassy Hardwrench (Quest Giver)
Sister Goldskimmer <Priest Trainer>
Slinky Sharpshiv <Rogue Trainer>
Warrior-Matic NX-01 <Warrior Trainer>

(3) KAJA'MITE CAVERN
Dead Orc Scout (Quest Giver)
Foreman Dampwick (Quest Giver)

(4) HORDE BASE CAMP
Aggra (Quest Giver)
Chawg <Armor Vendor>

(5) THE VICIOUS VALE
Kilag Gorefang

(6) WILD OVERLOOK
Kilag Gorefang (Quest Giver)

(7) THE LOST ISLES
Scout Brax

(8) WILD OVERLOOK
Ace
Aggra
Bamm Megabomb <Hunter Trainer>
Brett "Coins" McQuid <Recovered Supplies>
Candy Cane
Chawg <Armor Vendor>
Chip Endale
Coach Crosscheck
Doc Zapnozzle <First Aid Trainer>
Evol Fingers <Warlock Trainer>
Fizz Lighter <Mage Trainer>
Gobber
Grimy Greasefingers <Innkeeper>
Izzy
Kilag Gorefang
Maxx Avalanche <Shaman Trainer>
Megs Dreadshredder
Sally "Salvager" Sandscrew <Slightly Damp Salvage>
Sassy Hardwrench (Quest Giver)
Scout Brax
Sister Goldskimmer <Priest Trainer>
Slinky Sharpshiv <Rogue Trainer>
Thrall
Warrior-Matic NX-01 <Warrior Trainer>

(9) TOWN-IN-A-BOX
Assistant Greely
Bamm Megabomb <Hunter Trainer> (Quest Giver)
Coach Crosscheck
Doc Zapnozzle <First Aid Trainer>
Evol Fingers <Warlock Trainer>
Fizz Lighter <Mage Trainer>
Foreman Dampwick (Quest Giver)
Geargrinder Gizmo
Gobber <Banker>
Grimy Greasefingers <Innkeeper>
Hobart Grapplehammer (Quest Giver)
Izzy
Maxx Avalanche <Shaman Trainer>
Sally "Salvager" Sandscrew <Slightly Damp Salvage>
Sassy Hardwrench
Sister Goldskimmer <Priest Trainer>
Slinky Sharpshiv <Rogue Trainer>
Warrior-Matic NX-01 <Warrior Trainer>

(10) RUINS OF VASHJ'ELAN
Ace
Brett "Coins" McQuid <Recovered Supplies>
Megs Dreadshredder

(11) OOMLOT VILLAGE
Izzy (Quest Giver)

(12) LOST PEAK
Assistant Greely (Quest Giver)
Coach Crosscheck (Quest Giver)
Foreman Dampwick (Quest Giver)

(13) LOST CALDERA
Ace
Doc Zapnozzle <First Aid Trainer>
Gobber <Banker>
Hobart Grapplehammer (Quest Giver)
Izzy
Sally "Salvager" Sandscrew <Slightly Damp Salvage>

(14) VOLCANOTH'S LAIR
Sassy Hardwrench (Quest Giver)

(15) WARCHIEF'S OVERLOOK
Aggra (Quest Giver)
Chawg <Armor Vendor>
Sassy Hardwrench (Quest Giver)
Thrall (Quest Giver)

(16) TRANQUIL COAST
Kilag Gorefang (Quest Giver)

(17) SKY FALLS
Bamm Megabomb <Hunter Trainer>
Evol Fingers <Warlock Trainer>
Fizz Lighter <Mage Trainer>
KTC Train-a-Tron Deluxe <Profession Trainer & Vendor>
Maxx Avalanche <Shaman Trainer>
Sister Goldskimmer <Priest Trainer>
Slinky Sharpshiv <Rogue Trainer>
Warrior-Matic NX-01 <Warrior Trainer>

(18) GALLYWIX LABOR MINE
Ace
Assistant Greely (Quest Giver)
Gobber <Banker>
Izzy

(19) BILGEWATER LUMBER YARD
Ace
Assistant Greely (Quest Giver)
Coach Crosscheck (Quest Giver)
Gobber <Banker>
Izzy (Quest Giver)

(20) THE SLAVE PITS
Brett "Coins" McQuid
Chawg <Armor Vendor> (Quest Giver)
Geargrinder Gizmo
Hobart Grapplehammer (Quest Giver)
Megs Dreadshredder
Sassy Hardwrench (Quest Giver)

(21) GALLYWIX DOCKS
Thrall (Quest Giver)
Ace
Aggra
Assistant Greely
Bamm Megabomb <Hunter Trainer>
Brett "Coins" McQuid <Recovered Supplies>
Chawg <Armor Vendor>
Coach Crosscheck
Doc Zapnozzle <First Aid Trainer>
Evol Fingers <Warlock Trainer>
Fizz Lighter <Mage Trainer>
Foreman Dampwick
Geargrinder Gizmo
Gobber
Grimy Greasefingers <Innkeeper>
Hobart Grapplehammer
Izzy
Kilag Gorefang
KTC Train-a-Tron Deluxe <Profession Trainer & Vendor>
Maxx Avalanche <Shaman Trainer>
Megs Dreadshredder
Sally "Salvager" Sandscrew <Slightly Damp Salvage>
Sassy Hardwrench
Scout Brax
Sister Goldskimmer <Priest Trainer>
Slinky Sharpshiv <Rogue Trainer>
Trade Prince Gallywix
Warrior-Matic NX-01 <Warrior Trainer>

DEATH KNIGHT

Death Knights are the game's sole Hero class, able to utilize powerful spells and strikes, and manipulate dark energies to destroy their foes. Death Knights are capable tanks as well as excellent melee damage dealers. Since Death Knights begin at level 55, they have more abilities available to them initially than other classes. This is a melee class with a handful of ranged spells and the ability to summon short term combat pets.

Unlike other classes, where your starting area is determined by your character's race, all Death Knights begin in a special area in the Eastern Plaguelands. The quests in this area introduce you to the abilities and lore of the Death Knight class, so you initially acquire abilities and talents at a much quicker pace than other classes.

RACE AVAILABILITY

ALLIANCE

Draenei

Dwarf

Gnome

Human

Night Elf

Worgen

HORDE

Blood Elf

Goblin

Orc

Tauren

Troll

Undead

RACIAL ADVANTAGES

ALLIANCE

Race	Best for	Notes
Draenei	Any spec	Heroic Presence grants Draenei +1% Hit chance. Shadow spells are less likely to hit a Draenei.
Dwarf	Any spec	Mace Specialization grants Expertise to Dwarves who wield maces. Frost spells are less likely to hit a Dwarf. Stoneform removes all poison, disease, and bleed effects and increases armor for 8 seconds.
Gnome	Frost	Shortblade Specialization grants Expertise to Gnomes who wield daggers or one-hand sword.
Worgen	Frost/Unholy	Ferocity adds 1% Critical Strike chance.
Human	Any spec	Every Man For Himself allows the Death Knight to break fears, stuns, and CC. Sword and Mace Specializations grants Expertise to Humans who wield swords or maces.
Night Elf	Blood	Night Elves are less likely to be hit by any physical attack, or Nature spell.

HORDE

Race	Best for	Notes
Blood Elf	Blood	Arcane Torrent silences nearby enemies and restores some of the Blood Elf's runic power. All magic spells are less likely to hit a Blood Elf.
Goblin	Frost/Unholy	Time is Money boosts attack and casting speeds by 1%. Rocket Barrage is an extra damage ability.
Orc	Unholy	Axe Specialization grants Expertise to Orcs who wield axes and fist weapons. Blood Fury boost Attack Power for a Death Knight. Command increases damage done by your pets.
Tauren	Blood	War Stomp stuns nearby enemies. Endurance increases base health. Nature spells are less likely to hit a Tauren.
Troll	Frost/Unholy	Berserking increases attack and casting speed.
Undead	Blood	Will of the Forsaken breaks Charm, Fear, and Sleep effects. Shadow spells are less likely to hit an Undead Death Knight.

EQUIPMENT OPTIONS

Armor Type	Shield	Ranged Slot
Plate	No	Relic

WEAPON CHOICES

1 Hand Weapons	2 Hand Weapons
Axe	Axe
Mace	Mace
Sword	Sword
	Polearm

DEATH KNIGHT SPELLS

Level Learned	Ability Name		Tree	Description
55	Rune of Cinderglacier		Frost	Affixes your rune weapon with a rune that has a chance to increase the damage by 20% for your next 2 attacks that deal Frost or Shadow damage
55	Rune of Razorice		Frost	Affixes your weapon with a rune that causes 2% extra weapon damage as Frost damage and increases enemies' vulnerability to your Frost attacks
55	Icy Touch		Frost	Deals Frost damage modified by attack power and reduces the target's ranged, melee attack, and casting speed by 20% for 20 sec. 20 yd range, Instant, 6 sec cooldown
55	Icy Talons		Frost	Your melee attack speed is increased by 20%.
55	Frost Strike		Frost	Instantly strike the enemy, causing 110% weapon damage plus additional damage as Frost damage. 40 Runic Power, 5 yd range, Instant
55	Frost Presence		Frost	Strengthens the Death Knight with the presence of Frost, increasing damage by 10% and increasing Runic Power generation by 10%.
55	Death Strike		Blood	A deadly attack that deals damage plus and heals the Death Knight for a percent of damage done to him in the last 5 seconds.
55	Forceful Deflection		Blood	Increases your Parry Rating by 25% of your total Strength
55	Blood Strike		Blood	Instantly strike the enemy, causing 80% weapon damage plus additional damage, increased by an additional 10% for each of your diseases on the target.
55	Unholy Blight		Unholy	Causes the victims of your Death Coil to be surrounded by a vile swarm of unholy insects, taking 10% of the damage done by the Death Coil over 10 sec, and prevents diseases on the victim from being dispelled.
55	Scourge Strike		Unholy	An unholy strike that deals 100% of weapon damage as Physical damage plus additional damage. In addition, for each of your diseases on your target, you deal an additional 12% of the Physical damage done as Shadow damage.
55	Plague Strike		Unholy	A vicious strike that deals 100% weapon damage plus additional damage and infects the target with Blood Plague, a disease dealing Shadow damage over time.
55	Death Grip		Unholy	Harness the unholy energy that surrounds and binds all matter, drawing the target toward the death knight and forcing the enemy to attack the death knight for 3 sec. 8-30 yd range, Instant, 35 sec cooldown
55	Death Gate		Unholy	Opens a gate which the Death Knight can use to return to Ebon Hold. 10 sec cast, 1 min cooldown
55	Death Coil		Unholy	Fire a blast of unholy energy, causing Shadow damage to an enemy target or healing damage from a friendly Undead target. 40 Runic Power, 30/40 yd range, Instant
55	Acherus Deathcharger (Summon)		Unholy	Summons and dismisses your rideable Acherus Deathcharger. This is a very fast mount.
56	Pestilence		Blood	Spreads existing Blood Plague and Frost Fever infections from your target to all other enemies within 10 yards. Diseases spread this way deal 50% of normal damage.
56	Raise Dead		Unholy	Raises a Ghoul to fight by your side. You can have a maximum of one Ghoul at a time. Lasts 1 min. 30 yd range, Instant, 3 min cooldown
57	Mind Freeze		Frost	Smash the target's mind with cold, interrupting spellcasting and preventing any spell in that school from being cast for 4 sec. 20 Runic Power, 5 yd range, Instant, 10 sec cooldown
57	Blood Presence		Blood	The death knight takes on the presence of Blood, increasing Stamina by 8%, armor contribution from cloth, leather, mail and plate items by 60%, and reducing damage taken by 8%. Increases threat generated. Only one Presence may be active at a time.
58	Chains of Ice		Frost	Shackles the target with frozen chains, reducing their movement by 60% for 8 sec. Also infects the target with Frost Fever. 20 yd range, Instant
58	Blood Boil		Blood	Boils the blood of all enemies within 10 yards, dealing Shadow damage. Deals additional damage to targets infected with Blood Plague or Frost Fever.
59	Strangulate		Blood	Strangulates an enemy, silencing them for 5 sec. Non-player victim spellcasting is also interrupted for 3 sec. 30 yd range, Instant, 2 min cooldown

Level Learned	Ability Name		Tree	Description
60	Death and Decay		Unholy	Corrupts the ground targeted by the Death Knight, causing Shadow damage every sec that targets remain in the area for 10 sec. This ability produces a high amount of threat. 30 yd range, Instant, 30 sec cooldown
61	Path of Frost		Frost	The Death Knight's freezing aura creates ice beneath his or her feet, allowing him or her and his or her party or raid to walk on water for 10 min. Works while mounted. Any damage will cancel the effect.
61	Obliterate		Frost	A brutal instant attack that deals 160% weapon damage plus additional damage, total damage increased 12.5% per each of your diseases on the target.
62	Icebound Fortitude		Frost	The Death Knight freezes his or her blood to become immune to Stun effects and reduce all damage taken by 30% for 12 sec. 20 Runic Power, Instant, 2 min cooldown
64	Blood Tap		Blood	Immediately activates a Blood Rune and converts it into a Death Rune for the next 20 sec. Death Runes count as a Blood, Frost or Unholy Rune. 6% of base health, Instant, 1 min cooldown
65	Horn of Winter		Frost	The Death Knight blows the Horn of Winter, which generates 10 runic power and increases total Strength and Agility of all party or raid members within 45 yards. Lasts 2 min. Instant, 20 sec cooldown
65	Dark Command		Blood	Commands the target to attack you, but has no effect if the target is already attacking you. 30 yd range, Instant, 8 sec cooldown
66	Death Pact		Blood	Sacrifices an undead minion, healing the Death Knight for 40% of his or her maximum health. This heal cannot be a critical. 40 Runic Power, Instant, 2 min cooldown
67	Rune Strike		Frost	Strike the target for 200% weapon damage plus [20% of AP]. Only usable while in Blood Presence, or after the Death Knight dodges or parries. Can't be dodged, blocked, or parried. This attack causes a high amount of threat. 30 Runic Power, 5 yd range, Instant
68	Runic Empowerment		Frost	When you use your Death Coil, Frost Strike, or Rune Strike ability, you have a 45% chance to activate a random fully depleted rune.
68	Anti-Magic Shell		Unholy	Surrounds the Death Knight in an Anti-Magic Shell, absorbing 75% of the damage dealt by harmful spells (up to a maximum of 50% of the Death Knight's health) and preventing application of harmful magical effects. Lasts 5 sec. Instant, 45 sec cooldown
70	Unholy Presence		Unholy	Infuses the death knight with unholy fury, increasing attack speed and rune regeneration by 10%, movement speed by 15% and reducing the global cooldown on your abilities by 0.5 seconds. Only one Presence may be active at a time.
72	Raise Ally		Unholy	Raises the corpse of a raid or party member to fight by your side. The player will have control over the Ghoul for 5 min. 30 yd range, Instant, 10 min cooldown
74	Festering Strike		Frost	An instant attack that deals 150% weapon damage plus additional damage and increases the duration of your Blood Plague, Frost Fever, and Chains of Ice effects on the target by up to 6 sec.
75	Empower Rune Weapon		Frost	Empower your rune weapon, immediately activating all your runes and generating 25 runic power. Instant, 5 min cooldown
80	Army of the Dead		Unholy	Summons an entire legion of Ghouls to fight for the Death Knight. The Ghouls will swarm the area, taunting and fighting anything they can. While channelling Army of the Dead, the Death Knight takes less damage equal to his or her Dodge plus Parry chance. Channeled, 10 min cooldown
81	Outbreak		Unholy	Instantly applies Blood Plague and Frost Fever to the target enemy. 30 yd range, Instant, 1 min cooldown
83	Necrotic Strike		Unholy	A vicious strike that deals 100% weapon damage and absorbs the next [40% of AP] healing received by the target.
85	Dark Simulacrum		Blood	Places a dark ward on an enemy that persists for 8 sec, triggering when the enemy next spends mana on a single-target spell, and allowing the Death Knight to unleash an exact duplicate of that spell. Against nonplayers, only absorbs some harmful spells. 20 Runic Power, 40 yd range, Instant, 1 min cooldown

DEATH KNIGHT ABILITIES

RUNIC POWER

Runic Power is a resource that works similarly to Rage. Certain abilities grant Runic Power when used, and others drain Runic Power. Runic Power is gained by dealing auto-swing damage with your weapon, certain strikes, and other instant cast abilities. Using cooldown abilities expends the Death Knight's Runic Power. Examples of abilities that cost Runic Power are Death Coil, Icebound Fortitude, Frost Strike, Mind Freeze, and Death Pact. Runic Power is a resource that you need to which you must pay attention—if you drain your Runic Power but need to use by Mind Freeze to interrupt a spell, you are out of luck. There are abilities that grant Runic Power, such as Death and Decay, but you shouldn't rely on them for Runic Power management.

RUNES

Runes are a regularly replenishing resource, with some tools which allow you to manipulate them. Death Knights have a maximum of two of each type of Rune, meaning 2 Frost, 2 Unholy, and 2 Blood Runes. Examples of abilities that cost Runes are Icy Touch (1 Frost), Blood Strike (1 Blood), and Plague Strike (1 Unholy). Other abilities use more than one type of rune, such as Obliterate (1 Unholy, 1 Frost), or Death Strike (1 Unholy, 1 Frost). One way to manipulate Runes outside of their standard usage is through Blood Tap. Blood Tap has a one minute cooldown, and allows you to convert a Blood Rune into a Death Rune. A Death Rune counts as any type of Rune, so you can turn an excess Blood Rune into another type that may be more useful in a given situation.

Runes are the pacing mechanism for a Death Knight's damage potential. They also allow Death Knights to create a rotation of sorts when dealing damage. For example, a common opening to use your Runes effectively would be Icy Touch, Plague Strike, Blood Strike—which would take you down to 1 of each Rune available—then using that cycle again.

PRESENCES

Presences are the Death Knight version of Warrior stances. Death Knights gain certain benefits depending on which Presence is active. Blood Presence is the tanking presence. It bolsters health, armor, and threat generation, and reduces damage taken. Frost Presence causes Death Knights to deal 10% additional damage and generate 10% additional Runic Power. Frost Presence helps out when you're using many abilities that deal damage and cost Runic Power. Finally, Unholy Presence increases attack speed and rune regeneration rates by 10%, as well as the movement speed by 15%. This is the primary presence to use for dual wielding and using many abilities that fully drain all your Runes. You should always change to Unholy Presence whenever you need a movement speed boost.

Presence Bar

This shortcut bar appears in the lower left corner of your screen, just above your Action Bars. This bar allows you to switch between Presences quickly.

RUNEFORGING

Death Knights imbue their own weapons with specialized super enchantments. These do not stack with enchants that are already on the weapon. This means you save money on enchants, and still have access to excellent (and customizable) weapon enchantments. Runeforging requires a trip to Ebon Hold to use a forge there, however.

SUGGESTED PROFESSION FOR A FIRST-TIME DEATH KNIGHT

Blacksmithing is an excellent profession for a first-time Death Knight. Blacksmithing allows you to craft weapons and armor. You may be able to fill in holes in your gear with something you craft yourself! Mining pairs well with Blacksmithing, as you need raw ore and gems in order to craft weapons and armor. Mining also provides a Stamina benefit, which is a big help for Blood Death Knights.

PLAYING AS A BLOOD DEATH KNIGHT

Blood Death Knights are the primary tanking Death Knights. Nearly all talents in the tree specialize in bolstering the Death Knight's ability to take damage effectively, and heal themselves. They gain Attack Power from taking damage, their Stamina and Expertise are higher than Frost and Unholy Death Knights, and their Death Strike and Obliterate abilities allow them to use more Death Runes (making them more versatile with how they use their resources).

Heart Strike is the defining ability of this line. It instantly hits up to three enemies with a melee attack. Damage is highest for the first victim but decreases substantially for the other targets struck. Stacking diseases on the enemies ahead of time raises the total damage they take from Heart Strike. This attack helps to keep aggro from multiple enemies.

Passive talents in this line give Blood Death Knights more armor and better general survivability. Active abilities, like Bone Shield, Rune Tap, and Vampiric Blood, let the Death Knights endure enemies with extreme damage output.

At the end of the line is Dancing Rune Weapon. This summons a spare weapon to fight, deal adequate damage, and raise the Death Knight's Parry by 20%. When combined with other survivability abilities, this makes the tank quite hard to kill.

ABILITIES LEARNED IF YOU SELECT BLOOD

	Ability	Description
	Heart Strike	Instantly strike the target and up to two additional nearby enemies, causing 100% weapon damage plus additional damage on the primary target, with damage reduced by 25% on each subsequent target. Each target takes 10% additional damage for each of your diseases active on that target.
	Veteran of the Third War	Increases your total Stamina by 9% and your expertise by 6.
	Blood Rites	Whenever you hit with Death Strike or Obliterate, there is a 100% chance that the Frost and Unholy Runes will become Death Runes when they activate. Death Runes count as a Blood, Frost, or Unholy Rune.
	Vengeance	Each time you take damage, you gain 5% of the damage taken as Attack Power, up to a maximum of 10% of your health.
	Mastery: Blood Shield	Each time you heal yourself via Death Strike, you gain 50% of the amount healed as a damage absorption shield. Each point of Mastery increases the shield by an additional 6.25%.

DESIRABLE STATS

Since you're outfitting a tank, look for Plate armor with the highest Stamina and and armor values available. Defensive attributes such as Dodge Rating and Parry Rating are also desirable. When it comes to weapons, select a two handed sword, axe, or mace with the highest Stamina. Strength is generally better than Agility, but don't pass on a weapon that is a Stamina upgrade because it lacks Strength.

LEVELS 55 - 80

Playing Solo

A new Death Knight is unique from other classes in that they start at level 55, and thus you quickly have many abilities and talents to work with. Blood Death Knights playing are far more durable than most classes. You are capable of surviving for a long time against foes through judicious applications of Death Strike. Use the standard abilities to apply diseases and maximize your damage and healing potential, via Icy Touch and Plague Strike. When taking on many foes, be aware of your health and the diseases on your target to maximize Death Strike's healing, and use Pestilence, Blood Boil, and Death and Decay to maximize your AoE damage. Icebound Fortitude and Bone Shield are both cooldowns on a short duration (2 minutes and 1 minute respectively) that allow you to take significantly less damage for the duration. Remember that as a Blood Death Knight, your damage output may not be as high as a pure DPS class, but your survivability more than makes up for it, so use that to your advantage.

Playing in a Group

Blood Presence is required for Blood Death Knights to hold threat. Stick with Icy Touch, Blood Boil, Death Strike, Death and Decay and Plague Strike to hold the attention of nearby enemies. If you're using any AoE abilities to tank, communicate with your group every time crowd control spells are used. Your AoE damage abilities may break the CC on the target.

Speak with your healer to find out if you are taking too much damage. If the healer says they are having no problem keeping you alive, you can be more aggressive with the rate at which you pull and engage mobs, and most likely use less crowd control and more damage abilities. However, if the healer says you are taking excessive damage and keeping you alive is a chore, slow down your pace and use defensive cooldown abilities more frequently.

THE CATACLYSM: LEVELS 81 - 85

Not much changes for Blood Death Knights at higher levels, but you do gain Outbreak, which applies both Blood Plague and Frost Fever to a target at the same time, although you need to wait one minute between each use. Incoming damage takes steep upturn as you move through Cataclysm's new zones, so temper your expectations about continuing to face large groups of enemies at the same time.

Preparing Your Blood Death Knight
for Heroic Dungeons

Survivability comes before threat generation. Take the quest rewards that boost your Stamina whenever possible. Your next priorities are defensive stats such as Dodge Rating and Parry Rating. Hit Rating and Expertise Rating are valuable, but you may not get much of these stats on equipment on your starting heroic dungeon gear, although you could always Reforge Haste Rating and Critical Strike Rating as these stats are luxuries instead of necessities.

Blood Death Knights: Group Buffs and Debuffs

Blood Death Knights offer several buffs and debuffs that can greatly help their party or raid. Scarlet Fever, a talent applied by using Blood Boil, reduces the enemy's damage by 10% for 30 seconds. Abomination's Might boosts the entire raid's attack power by 10%. Icy Touch applies an attack speed reduction called Frost Fever, which is a huge benefit against melee-oriented enemies. Horn of Winter boosts the Strength and Agility of the entire raid.

PLAYING AS A FROST DEATH KNIGHT

Frost Death Knights specialize in dual wielding to deal their damage, and have many procs that result in bursts of damage between their constant dual weapon strikes. Frost Death Knights can also choose to stay with a single 2-handed weapon style if they desire. There are talents for both choices in this line.

Frost Death Knights get a 20% boost to melee attack speed and can use talents to gain 30 more maximum Runic Power. Their Blood Strikes and Pestilence cause a Blood Rune to become a Death Rune, giving them more versatility in what to do next.

Frost Strike is the defining ability of this line. It's an instant attack that deals moderate damage. Abilities like Pillar of Frost provide burst damage. Other talents make it harder to pin down these Death Knights. On a Pale Horse limits movement-slowing effects for these characters. Hungering Cold turns the tables, trapping nearby enemies.

ABILITIES LEARNED IF YOU SELECT FROST

	Ability	Description
	Frost Strike	Instantly strike the enemy, causing 110% weapon damage plus additional damage as frost damage.
	Icy Talons	Your melee attack speed is increased by 20%.
	Blood of the North	Increases Blood Strike and Frost Strike damage by 10%. In addition, whenever you hit with Blood Strike or Pestilence, there is a 100% chance that the Blood Rune will become a Death Rune when it activates. Death Runes count as a Blood, Frost, or Unholy Rune.
	Mastery: Frozen Heart	Increases all Frost damage done by 16%. Each point of Mastery increases Frost damage by an additional 2%.

DESIRED STATS

Look for Plate armor with Strength, Hit Rating, Expertise Rating, Haste Rating, and Critical Strike Rating. These are stats desired by a Frost Death Knight, in roughly that order of priority. Hit Rating requirements are much higher if you choose to dual wield. Haste Rating increases the rate at which Runes replenish and you swing your weapons, which increases the chance of having procs activate for you to do even more damage.

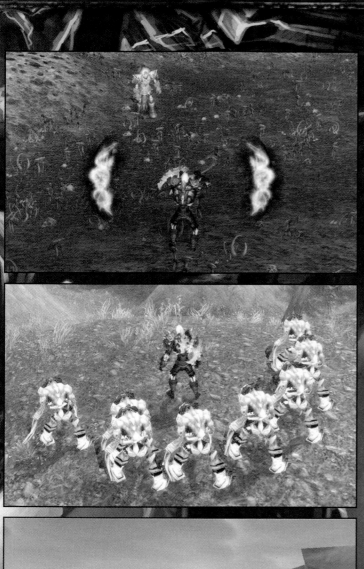

LEVELS 55 - 80

Playing Solo

Use standard abilities to apply diseases, which maximizes your damage and healing potential via Icy Touch and Plague Strike. Icebound Fortitude is a strong cooldown on a short duration (2 minutes) that allows you to take significantly less damage for the duration. Remember that as Frost Death Knight you have access to more snares and slowing effects than most classes, so use that to your advantage when fighting multiple foes or running away.

Playing in a Group

Frost Death Knights provide steady melee damage, and also has direct damage attacks with greater range than other melee classes. It is crucial to understand the different situations where you put your various abilities to use. If a creature is fleeing from the group when it is low on health, for example, use Death Coil on it, or use Chains of Ice to reduce the creature's movement speed. Death Knights have two interrupts. Mind Freeze is a short cooldown interrupt while Strangulate, which has a 2 minute cooldown, silences its target for 5 seconds. Strangulate's advantage is its range of 30 yards. Use Strangulate wisely, and your group will thank you for it!

When maximizing your damage on a single target, don't use AoE abilities. However, when there are larger pulls where you can use AoEs like Blood Boil, or Death and Decay, give the tank enough time to build up threat so you don't steal it away. Don't immediately panic if you do, however. Frost Death Knights can snare creatures they are attacking, so you may be able to kite around the mobs until your tank gets things under control. If you find a tank who is more than capable of sustaining threat, a Frost Death Knight becomes one of the most powerful AoE classes around. Between Howling Blast procs from Rime, Pestilence, and Death and Decay, you become a major asset to a group if there are many large pulls.

THE CATACLYSM: LEVELS 81 - 85

Not much changes for Frost Death Knights at higher levels, but you do gain Outbreak, which applies both Blood Plague and Frost Fever to a target at the same time, although you need to wait one minute between each use. Incoming damage takes steep upturn as you move through Cataclysm's new zones, so temper your expectations about continuing to face large groups of enemies at the same time.

Preparing Your Frost Death Knight for Heroic Dungeons

Grab gear with Strength, Hit Rating, Haste Rating, and Critical Strike Rating when possible. The amount of Hit Rating you need depends on whether you are dual-wielding weapons or using a single weapon. Expertise Rating is important as well. It increases your damage by reducing the enemy's chance to dodge or parry your attacks, but you only need a total of -6.5% reduction, which you can check in your character stats sheet. Don't shy away from equipment that puts you over the Expertise cap. You can always Reforge it into another secondary stat.

Frost Death Knights: Group Buffs and Debuffs

Frost Death Knights bring Improved Icy Talons, a passive aura which benefits the entire raid by increasing melee and ranged attack speeds by 20%. Icy Touch applies an attack speed reduction called Frost Fever. The talent Brittle Bones causes Frost Fever to increase the physical damage taken by the target by 4%. Horn of Winter boosts the Strength and Agility of the entire raid.

PLAYING AS AN UNHOLY DEATH KNIGHT

Unholy Death Knights are masters of plagues, diseases, and afflictions. They corrupt their foes and spread diseases to enemies with devastating effects. Unholy Death Knights get more tricks and abilities for peripheral damage. They don't do as much by themselves as the Frost Death Knights, instead they get a little help from their friends.

Master of Ghouls is a passive ability that lets Unholy Death Knights keep their Ghouls around until the pets are slain. Also, the cooldown on that ability is 1 minute shorter, so it's pretty common to have them run around with their undead minion. Summon Gargoyle gives the Death Knight more burst damage by calling on another pet.

Scourge Strike is the defining ability of this tree. This Unholy attack does moderate damage by itself, but it scales quite well if there are multiple diseases on the target. Blood Strike, Pestilence, and Festering Strike all trigger Death Runes to appear after they regenerate. This ensures that Unholy DKs have a wider variety of abilities to use.

Anti-Magic Zone is an AoE that protects the Unholy Death Knight and nearby allies for up to 10 seconds. This absorbs damage from enemy spells, so it's rather effective in PvP and group encounters.

ABILITIES LEARNED IF YOU SELECT UNHOLY

	Ability	Description
	Scourge Strike	An unholy strike that deals 100% of weapon damage as Physical damage plus additional damage. In addition, for each of your diseases on your target, you deal an additional 12% of the Physical damage done as Shadow damage.
	Master of Ghouls	Reduces the cooldown on Raise Dead by 60 sec, and the Ghoul summoned by your Raise Dead spell is considered a pet under your control. Unlike normal Death Knight Ghouls, your pet does not have a limited duration.
	Unholy Might	Whenever you hit with Blood Strike, Pestilence, or Festering Strike, the Runes spent will become Death Runes when they activate. Death Runes count as a Blood, Frost or Unholy Rune.
	Reaping	Dark power courses through your limbs, increasing your Strength by 10%.
	Mastery: Blightcaller	Increases the damage done by your diseases by 32%. Each point of Mastery increases disease damage by an additional 4%.

DESIRABLE STATS

Look for Strength, Hit Rating, Critical Strike Rating and Haste Rating. Hit Rating in particular becomes more valuable as you level up because you gain more spell-based abilities. Haste Rating increases the rate at which Runes replenish and you swing your weapons, which increases the chance of having procs activate for you to do even more damage.

LEVELS 55 - 80

Playing Solo

Unholy Death Knights are a true pet class in that your ghoul minion is always present. Your Ghoul can temporarily tank mobs, until you pull threat off of it with your damage. However, when engaging more than one enemy at a time, send your pet to attack an enemy that you are not, so that they take the damage rather than you. Your pet also has some stuns and other utility abilities you may find useful. As an Unholy Death Knight the biggest contribution to your damage is diseases, so you should maximize their uptime and spread them to any foes when possible.

Playing in a Group

Unholy Death Knights deal incredible damage over time (once diseases are applied and spread to every enemy) and they bring a pet to provide some stuns. These stuns add more choices as you face enemies, particularly if there's a spellcaster or a runner. Use your ghoul's leap and gnaw ability to stun either type of target. Don't forget you still have Mind Freeze and Strangulate for casters, and Death Grip for the runners.

If there are many large pulls, maximizing your damage involves spreading your diseases to all nearby targets, and while the damage may start off slowly, it will quickly ramp up and cause serious damage to all opponents. Before you do so, gauge the tank's ability to hold threat against large groups and check for any crowd controlled enemies who wander too close to the designated combat zone.

THE CATACLYSM: LEVELS 81 - 85

Not much changes for Unholy Death Knights at higher levels, but you do gain Outbreak, which applies both Blood Plague and Frost Fever to a target at the same time, although you need to wait one minute between each use. Incoming damage takes steep upturn as you move through Cataclysm's new zones, so temper your expectations about continuing to face large groups of enemies at the same time.

Preparing Your Unholy Death Knight for Heroic Dungeons

Look for Strength, Hit Rating, Haste Rating, and Critical Strike Rating. Don't neglect your Expertise Rating, but you can safely Reforge it into other stats once you have reduced the chances of enemies to dodge or parry your attacks. Hit Rating requirements for Unholy Death Knights are on par with a dual wielding Frost Death Knight due to the higher hit requirements for spells.

Unholy Death Knights: Group Buffs and Debuffs

Unholy Frenzy is a powerful temporary buff Unholy Death Knights grant to an ally. It lasts for 30 seconds and increases the melee and ranged attack speed of the affected ally by 20%, but at a cost of health over time. Don't use this on tanks unless you really know what you are doing. It's far better when used on damage dealers (such as Hunters, who are away from the fight and are less likely to need their health). Icy Touch applies an attack speed reduction called Frost Fever. Anti-Magic Zone is a unique ability that actually creates a bubble-like effect on the ground, and any players inside take 75% less damage from magic attacks. The damage absorbed is based on the Death Knight's attack power, and is most useful when used in smaller scale settings, as the damage absorbed is limited.

Ebon Plaguebringer, which inflicts Ebon Plague on targets, is a debuff that causes all targets to take an additional 15% damage from your diseases, as well as 8% extra damage from spells. Horn of Winter boosts the Strength and Agility of the entire raid.

DRUID

Druids are true hybrids and the masters of shapeshifting. They can learn up to eight different forms. Each of their forms grants unique bonuses, and has a purpose either in combat or outside of it. Unlike other classes, druids are able to play every role category efficiently. Feral Druids focus on melee combat, either as DPS or a tank. Balance Druids, or Moonkin, use spells to provide ranged DPS. Finally, Restoration Druids act as healers.

This flexibility makes them a perfect fit for those who wish to experience every aspect of combat in a single class. Because of their affinity to nature, Druids possess a great arsenal of nature-based spells, and they have delved into the arcane arts as well, further increasing their spell selection.

RACE AVAILABILITY

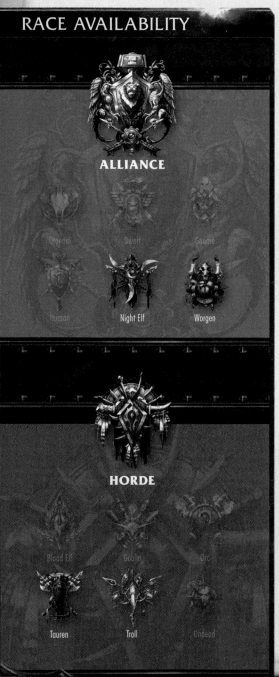

ALLIANCE

Draenei · Dwarf · Gnome

Human · Night Elf · Worgen

HORDE

Blood Elf · Goblin · Orc

Tauren · Troll · Undead

RACIAL ADVANTAGES

ALLIANCE

Race	Best for	Notes
Night Elf	Feral (tanking), Restoration (PvP)	Night Elves are less likely to be hit by any physical attack, or Nature spell. Shadowmeld cancels spells being cast by enemies on the Night Elf.
Worgen	Any spec	Viciousness increases Critical Strike chance by 1%.

HORDE

Race	Best for	Notes
Troll	Balance, Feral (DPS)	Berserking increases attack and casting speed.
Tauren	Feral (tanking), PvP	Endurance increases base health by 5%. Nature spells are less likely to hit a Tauren. War Stomp stuns nearby enemies.

EQUIPMENT OPTIONS

Armor Type	Shield	Ranged Slot
Leather	No	Relic

WEAPON CHOICES

1 Hand Weapon	2 Hand Weapon
Mace	Mace
Dagger	Staff
Fist Weapon	Polearm

DRUID ABILITIES

FORMS

Shapeshifting is the bread and butter of Druid combat and travel. At certain levels, starting at level 8, Druids are granted the ability to change their form into several different animals, each of which has a specific function.

Form	Level	Talent Tree of Proficiency	Function
Cat	8	Feral Combat	Melee DPS
Bear	15	Feral Combat	Tanking
Travel	16	None	Ground traveling
Aquatic	16	None	Water traveling
Moonkin	Talent	Balance	Ranged DPS
Tree of Life	50	Restoration	Short-term Healing boost
Flight	60	None	Flight
Swift Flight	70	None	Flight

While shapeshifted, Druids are immune to Polymorph effects. The act of shapeshifting also breaks any snares or roots. Forms are flexible; Druids can shift from one form to another without reverting to their original form first. With the help of macros (or quick fingers), Druids can even shift from a form to itself, which breaks snares and roots without changing the Druid's current form (do note, however, that any stored Rage of Energy is lost in the process). Mana is conserved across forms, and will continue to regenerate even while shapeshifted. Forms that don't have a special resource such as Energy or Rage show the Mana bar.

Shapeshifting Bar

After learning at least one shapeshifting form, a small bar with several blue icons appears above the Action Bar in the lower-left section of the screen. Each of these icons represents a different form; when a form is active, the icon turns into a white spark, signifying the Druid's current form (none displayed if the Druid is not shapeshifted).

Druids have three different ways to shapeshift: clicking on one of the icons in this bar, binding "Special Action" 1 through 6 in the Key Bindings menu, or simply opening the spellbook and dragging a form to an open slot in the Action Bar. Each combat form (Bear, Cat and Moonkin) has a different primary Action Bar, meaning it switches automatically when you change forms. When you're setting up your Action Bars, switch to each form and place abilities specific to that form into the appropriate Action Bar.

ENHANCED TRAVELING

Druids have three forms that increase their speed: Travel Form, Aquatic Form, and Flight Form (and its improved version, Swift Flight Form). These forms serve no purpose when it comes to tanking, healing or dealing damage; instead, they allow the Druid to escape unfavorable situations or simply travel faster. Flight Form cannot be used in combat, but it serves as a replacement for flying mounts with a slight edge—its instant casting time. Druids can prevent fall damage by shifting into Flight Form (in permitted areas) while falling.

HEALS OVER TIME

Druids have multiple tools available to them when it comes to keeping allies alive, but they are most known for their Heal over Time spells. Rejuvenation, Regrowth, Lifebloom, and Wild Growth all restore health over time. In addition, the effects of Nourish are enhanced when used on a target with one of those spells active on it.

TANKING IN BEAR FORM

While in Bear form, Druids use Rage to activate their abilities. Rage is generated by dealing damage with auto-attacks (most abilities consume rage instead of generating it) and taking damage in battle. The amount of Rage generated depends on the relative damage dealt and taken; when tanking bosses or several mobs at once, however, Druids should have sufficient rage to utilize all their abilities as often as possible. The Enrage ability, learned at level 22, allows Druids to gain 20 Rage instantly, and an additional 10 Rage over time, at the cost of some armor.

CAT FORM DPS

While in Cat form, Druids spend Energy to use their abilities. This resource constantly replenishes itself as time passes, usually in a speedier fashion than other resources (it's a matter of seconds for an Energy bar to go from empty to full). Maximum Energy is 100 by default, but that can be increased through equipment (set bonuses) and talents.

Certain abilities also generate Combo Points, which are visible around the character portrait. These points are required for other abilities—the more points, the stronger or more efficient these abilities become. Some abilities, like Swipe (Cat) and Faerie Fire (Feral), don't generate or spend Combo Points.

INNERVATE

This ability, trained at level 28, makes Druids incredibly popular among other classes which depend on mana. Innervate restores a big chunk of mana to the targeted ally over 10 seconds. While it's tempting to use this on yourself all the time, keep in mind that, while grouping, Innervate might be more valuable if cast on other players, particularly the healer.

ECLIPSE

Balance Druids have a UI element that shows a sun and a moon. Each time an Arcane spell is cast, the pointer in the UI moves closer to the sun, and increase your Nature damage. Each Nature spell cast moves the pointer closer to the moon, which increases Arcane damage output.

SUGGESTED PROFESSION FOR A FIRST-TIME DRUID

For first-time Druids, a combination of Skinning and Leatherworking is a good start. This allows you to skin defeated monsters and use the hides to create Leather armor. Since Druids are hybrids, however, they benefit from any profession; it mainly depends on your style of play.

⬤⬤⬤ DRUID SPELLS

Level Learned	Ability Name		Tree	Description
1	Wrath		Balance	Causes Nature damage to the target.
3	Healing Touch		Restoration	Heals a friendly character. 40 yd range, 3 sec cast.
4	Moonfire		Balance	Burns the enemy with Arcane damage and then additional Arcane damage over 12 sec. 30 yd range, Instant cast.
5	Thorns		Balance	Thorns sprout from the friendly target causing Nature damage to attackers when hit. Lasts 20 sec. 30 yd range, Instant cast, 45 sec. cooldown.
7	Entangling Roots		Balance	Roots the target in place and causes Nature damage over 30 sec. Damage caused may interrupt the effect. 35 yd range, 2 sec cast.
8	Starfire		Balance	Causes Arcane damage to the target. 40 yd range, 3.2 sec cast.
8	Rake		Feral Combat	Rake the target for bleed damage and additional bleed damage over 9 sec. Awards 1 combo point. 35 Energy, 5 yd range, Instant.
8	Ferocious Bite		Feral Combat	Finishing move that causes damage per combo point and consumes up to 35 additional energy to increase damage by up to 100%. Damage is increased by your attack power. 35 Energy, 5 yd range, Instant.
8	Claw		Feral Combat	Claw the enemy, causing additional damage. Awards 1 combo point. 40 Energy, 5 yd range, Instant.
8	Cat Form		Feral Combat	Shapeshift into cat form, increasing melee attack power and causing agility to increase attack power. Also protects the caster from Polymorph effects and allows the use of various cat abilities. The act of shapeshifting frees the caster of Polymorph and Movement Impairing effects. Instant.
8	Rejuvenation		Restoration	Heals the target for a moderate amount every 3 sec over 12 sec. 40 yd range, Instant.
10	Prowl		Feral Combat	Allows the Druid to prowl around, but reduces movement speed by 30%. Lasts until cancelled. 10 sec cooldown, Instant.
12	Revive		Restoration	Returns the spirit to the body, restoring a dead target to life with 35% of maximum health and mana. Cannot be cast when in combat. 40 yd range, 10 sec cast.
12	Regrowth		Restoration	Heals a friendly target for a moderate amount and an extra amount over 6 sec. 40 yd range, 1.5 sec cast.
15	Teleport: Moonglade		Balance	Teleports the caster to the Moonglade. 120 Mana, 10 sec cast
15	Maul		Feral Combat	An attack that instantly deals physical damage. Effects which increase Bleed damage also increase Maul damage. 35 Rage, 5 yd range, Instant, 3 sec cooldown.
15	Growl		Feral Combat	Taunts the target to attack you, but has no effect if the target is already attacking you. 30 yd range, Instant, 8 sec cooldown.
15	Demoralizing Roar		Feral Combat	The druid roars, reducing the physical damage caused by all enemies within 10 yards by 10% for 30 sec. 10 Rage, Instant.
15	Bear Form		Feral Combat	Shapeshift into bear form, increasing melee attack power, armor contribution from cloth and leather items, and Stamina. Causes agility to increase attack power. Also protects the caster from Polymorph effects and allows the use of various bear abilities. The act of shapeshifting frees the caster of Polymorph and Movement Impairing effects. Instant.
16	Travel Form		Feral Combat	Shapeshift into travel form, increasing movement speed by 40%. Also protects the caster from Polymorph effects. Only useable outdoors. The act of shapeshifting frees the caster of Polymorph and Movement Impairing effects. Instant.

Level Learned	Ability Name		Tree	Description
16	Aquatic Form		Feral Combat	Shapeshift into aquatic form, increasing swim speed by 50% and allowing the druid to breathe underwater. Also protects the caster from Polymorph effects. The act of shapeshifting frees the caster of Polymorph and Movement Impairing effects. Instant.
20	Insect Swarm		Balance	The enemy target is swarmed by insects, causing Nature damage over 12 sec. 30 yd range, Instant.
20	Feral Charge (Cat)		Feral Combat	Causes you to leap behind an enemy, dazing them for 3 sec. 10 Energy, 8-25 yd range, Instant, 30 sec cooldown.
20	Feral Charge (Bear)		Feral Combat	Causes you to charge an enemy, immobilizing them for 4 sec. 5 Rage, 8-25 yd range, Instant, 15 sec cooldown.
20	Rebirth		Restoration	Returns the spirit to the body, restoring a dead target to life with 20% health and mana. 40 yd range, 2 sec cast, 30 min cooldown, Reagent: Maple Seed.
20	Omen of Clarity (Passive)		Restoration	Your damage and healing spells have a small chance to cause you to enter a Clearcasting state. The Clearcasting state reduces the Mana, Rage or Energy cost of your next cast-time damaging or healing spell or offensive feral ability by 100%. If specialized as a Feral Druid, Omen of Clarity will also have a chance to occur on your auto-attacks.
22	Skull Bash		Feral Combat	You charge and skull bash the target, interrupting spellcasting and preventing any spell in that school from being cast for 5 sec. 15 Rage, 13 yd range, Instant, 1 min cooldown.
22	Ravage		Feral Combat	Ravage the target, causing a large amount of damage to the target. Must be prowling and behind the target. Awards 1 combo point. 60 Energy, 5 yd range, Instant.
22	Enrage		Feral Combat	Generates 20 rage, and then generates an additional 10 rage over 10 sec, but increases physical damage taken by 10%. Instant, 1 min cooldown.
24	Faerie Fire		Balance	Decrease the armor of the target by 4% for 5 min. While affected, the target cannot stealth or turn invisible. Stacks up to 3 times. 30 yd range, Instant cast.
24	Tiger's Fury		Feral Combat	Increases damage done by 15% for 6 sec. Instant, 30 sec cooldown.
24	Remove Corruption		Restoration	Nullifies corrupting effects on the friendly target, removing 1 curse and 1 poison effect. 40 yd range, Instant.
26	Feline Grace (Passive)		Feral Combat	Reduces damage from falling.
26	Dash		Feral Combat	Increases movement speed by 70% while in Cat Form for 15 sec. Does not break prowling. Instant, 3 min cooldown.
26	Cower		Feral Combat	Cower, causing no damage but lowering your threat by 10%, making the enemy less likely to attack you. 20 Energy, 5 yd range, Instant, 10 sec cooldown.
28	Soothe		Balance	Soothes the target, dispelling all enrage effects. 40 yd range, 1.5 second cast.
28	Innervate		Balance	Causes the target to regenerate mana equal to a percentage of the casting Druid's maximum mana pool over 10 sec. 30 yd range, Instant, 3 min cooldown.
28	Challenging Roar		Feral Combat	Forces all nearby enemies within 10 yards to focus attacks on you for 6 sec. 15 Rage, Instant, 3 min cooldown.
30	Mark of the Wild		Restoration	Increases the friendly target's Strength, Agility, Stamina, and Intellect by 5%, and all magical resistances by a moderate amount for 1 hr. If target is in your party or raid, all party and raid members will be affected. 30 yd range, Instant.

Level Learned	Ability Name		Tree	Description
32	Track Humanoids		Feral Combat	Shows the location of all nearby humanoids on the minimap. Only one type of thing can be tracked at a time. Instant, 1.5 sec cooldown.
32	Pounce		Feral Combat	Pounce, stunning the target for 3 sec and causing a moderate amount of damage over 18 sec. Must be prowling. Awards 1 combo point. 50 Energy, 5 yd range, Instant.
32	Bash		Feral Combat	Stuns the target for 4 sec. 10 Rage, 5 yd range, Instant, 1 min cooldown.
36	Swipe (Cat)		Feral Combat	Swipe nearby enemies, inflicting 125% weapon damage. 45 Energy, 5 yd range, Instant.
36	Swipe (Bear)		Feral Combat	Swipe nearby enemies, inflicting a small amount of damage. Damage increased by attack power. 30 Rage, 8 yd range, Instant, 6 sec cooldown.
40	Savage Defense		Feral Combat	Each time you deal a critical strike while in Bear Form or Dire Bear Form, you have a 50% chance to gain Savage Defense, reducing the damage taken from the next physical attack that strikes you by 65% of your attack power. Instant, 3 min cooldown.
44	Hurricane		Balance	Creates a violent storm in the target area causing Nature damage to enemies every 1 sec, and increasing the time between attacks of enemies by 20%. Lasts 10 sec. Druid must channel to maintain the spell. 30 yd range, Channeled.
46	Shred		Feral Combat	Shred the target, causing 225% damage plus extra damage to the target. Must be behind the target. Awards 1 combo point. Effects which increase Bleed damage also increase Shred damage. 40 Energy, 5 yd range, Instant.
48	Hibernate		Balance	Forces the enemy target to sleep for up to 40 sec. Any damage will awaken the target. Only one target can be forced to hibernate at a time. Only works on Beasts and Dragonkin. 30 yd range, 1.5 sec cast.
50	Tree of Life		Restoration	Shapeshift into the tree of life, increasing healing done by 15% and increasing your armor by 120% but reducing your movement speed by 50%. In addition, some of your spells are temporarily enhanced while shapeshifted. Lasts 45 sec. Enhanced spells: Lifebloom, Wild Growth, Regrowth, Entangling Roots, Thorns, Wrath. Instant, 5 min cooldown.
52	Nature's Grasp		Balance	While active, any time an enemy strikes the caster they have a 100% chance to become afflicted by Entangling Roots. 3 charges. Lasts 45 sec. Instant, 1 min cooldown.
52	Frenzied Regeneration		Feral Combat	Increases maximum health by 30%, increases health to 30% (if below that value), and converts up to 10 rage per second into health for 20 sec. Each point of rage is converted into 0.3% of max health. Instant, 3 min cooldown.
54	Rip		Feral Combat	Finishing move that causes damage over time. Damage increases per combo point and by your attack power. 30 Energy, 5 yd range, Instant.
58	Barkskin		Balance	The druid's skin becomes as tough as bark. All damage taken is reduced by 20%. While protected, damaging attacks will not cause spellcasting delays. This spell is usable while stunned, frozen, incapacitated, feared or asleep. Usable in all forms. Lasts 12 sec. Instant, 1 min cooldown.
60	Flight Form		Feral Combat	Shapeshift into flight form, increasing movement speed by 150% and allowing you to fly. Cannot use in combat. Can only use this form in Outland or Northrend. The act of shapeshifting frees the caster of Polymorph and Movement Impairing effects. Instant.

Level Learned	Ability Name		Tree	Description
62	Maim		Feral Combat	Finishing move that causes damage and stuns the target. Causes more damage and lasts longer per combo point. 35 Energy, 5 yd range, Instant, 10 sec cooldown.
64	Lifebloom		Restoration	Heals the target for a small amount over 10 sec. When Lifebloom completes its duration or is dispelled, the target instantly self-heals for a large amount. This effect can stack up to 3 times on the same target. Lifebloom can only be active one target at a time. 40 yd range, Instant.
66	Lacerate		Feral Combat	Lacerates the enemy target, dealing a very small amount of damage and making them bleed for a small amount of damage over 15 sec and causing a high amount of threat. Damage increased by attack power. This effect stacks up to 3 times on the same target. 15 Rage, 5 yd range, Instant.
68	Tranquility		Restoration	Heals 5 nearby lowest health party or raid targets within 40 yards every 2 sec for 8 sec. Stacks up to 3 times. The Druid must channel to maintain the spell. Channeled, 8 min cooldown.
70	Swift Flight Form		Feral Combat	Shapeshift into swift flight form, increasing movement speed by 280% and allowing you to fly. Cannot use in combat. Can only use this form in Outland or Northrend. The act of shapeshifting frees the caster of Polymorph and Movement Impairing effects. Instant.
74	Cyclone		Balance	Tosses the enemy target into the air, preventing all action but making them invulnerable for up to 6 sec. Only one target can be affected by your Cyclone at a time. 20 yd range, 2 sec cast.
76	Savage Roar		Feral Combat	Finishing move that consumes combo points on any nearby target to increase physical damage done by 30%. Only useable while in Cat Form. Lasts longer per combo point. 25 Energy, Instant.
78	Nourish		Restoration	Heals a friendly target for a large amount. Heals for an additional 20% if you have a Rejuvenation, Regrowth, Lifebloom, or Wild Growth effect active on the target. 40 yd range, 3 sec cast.
81	Thrash		Feral Combat	Deals a small amount of damage, and causes all nearby targets to bleed for a small amount of damage every 2 sec for 6 sec. 25 Rage, 8 yd range, Instant, 6 sec cooldown.
83	Stampeding Roar (Bear)		Feral Combat	The druid roars, increasing all nearby friendly players movement speed within 10 yards by 40% for 6 sec. 15 Rage, Instant, 2 min cooldown.
83	Stampeding Roar (Cat)		Feral Combat	The druid roars, increasing all nearby friendly players movement speed within 10 yards by 40% for 6 sec. 30 Energy, Instant, 2 min cooldown.
85	Wild Mushroom		Balance	Grow a magical Mushroom with 5 Health at the target location. After 6 sec, the Mushroom will become invisible. When detonated by the Druid, all Mushrooms will explode dealing a moderate amount of damage to all nearby enemies within 3 yards. Only 3 Mushrooms can be placed at one time. No cooldown. 40 yd range. Instant cast. Use Wild Mushroom - Detonate to detonate all Mushrooms. 40 yd range, 0.5 sec cast.

PLAYING AS A BALANCE DRUID

Balance is a caster DPS tree, focused on abilities that excel at dealing ranged, magical damage. Druids who specialize in Balance are able to stay at range and dish some serious damage through spells such as Wrath, Starfire and Moonfire. Nature's Majesty gives them more of a critical strike damage bonus with many of their pertinent spells, and Celesital Focus makes it easier for these Druids to cast while being attacked directly. Balance Druids use Starsurge as a class-defining ability. It's a hard-hitting spell that slaps damage on a target and throws them down as well.

Balance Druids assume a strange, antlered shape known as Moonkin Form. Druids in this form love to harp on their direct, instant damage. This has lead to the term "Boomkin" for Druids that stay in that form and toss damage constantly.

Of all three specs, this is the easiest one to play. You still need to know which abilities to use at what times, but there isn't nearly as much shapeshifting to worry about, and you won't have an entire group's survival in your hands.

ABILITIES LEARNED AT LEVEL 10 IF YOU SELECT BALANCE

	Ability	Description
	Starsurge	You fuse the power of the moon and sun, launching a devastating blast of energy at the target. Causes Spellstorm damage to the target and generates 15 Lunar or Solar energy, whichever is more beneficial to you. 40 yd range, 2 sec cast, 15 sec cooldown.
	Celestial Focus	Arcane and Nature spell damage increased by 15%. Increases the critical strike damage bonus of your Wrath, Moonfire, Starfire, Insect Swarm and Starfall spells by 100%.
	Mastery: Total Eclipse	Increases the bonus damage from Eclipse by 12%. Each point of Mastery increases the bonus by an additional 1.5%.

DESIRABLE STATS

Balance Druids benefit greatly from Intellect, Critical Strike Rating, Haste Rating, Spell Power (from weapons) and Mastery. Mana regeneration is usually not a problem as Innervate offsets the need for it, but players who seem to be running out of mana too quickly might want to use a few pieces with Spirit. When it comes to weapons, consider off-hand bonuses when choosing a two-handed weapon (usually a staff for Balance Druids) over a one-handed weapon. The most popular setups for Balance Druids are Dagger and an off-hand, One-Hand Mace and off-hand, or simply a Staff.

If you plan to raid, Hit Rating becomes increasingly important, up to the point at which missing spells on bosses is no longer an issue. When deciding between two attractive items for Balance, check the gear's item levels, as it will usually tell you which item is more powerful, as long as both items have stats from which spellcasting benefits.

LEVELS 1 - 80

Playing Solo

Starting at level 1, Druids are limited to using Wrath and melee attacks. At level 4, Moonfire provides a decent DoT to apply after the first Wrath. Level 7 provides Entangling Roots, which is useful for keeping foes at a distance. It is at level 10, however, that Balance becomes different from other specializations, with the introduction of Starsurge, a spell that deals damage to a target. From this point on, your rotation should consist of pulling with Wrath, applying the Moonfire effect, and keeping enemies at a distance with Entangling Roots and Starsurge.

At level 8, you learn Starfire, which is optimal for pulling as it deals a large amount of damage. Insect Swarm, a strong DoT, is added to the mix at level 20. The most efficient spell sequence usually requires casting Starfire first (if the mob is not likely to move out of range), followed by Moonfire and Insect Swarm. Keep an eye on your Eclipse meter, and cast Wrath and Starfire accordingly. For mobs with low health, you can skip some of these. Start with Starfire and Moonfire, skip Insect Swarm, and finish with Wrath.

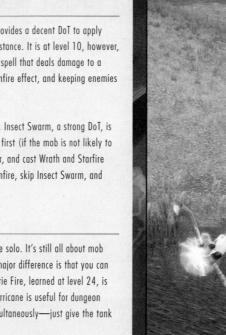

Playing in a Group

As a Balance druid, dealing damage while in a dungeon group is similar to dealing damage while solo. It's still all about mob health—plan out your spell selection so that DoTs are not wasted on mobs that die early. The major difference is that you can be more liberal about the use of Starfire, since mobs will likely be attacking someone else. Faerie Fire, learned at level 24, is a valuable tool to use on bosses, especially when your group has several melee DPS classes. Hurricane is useful for dungeon grouping, as it becomes your main AoE spell, capable of dealing damage to numerous mobs simultaneously—just give the tank time to build threat on all of them first!

At this point, your spell rotation is likely to remain the same while leveling all the way. As soon as you can learn Moonkin Form, do so; shifting to it increases your Spell Critical chance and grants an armor bonus.

THE CATACLYSM: LEVELS 81 - 85

At higher levels, Druids have a leveling advantage over other classes—Flight Form. This invaluable tool allows Druids to travel quickly from quest to quest without spending time to mount—some quests that require collecting items off the ground can be completed without ever leaving Flight Form. At level 78, you can start leveling in the first Cataclysm area (Mount Hyjal), which provides excellent gear rewards.

Preparing Your Balance Druid for Heroic Dungeons

For heroic dungeons, your focus is maximizing your DPS output. In order to accomplish this, select items with as much Intellect and Haste Rating as possible. Your Hit Rating may not be stellar when you begin running Heroics, but try to build it up as items become available. Critical Strike Rating falls behind Haste Rating for Balance Druids, but don't shy away from taking items with it if Haste Rating is unavailable (remember, you can always Reforge some stats into others!). Pick a weapon with a high amount of Spell Power. You can safely prioritize DPS-oriented stats over survivability for heroic dungeons when it comes to gems and enchants, as Druids are quite durable and can heal themselves in a bind.

Balance Druid: Group Buffs and Debuffs

Beyond the standard Druid abilities (Mark of the Wild, Insect Swarm, and Faerie Fire) Balance Druids provide the Moonkin Aura buff, and apply Earth & Moon to enemies just by casting damage spells. For bosses, it is important to cast Faerie Fire as soon as possible, as it boosts the raid's casters' hit rate significantly. On certain fights, you may need to use Innervate on yourself, while on others you should save it for healers. Keep a close eye on how fast your mana depletes in order to make this decision. You may need to use Rebirth (the only way to return non-Soul Stoned/non-Shaman characters back to life during combat) on a dead player in the middle of a fight—just communicate with other Druids to prevent wasted spells.

PLAYING AS A RESTORATION DRUID

Restoration is the healing line of the Druid's talent trees. They augment normal Druid healing with the addition of Swiftmend, an ability that consumes a heal over time effect to give someone a massive, sudden boost in their health. Resto Druids are harder to delay while casting their healing spells, and they regain mana quickly during combat. Critical heal chances are important to Resto Druids. Many of their talents cause additional effects to trigger when a spell critically heals a target.

While these Druids are fairly hard to kill (because of their many ways to keep casting and healing) they're not ideal soloers. This makes Restoration Druids popular as a secondary specialization after people reach level 40. These characters are extremely group friendly, and they rock the town as dedicated healers for a dungeon party.

ABILITIES LEARNED AT LEVEL 10 IF YOU SELECT RESTORATION

	Ability	Description
	Swiftmend	Consumes a Rejuvenation or Regrowth effect on a friendly target to instantly heal for a moderate amount. 40 yd range, Instant, 15 sec cooldown.
	Meditation	Allows 50% of your mana regeneration from Spirit to continue while in combat.
	Gift of Nature	Healing increased by 25%.
	Mastery: Symbiosis	Increases the potency of your healing spells by 10% on targets already affected by one of your heal over time spells. Each point of Mastery increases heal potency by an additional 1.25%.

DESIRABLE STATS

Restoration Druids mainly appear as part of a group, meaning stats that aid survivability can drop low on the priority list. Using Cloth armor is not completely out of the question, but keep in mind wearing a full set of Leather armor grants bonuses.

Restoration Druids should focus on stats such as Intellect, Critical Strike Rating (since it applies to HoTs), Haste Rating, Spell Power on weapons, and Spirit. Spirit is valuable to Restoration Druids due to the Meditation talent and the need for higher mana regeneration.

LEVELS 1 - 80

Playing Solo

Restoration is not the optimal talent tree to choose if you're going it alone. Keep in mind, however, that Restoration gear boosts the power of offensive spells as well, so it is entirely possible to level as Restoration using the essentially the same approach as a Moonkin. In the end, it's usually better to level as one of the damage-oriented trees if you plan to play on your own.

Playing in a Group

Restoration Druids are tasked with healing for dungeon and raid groups. There are different healing styles based on what gear approach and glyphs you choose, but it's basically narrowed to two methods: direct healing versus heals over time. One method does not disable the other; usually, either method will use some of the other, so take advantage of spells like Rejuvenation and Swiftmend even if you're using glyphs that boost Healing Touch. Because heals over time are relatively cheap, you can apply them on members that are likely to take damage in the future (even if they're near full health when you use the spell), then use Swiftmend on them when they take damage. Another aspect of healing is removing debuffs—your tool for this is Remove Corruption. Restoration Druids learn the ability to remove one magical effect in addition to the one curse/one poison effect that any Druid can remove. Most of the debuffs you encounter are magical, but keep an eye out for curses and poisons as well.

When players in your group die, you have two options: you can resurrect them immediately using Rebirth (which has a long cooldown), or wait until combat is over and use Revive on them. It depends on the situation; for long fights, if there is no immediate need for healing, consider using Rebirth to return the dead character to the battle.

THE CATACLYSM: LEVELS 81 - 85

Although Restoration Druids get no new spells after level 80, they remain powerful healers that are relatively gear independent. Innervate offsets the need for mana regeneration gear (for a while) and heals over time are quite mana efficient. For your secondary tree (after acquiring Tree of Life in Restoration), it's usually a good idea to spend points in Balance, as it provides more caster-oriented benefits. Feral Combat is not completely out of the question if you want to be a little more versatile, but having better spellcasting bonuses is more beneficial to your group most of the time.

Preparing Your Restoration Druid for Heroic Dungeons

Since Restoration Druids don't depend on gear as much as other healers, they might have an easier time in early heroic dungeons. Regardless, it's always a good idea to improve your gear before attempting a heroic dungeon for the first time. Start by gathering gear with Spirit, Intellect, and Critical Strike Rating. Haste Rating makes your healing output larger in relation to time, but too much of it might make you run out of mana quickly. Spell Power (which comes from Intellect and weapons) is the single biggest boost to your heals, so stack up as much of it as you can.

Restoration Druids: Group Buffs and Debuffs

Aside from Mark of the Wild and Faerie Fire, which is available to all talent trees, Restoration Druids offer no other raid buffs or debuffs.

HUNTER

Hunters are the sole non-magical, ranged damage-dealers. Hunters have a number of different shots and stings, which can do many things, such as making an enemy receive less healing from allies, and doing damage-over-time. They are also capable of laying traps to deal damage or otherwise slow or incapacitate an enemy.

Hunters also tame beasts and use them as a pet to aid them in combat. While they are not the only class which can use pet minions, the Hunter's pet is unique in that each species falls into a particular type, and each type has a talent tree. The hunter distributes the points into various skills and passive abilities for their pets.

RACE AVAILABILITY

ALLIANCE

Draenei | Dwarf | Gnome

Human | Night Elf | Worgen

HORDE

Blood Elf | Goblin | Orc

Tauren | Troll | Undead

RACIAL ADVANTAGES

ALLIANCE

Race	Best For	Notes
Draenei	Any Spec	Heroic Presence grants Draenei +1% Hit chance.
Dwarf	Any Spec	Gun Specialization grants Dwarves an additional 1% Critical Strike chance with Guns.
Human	Any Spec	Every Man For Himself allows the Hunter to break fears, stuns, and CC.
Night Elf	Any Spec	Night Elves are less likely to be hit by any physical attack, or Nature spell.
Worgen	Any Spec	Ferocity adds 1% Critical Strike chance.

HORDE

Race	Best For	Notes
Blood Elf	Any Spec	Arcane Torrent silences all enemies and restores some of the Blood Elf's focus.
Goblin	Any Spec	Time is Money boosts attack speeds by 1%.
Orc	Any Spec	Blood Fury boost Attack Power. Command increases damage dealt by your pet.
Tauren	Any Spec	War Stomp stuns nearby enemies. Endurance increases base health. Nature spells are less likely to hit a Tauren.
Troll	Any Spec	Berserking increases attack speed. Bow Specialization grants an additional 1% Critical Strike chance with Bows.
Undead	Any Spec	Will of the Forsaken breaks Charm, Fear, and Sleep effects. Shadow spells are less likely to hit an Undead Hunter.

EQUIPMENT OPTIONS

Armor Type	Shield	Ranged Slot
Leather until 40, then Mail	No	Bow, Crossbow, Gun, Thrown

WEAPON CHOICES

1 Hand Weapons	2 Hand Weapons
Axe	Axe
Sword	Sword
Dagger	Staff
Fist Weapon	Polearm

HUNTER SPELLS

Level Learned	Ability Name		Tree	Description
1	Auto Shot		Marksmanship	Automatically shoots the target until canceled.
1	Call Pet 1		Beast Mastery	Summons your first pet to you.
1	Revive Pet		Beast Mastery	Revives your pet, returning it to life with 15% base health. 35 Focus. 10 sec cast.
3	Steady Shot		Marksmanship	A steady shot that causes weapon damage plus more based on your attack power. Generates 9 Focus. 1.5 sec cast.
4	Track Beasts		Survival	Shows the location of all nearby beasts on the minimap.
6	Arcane Shot		Marksmanship	An instant shot that causes weapon damage plus more based on attack power as arcane damage. 25 Focus.
6	Raptor Strike		Survival	An attack that instantly deals melee damage based on your attack power. 6 sec cooldown.
8	Concussive Shot		Marksmanship	Dazes the target, slowing movement speed by 50% for 4 sec. 5 sec cooldown.
10	Aspect of the Hawk		Beast Mastery	Increases ranged attack power by an amount based on your level.
10	Beast Lore		Beast Mastery	Gather information about the target beast. The tooltip will display damage, health, armor, any special resistances, and diet. In addition, Beast Lore will reveal whether or not the creature is tameable and what abilities the tamed creature has.
10	Control Pet		Beast Mastery	Allows you to give commands to control your pet.
10	Dismiss Pet		Beast Mastery	Temporarily sends your active pet away. You can call it back later. 2 sec cast.
10	Kill Command		Beast Mastery	Give the command to kill, causing your pet to instantly inflict damage based on your attack power to the target. Your Pets happiness increases the damage done. 40 Focus. 6 sec cooldown.
10	Tame Beast		Beast Mastery	Begins taming a beast to be your companion. 10 sec channel.
12	Mend Pet		Beast Mastery	Heals your pet for an amount based on your level over 10 seconds.
12	Track Humanoids		Survival	Shows the location of all nearby humanoids on the minimap.
12	Wing Clip		Survival	Reduces the target's movement speed by 50% for 10 sec. Requires melee range.
14	Eagle Eye		Beast Mastery	Zooms in the hunter's vision. Only usable outdoors. 1 min channel.
14	Hunter's Mark		Marksmanship	Increases ranged attack power of all attackers against the marked target by an amount based on your level. In addition, the target of this ability can always be seen by the Hunter.
14	Scare Beast		Beast Mastery	Scares a beast, causing it to run in fear for up to 20 sec. 25 Focus. 1.5 sec cast.
15	Feed Pet		Beast Mastery	Feeds your pet the selected item. Feeding your pet increases happiness. 10 sec cooldown.
15	Scatter Shot		Marksmanship	A short-range shot that deals 50% weapon damage and disorients the target for 4 sec. 30 sec cooldown.
16	Aspect of the Cheetah		Beast Mastery	Increases movement speed by 30%. If the hunter is struck, he will be dazed for 4 sec.
18	Call Pet 2		Beast Mastery	Summons your second pet to you.
18	Track Undead		Survival	Shows the location of all nearby undead on the minimap.
22	Immolation Trap		Survival	Place a fire trap that will burn the first enemy to approach for damage based on your attack power over 15 sec. Trap will exist for 1 min. 1 min cooldown.
24	Multi-Shot		Marksmanship	Fires several missiles, hitting your current target and all enemies nearby for 55% weapon damage. 40 Focus.
24	Track Hidden		Survival	Greatly increases stealth detection and shows hidden units within detection range on the minimap.
26	Serpent Sting		Marksmanship	Causes nature damage based on your attack power over 15 sec. 25 Focus.
28	Freezing Trap		Survival	Place a frost trap that freezes the first enemy that approaches, preventing all action for up to 20 sec. Any damage caused will break the ice. Trap will exist for 1 min. 1 min cooldown.
30	Feign Death		Survival	Feign death which may trick enemies into ignoring you. 30 sec cooldown.
32	Track Demons		Survival	Shows the location of all nearby demons on the minimap.
34	Explosive Trap		Survival	Place a fire trap that explodes when an enemy approaches, causing fire damage and burning all enemies for additional fire damage over 20 sec to all within 10 yards. Trap will exist for 1 min. 1 minute cooldown.
34	Track Elementals		Survival	Shows the location of all nearby elementals on the minimap.
35	Kill Shot		Marksmanship	Deals 150% weapon damage plus extra based on your attack power. Can only be used on enemies that have 20% or less health. 10 sec cooldown.
35	Tranquilizing Shot		Marksmanship	Attempts to remove 1 Enrage and 1 Magic effect from an enemy target. 20 Focus.
36	Deterrence		Survival	When activated, increases parry chance by 100%, reduces the chance ranged attacks will hit you by 100%, and grats a 100% chance to deflect spells. While Deterrence is active, you cannot attack. Lasts 5 sec. 2 min cooldown.
38	Flare		Marksmanship	Exposes all hidden and invisible units within 10 yards of the targeted area for 20 sec. 20 sec cooldown.
40	Widow Venom		Beast Mastery	A venomous shot that reduces the effectiveness of any healing taken by 10% for 30 sec. 15 Focus.
42	Call Pet 3		Beast Mastery	Summons your third pet to you.
46	Ice Trap		Survival	Place a frost trap that creates an ice slick around itself for 30 sec when the first enemy approaches it. All enemies within 10 yards will be slowed by 50% while in the area of effect. Lasts for 1 min. 1 min cooldown.
46	Track Giants		Survival	Shows the location of all nearby giants on the minimap.
48	Trap Launcher		Survival	When used, your next Trap can be launched to a target location within 40 yards. 20 Focus.
50	Track Dragonkin		Survival	Shows the location of all nearby dragonkin on the minimap.
52	Distracting Shot		Marksmanship	Distracts the target to attack you. Has no effect if the target is already attacking you. 8 sec cooldown.
54	Rapid Fire		Marksmanship	Increases ranged attack speed by 40% for 15 sec. 5 min cooldown.
56	Aspect of the Pack		Beast Mastery	Increases move speed of all raid members within 40 yards of the hunter by 30%. If you are struck, you will be dazed for 4 sec.
62	Call Pet 4		Beast Mastery	Summons your fourth pet to you.
64	Aspect of the Wild		Beast Mastery	The hunter and his raid within 30 yards gain nature resistance that increases based on the Hunter's level.
68	Snake Trap		Survival	Place a nature trap that will release several venomous snakes to attack the first enemy to approach. Snakes will die after 15 sec. Trap will exist for 1 min. 1 min cooldown.
75	Master's Call		Beast Mastery	Your pet attempts to remove all root and movement impairing effects from itself and its target, and causes your pet and its target to be immune to all such effects for 4 sec. 1 min cooldown.
76	Misdirection		Survival	The current party or raid member targeted will receive the threat caused by your next damaging attack and all actions taken for 4 sec afterwards. Transferred threat will fade after 30 sec. 30 sec cooldown.
78	Disengage		Survival	You attempt to disengage from combat, leaping backwards. Can only be used while in combat. 25 sec cooldown.
81	Cobra Shot		Survival	Deals weapon damage plus extra based on attack power in the form of nature damage, and increases the duration of your Serpent Sting on the target by 6 sec. Generates 9 Focus. 2 sec cast.
82	Call Pet 5		Beast Mastery	Summons your fifth pet to you.
83	Aspect of the Fox		Beast Mastery	Allows you to shoot Steady and Cobra Shot while moving, and causes you to gain 2 Focus whenever you receive a melee attack.
85	Camouflage		Survival	You camouflage, blending into your surroundings, causing you and your pet to be untargetable and providing stealth while stationary. You can lay traps while camouflaged, but any damage done by you or your pet will cancel the effect. Cannot be cast while in combat. Lasts for 1 min. 20 Focus. 1 min cooldown.

PLAYING AS A BEAST MASTERY HUNTER

Beast Mastery Hunters focus their skills and abilities on making their pet faster and stronger. They also gain access to exotic pets with their 31-point talent. These Hunters can get their pets to use Intimidation, an ability that accrues massive Threat and Stuns the target. If that's not enough fun for you, Beast Masters also get to use Bestial Wrath, making their pet unstoppable for a brief period.

Because many Beast Mastery talent abilities are on a short cooldown, you get to bring these to almost every large fight. This is useful when soloing or taking groups through dungeons.

Your Hunter takes somewhat of a back seat because of this talent line. They act as baseline damage while almost all of the cool toys go to your pet. This is only a problem during encounters where pets are a liability (because of dangers from adds, AoEs, or whatever else). These problems have been ebbing in recent years, so Beast Mastery Hunters continue to gain traction as great group members as well as absurdly fun soloists.

ABILITIES LEARNED AT LEVEL 10 IF YOU SELECT BEAST MASTERY

	Ability	Description
	Intimidation	Command your pet to intimidate the target, causing a high amount of threat and stunning the target for 3 sec. Lasts 15 seconds.
	Animal Handler	Attack power increased by 15%.
	Mastery: Master of Beasts	Increases the damage done by your pets by 13%. Each point of Mastery increases pet damage by an additional 1.7%.

DESIRABLE STATS

Agility provides the most benefit to Hunters, making it the primary stat you want from your gear. Critical Strike Rating, Haste Rating, and even Hit Rating can wait until you start on heroic dungeons.

LEVELS 1 – 80

Playing Solo

Beast Mastery is a popular spec for leveling, because the primary goal of the tree at early levels is to make your pet a tank, effectively causing it to take all the damage and keep you relatively safe. The general sequence of events when fighting a monster is to send your pet in to attack, and you will start spending some of your focus on abilities like Arcane Shot or Kill Command. When you are low on focus, cast Steady Shot to regenerate some of it until you can start using your abilities again. Meanwhile, your pet will be dealing a hefty amount of damage by itself.

If the target is getting close to you, you can use Concussive Shot or Frost Trap to slow it while you gain some distance, while continuing to use abilities. You can use most abilities while moving, but your Auto-shot won't be active. If you stop moving for around half a second, it will fire your auto-shot as long as you are facing the target, and start the internal cooldown for the next shot, which will cool-down even if you continue moving again! This is called "kiting", and is an essential skill to learn when playing a Hunter.

Additionally if you engage multiple enemies, make sure your pet attacks and gets threat on all of the enemies. This will allow you to focus down one enemy so it isn't freely attacking you when it could be hitting your pet tanking instead.

Playing in a Group

Use Focus to activate abilities, switch to Steady Shot or Cobra Shot when you run low, then back to abilities and spending Focus as you see fit. Keep your pet on your target! You don't want it to wander off and cause more enemies to attack your party, and you don't want it to pull threat off the tank. Turn off your pet's Growl ability in a group, as players are much more suited for tanking mobs meant to be fought in groups than your pet is. Put your traps to use if you need to control additional mobs, or to protect your healer. If you ever draw aggro from the tank on a monster, use Feign Death. If it fails, use Deterrence so you don't take any damage while the tank gets the monster off you.

THE CATACLYSM: LEVELS 81 – 85

The Cataclysm levels play mostly the same as the early levels for Beast Mastery. Expect to keep Mend Pet up at all times, since the damage dealt by mobs over level 80 dramatically increases. Use some of your more powerful abilities such as Beastial Wrath when needed, since it allows you to kill high HP quest monsters much quicker than if you hadn't used them.

Preparing Your Beast Mastery Hunter for Heroic Dungeons

While Agility remains at the top of your want list, you need to collect enough Hit Rating to hit the high level bosses in heroic dungeons. Look for Mastery Rating, Critical Strike Rating and Haste Rating next, in that order. Don't forget about Reforging less desirable stats on gear you collect from quests or as drops. The item may not seem like an upgrade at first, but one trip to the Arcane Reforger should take care of that.

Group Buffs and Debuffs

Beast Mastery Hunters are the most versatile spec in the game when it comes to group buffs and debuffs they (although it's really their pets) can bring. There are many different types of buffs certain Hunter pets can learn. Look for the full list at the end of the Hunter section. When playing with others, try to select a pet that has an ability that will improve your group's performance the most. Beast Mastery also has access to Ferocious Inspiration, which increases your group's damage by 3%. This talent is a pre-requisite for Invigoration (which is quite powerful on its own), so it is always worth taking in any Beast Mastery spec.

PLAYING AS A SURVIVAL HUNTER

Attuned to nature, the Survival Hunter is a master of traps and poisons, and getting out of sticky situations. Survival Hunters use a complex set of tactics to gain the edge in both normal combat and PvP. Their focus on traps and disabling abilities is interesting, though it takes more time to master their use. Explosive Shot is a mean attack for direct damage with a damage over time chaser. This is their class-defining ability.

Survivalists' traps often act longer or have a stronger effect than other Hunters. They allows them to disable enemies well in dungeons, giving groups more time to fight major enemies without worrying about peripheral targets.

A major advantage to Survivalists is their ability called Wyvern Sting. This long-term disabling attacks lets them shoot an enemy at range and leave them out of a fight for quite some time. When it ends, the effect triggers damage over time as well. This is a great ability during dungeon runs because the Hunter can team up well with Mages to disable a couple enemies in a group before the fight begins even if those foes are at longer range. Poly one. Sting the other.

Survival Hunters are very group friendly. They've traded some of their damage potential for a bag of tricks that is a constant frustration to their enemies. In small groups, they shine their brightest.

ABILITIES LEARNED AT LEVEL 10 IF YOU SELECT SURVIVAL

	Ability	Description
	Explosive Shot	You fire an explosive charge into the enemy target, dealing Fire damage based on attack power. The charge will blast the target every second for an additional 2 sec. 50 Focus. 6 sec cooldown.
	Into the Wilderness	Agility increased by 15%.
	Mastery: Essence of the Viper	Increases all elemental damage you deal by 8%. Each point of Mastery increases elemental damage by an additional 1%.

DESIRABLE STATS

Agility provides the most benefit to Hunters, making it the primary stat you want on your gear. Critical Strike Rating, Haste Rating, and even Hit Rating can wait until you start on heroic dungeons.

LEVELS 1 – 80

Playing Solo

Survival Hunters tend to kill a little bit slower than Marksmanship Hunters, but have many tools to control mobs so they have an easier time dealing with them. Some talents you can pick up will increase the duration of your traps, let your traps root your enemy in place, and put your enemy to sleep and deal heavy damage when they awaken. Survival Hunters play much like Beast Mastery, except you will be much safer if you pull additional monsters.

If a target gets too close to you, use Concussive Shot or Frost Trap to slow it while you gain some distance, while continuing to use abilities. If you engage multiple enemies, let your pet build threat on them first. This allows you to focus on one enemy at a time while your pet keeps the rest occupied.

Playing in a Group

Survival Hunters bring nice utility to groups with their improved traps and all the tricks you can do with them.

THE CATACLYSM: LEVELS 81 – 85

With snares and roots, Survival Hunters should take next to no damage. When you get Cobra Shot at 81, stop using Steady Shot and use Cobra Shot instead. Its damage increases with your mastery since it deals pure Nature damage, which ignores armor. Aspect of the Fox makes kiting much easier, and it wasn't like you needed the help as a Survival Hunter!

Preparing Your Survival Hunter for Heroic Dungeons

While Agility remains at the top of your want list, you need to collect enough Hit Rating to hit the high level bosses in heroic dungeons. Look for Mastery Rating, Critical Strike Rating and Haste Rating next, in that order. Don't forget about Reforging less desirable stats on gear you collect from quests or as drops. The item may not seem like an upgrade at first, but one trip to the Arcane Reforger should take care of that.

Group Buffs and Debuffs

Survival brings Hunting Party, a talented ability that increases melee and ranged attack speed by 10%. All physical damage-dealers love this buff! The talent also gives you a 2% agility bonus, so there's no reason to skip it even if you're playing solo. Depending on the pet you bring, you may also be responsible for another group buff.

MAGE

Mages are known for dealing larges doses of direct damage from a distance, while also being capable of damaging multiple enemies at once with their numerous AoE spells. Mages are not without their share of utility, however, which includes teleportation spells (for the mage and group members), reliable crowd control and conjury of temporary items that replenish health and mana. Depending on the situation and the talents chosen, Mages can be fragile but powerful wizards (often referred to as "glass cannons") or durable masters of snares and crowd control. Although all of a Mage's talent trees are involved in dealing damage, they're vastly different in their purpose and the way they're played.

RACE AVAILABILITY

ALLIANCE

Draenei Dwarf Gnome

Human Night Elf Worgen

HORDE

Blood Elf Goblin Orc

Tauren Troll Undead

RACIAL ADVANTAGES

ALLIANCE

Race	Best for	Notes
Draenei	Any spec	Heroic Presence grants Draenei +1% Hit chance.
Dwarf	PvP	Stoneform removes poisons, diseases, bleed effects, and increases armor.
Gnome	Any spec	Escape Artist removes snares (including those that cannot be removed through Dispel). Gnomes enjoy a higher Intellect stat.
Human	PvP	Every Man For Himself allows the Mage to break fears, stuns, and CC.
Night Elf	PvP	Shadowmeld cancels spells being cast by enemies on the Night Elf. Nature spells are less likely to hit a Night Elf.
Worgen	PvP	Viciousness increases critical strike chance by 1%. Darkflight grants a 70% speed boost for 10 sec.

HORDE

Race	Best for	Notes
Blood Elf	Any spec	Arcane Torrent silences nearby enemies and restores some mana. All magic spells are less likely to hit a Blood Elf.
Goblin	PvP	Rocket Barrage deals instant fire damage. Rocket Jump allows the mage to leap forward instantly (acting as a second blink). Time is Money increases casting speeds by 1%.
Orc	Any spec	Blood Fury increases spell damage temporarily.
Troll	PvE	Berserking increases casting speeds.
Undead	PvP	Will of the Forsaken removes charm, fear and sleep effects. Shadow spells are less likely to hit Undead.

EQUIPMENT OPTIONS

Armor Type	Shield	Ranged Slot
Cloth	No	Wand

WEAPON CHOICES

1 Hand Weapons	2 Hand Weapons
1H Sword	Staff
Dagger	

MAGE SPELLS

Level Learned	Ability Name		Tree	Description
1	Fireball		Fire	Hurls a fiery ball that causes Fire damage. 40 yd range, 2.5 sec cast.
3	Arcane Missiles		Arcane	Launches waves of Arcane Missiles at the enemy, causing Arcane damage per wave. Each offensive spell you cast has a 40% chance to activate Arcane Missiles. 40 yd range, Channeled.
5	Fire Blast		Fire	Blasts the enemy for Fire damage. 30 yd range, Instant cast, 8 sec cooldown.
7	Frostbolt		Frost	Launches a bolt of frost at the enemy, causing Frost damage and slowing movement speed by 40% for 9 sec. 35 yd range, 2 sec cast.
8	Frost Nova		Frost	Blasts enemies near the caster for Frost damage and freezes them in place for up to 8 sec. Damage caused may interrupt the effect. Instant, 25 sec cooldown.
9	Counterspell		Arcane	Counters the enemy's spellcast, preventing any spell from that school of magic from being cast for 8 sec. Generates a high amount of threat. 40 yd range, Instant cast, 24 sec cooldown.
12	Evocation		Arcane	Gain 15% of your mana instantly and another 60% of your total mana over 6 sec. Channeled, 4 min cooldown.
14	Polymorph		Arcane	Transforms the enemy into a sheep, forcing it to wander around for up to 50 sec. While wandering, the sheep cannot attack or cast spells but will regenerate very quickly. Any damage will transform the sheep back into its normal form. Only one target can be polymorphed at a time. Only works on Beasts, Humanoids and Critters. 35 yd range, 2 sec cast.
16	Blink		Arcane	Teleports the caster 20 yards forward, unless something is in the way. Also frees the caster from stuns and bonds. Instant, 15 sec cooldown.
18	Cone of Cold		Frost	Targets in a cone in front of the caster take Frost damage and are slowed by 60% for 8 sec. Instant cast, 10 sec cooldown.
20	Arcane Blast		Arcane	Blasts the target with energy, dealing Arcane damage. Each time you cast Arcane Blast, the damage of additional Arcane Blasts is increased by 20% and mana cost of Arcane Blast is increased by 175%. Effect stacks up to 4 times and lasts 6 sec or until any Arcane damage spell except Arcane Blast is cast. 40 yd range, 2.5 sec cast.
22	Arcane Explosion		Arcane	Causes an explosion of arcane magic around the caster, causing Arcane damage to all targets within 10 yards. Instant.
24	Teleport		Arcane	Teleports the caster to Orgrimmar, Undercity, Thunder Bluff, Silvermoon, or Stonard. 10 sec cast. Horde Mages only.
24	Teleport		Arcane	Teleports the caster to Stormwind, Ironforge, Exodar, Darnassus, or Theramore. 10 sec cast, Alliance Mages only.
26	Scorch		Fire	Scorch the enemy, dealing Fire damage. 40 yd range, 1.5 sec cast.
28	Ice Lance		Frost	Deals Frost damage to an enemy target, or double Frost damage to a frozen enemy target. 35 yd range, Instant.
30	Remove Curse		Arcane	Removes 1 Curse from a friendly target. 40 yd range, Instant.
30	Ice Block		Frost	You become encased in a block of ice, protecting you from all physical attacks and spells for 10 sec, but during that time you cannot attack, move or cast spells. Also causes Hypothermia, preventing you from recasting Ice Block for 30 sec. Instant cast, 5 min cooldown.
32	Slow Fall		Arcane	Slows friendly party or raid target's falling speed for 30 sec. 40 yd range, Instant, Reagent: Light Feather.
34	Molten Armor		Fire	Causes Fire damage when hit and increases your critical strike chance by 3%. Only one type of Armor spell can be active on the Mage at any time. Lasts 30 min. Instant.
38	Conjure Refreshment		Arcane	Conjures mana food providing the mage and his or her allies with something to eat. Conjured items disappear if logged out for more than 15 minutes. 3 sec cast.
42	Portal		Arcane	Creates a portal, teleporting group members that use it to Orgrimmar, Undercity, Thunder Bluff, Silvermoon, or Stonard. 10 yd range, 10 sec cast, 1 min cooldown. Horde Mages only.
42	Portal		Arcane	Creates a portal, teleporting group members that use it to Ironforge, Stormwind, Darnassus, Exodar, or Theramore. 10 yd range, 10 sec cast, 1 min cooldown. Alliance Mages only.
44	Flamestrike		Fire	Calls down a pillar of fire, burning all enemies within the area for Fire damage and additional Fire damage over 8 sec. 40 yd range, 2 sec cast.
46	Mana Shield		Arcane	Absorbs damage, draining mana instead. Drains 1 mana per damage absorbed. Lasts 1 min. Instant, 12 sec cooldown.
48	Conjure Mana Gem		Arcane	Conjures a mana gem that can be used to instantly restore mana. 3 sec cast.
50	Mirror Image		Arcane	Creates 3 copies of the caster nearby, which cast spells and attack the mage's enemies. Lasts 30 sec. Instant, 3 min cooldown.
52	Blizzard		Frost	Ice shards pelt the target area doing Frost damage over 8 sec. 35 yd range, Channeled.
54	Frost Armor		Frost	Increases armor from items by 20% and Frost resistance. If an enemy strikes the caster, they may have their movement slowed by 30% and the time between their attacks increased by 25% for 5 sec. Only one type of Armor spell can be active on the Mage at any time. Lasts 30 min. Instant.
56	Frostfire Bolt		Fire	Launches a bolt of Frostfire at the enemy, causing Frostfire damage and slowing the target by 40% for 9 sec. This spell will be checked against the lower of the target's Frost and Fire resists. 40 yd range, 2.5 sec cast.
58	Arcane Brilliance		Arcane	Infuses all party and raid members with brilliance, increasing their spell power by 6% and maximum mana for 1 hr. If target is in your party or raid, all party and raid members will be affected. 30 yd range, Instant.
60	Polymorph: Pig / Rabbit / Turtle		Arcane	Transforms the enemy into a pig, rabbit, or turtle, forcing it to wander around for up to 50 sec. While wandering, the target cannot attack or cast spells but will regenerate very quickly. Any damage will transform the target back into its normal form. Only one target can be polymorphed at a time. Only works on Beasts, Humanoids and Critters. 35 yd range, 2 sec cast.
62	Teleport: Shattrath		Arcane	Teleports the caster to Shattrath. 10 sec cast, Reagent: Rune of Teleportation.
66	Portal: Shattrath		Arcane	Creates a portal, teleporting group members that use it to Shattrath. 10 yd range, 10 sec cast, 1 min cooldown, Reagent: Rune of Portals.
68	Mage Armor		Arcane	Increases your resistance to all magic and causes you to regenerate 3% of your maximum mana every 5 sec. In addition, the duration of all harmful Magic effects used against you is reduced by 50%. Only one type of Armor spell can be active on the Mage at any time. Lasts 30 min. Instant.
70	Ritual of Refreshment		Arcane	Begins a ritual that creates a refreshment table. Raid members can click the table to acquire conjured food. The table lasts for 3 min or 50 charges. Requires the caster and 2 additional party members to complete the ritual. In order to participate, all players must right-click the refreshment portal and not move until the ritual is complete. Channeled, 5 min cooldown, Reagents: Arcane Powder x 2.
72	Teleport: Dalaran		Arcane	Teleports the caster to Dalaran. 10 sec cast, Reagent: Rune of Teleportation.
74	Portal: Dalaran		Arcane	Creates a portal, teleporting group members that use it to Dalaran. 10 yd range, 10 sec cast, 1 min cooldown, Reagent: Rune of Portals.
76	Spellsteal		Arcane	Steals a beneficial magic effect from the target. This effect lasts a maximum of 2 min. 40 yd range, Instant.
78	Invisibility		Arcane	Fades the caster to invisibility over 3 sec, reducing threat each second. The effect is cancelled if you perform any actions. While invisible, you can only see other invisible targets and those who can see invisible. Lasts 20 sec. Instant cast, 3 min cooldown.
81	Flame Orb		Fire	Launches a Flame Orb forward from the Mage's position, dealing Fire damage every second to the closest enemy target for 15 secs. 40 yd range, Channeled, 1 min cooldown.
83	Ring of Frost		Frost	Summons a Ring of Frost, taking 3 sec to coalesce. Enemies entering the fully-formed ring will become frozen for 10 sec. Lasts 12 sec. 10 yd radius. 30 yd range, Channeled, 3 min cooldown.
85	Time Warp		Arcane	Warps the flow of time, increasing melee, ranged, and spell casting speed by 30% for all party and raid members. Lasts 40 sec. Allies receiving this effect will become unstuck in time, and be unable to benefit from Bloodlust, Heroism, or Time Warp again for 10 min. Instant, 5 min cooldown.
85	Portal: Tol Barad		Arcane	Creates a portal, teleporting level 85+ group members that use it to Tol Barad. 10 yd range, 10 sec cast, 1 min cooldown, Reagent: Rune of Portals.
85	Teleport: Tol Barad		Arcane	Teleports the caster to Tol Barad. 10 sec cast, Reagent: Rune of Teleportation.

PLAYING AS AN ARCANE MAGE

Arcane Mages specialize in mana conservation, utility and burst damage (with an emphasis on the latter). Along with some Fire builds, Arcane tends to resemble a glass cannon, meaning the damage output is great, but there are few extra escape or defense abilities. Mages who spec into this have great mobility options, primarily from their level 10 skill, Arcane Barrage. Arcane Barrage is the defining ability of this line. It's a fairly hard-hitting attack that can be thrown quite suddenly.

Presence of Mind has always been a major aspect of Arcane Mages. This ability lets them prepare for a single spell, making almost anything instant for the next casting. Arcane Mages can ambush people or monsters with a first attack, hit Presence of Mind, and then slam the targets again before the victim even knows what's going on.

ABILITIES LEARNED AT LEVEL 10 IF YOU SELECT ARCANE

	Ability	Description
	Arcane Barrage	Launches bolts of arcane energy at the enemy target, instantly causing Arcane damage.
	Arcane Specialization	Increases the damage of your Arcane spells by 25%.
	Mastery: Mana Adept	Increases all spell damage done by up to 12%, based on the amount of mana the Mage has unspent. Each point of Mastery increases damage done by up to an additional 1.5%.

DESIRABLE STATS

Arcane mages are particularly vulnerable to attack due to a lack of utility in favor of burst damage. Since there is not much defensive value in Cloth armor, building up a healthy stat pool is important. The stats that benefit your Mage the most while leveling up are Intellect, Spirit, and Stamina. When questing or exploring instances with a group, Intellect is your best friend, since a large mana pool allows you to keep casting when it's not always possible to stop and rest. For solo grinding, Stamina can give you a much-needed edge if you're ambushed by an enemy player or a wandering pack of gnolls. The important thing is to find a balance of the three stats when choosing your gear. While it may be tempting to stack Intellect at the expense of other stats, you may not live long enough, or regenerate mana quickly enough, to finish off a tough opponent.

LEVELS 1 - 80

Playing Solo

When it comes to speedy leveling specs for Mages, Arcane is king. It offers talents such as Arcane Concentration for mana efficiency, while Arcane Potency and Torment the Weak boost the overall damage of certain core spells. Though the initial cost of Arcane spells can be relatively high, the powerful Evocation ability is learned at level 12. This channeled spell instantly restores 15% of the mage's total mana pool, then 60% more over the course of 6 seconds. Overall, this talent tree provides plenty of opportunities to conserve mana while shelling out very good DPS.

Perhaps the most important change made in Cataclysm for Arcane mages is the removal of Arcane Missiles as a core ability. Instead, it now has a 40% chance to proc off any damage spell—and it costs no mana.

At level 10, Arcane mages gain the Arcane Barrage ability, which supplies a quick burst of damage on a short cooldown, to be used intermittently with another spell, such as Frostbolt or the harder-hitting Arcane Blast, which is available at level 20.

Arcane Blast is the Arcane mage's bread and butter. It has a 40 yard range, making it a great opener against a mob or player. By putting points into Slow and Nether Vortex, Arcane Blast has a 50% or 100% chance to slow any target it damages, provided the target is not already affected by Slow. This helpful effect keeps the mob off the Mage for a longer time, buying more time to score a kill before battle is joined.

Another useful core ability for solo play is Arcane Explosion, an AoE spell obtained at level 22. Arcane Explosion has no cooldown and deals moderate damage to groups of enemies. Don't try to engage a group of same-level mobs with Arcane Explosion alone, at least at low levels, because it is unlikely your mana pool will outlast the mobs' health, but it is an incredibly handy "clean-up" spell for multiple enemies with low health.

An optimal spell rotation for an Arcane mage at low levels would be Frostbolt to snare the mob, followed by Arcane Barrage, another Frostbolt or a Fireblast with the likelihood of Arcane Missile activating anywhere in the mix.

Playing in a Group

An Arcane mage in a dungeon is a thirsty creature. Conjure plenty of refreshments for yourself and your group before heading to an instance, because you'll likely need them. Fortunately, Mage Armor helps with mana regen, and the mana gained from your Mana Gems will be greater. Until you get Arcane Blast, your spell rotation will be the same: Frostbolt to proc Arcane Missiles, Fireblast if a mob is low, and Arcane Explosion to clean up any remaining low-HP mobs.

After you get Arcane Blast at level 34, however, you gain a bit more flexibility. Each cast of this spell boosts the damage done by additional Arcane Blasts by 20%, while also increasing the mana cost of subsequent Arcane Blast casts by 175%. This can be extremely taxing to your mana pool, but random procs such as Clearcasting and Arcane Missiles help offset the cost and skyrocket your damage output.

Be careful, though. Arcane mages are capable of incredible burst when using talents such as Presence of Mind and Arcane Power (an activated ability which does 20% more damage while costing 20% more mana). Holding back until your tank has generated sufficient threat is crucial to your survival, particularly in raids.

THE CATACLYSM: LEVELS 81 - 85

At higher level, Mages learn the invaluable skill Time Warp along with new Teleport and Portal spells that lead to Tol Barad. If you wish to raid, keep an eye out for gear that has hit rating on it, as you need to increase your Hit Rating in order to minimize misses on raid bosses. Luckily, Arcane Mages have access to talents that alleviate the need for hit gear, but not enough to ensure every spell will successfully damage a raid boss.

Preparing Your Arcane Mage for Heroic Dungeons

In order to maximize your damage output in heroic dungeons, you should look for high-quality gear that provides Intellect, Hit Rating and Haste Rating. Critical Strike Rating is slightly less beneficial than Haste Rating, but it's still a good idea to keep your Critical Strike chance as high as possible. Stamina shouldn't be completely ignored, as many encounters deal AoE damage that can kill you prematurely.

Arcane Mage: Group Buffs and Debuffs

In addition to Arcane Intellect and Time Warp, Arcane Mages buff allies with Arcane Tactics, which increases their damage output by 3%.

PLAYING AS A FIRE MAGE

Fire Mages initially lack much of the protection provided by the Frost tree, so staying at range is crucial to staying alive. The main source of Fire Mage damage comes from Fireball, Scorch, and Fireblast. Taking advantage of Fireball's long range to open on opponents, and Scorch's quick cast time, Fire mages can finish off a same level enemies with an instant, though mana-inefficient, Fireblast.

While Fire mages are capable of extreme burst damage, they must sometimes opt to use mana conservatively when leveling. In other words, just because you can kill a crocolisk in 3 seconds doesn't mean you should every time.

Fire Mages use Pyroblast, a spell with a lengthy cast time, to pummel enemies with upfront damage and a brutal damage over time

effect. This is a good way to ambush targets before they're aware of your Mage; the casting time doesn't mean much of the enemy isn't running toward you yet. It's also a great way start any encounter; get to your maximum range, hit Pyroblast to start the fight, and then move to faster, less-damaging Fire spells. When fighting in dungeons, the long casting time for Pyroblast means the tank has time to secure aggro before you blast the boss.

In addition, Fire Mages sometimes get an instant and free Pyroblast! This requires the Hot Streak talent (which trades the Arcane Missile proc for Pyroblast) and a fairly good critical hit percentage.

ABILITIES LEARNED AT LEVEL 10 IF YOU SELECT FIRE

	Ability	Description
	Pyroblast	Hurls an immense fiery boulder that causes direct Fire damage and additional Fire damage over 12 sec.
	Fire Specialization	Increases the damage of your Fire spells by 25%.
	Mastery: Flashburn	Increases the damage done by all your periodic fire damage effects by 20%. Each point of Mastery increases periodic damage done by an additional 2.5%.

DESIRABLE STATS

Remember that when choosing weapons, weapon damage and speed are not relevant, so focus on the weapon or weapon/offhand combo that provides the greatest stat bonus. At early levels, boosting Stamina and Intellect is the way to go. Spirit is less valuable since the idea with Fire Mages is to end fights quickly. Due to the effects of the talent Ignite, which causes your target to take heavy damage over time following a crit, Critical Strike chance is perhaps the most important stat to Fire Mages outside of a raid or PvP environment.

LEVELS 1 – 80

Playing Solo

Many Mages prefer Fire for early leveling, as the base damage of Fireball is wonderful. When paired with Scorch, you have a hard-hitting and low mana cost combo at your disposal at relatively early levels. At level 10, you gain the Pyroblast spell, which you should only use as an opening attack until you get the Hot Streak talent.

Though mana can be problem at times when soloing as a Fire mage, consider putting points in the Master of Elements talent. It refunds a portion of your spell's base mana cost upon scoring a critical strike. Add Ignite and Hot Streak, then stack Critical Strike Rating.

Burning Soul, now found at the top of the Fire talent tree, is a nice choice when you're on your own. Fireball can be tricky to cast with enemies in your face. Burning Soul reduces the pushback on casting time due to taking damage, which allows you to cast your spells faster.

At higher levels, you gain access to abilities invaluable to solo players: Blast Wave and Dragon's Breath. Blast Wave is a powerful instant AoE wave of flame, which slows all targets caught in its radius. Dragon's Breath is a cone attack (meaning it spreads out into an area in front of the caster) which deals moderate damage and disorients all targets for 5 seconds. Dragon's Breath is a great way to buy yourself a moment's respite from attackers.

Playing in a Group

In group settings, your single-target DPS rotation should consist of Fireballs, and using Fireblast depending on an enemy's health. Scorch, however, may become your main nuke of choice if you value mana efficiency over raw damage. Talents reduce the mana cost of Scorch and allow you to cast it while on the move.

In dungeons and raids, Frostfire Bolt (a dual-element ability gained at level 56) provides excellent single target DPS and a means of triggering Hot Streak. Your rotation against bosses should consist either of Frostfire Bolt or Fireball, and Pyroblast when Hot Streak activates. Use Scorch and Fireblast only when crunched for time (or on the move), and Blast Wave or Dragon's Breath only for up-close AoE of enemies.

Don't forget the ultimate talent of the Fire tree, Living Bomb. Think of it as a timed bomb—it ticks for 12 seconds on its target before exploding and dealing damage to enemies in a 10-yard radius. There is no better spell for heavily damaging a boss mob and its cohorts. Refresh it every time it explodes for maximum damage output.

THE CATACLYSM: LEVELS 81 – 85

At level 81, Mages learn the spell Flame Orb. This channeled spell is cheap, but has a considerable cooldown period. It deals fire-based damage to the closest enemy, starting from the Mage's position. This is best used as an emergency cooldown, or in instance groups.

Preparing Your Fire Mage for Heroic Dungeons

For heroic dungeons and beyond, Critical Strike Rating remains important, but you also need Hit Rating and Spirit. Because raid bosses are several levels higher than you, fully resisted nukes are common so Hit Rating takes precedence over Critical Strike Rating up to a certain point. Look for weapons with as much Spell Power as possible. Haste Rating is also beneficial, but if you find yourself owning gear that is mostly haste-based, consider Reforging it, or trying out an Arcane build.

Fire Mages: Group Buffs and Debuffs

Fire Mages offer Arcane Intellect and Time Warp, but no other additional buffs or debuffs.

PALADIN

Paladins are survivors and protectors, able to fulfill any role in the World of Warcraft. Retribution Paladins are the damage dealers, applying Holy magic to boost their physical damage. Holy Paladins restore and mend fallen or injured allies during battle. Protection Paladins excel at holding threat in any size group.

When you first start your paladin, you have access to one core Paladin ability: Crusader Strike. By the time you reach level 10, you have access to additional skills such as Seal of Righteousness, Judgement, Devotion Aura, Hammer of Justice, and your first heal, Word of Glory. Use Crusader Strike and Judgement with Seal of Righteousness active while taking down enemies. Crusader Strike builds Holy Power, which you can expend to heal yourself with Word of Glory. Don't forget about Divine Shield! It's always there to give you time to heal your injuries, or in some cases, flee from the scene.

RACE AVAILABILITY

ALLIANCE

Draenei | Dwarf | Gnome

Human | Night Elf | Worgen

HORDE

Blood Elf | Goblin | Orc

Tauren | Troll | Undead

RACIAL ADVANTAGES

ALLIANCE

Race	Best for	Notes
Draenei	Retribution	Heroic Presence adds 1% Hit for a Draenei.
Dwarf	Retribution/Protection	Mace Specialization grants Expertise to Dwarves who wield maces. Stoneform removes all poison, disease, and bleed effects and increases armor for 8 seconds.
Human	Any spec	Mace and Sword Specializations grant Expertise to humans who wield maces and swords. Every Man For Himself allows the player to break fears, stuns, and CC.

HORDE

Race	Best for	Notes
Blood Elf	Protection	Arcane Torrent silences nearby enemies and restores some of the Blood Elf's mana, energy or runic power. All magic spells are less likely to hit a Blood Elf.
Tauren	Protection	War Stomp stuns nearby enemies. Endurance increases base health by 5%. Nature spells are less likely to hit a Tauren.

EQUIPMENT OPTIONS

Armor Type	Shield	Ranged Slot
Mail until 40, then Plate	Yes	Relic

WEAPON CHOICES

1 Hand Weapons	2 Hand Weapons
Axe	Axe
Mace	Mace
Sword	Sword
	Polearm

PALADIN SPELLS

Level Learned	Ability Name		Tree	Description
1	Crusader Strike		Retribution	An instant strike that causes 100% weapon damage and grants a charge of Holy Power.
3	Seal of Righteousness		Protection	Fills the paladin with holy spirit for 30 min, granting each single-target melee attack additional Holy damage.
4	Judgement		Retribution	Unleashes the energy of a Seal to judge an enemy for Holy damage.
5	Devotion Aura		Protection	Gives additional armor to party and raid members within 40 yards.
7	Hammer of Justice		Protection	Stuns the target for 6 sec.
9	Word of Glory		Holy	Consumes all Holy Power to heal a friendly target for a certain amount per charge of Holy Power.
12	Righteous Fury		Protection	Increases your threat generation while active, making you a more effective tank.
14	Hand of Reckoning		Protection	Taunts the target to attack you, but has no effect if the target is already attacking you.
14	Holy Light		Holy	Heals a friendly target.
16	Flash of Light		Holy	A quick, expensive heal that heals a friendly target.
16	Lay on Hands		Holy	Heals a friendly target for an equal amount of the Paladin's maximum health.
18	Hand of Protection		Protection	A targeted party or raid member is protected from all physical attacks for 10 sec, but during that time they cannot attack or use physical abilities.
18	Exorcism		Holy	Causes holy damage to an enemy target. If the target is Undead or Demon, it will always critically hit.
22	Blessing of Kings		Protection	Places a Blessing on the friendly target, increasing Strength, Agility, Stamina, and Intellect by 5% and all magic resistances by a certain amount for 1 hour. If the target is in your party or raid, all party and raid members will be affected.
24	Consecration		Holy	Consecrates the land beneath the Paladin, doing Holy damage over 10 sec to enemies who enter the area.
26	Retribution Aura		Retribution	Causes Holy damage to any enemy that strikes a party of raid member within 40 yards.
28	Holy Wrath		Holy	Sends bolts of holy power in all directions, causing Holy damage divided among all targets within 10 yards and stunning all Demons and Undead for 3 sec.
28	Redemption		Holy	Brings a dead ally back to life with 35% of maximum health and mana. Cannot be cast when in combat.
30	Divine Protection		Protection	Reduces all damage taken by 20% for 10 sec.
32	Seal of Insight		Holy	Fills the Paladin with divine power for 30 min, giving each single-target melee attack a chance to heal the Paladin and restore 4% of the paladin's maximum mana.
34	Cleanse		Holy	Cleanses a friendly target, removing 1 Poison effect and 1 Disease effect.
36	Righteous Defense		Protection	Come to the defense of a friendly target, commanding up to 3 enemies attacking the target to attack the Paladin instead.
42	Concentration Aura		Holy	All party and raid members within 40 yards lose 35% less casting or channeling time when damage.
44	Seal of Truth		Retribution	Fills the Paladin with holy power, causing single-target attacks to Censure the target, which deals additional holy damage over 15 sec. Censure can stack up to 5 times. Once stacked to 5 times, each of the Paladin's attacks also deals 15% weapon damage as addition Holy damage.
44	Divine Plea		Holy	You gain 10% of your total mana over 15 sec, but the amount healed by your healing spells is reduced by 50%.
46	Hammer of Wrath		Retribution	Hurls a hammer that strikes the enemy for Holy damage. Only usable on enemies that have 20% or less health.
48	Divine Shield		Protection	Protects the paladin from all damage and spells for 8 sec, but reducing all damage you deal by 50%.
52	Hand of Freedom		Protection	Places a Hand on the friendly target, granting immunity to movement impairing effects for 6 sec.
56	Blessing of Might		Retribution	Places a Blessing on the friendly target, increasing attack power by 10% and restores mana every 5 seconds for 1 hour.
62	Crusader Aura		Retribution	Increases the mounted speed by 20% for all party and raid members within 40 yards.
62	Divine Light		Holy	A large heal that heals a friendly target. Good for periods of heavy damage.
64	Seal of Justice		Protection	Fills the Paladin with the spirit of justice for 30 min, causing each single-target melee attack to limit the target's maximum run speed for 5 sec and deal additional Holy damage.
66	Hand of Salvation		Protection	Places a Hand on the party of raid member, reducing their total threat by 2% every 1 sec. for 10 sec.
72	Avenging Wrath		Retribution	Increases all damage and healing by 20% for 20 sec.
76	Resistance Aura		Holy	Gives additional Fire, Frost and Shadow resistance to all raid members within 40 yards.
78	Turn Evil		Holy	The targeted undead or demon enemy will be compelled to flee for up to 20 sec. Damage caused may interrupt the effect. Only one target can be turned a time.
80	Hand of Sacrifice		Protection	Places a Hand on the party or raid member, transferring 30% damage taken to the caster. Lasts 12 sec or until the caster has transferred 100% of their maximum health.
81	Inquisition		Retribution	Consumes all Holy Power to increase your Holy Damage by 30%. Lasts 4 sec per charge of Holy Power consumed.
83	Holy Radiance		Holy	Heals all friendly targets within 10 yards every sec. Lasts 10 sec.
85	Guardian of Ancient Kings			Holy: Summons a Guardian of Ancient Kings to protect you for 30 sec. While active, your next 5 heals will cause the Guardian to heal the same target for the amount healed by your heal, and friendly targets within 10 yards of the target for 10% of the amount healed. Protection: Summons a Guardian of Ancient Kings to protect you for 12 sec. While the Guardian is active, all incoming damage is reduced by 60%. Retribution: Summons a Guardian of Ancient Kings to attack your current target for 12 sec. While active, your and your Guardian's attacks cause you to be infused with Ancient Power, increasing your Strength by 20 per application. After 12 sec or when your Guardian is killed, you will release Ancient Fury, causing damage and additional damage per application of Ancient Power, divided amongst all targets within 10 yards.

PLAYING AS A HOLY PALADIN

Holy Paladins are group-friendly healers that are hard to take down. Most people expect healers to be kind of squishy, but that isn't the case when said healer is wearing plate armor and can carry a shield.

Holy Paladins have increased mana regeneration in combat compared with their rivals. They also gain a bonus to all of their healing spells, and they don't suffer as much pushback when being attacked in melee during healing.

Holy Shock is the defining ability of this line. It's either an attack (if targeting an enemy) or a healing spell (when targeting a friend). This instant ability gives the Paladin a bit more offense during easy encounters and the chance to restore health to someone quickly if they're under fire themselves.

Almost everything a Holy Paladin learns is about better healing, critical heals, or other survivability issues. You won't have much damage to offer a party, and this is a slow selection for solo leveling. Holy Paladins are awesome when taken as a backup specialization after you learn Dual Specialization.

ABILITIES LEARNED AT LEVEL 10 IF YOU SELECT HOLY

	Ability	Description
	Holy Shock	Blasts the target with Holy energy, causing Holy damage to an enemy, or healing to an ally, and grants a charge of Holy Power.
	Walk in the Light	Increases the effectiveness of your healing spells by 15%.
	Meditation	Allows 50% of your mana regeneration from Spirit to continue while in combat.
	Mastery: Illuminated Healing	Your healing spells also place an absorb shield on your target for 10% of the amount healed lasting 8 seconds. Each point of Mastery increases the absorb amount by an additional 1%.

DESIRABLE STATS

Holy Paladin gear should be a one-hand weapon, a shield, and Plate armor, all loaded with Intellect and Spirit. Plate Specialization for Holy Paladins grants a 5% Intellect boost when they wear Plate armor in all armor slots. The type of weapon isn't as important as its stats (in particular, don't worry about racial Expertise bonuses for healing weapons) when considering them.

Holy Paladins are concerned with two aspects of healing: throughput and mana regeneration. Intellect provides both throughput (with increased Spell Power), and mana regeneration through the use of Divine Plea and Replenishment (a buff provided by other party members) which restores mana based on your total mana pool. Spirit also provides mana regeneration and it is wise to consider both attributes when choosing equipment.

Aside from Intellect and Spirit, look for Haste Rating and Critical Strike Rating on gear. Both stats help increase throughput, with Haste being the stronger of the two. However, Haste causes your rate of mana regeneration to suffer because of the increased usage of spells so don't pile it on too high.

LEVELS 1 - 80

Playing Solo

Upon reaching level 10, you gain the ability Holy Shock. It has two uses: an instant heal or a single-target holy blast against enemies. Holy Shock generates Holy Power for the use of Word of Glory. At higher levels, Paladins gain access to more offensive and defensive tools. Use Offensive abilities such as Exorcism, Holy Wrath, Hammer of Wrath, and Consecration to take down enemies, while using heals such as Flash of Light and Holy Light to keep yourself alive.

Playing in a Group

It's hard to make a Paladin that isn't group friendly. Holy Paladins get better Auras, so they can protect casters from Silence/Interruption with their Concentration Aura or add more to everyone's stats with other auras. For example, use Enlightened Judgements to heal yourself, or instant Exorcisms through the talent Denounce. Beacon of Light allows you to heal multiple targets. You may also want to consider Seal of Insight to help restore your mana. Spells like Judgement and Crusader Strike are single-target melee attacks and both have a chance to restore mana through this Seal.

Use an Aura that best suits the situation and keep your party buffed with a Blessing. Employ the other offensive or defensive abilities that help reduce the amount of damage your party takes. Hammer of Justice works well for this, although many Bosses are not affected by it.

THE CATACLYSM: LEVELS 81 - 85

Many quests in this level range will offer you a choice of items that may be something you use in introductory dungeons or raids. Keep that in mind when you decide to skip or abandon a quest line. Also, because of the increases in level, your Critical Strike Rating and Haste percentage may have dropped substantially. Try to complete as many of the difficult or group quests as possible, as they reward some of the best items you can obtain before getting in to dungeon content.

Preparing Your Holy Paladin for Heroic Dungeons

Remember you're interested in high Intellect and Spirit items with as much Haste Rating and Critical Strike Rating as possible. All your gear should be appropriately gemmed and enchanted to improve your healing throughput and mana regeneration. Your gear doesn't need to be absolutely perfect just to start heroics, but it needs to illustrate to your group that you put some time and thought into your character. Since only one class uses Plate armor with Intellect and Spirit, you shouldn't need to worry about if a drop is appropriate for your class and spec, only if it's a better option than what you have already.

Holy Paladin: Group Buffs

Always have the appropriate Aura active and place a Blessing on everyone in the group or raid. Depending on how you have spent your talent points, you may have Protector of the Innocent. This talent boosts the armor bonus of Devotion Aura and increases the healing on all allies affected by the aura by 3%. If there are multiple Paladins in the group, coordinate Auras and Blessings so there's no overlap.

PLAYING AS A PROTECTION PALADIN

Protection Paladins are tanks that can hold aggro against large clusters of enemies using abilities such as Consecration. They ensure that even targets that aren't being hit stay focused on the Paladin instead of the damage dealers or a primary healer.

With Vengeance, these Paladins reach much higher Attack Power when tanking powerful enemies. They also receive massive bonuses to Stamina, and their Spell Power benefits from high Strength, making it easy for them to gear up without giving up on standard tanking equipment.

Avenger's Shield is the defining ability of this line. It gives the Paladin a ranged attack that can hit multiple foes, silence them, and do heavy damage in the process. This forces melee enemies and casters over to the Paladin in a direct assault. That's exactly what the Protection Paladin wants, so it's a perfect starter for every major battle.

Protection Paladins have higher damage than Holy Paladins, and they're much harder to kill. Anyone who takes both specializations is practically guaranteed to have a slot in a dungeon group. Tanks and healers are the hardest roles to fill, and Paladins can do either with finesse.

ABILITIES LEARNED AT LEVEL 10 IF YOU SELECT PROTECTION

	Ability	Description
	Avenger's Shield	Hurls a holy shield at the enemy, dealing Holy damage, silencing them, interrupting for 3 sec, and then jumping to additional nearby enemies. Affects 3 total targets.
	Vengeance	Each time you take damage, you gain 5% of the damage taken as attack power, up to a maximum of 10% of your health.
	Touched by the Light	Increases your total Stamina by 15%, increases your spell hit by 8%, and increases your spell power by an amount equal to 60% of your strength.
	Judgements of the Wise	Your Judgement grants you 30% of your base mana over 10 seconds.
	Mastery: Divine Bulwark	Increases your chance to block melee attacks by 24%. Each point of Mastery increases block chance by an additional 3%.

DESIRABLE STATS

Protection Paladins want gear with defensive attributes such as Stamina, Dodge Rating, and Parry Rating. You need some Strength for threat generation, but it's typically found on defensive gear already; you shouldn't need to anything beyond what you get with the rest of your gear. Protection Paladins also need a suitable melee-oriented one-hand weapon; however, their biggest need is a quality shield with a high armor value and defensive stats. When you get deeper into heroic dungeons and raiding, you should collect a bit of Hit Rating and Expertise Rating, but stock up on as much health and avoidance as you can muster before you worry about threat generation.

LEVELS 1 - 80

Playing Solo

At level 10, you gain the ability Avenger's Shield. Use your assortment of offensive abilities such as Exorcism, Holy Wrath, Divine Storm, Hammer of Wrath, and Consecration to take down enemies. Defensive cooldowns like Divine Protection reduce the time you spend between battles restoring your health.

Playing in a Group

You are expected to fulfill the tank role, which means keeping everyone in the group safe. You are responsible for keeping the focus of every enemy on you, and not on other party members. The group may also rely on your support abilities such as the Hand spells, Word of Glory and Lay on Hands. In some circumstances you may be required to help heal or cleanse debuffs, so have these spells easily accessible.

THE CATACLYSM: LEVELS 81 - 85

Not much changes for playing as a Protection Paladin in the high level zones. Incoming damage scales up quickly as you progress through Cataclysm's zones, so you may need to reduce the number of enemies you take on at once compared to how many you were able to handle in Azeroth, Outlands, and even Northrend.

Preparing Your Protection Paladin for Heroic Dungeons

If you skipped Sanctuary in the Protection talent tree while leveling up, you must spend points in it now (respec if necessary). Without it, you won't be able to stand up to the damage from heroic dungeon bosses or raid bosses. Grab any equipment that is clearly for tanking: high Stamina, Dodge Rating, Parry Rating, and so on. They may not help you in the short term as you finish the last few levels to 85, but once you are given the responsibility of tanking for a group or raid and need to survive the incoming damage, you need that gear. You're competing with Warriors and Death Knights for gear, so you can't depend on getting items dropped by bosses in dungeons. Complete the more difficult quests, as they reward the best items you can obtain before getting in to dungeon content. Look for crafted items or reputation rewards to fill out your gear.

Threat generation is your secondary concern. Strength, Hit Rating, and Expertise Rating all contribute to threat generation but they're less necessary when you're just starting out.

Protection Paladins: Group Buffs and Debuffs

Always have the appropriate Aura active and place a Blessing on everyone in the group or raid. Judgements of the Just is an important talent for Protection Paladins. It reduces the melee attack speed of your target, which makes the healer's life much easier. You should also consider Vindication. This talent reduces the amount of damage you take from physical attacks by 10%.

PRIEST

Priests harness the power of Holy and Shadow magic. Although Priests may seem like a pure healing class, they're able to use many spells that deal damage directly or over time. Priests are versatile healers, with many instant spells that can save group members from certain death. They're also the only class with two different healing specializations, both with very different playstyles, each excelling at restoring or preventing different kinds of damage. Among a priest's repertoire are many other utility spells, such as Mind Control, Levitate and Mind Vision. Although these might not necessarily be fit for typical combat, they're usually considered fun novelties to play with.

RACE AVAILABILITY

ALLIANCE

- Draenei
- Dwarf
- Gnome
- Human
- Night Elf
- Worgen

HORDE

- Blood Elf
- Goblin
- Orc
- Tauren
- Troll
- Undead

RACIAL ADVANTAGES

ALLIANCE

Race	Best for	Notes
Draenei	Shadow	Heroic Presence grants Draenei +1% Hit chance. Gift of the Naaru heals the Draenei or any ally.
Dwarf	Holy or Discipline PvP	Stoneform removes poisons, diseases, bleed effects, and increases armor.
Gnome	Any spec	Expansive Mind increases Intellect.
Human	PvP	Every Man For Himself allows the Priest to break fears, stuns, and CC.
Night Elf	PvP	Night Elves are less likely to be hit by any physical attack, or Nature spell. Shadowmeld cancels spells being cast by enemies on the Night Elf.
Worgen	Discipline, PvP	Viciousness increases critical strike chance by 1%. Darkflight grants a 70% speed bost for 10 sec.

HORDE

Race	Best for	Notes
Blood Elf	Any spec	Arcane Torrent silences nearby enemies and restores some of the Blood Elf's mana. Magic spells are less likely to hit a Blood Elf.
Goblin	Shadow	Time is Money boosts attack and casting speeds by 1%. Rocket Barrage is an extra damage ability.
Tauren	PvP	War Stomp stuns nearby enemies. Endurance increases base health. Nature spells are less likely to hit a Tauren.
Troll	Shadow PvE	Berserking increases attack and casting speeds.
Undead	PvP	Will of the Forsaken breaks Charm, Fear, and Sleep effects. Shadow spells are less likely to hit an Undead Priest.

EQUIPMENT OPTIONS

Armor Type	Shield	Ranged Slot
Cloth	No	Wand

WEAPON CHOICES

1 Hand Weapons	2 Hand Weapons
Mace	Staff
Dagger	

PRIEST SPELLS

Level Learned	Ability Name		Tree	Description
1	Smite		Holy	Smite an enemy, dealing Holy damage. 30 yd range, 2.5 sec cast.
3	Flash Heal		Holy	Heals a friendly target. 40 yd range, 1.5 sec cast.
4	Shadow Word: Pain		Shadow	A word of darkness that causes Shadow damage over 18 sec. 40 yd range, Instant.
5	Power Word: Shield		Discipline	Draws on the soul of the friendly target to shield them. Lasts 30 sec. While the shield holds, spellcasting will not be interrupted by damage. Once shielded, the target cannot be shielded again for 15 sec. 40 yd range, Instant, 3 sec cooldown.
7	Inner Fire		Discipline	A burst of Holy energy fills the caster, increasing the armor value from items by 60% and spell power by a moderate amount. Lasts 30 min. Instant.
8	Renew		Holy	Heals the target every 3 sec over 12 sec. 40 yd range, Instant.
9	Mind Blast		Shadow	Blasts the target for Shadow Damage. 40 yd range, 1.5 sec cast, 8 sec cooldown.
12	Psychic Scream		Shadow	The caster lets out a psychic scream, causing 5 enemies within 8 yards to flee for 8 sec. Damage caused may interrupt the effect. Instant, 30 sec cooldown.
14	Power Word: Fortitude		Discipline	Power infuses all party and raid members, increasing their Stamina for 1 hr. If target is in your party or raid, all party and raid members will be affected. 40 yd range, Instant.
14	Resurrection		Holy	Brings a dead ally back to life with 35% health and mana. Cannot be cast when in combat. 30 yd range, 10 sec cast.
16	Heal		Holy	Heals your target. 40 yd range, 3 sec cast.
18	Holy Fire		Holy	Consumes the enemy in Holy flames that cause Holy damage and additional Holy damage over 7 sec. 30 yd range, 2 sec cast, 10 sec cooldown.
22	Cure Disease		Holy	Removes 1 disease from a friendly target. 40 yd range, Instant.
24	Fade		Shadow	Fade out, temporarily reducing all your threat for 10 sec. Instant, 30 sec cooldown.
26	Dispel Magic		Discipline	Dispels magic on the target, removing 2 harmful spells from a friend of 2 beneficial spells from an enemy. 30 (enemy)/40 (friend) yd range, Instant.
28	Devouring Plague		Shadow	Afflicts the target with a disease that causes Shadow damage over 24 sec. 15% of damage caused by the Devouring Plague heals the caster. This spell can only affect one target at a time. 40 yd range, Instant.
32	Shackle Undead		Discipline	Shackles the target undead enemy for up to 50 sec. The shackled unit is unable to move, attack or cast spells. Any damage caused will release the target. Only one target can be shackled at a time. 30 yd range, 1.5 sec cast.
32	Shadow Word: Death		Shadow	A word of dark binding that inflicts Shadow damage to the target. If the target is not killed by Shadow Word: Death, the caster takes damage equal to the damage inflicted upon the target. 40 yd range, Instant.
34	Levitate		Discipline	Allows the friendly party or raid target to levitate, floating a few feet above the ground. While levitating, the target will fall at a reduced speed and travel over water. Any damage will cancel the effect. Lasts 2 min. 30 yd range, Instant, Reagent: Light Feather.
36	Mind Vision		Shadow	Allows the caster to see through the target's eyes for 1 min. Will not work if the target is in another instance or on another continent.
38	Greater Heal		Holy	A slow casting spell that heals a single target. 40 yd range, 3 sec cast.
38	Mind Control		Shadow	Controls a humanoid mind, but increases the time between its attacks by 25%. Lasts up to 30 sec. 20 yd range, 2.5 sec cast, Channeled.
44	Prayer of Healing		Holy	A powerful prayer heals the friendly target's party members within 30 yards. 40 yd range, 2.5 sec cast.
48	Binding Heal		Holy	Heals a friendly target and the caster. Low threat. 40 yd range, 1.5 sec cast.
50	Mysticism			Increases your Intellect by 5%.
52	Shadow Protection		Shadow	Power infuses the target's party and raid members, increasing their Shadow resistance for 1 hr. If target is in your party or raid, all party and raid members will be affected. 40 yd range, Instant.
54	Fear Ward		Discipline	Wards the friendly target against Fear. The next Fear effect used against the target will fail, using up the ward. Lasts 3 min. 30 yd range, Instant, 3 min cooldown.
56	Mind Soothe		Shadow	Soothes the target, reducing the range at which it will attack you by 10 yard. Only affects Humanoid and Dragonkin targets. Lasts 15 sec. 40 yd range, Instant.
58	Mana Burn		Discipline	Destroy 10% of the target's mana (up to a maximum of 20% of your own maximum mana). For each mana destroyed in this way, the target takes 0.5 Shadow damage. 30 yd range, 2.5 sec cast.
62	Holy Nova		Holy	Causes an explosion of holy light around the caster, causing Holy damage to all enemy targets within 10 yards and healing all party and raid members within 10 yards. These effects cause no threat. Instant.
64	Hymn of Hope		Holy	Restores 2% mana to 3 nearby low mana friendly party or raid targets every 2 sec for 8 sec, and increases their total maximum mana by 15% for 8 sec. The Priest must channel to maintain the spell. 40 yd range, Instant.
66	Shadowfiend		Shadow	Creates a shadowy fiend to attack the target. The caster receives 3% mana when the Shadowfiend attacks. Damage taken by area of effect is reduced. Lasts 15 sec. 30 yd range, Instant, 5 min cooldown.
68	Prayer of Mending		Holy	Places a spell on the target that heals them the next time they take damage. When the heal occurs, Prayer of Mending jumps to a party or raid member within 20 yards. Jumps up to 5 times and lasts 30 sec after each jump. This spell can only be placed on one target at a time. 40 yd range, Instant, 10 sec cooldown.
72	Mass Dispel		Discipline	Dispels magic in a 15 yard radius, removing 1 harmful spell from each friendly target and 1 beneficial spell from each enemy target. Affects a maximum of 10 friendly targets and 10 enemy targets. This dispel is potent enough to remove Magic effects that are normally undispellable. 30 yd range, 1.5 sec cast.
74	Mind Sear		Shadow	Causes an explosion of Shadow magic around the enemy target, dealing Shadow damage every 1 sec for 5 sec to all enemies within 10 yards around the target. 30 yd range, Channeled.
78	Divine Hymn		Holy	Heals 3 nearby lowest health friendly party or raid targets within 40 yards every 2 sec for 8 sec, and increases healing done to them by 10% for 8 sec. The Priest must channel to maintain the spell. 40 yd range, Channeled, 8 min cooldown.
81	Mind Spike		Shadow	Blasts the target, dealing Shadowfrost damage, and increases the critical strike chance of your next Mind Blast on the target by 30%. Stacks up to 3 times. Causes a high amount of threat. 35 yd range, 1.5 sec cast.
83	Inner Will		Discipline	A burst of Holy energy fills the caster, reducing the mana cost of instant cast spells by 15% and increasing your movement speed by 10%. Lasts 30 min. Instant.
85	Leap of Faith		Holy	You pull the spirit of the friendly party or raid target to you, instantly moving them directly in front of you. 40 yd range, Instant, 1.5 min cooldown.

PLAYING AS A DISCIPLINE PRIEST

Discipline is one of the Priest's healing specializations. It excels at mobile restoration, agile casting, defensive abilities and, perhaps most importantly, damage prevention. Discipline is all about instant or quick casts, which allow the priest to be constantly on the move. This, paired with the fact that discipline boosts the priest's defenses in several ways, makes Discipline a very good PvP specialization. This doesn't mean that Discipline is PvP-exclusive by any means, however—as mentioned before, their niche is damage prevention, which can be invaluable in both PvP and PvE.

Discipline Priests are a complex molding of damage casters and healers. They're deadlier than a Holy Priest but lack the raw aggression of a Shadow Priest. They're given more abilities that get them out of trouble, so they're actually somewhat defensive, especially for this class. Penance is the defining ability from this line; it's a long-range spell that can damage an enemy somewhat or heal an ally.

Look through the Discipline talent line and you're bound to notice the volume of improvements to Power Word: Shield and other defensive abilities. These Priests augment their class' weak armor with these shield perks. At the end of the tree, Power Word: Barrier allows the Priests to protect an entire area with this type of effect.

Discipline Priests are fairly self-sufficient, and they can outlast many threats. They're still slower killers compared with Shadow Priests and members of most other classes, so it's an okay leveling specialization as long as you're patient.

ABILITIES LEARNED AT LEVEL 10 IF YOU SELECT DISCIPLINE

	Ability	Description
	Penance	Launches a volley of holy light at the target, causing Holy damage to an enemy, or healing to an ally instantly and every 1 sec for 2 sec.
	Enlightenment	Healing is increased by 15%.
	Meditation	Allows 50% of mana regeneration to continue while in combat.
	Mastery: Shield Discipline	Increases the potency of all your damage absorption spells by 20%. Each point of Mastery increases the potency of absorbs by an additional 2.5%.

DESIRABLE STATS

Being casters, Discipline priests benefit most from stats and ratings that help them cast faster and stronger spells while keeping their mana pool healthy. This being the case, it's hard to simply stack a single stat for Discipline. The first thing to keep in mind when gearing a Discipline priest is mana regeneration. Since Meditation is one of Discipline's core abilities, Spirit becomes valuable and should be considered before everything else until mana regeneration is no longer an issue. Remember instant spells are expensive, even after the discounts granted by talents. Following Spirit, other stats and ratings are similarly beneficial (depending on what the gear set will be used for, naturally): Intellect increases the potency of your spells (along with mana and critical hit chance), Critical Hit Rating occasionally makes your direct heals bigger and triggers effects like Divine Aegis, and Mastery Rating contributes to your absorption effects.

LEVELS 1 - 80

Playing Solo

Discipline isn't the fastest choice for priest leveling, but it's decent when compared to other classes' healing specializations. Needless to say, Discipline Priests are durable; with all the boosts granted to Power Word: Shield, this might be the only healing (or damage prevention in this case) needed while leveling.

The level 10 bonuses are actually solo-friendly: Penance deals damage to a single target, Meditation helps reduce downtime by accelerating mana regeneration, and the Discipline passive reduces spell pushback, which is great should mobs get too close.

At low levels, Smite, Penance and your wand will be your bread and butter when it comes to dealing damage. At level 17, start investing points into Evangelism, a great talent that will immediately grant a respectable boost to your damage output. Archangel, the following talent, will help if you start having mana issues. Soon after that, you'll learn Holy Fire, which will likely see a place in your damage rotation.

Your rotation will often depend on the strength of the mob being fought. You could save mana on weaker mobs by simply using your wand (perhaps after applying a shadow DoT) and using Power Word: Shield on yourself. On stronger mobs, you might have to go all out and charge your Evangelism through Smite. If you accidentally pull more mobs than necessary, consider the use of Power Infusion, Power Word: Shield yourself, cast Psychic Scream (if it's safe), and kill the pack one by one. Remember to keep casting your buffs when they wear off (or before), especially Inner Fire.

Playing in a Group

The Discipline healing style is a little less straightforward than other classes, but it's plenty of fun. Instead of simply healing through damage, the idea is to prevent it as much as possible, and then heal through what couldn't be prevented. The prime tool for this, naturally, is Power Word: Shield. Many Discipline talents boost the effects of Power Word: Shield in some way. It's practically impossible to spend talent points in the Discipline tree without taking some of these Shield-enhancing talents, so you're likely to be set without having to take extra Shield talents in your solo spec.

Being a successful Discipline healer involves predicting which party members will take damage, then using Power Word: Shield on them. The tank of your group often requires additional healing, for which Penance is a great tool. Flash Heal is also a great asset if Penance is still on Cooldown and one of your group members needs quick healing. Pain Suppression serves as a sizable damage dampener on a friendly target, but make sure threat is not an issue for the tank if casting it on him or her. Lastly, Power Word: Barrier is a great spell to use in situations where the group is taking heavy AoE damage.

THE CATACLYSM: LEVELS 81 - 85

Higher levels will make Discipline better at damage prevention with the introduction of Absorption and the Mastery stat. That aside, your leveling rotation will be the same as before; keep taking full advantage of Evangelism if necessary.

Preparing Your Discipline Priest for Heroic Dungeons

Like other healers, it's imperative that your mana regeneration is sufficient to keep entire groups alive against the tough bosses encountered in heroic dungeons. To accomplish this, prioritize Spirit and Intellect for more mana regeneration and a larger mana pool. Reforge pieces with Hit Rating and Haste Rating to boost your Spirit or Critical Strike Rating. Luckily, Discipline is mana efficient when it comes to smaller groups, and damage prevention really shines in dungeons of this size. Because Discipline Priests are one of the hardest healers to master, practice your healing skills on normal dungeons and groups before attempting to heal a heroic dungeon.

Discipline Priest: Group Buffs and Debuffs

All Priests add extra health through Power Word: Fortitude, and extra Shadow Protection. Discipline Priests also provide Grace, a Discipline-exclusive talent, which increases healing received by targets healed by the priest, which can be really useful when healing the same targets frequently (such as a tank).

PLAYING AS A SHADOW PRIEST

Shadow is a damage-oriented Priest specialization. Like other spellcasters, Shadow Priests prefer to stay at range, especially considering Mind Flay, one of the primary Shadow spells, is channeled and suffers from spell pushback. Note that Dark Thoughts helps reduce this penalty, and a quick self-cast Power Word: Shield can temporarily eliminate it. Shadow talents greatly increase a Priest's damage output, downtime and survivability.

A Shadow Priest's drawbacks depend on the situation. When soloing (depending on level), mana might be a problem, and you might often see yourself forced to use your wand to finish enemies off. In groups, it is important to keep watch on your threat levels, especially if your gear is greater than the tank's in level and quality.

Shadow Priests have more access to disabling abilities than their rivals. They can Terrify enemies with Psychic Horror! It's also dangerous to Dispel their Vampiric Touch debuff, because that can trigger Fear effects.

ABILITIES LEARNED AT LEVEL 10 IF YOU SELECT SHADOW

Ability	Description
Mind Flay	Assaults the target's mind with Shadow energy, causing 18 Shadow damage over 3 sec and slowing their movement speed by 50%.
Shadow Power	Spell damage is increased by 25%. Increases the critical damage of your Shadow spells by 100%.
Mastery: Shadow Orbs	You have a 10% chance for your Shadow Word: Pain and Mind Flay spells to grant you a Shadow Orb each time they deal damage. Each Shadow Orb increases the damage done by your Mind Blast and Mind Spike spells by 34%. Each point of Mastery increases damage by an additional 4.3%. You can have up to a maximum of 3 orbs.

DESIRABLE STATS

Look for Intellect and Spirit, while keeping a healthy balance of Haste Rating, and Critical Strike Rating. Hit Rating is less useful in this scenario, as you will usually be fighting enemies slightly above or below your level, and the base chance to miss is very small.

When leveling solo, Shadow Priests benefit from having a wand with high DPS values, as this can reduce downtime by finishing enemies off with the wand instead of casting an extra spell. When fighting lower-level enemies, it is viable to defeat them by simply applying a DoT and using your wand as a melee replacement.

LEVELS 1 - 80

Playing Solo

Shadow is the optimal Priest specialization for leveling. Keep in mind, however, that talents significantly boost a Shadow Priest's damage, which means you might have some downtime at early levels, and accidental pulls with numerous enemies might make quick work of you since there's nothing from talents that helps keep you alive until you get Shadowform.

At level 10, you learn Mind Flay which becomes the bread and butter ability of leveling, with a touch of DoT spells like Shadow Word: Pain and Devouring Plague. Your basic rotation should vary depending on the enemy's difficulty, but it is usually a good idea to start a fight with Mind Blast (which has exceptional range) and Shadow Word: Pain (which has a smaller range, but the enemy will usually run toward you after Mind Blast). Take down weaker enemies with your wand and cast Mind Blast as often as possible. Stronger enemies often require the use of Mind Flay (to slow their advance toward you) instead of the wand. Mind Blast is a huge chunk of damage, so it's usually a good idea to use it as soon as it's ready. If an enemy is quickly nearing you, and you're planning on using Mind Flay instead of your wand, self-cast Power Word: Shield to avoid spell interruption or pushback. Because Power Word: Shield is a Discipline spell, this method can be used in Shadowform as well.

Psychic Scream is a great tool for catching your breath. Be careful when using this, however, as enemies will run in terror randomly and might get too close to others, which will then aggro you. When fighting just one enemy, Psychic Scream can be used along with Mind Flay, which will slow the enemy and prevent it from wandering away too far. As you level, your talents provide great boosts to your health, mana regeneration and survivability. Shadowform increases your Shadow damage and Spell Haste, and reduces incoming damage (and far more importantly, it makes you look awesome). Take this talent as soon as it becomes available, but remember you cannot cast Holy spells while Shadowform is active.

Use Shadow Word: Death with caution. It's best used when an enemy is about to die, but missing it is usually not a big deal unless you're low on health and there are more enemies. Remember you can always Renew yourself (when not in Shadowform) to make up for the damage inflicted on yourself. Shadowfiend makes mana problems become less pervasive, especially when leveling alone. Since your wand damage steadily decreases in relation to your enemies' health, you rely on Mind Flay much more often. Your rotation should be similar throughout the levels, but use situational spells such as Devouring Plague and Fade to your advantage.

Playing in a Group

Grouping as a Shadow Priest is similar to playing solo as one. Gauge how long enemies will last in a battle to determine whether or not to use Shadow Word: Pain. You will likely use Mind Blast and Mind Flay the most, mixed with situational spells like Vampiric Touch (if the group is taking AoE damage), Mind Sear (if several enemies are present and the tank has built enough threat on all of them), Fade (if your threat level becomes an issue) and Dispersion (if you accidentally pull aggro from the tank). If the group is in trouble, running up to the enemies and using Psychic Scream might save the day, but keep in mind this is incredibly dangerous if the vicinity is not entirely clear. Keep in mind that Vampiric Touch is an excellent group buff, but it only activates when you cast Mind Blast. At times, you might be tempted to AoE everything down using Mind Sear or repeatedly cast Mind Flay on every enemy you face.

A big part of playing a Shadow Priest is providing group buffs, so prioritize this over your own damage. On bosses, you can usually get away with casting Shadow Word: Death as soon as it's ready, even if the boss is above 25% health (which makes the talent Mind Melt activate). Healers will have no problem healing through the recoil damage caused by Shadow Word: Death unless an encounter deals heavy damage to the tank or everyone at once.

THE CATACLYSM: LEVELS 81 – 85

At high levels, Shadow Priests benefit from Mind Spike, which is a short cast damage spell that stores 30% of the damage dealt on a mob. This damage can be detonated by using Mind Blast on the same mob, which makes it great for soloing enemies with high health values. In groups, this spell increases your damage output, but keep in mind that the act of detonating stored damage generates a high amount of threat, so use it only when your tank is well ahead of your threat level.

After obtaining the desired amount of talents in the Shadow tree, spend points on the Discipline tree for Evangelism and several bonuses to instant spells (such as Mental Agility and Twin Disciplines).

Preparing Your Shadow Priest for Heroic Dungeons

Because Power Word: Shield can still be cast in Shadowform, prioritize raw damage over survival. It's important that you learn how to manage your threat, however, preferably on the normal versions of the dungeons you wish to enter. Mana shouldn't be a problem due to your Shadowfiend ability and constant Replenishment uptime, but take a few mana potions to your first few runs if your gear is lacking.

The dungeons introduced in Cataclysm drop excellent rewards, and most of the cloth gear has a nice balance of stats and ratings. Keep an eye out for gear with Mastery Rating, which will boost the efficiency of your Shadow Orbs. If raiding is in your future, save (or Reforge) some gear with Hit Rating, which will be useful against the high-level creatures that lurk raid dungeons. The bad news is that you're competing with Mages and Warlocks for most of the same gear.

Prioritize Intellect, Spell Power (from weapons) and Spirit, while keeping a healthy balance of Haste Rating, Critical Strike and Mastery Ratings. Shadow Priests don't need as much Spell Hit as other casters due to hit-increasing talents like Twisted Faith. Because Mind Flay (a channeled spell) can cause critical damage, Critical Strike Rating is comparable to Haste Rating and Mastery Ratings.

Shadow Priests: Group Buffs and Debuffs

Shadow Priest provides the most group buffs out of the three Priest specialization trees. Beyond the standard Priest buffs to Shadow Protection and Stamina, Shadow Priests bring Vampiric Embrace, which heals nearby party members as you deal damage, and Replenishment in the form of 1% of mana every 5 seconds to up to 10 allies after you use Mind Blast on a target with Vampiric Touch on it.

ROGUE

Rogues specialize in melee combat. Whether it's through steady doses of controlled damage or spiky bursts of damage, all three talent trees are dedicated to creating a dual-wielding killing machine. Through the various talent trees, Rogue enhance their weapon expertise, poison potency, or the usage of subtlety and stealth.

Rogues are usually the ones to get in the first hit (thanks to abilities like Stealth and Sap), and they use stealth and stuns to keep their advantage. They kill dependably as long as those abilities last. A Rogue caught flat footed dies quickly. A Rogue that's played well can kill just as quickly. If high risk and high reward intrigue you, this is a class that's worth your time and attention.

RACE AVAILABILITY

ALLIANCE

Orgrimer · Dwarf · Gnome

Human · Night Elf · Worgen

HORDE

Blood Elf · Goblin · Orc

Tauren · Troll · Undead

RACIAL ADVANTAGES

ALLIANCE

Race	Best for	Notes
Dwarf	Any spec	Mace Specialization grants Expertise to Dwarves who wield maces.
Gnome	Any spec	Escape Artist allows the Rogue to break snare or slow effects. Shortblade Specialization grants Expertise to Gnomes who wield daggers or one-hand sword.
Worgen	Any spec	Ferocity adds 1% Critical Strike chance.
Human	Any spec	Sword and Mace Specializations grants Expertise to Humans who wield swords or maces.
Night Elf	Any spec	Quickness grants the Rogue 2% additional chance to be missed by any physical attacks.

HORDE

Race	Best for	Notes
Blood Elf	Any spec	Arcane Torrent silences nearby enemies and restores some of the Blood Elf's energy.
Goblin	Any spec	Time is Money boosts attack speeds by 1%.
Orc	Any spec	Axe Specialization grants Expertise to Orcs who wield axes and fist weapons. Blood Fury boost Attack Power.
Troll	Any spec	Berserk increases attack speed.
Undead	Any spec	Will of the Forsaken breaks Charm, Fear, and Sleep effects.

EQUIPMENT OPTIONS

Armor Type	Shield	Ranged Slot
Leather	No	Bow, Crossbow, Gun, Thrown

WEAPON CHOICES

1 Hand Weapons	2 Hand Weapons
Axe	
Mace	
Sword	
Dagger	
Fist Weapon	

ROGUE SPELLS

Level Learned	Ability Name		Tree	Description
1	Sinister Strike		Combat	An instant strike that causes damage. Awards 1 combo point. 45 Energy
1	Eviscerate		Assassination	Finishing move that causes more damage per combo point.
5	Stealth		Subtlety	Allows the rogue to sneak around, but reduces your speed by 30%. Lasts until cancelled. 10 Second cooldown.
7	Pick Pocket		Subtlety	Pick the target's pocket.
8	Ambush		Assassination	Ambush the target, causing 190% weapon damage plus additional damage, and further bonus damage if using a dagger. Must be stealthed and behind the target. Awards 2 combo points.
9	Evasion		Combat	Increases the rogue's dodge chance by 50% and reduces the chance ranged attacks hit the rogue by 25%. Lasts 15 seconds. 3 minute cooldown
10	Sap		Subtlety	Incapacitates the target for up to 1 min. Must be stealthed. Only works on Humanoids, Beasts, Demons and Dragonkin that are not in combat. Any damage caused will revive the target. Only 1 target may be sapped at a time. 35 Energy
12	Recuperate		Combat	Finishing move that consumes combo points on any nearby target to restore 3% of maximum health every 3 seconds. Lasts longer per combo point, up to a maximum of 30 seconds. 30 Energy
14	Kick		Combat	A quick kick that interrupts spellcasting and prevents any spell in that school from being cast for 5 seconds. 25 Energy, 10 second cooldown
16	Sprint		Combat	Increases the rogue's movement speed by 70% for 15 seconds. Does not break stealth. 3 Minute cooldown
16	Gouge		Combat	Causes minor damage, incapacitating the opponent for 4 seconds, and turns off your attack. Target must be facing you. Any damage caused will revive the target. Awards 1 combo point. 45 Energy, 10 sec cooldown.
18	Backstab		Combat	Backstab the target, causing 200% weapon damage plus additional damage to the target. Must be behind the target. Requires a dagger in the main hand. Awards 1 combo point.
22	Slice and Dice		Assassination	Finishing move that consumes combo points on any nearby target to increase melee attack speed by 40%. Lasts longer per combo point. 25 Energy
24	Vanish		Subtlety	Allows the rogue to vanish from sight, entering an improved stealth mode for 3 sec. For the first 3 sec seconds after vanishing, damage and harmful effects received will not break stealth. Also breaks movement impairing effects. 3 min cooldown
26	Cheap Shot		Assassination	Stuns the target for 4 seconds. Must be stealthed. Awards 2 combo points. 40 Energy
28	Distract		Subtlety	Throws a distraction, attracting the attention of all nearby monsters for 10 seconds. Does not break stealth. 30 Energy, 30 yard range, 30 second cooldown.
30	Kidney Shot		Assassination	Finishing move that stuns the target. Lasts longer per combo point, up to a maximum of 6 seconds. 25 Energy, 20 second cooldown.
32	Detect Traps		Subtlety	Greatly increases your chance to detect traps. Passive.
34	Blind		Subtlety	Blinds the target, causing it to wander disoriented for up to 10 sec. Any damage caused will remove the effect. 15 Energy, 10 yard range, 3 minute cooldown.
36	Expose Armor		Assassination	Finishing move that exposes the target, reducing armor by 12% and lasting longer per combo point, up to a maximum of 50 seconds. 25 Energy

Level Learned	Ability Name		Tree	Description
38	Dismantle		Assassination	Disarm the enemy, removing all weapons, shield, or other equipment carried for 10 seconds. 25 Energy, 1 minute cooldown.
40	Mutilate		Assassination	Instantly attacks with both weapons for high damage. Damage is increased by 20% against poisoned targets. Awards 2 combo points. 60 Energy
40	Garrote		Assassination	Garrote the enemy, silencing them for 3 seconds and causing damage over 18 seconds, increased by your attack power. Must be stealthed and behind the target. Awards 1 combo point.
42	Feint		Combat	Performs a feint, causing no damage but lowering your threat by 5%, making the enemy less likely to attack you. In addition, reduces the damage you take from area of effect attacks by 50% for 6 seconds. 20 Energy, 10 sec cooldown.
44	Disarm Trap		Subtlety	Disarm a hostile trap.
46	Rupture		Assassination	Finishing move that causes damage over time, increased by your attack power. Lasts longer per combo point. 25 Energy
48	Safe Fall		Subtlety	Reduces damage from falling. Passive.
54	Envenom		Assassination	Finishing move that consumes your deadly poison DoT on the target and deals instant poison damage. Following the Envenom attack your Deadly Poison application chance is increased by 15%, and your Instant Poison application frequency by 75%, for 1 second plus 1 second per combo point. 35 Energy
58	Cloak of Shadows		Subtlety	Instantly removes all existing harmful spell effects, provides momentary immunity against all damage and harmful effects, and increases your chance to resist all spells by 100% for 5 seconds. Does not remove effects that prevent you from using Cloak of Shadows. 1.5 Minute cooldown.
62	Deadly Throw		Assassination	Finishing move that reduces the movement speed of the target by 50% for 6 seconds and causes more damage per combo point. 35 Energy, 30 yard range.
70	Shiv		Combat	Strikes an enemy's pressure point with your offhand weapon, guaranteeing poison application from that weapon and dispelling an Enrage effect on the target. Slower weapons require more Energy. Neither Shiv nor the poison it applies can be a critical strike. Awards 1 combo point. 20 base energy cost.
75	Tricks of the Trade		Subtlety	The current party or raid member becomes the target of your Tricks of the Trade. The threat caused by your next damaging attack and all actions taken for 6 sec afterwards will be transferred to the target. In addition, all damage caused by the target is increased by 15% during this time. 15 Energy, 20 yd range, 30 sec cooldown.
80	Fan of Knives		Combat	Instantly whirl around, releasing a spray of throwing knives at all targets within 8 yards, causing 80% thrown weapon damage. Requires a throwing weapon. 35 Energy
81	Redirect		Subtlety	Transfers any existing combo points to the current enemy target. 40 yard range, 1 minute cooldown.
83	Combat Readiness		Combat	Enter into a state of heightened awareness, deflecting enemy weapon strikes with increasing effectiveness. Successive attacks will deal 10% less damage per application, stacking 5 times. Lasts for 30 sec, but if 6 sec elapse without any incoming weapon strikes, this state will end. 2 min cooldown
85	Smoke Bomb		Subtlety	Creates a cloud of thick smoke in a 10 yard radius around the Rogue for 10 sec. Enemies are unable to target into or out of the smoke cloud. 3 min cooldown

PLAYING AS AN ASSASSINATION ROGUE

Assassination Rogues wield daggers, slam home with poisons, and build Combo Points quickly. Their base damage with daggers is raised by 15%, and they have access to 120 Energy as long as daggers are equipped. Deadly Poison affects their targets 20% more often, and Instant Poison has a 50% higher bonus.

This lets these Rogues do extreme damage and have enough Combo Points to use their finishers more often. They also get improvements to Backstab (which has become an even better ability in recent times). They're superb at picking a single target and making that victim suffer and then die. They're pretty much useless for AoE fights, but that's a common problem for most Rogues.

When you want to have a character that does lethal damage over time, Assassination Rogues are a great choice. They're easier to play than they used to be, and their survivability has being going up recently, with Deadened Nerves being a must-have talent.

ABILITIES LEARNED AT LEVEL 10 IF YOU SELECT ASSASSINATION

Ability	Description
Mutilate	Instantly attacks with both weapons for 150% weapon damage plus additional damage. Damage is increased by 20% against Poisoned targets. Awards 2 combo points.
Improved Poisons	Increases the chance to apply Deadly Poison to your target by 20% and the frequency of applying Instant Poison to your target by 50%.
Assassin's Resolve	Increases maximum energy and damage dealt while wielding a dagger.
Mastery: Potent Poisons	Increases the damage done by your poisons by 28%. Each point of Mastery increases damage by an additional 3.5%.

DESIRABLE STATS

Assassination Rogues want fast daggers in both hands for maximum efficiency. This helps both their abilities and maximizing the chance of poison procs. After Agility, look for Hit Rating, Expertise Rating, Haste Rating, and Critical Strike Rating. They are the stats an Assassination Rogue wants, in roughly that order of priority.

LEVELS 1 - 80

Playing Solo

At first, Assassination Rogues generally use Sinister Strike exclusively, and sometimes Eviscerate. As you gain access to abilities such as Slice and Dice and more powerful attacks such as Mutilate, mix them into your rotation. Regardless of the setting, you always want to keep Slice and Dice active. Initiate combat with a 1-point Slice and Dice to get the attack speed boost, then refresh it with a higher stack of the buff when you have the chance.

Hastened melee swings proccing poisons is effective for killing most foes, while Backstab, Mutilate, and Eviscerate deal the bulk of your damage. You can open with either Cheap Shot or Garrote (or even Ambush) to either stun, silence, or do high burst damage to your foe.

Playing in a Group

Rogues provide top-notch DPS for groups, but you may need to do more than just maximum damage. Sap works on nearly every enemy type, and your group may ask you to Sap a particular creature before you start combat. If the group doesn't ask, don't be shy about volunteering if you feel the encounter calls for some crowd control. However, keep in mind that it takes extra time to stealth and set up a Sap before each pull, so if the group has no trouble dealing with all of the enemies, they may be bothered by the extra time it takes for you to Sap. Besides crowd control, Rogues have Kick, and stuns to deal with spellcasters, and crippling poison keeps enemies from running away too quickly. Work with your group and analyze the enemies to find if you should focus purely on maximum damage output, or lockdown and control.

THE CATACLYSM: LEVELS 81 - 85

Combat Readiness makes it easy to take on melee enemies but you must be extra careful about facing enemies individually due to the increased damage done by enemies in Cataclysm's zones. Redirect is a big help in case an enemy dies before you get a chance to use up all the combo points you managed to build up. However, you may need to use those combo points on Recuperate depending on how damaged the previous fight left you.

Preparing Your Assassination Rogue for Heroic Dungeons

Rogues want Agility, Hit Rating, Haste Rating, and Critical Strike Rating where possible. Expertise Rating also increases your damage by reducing the enemy's chance to dodge or parry your attacks, but you only need a total of -6.5% reduction, which you can check in your character stats sheet. Your gear doesn't need to be absolutely perfect to start heroics, but it needs to illustrate to your group that you have put some time and thought into your character.

Assassination Rogues: Group Buffs and Debuffs

Assassination Rogues provide the 8% spell damage vulnerability debuff to any enemies with the talent Master Poisoner. This covers that slot for the raid or group, and other classes will not need to apply their own 8% spell damage debuff because of it. Rogues should use the combo Finisher Expose Armor as a finishing move if the group has no other means to apply the 12% armor reduction.

PLAYING AS A COMBAT ROGUE

Combat Rogues have a 25% higher Energy regeneration rate than other Rogues. They also get a 75% damage bonus to offhand and thrown weapon attacks, but this isn't nearly as high as it sounds. Other Rogue damage bonuses (like the 15% dagger boost for Assassination) affect normal and special attacks. The offhand bonus is primarily a boost to normal attacks, meaning that it isn't nearly as substantial.

Blade Flurry is a defining ability in this talent line. It causes Rogues to be able to hit a second target with their attacks. It has a trivial cooldown, so it can be used often (though it slows Energy regeneration somewhat).

Combat Rogues often use larger, slower weapons than their rivals. Expect to see these guys wandering around with swords in their main hand instead of daggers. Because simple attacks like Sinister Strike dominate the Combat playstyle, this is one of the easier ways to play a Rogue. Combat is not the most damaging or survivable line, but it gets the job done without much preparation or hassle.

With abilities like Adrenaline Rush and Killing Spree, Combat Rogues end up being cooldown-dependent for their best damage.

ABILITIES LEARNED AT LEVEL 10 IF YOU SELECT COMBAT

	Ability	Description
	Blade Flurry	Increases your attack speed by 20%. In addition, attacks strike an additional nearby opponent. Lasts 15 sec.
	Vitality	Increases your Energy regeneration rate by 25%.
	Ambidexterity	Increases the damage done by your offhand and thrown weapons by 75%.
	Mastery: Main Gauche	Your main hand attacks have a 16% chance to grant you an extra off hand attack. Each point of Mastery increases the chance by an additional 2%.

DESIRABLE STATS

Combat Rogues should wield the two weapons with the highest upper damage score available. This can be a sword and a mace, perhaps two axes, or even a sword and a dagger. Place the slowest, most powerful weapon available in your main hand. Agility, Hit Rating, Haste, and Critical Strike Rating are the stats a Combat Rogue wants, in roughly that order of priority.

LEVELS 1 - 80

Playing Solo

As a Rogue, regardless of the setting, you always want to keep Slice and Dice active. As you gain levels, Sinsiter Strike is complemented by abilities such as Revealing Strike and Blade Flurry. Alternatively you can pop multiple cooldowns and damage many enemies at once, using a combination of Adrenaline Rush, Blade Flurry, Fan of Knives, and Killing Spree. This allows you to take on many enemies at once, whenever all cooldowns are ready. Judicious use of Stealth is an excellent way for you to pick and choose your fights, or the ideal time to start a fight.

Playing in a Group

Rogues provide top-notch DPS for groups, but you may need to do more than just maximum damage. Sap works on nearly every enemy type, and your group may ask you to Sap a particular creature before you start combat. If the group doesn't ask, don't be shy about volunteering if you feel the encounter calls for some crowd control. However, keep in mind that it takes extra time to stealth and set up a Sap before each pull, so if the group has no trouble dealing with all of the enemies, they may be bothered by the extra time it takes for you to Sap. Besides crowd control, Rogues have Kick, and stuns to deal with spellcasters, and crippling poison keeps enemies from running away too quickly. Work with your group and analyze the enemies to find if you should focus purely on maximum damage output, or lockdown and control.

The Cataclysm: Levels 81 - 85

Combat Readiness makes it easy to take on melee enemies but you must be extra careful about facing enemies individually due to the increased damage done by enemies in Cataclysm's zones. Redirect is a big help in case an enemy dies before you get a chance to use up all the combo points you managed to build up. However, you may need to use those combo points on Recuperate depending on how damaged the previous fight left you.

Preparing Your Assassination Rogue for Heroic Dungeons

Get gear, gems and enchants that provide Agility, Hit Rating, Expertise Rating, Haste Rating, and Critical Strike Rating where possible. Keep in mind that a Combat Rogue has access to the talent Precision, which increases your chance to hit and provides a bit of room with how much Hit Rating you need from gear, gems, and enchants. Most importantly, get a slow, hard-hitting weapon for your main hand.

Combat Rogues: Group Buffs and Debuffs

A Combat Rogue with Savage Combat causes any enemy that is afflicted with their poisons to suffer an additional 4% physical damage. Any Rogue can also use Expose Armor to apply the 12% armor reduction. If you're running with a Warrior tank, don't bother with Expose Armor as the Warrior should be using Sunder Armor to help generate threat.

PLAYING AS A SUBTLETY ROGUE

Subtlety causes Rogues to deal 10% extra damage when coming out of Stealth and for several seconds afterward. They also get a massive 25% bonus to Agility and a similar bonus to Backstab and Hemorrhage damage. This is a substantial foundation for the specialization's damage. A higher Agility than other Rogues ensures that Subtlety players have high base damage; this is something that the talent line didn't have during earlier expansions, so it's a welcome change.

Shadowstep is the defining ability for this tree. This ability raises movement speed for a short time and gets the Rogue behind a target. In addition, this buffs the next Ambush or Garrote delivered within 10 seconds. With a short cooldown, this ability acts as a great way to keep massive damage on targets even in the middle of a fight. Subtlety Rogues love their sudden attacks out of stealth, so this ability keeps them from languishing in a longer fight even after they've used Vanish, Preparation, and other fun toys.

Speaking of Preparation, that is another beauty in this talent line. Using this resets the cooldowns for Evasion, Sprint, Vanish, and Shadowstep. With a second bite at all of these apples, a Subtlety Rogue can give themselves much higher survivability and damage in an important fight. It's on a 5-minute cooldown, so this should be reserved for semi-major battles.

Shadow Dance is at the end of the tree. It lets these Rogues use a number of abilities that require stealth even if they're fighting out in the open.

The general theme of this tree is that Subtlety Rogues start fights with a huge advantage and then try to kill their target before this is used up. They get a ton of Combo Points early on to aid in this. If you like frontloading your damage, this is a good choice.

ABILITIES LEARNED AT LEVEL 10 IF YOU SELECT SUBTLETY

	Ability	Description
	Shadowstep	Attempts to step through the shadows and reappear behind your enemy and increases movement speed by 70% for 3 sec. The damage of your next ability is increased by 30%. Lasts 10 sec.
	Master of Subtlety	Attacks made while stealthed and for 6 seconds after breaking stealth cause an additional 10% damage.
	Sinister Calling	Increases your total Agility by 25% and increases the percentage damage bonus of Backstab and Hemorrhage by an additional 25%.
	Mastery: Executioner	Increases the damage done by all your finishing moves by 20%. Each point of Mastery increases damage by an additional 2.5%.

DESIRABLE STATS

Agility is top priority due to Sinister Calling and all the benfits Agility provides. Hit Rating and Critical Strike Rating are next in line. Subtlety Rogues need to load up on early hits to take advantage of Master of Subtlety. Subtlety Rogues get the most use out of a fast dagger in their main hand (in order to utilize Ambush) but can wield any type of weapon to great effect.

LEVELS 1 - 80

Playing Solo

Subtley Rogues really start to shine when they gain abilities such as Hemorrhage and Ghostly Strike. Subtlety Rogue talents and increased Stealth proficiency allow you to deal massive damage and potentially kill foes outright with just Ambush. Always keep Slice and Dice active. Use Backstab, Hemorrhage and Ghostly Strike to deal most of your damage. Subtlety Rogues have many talents and abilities that can be used more frequently than usual (due to increased Energy regeneration) to disrupt enemies and enhance your combat prowess. When things get out of hand, or when you really need all your tricks for a fight, using Shadowstep, Preparation, and Shadow Dance in a battle quickly tips the scales in your favor.

Playing in a Group

Rogues provide top-notch DPS for groups, but you may need to do more than just maximum damage. Sap works on nearly every enemy type, and your group may ask you to Sap a particular creature before you start combat. If the group doesn't ask, don't be shy about volunteering if you feel the encounter calls for some crowd control. However, keep in mind that it takes extra time to stealth and set up a Sap before each pull, so if the group has no trouble dealing with all of the enemies, they may be bothered by the extra time it takes for you to Sap. Besides crowd control, Rogues have Kick, and stuns to deal with spellcasters, and crippling poison keeps enemies from running away too quickly. When it comes to maximizing your damage as a Subtlety Rogue, stay behind enemies at all times if you are using a dagger, which allows you to Backstab freely. With Honor Among Thieves, playing in a group provides many extra combo points. Don't let any combo points go to waste; refresh Slice and Dice, and use Rupture on multiple enemies at once.

THE CATACLYSM: LEVELS 81 - 85

Combat Readiness makes it easy to take on melee enemies but you must be extra careful about facing enemies individually due to the increased damage done by enemies in Cataclysm's zones. Redirect is a big help in case an enemy dies before you get a chance to use up all the combo points you managed to build up. However, you may need to use those combo points on Recuperate depending on how damaged the previous fight left you.

Preparing Your Subtlety Rogue for Heroic Dungeons

You want Agility, Expertise Rating (up to -6.5% reduction in Parry and Dodge chances), Hit Rating, Haste Rating, and Critical Strike Rating from your gear, gems and enchants. Get a good dagger for your main hand since Backstab is a great way to boost your damage output.

Subtlety Rogues: Group Buffs and Debuffs

Subtlety Rogues provide the 5% physical Critical Hit chance buff if they are specced into Honor Among Thieves. This is a passive aura that the Rogue applies to the entire party or raid as long as they are alive. Waylay cause the Subtlety Rogue's Ambush and Backstab abilities to increase the time between melee swings and movement speed of the target. As long as the rogue is using one of these abilities every 8 seconds, the debuff is always active. Hemorrhage applies a debuff that causes the target to take 30% additional damage from bleeds for one minute. Use Expose Armor to apply a 12% armor reduction to an enemy.

SHAMAN

Shamans are masters of Nature and Elemental magic. They are a hybrid class that can play multiple roles with vastly different playstyles. While Shamans are mainly spellcasters, they can excel at melee combat if the proper talents are chosen. Shamans are also capable of deploying totems, which will grant significant benefits to the Shaman and his or her allies. Totems are invaluable for grouping, and other Shaman buffs add to the desirability to group with a Shaman.

Because they can heal, Shamans are a great class for solo play as well. There are numerous totems across the four elements; choosing the right one for every situation is part of the fun of playing a Shaman. After all, when things go poorly in a fight, what other class has the ability to throw a stick into the ground that grabs everyone's attention, then turn into a wolf and leave everyone in the dust?

RACE AVAILABILITY

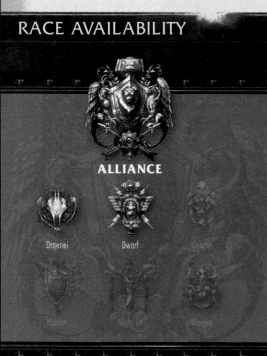

ALLIANCE

Draenei

Dwarf

Gnome

Human

Night Elf

Worgen

HORDE

Blood Elf

Goblin

Orc

Tauren

Troll

Undead

RACIAL ADVANTAGES

ALLIANCE

Race	Best for	Notes
Draenei	Elemental, Enhancement	Heroic Presence grants Draenei +1% Hit chance.
Dwarf	Enhancement, PvP	Mace Specialization grants Expertise to Dwarves who wield maces. Stoneform removes poisons, diseases, bleed effects, and increases armor.

HORDE

Race	Best for	Notes
Goblin	Any spec	Time is Money increases attack and casting speeds by 1%. Rocket Barrage deals fire damage.
Orc	Elemental, Enhancement	Axe Specialization grants Expertise to Orcs who wield axes and fist weapons. Blood Fury boosts Attack Power or Spell Power.
Tauren	PvP	War Stomp stuns nearby enemies. Endurance increases base health.
Troll	Any	Berserking increases attack and casting speeds by 20% for 10 sec.

EQUIPMENT OPTIONS

Armor Type	Shield	Ranged Slot
Leather until 40, then Mail	Yes	Relic

WEAPON CHOICES

1 Hand Weapons	2 Hand Weapons
Axe	Axe
Mace	Mace
Dagger	Staff
Fist Weapon	

SHAMAN SPELLS

Level Learned	Ability Name	Tree	Description
1	Lightning Bolt	Elemental	Casts a bolt of lightning at the target that deals Nature damage. 30 yd range, 2.5 sec cast.
3	Primal Strike	Enhancement	An instant weapon strike that causes additional damage. 5 yd range, Instant, 8 sec cooldown.
4	Strength of Earth Totem	Enhancement	Summons a Strength of Earth Totem with 5 health at the feet of the caster. The totem increases the strength and agility of all party and raid members within 40 yards. Lasts 5 min. Instant.
5	Earth Shock	Elemental	Instantly shocks the target with concussive force, causing Nature damage and reducing melee attack speed by 20% for 8 sec. 25 yd range, Instant, 6 sec cooldown.
7	Healing Wave	Restoration	Heals a friendly target. 40 yd range, 3 sec cast.
8	Lightning Shield	Enhancement	The caster is surrounded by 3 balls of lightning. When a spell, melee or ranged attack hits the caster, the attacker will be struck for Nature damage. This expends one lightning ball. Only one ball will fire every few seconds. Lasts 10 min. Only one Elemental Shield can be active on the Shaman at any one time. Instant.
10	Flametongue Weapon	Enhancement	Imbue the Shaman's weapon with fire, increasing total spell damage. Lasts 30 minutes. Unleashing this enchantment deals Fire damage to an enemy target and increases the damage dealt by the Shaman's next Fire spell by 20%. Instant.
10	Searing Totem	Elemental	Summons a Searing Totem with 5 health at your feet for 1 min that repeatedly attacks an enemy within 20 yards for Fire damage. The totem will prefer to target enemies that are afflicted by your Flame Shock or Stormstrike effects. Instant.
12	Flametongue Totem	Enhancement	Summons a Flametongue Totem with 5 health at the feet of the caster. The totem increases the spell power of all party and raid members within 40 yards by 6%. Lasts 5 min. Instant.
12	Purge	Elemental	Purges the enemy target, removing 2 beneficial magic effects. 30 yd range, Instant.
12	Ancestral Spirit	Restoration	Returns the spirit to the body, restoring a dead target to life with 35% of maximum health and mana. Cannot be cast when in combat. 30 yd range, 10 sec cast.
14	Flame Shock	Elemental	Instantly sears the target with fire, causing Fire damage immediately and additional Fire damage over 18 sec. 25 yd range, Instant, 6 sec cooldown.
15	Ghost Wolf	Enhancement	Turns the Shaman into a Ghost Wolf, increasing speed by 30%. As a Ghost Wolf, the Shaman is less hindered by effects that would reduce movement speed. 2 sec cast.
16	Wind Shear	Elemental	Disrupts the target's concentration with a burst of wind, interrupting spellcasting and preventing any spell in that school from being cast for 2 sec. Also lowers your threat, making the enemy less likely to attack you. 25 yd range, Instant, 6 sec cooldown.
18	Earthbind Totem	Elemental	Summons an Earthbind Totem with 5 health at the feet of the caster for 45 sec that slows the movement speed of enemies within 10 yards. Instant, 15 sec cooldown.
18	Cleanse Spirit	Restoration	Removes one Curse effect from a friendly target. 40 yd range, Instant.
20	Water Shield	Restoration	The caster is surrounded by 3 globes of water, granting mana per 5 sec. When a spell, melee or ranged attack hits the caster, mana is restored to the caster. This expends one water globe. Only one globe will activate every few seconds. Lasts 10 min. Only one Elemental Shield can be active on the Shaman at any one time. Instant.
20	Healing Surge	Restoration	Heals a friendly target. 40 yd range, 1.5 sec cast.
20	Healing Stream Totem	Restoration	Summons a Healing Stream Totem with 5 health at the feet of the caster for 5 min that heals group members within 30 yards every 2 seconds. Instant.
22	Frost Shock	Elemental	Instantly shocks the target with frost, causing Frost damage and slowing movement speed by 50%. Lasts 8 sec. Causes a high amount of threat. 25 yd range, Instant, 6 sec cooldown.
24	Water Walking	Enhancement	Allows a friendly target to walk across water for 10 min. Any damage will cancel the effect. 30 yd range, Instant, Reagent: Fish Oil.
26	Frostbrand Weapon	Enhancement	Imbue the Shaman's weapon with frost. Each hit has a chance of causing additional Frost damage and slowing the target's movement speed by 50% for 8 sec. Lasts 30 minutes. Unleashing this enchantment deals Frost damage to a target enemy and reduces their movement speed by 50% for 5 sec. Increased in effectiveness if the target is already afflicted by a movement-reducing Frost effect. Instant.
28	Fire Nova	Elemental	Causes the shaman's active Flametongue, Magma, or Fire Elemental Totem to emit a wave of flames, inflicting Fire damage to enemies within 10 yards of the totem. 30 yd range, Instant, 10 sec cooldown.
28	Chain Lightning	Elemental	Hurls a lightning bolt at the enemy, dealing damage and then jumping to additional nearby enemies. Each jump reduces the damage by 30%. Affects 3 total targets. 30 yd range, 2 sec cast, 3 sec cooldown.
30	Totemic Recall	Restoration	Returns your totems to the earth, giving you 25% of the mana required to cast each totem destroyed by Totemic Recall. Instant.
30	Reincarnation	Restoration	Allows you to resurrect yourself upon death with 20% health and mana. 30 min cooldown, Reagent: Ankh.
30	Windfury Totem	Enhancement	Summons a Windfury Totem with 5 health at the feet of the caster. The totem increases the melee and ranged attack speed of all party and raid members within 40 yards by 10%. Lasts 5 min. Instant.
30	Astral Recall	Enhancement	Yanks the caster through the twisting nether back to his or her home location. Speak to an Innkeeper in a different place to change your home location. 10 sec cast, 15 min cooldown.
32	Windfury Weapon	Enhancement	Imbue the Shaman's weapon with wind. Each hit has a 20% chance of dealing additional damage equal to two extra attacks with extra attack power. Lasts 30 minutes. Unleashing this enchantment deals 20% of weapon damage to the target enemy and increases the Shaman's melee attack speed for the next 6 swings or until 12 sec have elapsed. Instant.
34	Lava Burst	Elemental	You hurl molten lava at the target, dealing Fire damage. If your Flame Shock is on the target, Lava Burst will deal a critical strike. 30 yd range, 2 sec cast, 8 sec cooldown.
36	Magma Totem	Elemental	Summons a Magma Totem with 5 health at the feet of the caster for 20 sec that causes Fire damage to creatures within 8 yards every 2 seconds. Instant.
38	Grounding Totem	Enhancement	Summons a Grounding Totem with 5 health at the feet of the caster that will redirect one harmful spell cast on a nearby party member to itself, destroying the totem. Will not redirect area of effect spells. Lasts 45 sec. Instant, 15 sec cooldown.
40	Chain Heal	Restoration	Heals the friendly target, then jumps to heal additional nearby targets. If cast on a party member, the heal will only jump to other party members. Prioritizes healing most injured party members. Each jump reduces the effectiveness of the heal by 30%. Heals 4 total targets. 40 yd range, 2.5 sec cast.
42	Mana Spring Totem	Restoration	Summons a Mana Spring Totem with 5 health at the feet of the caster for 5 min that restores mana every 5 seconds to all party and raid members within 40 yards. Instant.
44	Wrath of Air Totem	Enhancement	Summons a Wrath of Air Totem with 5 health at the feet of the caster. The totem provides 5% spell haste to all party and raid members within 40 yards. Lasts 5 min. Instant.
46	Water Breathing	Enhancement	Allows the target to breathe underwater for 10 min. 30 yd range, Instant, Reagent: Shiny Fish Scales.
48	Stoneskin Totem	Enhancement	Summons a Stoneskin Totem with 5 health at the feet of the caster. The totem protects party and raid members within 40 yards, increasing their armor. Lasts 5 min. Instant.
52	Tremor Totem	Restoration	Summons a Tremor Totem with 5 health at the feet of the caster that shakes the ground around it, removing Fear, Charm and Sleep effects from party members within 30 yards. Lasts 5 min. Instant.
54	Earthliving Weapon	Restoration	Imbue the Shaman's weapon with earthen life. Increases healing done and each heal has a 20% chance to proc Earthliving on the target, healing them over 12 sec. Lasts 30 minutes. Unleashing this enchantment heals a friendly target and increases the effect of the Shaman's next direct heal by 20%. Instant.
56	Earth Elemental Totem	Enhancement	Summon an elemental totem that calls forth a greater earth elemental to protect the caster and his or her allies. Lasts 2 min. Instant, 10 min cooldown.
58	Stoneclaw Totem	Elemental	Summons a Stoneclaw Totem at the feet of the caster for 15 sec that taunts creatures within 8 yards to attack it. Enemies attacking the Stoneclaw Totem have a 50% chance to be stunned for 3 sec. Stoneclaw totem also protects all your totems, causing them to absorb damage. Instant, 30 sec cooldown.
66	Fire Elemental Totem	Elemental	Summons an elemental totem that calls forth a greater fire elemental to rain destruction on the caster's enemies. Lasts 2 min. Instant, 10 min cooldown.
68	Bind Elemental	Elemental	Binds the target hostile elemental for up to 50 sec. The bound unit is unable to move, attack or cast spells. Any damage caused will release the target. Only one target can be bound at a time. 30 yd range, 1.5 sec cast.
68	Greater Healing Wave	Restoration	Heals a friendly target. 40 yd range, 3 sec cast.
70	Heroism (Alliance)	Enhancement	Increases melee, ranged, and spell casting speed by 30% for all party and raid members. Lasts 40 sec. Allies receiving this effect will become Exhausted and be unable to benefit from Heroism or Time Warp again for 10 min. Instant, 5 min cooldown.
70	Bloodlust (Horde)	Enhancement	Increases melee, ranged, and spell casting speed by 30% for all party and raid members. Lasts 40 sec. Allies receiving this effect will become Sated and be unable to benefit from Bloodlust or Time Warp again for 10 min. Instant, 5 min cooldown.
74	Totem of Tranquil Mind	Restoration	Summons a Totem of Tranquil Mind with 5 health at the feet of the caster for 5 min, causing party or raid members within 30 yards to lose 30% less casting or channeling time when damaged. Instant.
75	Rockbiter Weapon	Enhancement	Imbue the Shaman's weapon with the fury of the earth, increasing all threat generation by 30% and reducing damage taken by 5%. Lasts 30 minutes. Unleashing this enchantment forces the target enemy to attack you for 5 sec. Instant.
80	Hex	Elemental	Transforms the enemy into a frog. While hexed, the target cannot attack or cast spells. Damage caused may interrupt the effect. Lasts 1 min. Only one target can be hexed at a time. Only works on Humanoids and Beasts. 20 yd range, 1.5 sec cast, 45 sec cooldown.
81	Unleash Elements	Enhancement	Focuses the elemental force imbued in the Shaman's weaponry, with the concentrated effects depending on the enchantment unleashed. 40 yd range, Instant, 15 sec cooldown.
83	Healing Rain	Restoration	Calls forth healing rains to blanket the area targeted by the Shaman, restoring health to allies in the area every 2 sec for 10 sec. 30 yd range, 2 sec cast, 10 sec cooldown.
85	Spiritwalker's Grace	Elemental	Calls upon spiritual guidance, permitting movement while casting non-instant Shaman spells. This spell may be cast while casting other spells. Lasts 10 sec. Instant, 2 min cooldown.

SHAMAN ABILITIES

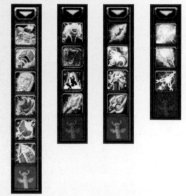

TOTEMS

Placing totems is a Shaman's signature ability. As you level, you learn to place different totems, each of which has a specific function for solo or group play. Take some time to learn the ins and outs of your totems. Knowing which one to use in a given situation often means more than all the healing or damage you can do. Set up your various abilities that drop sets of totems at once so you're ready to switch which totems you use quickly.

Totems are small, friendly units that grant you (and your group) a buff, or inflict negative effects on hostile targets. They are very fragile and can usually be killed with one swing of an enemy's weapon. Because they are unaffected by AoE, however, enemies must manually target your totems if they wish to destroy them.

Totems are grouped into four categories, each corresponding to one of the elements of nature: Earth, Fire, Water, and Wind. Their classification is relevant, because you can only drop one totem per element at a time. This means that, if you have an earth-based totem on the ground, and you drop a different one, the first one instantly vanishes. Totems are considered spells, and as such, cost mana, so constantly replacing a totem in order to attempt to grant two buffs of the same category to your group is not always viable.

At times, you might want to purposefully destroy all your totems (perhaps to avoid an enemy from spotting them). Totemic Recall does just that—it instantly recalls all your totems, granting you a fraction of the mana spent to summon them. It's good practice to recall your totems whenever you move to a new spot, as wandering enemies might run toward you after spotting and killing your abandoned totems.

ELEMENTAL SHIELDS

As a Shaman, you learn several different elemental shields that grant diverse bonuses passively or when struck in battle. You can only have one shield active at a time, but as a rule of thumb, Enhancement Shamans prefer Lightning Shield (unless mana is a problem), and both Elemental and Restoration Shamans use Water Shield. Earth Shield can be cast on others, but you can cast it on yourself when survivability is an issue, such as PvP encounters.

Lightning Shield is the simplest form of this spell category. It creates several lightning orbs that surround you and deal damage to any enemy that attacks you. The orbs only detonate every few seconds, so fast attackers will not deplete all your lightning orbs instantly.

Certain Enhancement talents increase the usefulness of this skill by increasing the number of orbs and granting other bonuses.

Water Shield is for a spellcasting Shaman. It creates three water globes that surround you and passively grant you mana regeneration for as long as the spell is active. If you're struck in combat, one of the globes detonates and grants a slightly larger burst of mana.

Earth Shield, exclusive to Restoration Shamans, is an outstanding skill for survivability. It surrounds the target with numerous earthen orbs, each of which will provide a small heal upon detonation (when the target is struck). Earth Shield also passively reduces spell pushback by 30%, which, in combination with one of the talents that reduces it by 70%, can grant the target immunity to spell pushback (do note that spells can still be interrupted through other means, such as stuns).

WEAPON IMBUES

Like elemental shields, weapon imbues are self-cast buffs that enhance your abilities or hinder enemies. The main difference is that these imbues are cast on your weapon, and remain active until they expire or they're cancelled.

Flametongue Weapon increases your spell damage when active. Upon striking an enemy with the enchanted weapon, you deal additional Fire damage. This imbue is primarily aimed at offensive casters.

Frostbrand Weapon deals additional Frost damage and has a chance to snare enemies struck by the enchanted weapon. This imbue is great for slowing enemies in PvP, or enemies who run away in PvE.

Rockbiter Weapon increase threat generation by 30%, while reducing damage taken by 5%. Shaman aren't tanks so only use this imbue for its reduction in damage in PVP environments.

Earthliving Weapon increases healing done and gives the Shaman a chance to apply Earthliving (a small heal over time) on the target of any heals from the Shaman. Because Earthliving has a chance to activate on every heal, this enchantment considerably boosts the usefulness of Chain Heal, which affects multiple targets.

SUGGESTED PROFESSION FOR A FIRST-TIME SHAMAN

Leatherworking is the profession of choice when it comes to crafting mail items. Because it also gives sizable stat bonuses through bracer enchants, it is all-around useful for Shamans. Leatherworking can be expensive to level, so pairing it with Skinning (which also grants a small bonus to Critical Strike Rating, good all three specializations) is usually a good idea.

PLAYING AS AN ELEMENTAL SHAMAN

If you're looking to stay at range and deal magical damage, Elemental is the talent tree for you. It boosts your offensive spells, and grants you bonuses to mana regeneration along with improvements to totems that grant spell benefits. Although they lack the mobility of the more fragile cloth users, Elemental Shamans are a durable caster class as they can wear mail gear and equip a shield. The spells boosted by the Elemental tree are primarily Nature-based, with Lightning Bolt and Chain Lightning as the main sources of damage, but Shock spells of different elements, along with Lava Burst, benefit as well.

Elemental Fury raises critical hit damage by Fire, Frost, and Nature spells by 100%. It also makes Searing and Magma Totems have a more substantial bonus. This makes Elemental Shamans extremely spiky in their damage output. In a good fight they can burst an amazing amount of damage in a short period.

To define the talent line, Elemental Shamans learn Thunderstorm. This attack gives your Shaman mana, damages all nearby enemies, and throws attackers back quite a ways. This is a great way to get out of trouble if too many enemies close the gap and start exploiting your weaker melee defenses.

ABILITIES LEARNED AT LEVEL 10 IF YOU SELECT ELEMENTAL

	Ability	Description
	Thunderstorm	You call down a bolt of lightning, energizing you and damaging nearby enemies within 10 yards. Restores 8% mana to you and deals Nature damage to all nearby enemies, knocking them back 20 yards. This spell is usable while stunned.
	Elemental Fury	Increases the critical strike damage bonus of your Searing and Magma Totems and your Fire, Frost, and Nature spells by 100%.
	Shamanism	Your Lightning Bolt, Chain Lightning, and Lava Burst spells gain an additional 20% benefit from your spell power, and their casting time is reduced by 0.5 sec.
	Mastery: Elemental Overload	Grants a 16% chance for Elemental Overload to occur. Elemental Overload causes a Lightning Bolt, Chain Lightning, or Lava Burst spell you cast to trigger a second, similar spell on the same target at no additional cost that causes 75% of normal damage and no threat. Each point of Mastery increases the chance of Elemental Overload by an additional 2%.

DESIRABLE STATS

Elemental Shamans greatly benefit from Intelligence, like most other casters. This increases their spell damage, mana pool and Critical Strike rating. Gear with Spirit initially benefits Elemental Shamans less than it would other casters but if you take the talent Element Precision, suddenly Spirit becomes an incredibly solid stat. Once Lava Burst is learned, Critical Strike Rating loses some appeal, as it is guaranteed to crit if the Flame Shock debuff is on a target.

LEVELS 1 - 80

Playing Solo

With outstanding armor, a shield, and healing spells, keeping your distance from mobs isn't as important as it is for other caster classes. As an Elemental Shaman, you are durable and capable of withstanding blows from several enemies at once. Your level 10 spell, Thunderstorm, knocks back enemies and restores mana. This particular spell shouldn't be saved for a rainy day (unless you suspect there will be some PvP action), so use it often to keep your mana pool healthy. Your basic rotation will change throughout the levels, but it's safe to assume Lightning Bolt will be your main source of damage.

Use Earth Shock as an effective, albeit expensive in mana terms, instant finisher. When you get Flame Shock, start using that immediately. Cast it early in a fight so it completes its duration. When you pick up Chain Lightning, consider using it, even on single enemies, since it has a fast cast time. Granted, more enemies means more damage, but keep in mind the effectiveness of Chain Lightning is reduced with each bounce. Your rotation changes again with the addition of Lava Burst, a fast-casting sizable damage spell with a small cooldown. You continue to gain more abilities as you level up, but these are your main tools.

Playing in a Group

Elemental Shamans really shine in groups, as their totems will benefit melee classes and casters alike. Don't be afraid to ask whether certain group members have a totem preference, as this will be part of your group playstyle.

Your rotation in groups will be similar to your solo rotation, with the advantage that certain mobs (usually bosses) have large health pools, which means your Flame Shock can complete its duration several times. Always try to start with Flame Shock, followed by Lava Burst and several Lightning Bolts. Refresh Flame Shock whenever it expires, and cast Lava Burst as soon as its cooldown has finished. If enemies use magic-based beneficial effects on themselves, use Purge to remove them. If your threat seems unusually high and you foresee you're about to pull aggro, use Wind Shear instead of Flame Shock in order to shed some of it.

THE CATACLYSM: LEVELS 81 - 85

Higher levels mean more mana efficiency for Elemental Shamans. These higher levels can be perilous, but at this point, your Shaman should be powerful enough to handle most situations. Remember Shamans have many escape routes should they get in trouble, and there's almost certainly a spell that can help you overcome dire circumstances.

Preparing Your Elemental Shaman for Heroic Dungeons

The first piece of equipment you should try to upgrade when nearing the level cap is your weapon, as it's a big boost to your Spell Power. Following that, look for gear with Intellect and Haste Rating, followed by Mastery Rating and Critical Strike Rating. Don't neglect Hit Rating, but don't use too much of it either—heroic bosses are usually one or two levels higher than you, so some Hit minimizes the amount of spell misses, but it's good only up to a certain point.

Elemental Shaman: Group Buffs and Debuffs

All Shaman provide Heroism/Bloodlust, and a host of possible buffs from their totems. There are two buffs exclusive to Elemental Shaman. Totemic Wrath grants additional spell power to your group so long as you have a Fire Totem up. Elemental Oath increases the Critical Strike chance for other people in your group by 3%.

PLAYING AS AN ENHANCEMENT SHAMAN

Enhancement Shaman get up close with enemies and damage them using weapons and spells. Enhancement is a tree primarily dedicated to boosting your melee prowess, while using your mana pool to increase your damage through various spells. Enhancement is one of the few specialization trees that delves into the art of wielding two one-handed weapons at once. Even though they lack the shield that Elemental and Restoration Shamans use, Enhancement Shamans remain durable as they are still able to wear mail armor and heal themselves in a pinch.

Mental Quickness ensures that Enhancement Shamans benefit from extra Attack Power. Stacking Agility gives them a Spell Power benefit as well, helping to get their melee and magic damage as high as possible.

Enhancement Shamans also learn how to summon wolves to aid them in combat with the Feral Spirit talent. This doesn't happen until the end of the tree, but it's a fun way to finish things off. This gives the steady damage dealers an extra burst for larger encounters.

ABILITIES LEARNED AT LEVEL 10 IF YOU SELECT ENHANCEMENT

	Ability	Description
	Lava Lash	You charge your off-hand weapon with lava, instantly dealing 200% of that weapon's damage to an enemy target. Damage is increased by 40% if your off-hand weapon is enchanted with Flametongue.
	Mental Quickness	Increases your spell power by an amount equal to 50% of your attack power, and reduces the mana cost of your instant spells by 75%.
	Dual Wield	Allows one-hand and off-hand weapons to be equipped in your off-hand, allows you to parry frontal melee attacks, and and increases your chance to hit by an additional 6%.
	Primal Wisdom	Your melee attacks have a 40% chance to immediately restore 5% of your base mana.
	Enhanced Elements	Increases all Fire, Frost, and Nature damage done by 20%. Each point of Mastery increases damage by an additional 2.5%

DESIRABLE STATS

Because a fraction of your Attack Power is converted into spellpower, forget about picking up mail armor designed for spell casting and stack as much Agility as you can. Hit Rating is important because you dual wield and you need to hit with spells to inflict the most damage. Find a healthy balance between Agility and Hit Rating and you'll be killing mobs at a decent pace. Weapon damage is important for Enhancement Shaman, so look for weapons with the highest damage per second value, even if the stat boosts granted by such weapon aren't ideal. This usually means a slow weapon for both hands.

LEVELS 1 - 80

Playing Solo

As Enhancement, you kill enemies quickly while keeping your health and mana pools topped off through healing spells and mana-regenerating abilities. Weapon imbues are particularly useful for Enhancement Shamans, as they provide a sizable damage boost just by being active on a weapon.

Lava Lash is an instant ability which must be used in melee range. If your off-hand weapon is imbued with Flametongue Weapon, Lava Lash becomes considerably more powerful. For your main weapon, go with Windfury Weapon.

Use Shock spells that fit the situation. Flame Shock is normally the most damage if battles last long enough. Use your instant strikes (Lava Lash and Primal Strike until you get Stormstrike, at which point you dump Primal Strike) and maintain your Lightning Shield.

Generally, you won't need to drop totems to kill normal enemies, as you'll be taking down their health quickly. You should get in the habit of using them since you'll need the help against tougher enemies.

When in a bind, use Shamanistic Rage or long cooldowns such as Heroism/Bloodlust or Greater Earth Elemental. Feral Spirit works twofold: the wolves spawned by it can save your life (by healing you) and increase your damage simultaneously. This talent is a great cooldown in both PvE and PvP, and will make it much easier to go up against tough enemies.

Playing in a Group

Enhancement grouping is similar to solo play. The same rotation and weapon enchantments apply, but there are two major differences: you may need to change which totems you use and you must be wary of threat levels. Drop totems that won't duplicate buffs provided by other classes. For example, Strength of Earth isn't necessary with a Warrior or Death Knight in the group so go with Stoneskin Totem instead. Since many fights should last longer in groups, you are likely to get more benefit out of the Maelstrom Weapon talent, meaning Lightning and Chain Lightning become a bigger slice of your overall damage output.

THE CATACLYSM: LEVELS 81 - 85

Monsters become significantly tougher in Cataclysm areas, so watch your totems carefully. Taking one or two enemies at a time is still possible, but don't push your luck beyond that unless your Spirit Wolves are ready to go. Unleash Elements should work its way into your damage rotation at some point as well.

Preparing Your Enhancement Shaman for Heroic Dungeons

Since they dual wield and use spells as a significant portion of their damage, Enhancement Shamans have rough statistical requirements to meet. Agility is vital, but you need to get your Expertise Rating and Hit Rating built up first. Once you have enough Expertise and Hit, stack Agility and look for Mastery Rating, Critical Strike Rating, and Haste Rating. Weapon damage is important as well. Look for slow weapons with high top-end damage numbers. A weapon's damage is more important than its stats (especially now that you can Reforge some stats), meaning that you shouldn't necessarily wait for a one-handed axe with perfect stats. If it hits hard, you want it.

Enhancement Shaman: Group Buffs and Debuffs

All Shaman provide Heroism/Bloodlust, and a host of possible buffs from their totems. An Enhancement Shaman provides Unleashed Rage, which increase the melee attack power of everyone in the party or raid.

PLAYING AS A RESTORATION SHAMAN

Restoration is the healing-oriented specialization tree available to Shamans. It specializes in boosting Shaman abilities that restore health to the caster or other friendly units. Restoration Shamans, like Druids, use Nature-based heals. They are one of the most resilient healer classes due to the ability to use mail armor and a shield.

The defining ability of this talent line is called Earth Shield. This lovely spell protects a target from nine hits, healing them a little each time they're struck. Only one Shaman at a time can give a person this effect, but it's an awesome way to send a tank into battle. You won't need to start healing them as quickly or as aggressively during the early stage of the encounter. As such, the Shaman doesn't risk getting threat from as many enemies before the tank has had time to get their attention.

Mana Tide Totem is a totem unique to this talent tree. It's used to restore mana to nearby group members during a make-or-break battle. For caster-heavy groups, it's a gift from the Earthmother.

Restoration Shamans are incredibly popular as a secondary specialization line. They don't level as well as Elemental or Enhancement Shamans, but they're easier to find groups for and contribute tremendously in dungeons. They're also a skilled PvP class, being able to heal well and still survive (an important thing to note because healers draw attention during PvP).

ABILITIES LEARNED AT LEVEL 10 IF YOU SELECT RESTORATION

	Ability	Description
	Earth Shield	Protects the target with an earthen shield, reducing casting or channeling time lost when damaged by 30% and causing attacks to heal the shielded target. This effect can only occur once every few seconds. 9 charges. Lasts 10 min. Earth Shield can only be placed on one target at a time and only one Elemental Shield can be active on a target at a time.
	Purification	Increases the effectiveness of your healing spells by 10%, and reduces the casting time of your Healing Wave and Greater Healing Wave spells by 0.5 sec.
	Meditation	Allows 50% of your mana regeneration from Spirit to continue while in combat.
	Mastery: Deep Healing	Increases the potency of your direct healing spells by up to 20%, based on the current health level of your target (lower health targets are healed for more). Each point of Mastery increases direct heals by up to an additional 2.5%.

DESIRABLE STATS

Restoration Shamans should be more concerned about mana than Elemental Shamans. Try to build up as much Spirit and Intellect as possible, before considering other stats. Critical Strike Rating offers additional help through Ancestral Healing (which reduces physical damage taken on a critically healed target). While you typically use a weapon and shield for your equipment, don't dismiss two-handed items (staffs for the most part) without seeing which set up provides more benefit. You shouldn't be taking any hits, so you shouldn't miss the protection of a shield.

LEVELS 1 - 80

Playing Solo

Restoration is not the optimal choice for Shaman Leveling, as it lacks the offensive capability of Enhancement or Elemental. If you want to be a viable dungeon healer at low levels, choose Elemental as your primary leveling specialization, as it's easier to collect gear that works for Elemental and Restoration at the same time.

At level 40, however, it's best to purchase the dual talent specialization and spend your secondary set of talents on Restoration. That way, you can level at an optimal speed while occasionally being very proficient at group healing.

Playing in a Group

Restoration is one of the most straightforward specializations when it comes to healing. In groups, your primary heals are direct, and you have your trusty Earth Shield. As the healer, you should drop totems that provide you the most benefit. Use Totemic Recall whenever your group is relocating so you can regain some of the mana spent, and your group can move along quicker.

Your main heals are Lesser Healing Wave, Healing Wave, and Greater Healing Wave. These go from fastest and most mana inefficient to slowest and most mana efficient. Gauge the danger of the situation and react accordingly, while keeping Earth Shield on a target that takes constant damage (usually the tank). At times, there will be heavy incoming area of effect damage, which should be countered with Chain Heal. Remember to keep Earthliving Weapon active when possible, especially when using Chain Heal, as it'll often place a small heal over time on affected targets. Since conserving mana is important, keep Water Shield active at all times, and use Mana Tide Totem whenever mana runs low. In an emergency, activate Nature's Swiftness to make your next heal instant. This is best used on Greater Healing Wave or Chain Heal, which have considerable cast times. The highest Restoration talent, Riptide, provides an instant heal, which is an alternative to using Nature's Swiftness.

THE CATACLYSM: LEVELS 81 – 85

If you remained a dedicated healer up to this point, you should have plenty of friends eager to keep you on that path. At level 83, Shamans learn Healing Rain, which is a spell with a relatively short cast time. Healing Rain creates an area that constantly heals affected targets over 10 seconds, which is very good for encounters with heavy area of effect damage. Keep in mind that, although it has a short cooldown, Healing Rain is expensive, so it is best used when several friendly targets are missing considerable amounts of health.

Preparing Your Restoration Shaman for

Heroic Dungeons

Grab gear with Intellect and Spirit. Look for a weapon with the highest amount of Spell Power. The most important factor to consider as a healer is mana regeneration, however—you're no good to your group if you're out of mana and can't heal. Sometimes raw healing power will save you mana because you don't need to heal as often, but the benefit granted by Spirit usually outperforms straight Haste Rating or Critical Strike Rating. Remember that gear beneficial to Elemental Shamans is usually good for Restoration, so don't be afraid to roll on pieces that might seem DPS caster-oriented; there's always Reforging to consider.

Restoration Shamans: Group Buffs and Debuffs

All Shaman provide Heroism/Bloodlust, and a host of possible buffs from their totems. Unique buffs from the Restoration tree include Ancestral Healing, which provides damage reduction to targets critically healed by the Shaman, and Mana Tide Totem, which provides a burst of mana regeneration.

WARLOCK

Warlocks are powerful casters who delve into the arts of dark magic. They are primarily damage-oriented magic users with the ability to summon powerful pets to aid them. Among a warlock's niches are hefty damage-over-time spells, summoning and controlling demons, applying various curses and instilling fear on enemies.

Like Mages, Warlocks lack on physical defense, but they still manage to be durable thanks to Demon Armor, their ability to control crowds, and reduce overall incoming damage. Warlock specialization trees range from pure burst damage dealing, to slow and steady damage over time to summoning more powerful demonic pets. Though a Warlock's primary source of damage is Shadow spells, they can make use of Fire spells, which makes them versatile against enemies that are resistant to Shadow.

Warlocks offer a variety of utility spells, including the ability to summon other players, which can be invaluable when a group member is far away or even too lazy to travel to the group! They also conjure and distribute magical candy (although they're called Healthstones in the game) which acts as a back-up healing potion.

RACE AVAILABILITY

ALLIANCE

Dwarf   Gnome

Human   Night Elf   Worgen

HORDE

Blood Elf   Goblin   Orc

Tauren   Troll   Undead

RACIAL ADVANTAGES

ALLIANCE		
Race	Best for	Notes
Dwarf	PVP	Stoneform removes all poison, disease, and bleed effects and increases armor.
Gnome	Any spec	Escape Artist removes snares (including those that cannot be removed through Dispel). Expansive Mind increases Intellect.
Human	PvP	Every Man For Himself allows the Warrior to break fears, stuns, and CC.
Worgen	Any spec	Viciousness increases Critical Strike Chance by 1%. Darkflight grants a 70% speed boost for 10 sec.

HORDE		
Race	Best for	Notes
Blood Elf	Any spec	Arcane Torrent silences nearby enemies and restores some of the Blood Elf's mana.
Goblin	Any spec	Time is Money boosts attack and casting speeds by 1%. Rocket Barrage is an extra damage ability.
Orc	Any spec	Command increases damage dealt by your pet. Blood Fury increases spell damage temporarily.
Troll	Any spec	Berserking increases spell casting speed.
Undead	PvP	Will of the Forsaken removes charm, fear and sleep effects.

EQUIPMENT OPTIONS

Armor Type	Shield	Ranged Slot
Cloth	No	Wand

WEAPON CHOICES	
1 Hand Weapons	2 Hand Weapons
Sword	Staff
Dagger	

WARLOCK SPELLS

Level Learned	Ability Name		Tree	Description
1	Summon Imp		Demonology	Summons an Imp under the command of the Warlock. 6 sec cast.
1	Shadow Bolt		Destruction	Sends a shadowy bolt at the enemy, causing Shadow damage. 40 yd range, 3 sec cast.
3	Immolate		Destruction	Burns the enemy for Fire damage and then additional Fire damage over 15 sec. 40 yd range, 2 sec cast.
4	Corruption		Affliction	Corrupts the target, causing Shadow damage over 18 sec. 30 yd range, Instant.
6	Drain Life		Affliction	Drains the life from the target, causing Shadow damage and restoring 2% of the caster's total health every 1 sec. Lasts 3 sec. 40 yd range, Channeled.
8	Summon Voidwalker		Demonology	Summons a Voidwalker under the command of the Warlock. 6 sec cast.
8	Demon Armor		Demonology	Protects the caster, increasing armor, and increasing the amount of health generated through spells and effects by 20%. Only one type of Armor spell can be active on the Warlock at any time. Lasts 30 min.
9	Create Healthstone		Demonology	Creates a Healthstone that can be used to instantly restore health equal to 45% of the creator's base health. Conjured items disappear if logged out for more than 15 minutes. 3 sec cast.
10	Soulburn		Demonology	Consumes a Soul Shard, allowing you to use the secondary effects on some of your spells. Lasts for 15 sec. The spells empowered are Drain Life, Summon Imp, Voidwalker, Succubus, Felhunter, Felguard, Demonic Circle: Teleport, Soul Fire, Healthstone and Searing Pain. Instant, 45 sec cooldown.
10	Drain Soul		Affliction	Drains the soul of the target, causing Shadow damage over 15 sec. If the target is at or below 25% health, Drain Soul causes four times the normal damage. If the target dies while being drained, and yields experience or honor, the caster gains 3 Soul Shards. Soul Shards are required for Soulburn. 40 yd range, Channeled.
12	Soul Harvest		Demonology	You seek out nearby wandering souls, gaining 1 soul shard and regenerating 15% of your health every 3 sec for 9 sec. Cannot be cast when in combat. Channeled, 30 sec cooldown.
12	Health Funnel		Demonology	Sacrifices 1% of your total health to restore 6% of your summoned Demon's total health every 1 sec. Channeled.
12	Bane of Agony		Affliction	Banes the target with agony, causing Shadow damage over 24 sec. This damage is dealt slowly at first, and builds up as the Curse reaches its full duration. Only one Bane per Warlock can be active on any one target. 40 yd range, Instant.
14	Fear		Affliction	Strikes fear in the enemy, causing it to run in fear for up to 20 sec. Damage caused may interrupt the effect. Only 1 target can be feared at a time. 30 yd range, 2 sec cast.
16	Unending Breath		Demonology	Allows the target to breathe underwater for 10 min. 30 yd range, Instant.
16	Curse of Weakness		Affliction	Target's physical damage done is reduced by 10% for 2 min. Only one Curse per Warlock can be active on any one target. 40 yd range, Instant.
18	Create Soulstone		Demonology	Creates a Soulstone. The Soulstone can be used to store one target's soul. If the target dies while his soul is stored, he will be able to resurrect with 30% health and 30% mana. Conjured items disappear if logged out for more than 15 minutes. 3 sec cast.
18	Searing Pain		Destruction	Inflict searing pain on the enemy target, causing Fire damage. Causes a high amount of threat. 40 yd range, 1.5 sec cast.
18	Rain of Fire		Destruction	Calls down a fiery rain to burn enemies in the area of effect, dealing Fire damage over 8 sec. 35 yd range, Channeled.
20	Summon Succubus		Demonology	Summons a Succubus under the command of the Warlock. 6 sec cast.
20	Felsteed		Demonology	Summons a Felsteed, which serves as a mount. 1.5 sec cast.
20	Bane of Doom		Affliction	Banes the target with impending doom, causing Shadow damage every 15 sec. When Bane of Doom deals damage, it has a 20% chance to summon a Demon guardian. Only one target can have Bane of Doom at a time, only one Bane per Warlock can be active on any one target. 40 yd range, Instant.
24	Drain Mana		Affliction	Transfers 3% of target's maximum mana every 1 sec from the target to the caster (up to a maximum of 6% of the caster's maximum mana every 1 sec). Lasts 3 sec. 40 yd range, Channeled.
26	Curse of Tongues		Affliction	Forces the target to speak in Demonic, increasing the casting time of all spells by 30%. Only one Curse per Warlock can be active on any one target. Lasts 30 sec. 40 yd range, Instant.
30	Summon Felhunter		Demonology	Summons a Felhunter under the command of the Warlock. 6 sec cast.
30	Enslave Demon		Demonology	Enslaves the target demon, forcing it to do your bidding. While enslaved, the time between the demon's attacks is increased by 30% and its casting speed is slowed by 20%. Lasts up to 5 min. 30 yd range, 3 sec cast.
30	Hellfire		Destruction	Ignites the area surrounding the caster, causing Fire damage to himself or herself and Fire damage to all nearby enemies every 1 sec. Lasts 15 sec. Channeled.
32	Banish		Demonology	Banishes the enemy target, preventing all action but making it invulnerable for up to 30 sec. Only one target can be banished at a time. Casting Banish on a banished target will cancel the spell. Only works on Demons and Elementals. 30 yd range, 1.5 sec cast.
34	Shadow Ward		Demonology	Absorbs shadow damage. Lasts 30 sec. Instant, 30 sec cooldown.
40	Dreadsteed		Demonology	Summons a Dreadsteed, which serves as a mount. This is a very fast mount. 1.5 sec cast.
42	Ritual of Summoning		Demonology	Begins a ritual that creates a summoning portal. The summoning portal can be used by 2 party or raid members to summon a targeted party or raid member. The ritual portal requires the caster and 2 additional party or raid members to complete. In order to participate, all players must be out of combat and right-click the portal and not move until the ritual is complete. 30 yd range, Channeled, 2 min cooldown.
44	Howl of Terror		Affliction	Howl, causing 5 enemies within 10 yds to flee in terror for 8 sec. Damage caused may interrupt the effect. 1.5 sec cast, 40 sec cooldown.
50	Summon Infernal		Demonology	Summons a meteor from the Twisting Nether, causing Fire damage and stunning all enemy targets in the area for 2 sec. An Infernal rises from the crater, under the command of the caster for 45 sec. The Infernal deals strong area of effect damage, and will be drawn to attack targets afflicted by your Bane of Agony or Bane of Doom spells. 30 yd range, 1.5 sec cast, 10 min cooldown.
52	Curse of the Elements		Affliction	Curses the target for 5 min, reducing Arcane, Fire, Frost, Nature, and Shadow resistances and increasing magic damage taken by 8%. Only one Curse per Warlock can be active on any one target. 40 yd range, Instant.
54	Soul Fire		Destruction	Burn the enemy's soul, causing Fire damage. 40 yd range, 4 sec cast.
58	Summon Doomguard		Demonology	Summons a Doomguard to fight beside you for 45 sec. The Doomguard will assist you by attacking the target which is afflicted by your Bane of Doom or Bane of Agony spell. Instant, 10 min cooldown.
62	Fel Armor		Demonology	Surrounds the caster with fel energy, increasing spell power. In addition, you regain 2% of your maximum health every 5 sec. Only one type of Armor spell can be active on the Warlock at any time. Lasts 30 min. Instant.
64	Incinerate		Destruction	Deals Fire damage to your target and additional Fire damage if the target is affected by an Immolate spell. 40 yd range, 2.5 sec cast.
66	Soulshatter		Demonology	Reduces threat by 90% for all enemies within 50 yards. Instant, 2 min cooldown.
68	Ritual of Souls		Demonology	Begins a ritual that creates a Soulwell. Raid members can click the Soulwell to acquire a Healthstone. The Soulwell lasts for 3 min or 25 charges. Requires the caster and 2 additional party members to complete the ritual. In order to participate, all players must right-click the soul portal and not move until the ritual is complete. 30 yd range, Channeled, 5 min cooldown.
72	Seed of Corruption		Affliction	Imbeds a demon seed in the enemy target, causing Shadow damage over 18 sec. When the target takes a certain amount of damage or dies, the seed will inflict Shadow damage to all enemies within 15 yards of the target. Only one Corruption spell per Warlock can be active on any one target. 35 yd range, 2 sec cast.
76	Shadowflame		Destruction	Targets in a cone in front of the caster take Shadow damage and feared in horror while taking additional Fire damage over 6 sec. Instant, 25 sec cooldown.
78	Demonic Circle: Teleport		Demonology	Teleports you to your Demonic Circle and removes all snare effects. 40 yd range, Instant, 30 sec cooldown.
78	Demonic Circle: Summon		Demonology	You summon a Demonic Circle at your feet, lasting 6 min. You can only have one Demonic Circle active at a time. 0.5 sec cast.
81	Fel Flame		Destruction	Deals Shadowflame damage to an enemy target, increasing the duration of Immolate or Unstable Affliction by 6 sec. 35 yd range, Instant.
83	Dark Intent		Affliction	You link yourself with the targeted friendly target, increasing both of your haste by 3%. When you or the linked target gains a critical periodic damage or healing effect, the other gains an increased 3% increased periodic damage and healing lasting for 7 sec. Stacks up to 3 times. Dark Intent lasts for 30 min. 30 yd range, Instant.
85	Demon Soul		Demonology	You and your summoned demon fuse souls, granting the Warlock a temporary power depending on the demon currently enslaved. Imp: Critical Strike damage on cast time Destruction spells increased by 60% for 30 sec. Each spell cast benefitting from this effect reduces the bonus by 20% until the bonus expires after 3 casts. Voidwalker: All threat generated by you transferred to your Voidwalker for 15 sec. Succubus: Shadow Bolt damage increased by 10% for 20 sec. Felhunter: Periodic shadow damage increased by 20% for 20 sec. Felguard: Spell haste increased by 15% and fire and shadow damage done increased by 10% for 20 sec. 100 yd range, Instant, 2 min cooldown.

WARLOCK ABILITIES

MINIONS

Warlocks are often identified by their ability to summon demonic minions. Although the Demonology tree is dedicated to enhancing your summoned pet's abilities, it's not necessary to make the summoned demons useful. There are few situations where a summoned demon doesn't contribute to a fight, so regardless of the specialization you choose, always keep a pet at your side. The process of summoning is usually lengthy in relation to other spells, but can be shortened through some of the talents available in the Demonology tree. There are numerous demons that can be summoned, each useful depending on the scenario. It often boils down to personal taste, however.

Demon	Description
Imp	Fragile caster with the ability to become untargetable by foes. The Imp is capable of casting fire spells quickly to add to your damage.
Voidwalker	Durable demon with the ability to taunt enemies to keep them away from the Warlock. The Voidwalker is preferable against numerous enemies, or enemies who deal high amounts of physical damage.
Succubus	Fragile seductress with the ability to deal melee damage and crowd control enemies. The Succubus is best used in situations where a foe must be kept at bay, such as PvP.
Felhunter	Melee-range demon adept at silencing and dispelling enemies. Because Warlocks don't have an innate dispel (or silence), Felhunters serve as a nice complement to their abilities. They are frequently used for PvP encounters where an enemy must be dispelled or silenced.
Felguard	Powerful and well-rounded demon exclusive to the Demonology tree. The Felguard serves as a replacement for the Voidwalker in the sense that it is durable and can taunt enemies, in addition to dealing superb melee damage.

DEALING DAMAGE OVER TIME

Regardless of what talent tree is chosen, a Warlock's offensive spell arsenal and rotation includes damage over time (DoT) spells. Such spells don't deal burst damage; instead, they place a debuff on an enemy target, slowly chipping away at their health. Don't be fooled by the relatively small numbers, however—DoT spells are among the most powerful damage dealing abilities in the game! To get the most out of DoTs, apply them early in the fight so that they last for their entire duration.

The Affliction tree, in particular, hosts many talents that increase the damage or duration of DoT spells, making it prime for those who wish to deal large amounts of damage as time passes. One big advantage DoT spells have over direct damage is that they're usually fast casts (and are often instant), granting the Warlock some freedom to move around while still dealing damage.

SUMMONING

Among a Warlock's utility spells is the ability to summon group members. Warlocks can't exactly do this on their own. Two other allies must assist in the creation of a Summoning Portal. Once placed near the Warlock, the Portal has unlimited ability to summon group or raid members before it disappears. This is an invaluable time saver, especially for large groups. Its uses are only limited by the players' imagination—if any players left important items in the bank before entering a raid instance, for example, they could simply use their Hearthstone and be summoned back.

SOUL SHARDS

Soul Shards are items used by Warlocks to activate the Soulburn ability, which grants various bonuses to certain spells. Upon activation, the Soulburn effect lasts 15 seconds and consumes a single Soul Shard. There are three methods for acquiring Soul Shards: Drain Soul, Soul Harvest or Shadowburn.

Drain Soul deals channeled damage to an enemy, generating up to three Soul Shards should the enemy die while the spell is still in place, provided the target would normally yield experience or honor. Shadowburn works the same way without being a channeled spell; however, the target must die within 5 seconds of the spell for the Warlock to obtain the three Shards. Soul Harvest ultimately creates three Soul Shards as well, but it cannot be used in combat and it must run its entire nine-second channeled duration.

Generally, using Drain Soul consistently keeps your Shard supply healthy, but Soul Harvest serves as a buffer should you run out inadvertently.

SUGGESTED PROFESSION FOR A FIRST-TIME WARLOCK

Warlocks benefit greatly from Tailoring, which allows them to craft their own gear, and eventually obtain a hefty Spell Power bonus. Because there's no gathering profession that directly benefits Tailoring, you have more freedom in selecting a second Profession. Enchanting provides great bonuses to Warlocks, and the ability to enchant your own gear on the fly is always a plus! If leveling up two crafting Professions at once proves to be difficult on your gold reserves, don't be afraid to pick up Mining instead. It grants a Stamina bonus suitable for Warlocks.

PLAYING AS AN AFFLICTION WARLOCK

Affliction Warlocks are the masters of Damage over Time (DoT) spells. They have talents that boost the damage, duration or effectiveness of DoT spells, while helping other aspects like survivability. They cast Bane, Curse, and Corruption spells as fast as possible, suffering from only a 1-second cooldown between each casting. The normal global cooldown is 50% longer than that, so the difference is quite noticeable.

Affliction Warlocks suffer only a minor setup from damage taken while casting, which makes it possible for them to cast through damage without losing as much of their damage potential. Unstable Affliction is the defining ability of this line. It's a damage over time ability, like so many others in Affliction. This DoT is also a trap. Anyone who tries to save your target by dispelling the effect gets hit hard and Silenced as well. Take that, good Samaritan!

ABILITIES LEARNED AT LEVEL 10 IF YOU SELECT AFFLICTION

	Ability	Description
	Unstable Affliction	Shadow energy slowly destroys the target, causing damage over 15 sec. In addition, if the Unstable Affliction is dispelled it will cause extra damage to the dispeller and silence them for 5 sec. Only one Unstable Affliction or Immolate per Warlock can be active on any one target.
	Shadow Mastery	Increases Shadow spell damage by 25%.
	Mastery: Potent Afflictions	Increases all periodic shadow damage you deal by 13%. Each point of Mastery increases periodic shadow damage by an additional 1.6%.

DESIRABLE STATS

Affliction Warlocks benefit from typical spellcasting stats such as Spell Power, Intellect, Critical Strike rating and Haste Rating. Spirit, although technically a caster stat, is better suited for healers, as Warlocks recover mana via Life Tap. Life Tap makes Stamina an exciting stat, even for Warlocks who don't expect to get hit because they spend most of their time in a group.

LEVELS 1 - 80

Playing Solo

Affliction solo is all about tossing out DoT spells and letting them do most of the work for you. This is not to say you should simply apply your DoT spells and wait for the mobs to die—there are many things to do to fill the gaps, such as using your wand, casting Shadow Bolt or using Drain abilities. Your primary spells are Corruption, Bane of Agony (or Doom), Unstable Affliction, Drain Life and Drain Soul. Your rotation usually consists of applying Unstable Affliction, followed by Corruption and a Bane, then using Drain Life if necessary (if not, use Drain Soul).

There are several ways to solo as an Affliction Warlock, depending on the mobs' difficulty and your gear. A common method is to use the Voidwalker minion, which serves as your personal tank, and cast your spell rotation. Usually, the Voidwalker will be able to hold aggro until your DoT spells have dealt too much damage to the enemy, at which point it'll lunge for you. Another method involves purposefully pulling several enemies at once and applying several DoT spells on all of them. This is risky if the enemies are too tough, have too much health or you accidentally pull too many. If executed correctly, however, you can kill several enemies simultaneously, making quests quicker! Key talents for this method include Siphon Life (which will keep your health up), Haunt (an extra DoT spell that increases your overall damage) and Improved Howl of Terror (which makes it instant - a complete life-saver if mobs are chipping at your health too quickly). You should use a damage-oriented pet such as an Imp.

Playing in a Group

Grouping as Affliction can be tricky, especially depending on group composition, but it's fun once you get the hang of it. The tricky part is that, in order to maximize your damage, your DoT spells should last their entire duration. Because mobs usually die quickly in dungeons, Affliction Warlocks can apply their DoTs on multiple enemies at a time. If your tank is focusing on keeping the attention of only one mob, let him know that you're going to be dealing damage to several enemies for pulls with multiple mobs. For weaker packs, it's usually best to simply use your AoE spells rather than try to apply DoTs on everything.

On bosses, the idea is to apply your DoTs early and reapply them as they wear off, using other abilities to fill the gaps. One disadvantage Affliction Warlocks have is that they can't stop their damage on demand, so if you're close to pulling aggro and your DoTs are still ticking on a boss, chances are the boss ends up punching you in the face. Plan accordingly on your first batch of DoT applications, and hold back on the gap-filling abilities if you feel like you're likely to pull aggro. At higher levels, Soulshatter alleviates this problem, significantly reducing your threat on a whim.

THE CATACLYSM: LEVELS 81 - 85

In Cataclysm areas, mobs will have much more health than you're used to, so test the waters before attempting to make multiple pulls. Fortunately, Cataclysm gear pieces have hefty amounts of Stamina and Intellect, so you should gear up quickly. The new Affliction spell is Dark Intent, which can be applied to a friendly target in order to increase their haste (and yours). Dark Intent also increases a player's periodic effectiveness (DoT or HoT) by 3% when the other player crits, making other Warlocks or a Druid the ideal targets.

Preparing Your Affliction Warlock for Heroic Dungeons

Grab gear with Intellect and as much Spell Power as possible. Next, look for Stamina (remember, you don't rely on Spirit for mana regeneration), Critical Strike Rating (which helps proc Dark Intent) Mastery Rating, and Haste Rating. You need some Hit Rating as well, but with so many instant casts you don't lose much uptime in your spells if you miss once in a while.

Affliction Warlock: Group Buffs and Debuffs

All Warlocks are capable of making a wipe less painful by applying a Soulstone to a character capable of returning others to life. Beyond bringing standard Warlock debuffs (mainly various Cruses) to the table, Affliction Warlocks add Jinx, which makes Curse of the Elements an AoE spell. Curse of Elements goes from a good spell to a great one for use against large packs of enemies.

PLAYING AS A DESTRUCTION WARLOCK

Destruction Warlocks are burst-heavy casters that function like a demonic version of a mage. They use Shadow and Fire to destroy their targets. Their defining ability is called Conflagrate; it uses an Immolate or Shadowflame effect to deal instant damage and slap a new DoT on the victim as well.

Destruction Warlocks have a more predictable rotation of spells than their cousins. They're also less mobile. Expect them to set up shop where they can see their targets. Once in place, they pummel the person with slow but high-damage spells. They then get to slip in a few instant spells to finish off any threats.

ABILITIES LEARNED AT LEVEL 10 IF YOU SELECT DESTRUCTION

	Ability	Description
	Conflagrate	Instantly deals fire damage equal to 60% of your Immolate's periodic damage on the target.
	Cataclysm	Increases Fire spell damage by 25%.
	Mastery: Fiery Apocalypse	Increases all fire damage you deal by 10%. Each point of Mastery increases fire damage by an additional 1.25%

DESIRABLE STATS

Unlike the other two Warlock specs survivability is a concern when soloing on a Destruction Warlock. Having a healthy balance of Spell Power and survivability is key to soloing as Destruction; most cloth gear will give you the stats you need, but don't neglect extra Stamina if you're likely to be in a situation where there's nobody to take the brunt of the damage for you. You should definitely go for spellcasting stats (Intellect, Critical Strike Rating and Haste rating) if you're not likely to take much damage.

LEVELS 1 - 80

Playing Solo

Destruction is better suited as a secondary spec (after learning Dual Specialization) for leveling, as it has significant downtime when soloing, along with an increased risk of dying. Your Voidwalker will have a hard time keeping enemies off you, as you'll be dishing out some serious damage in short amounts of time. Unfortunately, aside from Soul Leech (which grants you the Replenishment effect), Destruction is not very good at conserving mana, and Life Tap might not be enough to minimize the downtime presented by this problem.

If you like challenges or you're simply very passionate about playing Destruction all the way, get ready to play like a Mage—blast enemies, defeating them before they can defeat you, and patch yourself up after fights. Depending on your gear, you might even kill enemies before they reach you. Even with so many spells that require you to stand still, Destruction is still a mobile spec, considering instant spells like Conflagrate and Shadowburn. The real problem lies in the downtime involved, but gear could make up for it by reducing the amount of spells needed to kill a single enemy.

Playing in a Group

Groups are where Destruction Warlocks shine, allowing them to blast away at enemies with their powerful spells. Unlike Demonology and Affliction, you shouldn't necessarily apply DoTs on everything; it's usually best to use the time to keep casting your primary spells (Shadow Bolt and Incinerate). The one DoT you should always try to apply is Immolate, which enables the use of Conflagrate. On numerous enemy packs, Demonology Warlocks can have some fun by using Shadowfury (which stuns enemies), followed by Rain of Fire, causing large amounts of damage in a short time. The talent Bane of Havoc allows you to deal partial damage to an additional enemy, making it useful for boss encounters with more than one target. In group settings, you should use your Imp, as it gets several bonuses from talents, such as the ability to make your Soulfire spell instant. In conjunction with Improved Soul Fire, this makes a great combo to use when a boss is above 80% health—just watch your threat to avoid getting killed!

THE CATACLYSM: LEVELS 81 - 85

The new Destruction ability is called Fel Flame, which is an instant cast spell akin to Shadowburn. In addition to dealing damage, it increases the duration of your Immolate ability by 6 sec (or Unstable Affliction for Affliction Warlocks using this ability), making it useful for mobile encounters. If you found soloing difficult before Cataclysm areas, you could be in trouble here! Enemies have much more health than previously, and they can make quick work of an unprepared Destruction Warlock. If your gear isn't allowing you to quickly defeat enemies, consider using an alternate spec until you acquire better loot.

Preparing Your Destruction Warlock for Heroic Dungeons

Destruction is the most gear-dependent Warlock specialization, meaning you'll become much more powerful as you acquire upgrades. This means you should devote some time running the normal version of dungeons, along with questing for gear rewards. Focus on Spell Power (from your weapons), Intellect and Mastery Ratings. With enough Mastery (or the Shadow and Flame talent), which boosts your Fire-based spells, Incinerate gains an edge over Shadow Bolt.

Destruction Warlocks: Group Buffs and Debuffs

All Warlocks are capable of making a wipe less painful by applying a Soulstone to a character capable of returning others to life. Beyond bringing standard Warlock debuffs (mainly various Cruses) to the table, Destruction Warlocks add the Soul Leech talent, which grants the Replenishment buff to up to 10 party or raid members, significantly increasing their mana regeneration. Additionally, Shadow and Flame makes your Shadow Bolt spell place a debuff, increasing spell critical chance against the target by 5%.

WARRIOR

Warriors are the masters of melee combat. Warriors can be either disciplined, versatile combat fighters, furious raging berserkers, or the stalwart protector of your forces. Warriors can use nearly all weapon types, and don heavy plate armor and shields.

When you are playing a Warrior, you must be flexible and know which abilities are best suited to any situation. Have in plan in mind when you start a fight so you have enough Rage, your primary resource, available to fuel your abilities. It may be tempting to use solely high damage abilities, but other abilities may serve you better. You may need to interrupt a spell being cast, particularly from an enemy known to have healing abilities. This also applies to other situations such as fleeing from a fight, which may call for abilities like Intimidating Shout and Enraged Regeneration.

RACE AVAILABILITY

ALLIANCE

Draenei | Dwarf | Gnome

Human | Night Elf | Worgen

HORDE

Blood Elf | Goblin | Orc

Tauren | Troll | Undead

RACIAL ADVANTAGES

ALLIANCE

Race	Best for	Notes
Draenei	Arms/Fury	Heroic Presence grants Draenei +1% Hit chance. Shadow spells are less likely to hit a Draenei.
Dwarf	Any spec	Mace Specialization grants Expertise to Dwarves who wield maces. Frost spells are less likely to hit a Dwarf. Stoneform removes all poison, disease, and bleed effects and increases armor.
Gnome	Any spec	Shortblade Specialization grants Expertise to Gnomes who wield daggers or one-hand sword. Arcane spells are less likely to hit a Gnome.
Worgen	Arms/Fury	Ferocity adds 1% Critical Strike chance.
Human	Protection	Every Man For Himself allows the Warrior to break fears, stuns, and CC. Sword and Mace Specializations grants Expertise to Humans who wield swords or maces.
Night Elf	Protection	Night Elves are less likely to be hit by any physical attack, or Nature spell.

HORDE

Race	Best for	Notes
Blood Elf	Any spec	Arcane Torrent silences nearby enemies and restores some of the Blood Elf's rage. Magic spells are less likely to hit a Blood Elf.
Goblin	Any spec	Time is Money boosts attack and casting speeds by 1%. Rocket Barrage is an extra damage ability.
Orc	Arms/Fury	Axe Specialization grants Expertise to Orcs who wield axes and fist weapons. Blood Fury boosts Attack Power.
Tauren	Any spec	War Stomp stuns nearby enemies. Endurance increases base health. Nature spells are less likely to hit a Tauren.
Troll	Arms/Fury	Berserking increases attack speed.
Undead	Any spec	Will of the Forsaken breaks Charm, Fear, and Sleep effects. Shadow spells are less likely to hit an Undead Warrior.

EQUIPMENT OPTIONS

Armor Type	Shield	Ranged Slot
Mail until 40, then Plate	Yes	Bow, Crossbow, Gun, Thrown

WEAPON CHOICES

1 Hand Weapon	2 Hand Weapon
Axe	Axe
Mace	Mace
Sword	Sword
Dagger	Staff
Fist Weapon	Polearm

WARRIOR SPELLS

Level Learned	Ability Name	Tree	Description
1	Battle Stance	Arms	A balanced combat stance that increases damage done by 5%. Decreases damage taken by 5%. Instant, 1 second cooldown
1	Strike	Arms	An simple weapon strike that deals 52% of weapon damage. 20 Rage, 3 second cooldown
3	Charge	Arms	Charge an enemy, generate 15 rage, and stun it for 1.5 sec. Cannot be used in combat. 8-25 yd range, instant, 15 sec cooldown
5	Victory Rush	Fury	Instantly attack the target causing [45% of AP] damage and healing you for 20% of your maximum health. Can only be used within [20 sec after you kill an enemy that yields experience or honor. 5 yd range, Instant
7	Rend	Arms	Wounds the target causing them to bleed for 25 damage plus additional damage based on your weapon's damage over 15 sec. 10 Rage, 5 yd range, instant
9	Thunder Clap	Arms	Blasts nearby enemies, increasing the time between their attacks by 20% for 30 sec and causing damage. Damage increased by attack power. 20 Rage, Instant, 6 sec cooldown
10	Taunt	Protection	Taunts the target to attack you, but has no effect if the target is already attacking you. 30 yd range, Instant, 8 sec cooldown
10	Shield Slam	Protection	Slam the target with your shield, causing damage plus 100% of your attack power in additional damage and dispelling 1 magic effect on the target. Also causes a high amount of threat. 20 Rage, 5 yd range, Instant, 6 sec cooldown
10	Defensive Stance	Protection	A defensive combat stance. Decreases damage taken by 10%. Increases threat generated. Instant, 1 sec cooldown
12	Sunder Armor	Protection	Sunders the target's armor, reducing it by 4% per Sunder Armor and causes a high amount of threat. Threat increased by attack power. Can be applied up to 3 times. Lasts 30 sec. 15 Rage, 5 yd range, Instant
14	Execute	Fury	Attempt to finish off a wounded foe, causing [25% of AP] physical damage and consumes up to 20 additional rage to deal up to [50% of AP] additional damage. Only usable on enemies that have less than 20% health. 10 Rage, 5 yd range, Instant
16	Revenge	Protection	Instantly counterattack an enemy for moderate damage. Revenge is only usable after the warrior blocks, dodges or parries an attack. 5 Rage, 5 yd range, instant, 5 sec cooldown
18	Shield Block	Protection	Increases your chance to block by 100% for 10 sec. 10 Rage, Instant, 30 sec cooldown
19	Piercing Howl	Fury	Causes all enemies within 10 yards to be dazed, reducing movement speed by 50% for 6 sec. 10 rage
20	Shield Bash	Protection	Bash the target with your shield dazing them and interrupting spellcasting, which prevents any spell in that school from being cast for 6 sec. 10 Rage, 5 yd range, instant, 12 sec cooldown
22	Overpower	Arms	Instantly overpower the enemy, causing weapon damage. Only useable after the target dodges. The Overpower cannot be blocked, dodged or parried. 5 Rage, 5 yd range, Instant, 5 sec cooldown
24	Disarm	Protection	Disarm the enemy's main hand and ranged weapons for 10 sec. 15 Rage, 5 yd range, instant, 1 min cooldown
26	Hamstring	Arms	Maims the enemy, reducing movement speed by 50% for 15 sec. 10 Rage, 5 yd range, Instant
26	Cleave	Fury	A sweeping attack that strikes the target and the target's physical damage and consuming up to 20 additional rage to deal up to additional damage per point of rage consumed. 10 Rage, 5 yd range, instant
29	Sweeping Strikes	Arms	Your melee attacks strike an additional nearby opponent. Lasts 10 sec. 1 minute cooldown. 30 rage
29	Last Stand	Protection	Temporarily grants you 30% of your max health for 20 sec. After the effect expires, the additional health is lost. 3 minute cooldown
29	Concussion Blow	Protection	Stuns the opponent for 5 sec and deals moderate damage based on attack power. 15 rage. 30 sec cooldown.
29	Death Wish	Fury	When activated you become Enraged, increasing your physical damage by 20%, but increasing all damage you take by 5%. Lasts 30 sec. 10 rage. 3 min cooldown
30	Berserker Stance	Fury	An aggressive stance. Increases damage done by 10%. Instant, 1 sec cooldown
32	Battle Shout	Fury	The warrior shouts, increasing strength and agility of all raid and party members within 30 yards by 15 and gaining 10 rage. Lasts 2 min. Instant, 1 min cooldown
36	Whirlwind	Fury	In a whirlwind of steel you attack all enemies within 8 yards, causing 75% weapon damage from both melee weapons to each enemy. 25 Rage, Instant, 10 sec cooldown
38	Pummel	Fury	Pummel the target, interrupting spellcasting and preventing any spell in that school from being cast for 4 sec. 10 Rage, 5 yd range, Instant, 10 sec cooldown
39	Deadly Calm	Arms	For the next 10 sec, none of your abilities cost rage, but you continue to generate rage. Cannot be used during Inner Rage. 2 minute cooldown.
39	Raging Blow	Fury	A mighty blow that deals 100% weapon damage from both weapons. Can only be used while enraged. 20 rage. 6 sec cooldown.
39	Devastate	Protection	Sunders the target's armor causing the Sunder Armor effect. In addition, cause 150% weapon damage and additional damage for each application of Sunder Armor on the target.
39	Heroic Fury	Fury	Removes any immobilization effects and resets the cooldown on your Intercept ability. 30 second cooldown.
42	Intimidating Shout	Fury	The warrior shouts, causing up to 5 enemies within 8 yards to cower in fear. The targeted enemy will be unable to move while cowering. Lasts 8 sec. 25 Rage, 18 yd range, Instant, 2 min cooldown
44	Slam	Fury	Slams the opponent, causing weapon damage plus additional damage. 20 Rage, 18 yd range, 1.5 sec cast
46	Challenging Shout	Fury	Forces all enemies within 10 yards to focus attacks on you for 6 sec. 5 Rage, Instant, 3 min cooldown
48	Shield Wall	Protection	Reduces all damage taken by 40% for 12 sec. Instant, 5 min cooldown
49	Vigilance	Protection	Focus your protective gaze on a group or raid target, reducing their damage taken by 3%. In addition, each time they are hit by an attack your Taunt cooldown is refreshed and you gain Vengeance as if 20% of the damage was done to you. Lasts 30 min. This effect can only be on one target at a time.
50	Intercept	Fury	Charge an enemy, causing [12% of AP] damage and stunning it for 3 sec. 10 Rage, 8-25 yd range, Instant, 30 sec cooldown
52	Demoralizing Shout	Fury	Reduces the physical damage caused by all enemies within 10 yards by 10% for 30 sec. 10 Rage, Instant
54	Berserker Rage	Fury	The warrior enters a berserker rage, removing and granting immunity to Fear, Sap and Incapacitate effects and generating extra rage when taking damage. Lasts 10 sec. Instant, 30 sec cooldown
56	Retaliation	Arms	Instantly counterattack any enemy that strikes you in melee for 12 sec. Melee attacks made from behind cannot be counterattacked. A maximum of 20 attacks will cause retaliation. Instant, 5 min cooldown
59	Throwdown	Arms	Knocks the target to the ground and stuns it for 5 sec. 15 rage. 45 second cooldown
64	Recklessness	Fury	Your next 3 special ability attacks have an additional 100% to critically hit but all damage taken is increased by 20%. Lasts 12 sec. Instant, 5 min cooldown
66	Spell Reflection	Protection	Raise your shield, reflecting the next spell cast on you. Lasts 5 sec. 15 Rage, Instant, 10 sec cooldown
68	Commanding Shout	Protection	Increases Stamina of all party and raid members within 30 and grants 10 rage to you. Lasts 2 min. Instant, 1 min cooldown
69	Bladestorm	Arms	You become a whirling storm of destructive force, instantly striking all nearby targets with your weapon and continuing to perform a whirlwind attack every 1 sec for 6 sec. While under the effects of Bladestorm, you do not feel pity or remorse or fear and you cannot be stopped unless killed or disarmed, but you cannot perform any other abilities. 25 rage. 1.5 min cooldown
69	Shockwave	Protection	Sends a wave of force in front of you, inflicting high damage based on attack power and stunning all targets within a 10 yard frontal cone.
72	Intervene	Protection	Run at high speed towards a party member, intercepting the next melee or ranged attack made against them as well as reducing their total threat by 10%. 10 Rage, 8-25 yd range, Instant, 30 sec cooldown
74	Shattering Throw	Arms	Throws your weapon at the enemy causing [50% of AP + 12] damage, reducing the armor on the target by 20% for 10 sec or removing any invulnerabilities. 25 Rage, 30 yd range, 1.5 sec cast, 5 min cooldown
76	Enraged Regeneration	Fury	You regenerate 30% of your total health over 10 sec. Can only be used while Enraged. 15 Rage, Instant, 3 min cooldown
78	Heroic Throw	Arms	Throws your weapon at the enemy causing [50% of AP + 12] damage. This ability causes high threat. 30 yd range, Instant, 1 min cooldown
81	Colossus Smash	Arms	Smashes a target for 150% weapon damage plus additional damage, and weakens their defenses. Your attacks bypass armor entirely for 6 seconds. 20 Rage, 20 second cooldown.
81	Inner Rage	Fury	Whenever you have over 75 Rage you enter an Enraged state, increasing damage caused by all abilities by 15% and increasing Rage cost by 50%. Lasts for 15 seconds. Instant
85	Heroic Leap	Fury	Leap through the air towards a targeted location, slamming down with destructive force to deal 100% weapon damage to all enemies within 5 yards, stunning them for 2 sec. 8-25 yd range, Instant, 1 min cooldown

WARRIOR ABILITIES

RAGE

Rage is the resource by which a Warrior lives and dies. Rage is generated both from dealing damage with your auto attacks, and by receiving damage. You also receive rage if you avoid an attack that would have otherwise hit you. Nearly all abilities cost Rage, some have a variable rage cost (such as Execute), and a few of them help you generate Rage.

SHOUTS

Shouts are temporary buffs and debuffs. There are five shouts, but some come from talents and aren't available to all Warriors. The shouts are Commanding Shout, Battle Shout, Intimidating Shout, Demoralizing Shout, and Piercing Howl.

Commanding Shout boosts the Stamina of everyone in your party or raid. Battle Shout increases Strength and Agility. These two shouts actually grant you 10 rage when using them, but they are also on a shared 1-minute cooldown.

The remaining shouts are debuffs and cost Rage to use. Intimidating Shout causes nearby enemies to flee in terror for a short time. Demoralizing Shout reduces physical damage done by any enemy affected by it, while Piercing Howl's effect reduces the movement speed of enemies within its range.

Stance Bar

The Stance Bar appears just above your Action Bars in the lower left-hand corner of the screen. The Stance Bar provides quick access to switching Battle Stance, Defensive Stance, and Berserker stance.

STANCES

Warriors begin with only Battle Stance, but eventually learn Defensive Stance and Berserker Stance. You can switch between stances freely, but only one stance is active at a time. They are on an independent global cooldown from the rest of your class abilities, and have no cost or restriction. You need to set your Action Bars for each Stance, so before you enter battle set your Action Bars for one stance, switch to another and repeat the process.

For nearly all intents and purposes Arms Warriors spend their time in Battle Stance, while Protection Warriors stay in Defensive Stance, and Fury Warriors in Berserker Stance. Certain abilities are restricted to some stances only, which require "Stance Dancing" between the various stances to fully utilize their arsenal.

SUGGESTED PROFESSION FOR A FIRST-TIME WARRIOR

Blacksmithing is an excellent choice. It allows Warriora to craft their own weapons and armor, which is a great benefit, since there is no guarantee you will always get lucky with drops. You may be able to fill in holes in your gear with something you craft yourself! Blacksmiths can craft both Mail and Plate, as well as a wide array of weapons. Mining is the natural complement to Blacksmithing, as it calls for the metals and gems harvested by Miners to craft weapons and armor. Mining also provides a Stamina benefit, which helps any class, but tanks, like Protection Warriors, always need more Stamina.

PLAYING AS AN ARMS WARRIOR

Arms Warriors are designed to deal controlled, methodical melee damage with a single powerful weapon and bleed effects. Arms Warriors generate Rage over time because of Anger Management. These are the slow-hitting, big number version of damage Warriors. They primarily dance between Battle and Berserk Stance in a given encounter, with Battle Stance being their home. Take Arms if you want to see big numbers and don't mind waiting a moment or two between swings.

Mortal Strike is the defining ability of this line. This used to be one of the only healing debuffs in the game, but abilities of this type have become much more commonplace over the last few years. As such, Arms has shifted from being the only PvP spec for Warriors into being a strong choice that isn't necessarily the only one.

Arms Warriors benefit from having multiple targets to attack. Their use of Sweeping Strikes, and later Bladestorm, allows for far more damage output when there are more people to hit.

Overpower is one of the most important parts of using heavy weapons in this line. Taste for Blood lets Warriors use Overpower quite often, making it possible to raise their damage without only a pittance of Rage expended.

ABILITIES LEARNED AT LEVEL 10 IF YOU SELECT ARMS

	Ability	Description
	Mortal Strike	A vicious strike that deals 185% weapon damage plus additional damage and wounds the target, reducing the effectiveness of any healing by 10% for 10 sec. 25 Rage, 5 yd range, Instant, 4.5 sec cooldown
	Anger Management	Generates 1 rage per 3 seconds in combat and 25% extra Rage from damage dealt.
	Two-Handed Weapon Specialization	Increases the damage you deal with two-handed melee weapons by 10%
	Mastery: Strikes of Opportunity	Grants at 16% chance for your melee attacks to instantly trigger an additional melee attack for 115% of normal damage. Each point of Mastery increases this chance by 2%

DESIRABLE STATS

The stats you want are Strength and Critical Strike Rating. Hit Rating has some value if you are in a situation where your abilities must land (such as interrupts, stuns, or snares). Most importantly, get a two-handed weapon that has a high top-end damage number. If a weapon with lower DPS has more desirable overall stats, that may outweigh the effect of the higher base weapon damage of another weapon, but that usually only happens if there's a noticeable disparity in item levels.

LEVELS 1 - 80

Playing Solo

For the first few dozen levels, open up with Charge, then use Rend and Thunder Clap. Use excess Rage on Strike at first, then Mortal Strike as soon as you get it at level 10. If you are moving between targets quickly, use Victory Rush. It greatly reduces your downtime because of its healing component. Against groups of enemies, start out with Thunder Clap and Demoralizing Shout to reduce incoming damage, then use Sweeping Strikes and Cleave to hit multiple targets.

At higher levels Warriors gain access to more tools that allow them to take on tougher opponents or larger groups of enemies. Which abilities you use depends on the situation. If the enemies rely on physical damage, Charge into the group and activate Retaliation. If there are more caster-types, Recklessness may be a better choice. If you get in to a bad situation, you can always switch to a shield, activate Defensive Stance, and use Shield Wall and Shield Block to give yourself a bit more protection.

Playing in a Group

Arms Warriors fill the damage role in groups, but there is a good chance you may be asked to supply more than simply high DPS. Demoralizing Shout and Thunder Clap won't boost your DPS, but they make life easier for tanks and healers. Enemies fleeing from battle are a concern, and Arms Warriors provide a snare in the form of Hamstring (especially in its improved form from Arms talents) to prevent runners pulling in adds. You have a few ways to interrupt spells, such as stuns from Charge or Intercept, and Pummel, though you may need to change stances to use it.

THE CATACLYSM: LEVELS 81 - 85

While you get abilities like Bladestorm and Throwdown before level 81, expect to rely on them more heavily in the high level zones in Cataclysm. Save Throwdown for abilities that can't be interrupted through normal means (their cast bars have a silver shield around the icon). The damage from enemies in Cataclysm's new zones ramps up significantly, and you don't want to get hit by the special abilities of these powerful creatures if you're running around alone.

Preparing Your Arms Warrior for Heroic Dungeons

Look for Strength, Hit Rating, and Critical Strike Rating on your gear. Expertise Rating increases your damage by reducing the enemy's chance to dodge or parry your attacks, but there's a cap on how much you need. Check your character stats sheet and add just enough to make all the dodge values equal to 0.00%; anything beyond that serves no purpose.

Haste Rating isn't a particularly valuable statistic, so consider Reforging as much of it into another stat that is more valuable to you. Remember, your gear doesn't need to be absolutely perfect to start heroics, but it needs to illustrate to your group that you have put some time and thought into your character.

Arms Warriors: Group Buffs and Debuffs

Beyond Battle Shout, Commanding Shout and Demoralizing Shout, Arms Warriors also provide the Blood Frenzy debuff, which causes targets to take 4% additional physical damage, as well as increasing the potency of all bleed damage by 30%. Sunder Armor reduces an enemy's armor by up to 12%. Thunder Clap reduces the attack speed enemies by 20%. Mortal Strike provides a healing debuff on enemies.

PLAYING AS A FURY WARRIOR

Fury Warriors are designed to deal massive, constant melee damage with either two one-handed weapons, or two two-handed weapons. Fury Warriors gain a 3% bonus to hit and do 25% more damage with their off-hand weapon. Essentially, this mitigates half the penalties for using this weapon combination. As such, Fury Warriors still have a lower overall Hit rate, but their higher number of attacks lead to substantial Rage accrual and high total damage output.

Bloodthirst is their defining ability. This attack deals instant damage and then lets the Warrior's next few attacks heal them. It's a way to keep yourself topped off on health while going crazy on the frontlines. That's good, because Fury Warriors take much more damage than either of their rivals. They spend more time in Berzerk Stance, and they rarely stack on anything that gives them more survivability.

Fury Warriors often trade their safety for increased damage output. They're more likely to die in groups, so that's a problem. However, when played well, you can learn to avoid stealing threat and let the tanks do their job. Avoid monster aggro, kill your targets, and know how to get out of trouble.

ABILITIES LEARNED AT LEVEL 10 IF YOU SELECT FURY WARRIOR

	Ability	Description
	Bloodthirst	Instantly attack the target. In addition, the next 3 successful melee attacks will restore 0.5% of max health. This effect lasts 8 sec. Damage is based on your attack power. 20 Rage, 5 yd range, Instant, 3 sec cooldown
	Precision	Increases your chance to hit with melee weapons by 3%.
	Dual Wield Specialization	Allows you to equip one-hand and off-hand weapons in your off-hand. Increases all Physical damage by 10% and raises of your off-hand attacks by an additional 25%.
	Mastery: Unshackled Fury	Increases the benefit of abilities that cause or require you to be enranged by 25%. Each point of Mastery increases enrage effects by an additional 3.13%.

DESIRABLE STATS

Strength, Hit Rating, and Critical Strike Rating are the stats an Arms Warrior wants, in roughly that order of priority. Hit Rating may be more valuable than Strength at times since, compared to using a single weapon, dual wielding requires more Hit Rating to remain as effective. Until you start facing enemies that are higher level than your character, however, Hit Rating falls well behind Strength.

LEVELS 1 - 80

Playing Solo

Fury Warriors have little regard for their well-being and are designed to fight almost non-stop against single targets. Who needs to sit and eat to restore health when you have Bloodthirst and Blood Craze to restore health gradually (although one requires foes to hit, and the other calls for enemies to hit you!), and Victory Rush to get back health in bigger chunks?

That doesn't mean you should try taking on large groups of enemies at once. Fury Warriors really only have Cleave for hitting multiple targets at once (until you get Whirlwind at level 36). Consider Death Wish (the talent, not the attitude of Fury Warriors), which trades improved damage output for increased damage taken. Against one enemy increased damage isn't a big concern, but in a group setting it could spell a quick death.

Playing in a Group

Fury Warriors offer damage and a handful of utility abilities that are nice additions to any group outing. With points in Rude Interruption, you should always volunteer to be the first person to interrupt spells (just remember to use Pummel). Everyone's happy when enemy spells are stopped and you get a nice boost to your damage output. Don't forget to apply your shouts as needed, and use Hamstring to keep an individual enemy from fleeing, or Piercing Howl if there are multiple enemies trying to scatter at once.

THE CATACLYSM: LEVELS 81 - 85

Since the damage output from enemies in the high-level Cataclysm zones increases quite a bit as you move to higher level zones, so it's even more important that you limit just how many enemies you face at the same time. You should still win a DPS race against most enemies solo, but Fury Warriors just aren't built to stand up to multiple enemies pounding on them at once. You can try to take talents from the other trees that help keep you alive (such as Field Dressing in the Arms tree) but even that won't help you survive a bad pull. Set up your fights methodically by planning a string of targets you can face alone (or two at a time if there's no other choice), turn into a whirlwind of weapons once the combat starts, then quickly jump to the next target to take advantage of Victory Rush's healing.

Preparing Your Fury Warrior for Heroic Dungeons

Look for Strength, Hit Rating and Expertise Rating first. You need quite a bit more Hit Rating than Arms or Protection Warriors due to dual wielding weapons, but the Expertise requirements for Fury are the same. Build up your Critical Strike Rating only after you're comfortable with your Hit and Expertise scores. Haste Rating isn't a particularly valuable statistic so Reforge it for other stats that provide you with greater benefit.

Fury Warriors: Group Buffs and Debuffs

Fury Warriors bring the standard Warrior buffs (Battle Shout, Commanding Shout) and debuffs (Demoralizing Shout, Thunderclap, Sunder Armor) to a raid. In addition, they can talent into Rampage, which boosts the physical Critical Strike chance of all raid members by 5%, and the Warrior gains an extra 2% on top of that from the talent.

PLAYING AS A PROTECTION WARRIOR

Protection Warriors are pure tanks. They get a 15% bonus to Stamina, a 15% higher chance to block, and an Attack Power buff when taking damage from enemies. This lets them hold onto monster aggro even when everyone in a group is going all out to kill the target. Shield Slam is the defining ability of this line. It's a shield attack that does high damage, accrues substantial Threat, and removes a positive magical effect from the target.

Protection Warriors do decent enough damage, especially if they're absorbing incoming attacks. They rely on enemy attacks to get a fair amount of their Rage, so these are characters are awful damage dealers if anyone else is taking the hits. To avoid that problem, Protection Warriors can learn how to generate Rage when blocking attacks or deflecting spells. They also use their Rage quite efficiently. Their Thunderclap gains a DoT component, and it can be trained to spread Rend to nearby targets. This gets all monsters to start taking damage early in a fight (when Warriors traditionally have trouble holding AoE aggro).

Instead of Sundering enemy armor, Protection Warriors get the Devastate ability, letting them continue to do some damage while ripping off enemy armor. They also get more Stuns than other Warriors, including Shockwave (an AoE damage and Stun ability) and Concussion Blow.

Protection Warriors can temporarily boost their health and survive through even the foulest group and raid encounters. They have no real downsides for these situations. When soloing they're slow killers, but it's almost impossible to kill them. Expect the majority of Warrior players to keep this as at least a secondary specialization.

ABILITIES LEARNED AT LEVEL 10 IF YOU SELECT PROTECTION

Ability	Description
Shield Slam	Slam the target with your shield, causing damage plus 100% of your attack power and dispelling 1 magic effect on the target. Also causes a high amount of threat.
Sentinel	Increases your total Stamina by 15% and your block chance by 15%. You also generate 50% additional Rage from attacking targets that are not targetting you.
Vengeance	Increases attack power by a percentage of damage taken, up to a maximum of a percentage of the character's health.
Mastery: Critical Block	Increases your chance to block by 10% and your chance to critically block by 20%. Each point of Mastery increases your block and critical block chances by an additional 2.5%.

DESIRABLE STATS

Protection Warriors want Stamina, armor value, and avoidance stats (Dodge and Parry), then Strength. However, a Protection Warrior's biggest asset is a good shield. Look for Shields with the highest armor value possible, but it should have appropirate stats on it. Don't steal a spell caster's shield simply because it has more armor than what you're using currently!

LEVELS 1 - 80
Playing Solo

Tank specs, like Protection Warriors, need a completely different mindset than damage specs when it comes to playing solo. Plan to wear down enemies and win battles through attrition. Even low level Protection Warriors can pull multiple enemies at once, but don't expect them to die quickly. Use Rend and Thunder Clap to spread damage (Thunder Clap should apply Rend to all of the enemies assuming you picked up the Blood and Thunder talent), and use Victory Rush to heal up after each enemy dies. Protection Warriors can often solo many group quests through clever use of stuns (Concussion Blow, Shockwave), snares and kiting. For Example, Hamstring or a stun plus Intercept or Charging away to a different enemy. Use bandages and heavy defensive abilities to keep yourself up. It's easier to face melee enemies in larger groups since they're losing health to Rend, Thunder Clap, Revenge (with its accompanying talent), Cleave and Shockwave. It's not impossible to take down spell casters (Gag Order is a big help here), it's just tougher to get them to bunch up for you.

Playing in a Group

Your job in groups is to keep all the attention of every enemy squarely on you. Depending on the size of the encounter, you may need to be concerned about positioning. If any crowd control is necessary, you need to move the pile away from CC'ed enemies so you're still free to use your AoE abilities such as Cleave, Thunder Clap, and Shockwave.

Tanks are often looked to for leadership in groups. A great tank is vocal with their group and never lets stray mobs beat on the healer. Don't be afraid to ask your group if you should be pulling faster (which would generally be if your healer has plenty of mana left after a pack of enemies), or slower (if the healer is having trouble keeping up). As long as the group stays alive and clears gradually with minimal problems, things are going ok.

THE CATACLYSM: LEVELS 81 - 85

Enemies in the world in Cataclysm are much more potent than what you faced on the path from level 1 to 80. Cataclysm mobs deal much more damage compared to your effective health pool, and they have more health in addition. Because of this, you may struggle against groups of enemies if you get too many at once. Protection Warriors can go still go toe-to-toe with multiple foes at once, though. The basic routine when leveling and fighting multiple enemies should be to apply Rend immediately, then Thunder Clap as soon as all of the mobs are in range. Continue with Cleave and Shockwave until the mobs are dead, refreshing Thunder Clap every 6 seconds for the damage and to keep Rend rolling.

With any spare global cooldowns to use on other abilities, focus on only one mob at a time with abilities like Shield Slam and Devastate. Every time you kill a mob, immediately use Victory Rush. Keep in mind that Victory Rush heals based on your maximum health, so you can use health buffs such as Commanding Shout and Last Stand to actually increase how much healing you receive.

Preparing Your Protection Warrior for Heroic Dungeons

Bastion of Defense is a must-have talent from the Protection Tree. If you skipped it while leveling up, you must get it now. If that means a respec, then get ready to shell out some gold at the Warrior trainer. When leveling in Cataclysm, you need to keep a few things in mind from the get-go. Quest rewards have much higher item level than what you started leveling with, and, with only five levels to gain, any Superior quest rewards or dungeon drops could last a long time. Keep an eye out for any quest rewards that have tank-friendly statistics, and hold on to them until you have an item that is better in every way.

Look for items that greatly bolster your ability to survive encounters with heroic enemies. Snag gear with high Stamina, Dodge Rating, and Parry Rating. You eventually need to build up a bit of Expertise Rating and Hit Rating, but you don't need to go all out for these stats until you're getting ready to raid. A new tank needs a smattering of all defensive stats, so don't shy away from using Green, Orange, and Purple gems in your gear.

Protection Warriors: Group Buffs and Debuffs

Devastate makes Sunder Armor just a little bit better, and it's nearly effortless for Protection Warriors to maintain the 12% armor debuff the raid needs. Use Commanding Shout, or Battle Shout as necessary to boost the raid and Demoralizing Shout and Thunder Clap to make it tougher for melee enemies to deal damage.

Keep in mind that if you're the tank, and you have a debuff ability (or an effect that is similar to an ability from another class) you need to be the one applying that debuff! Everything you can slap on enemies makes the task of holding their attention that much easier.

PVP COMBAT

PvP combat can be an excellent focal point for roleplaying, but that's not all that you can do with this medium. PvP is fun for practicing advanced character use, for blowing off steam, and for getting special rewards and achievements.

DUELING

Dueling another player is a safe way of practicing your PvP skills. You can duel on any kind of server, and you can duel players from either faction.

To start a duel, right-click on a player's portrait and click "Duel." A duel flag appears, and your opponent can choose to accept or decline. If they accept, a countdown begins, indicating when the duel will start.

A duel ends when one player's health is reduced to 1. The other player is declared the winner, and the results are broadcast in your region. Anyone who runs too far away from the duel flag loses by default, so that is another way that the match can end.

Outside of an achievement, there are no tangible rewards to dueling other players. You cannot gain Honor in this way, nor can you loot anything from your opponents. The person who loses the duel doesn't actually die, so they won't have to deal with durability loss or reclaiming their body. Rather, dueling is a way to practice using your abilities or just goofing off with others.

PVP SERVERS

On PvP servers, Horde and Alliance players are actively at war. Anytime you enter neutral, contested, or enemy territory, you can be attacked by players of the opposite faction. This completely changes the nature of the game; while you are completing quests, you must also look for and defend against the enemy. Most players on PvP servers game with regular groups for protection.

PvP kills of the opposite faction yield Honor. This isn't a great way to beef up your character, but it's exciting stuff. You never know what's ahead. Even if you find a soloing character and kill them, there could be all kinds of trouble heading your way as a result!

PvP deaths that don't involve damage from monsters or falling won't cost you money. There isn't a durability loss as a result of these fights. You must still run back and claim your body or resurrect at a graveyard, though.

PVE SERVERS

If you are on a PvE server, you can choose to engage in PvP combat. Right-click your own character portrait and click PvP-Enable. You can now engage in PvP with other players who have turned on their PvP flags. When you click Disable, your PvP flag remains on for another 5 minutes.

You can tell that another player is flagged for PvP because their colors change. Someone flagged (when you are not) will look like a neutral target. As soon as you flag, they become red, signaling that combat can initiate at any time. Honor rewards and combat dynamics are exactly that same on PvE and PvP servers. Needing to flag for combat is the only difference between them.

If you get in over your head, enemies might kill you and corpse camp your character. That means that they wait for you to resurrect near your body, hoping to kill you again. Wait for 5 minutes, if necessary, and let your PvP flag fall. Doing so allows you to come back to life safely.

As an alternative, call for help from buddies or from people in the region. Use /general chat to let other players know that flagged targets are in a certain area. Someone will show up for a free fight!

PVP CURRENCY

You earn Honor Points by killing players from the opposing faction or by participating in Battlegrounds. If you accumulate enough points, you can use them to purchase special Honor Rewards, including unique gear. Honor Points are listed in the Currency tab of your Character window. While there's no limit on how many Honor Points you earn each week, there is a limit on how many you can store at any given time. If you hit the cap, you just need to spend some Honor Points and you can start earning additional points immediately.

Conquest Points work similarly to Honor Points, but are a bit harder to obtain. Conquest Points come from participating in Arenas and Rated Battlegrounds. There is a weekly cap on how many Conquest Points you can earn, and how many you can store at any given time.

When a new Arena season begins, all your Conquest Points are converted to Honor Points, and some of the Honor Rewards from the previous season are made available for purchase with Honor Points.

Honor Rewards are found in the capital city for your faction. Talk to guards to find out where you need to go, and then peruse the rewards to decide what you want. It takes a great deal of combat to earn the best items.

PVP TIPS BY CLASS

PVP tactics change considerably depending on the situation, and the goals of the battleground or arena in which you find yourself. They also change constantly as new abilities and talents are introduced to the game, or existing abilities and talents are modified. If you want to remain at the top of the PVP heap, look for active discussion boards, find the other top PVP players on your server or battlegroup and stay current.

The following pages provide the tools available to each class and should serve only as a starting point for your journey to the top of the rankings. They are broken down into broad categories so you can easily find the tools you need for your character, or the abilities of other classes you may need to counter.

DEATH KNIGHT

Death Knights have an impressive array of tools available to them, so you must be proficient with their proper use. Additionally, you need to be incredibly familiar with your keybindings. Death Knights are predominantly a melee class with a handful of utility spells that work at range. Regardless, keep the fight up close and personal or you won't enjoy much success.

HEALING REDUCTIONS

Necrotic Strike isn't a true healing reduction like Mortal Strike, but it has a very similar functionality. Necrotic Strike actually absorbs the next healing the target receives, up to 75% of the death knight's attack power. This is effectively the same thing as a healing reduction, and can even be better, if only small incremental heals are able to be used on the target—causing them to be fully absorbed.

IMMUNITIES

Anti-magic Shell isn't a true immunity, but it does allow the Death Knight to absorb magical damage (up to 75% of it, or 50% of the Death Knight's total health, whichever is more). Additionally, it removes and prevents the application of many harmful debuffs for five seconds. Icebound Fortitude also grants immunity to stuns, and incoming damage is reduced by 30%. Bone Shield is exclusive to the Blood tree which reduces damage taken by 20%, and lasts for one minute, or until all of its three charges are consumed.

INTERRUPTS

Mind Freeze is the standard Death Knight interrupt, but its range is limited. Strangulate is an interrupt which also silences the target for five seconds. Its 30 yard range is nice, but its two minute cooldown means you must use it judiciously.

Unholy Death Knights gain Shambling Rush, a Dark Transformation ability of a ghoul pet. It replaces Leap and gives the pet the ability to charge enemies, root them in place, and interrupt spellcasting.

QUICK MOVES

Think of Death Grip as a quick move in reverse. Every 35 seconds, Death Knights can target an enemy and pull the target into melee range. Death Grip is extremely powerful in PvP, as your entire team can, for example, hide behind a pillar or wall while the Death Knight peeks out and yanks someone from the opposing team into the area for a quick kill.

SLOWS/SNARES

Chains of Ice is one of the most feared and effective snares in World of Warcraft. Chais of Ice has a range of 20 yards, reduces movement speed by 60%, and due to Death Knight rune mechanics can be active on multiple targets simultaneously.

Chillblains is a talent in the Frost talent tree that causes Frost Fever to slow the target by 50%. With one application of Pestilence after hitting a target with Frost Fever, it's possible to snare an entire group at the same time.

STUNS

Death Knight stuns come only from talents in the Frost and Unholy Trees. Hungering Cold is a Frost talent that freezes any enemy within 10 yards, and also adds Frost Fever. The effect lasts for 10 seconds, or until the target suffers any damage, save diseases.

The stuns from the Unholy tree are all tied to the Death Knight's ghoul pet. Gnaw is a 3 second stun available to a standard ghoul, while Dark Transformation is needed for Shambling Rush, and Monstrous Blow, which is an improved Gnaw.

DRUID

Druids are a favorite opening target for opposing teams. Druids are effective healers (being a Druid healer is a double whammy if you want to avoid notice in PVP situations), and damage dealers, but leather armor doesn't make for the greatest protection. If you're a spellcaster, learn how to run and gun (or heal) and shapeshift to stay mobile.

DEBUFF REMOVAL

Remove Corruption takes away Curse and Poison effects, and Restoration Druids also gain the ability to remove Magic effects.

CROWD CONTROL

Cyclone is a short-term solution (6 seconds) for removing an enemy from the game, but it's incredibly effective. Hibernate gets less use, but you can take out a Hunter's pet or another Druid in an animal form so don't completely discount it.

IMMUNITIES

Barkskin reduces incoming damage by 20%, but more importantly for Balance and Resto Druids, they are immune to pushback on spellcasting due to damaging attacks. A Balance Druid talent, Owlkin Frenzy, has a similar effect but it's not an active ability.

INTERRUPTS

While you don't need to be a Feral Druid to use Skull Bash, you must be in Bear or Cat form to use it. It interrupts spellcasting and prevents spells from the same school from being cast for 5 sec.

KNOCKBACKS

Typhoon is exclusive to Balance Druids and knocks back enemies, but has a limitation. It is a cone attack, meaning it hits only enemies in front of your character, so you may need to move to make it work the way you want.

QUICK MOVES

Feral Charge is a Feral Combat talent that is available in both Bear form and Cat form. Bears charge into an enemy and root them in place for 4 seconds. Cats actually leap behind their target, and apply a daze effect.

SLOWS/SNARES

Entangling Roots is a snare which can be applied on enemies in one of two ways. First, it's a targeted spell that can hold one target in place. Second, Druids can apply Nature's Grasp to themselves. Any enemy who strikes that Druid could be wrapped up by Entangling Roots. Feral Combat Druids who spec into Infected Wounds can slow their target's movement speed by using Shred, Maul, Rage, or Mangle.

STUNS

Druids in Bear form can Bash a target for a 4 second stun. Druids in Cat form get two abilities that stun a target. Pounce must be done while prowling, but provides a 3 second stun. Maim is a finishing move that stuns the target based on how many combo points have been applied.

HUNTER

While all Hunters fight best at range, you must become familiar with aspects of melee combat since that's where your pet spends most of its PVP time. Pet choice is important but picking the right one depends on many factors. The time you spend learning about everything pets add to your pool of abilities, the more rounded (and tougher) you become in PVP.

BUFF REMOVAL

Tranquilizing Shot removes Enrage effects from a target (meaning abilities like Death Wish). Additionally, it dispels one magical effect on the target, so this can be used to strip off buffs such as Bloodlust/Heroism or Power Word: Shield.

CROWD CONTROL

Place Freezing Traps on the ground to capture the character who triggers it for up to 20 seconds. Any damage breaks the effect, but these traps are a great way to keep the heat off you (or a healer) for a short time.

FEARS

Scare Beast allows the Hunter to fear a beast opponent, which in many cases is simply another Hunter's pet. However, it also works against Druids in a Beast form.

HEALING REDUCTIONS

Widow Venom reduces any healing the target receives by 10%, lasting for 30 seconds. Like most Hunter shots, this has a very long (40 yard) range.

IMMUNITIES

While not a true immunity, Deterrence is the next best thing. The Hunter's parry chance is increased by 100%, the chance of being hit by a ranged attacks is reduced by 100%, and the Hunter has a 100% chance to deflect enemy spells. What this means is that as long as the hunter faces the melee attackers (in order to parry), nothing can hit over the 5 second duration. Spells and ranged attacks are avoided regardless of direction faced.

INTERRUPTS

Scatter Shot isn't an interrupt, but serves nearly the same purpose. Scatter Shot causes targets to become disoriented for 4 seconds, which stops any attacks or spells. Silencing Shot is a Marksmarnship-exclusive talent that silences its target for 3 seconds.

QUICK MOVES

Disengage is a quick escape move. Upon triggering it, the Hunter immediately leaps backwards many yards. This can be used in conjunction with jumping at the same time to travel farther, and even while leaping off of something. This can be used both as an escape tool or to close distance, if you face the other direction before using it.

SLOWS/SNARES

Concussive Shot is a long-range snare, with a short duration; for 4 seconds, the target's movemeent suffers a 50% movement reduction and is considered dazed. Wing Clip is a melee range snare, reducing the target's movement speed by 50% for 10 seconds. Wing Clip should be your back-up escape plan, for the times Disengage is on cooldown.

When an enemy triggers an Ice Trap, a 10 yard area becomes covered with snow-like effect. Opponents caught or entering this area lose 50% of their movement speed.

STUNS

Sting and Sonic Blast are two pet abilities, obtained by taming a Wasp or a Bat pet respectively. These are short, 2 second stuns. Sting has a 45 second cooldown and must be used in melee range, while Sonic Blast has a minute cooldown, but can be used up to 20 yards away.

Beast Mastery Hunters can command their pet to stun their opponent using Intimidation. It only lasts for 3 seconds and has a minute cooldown, however, so avoid using it capriciously.

MAGE

BUFF REMOVAL

Mages not only remove magical buffs from a target, but they actually take its benefits for themselves with Spellsteal. The downside is that any buff stolen in this way has its duration decreased to 2 minutes regardless of its normal duration.

DEBUFF REMOVAL

Mages are the only class without a healing spell who have the capability to remove a debuff from others. It's limited to Curses, but it's better than nothing.

CROWD CONTROL

Polymorph comes in many flavors, but the end result is the same: your Humanoid or Beast target is transformed into a small animal. The affected character loses all control and remains in that form until the spell expires or becomes damaged in any way.

HEALING REDUCTIONS

Permafrost is a Frost-based talent, but any Mage can reach it in the Frost tree. Any spell which applies the Chill effect also adds a healing debuff (up to 25%) to the target.

IMMUNITIES

Ice Block protects the Mage from harm for up to 10 sec, but the Mage cannot move or cast spells for the duration of the effect. Unless you have help in the area, or are simply waiting on a cooldown, Ice Block just delays the inevitable.

Frost Mages also get Ice Barrier deep in their talent tree. Ice Barrier absorbs a good chunk of damage and also allows you to ignore pushback on spellcasting due to damage. Use it early. Use it often.

INTERRUPTS

Counterspell interrupts an enemy cast. If successful, it also prevents the enemy from casting a spell from the same school of magic for up to 8 seconds. Improved Counterspell, found at the top of the Arcane talent tree, adds a silencing component to the spell meaning it's no longer necessary to time the spell to keep someone from casting.

QUICK MOVES

Blink teleports you away a short distance, and also removes snare and stun effects. Keep it somewhere easy to remember as Bilnk should get quite a bit of use in PVP.

SLOWS/SNARES

Various Frost-based spells such as Frostbolt and Cone of Cold have a chance to apply the Chill effect. Chill slows enemies movement speed significantly. Frost Nova is a great way to escape multiple melee attackers. For 8 seconds (unless they take damage) anyone near the caster becomes snared in ice. Ring of Frost is a slower version of Frost Nova, but lasts longer. Almost every Frost spell cast by Frost Mages either slows or snares its targets more effectively than what Fire or Arcane mages can manage. Fire Mages can talent into Blast Wave, which slows anyone near the mage by 70%. Slow is available deep in the Arcane tree. It reduces its target movement speed, and slows ranged attacks and spell casting.

STUNS

The ultimate Frost talent, Deep Freeze, stuns targets for 5 seconds if they were Frozen already. Targets immune to stun effects take additional damage. Fire Mages get one true stun from Impact (any spell that causes damage has a chance to make the next Fire Blast stun your target). Dragon's Breath isn't really a stun, but its disorienting effect works about the same. Targets in a cone in front of the Mage lose control of their character for up to 5 seconds.

If you plan to PVP as a Mage, you must become familiar with all the ways to escape melee attackers at your disposal. You have a few tricks to combat other spellcasters, but your only defense against melee classes is range. Freeze them in place, Blink away, it doesn't matter. Just get away and take them down before they reach you again.

PALADIN

Paladins can be a handful for other melee classes to take down due to their thick armor, shields, and a frustrating bag of tricks. In many situations, Paladins are initially CC'ed while other, softer, targets are taken down. As a Paladin, you must become familiar with the effects of Hands and the best times to put them to use.

FEARS

Turn Evil is a niche spell, only working on demon or undead targets. However, two of the most irritating aspects of PvP are Warlock pets and Death Knight pets! Turn Evil causes these pets to run in fear for up to 20 seconds.

IMMUNITIES

Divine Shield completely protects the Paladin from all damage and abilities for 8 seconds. However, any damage the paladin deals while under this effect is reduced by 50%. Divine Shield should be saved for absolute emergencies, such as when you are about to die, or when you absolutely need to cast a spell.

Hand of Protection causes the target to become immune to physical attacks and abilities for 10 seconds. While protected, the target cannot attack or use physical abilities, however, they can still cast spells. Hand of Protection also removes any physical debuff that was active before the buff was gained.

INTERRUPTS

Rebuke is a talented interrupt for Retribution Paladins that stops casting for 4 seconds. This is a melee range interrupt, and it deals no damage.

SLOWS/SNARES

While not true snare, Seal of Justice causes the Paladin's melee swings to limit the movement speed of the target. The debuff lasts 5 seconds (but each swing re-applies it), and causes the target to be unable to move faster than the default 100% movement speed. This means any effect such as sprint, run speed enchants, and so on, will not work on the target.

STUNS

Hammer of Justice stuns a target for 6 seconds and has a 10 yard range. Use Hammer of Justice to set up a target to be killed, as its duration ensures it can't escape. Alternatively use it on healers to stop casting for a while, or even on someone who's about to kill you, so you have time to heal.

PRIEST

BUFF REMOVAL

Dispel Magic removes two magic debuffs from an ally, or two magic buffs from an enemy. Mass Dispell removes one magic debuff from allies, or one magic buff from enemies in a wide area. Mass Dispel is the only way to remove player invulnerabilities such as Ice Block and Divine Shield.

DEBUFF REMOVAL

Beyond Remove Magic and Mass Dispell, Priests are also able to Cure Disease. You only need this ability when Death Knights are on the other team.

CROWD CONTROL

Speaking of Death Knights, Shackle Undead comes in handy against them. Their pets are considered Undead targets, so you can lock them into place with this ability. Mind Control is a fun toy in PVP. You possess a target humanoid, taking control of their actions. When successful, you gain access to a limited number of their abilities, and can control their movement, such as running them off a cliff.

FEARS

Psychic Scream causes up to 5 enemies close to the Priest to flee in terror for up to 8 seconds. Use Psychic Scream to catch your breath when you're in trouble.

Psychic Horror is a Shadow talent which fears one target for 3 seconds, and also disarms them for 10 seconds. Melee characters are much easier to handle when they're down a weapon.

HEALING REDUCTIONS

Improved Mind Blast Causes Mind Blast to apply a 10% healing reduction for 10 sec while in Shadowform, so it's limited to Shadow Priests.

IMMUNITIES

Power Word: Shield blocks incoming damage, and there are talents in the Discipline tree that make it even better. You can put it on any friendly character, including your Priest.

Pain Suppression, a Discipline talent, reduces the damage taken by its target by 40%. Not a true immunity, but it does a passable job at keeping someone alive a bit longer.

Dispersion is a Shadow talent that reduces incoming damage by 90% of 6 seconds. Dispersion's added benefits include mana regeneration, and the removal of stuns, fears, snares, and silence effects. You can't really do anything while Dispersed, but nothing can really harm you either.

It may be a stretch to call Spirit of Redemption an immunity, so think of it as a contingency plan for Holy Priests. Yes, you must die before this kicks in, but for 15 seconds you're free to continue healing and there's nothing anyone can do about it.

INTERRUPTS

Shadow Priests learn how to Silence targets. It works whether your targets are in the middle of casting a spell or if they're simply standing around.

SLOWS/SNARES

Mind Flay is a core Shadow Priest ability learned at level 10. In addition to the damage it deals, Mind Flay slows its target's movement speed by 50% during its duration.

Paralysis, a Shadow talent, causes critical strikes from Mind Blast to snare the target for up to 4 seconds. Holy Word: Chastise, a core Holy talent picked up at level 10, disorients its target for 3 seconds.

Priests are fragile, and Shadow (even with extra defensive abilities) is not exempt. Coupled with the "healer dies first" mindset prevelant in PVP encounters, you need to keep your friends much, much closer than your enemies.

ROGUE

Rogues must keep fights at melee range. While you might think a Rogue's answer to every PVP situation is some form of stun, they do have a bit more versatility than that.

BUFF REMOVAL

Shiv dispels Enrage effects off targets only. There aren't many classes with Enrage effects, but it's a powerful buff for those classes that you can remove.

CROWD CONTROL

Sap is a long-term Crowd Control ability (although in PVP its effect is diminished to 10 seconds) that essentially removes one character from the battle. The only catches are that the target can't be in combat already, and you must be stealthed to use Sap.

HEALING REDUCTIONS

Wound Poison is a standard PvP poison. It inflicts damage, and reduces all healing the target receives by 10%. It has a high proc on any damaging swing, meaning this debuff is almost always up on the Rogue's target of choice.

IMMUNITIES

Cloak of Shadows is a short but powerful immunity from magic. It removes magical debuffs from the Rogue and any further magical spells cast for its brief (5 seconds) duration are similarly ineffective.

Evasion is not total immunity, but it does provide a 50% chance to dodge melee attacks, and a 25% chance for ranged attacks to miss. Save it for fights against melee classes (who aren't Warriors) and Hunters.

INTERRUPTS

Kick is and effective melee interrupts, which is a 5 second spell lockout, rather than the more common 4 seconds. With a short (10 seconds) cooldown, Kick is a Rogue's primary means of stopping spells from being cast.

QUICK MOVES

Use Sprint to catch up to an escaping enemy, come to the aid of an ally, or to flee to fight another day. Sprint increases movement speed by 70% for 8 seconds, and can be used while stealthed. Only available to Subtlety Rogues, Shadowstep acts like a teleport. When used, Rogues instantly appear behind their target, and increases the damage of the next Ambush or Garrote by 30%. The Rogue's movement speed is increased by 70% for 3 seconds as well.

Use Vanish to disappear in a cloud of smoke. Use Vanish to escape being targeted, avoid magical spells, and more importantly, break out of movement impairing effects. Vanish automatically puts you into stealth.

SLOWS/SNARES

Another weapon coating, and often paired with Wound Poison, Crippling Poison is one of the most effective snares in the game. Each strike has a high chance of reducing a target's movement speed by 70% for 12 seconds. Deadly Throw requires combo points and a Thrown Weapon to use, but it deals good damage and reduces the movement speed of the target by 50% for 6 seconds. This is an excellent ability to use if a target gets out of melee range, but still has combo points still active on it.

Waylay is a Subtlety talent, but can be obtained by other specs. Waylay causes Ambush and Backstab to reduce the target's attack speed by 20%, and movement speed by 50%. Blade Twisting, a talent deep in the Combat tree, gives Rogues the unique ability to daze enemies constantly with their melee swings, reducing their movement speed by a whopping 70% for 8 seconds.

STUNS

Kidney Shot is tied with Hammer of Justice for being the most effective stun in the game. The duration varies based on the number combo points on the target, with a 1 point-stun lasting for 2 seconds, and a 5 pointer lasting 6 seconds. Cheap Shot is an inexpensive, effective opener for Rogues. It must be used from stealth, meaning you must decide if it's a better opener than the damaging effects of Ambush or Garrote. Blind disorients instead of stuns, but the effect is essentially the same for the target: loss of control for a short time.

SHAMAN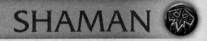

While your approach to PVP as a Shaman changes considerably depending on your talent tree choice, there are many elements to PVP that are universal. You must become proficient at totem selection and quick replacement (totems are an easy target for your opponents). Many of your situational abilities are tied to totems, so it's in your best interest to know when to drop a certain totem.

BUFF REMOVAL

All Shaman have access to Purge, which removes up to two magic-based buffs from an enemy target per application.

DEBUFF REMOVAL

Cleanse Spirit is available to all Shaman and removes magic debuffs that have been applied to you or an ally. Restoration Shaman can talent into Cleanse Spirit to also remove Curses. There are two totems designed to keep you safe proactively. Tremor Totem removes Fear, Charm, and Sleep effects in pulses, so long as the totem is active and you are within range. Grounding Totem absorbs a single, targeted (it's not effective against AoE spells) damage or debuff spell. It only works once, so you need to drop a new one to block additional spells.

CROWD CONTROL

In PVP situations, the only applicable Crowd Control spell for Shaman is Hex. It turns its target into a frog, which is unable to attack or cast spells, although it does nothing to restrict movement.

IMMUNITIES

Outside of what Grounding Totem provides, Shaman lack a true immunity. Enhancement Shaman have the closest thing to an immunity in Shamanistic Rage. When active, it reduces all incoming damage by 30%.

INTERRUPTS

While Wind Shear's reduction in threat has no PVP value, its ability to interrupt an enemy's spellcasting and prevent that enemy from casting spells from the same school for 2 seconds is invaluable. Elemental Shaman can talent into Earthquake, which isn't designed exactly as an interrupt, but since it knocks down enemies it is as effective as anything else.

KNOCKBACKS

Elemental Shaman have a trick up their sleeves for keeping enemies at a safe distance. Thunderstorm is a base Elemental spell learned at level 10 that knocks back enemies 20 yards.

QUICK MOVES

Shaman lack a true quick move ability, but their travel form, Ghost Wolf, is usable in combat. The better news is that any Shaman can (and should, for PVP) get the Enhancement talent, Ancestral Swiftness which makes Ghost Wolf an instant cast. Enhancement Shaman get an additional speed boost (and snare removal) when they activate Feral Spirit, so save it for tricky PVP battles when you need to reach enemies in a hurry.

SLOWS/SNARES

Shaman have multiple tools when it comes to slowing enemies. Frostbrand Weapon and Frost Shock both apply a magic debuff that can be removed, and Earthbind Totem has a limited range but its effect can only be removed by destroying the totem or moving out of its range. Only Elemental Shaman get a true snare in the form of the talent, Earth's Grasp.

WARLOCK

With fears and pets and a variety of instant-cast spells, Warlocks are often near the top of most hated classes to fight against in PVP. As a Warlock, you should spend time with each pet and learn how to use it effectively based on different situations.

BUFF REMOVAL

Felhunters love the taste of magic and can consume one buff (at a time) from a target. The bonus is that doing so heals the Felhunter.

DEBUFF REMOVAL

Imps use Singe Magic to remove one Magic effect from a friendly target.

CROWD CONTROL

A Succubus can Charm a target, making it unable to move or act until the effect expires or it takes damage.

FEARS

Fear causes an enemy to flee in terror until the effect expires. Damage may interrupt the effect early, so let others know who you plan to target.

Howl of Terror causes up to five enemies to flee in terror until the effect expires. You don't need to target anyone for the effect to take hold. Damage may interrupt the effect early.

INTERRUPTS

Felhunters can Spell Lock targets, which silences them for 3 seconds, and if a spell was being cast, locks out that school of magic for 6 seconds.

QUICK MOVES

Demonic Circle: Teleport requires some set up, but is an invaluable escape from potentially hazardous situations. Set up your circle in a safe spot, then go out and fight. When things look bad, use the Teleport to escape to the location of the circle.

SLOWS/SNARES

Curse of Exhaustion reduces an enemy's movement speed by 50%. Unfortunately, only one Curse can be active on an enemy at a time, so you must decide if it's worth the loss of another Curse's effects to apply this.

STUNS

Felguards are Demonology only pets, but their Axe Toss ability acts a 4 second stun. Destruction Warlocks get Shadowfury, which deals damage in addition to the 3 second stun on any enemy caught within its area of effect.

WARRIOR

BUFF REMOVAL

A Protection Warrior exclusive, Shield Slam removes Magical buffs only, but this does apply to nearly every buff including critical spells such as Power Word: Shield and Heroism/Bloodlust!

FEARS

Intimidating Shout is a unique fear in that it's not considered a magical effect. However, it does have a lengthy cooldown and works against a maximum of only five nearby enemies.

HEALING REDUCTIONS

Mortal Strike was the original ability Healing Reduction debuff. Restricted to Arms Warriors, Mortal Strike deals hefty damge in addition to a 10% healing reduction. Furious Attacks is a talent that causes a Fury Warrior's default swings to apply a healing reduction debuff. It's a 10% reduction, but remains effective since any swing applies the debuff.

INTERRUPTS

Shield Bash requires Defensive or Battle stance and, of course, a shield. It is the most effective in the Warrior arsenal. Shield Bash stops the current spell cast and locks out that tree for 6 seconds. Pummel doesn't require a shield, and is available in Battle and Berserker Stances. Interruption a spell also locks out that tree of spells for 4 seconds.

QUICK MOVES

Charge is learned early and is an integral part of Warrior play. You get extra Rage and briefly stun your target, so what's not to love about Charge?. Only Fury warriors cannot use Charge in combat, making it an effective way for Protection and Arms Warriors to move quickly between targets.

Intercept requires Berserker Stance, unless you're a Protection Warrior with the Warbringer talent. Intercept works the same as Charge, but has a different cooldown. Heroic Leap is a quick, 40 yard move where you target an area instead of another character.. Use it to escape or to stun and deal damage to the enemies in the targeted area. Intervene works a bit differently, since you actually target an ally. You rush to your target and absorb the next melee swing intended for that target.

SLOWS/SNARES

Hamstring has no cooldown and only a low Rage cost, meaning you can apply it to nearly any enemy you encounter. Snaring your opponents ensures both that they cannot escape you if you are focusing them, and that they will not be able to chase you or your allies if you need to escape. Arms Warriors can turn Hamstring into a full Snare with points in Improved Hamstring.

While Piercing Howl is a Fury talent, any Warrior could talent into it. Piercing Howl is one of the most powerful snares in the game, as it has no cooldown, and unlimited targets within its effective range. Any enemy within 10 yards is instantly slowed by 50% for 6 seconds.

STUNS

Beyond the effects provided by Charge, Intercept, and Heroic Leap, Warrior stuns are limited. Protection Warriors get Concussion Blow through talents. It deals damage and provides a 5 second stun on its target. Throwdown is exclusive to Arms Warriors. It causes no damage, but does knock down its target and stuns it for 5 seconds.

Where Rogues control range with stuns and other disorientnig effects, Warriors use a number of quick move abilities and Hamstring to keep enemies within the range of their weapons. Get used to switching between your Warrior stances since some of your situational abilities are exclusive to one stance or another.

BATTLEGROUNDS

Battlegrounds are instanced PvP combat areas for players of all levels. Players fight Horde versus Alliance in a structured game setting. You can enter a battleground alone or with a group of comrades. To get the most out of your time in Battlegrounds, try random Battlegrounds and spend time in the featured Battleground during the weekends. The featured Battleground changes every week, and the schedule appears on the in-game calendar.

WAR GAMES

If you're looking to challenge a specific guild, or group of friends, and face them in a Battleground, it's now possible to face off in War Games! While the rewards for War Games are reduced from what you could earn from regular Battlegrounds (no honor from killing other players and no Achievements are possible), you still earn points for meeting the objectives of the Battleground. Of course, War Games is more about bragging rights than rewards!

War Games ignores faction ties, which means you can challenge any other similarly-sized group, even if that group is comprised of other people from your guild! The groups can agree on a Battleground, or they can let the game pick one for them.

Battleground Marks of Honor

If you've heard about these from earlier times in World of Warcraft, have no worry. It is no longer required that you participate in specific battlegrounds to get the items you need.

RATED BATTLEGROUNDS

Rated Battlegrounds are new for Cataclysm and offer a way for players who enjoy PVP, but not Arena matches, to obtain the best gear possible. Rated Battlegrounds are divided into three groups: 10 vs. 10, 15 vs. 15, and 25 vs. 25. The 25 vs. 25 Rated Battlegrounds use the 40 vs. 40 Battleground maps Alterac Valley and Isle of Conquest.

Only fully premade groups can take part in Rated Battlegrounds. Just as with Arenas, your group will be matched up with teams of similar ranking, and level of gear. Good Premades aren't just going to know each other. They're going to use voice chat extensively, tactics that they've played before, and use every trick in the book. They're almost undefeatable if your team isn't similarly prepared.

Other than improved equipment, rewards from participation in Rated Battlegrounds include mounts, titles for your character, and Achievements.

ARENA

Arena combat offers unstructured, highly competitive PvP. Teams of 2, 3, or 5 compete against each other in a ranked series of tournaments. There are seasons for this, and the rewards that come from Arena are now with what you can get from Ranked Battleground matches.

There is no forum more competitive than the Arena. People must specialize their characters extremely well. They really must know all the ins and outs of their class and be able to use them at just the right moment. They must also find partners who complement their playstyle and skill as well as possible. Tactics and strategies for the Arena change constantly, and the best way to stay on top of things is to read forums and visit websites dedicated to Arena tactics.

10 VS. 10

WARSONG GULCH

Style of Play	Capture the Flag
Level Brackets	10-19; 20-29; 30-39; 40-49; 50-59; 60-69; 70-79; 80-85

NEW BATTLEGROUND

TWIN PEAKS

Style of Play	Capture the Flag
Level Brackets	85

Twin Peaks is a classic capture the flag competition where you must steal the opposing faction's flag and return it to your own base when your team's flag is safely held in your team's base. The Alliance works with the Wildhammer Clan of Dwarves, using their Longhouse as a base, while the Dragonmaw Clan of Orcs lend their Compound to the Horde.

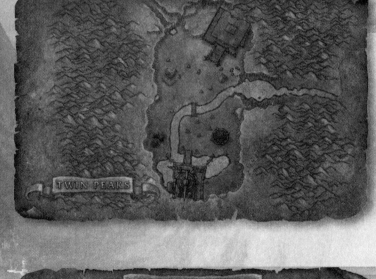

NEW BATTLEGROUND

BATTLE FOR GILNEAS

Style of Play	Capture Territory
Level Brackets	85

The Battle for Gilneas pits level 85 Horde and Alliance characters against each other in a struggle to control strategic points around Gilneas City. The goal of the game is to gather 2000 resources before the other faction. The game works similarly to Arathi Basin, but the set up of the map is considerably different. There are three strategic points to capture and hold, and each gives your faction access to new graveyard spawning points.

ARATHI BASIN

Style of Play	Hold Territory
Level Brackets	20-29; 30-39; 40-49; 50-59; 60-69; 70-79; 80-85

EYE OF THE STORM

Style of Play	Hold Territory and Capture the Flag Hybrid
Level Brackets	61-69; 71-79; 80-85

STRAND OF THE ANCIENTS

Style of Play	Siege and Vehicle Combat
Level Brackets	71-79; 80-85

ALTERAC VALLEY

Style of Play	Massive Siege Warfare
Level Brackets	51-59; 60-69; 70-79; 80-85

ISLE OF CONQUEST

Style of Play	Massive Siege Warfare
Level Brackets	71-79; 80-85

OUTDOOR PVP ZONE: TOL BARAD PENINSULA

Tol Barad Peninsula is an outdoor PVP zone located off the coast of Hillsbrad Foothills. There are two warring factions in Tol Barad, Baradin's Wardens and Hellscream's Reach.

The battleground is always available for exploration, but any character inside is automatically flagged as PVP-enabled. At set intervals a huge battle, which includes up to 100 combatants from each faction, commences. The number of total participants is determined by the side with fewer players, which keeps the battle from being too one-sided.

The objective for the battle depends on whether you are the attacking side or the defending team. The defending faction must maintain control of three buildings located at the center of the zone. The attacking team must wrest control of the towers from the defenders. There are other buildings on Tol Barad which the attackers can destroy to extend the duration of the battle.

The rewards for controlling Tol Barad include additional daily quests, and a specialized raid zone called Baradin Hold.

PROFESSIONS

LEARNING A PROFESSION

To learn a Profession, you must follow a process:

1. Learn the Apprentice level from a Profession Trainer.

2. Learn specific recipes from the trainer.

3. Acquire any necessary tools or ingredients in the recipes.

4. Create items from the recipes, which will also increase your skill level in your chosen profession.

5. Return to #2. Repeat.

6. Every 75 points, you need to find a trainer so that your character can advance to a new grade of that profession. Not all trainers teach every recipe, so you may need to search out new trainers as you reach higher levels.

Each character can learn two major Professions and as many secondary Professions as are available in the game. These modes of character progression are optional; you can avoid them entirely if you want. However, there are advantages to having these skills.

Many Professions let you craft items for yourself and others. Making your own gear can be kind of fun. Mastering various tiers of a Profession also grant various bonuses, so even heavy combat characters have something to gain.

BECOMING AN APPRENTICE

You can receive Apprentice training from any Profession trainer in the beginning regions of the game. Some of them are found near or in starting villages, but trainers for every Profession are found in each capital city (and if you don't know where to find one, ask a guard). For most Professions, you need to learn a variety of recipes. When you train to be an Apprentice, you automatically learn several initial recipes, patterns, or schematics. Each Profession has its own term for a new type of item, so you know what to search for in the Auction House or when researching things online.

To learn a new Profession, right-click on the trainer that is teaching the skill you want to learn. This is identified by the tag under the Trainer's name. It might say "Journeyman Cook" or something to that effect. Train with that person and pay the cost associated with it. Except in the very beginning of the game, these expenses are moderate but entirely affordable if you put in some effort.

Your General Chat Log records everything that you learn from your trainer. These abilities are added to your Profession menu. Like other spells and abilities, you can add shortcuts to one of your Action Bars. You should add the Profession and any associated Abilities—but not the individual recipes. The recipes themselves can be chosen from the Profession menu when you are creating items. If you need basic tools as an Apprentice, look for a trade vendor near the trainer.

Changing Professions

The game limits to you two Primary Professions, but you aren't locked into the first two you select. You can drop a Profession and learn a new one. The bad news is that you lose everything about your old Profession, so this only is useful if you find that you don't like the way a Profession progresses. When that happens, don't lament. Drop the Profession you dislike and try something new; it's better than having a slot taken up by something that you never plan on using again!

To drop a Profession, open the Spellbook (with "p") and click on the Professions Tab. Look for small red symbols that look like Do Not Enter signs. These are the unlearn buttons for each Profession. Don't click on them unless you are absolutely sure that you know what you're doing. You lose everything as soon as you say "yes" to the final query.

INCREASING YOUR SKILL LEVEL

The Apprentice level of a Profession covers your skill from 1 to 75. Using your profession advances it until it hits each cap (every 75 points). Whether you're gathering materials or creating them, the color of the activity is your guide to its difficulty.

Green recipes are easy, yellow are moderate, and orange are harder. The harder the recipe, the more likely it is to boost your level. The following colors apply to both gathering and non-gathering Profession recipes.

As a crafter, you'll always have limited resources; you can only carry so much metal or leather or herbs. To get access to the next recipe, you must raise your Profession level. If you need to raise your level, it's important to decide what you make. Look for pieces that require the least amount of material components but are almost certain to give you a point (orange recipes or those have just turned yellow). That way, you get the most out of your materials.

Red	Your character isn't high enough in the profession to make an attempt to gather an item or learn a crafting recipe
Orange	Success will increase your skill points every single time you complete this activity
Yellow	There is a high chance of increasing your skill points
Green	This activity is too easy; you aren't likely to gain points from completing it
Grey	There isn't a chance of gaining any skill points whether you complete this activity or not

Once you reach 75, you cannot increase your points until you train again as a Journeyman. Each proficiency level also has a character level requirement.

As your points increase, you can train in more recipes. Returning to your Profession trainer tells you when you can get more recipes or when you can train a higher proficiency. There are also many recipes hidden throughout the world, as a reward from certain quests, or as random drops. Check the Auction House for any new finds!

You might notice that the skill points for professional tiers don't add up evenly. Apprentices go from 1-75, but Journeyman can start as low as 50? This is because you can train a new tier in a Profession a bit early. That's a good idea because you don't want to hit the cap and waste any skill points. Train early as long as you have the money; there are no downsides in completing your training ahead of schedule.

PROGRESSION FOR CRAFTING PROFESSIONS

Proficiency Level name	Character Level minimum	Skill Level minimum	Skill level maximum
Apprentice	5	0	75
Journeyman	10	50	150
Expert	20	125	225
Artisan	35	200	300
Master	50	275	375
Grand Master	Varies by profession	350	450
Illustrious Grand Master	75	425	525

PROGRESSION FOR GATHERING PROFESSIONS

Proficiency Level name	Character Level minimum	Skill Level minimum	Skill level maximum
Apprentice	1	0	75
Journeyman	1	50	150
Expert	10	125	225
Artisan	25	200	300
Master	40	275	375
Grand Master	55	350	450
Illustrious Grand Master	Varies by profession	425	525

Secondary Profession Progressions

Secondary Professions follow their own progression paths, so the information is included in the individual sections that follow.

COMPLEMENTARY PROFESSIONS

Following is a list of Professions and classes that complement each other:

Profession	Good Additional Professions To Take
Alchemy	Herbalism, Fishing
Blacksmithing	Mining
Enchanting	Tailoring
Engineering	Mining
Herbalism	Alchemy or Inscription
Inscription	Herbalism
Jewelcrafting	Mining
Leatherworking	Skinning
Mining	Blacksmithing, Engineering, or Jewelcrafting
Skinning	Leatherworking
Tailoring	Anything

Fishing and Alchemy

Fishing is a great Profession to pick up if you plan on being an Alchemist. Some ingredients for Alchemy are obtained through Fishing. What's even better is that Fishing is a Secondary Profession, so you're still able to take Herbalism as your second Primary Profession.

ALCHEMY

BASICS OF ALCHEMY

Alchemy is one of the easier crafting professions to pick up and learn. If you want to be self-sufficient, pair Alchemy with Herbalism so that you can gather your own materials. The main components to Alchemy are herbs, and vials. Other items are required for specific creations, but for the most part it's herbs and flasks.

Alchemists also learn how to transmute certain items into other items. This ability often involves changing element-based items (such as Primals and Eternals) but also covers meta gems and certain ores. A Philosopher's Stone (a trinket created through Alchemy) is required for transmuting items. Transmuting an item sometimes leads to the discovery of a new recipe.

HERB PROGRESSION

Peacebloom
Silverleaf
Earthroot
Mageroyal
Swiftthistle
Briarthorn
Stranglekelp
Bruiseweed
Wild Steelbloom
Grave Moss
Kingsblood
Liferoot
Fadeleaf
Goldthorn
Khadgar's Whisker
Dragon's Teeth
Wintersbite
Firebloom
Purple Lotus
Wildvine
Arthas' Tears
Sungrass
Blindweed
Ghost Mushroom
Gromsblood
Golden Sansam
Dreamfoil
Mountain Silversage
Sorrowmoss
Icecap
Black Lotus

Herbs from Outland

Felweed
Dreaming Glory
Terocone
Ragveil
Flame Cap
Ancient Lichen
Netherbloom
Nightmare Vine
Mana Thistle
Fel Lotus

Herbs from Northrend

Goldclover
Tiger Lily
Talandra's Rose
Deadnettle
Firethorn
Adder's Tongue
Lichbloom
Icethorn
Frost Lotus

Herbs from Cataclysm's New Zones

Cinderbloom
Stormvine
Azshara's Veil
Heartblossom
Whiptail
Twilight Jasmine

PRACTICING ALCHEMY

Clicking on the Alchemy icon opens a menu of all potions you know. Alchemists don't need to be in a special place or to have a specific item in their inventory to do their work; they just need their herbs and purchasable vials. Good Alchemists carry spare vials around if they plan on making any new potions out in the field. More extensive creations (like elixirs and flasks) are better to do in town, where you can be certain to have what you need.

Goblin Bonus

Goblins have a racial ability—Better Living Through Chemistry—which increases their Alchemy skill by 15.

ALCHEMY BONUSES

Upon reaching skill level 50, Alchemists gain a bonus known as Mixology. With Mixology, you receive an increased effect and duration when you drink any elixir or flask you are able to make. For example, when you consume an elixir or flask with a 1 hour duration, you gain the benefit for 2 hours.

Additionally, you are able to create special trinkets at various levels. There are trinkets that apply to every role, so there's a solid choice for everyone.

Making Money as an Alchemist

Healing and mana potions are constant points of sales because people go through them at a considerable pace. Later on, you start to see an expanding market for elixirs and their longer-term buffs. In the late game, flasks become important as well. These products are very expensive, but their effects are the strongest and they last through death (making them essential tools for raiders focusing on new content or very difficult dungeon runs).

ALCHEMY SPECIALTIES

When you reach level 68 and have an Alchemy skill of at least 325, you are given the opportunity to complete a quest that allows you to select an Alchemy specializion. Your choices are Potion Mastery, Elixir Mastery, and Transmutation Mastery.

Potion Mastery and Elixir Mastery work the same way. When you create a potion or an elixir (depending on your specialty), there is a chance you will create additional potions or elixirs of the same type with the same number of reagents. Transmutation Mastery does the same for materials that are created by any recipe tagged as a Transmute. When you transmute any item, there is a chance you will create an additional item at no additional reagent cost.

If you wish to change your specialization at any time, speak with the NPC who granted you the ability, then complete the quest for one of the other specialists. Keep in mind that there is a cost associated with dropping a specialization.

NEW RECIPES FOR CATACLYSM

Item	Skill Level	Reagents
Draught of War	425	Cinderbloom x1, Crystal Vial x1
Earthen Potion	450	Stormvine x1, Heartblossom x1, Crystal Vial x1
Ghost Elixir	450	Cinderbloom x2, Crystal Vial x1
Deathblood Venom	455	Stormvine x1, Crystal Vial x1
Elixir of the Naga	455	Stormvine x1, Azshara's Veil x1, Crystal Vial x1
Potion of Illusion	460	Volatile Life x3, Azshara's Veil x1, Crystal Vial x1
Volcanic Potion	460	Cinderbloom x1, Azshara's Veil x1, Crystal Vial x1
Elixir of the Cobra	465	Azshara's Veil x1, Cinderbloom x1, Crystal Vial x1
Potion of Concentration	465	Azshara's Veil x2, Crystal Vial x1
Deepstone Oil	470	Albino Cavefish x1
Mysterious Potion	470	Deepstone Oil x2, Crystal Vial x1
Elixir of Deep Earth	475	Heartblossom x2, Crystal Vial x1
Mighty Rejuvenation Potion	475	Whiptail x2, Crystal Vial x1
Elixir of Impossible Accuracy	480	Heartblossom x1, Crystal Vial x1
Prismatic Elixir	480	Cinderbloom x1, Whiptail x1, Crystal Vial x1
Mythical Mana Potion	485	Cinderbloom x1, Whiptail x2, Crystal Vial x1
Potion of the Tol'vir	485	Stormvine x1, Whiptail x1, Crystal Vial x1
Transmute: Living Elements	485	Volatile Fire x15, Volatile Water x15, Volatile Shadow x15, Volatile Life x15, Volatile Air x15, Volatile Earth x15
Elixir of Mighty Speed	490	Stormvine x1, Twilight Jasmine x1, Crystal Vial x1
Golemblood Potion	490	Volatile Life x1, Heartblossom x1, Crystal Vial x1
Elixir of the Master	495	Twilight Jasmine x1, Heartblossom x1, Crystal Vial x1
Mythical Healing Potion	495	Volatile Life x1, Twilight Jasmine x2, Crystal Vial x1
Flask of Enhancement	500	Volatile Life x40, Stormvine x6, Whiptail x6, Twilight Jasmine x8, Azshara's Veil x8, Melted Vial x1
Flask of Flowing Water	500	Volatile Life x6, Stormvine x12, Heartblossom x12, Crystal Vial x1
Flask of Steelskin	500	Volatile Life x20, Cinderbloom x8, Twilight Jasmine x8, Melted Vial x1
Flask of the Draconic Mind	505	Volatile Life x20, Azshara's Veil x8, Twilight Jasmine x8, Melted Vial x1
Transmute: Dream Emerald	505	Jasper x3, Stormvine x3
Flask of the Winds	510	Volatile Life x20, Azshara's Veil x8, Whiptail x8, Melted Vial x1
Flask of Titanic Strength	510	Volatile Life x20, Cinderbloom x8, Whiptail x8, Melted Vial x1
Transmute: Ember Topaz	510	Hessonite x3, Cinderbloom x3
Transmute: Demonseye	515	Nightstone x3, Twilight Jasmine x3
Transmute: Ocean Sapphire	515	Zephyrite x3, Azshara's Veil x3
Transmute: Amberjewel	520	Alicite x3, Whiptail x3
Transmute: Pyrium Bar	520	Elementium Bar x4, Volatile Earth x8
Big Cauldron of Battle	525	Flask of Steelskin x3, Flask of the Draconic Mind x3, Flask of the Winds x3, Flask of Titanic Strength x3
Cauldron of Battle	525	Flask of Steelskin, Flask of the Draconic Mind, Flask of the Winds, Flask of Titanic Strength, Deathblood Venom x8
Potion of Deepholm	525	Heartblossom x5, Crystal Vial x1
Potion of Treasure Finding	525	Cinderbloom x8, Stormvine x4, Whiptail x4, Heartblossom x6, Melted Vial x1
Transmute: Inferno Ruby	525	Carnelian x3, Heartblossom x3
Transmute: Shadowspirit Diamond	525	Alicite x3, Nightstone x3, Jasper x3, Hessonite x3, Zephyrite x3, Carnelian x3
Transmute: Truegold	525	Pyrium Bar x8
Vial of the Sands	525	Sands of Time x8, Truegold x12, Flask of the Winds x8, Flask of Titanic Strength x8, Deepstone Oil x8, Pyrium-Laced Crystalline Vial x1

BLACKSMITHING

BASICS OF BLACKSMITHING

Blacksmithing is the shaping of bars, gems, stones and trade goods into armor and melee weapons. At low levels, Blacksmiths also turns stones uncovered by miners into temporary weapon enhancements. Many unique weapons and armor pieces can be created only by player blacksmiths for their own use. To be a self-sufficient Blacksmith, take Mining for a second Profession.

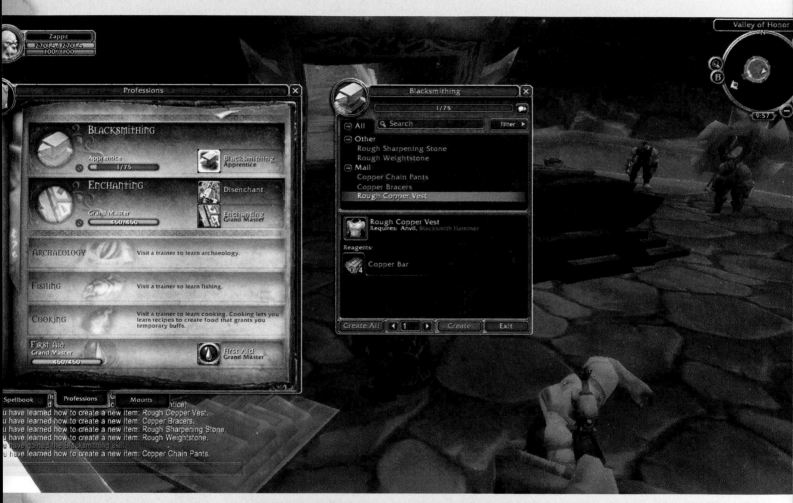

METAL PROGRESSION	Metals from Outland	Metals from Northrend	Metals from Cataclysm's New Zones
Copper Bars	Fel Iron Bars	Cobalt Bars	Obsidium Bars
Tin Bars	Adamantite Bars	Saronite Bars	Elementium Bars
Bronze Bars	Eternium Bars	Titanium Bars	Pyrium Bars
Silver Bars	Felsteel Bars	Titansteel Bars	Hardened Elementium Bars
Iron Bars	Khorium Bars		
Gold Bars	Hardened Adamantite Bars		
Steel Bars	Hardened Khorium Bars		
Mithril Bars			
Truesilver Bars			
Thorium Bars			
Dark Iron Bars			

PRACTICING BLACKSMITHING

Clicking on the Blacksmithing icon opens a menu of all the recipes you know. Most Blacksmithing items require a Blacksmithing Hammer to be in your inventory. In addition, work must be completed near an anvil. Anvils are found in any town or city, most often near the Blacksmithing trainers. Some recipes call for items available only from a trade vendor as well, so don't head for the anvil until you're sure you have everything you need for your creation.

BLACKSMITHING BONUSES

At higher levels, Blacksmiths learn how to add extra gem sockets to their bracers and gloves. Enchantments can be applied to these pieces in addition to the gem sockets placed on the gloves and bracers.

Making Money as a Blacksmith

Blacksmithing is a brutal profession on your bank account. It's hard to find a market for your created items too because most of these items are only on par with green drops that are cheap and plentiful. Only specific Blacksmithing gear at high levels warrants the higher investment in time and materials. To cut down on the price, take Mining and gather your own ore. Even here you should be careful. Someone joining a guild is likely to have access to their own Blacksmith. Only take this Profession if you know what you're getting into.

NEW RECIPES FOR CATACLYSM

Item	Skill Level	Reagents
Cold-forged Shank	425	Volatile Earth x5, Obsidium Bar x36
Decapitator's Razor	425	Volatile Earth x5, Obsidium Bar x30
Fire-etched Dagger	425	Volatile Fire x6, Obsidium Bar x30, Pyrium Bar x9
Folded Obsidium Bar	425	Obisidum Bar x2
Hardened Obsidium Belt	425	Obsidium Bar x10
Hardened Obsidium Boots	425	Obsidium Bar x12
Hardened Obsidium Breastplate	425	Obsidium Bar x4, Pyrium Bar x8
Hardened Obsidium Gauntlets	425	Elemental Flux x1, Obsidium Bar x6
Hardened Obsidium Helm	425	Volatile Earth x6, Obsidium Bar x12, Pyrium Bar x18
Hardened Obsidium Legguards	425	Obsidium Bar x6, Pyrium Bar x5
Hardened Obsidium Shield	425	Elemental Flux x1, Obsidium Bar x6
Hardened Obsidium Shoulders	425	Volatile Earth x5, Obsidium Bar x36, Pyrium Bar x6

NEW RECIPES FOR CATACLYSM

Item	Skill Level	Reagents
Lifeforce Hammer	425	Volatile Water x6, Obsidium Bar x30, Pyrium Bar x9
Obsidium Bladespear	425	Volatile Earth x5, Obsidium Bar x36
Obsidium Executioner	425	Volatile Earth x6, Obsidium Bar x30, Pyrium Bar x9
Obsidium Skeleton Key	425	Obsidium Bar x5
Redsteel Belt	425	Obsidium Bar x10
Redsteel Boots	425	Volatile Earth x5, Obsidium Bar x36
Redsteel Bracers	425	Elemental Flux x1, Obsidium Bar x5
Redsteel Breastplate	425	Volatile Fire x6, Pyrium Bar x30
Redsteel Gauntlets	425	Elemental Flux x1, Obsidium Bar x6
Redsteel Helm	425	Pyrium Bar x10
Redsteel Legguards	425	Obsidium Bar x6, Pyrium Bar x5
Redsteel Shoulders	425	Obsidium Bar x8, Pyrium Bar x4
Stormforged Belt	425	Obsidium Bar x10
Stormforged Boots	425	Obsidium Bar x12
Stormforged Bracers	425	Elemental Flux x1, Obsidium Bar x5
Stormforged Breastplate	425	Pyrium Bar x10
Stormforged Gauntlets	425	Volatile Earth x2, Obsidium Bar x18
Stormforged Helm	425	Volatile Water x6, Obsidium Bar x18, Pyrium Bar x15
Stormforged Legguards	425	Obsidium Bar x10, Pyrium Bar x3
Stormforged Shield	425	Obsidium Bar x12
Stormforged Shoulders	425	Volatile Earth x5, Obsidium Bar x30, Pyrium Bar x9
Hardened Obsidium Bracers	440	Elemental Flux x1, Obsidium Bar x5
Bloodied Pyrium Bracers	500	Volatile Earth x10, Pyrium Bar x10
Ornate Pyrium Bracers	500	Volatile Water x10, Pyrium Bar x10
Bloodied Pyrium Gauntlets	505	Volatile Earth x10, Pyrium Bar x10
Ornate Pyrium Gauntlets	505	Volatile Water x10, Pyrium Bar x10
Bloodied Pyrium Belt	510	Volatile Earth x10, Pyrium Bar x10
Hardened Elementium Girdle	510	Hardened Elementium Bar x5, Elementium Bar x1
Light Elementium Belt	510	Hardened Elementium Bar x5, Elementium Bar x1
Ornate Pyrium Belt	510	Volatile Water x10, Pyrium Bar x10
Bloodied Pyrium Boots	515	Volatile Earth x10, Pyrium Bar x12
Elementinum Gutslicer	515	Hardened Elementium Bar x25, Truegold x5, Chaos Orb x1
Elementium Bonesplitter	515	Hardened Elementium Bar x6, Elementium Bar x1
Elementium Deathplate	515	Hardened Elementium Bar x6, Elementium Bar x1
Elementium Hammer	515	Hardened Elementium Bar x6, Elementium Bar x1
Hardened Elementium Hauberk	515	Hardened Elementium Bar x6, Elementium Bar x1
Light Elementium Chestguard	515	Hardened Elementium Bar x6, Elementium Bar x1
Ornate Pyrium Boots	515	Volatile Water x10, Pyrium Bar x12
Bloodied Pyrium Shoulders	520	Volatile Earth x10, Pyrium Bar x16
Elementium Earthguard	520	Hardened Elementium Bar x8, Elementium Bar x1
Elementium Girdle of Pain	520	Hardened Elementium Bar x5, Elementium Bar x1
Elementium Poleaxe	520	Hardened Elementium Bar x8, Elementium Bar x1
Elementium Shank	520	Hardened Elementium Bar x8, Elementium Bar x1
Elementium Spellblade	520	Hardened Elementium Bar x8, Elementium Bar x1
Elementium Stormshield	520	Hardened Elementium Bar x8, Elementium Bar x1
Forged Elementium Mindcrusher	520	Hardened Elementium Bar x5, Truegold x6, Chaos Orb x3
Ornate Pyrium Shoulders	520	Volatile Water x10, Pyrium Bar x16
Bloodied Pyrium Breastplate	525	Volatile Earth x10, Pyrium Bar x20
Bloodied Pyrium Helm	525	Volatile Earth x10, Pyrium Bar x20
Bloodied Pyrium Legguards	525	Volatile Earth x10, Pyrium Bar x20
Ornate Pyrium Breastplate	525	Volatile Water x10, Pyrium Bar x20
Ornate Pyrium Helm	525	Volatile Water x10, Pyrium Bar x20
Ornate Pyrium Legguards	525	Volatile Water x10, Pyrium Bar x20

ENCHANTING

BASICS OF ENCHANTING

Enchanting recipes add various buffs to your weapons and armor, such as improved statistics for your character or procs with random effects to your weapons. They also create low-level wands, and oils (which are short term buffs to weapons).

Enchanters learn a second ability, known as Disenchanting, which they use to create their own materials. That sounds like a great deal, right? You get to make the materials that you need to advance your craft. There's a catch. You can't gather Enchanting materials without destroying magical items. Green, blue, and purple items each have their own types of Enchanting reagents stored inside them. Beyond that, you need to destroy higher level equipment of these quality levels to complete higher level enchantments.

ENCHANTING MATERIALS OBTAINED THROUGH DISENCHANTING

There are four types of enchanting materials: Dust, Essences, Shards, and Crystals. The types of materials that come from Disenchanting items is based on the item level of the object.

Essences are more commonly obtained from weapons than armor of Uncommon quality. Dust is more commonly obtained from armor than weapons of Uncommon quality. Essences can be either Lesser or Greater. Three Lesser Essences can combine to become one Greater Essence, and one Greater Essence breaks down into three Lesser Essences.

Shards come from Superior quality items, or rarely from Uncommon quality items. You could get either Small or Large Shards when disenchanting an item. In some cases, three Small Shards can be combined into one Large Shard, and one Large Shard can be broken down into three Small Shards.

Crystals come from Epic quality items, and rarely from Superior quality items. At higher skill levels, you can learn how to convert these Crystals into other types of Enchanting material.

Item Levels	Dust	Essence	Shard	Crystal
5-25	Strange	Magic	Glimmering	—
26-35	Soul	Astral	Glimmering, Glowing	—
36-45	Vision	Mystic	Glowing, Radiant	—
46-55	Dream	Nether	Radiant	—
56-65	Illusion	Eternal	Brilliant	Nexus
66-120	Arcane	Planar	Prismatic	Void
121-277	Infinite	Cosmic	Dream	Abyss
278 and up	Hypnotic	Celestial	Heavenly	Maelstrom

Blood Elf Bonus

Blood Elves have a racial ability—Arcane Affinity—which increases their Enchanting skill by 10.

PRACTICING ENCHANTING

Add the Enchanting and Disenchant abilities to one of your Action Bars. Clicking the Enchanting icon opens a menu of all the magic recipes you know. Clicking the Disenchant icon enables you to extract magical elements from targeted items by destroying them forever. To enchant any item, you must have the proper Enchanting Rod in your inventory.

Up until skill level 60 or so, you can get points from destroying magical items. That trails off fairly soon, and then you need to use Enchanting to get skill points. Some Enchanting suppliers sell components necessary for lowest level enchanting recipes. As long as you have the materials, you can enchant the same item multiple times, but an item can only retain one Enchantment at a given time (you "overwrite" the Enchantment). There are also vellums created via Inscription which can hold enchants for later use.

ENCHANTING ROD PROGRESSION

Runed Copper Rod
Runed Silver Rod
Runed Golden Rod
Runed Truesilver Rod
Runed Arcanite Rod
Runed Fel Iron Rod
Runed Adamantite Rod
Runed Eternium Rod
Runed Titanium Rod
Runed Elementium Rod

ENCHANTING BONUSES

Enchanters are able to improve their own rings with a number of enchantments. Some add extra Stamina, while others help with melee damage output or boost spell power.

Making Money as an Enchanter

Enchanting is in high demand as many players are always striving to collect better and better gear. Buying cheap greens off of the auction house is one way to stockpile materials, but it's still not the best way to get everything you need. Enchanters frequently run dungeons to scoop up "crummy" blue and green items. You might even find an Enchanter running lower level dungeons by themselves for this exact purpose.

The other option is to take another Profession that creates destructable items. The best one for this is Tailoring; because it doesn't have its own gathering Profession (anyone can get cloth). You can make any number

of simple green cloth armor pieces and then Disenchant them to make your Enchanting ingredients. It's expensive, time consuming, you need to level up two Professions at the same time, and sometimes you won't be able to easily (or cheaply) make the items you need, but it's an option for a self-sufficient Enchanter.

Enchanters, through the use of vellums, have the ability to distribute their enchantments on the Auction House. You no longer need to wait around for other players to buy your Enchantments, which means more time for you to do other activities.

NEW RECIPES FOR CATACLYSM

Spell Name	Skill Level	Reagents
Enchant Boots - Earthen Vitality	425	Hypnotic Dust x2
Enchant Chest - Mighty Stats	425	Lesser Celestial Essence x2
Enchant Gloves - Mastery	425	Hypnotic Dust x1, Lesser Celestial Essence x1
Enchant Bracer - Speed	435	Hypnotic Dust x2, Lesser Celestial Essence x1
Enchant Cloak - Greater Spell Piercing	435	Hypnotic Dust x3
Enchant Weapon - Avalanche	450	Greater Celestial Essence x4
Enchant Weapon - Mending	450	Hypnotic Dust x1, Greater Celestial Essence x1
Enchant Boots - Haste	455	Hypnotic Dust x2, Greater Celestial Essence x1
Enchant Gloves - Haste	455	Hypnotic Dust x4, Lesser Celestial Essence x1
Enchant Bracer - Critical Strike	460	Hypnotic Dust x4, Lesser Celestial Essence x2
Enchant Chest - Stamina	460	Hypnotic Dust x5, Lesser Celestial Essence x1
Enchant Cloak - Intellect	465	Hypnotic Dust x6
Enchant 2H Weapon - Mighty Agility	470	Hypnotic Dust x3, Greater Celestial Essence x3, Heavenly Shard x3
Enchant Ring - Agility	475	Heavenly Shard x1
Enchant Ring - Greater Stamina	475	Heavenly Shard x1
Enchant Ring - Intellect	475	Heavenly Shard x1
Enchant Ring - Strength	475	Heavenly Shard x1
Enchant Shield - Protection	475	Greater Celestial Essence x1, Volatile Earth x15
Enchant Gloves - Exceptional Strength	480	Hypnotic Dust x3, Greater Celestial Essence x2
Enchant Weapon - Elemental Slayer	480	Hypnotic Dust x5, Greater Celestial Essence x1
Enchant Boots - Major Agility	485	Hypnotic Dust x4, Greater Celestial Essence x2
Enchant Chest - Mighty Resilience	485	Hypnotic Dust x9
Enchant Gloves - Greater Expertise	490	Hypnotic Dust x5, Greater Celestial Essence x2
Enchant Weapon - Hurricane	490	Hypnotic Dust x7, Heavenly Shard x1
Enchant Shield - Blocking	495	Volatile Fire x10, Volatile Earth x10, Heavenly Shard x1
Enchant Weapon - Heartsong	495	Hypnotic Dust x2, Greater Celestial Essence x3, Heavenly Shard x1
Enchant Bracer - Dodge	500	Hypnotic Dust x6, Volatile Air x15
Enchant Cloak - Critical Strike	500	Hypnotic Dust x8, Greater Eternal Essence x2
Enchant Bracer - Precision	505	Hypnotic Dust x12, Greater Celestial Essence x1
Enchant Chest - Exceptional Spirit	505	Hypnotic Dust x10, Greater Eternal Essence x2
Enchant Boots - Precision	510	Hypnotic Dust x8, Greater Celestial Essence x4
Enchant Cloak - Greater Intellect	510	Hypnotic Dust x9, Greater Celestial Essence x4
Enchant Cloak - Protection	510	Hypnotic Dust x8, Volatile Earth x15
Enchant Off-Hand - Superior Intellect	510	Greater Celestial Essence x3, Volatile Water x18
Enchant Bracer - Exceptional Spirit	515	Hypnotic Dust x9, Greater Celestial Essence x3
Runed Elementium Rod	515	Runed Titanium Rod x1, Hypnotic Dust x10, Greater Celestial Essence x6, Heavenly Shard x6, Elementium Rod x1
Enchant Boots - Mastery	520	Hypnotic Dust x10, Greater Celestial Essence x3
Enchant Bracer - Greater Expertise	520	Hypnotic Dust x4, Greater Celestial Essence x6
Enchant Boots - Assassin's Step	525	Hypnotic Dust x3, Greater Celestial Essence x9, Maelstrom Crystal x1
Enchant Boots - Lavawalker	525	Greater Celestial Essence x10, Maelstrom Crystal x1
Enchant Bracer - Greater Critical Strike	525	Hypnotic Dust x15, Greater Celestial Essence x3, Maelstrom Crystal x1
Enchant Bracer - Greater Speed	525	Hypnotic Dust x13, Greater Celestial Essence x4, Maelstrom Crystal x1
Enchant Chest - Greater Stamina	525	Hypnotic Dust x10, Heavenly Shard x4, Maelstrom Crystal x1
Enchant Chest - Peerless Stats	525	Maelstrom Crystal x3
Enchant Cloak - Greater Critical Strike	525	Hypnotic Dust x20, Maelstrom Crystal x1
Enchant Gloves - Greater Mastery	525	Hypnotic Dust x10, Greater Celestial Essence x5, Maelstrom Crystal x1
Enchant Gloves - Mighty Strength	525	Hypnotic Dust x4, Greater Celestial Essence x8, Maelstrom Crystal x1
Enchant Weapon - Landslide	525	Hypnotic Dust x6, Greater Celestial Essence x4, Maelstrom Crystal x4, Heavenly Shard x2
Enchant Weapon - Power Torrent	525	Hypnotic Dust x12, Heavenly Shard x2, Maelstrom Crystal x4
Enchant Weapon - Windwalk	525	Greater Celestial Essence x6, Heavenly Shard x2, Maelstrom Crystal x4
Enchanted Lantern	525	Hypnotic Dust x8, Heavenly Shard x8, Maelstrom Crystal x1
Magic Lamp	525	Greater Celestial Essense x4, Heavenly Shard x8, Maelstrom Crystal x1

ENGINEERING

BASICS OF ENGINEERING

Engineering creates a variety of items such as goggles, explosives, ranged weapon scopes, bombs, and mechanical animals. Creating different items with Engineering requires a handful of tools, most of which are created by the Engineer. Many (but not all) of the items created by Engineers require Engineering skill to use. One of the fun things about being an Engineer is that you never know when some of your creations will misfire, often leading to unexpected results.

Mining is a perfect way to make an Engineer self-sufficient. Pretty much everything an Engineer needs is found while you're out hunting for metal veins.

METAL PROGRESSION	Metals from Outland	Metals from Northrend	Metals from Cataclysm's New Zones
Copper Bars			
Tin Bars	Fel Iron Bars	Cobalt Bars	Obsidium Bars
Bronze Bars	Adamantite Bars	Saronite Bars	Elementium Bars
Silver Bars	Eternium Bars	Titanium Bars	Pyrium Bars
Iron Bars	Felsteel Bars	Titansteel Bars	Hardened Elementium Bars
Gold Bars	Khorium Bars		
Steel Bars	Hardened Adamantite Bars		
Mithril Bars	Hardened Khorium Bars		
Truesilver Bars			
Thorium Bars			
Dark Iron Bars			

PRACTICING ENGINEERING

Clicking the Engineering icon opens a menu of all the schematics you know. Engineers have a few tools that are needed to make various items, so you might want to carry them around with you if you prefer crafting on the fly (or just get a Gnomish Army Knife!). Otherwise, it's better to work when you're back in town, near a Bank.

Gnome Bonus

Gnomes have a racial ability—Engineering Specialization—which increases their Engineering skill by 15.

ENGINEERING BONUSES

Engineers are able to create specialized mounts. They aren't any faster than other mounts, but who cares when you're flying in a steam-powered helicopter!

Engineers also get a few Engineering-only trinkets, but the big boost for Engineers comes in the form of specialized enchantments for Gloves, Belts, Cloaks, and Boots. These enchantments range from Hand-Mounted Pyro Rockets to turning your cloak into a parachute.

Making Money as an Engineer

Engineering is not the best way to go when you're trying to make gold off your Profession. Because many items created with Engineering require Engineering to use them, your market is reduced. However, some of an Engineer's products are viable for selling. Selling various explosives and scopes is a decent way to make up for the expense of new schematics and materials. There are some big-ticket items (such as the Mechano-hog) that provide some nice income; you just can't depend on selling these items consistently.

ENGINEERING SPECIALTIES

When you reach an Engineering skill of 200, you are given a choice to specialize in Gnomish Engineering or Goblin Engineering. For the most part, items created by one specialization are usable by any Engineer with a high enough skill level. The main difference is that Goblin Enginners are able to teleport to Everlook (in Winterspring) and Area 52 (in Netherstorm), while Gnomes can travel instantly to Gadgetzan (in Tanaris) or Toshley's Station (in Blade's Edge Mountains).

You can change your specialization if you like. There is a fee involved with dropping on specialization, so you may not want to do this too often.

NEW RECIPES FOR CATACLYSM

Name	Skill Level	Reagents
Explosive Bolts	425	Handful of Obsidium Bolts x1
Handful of Obsidium Bolts	425	Obsidium Bar x2
Authentic Jr. Engineer Goggles	440	Obsidium Bar x8, Hessonite x2, Savage Leather x2
Electrostatic Condenser	440	Obsidium Bar x4, Handful of Obsidium Bolts x6, Volatile Earth x4
Electrostatic Condenser	440	Obsidium Bar x4, Handful of Obsidium Bolts x6, Volatile Earth x4
Electrified Ether	445	Volatile Air x2
R19 Threatfinder	450	Obsidium Bar x6, Handful of Obsidium Bolts x6, Alicite x2
Safety Catch Removal Kit	450	Obsidium Bar x10, Handful of Obsidum Bolts x10
Volatile Seaforium Blastpack	455	Handful of Obsidium Bolts x1, Electrified Ether x2
De-Weaponized Mechanical Companion	475	Obsidium Bar x12, Handful of Obsidium Bolts x4, Electrified Ether x8, Jasper x2
Elementium Dragonling	475	Handful of Obsidium Bolts x2, Electrified Ether x8, Elementium Bar x16, Embersilk Cloth x20
Elementium Toolbox	475	Elementium Bar x15, Volatile Earth x12
Lure Master Tackle Box	475	Elementium Bar x20, Handful of Obsidium Bolts x4
Personal World Destroyer	475	Obsidium Bar x10, Handful of Obsidium Bolts x8, Electrified Ether x8
High-Powered Bolt Gun	480	Obsidum Bar x10, Handful of Obsidium Bolts x8, Electrified Ether x4
Goblin Barbecue	490	Elementium Bar x2, Toughened Flesh x2, Lavascale Fillet x2
Loot-a-Rang	490	Hardened Elementium Bar x5, Electrified Ether x5
Volatile Thunderstick	495	Electrified Ether x2, Hardened Elementium Bar x5, Volatile Fire x5
Finely-Tuned Throat Needler	510	Obsidium Bar x4, Electrified Ether x2, Hardened Elementium Bar x5
Heat-Treated Spinning Lure	510	Handful of Obsidium Bolts x1, Elementium Bar x4, Volatile Fire x1
Agile Bio-Optic Killshades	525	Handful of Obsidium Bolts x6, Electrified Ether x6, Hardened Elementium Bar x2, Truegold x1, Chaos Orb x1, Dream Emerald x2
Camouflage Bio-Optic Killshades	525	Handful of Obsidium Bolts x6, Electrified Ether x6, Hardened Elementium Bar x2, Truegold x1, Chaos Orb x1, Ocean Sapphire x2
Deadly Bio-Optic Killshades	525	Handful of Obsidium Bolts x6, Electrified Ether x6, Hardened Elementium Bar x2, Truegold x1, Chaos Orb x1, Dream Emerald x2
Energized Bio-Optic Killshades	525	Handful of Obsidium Bolts x6, Electrified Ether x6, Hardened Elementium Bar x2, Truegold x1, Chaos Orb x1, Ocean Sapphire x2
Gnomish X-Ray Scope	525	Hardened Elementium Bar x2, Dream Emerald x2
Grounded Plasma Shield	525	Electrified Ether x3
Invisibility Field	525	Handful of Obsidium Bolts, Electrified Ether
Kickback 5000	525	Hardened Elementium Bar x9, Truegold x3, Hair Trigger x1, Walnut Stock x1, Chaos Orb x1
Lightweight Bio-Optic Killshades	525	Handful of Obsidium Bolts x6, Electrified Ether x6, Hardened Elementium Bar x2, Truegold x1, Chaos Orb x1, Ocean Sapphire x2
Overpowered Chicken Splitter	525	Hardened Elementium Bar x12, Truegold x2, Handful of Obsidium Bolts, Electrified Ether x8, Chaos Orb x1
Reinforced Bio-Optic Killshades	525	Handful of Obsidium Bolts x6, Electrified Ether x6, Hardened Elementium Bar x2, Truegold x1, Chaos Orb x1, Inferno Ruby x2
Specialized Bio-Optic Killshades	525	Handful of Obsidium Bolts x6, Electrified Ether x6, Hardened Elementium Bar x2, Truegold x1, Chaos Orb x1, Ocean Sapphire x2
Z50 Mana Gulper	525	Handful of Obsidium Bolts, Electrified Ether

INSCRIPTION

BASICS OF INSCRIPTION

Scribes create Glyphs, scrolls, cards, and other paper and book items with paper purchased from Trade vendors, and inks. To create inks, Scribes automatically learn Milling, which turns herbs into pigments, and other Inscription abilities turn the pigements into ink. While Inscription creates many items, it's best known for making Glyphs. Glyphs are class-specific recipes that enhance characters' abilities. There are three types of glyphs: Minor, Major, and Prime.

Inscription is an expensive profession, unless you take Herbalism as well. Scribes need a Virtuoso Inking Set in their inventory to create many of their goods. The set isn't expensive, and it never wears out. Keep one in your inventory and your character will be able to Inscribe anywhere in the world.

PARCHMENT PROGRESSION

Light Parchment
Common Parchment
Heavy Parchment
Resilient Parchment

PIGMENT PROGRESSION

Herb	Milled Into
Peacebloom, Silverleaf, Earthroot	Alabaster Pigment
Mageroyal, Stranglekelp, Briarthorn, Swiftthistle, Bruiseweed	Dusky Pigment, Verdant Pigment
Wild Steelbloom, Grave Moss, Kingsblood, Liferoot	Golden Pigment, Burnt Pigment
Fadeleaf, Goldthorn, Khadgar's Whisker, Wintersbite	Emerald Pigment, Indigo Pigment
Firebloom, Purple Lotus, Arthas' Tears, Sungrass, Blindweed, Ghost Mushroom, Gromsblood	Violet Pigment, Ruby Pigment
Golden Sansam, Dreamfoil, Mountain Silversage, Sorrowmoss, Icecap	Silvery Pigment, Sapphire Pigment

Pigment from Outland

Herb	Milled Into
Felweed, Dreaming Glory, Ragveil, Flame Cap, Terocone, Ancient Lichen, Netherbloom, Nightmare Vine, Mana Thistle	Nether Pigment, Ebon Pigment

Pigment from Northrend

Herb	Milled Into
Goldclover, Deadnettle, Firethorn, Tiger Lily, Talandra's Rose, Adder's Tongue, Lichbloom, Icethorn	Azure Pigment, Icy Pigment

Pigment from Cataclysm's New Zones

Herb	Milled Into
Cinderbloom, Stormvine, Azshara's Veil, Heartblossom, Twilight Jasmine, Whiptail	Ashen Pigment, Burning Embers

INK TYPES

Pigment	Ink
Alabaster Pigment	Ivory Ink, Moonglow Ink
Dusky Pigment	Midnight Ink
Verdant Pigment	Hunter's Ink
Golden Pigment	Lion's Ink
Burnt Pigment	Dawnstar Ink

INK TYPES

Pigment	Ink
Emerald Pigment	Jadefire Ink
Indigo Pigment	Royal Ink
Violet Pigment	Celestial Ink
Ruby Pigment	Fiery Ink
Silvery Pigment	Shimmering Ink

INK TYPES

Pigment	Ink
Sapphire Pigment	Ink of the Sky
Nether Pigement	Etheral Ink
Ebon Pigment	Darkflame Ink
Azure Pigment	Ink of the Sea
Icy Pigment	Snowfall Ink

INK TYPES

Pigment	Ink
Ashen Pigment	Blackfallow Ink
Burning Pigment	Inferno Ink

PRACTICING INSCRIPTION

Add the Inscription and Milling icons to one of your Action Bars. Clicking the Inscription icon opens a menu of all the Inscription patterns you know. Milling turns five similar herbs into one of two types of pigments (most herbs have a common pigment result and an uncommon pigment result). You must have five of the same herb in order to Mill them for pigments. The herbs are used up, but you get the pigments necessary to create inks. Creating ink is a good way to skill up Inscription each time you learn a new type of ink.

Making Money as a Scribe

Since everyone needs Glyphs, there's a large market for your goods. When it comes time to switch Glyphs, players need a steady supply of Dust of Disappearance, which can be created with Inscription. Finally, the sets of Darkmoon Cards draw quite a bit of interest. The downside to these cards is the random nature of its creation. You never know which card you'll create. Hit the right ones, though, and you could make a small fortune selling them to other players.

INSCRIPTION BONUSES

There are two bonuses for Inscription. First, there are a number of Epic quality bind on pickup Relics you can create for level 85. They're powerful pieces since each includes a Prismatic Socket, allow you to place any non-meta gem and still get the bonus. The other bonus is shoulder armor Inscriptions which are superior to what is available to anyone else in the game. There are shoulder armor Inscriptions for every role, meaning any class and spec benefit from them.

NEW RECIPES FOR CATACLYSM

Item	Skill Level	Reagents
Vanishing Powder	75	Midnight Ink x1
Blackfallow Ink	425	Ashen Pigment x2
Scroll of Intellect IX	445	Resilient Parchment x2, Blackfallow Ink x1
Mysterious Fortune Card	450	Resilient Parchment x1, Blackfallow Ink x1
Scroll of Protection IX	450	Resilient Parchment x2, Blackfallow Ink x1
Scroll of Spirit IX	455	Resilient Parchment x2, Blackfallow Ink x1
Adventurer's Journal	460	Resilient Parchment x4, Blackfallow Ink x1
Scroll of Stamina IX	460	Resilient Parchment x2, Blackfallow Ink x1
Scroll of Strength IX	465	Resilient Parchment x2, Blackfallow Ink x1
Scroll of Agility IX	470	Resilient Parchment x2, Blackfallow Ink x1
Book of Blood	475	Resilient Parchment x10, Inferno Ink x3, Volatile Life x6
Dust of Disappearance	475	Blackfallow Ink x2
Lord Rottington's Pressed Wisp Book	475	Resilient Parchment x2, Volatile Life x20
Etched Horn	480	Inferno Ink x4, Scavenged Dragon Horn x1
Inferno Ink	480	Burning Pigment x2
Origami Slime	480	Resilient Parchment x3
Manual of the Planes	490	Resilient Parchment x1, Inferno Ink x2, Volatile Water x2, Volatile Air x2, Volatile Earth x2, Volatile File x2
Origami Rock	490	Resilient Parchment x3
Felfire Inscription	500	Blackfallow Ink x4
Forged Documents	500	Resilient Parchment x1, Blackfallow Ink x3
Inscription of the Earth Prince	500	Blackfallow Ink x4
Lionsmane Inscription	500	Blackfallow Ink x4
Origami Beetle	500	Resilient Parchment x3
Runed Dragonscale	500	Inferno Ink x8, Volatile Life x24, Volatile Fire x6, Deathwing Scale Fragment x1
Runescroll of Fortitude II	500	Inferno Ink x5, Resilient Parchment x5
Swiftsteel Inscription	500	Blackfallow Ink x4
Battle Tome	510	Resilient Parchment x10, Inferno Ink x8, Volatile Life x24, Volatile Fire x6
Divine Companion	510	Resilient Parchment x10, Inferno Ink x8, Volatile Life x24, Volatile Air x6
Dungeoneering Guide	510	Resilient Parchment x10, Inferno Ink x8, Volatile Life x24, Volatile Water x6
Darkmoon Card of Destruction	525	Inferno Ink x10, Volatile Life x30, Resilient Parchment x1
Notched Jawbone	525	Inferno Ink x12, Volatile Life x36, Volatile Earth x12, Bleached Jawbone x1
Silver Inlaid Leaf	525	Inferno Ink x12, Volatile Life x36, Volatile Air x12, Silver Charm Bracelet x1
Tattooed Eyeball	525	Inferno Ink x12, Volatile Life x36, Volatile Water x12, Preserved Ogre Eye x1

JEWELCRAFTING

BASICS OF JEWELCRAFTING

Initially, Jewelcrafters create the wire and settings necessary to craft low level rings and necklaces, then start making rings, necklaces, and other random items. A Jeweler's Kit is required, but it is available at a trivial cost from a Trade vendor. At higher skill levels, Jewelcrafters learn how to cut gems that provide statistical bonuses to socketed equipment. Even at higher skill levels, Jewelcrafters continue to create rings and necklaces for anyone to use.

Jewelcrafting can be an expensive Profession to skill up, so strongly consider Mining as a second Profession, to find your own ore. Jewelcrafters learn a second ability, called Prospecting, which allows them to break down raw ore and extract different minerals and gems that are otherwise available only through mining.

PROSPECTING

The following tables list the possible gems that come from Prospecting (remember, you need five of the same ore type in order to Prospect). These results are identical to the types of gems that may be obtained from Mining the ore's vein or node.

GEM PROGRESSION BY COLOR

Gem Color	Outland Gems	Northrend Gems	Cataclysm Gems
Blue Gems	Azure Moonstone, Star of Elune, Empyrean Sapphire	Chalcedony, Sky Sapphire, Majestic Zircon	Zephyrite, Ocean Sapphire
Red	Blood Garnet, Living Ruby, Crimson Spinel	Bloodstone, Scarlet Ruby, Cardinal Ruby	Carnelian, Inferno Ruby
Yellow	Golden Draenite, Dawnstone, Lionseye	Sun Crystal, Autumn's Glow, King's Amber	Alicite, Amber Jewel
Green	Deep Peridot, Talasite, Seaspray Emerald	Dark Jade, Forest Emerald, Eye of Zul	Jasper, Dream Emerald
Orange	Flame Spessarite, Noble Topaz, Pyrestone	Huge Citrine, Monarch Topaz, Amertine	Hessonite, Ember Topaz
Purple	Shadow Draenite, Nightseye, Shadowsong Amethyst	Shadow Crystal, Twilight Opal, Dreadstone	Nightstone, Demonseye
Prismatic	—	Enchanted Pearl, Enchanted Tear, Nightmare Tear	
Meta Gems	Earthstorm Diamond, Skyfire Diamond	Earthsiege Diamond, Skyflare Diamond	Shadowspirit Diamond

ORE PROGRESSION

Ore Type	Gems Prospected
Copper Ore	Malachite, Shadowgem, and Tigerseye
Tin Ore	Moss Agate, Shadowgem, Lesser Moonstone, Jade
Iron Ore	Jade, Lesser Moonstone, Citrine, Aquamarine
Mithril Ore	Aquamarine, Citrine, Star Ruby
Thorium Ore	Star Ruby, Azerothian Diamond, Blue Sapphire, Huge Emerald, Large Opal

Ore From Outland

Ore Type	Gems Prospected
Fel Iron Ore, Adamantite Ore	Azure Moonstone, Blood Garnet, Deep Peridot, Flame Spessarite, Golden Draenite, Shadow Draenite, Noble Topaz, Talasite, Dawnstone, Living Ruby, Nightseye, Star of Elune

Ore From Northrend

Ore Type	Gems Prospected
Coblat Ore, Saronite Ore	Chalcedony, Bloodstone, Dark Jade, Huge Citrine, Sun Crystal, Shadow Crystal, Sky Sapphire, Scarlet Ruby, Forest Emerald, Monarch Topaz, Autumn's Glow, Twilight Opal
Titanium Ore	Sky Sapphire, Scarlet Ruby, Forest Emerald, Monarch Topaz, Autumn's Glow, Twilight Opal, Majestic Zircon, Cardinal Ruby, Eye of Zul, Amertine, King's Amber, Dreadstone

Ore From Cataclysm's New Zones

Ore Type	Gems Prospected
Obsidium Ore, Elementium Ore	Zephyrite, Carnelian, Alicite, Jasper, Hessonite, Nightstone, Ocean Sapphire, Inferno Ruby, Amber Jewel, Dream Emerald, Ember Topaz, Demonseye
Pyrite	Zephyrite, Carnelian, Alicite, Jasper, Hessonite, Nightstone, Ocean Sapphire, Inferno Ruby, Amber Jewel, Dream Emerald, Ember Topaz, Demonseye

PRACTICING JEWELCRAFTING

Clicking the Jewelcrafting icon opens a menu of all known recipes. Clicking Prospecting enables you to search five ore of the same type to find gems. Some types of ore of Uncommmon quality, such as Silver, cannot be Prospected. The ore is destroyed in the process, but you gain your shiny ingredients.

For high-level Jewelcrafting, you need a base set of gems to work with. These are then turned into finished cut gems that provide bonuses when slotted into equipment. Note that you don't gain points in Jewelcrafting for slotting equipment, only for making the gems.

Draenei Bonus

Draenei have a racial ability—Gemcutting—which increases their Jewelcrafting skill by 10.

JEWELCRAFTING BONUSES

Jewelcrafters, at many skill levels, create bind on pick up trinkets that work for any role, making them useful to every class and spec. Jewelcrafters also have access to specialty gems that are superior to Epic quality gems available to other players. There are two types of these gems, Dragon's Eyes (from Northrend), and Chimera's Eyes (from Cataclysm). There is a limit to how many of these specialty gems can be socketed into the Jewelcrafter's gear.

Making Money as a Jewelcrafter

After reaching high skill levels in this profession, Jewelcrafting turns from a major money sink into a considerable money maker. There's constant demand for high-end gems as many players are striving to collect better gear.

WHAT CUT GEM NAMES MEAN

The following table provides the names for the cuts for each gem of a specific color. For example, cutting a Rigid blue gem, whether it's Azure Moonstone or Ocean Sapphire, provides Hit Rating when it is placed into a socket. As you progress from Outland to Northrend and into Cataclysm, the statistical boost from the gems increases.

Color	Cut Name	Stat(s) Provided
Blue	Rigid	Hit Rating
	Solid	Stamina
	Sparkling	Spirit
	Stormy	Spell Penetration
Red	Bold	Strength
	Brilliant	Intellect
	Delicate	Agility
	Flashing	Parry Rating
	Precise	Expertise Rating
Yellow	Mystic	Resilience
	Quick	Haste Rating
	Smooth	Critical Strike Rating
	Subtle	Dodge Rating
Green	Energized	Haste Rating and Spirit
	Forceful	Haste Rating and Stamina
	Jagged	Critical Strike Rating and Stamina
	Lightning	Hit Rating and Haste Rating
	Misty	Critical Strike Rating and Spirit
	Nimble	Hit Rating and Dodge Rating
	Radiant	Critical Strike Rating and Spell Penetration
	Regal	Dodge Rating and Stamina
	Shattered	Haste Rating and Spell Penetration
	Steady	Resilience Rating and Stamina
	Turbid	Resilience Rating and Spirit
Orange	Champion's	Strength and Dodge Rating
	Deadly	Agility and Critical Strike Rating
	Deft	Agility and Haste Rating
	Fierce	Strength and Haste Rating
	Inscribed	Strength and Critical Strike Rating
	Lucent	Agility and Resilience Rating
	Potent	Intellect and Critical Strike Rating
	Reckless	Intellect and Haste Rating
	Resolute	Expertise Rating and Dodge Rating
	Resplendent	Strength and Resilience
	Stalwart	Parry Rating and Dodge Rating
	Willful	Intellect and Resilience Rating
Purple	Accurate	Expertise Rating and Hit Rating
	Defender's	Parry Rating and Stamina
	Etched	Strength and Hit Rating
	Glinting	Agility and Hit Rating
	Guardian's	Expertise Rating and Stamina
	Mysterious	Intellect and Spell Penetration
	Purified	Intellect and Spirit
	Shifting	Agility and Stamina
	Sovereign	Strength and Stamina
	Timeless	Intellect and Stamina
	Veiled	Intellect and Hit Rating

Two Special Cases: Prismatic and Meta Gems

Prismatic gems are considered Unique (meaning you can have only one socketed in all your equipment at a time), provide a boost to all stats, and don't have a defined color. These gems count as every color when it comes to a socket bonus.

Meta gems are a special gem that provide bonuses beyond simple statistical boosts. These gems fit only into meta sockets, and no other gem can go into a meta socket; meta sockets appear only in hats or helmets. Before you choose a meta gem, carefully read what other gems are required for its effect to be active. Raw meta gems are created by Alchemists, then cut by Jewelcrafters.

NEW RECIPES FOR CATACLYSM

Name	Skill Level	Reagents
Jasper Ring	425	Jeweler's Setting, Jasper x1
Alicite Pendant	435	Jeweler's Setting, Alicite x2
Jeweler's Ruby Monocle	450	Inferno Ruby x3, Elementium Bar x2, Volatile Fire x50
Jeweler's Emerald Monocle	460	Dream Emerald x3, Elementium Bar x2, Volatile Life x50
Jeweler's Sapphire Monocle	460	Elementium Bar x6
Nightstone Choker	460	Jeweler's Setting, Nightstone x2
Carnelian Spikes	470	Carnelian x3, Jeweler's Setting x3
Figurine - Demon Panther	485	Volatile Earth x40, Elementium Bar x4
Figurine - Dream Owl	485	Volatile Earth x40, Elementium Bar x4
Figurine - Earthen Guardian	485	Volatile Earth x40, Elementium Bar x4
Figurine - Jeweled Serpent	485	Volatile Earth x40, Elementium Bar x4
Figurine - King of Boars	485	Volatile Earth x40, Elementium Bar x4
Hessonite Band	485	Jeweler's Setting, Hessonite x2
Stardust	490	Nightstone x1
The Perforator	500	Amberjewel x1, Demonseye x1, Ember Topaz x1, Dream Emerald x1, Ocean Sapphire x1, Inferno Ruby x1
Rhinestone Sunglasses	510	Elementium Bar x2, Chimera's Eye x2, Stardust x6, Dream Emerald x2
Fire Prism	515	Carnelian x3, Alicite x3, Jasper x3, Hessonite x3, Nightstone x3, Zephyrite x3
Band of Blades	525	Elementium Bar x4, Chimera's Eye x4, Stormlord's Favor, Demonseye x4
Brazen Elementium Medallion	525	Elemenium Bar x4, Chimera's Eye x4, Azsharaen Sphere x1, Amberjewel x4
Elementium Destroyer's Ring	525	Elemenium Bar x4, Chimera's Eye x4, Stormlord's Favor x1, Demonseye x4
Elementium Guardian	525	Elemenium Bar x4, Chimera's Eye x4, Earthen Might x1, Ocean Sapphire x4
Elementium Moebius Band	525	Elemenium Bar x4, Chimera's Eye x4, Lifegivnig Seed x1, Dream Emerald x4
Entwined Elementium Choker	525	Elemenium Bar x4, Chimera's Eye x4, Azsharaen Sphere x1, Amberjewel x4
Eye of Many Deaths	525	Elemenium Bar x4, Chimera's Eye x4, Death Vortex x1, Inferno Ruby x4
Ring of Warring Elements	525	Elemenium Bar x4, Chimera's Eye x4, Spark of Ragnaros x1, Ember Topaz x4

LEATHERWORKING

BASICS OF LEATHERWORKING

Leatherworking uses leather and hides gathered from slain beasts to create different pieces of armor, and kits that boost armor in different ways. There are no special tools required for Leatherworking, save for the Salt Shaker needed to cure certain lower level hides. Some Leatherworking patterns require items purchased from trade vendors.

PROGRESSION OF SKINS AND HIDES

Leather scraps
Light Leather
Light Hide
Thin Kodo Leather
Medium Leather
Medium Hide
Deviate Scales
Perfect Deviate Scales
Scorpid Scale
Heavy Scorpid Scale
Silithid Chitin
Heavy Leather
Heavy Hide
Black Whelp Scale
Red Whelp Scale
Green Whelp Scale
Turtle Scales
Thick Leather
Thick Hide
Rugged Leather
Rugged Hide
Worn Dragonscale
Red Dragonscale
Blue Dragonscale
Green Dragonscale
Black Dragonscale
Devilsaur Leather
Warbear Leather
Dreamscale
Chromatic Dragonscale
Scale of Onyxia
Brilliant Chromatic Scale

Skins and Hides from Outland

Knothide Leather Scraps
Knothide Leather
Crystal Infused Leather
Fel Scale
Cobra Scale
Wind Scale
Nether Dragonscale

Skins and Hides from Northrend

Borean Leather Scraps
Borean Leather
Icy Dragonscale
Nerubian Chitin
Jormungar Scales
Arctic Fur

Skins and Hides from Cataclysm's New Zones

Savage Leather Scraps
Savage Leather
Heavy Savage Leather
Charred Dragonscale
Blackened Dragonscale
Pristine Hide

PRACTICING LEATHERWORKING

Clicking the Leatherworking icon opens a menu of all the patterns you know. It's best to do this near a Bank, because you need to carry around a huge amount of leather as well as any products that you're creating.

Making Money as a Leatherworker

Leatherworkers don't have extensive sales, but they also don't need to invest as heavily in their Profession. Anyone with Leatherworking and Skinning should have an easy time, especially due to the nature of Skinning. It's easy to find creatures that are skinnable, so reagents are somewhat cheap and plentiful. The problem is that Leatherworking is a poor money maker until you skill up to high-end armor kits, in the expansion areas. These are some of the few products in Leatherworking that have widespread appeal. Otherwise, this is more of a niche market.

LEATHERWORKING BONUSES

Leatherworkers get to apply Fur Lining to their wrist slot items. There are many types of Fur Lining, and there's at least one for each role. That means there's a solid choice regardless of your class or spec. In addition, Leatherworkers can create kits for their leg armor at a greatly reduced price and at a lower level than what is available for non-Leatherworkers.

COMBINING SCRAPS AND LEATHER

Leatherworkers are able to take a number of lesser leather and combine it into a better quality of leather. The following table shows what they can make and what skill level is required to make it.

Start with	Turns into	Skill Required
3 Ruined Leather scraps	Light Leather	1
4 Light Leather	Medium Leather	100
5 medium Leather	Heavy Leather	150
6 heavy Leather	Thick Leather	200
6 Thick Leather	Rugged Leather	250
5 Knothide Leather scraps	Knothide Leather	300
5 Knothide Leather	Heavy Knothide Leather	325
5 Borean Leather Scraps	Borean Leather	350
6 Borean Leather	Heavy Borean Leather	390
5 Savage Leather Scraps	Savage Leather	425
5 Savage Leather	Heavy Savage Leather	485

NEW RECIPES FOR CATACLYSM

Name	Skill Level	Reagents
Savage Armor Kit	450	Savage Leather x5
Razorshell Bracers	455	Savage Leather x6, Blackened Dragonscale x1
Razorshell Shoulders	455	Savage Leather x6, Blackened Dragonscale x1
Windbound Bracers	455	Savage Leather x10, Blackened Dragonscale x10
Windbound Gloves	455	Savage Leather x6, Blackened Dragonscale x1
Darkbrand Bracers	460	Savage Leather x7
Hardened Scale Cloak	460	Blackened Dragonscale x7
Razorshell Boots	460	Savage Leather x6, Blackened Dragonscale x1
Tsunami Boots	460	Savage Leather x10
Windbound Boots	460	Savage Leather x6, Blackened Dragonscale x1
Charscale Leg Reinforcements	465	Blackened Dragonscale x2
Darkbrand Belt	465	Savage Leather x10
Dragonbone Leg Reinforcements	465	Blackened Dragonscale x2
Razorshell Gloves	465	Savage Leather x10, Blackened Dragonscale x1
Tsunami Shoulders	465	Savage Leather x10
Windbound Belt	465	Savage Leather x10, Blackened Dragonscale x1
Razorshell Belt	470	Savage Leather x10, Blackened Dragonscale x1
Savage Cloak	470	Savage Leather x7
Tsunami Bracers	470	Savage Leather x7
Windbound Shoulders	470	Savage Leather x10, Blackened Dragonscale x1
Darkbrand Boots	475	Savage Leather x21
Darkbrand Gloves	475	Savage Leather x7
Razorshell Helm	475	Savage Leather x15, Blackened Dragonscale x1
Windbound Leggings	475	Savage Leather x15, Blackened Dragonscale x1
Razorshell Leggings	480	Savage Leather x15, Blackened Dragonscale x1
Tsunami Belt	480	Savage Leather x21

NEW RECIPES FOR CATACLYSM

Name	Skill Level	Reagents
Windbound Chest	480	Savage Leather x15, Blackened Dragonscale x1
Darkbrand Shoulders	485	Savage Leather x10
Heavy Savage Leather	485	Savage Leather x10, Blackened Dragonscale x1, Pristine Hide x1, Volatile Life x1, Volatile Water x1, Volatile Fire x1
Razorshell Chest	485	Savage Leather x10, Blackened Dragonscale x1, Pristine Hide x1, Volatile Life x1, Volatile Water x1, Volatile Fire x1
Scorched Leg Armor	485	Savage Leather x10
Tsunami Gloves	485	Savage Leather x7
Windbound Helm	485	Savage Leather x20, Blackened Dragonscale x1
Darkbrand Chestguard	490	Savage Leather x15
Heavy Savage Armor Kit	490	Savage Leather x10, Blackened Dragonscale x1, Pristine Hide x1, Volatile Life x1, Volatile Water x1, Volatile Fire x1
Tsunami Leggings	490	Savage Leather x15
Twilight Leg Armor	490	Savage Leather x10
Darkbrand Leggings	495	Savage Leather x20
Tsunami Helm	495	Savage Leather x20
Darkbrand Helm	500	Savage Leather x15
Draconic Embossment - Agility	500	Volatile Air x2
Draconic Embossment - Intellect	500	Volatile Water x2
Draconic Embossment - Stamina	500	Volatile Earth x2
Draconic Embossment - Strength	500	Volatile Fire x2
Tsunami Chestguard	500	Savage Leather x15
Cloak of Beasts	505	Savage Leather x10, Blackened Dragonscale x1, Pristine Hide x1, Volatile Life x1, Volatile Water x1, Volatile Fire x1
Cloak of War	505	Savage Leather x10, Blackened Dragonscale x1, Pristine Hide x1, Volatile Life x1, Volatile Water x1, Volatile Fire x1
Bloodied Dragonscale Bracers	515	Savage Leather x10, Blackened Dragonscale x1, Pristine Hide x1, Volatile Life x1, Volatile Water x1, Volatile Fire x1
Bloodied Dragonscale Shoulders	515	Savage Leather x10, Blackened Dragonscale x1, Pristine Hide x1, Volatile Life x1, Volatile Water x1, Volatile Fire x1
Bloodied Leather Bracers	515	Savage Leather x10, Blackened Dragonscale x1, Pristine Hide x1, Volatile Life x1, Volatile Water x1, Volatile Fire x1
Bloodied Leather Gloves	515	Savage Leather x10, Blackened Dragonscale x1, Pristine Hide x1, Volatile Life x1, Volatile Water x1, Volatile Fire x1
Bloodied Scale Bracers	515	Savage Leather x10, Blackened Dragonscale x1, Pristine Hide x1, Volatile Life x1, Volatile Water x1, Volatile Fire x1
Bloodied Scale Gloves	515	Savage Leather x10, Blackened Dragonscale x1, Pristine Hide x1, Volatile Life x1, Volatile Water x1, Volatile Fire x1
Bloodied Wyrmhide Belt	515	Savage Leather x10, Blackened Dragonscale x1, Pristine Hide x1, Volatile Life x1, Volatile Water x1, Volatile Fire x1
Bloodied Wyrmhide Bracers	515	Savage Leather x10, Blackened Dragonscale x1, Pristine Hide x1, Volatile Life x1, Volatile Water x1, Volatile Fire x1
Belt of Nefarious Whispers	520	Savage Leather x10, Blackened Dragonscale x1, Pristine Hide x1, Volatile Life x1, Volatile Water x1, Volatile Fire x1
Bloodied Dragonscale Boots	520	Savage Leather x10, Blackened Dragonscale x1, Pristine Hide x1, Volatile Life x1, Volatile Water x1, Volatile Fire x1
Bloodied Dragonscale Gloves	520	Savage Leather x10, Blackened Dragonscale x1, Pristine Hide x1, Volatile Life x1, Volatile Water x1, Volatile Fire x1
Bloodied Leather Boots	520	Savage Leather x10, Blackened Dragonscale x1, Pristine Hide x1, Volatile Life x1, Volatile Water x1, Volatile Fire x1
Bloodied Leather Shoulders	520	Savage Leather x10, Blackened Dragonscale x1, Pristine Hide x1, Volatile Life x1, Volatile Water x1, Volatile Fire x1
Bloodied Scale Belt	520	Savage Leather x10, Blackened Dragonscale x1, Pristine Hide x1, Volatile Life x1, Volatile Water x1, Volatile Fire x1
Bloodied Scale Boots	520	Savage Leather x10, Blackened Dragonscale x1, Pristine Hide x1, Volatile Life x1, Volatile Water x1, Volatile Fire x1
Bloodied Wyrmhide Boots	520	Savage Leather x10, Blackened Dragonscale x1, Pristine Hide x1, Volatile Life x1, Volatile Water x1, Volatile Fire x1
Bloodied Wyrmhide Gloves	520	Savage Leather x10, Blackened Dragonscale x1, Pristine Hide x1, Volatile Life x1, Volatile Water x1, Volatile Fire x1
Corded Viper Belt	520	Savage Leather x10, Blackened Dragonscale x1, Pristine Hide x1, Volatile Life x1, Volatile Water x1, Volatile Fire x1
Lightning Lash	520	Savage Leather x10, Blackened Dragonscale x1, Pristine Hide x1, Volatile Life x1, Volatile Water x1, Volatile Fire x1
Stormleather Sash	520	Savage Leather x10, Blackened Dragonscale x1, Pristine Hide x1, Volatile Life x1, Volatile Water x1, Volatile Fire x1
Bloodied Dragonscale Belt	525	Savage Leather x10, Blackened Dragonscale x1, Pristine Hide x1, Volatile Life x1, Volatile Water x1, Volatile Fire x1
Bloodied Dragonscale Helm	525	Savage Leather x10, Blackened Dragonscale x1, Pristine Hide x1, Volatile Life x1, Volatile Water x1, Volatile Fire x1
Bloodied Leather Belt	525	Savage Leather x10, Blackened Dragonscale x1, Pristine Hide x1, Volatile Life x1, Volatile Water x1, Volatile Fire x1
Bloodied Leather Helm	525	Savage Leather x10, Blackened Dragonscale x1, Pristine Hide x1, Volatile Life x1, Volatile Water x1, Volatile Fire x1
Bloodied Scale Legs	525	Savage Leather x10, Blackened Dragonscale x1, Pristine Hide x1, Volatile Life x1, Volatile Water x1, Volatile Fire x1
Bloodied Scale Shoulders	525	Savage Leather x10, Blackened Dragonscale x1, Pristine Hide x1, Volatile Life x1, Volatile Water x1, Volatile Fire x1
Bloodied Wyrmhide Chest	525	Savage Leather x10, Blackened Dragonscale x1, Pristine Hide x1, Volatile Life x1, Volatile Water x1, Volatile Fire x1
Bloodied Wyrmhide Shoulders	525	Savage Leather x10, Blackened Dragonscale x1, Pristine Hide x1, Volatile Life x1, Volatile Water x1, Volatile Fire x1
Assassin's Chestplate	530	Savage Leather x10, Blackened Dragonscale x1, Pristine Hide x1, Volatile Life x1, Volatile Water x1, Volatile Fire x1
Bloodied Dragonscale Chest	530	Savage Leather x10, Blackened Dragonscale x1, Pristine Hide x1, Volatile Life x1, Volatile Water x1, Volatile Fire x1
Bloodied Dragonscale Legs	530	Savage Leather x10, Blackened Dragonscale x1, Pristine Hide x1, Volatile Life x1, Volatile Water x1, Volatile Fire x1
Bloodied Leather Chest	530	Savage Leather x10, Blackened Dragonscale x1, Pristine Hide x1, Volatile Life x1, Volatile Water x1, Volatile Fire x1
Bloodied Leather Legs	530	Savage Leather x10, Blackened Dragonscale x1, Pristine Hide x1, Volatile Life x1, Volatile Water x1, Volatile Fire x1
Bloodied Scale Chest	530	Savage Leather x10, Blackened Dragonscale x1, Pristine Hide x1, Volatile Life x1, Volatile Water x1, Volatile Fire x1
Bloodied Scale Helm	530	Savage Leather x10, Blackened Dragonscale x1, Pristine Hide x1, Volatile Life x1, Volatile Water x1, Volatile Fire x1
Bloodied Wyrmhide Helm	530	Savage Leather x10, Blackened Dragonscale x1, Pristine Hide x1, Volatile Life x1, Volatile Water x1, Volatile Fire x1
Bloodied Wyrmhide Legs	530	Savage Leather x10, Blackened Dragonscale x1, Pristine Hide x1, Volatile Life x1, Volatile Water x1, Volatile Fire x1
Charscale Leg Armor	530	Savage Leather x10, Blackened Dragonscale x1, Pristine Hide x1, Volatile Life x1, Volatile Water x1, Volatile Fire x1
Chestguard of Nature's Fury	530	Savage Leather x10, Blackened Dragonscale x1, Pristine Hide x1, Volatile Life x1, Volatile Water x1, Volatile Fire x1
Dragonkiller Tunic	530	Savage Leather x10, Blackened Dragonscale x1, Pristine Hide x1, Volatile Life x1, Volatile Water x1, Volatile Fire x1
Dragonscale Leg Armor	530	Savage Leather x10, Blackened Dragonscale x1, Pristine Hide x1, Volatile Life x1, Volatile Water x1, Volatile Fire x1
Razor-Edged Cloak	530	Savage Leather x10, Blackened Dragonscale x1, Pristine Hide x1, Volatile Life x1, Volatile Water x1, Volatile Fire x1
Twilight Dragonscale Cloak	530	Savage Leather x10, Blackened Dragonscale x1, Pristine Hide x1, Volatile Life x1, Volatile Water x1, Volatile Fire x1
Twilight Scale Chestguard	530	Savage Leather x10, Blackened Dragonscale x1, Pristine Hide x1, Volatile Life x1, Volatile Water x1, Volatile Fire x1

TAILORING

BASICS OF TAILORING

Tailoring creates cloth armor, shirts, bags, and other items out of different types of cloth. Cloth is available as drops from humanoid and many undead enemies, and the silks dropped by spiders are often required for some patterns as well. Tailors also learn how to improve various types of cloth. These improved pieces of cloth are then used to create more powerful equipment, including special types of Spellthreads that act as Enchantments for leg armor.

CLOTH PROGRESSION

Cloth	Where Found
Linen	Level 1-15 enemies
Wool	Level 14-26 enemies
Silk	Level 25-41 enemies
Mageweave	Level 40-51 enemies
Runecloth	Level 50-60 enemies
Felcloth	Level 48-60 Demons

Cloth from Outland

Cloth	Where Found
Netherweave	Any Humanoid enemy in Outland

Cloth from Northrend

Cloth	Where Found
Frostweave	Any Humanoid enemy in Northrend

Cloth from Cataclysm's New Zones

Cloth	Where Found
Embersilk	Any Humanoid enemy in Cataclysm's new zones

SPIDER SILKS PROGRESSION

Silk	Where Found
Spider's Silk	Level 16-36 spiders
Thick Spider's Silk	Level 32-60 spiders
Shadow Silk	Level 45-60 spiders
Ironweb Spider Silk	Level 50-60 spiders

Spider Silks from Outland

Silk	Where Found
Netherweb Spider Silk	Any spider in Outland

Spider Silks from Northrend

Silk	Where Found
Iceweb Spider Silk	Any spider in Northrend

Spider Silks from Cataclysm's New Zones

Silk	Where Found
Fiery Silk Gland	Any spider in Cataclysm's high-level zones

CREATED CLOTHS PROGRESSION

Cloth	Materials Required
Mooncloth	Felcloth x2

Created Cloths from Outland

Cloth	Materials Required
Imbued Netherweave	Bolt of Netherweave x3, Arcane Dust x2
Primal Mooncloth	Bolt of Imbued Netherweave x1, Primal Water x1, Primal Life x1
Shadowcloth	Bolt of Imbued Netherweave x1, Primal Shadow x1, Primal Fire x1
Soulcloth	Bolt of Netherweave x1, Soul Essence x8
Spellcloth	Bolt of Imbued Netherweave x1, Primal Mana x1, Primal Fire x1

Created Cloths from Northrend

Cloth	Materials Required
Ebonweave	Bolt of Imbued Frostweave x1, Eternal Shadow x2
Imbued Frostweave	Bolts of Frostweave x2, Infinite Dust x2
Moonshroud	Bolt of Imbued Frostweave x1, Eternal Life x2
Spellweave	Bolt of Imbued Frostweave x1, Eternal Fire x2

Created Cloths from Cataclysm's New Zones

Cloth	Materials Required
Dreamcloth (Dream of Azshara)	Bolt of Embersilk x8, Volatile Water x 30
Dreamcloth (Dream of Ragnaros)	Bolt of Embersilk x8, Volatile Fire x 30
Dreamcloth (Dream of Skywall)	Bolt of Embersilk x8, Volatile Air x 30
Dreamcloth (Dream of Deepholm)	Bolt of Embersilk x8, Volatile Earth x 30
Dreamcloth (Dream of Hyjal)	Bolt of Embersilk x8, Volatile Life x 30
Dreamcloth (Dream of Destruction)	Bolt of Embersilk x8, Chaos Orb x5

All Dreamcloth recipes, save Dream of Destruction, have a 1 week dooldown. Dream of Destruction has no cooldown.

PRACTICING TAILORING

Click on the Tailoring icon to bring up your list of patterns. This can be done at many locations, but like Leatherworking it's best to do near a Bank or trade vendor because these might be additional reagents involved in the creation process.

TAILORING BONUSES

Tailors have the ability to enhance their own cloaks with specialized embroidery patterns. These embroidery patterns help out damage dealing and healing specs. In Northrend, Tailors eventually learn the Northrend Cloth Scavenging ability, which allows them to obtain additional Frostweave from defeated enemies. If you're a fan of flying carpets, Tailoring has what you want. There are three patterns for flying carpets that only Tailors can to fly around the world.

Making Money with Tailoring

Bags are the most widespread product from this Profession. Tailors have a long-term market for these, especially once they start getting into bags from the later game. In addition, Tailors can create a variety of shirts and other specialized clothing for fun and role-playing purposes. The high level enchantment threads are also in high demand as players earn better and better leg armor pieces.

NEW RECIPES FOR CATACLYSM

Name	Skill Level	Reagents
Deathsilk Belt	455	Bolt of Embersilk Cloth x3, Eternium Thread x1
Deathsilk Bracers	455	Bolt of Embersilk Cloth x3, Eternium Thread x1
Deathsilk Boots	460	Bolt of Embersilk Cloth x3, Volatile Fire x2
Deathsilk Shoulders	460	Bolt of Embersilk Cloth x3, Volatile Water x2
Deathsilk Leggings	465	Bolt of Embersilk Cloth x3, Volatile Fire x4
Enchanted Spellthread	465	Bolt of Embersilk Cloth x3, Volatile Fire x8
Deathsilk Cowl	470	Bolt of Embersilk Cloth x3, Volatile Fire x6
Deathsilk Gloves	470	Bolt of Embersilk Cloth x10, Volatile Fire x8
Ghostly Spellthread	470	Bolt of Embersilk Cloth x3, Volatile Fire x8
Deathsilk Robes	475	Bolt of Embersilk Cloth x10, Volatile Fire x6
Spiritmend Belt	475	Bolt of Embersilk Cloth x3, Volatile Fire x8
Spiritmend Bracers	475	Bolt of Embersilk Cloth x3, Volatile Fire x 8
Spiritmend Boots	480	Bolt of Embersilk Cloth x4, Volatile Water x8
Spiritmend Gloves	485	Bolt of Embersilk Cloth x4, Volatile Water x10
Spiritmend Leggings	485	Bolt of Embersilk Cloth x4, Volatile Water x10
Spiritmend Shoulders	485	Bolt of Embersilk Cloth x12, Volatile Water x25
Embersilk Bag	490	Bolt of Embersilk Cloth x20, Volatile Fire x50
Otherworldly Bag	490	Bolt of Embersilk Cloth x12, Volatile Fire x30
Hyjal Expedition Bag	500	Bolt of Embersilk Cloth x12, Volatile Fire x40
Spiritmend Cowl	500	Bolt of Embersilk Cloth x12, Volatile Fire x30
Spiritmend Robe	500	Bolt of Embersilk Cloth x4, Volatile Fire x10
Swordguard Embroidery	500	Bolt of Embersilk Cloth x4, Volatile Fire x4
Darkglow Embroidery	500	Bolt of Embersilk Cloth x4, Volatile Water x4
Lightweave Embroidery	500	Bolt of Embersilk Cloth x4, Volatile Life x4
Black Embersilk Gown	505	Bolt of Embersilk Cloth x5
Emberfire Bracers	505	Bolt of Embersilk Cloth x4, Volatile Fire x12
Fireweave Bracers	505	Bolt of Embersilk Cloth x4, Volatile Fire x15
Emberfire Shoulders	510	Bolt of Embersilk Cloth x4, Volatile Water x15
Emberfire Belt	515	Bolt of Embersilk Cloth x5, Volatile Water x15
Fireweave Belt	515	Bolt of Embersilk Cloth x4, Volatile Fire x12
Fireweave Shoulders	515	Bolt of Embersilk Cloth x5, Volatile Fire x15
Emberfire Gloves	520	Bolt of Embersilk Cloth x5, Volatile Water x20
Fireweave Boots	520	Bolt of Embersilk Cloth x5, Volatile Fire x20
Belt of the Depths	525	DreamCloth x2
Breeches of Mended Nightmares	525	DreamCloth x2
Dreamless Belt	525	DreamCloth x2
Emberfire Boots	525	Bolt of Embersilk Cloth x6, Volatile Water x20
Emberfire Cowl	525	Bolt of Embersilk Cloth x8, Volatile Water x20
Emberfire Pants	525	Bolt of Embersilk Cloth x8, Volatile Water x20
Emberfire Robe	525	Bolt of Embersilk Cloth x8, Volatile Water x20
Fireweave Cowl	525	Bolt of Embersilk Cloth x8, Volatile Fire x20
Fireweave Gloves	525	Bolt of Embersilk Cloth x6, Volatile Fire x20
Fireweave Pants	525	Bolt of Embersilk Cloth x8, Volatile Fire x20
Fireweave Robe	525	Bolt of Embersilk Cloth x8, Volatile Fire x20
Flame-Ascended Pantaloons	525	DreamCloth x2
Illusionary Bag	525	DreamCloth x5
Powerful Enchanted Spellthread	525	DreamCloth x1
Powerful Ghostly Spellthread	525	DreamCloth x1
High Society Top Hat	530	Bolt of Embersilk Cloth x5

HERBALISM

BASICS OF HERBALISM

Herbalism is the harvesting of herbs from plant nodes, and from some enemies (usually Elemental enemies that look like walking vegetation) which have some affinity with nature. These herbs are primarily used by Alchemists and Scribes. When you learn Herbalism, you gain the Find Herbs skill. When this skill is active, herb nodes appear on your mini-map. Watch for these icons while hunting and questing and you should see your skill increase rapidly. When you find a node, the herb will sparkle and your mouse cursor changes into a flower blossom. To gather, right-click on the herb in question. The same thing applies when you find harvestable enemies. When you mouse over a corpse, your mouse cursor changes to a flower blossom if you can harvest from it.

HERB NODE PROGRESSION

EASTERN KINGDOMS AND KALIMDOR

Node	Required Skill	Loot
Peacebloom	1	Peacebloom
Silverleaf	1	Silverleaf
Bloodthistle	1	Bloodthistle
Earthroot	15	Earthroot
Mageroyal	50	Mageroyal, Swiftthistle
Briarthorn	70	Briarthorn, Swiftthistle
Stranglekelp	85	Stranglekelp
Bruiseweed	100	Bruiseweed
Wild Steelbloom	115	Wild Steelbloom
Grave Moss	120	Grave Moss
Kingsblood	125	Kingsblood
Liferoot	150	Liferoot
Fadeleaf	160	Fadeleaf
Goldthorn	170	Goldthorn
Khadgar's Whisker	185	Khadgar's Whisker
Wintersbite	195	Wintersbite
Firebloom	205	Firebloom
Purple Lotus	210	Purple Lotus, Wildvine
Arthas' Tears	220	Arthas' Tears
Sungrass	230	Sungrass
Blindweed	235	Blindweed
Ghost Mushroom	245	Ghost Mushroom
Gromsblood	250	Gromsblood
Golden Sansam	260	Golden Sansam
Dreamfoil	270	Dreamfoil
Mountain Silversage	280	Mountain Silversage
Plaguebloom	285	Plaguebloom
Icecap	290	Icecap
Black Lotus	300	Black Lotus

OUTLAND

Node	Required Skill	Loot
Felweed	300	Felweed, Mote of Life, Fel Blosssom, Fel Lotus
Dreaming Glory	315	Dreaming Glory, Mote of Life, Fel Lotus
Ragveil	325	Ragveil, Mote of Life, Fel Lotus
Flame Cap	335	Flame Cap, Fel Lotus
Terocone	325	Terocone, Mote of Life, Fel Lotus
Ancient Lichen	340	Ancient Lichen, Fel Lotus
Netherbloom	350	Netherbloom, Mote of Mana,
Netherdust Bush	350	Netherdust Pollen, Mote of Mana, Fel Lotus, Netherwing Egg
Nightmare Vine	365	Nightmare Vine, Nightmare Seed, Fel Lotus
Mana Thistle	375	Mana Thistle, Mote of Life, Fel Lotus

NORTHREND

Node	Required Skill	Loot
Goldclover	350	Goldclover, Deadnettle, Crystallized Life, Frost Lotus
Firethorn	360	Fire Leaf, Crystallized Life, Frost Lotus
Tiger Lily	375	Tiger Lily, Deadnettle, Crystallized Life, Frost Lotus
Talandra's Rose	385	Talandra's Rose, Deadnettle, Crystallized Life, Frost Lotus
Frozen Herb	400	Goldclover, Talandra's Rose, Tiger Lily
Adder's Tongue	400	Adder's Tongue, Crystallized Life, Frost Lotus
Lichbloom	425	Lichbloom, Crystallized Life, Frost Lotus
Icethorn	435	Icethorn, Crystallized Life, Frost Lotus
Frost Lotus	450	Frost Lotus, Deadnettle, Crystallized Life

CATACLYSM'S NEW ZONES

Node	Required Skill	Loot
Cinderbloom	425	Cinderbloom, Volatile Life
Stormvine	450	Stormvine, Volatile Life
Azshara's Veil	450	Azshara's Veil, Volatile Life
Heartblossom	475	Heartblossom, Volatile Life
Whiptail	500	Whiptail, Volatile Life
Twilight Jasmine	525	Twilight Jasmine, Volatile Life

Tauren Bonus

Taurens have a racial ability—Cultivation—which increases their Herbalism skill by 15 and allows them to harvest herbs faster than other races.

HERBALISM BONUSES

Herbalists gain an ability known as Lifeblood. Lifeblood restores health to the Herbalist over time and also provides a boost to Haste. Lifeblood has a two minute cooldown, and its effects scales with your skill in Herbalism.

Making Money with Herbalism

Herbalism is a good Profession for making money. People buy herbs at lucrative prices, even from the beginning levels forward. There is always a market for most of these herbs, and a new player stands to make plenty of cash if they harvest and sell herbs with the Auction House.

MINING

BASICS OF MINING

With Mining, you extract ore, gems, and (in lower level zones) stones from raw metal veins, deposits, and from some enemies (usually rocky Elemental creatures). These materials are used primarily in Jewelcrafting, Blacksmithing, and Engineering. A Mining Pick (or any item that acts as a Mining Pick) is required to mine. You do not need to equip the Mining Pick; just keep it in your Backpack. Miners learn a second ability, Smelting, which turns the ore into metal bars. Mining also imparts the ability to Find Minerals. When it is active, mineral nodes appear on your mini-map. When you find a node, it will sparkle and the cursor changes into a pick axe. To mine, right-click on the node. The same thing applies when you find harvestable enemies. When you mouse over a corpse, your mouse cursor changes to a pick axe if you can harvest from it. Another way to increase you Mining skill level is to Smelt ore. To smelt, you need access to a forge and ore. Click on the Smelting icon to see you what you can currently smelt. Gaining skill ups from Smelting varies wildly with each new ore you learn to smelt. Any time you work with a new metal, Smelt as much of it as you can as soon as you can. The skill ups from Smelting dry up much faster than the skill ups you get from mining.

MINING NODE PROGRESSION

EASTERN KINGDOMS AND KALIMDOR

Node	Required Skill	Loot
Copper Vein	1	Copper Ore, Rough Stone, Malachite, Shadowgem, and Tigerseye
Tin Vein	65	Tin Ore, Coarse Stone, Moss Agate, Shadowgem, Lesser Moonstone, Jade
Silver Vein	75	Silver Ore, Shadowgem, Moss Agate, Lesser Moonstone
Iron Deposit	125	Iron Ore, Heavy Stone, Jade, Lesser Moonstone, Citrine, Aquamarine
Gold Vein	155	Gold Ore, Jade, Lesser Moonstone, Citrine
Mithril Deposit	175	Mithril Ore, Solid Stone, Aquamarine, Black Vitriol, Citrine, Star Ruby
Truesilver Deposit	205	Truesilver Ore, Aquamarine, Citrine, Star Ruby
Dark Iron Vein	230	Dark Iron Ore, Black Diamond, Black Vitriol, Blood of the Mountain
Small Thorium Vein	230	Thorium Ore, Dense Stone, Arcane Crystal, Black Vitriol, Star Ruby, Azerothian Diamond, Blue Sapphire, Huge Emerald, Large Opal
Rich Thorium Vein	255	Thorium Ore, Dense Stone, Arcane Crystal, Black Vitriol, Star Ruby, Azerothian Diamond, Blue Sapphire, Huge Emerald, Large Opal

OUTLAND

Node	Required Skill	Loot
Fel Iron Deposit	275	Fel Iron Ore, Mote of Fire, Mote of Earth, Eternium Ore, Azure Moonstone, Blood Garnet, Deep Peridot, Flame Spessarite, Golden Draenite, Shadow Draenite, Noble Topaz, Talasite, Dawnstone, Living Ruby, Nightseye, Star of Elune, Nether Residue
Adamantite Deposit	325	Adamantite Ore, Mote of Earth, Eternium Ore, Azure Moonstone, Blood Garnet, Deep Peridot, Flame Spessarite, Golden Draenite, Shadow Draenite, Noble Topaz, Talasite, Dawnstone, Living Ruby, Nightseye, Star of Elune, Nether Residue
Rich Adamantite Deposit	350	Adamantite Ore, Mote of Earth, Eternium Ore, Azure Moonstone, Blood Garnet, Deep Peridot, Flame Spessarite, Golden Draenite, Shadow Draenite, Noble Topaz, Talasite, Dawnstone, Living Ruby, Nightseye, Star of Elune, Nether Residue
Khorium Vein	375	Khroium Ore, Mote of Fire, Mote of Earth, Eternium Ore, Azure Moonstone, Blood Garnet, Deep Peridot, Flame Spessarite, Golden Draenite, Shadow Draenite, Noble Topaz, Talasite, Dawnstone, Living Ruby, Nightseye, Star of Elune, Nether Residue

NORTHREND

Node	Required Skill	Loot
Cobalt Deposit	350	Cobalt Ore, Crystallized Water, Crystallized Earth, Chalcedony, Bloodstone, Dark Jade, Huge Citrine, Sun Crystal, Shadow Crystal, Sky Sapphire, Scarlet Ruby, Forest Emerald, Monarch Topaz, Autumn's Glow, Twilight Opal
Rich Cobalt Deposit	375	Cobalt Ore, Crystallized Water, Crystallized Earth, Chalcedony, Bloodstone, Dark Jade, Huge Citrine, Sun Crystal, Shadow Crystal, Sky Sapphire, Scarlet Ruby, Forest Emerald, Monarch Topaz, Autumn's Glow, Twilight Opal
Saronite Deposit	400	Saronite Ore, Impure Saronite Ore, Crystallized Earth, Crystallized Shadow, Chalcedony, Bloodstone, Dark Jade, Huge Citrine, Sun Crystal, Shadow Crystal, Sky Sapphire, Scarlet Ruby, Forest Emerald, Monarch Topaz, Autumn's Glow, Twilight Opal
Rich Saronite Deposit	425	Saronite Ore, Impure Saronite Ore, Crystallized Earth, Crystallized Shadow, Chalcedony, Bloodstone, Dark Jade, Huge Citrine, Sun Crystal, Shadow Crystal, Sky Sapphire, Scarlet Ruby, Forest Emerald, Monarch Topaz, Autumn's Glow, Twilight Opal
Pure Saronite Deposit	450	Saronite Ore, Impure Saronite Ore, Crystallized Earth, Crystallized Shadow, Chalcedony, Bloodstone, Dark Jade, Huge Citrine, Sun Crystal, Shadow Crystal, Sky Sapphire, Scarlet Ruby, Forest Emerald, Monarch Topaz, Autumn's Glow, Twilight Opal
Titanium Vein	450	Titanium Ore, Crystallized Water, Crystallized Fire, Crystallized Earth, Crystallized Air, Sky Sapphire, Scarlet Ruby, Forest Emerald, Monarch Topaz, Autumn's Glow, Twilight Opal, Majestic Zircon, Cardinal Ruby, Eye of Zul, Amertine, King's Amber, Dreadstone

CATACLYSM'S NEW ZONES

Node	Required Skill	Loot
Obsidium Deposit	425	Obsidium Ore, Volatile Earth, Volatile Air, Zephyrite, Carnelian, Alicite, Jasper, Hessonite, Nightstone, Ocean Sapphire, Inferno Ruby, Amber Jewel, Dream Emerald, Ember Topaz, Demonseye, Volatile Fire, Volatile Shadow
Rich Obsidium Deposit	425	Obsidium Ore, Volatile Earth, Volatile Air, Zephyrite, Carnelian, Alicite, Jasper, Hessonite, Nightstone, Ocean Sapphire, Inferno Ruby, Amber Jewel, Dream Emerald, Ember Topaz, Demonseye, Volatile Fire, Volatile Shadow
Elementium Vein	475	Elementium Ore, Elementium Geode, Zephyrite, Carnelian, Alicite, Jasper, Hessonite, Nightstone, Ocean Sapphire, Inferno Ruby, Amber Jewel, Dream Emerald, Ember Topaz, Demonseye, Volatile Earth, Volatile Fire, Volatile Water
Rich Elementium Vein	500	Elementium Ore, Elementium Geode, Zephyrite, Carnelian, Alicite, Jasper, Hessonite, Nightstone, Ocean Sapphire, Inferno Ruby, Amber Jewel, Dream Emerald, Ember Topaz, Demonseye, Volatile Earth, Volatile Fire, Volatile Water
Pyrite Deposit	525	Pyrite Ore, Zephyrite, Carnelian, Alicite, Jasper, Hessonite, Nightstone, Ocean Sapphire, Inferno Ruby, Amber Jewel, Dream Emerald, Ember Topaz, Demonseye, Volatile Fire
Rich Pyrite Deposit	525	Pyrite Ore, Zephyrite, Carnelian, Alicite, Jasper, Hessonite, Nightstone, Ocean Sapphire, Inferno Ruby, Amber Jewel, Dream Emerald, Ember Topaz, Demonseye, Volatile Fire

MINING BONUSES

Miners gain extra Stamina due to Toughness. The extra Stamina provided by Toughness increases as your skill level in Mining increases.

Making Money with Mining

Mining can be incredibly profitable. With three distinct Professions all requiring ore, you have a large potential market. Try selling your metal in both bar and ore form as some people want the refined bars, while others (particularly Jewelcrafters) want the raw ore.

SKINNING

BASICS OF SKINNING

Skinners are able to harvest the leather and hides from slain beasts. After slaying a beast and looting it (assuming it's a skinnable creature) your mouse cursor changes into an animal hide when you mouse over it. A Skinning Knife (or another item that acts as a Skinning Knife) is required for Skinning; however, you don't need to equip the item, just keep it in your Backpack. To skin, right-click on a skinnable beast. You can also skin another player's looted corpses, but it's good form to ask for permission first unless the other player leaves the area. The leathers and hides are primarily used by Leatherworkers. Skinning is faster to advance than Herbalism or Mining, due to the prevalence of beasts in the game. When you first learn Skinning, you can skin any creature level 10 or lower. For creatures from levels 11 through 20, your skinning must be [10 x (Creature's Level - 10)], meaning your Skinning skill must be 20 if you wish to skin a level 12 beast, while a level 20 beast calls for a skill of 100. For creatures from levels 21 through 79, your Skinning skill must be equal to five times the creature's level to skin it successfully. That means your Skinning skill must be at 300 to skin level 60 beasts, and 350 for level 70 beasts. When you reach level 80 enemies, use the following table to determine what skill level you need to skin beasts.

Worgen Bonus

Worgen have a racial ability—Flayer—which increases their Skinning skill by 15 and allows them to skin faster than other races. They also do not need a Skinning Knife.

Enemy Level	Skinning Needed
80	425
81	440
82	455
83	470

Enemy Level	Skinning Needed
84	485
85	500
86	515
87	530

PROGRESSION OF SKINS AND HIDES

Loot	Enemy Types
Leather Scraps	Skinnable Enemies, Level 5-15
Light Leather	Skinnable Enemies, Level 5-27
Light Hide	Skinnable Enemies, Level 5-27
Medium Leather	Skinnable Enemies, Level 15-38
Medium Hide	Skinnable Enemies, Level 15-38
Heavy Leather	Skinnable Enemies, Level 26-46
Heavy Hide	Skinnable Enemies, Level 26-46
Thick Leather	Skinnable Enemies, Level 35-58
Thick Hide	Skinnable Enemies, Level 35-58
Rugged Leather	Skinnable Enemies, Level 45-60
Rugged Hide	Skinnable Enemies, Level 45-60

SPECIALTY LEATHER

Loot	Enemy Types
Thin Kodo Leather	Kodos in Northern Barrens
Deviate Scales	Deviate Enemies in Wailing Caverns
Perfect Deviate Scales	Deviate Enemies in Wailing Caverns
Scorpid Scale	Scorpids, Level 37-47
Heavy Scorpid Scale	Scorpids, Level 52-60
Silithid Chitin	Silithids, Level 55-60
Black Whelp Scale	Black Dragon Whelps in Redridge Mountains
Red Whelp Scale	Red Dragon Whelps in Wetlands
Green Whelp Scale	Green Dragon Whelps in Swamp of Sorrows
Turtle Scales	Turtles, Level 30-50
Worn Dragonscale	Any Dragonkin
Red Dragonscale	Red Dragonkin
Blue Dragonscale	Blue Dragonkin
Green Dragonscale	Green Dragonkin
Black Dragonscale	Black Dragonkin
Devilsaur Leather	Devilsaurs in Un'Goro Crater
Warbear Leather	Bears, Level 50-60

BASIC LEATHER - OUTLAND

Loot	Enemy Types
Knothide Leather Scraps	Skinnable Enemies, Level 58-70
Knothide Leather	Skinnable Enemies, Level 58-70

SPECIALTY LEATHER - OUTLAND

Loot	Enemy Types
Crystal Infused Leather	Any Ravager or Basilisk
Fel Scale	Any Ravager or Basilisk
Cobra Scale	Coilskar Cobras, Shadow Serpents, or Twilight Serpents
Thick Clefthood Leather	Any Clefthoof
Wind Scale	Wind Serpents and Dragonhawks, Level 66-70
Nether Dragonscale	Any Nether Drake

BASIC LEATHER - NORTHREND

Loot	Enemy Types
Borean Leather Scraps	Skinnable Enemies, Level 68-80
Borean Leather	Skinnable Enemies, Level 68-80
Arctic Fur	Any skinnable creature in Northrend

SPECIALTY LEATHER - NORTHREND

Loot	Enemy Types
Icy Dragonscale	Any Dragonkin or Whelp
Nerubian Chitin	Any Nerubian
Jormungar Scales	Any Jormungar

CATACLYSM'S NEW ZONES

Loot	Enemy Types
Savage Leather Scraps	Skinnable Enemies, Level 81-85
Savage Leather	Skinnable Enemies, Level 81-85
Pristine Hide	Any Skinnable creature, Level 81-85

SPECIALTY LEATHER - CATACLYSM'S NEW ZONES

Loot	Enemy Types
Blackened Dragonscale	Dragonkin, Level 81-85

SKINNING BONUSES

Skinners gain extra Critical Strike chance through Master of Anatomy. The extra Critical Strike chance provided by Master of Anatomy increases as you improve you Skinning skill level.

Making Money with Skinning

Hides are always in demand at the Auction House, but they don't fetch as much as the materials from herbalism and mining. Skins are arguably easier to acquire than ore and herbs since those nodes often appear alone, and you can find packs of beasts for Skinning, which leads to a greater supply, and lower prices.

ARCHAEOLOGY

BASICS OF ARCHAEOLOGY

The newest secondary Profession, Archaeology, is all about exploration and uncovering the past. There are two steps in the Archaeological process. First, you visit digsites around Azeroth and Draenor and use Surveying to locate and unearth artifact fragments of items from various cultures. After collecting enough pieces, you assemble them into a restored piece.

Unlike other gathering skills, digsites are player-specific. There is no competition for artifact fragments between players. Other players searching at the same digsite are uncovering their own fragments.

ARCHAEOLOGY PROGRESSION

Proficiency Level Name	Character Level Minimum	Skill Level Minimum	Skill level Maximum
Apprentice	20	0	75
Journeyman	20	50	150
Expert	20	125	225
Artisan	35	200	300
Master	50	275	375
Grand Master	65	350	450
Illustrious Grand Master	75	425	525

Most of the items uncovered with Archaeology are not for combat purposes. There are a few special pieces here and there, but mostly this Profession leads to more peripheral elements, like fun pets and mounts.

PRACTICING ARCHEOLOGY

Open your world map and look for the small shovel icons that appear around the world. There should be up to four zones appropriate to your character's level per continent (Eastern Kingoms, Kalimdor, Draenor, and Northrend) that include active digsites for you. When you zoom into a zone with an active digsite, the area shaded red on the map provides the exact location for you to visit. There's an option at the bottom of the map frame to toggle the red-shading at the dig sites.

When you reach the area, use the Survey ability to get directions to the exact location of the fragments. The survey instrument that appears indicates both the direction of, and distance to, the fragments. A red light means the fragments are far away, the yellow light indicates you are getting closer and the green light means you are very close to the fragments. When you are close enough to the fragments, a container of some sort appears instead of your survey tools. Right-click on the item to collect the fragments. You don't carry these items around in your Backpack. Instead, they're stored as currency. Each new cache of fragments found provides a skill up for you.

Dwarf Bonus

Dwarves have a racial ability—Explorer—which increases their Achaeology skill by 15, and allows them to Survey faster than other races.

Click on the appropriate Archaeology crest to watch your progress. After you collect enough fragments, click on the Solve button to create the listed item. The item goes into your backpack, you get a skill up, and you start on the next object. Any leftover fragments are applied to the new item, so you don't need to worry about wasted pieces.

COOKING

BASICS OF COOKING

Cooking turns various items (raw meat and fish, flour, and spider parts to name a few) into food which restores health and even conveys short term buffs to various statistics. Cooking requires a heat source of some type, such as a stove or cooking fire. Fortunately, when you first train cooking you also gain the ability to create a fire anywhere with Basic Campfire. You don't need any tools to create a Basic Campire.

At higher levels, Cooking buffs go beyond Stamina improvements and start to provide bonuses to a couple stats at once. These are very nice, especially considering the low cost involved in creating them. Food isn't hard to gather, and it takes only a few moments to start a fire.

Any character benefits from Cooking. It's easiest to keep up with when you start as soon as possible and use the materials you get from looting enemies. If you are also working on Fishing, there are many recipes available that allow you to cook your catches.

COOKING PROGRESSION

Proficiency Level name	Skill Level minimum	Skill level maximum
Apprentice	0	75
Journeyman	50	150
Expert	125	225
Artisan	200	300
Master	275	375
Grand Master	350	450
Illustrious Grand Master	425	525

PRACTICING COOKING

Put Cooking and Basic Campfire abilities on an Action Bar. Clicking Cooking opens a menu of all the recipes you know. Clicking Basic Campfire creates a fire should you need a heat source. Some recipes call for special spices or other items, but these are available from Cooking vendors, and most Trade vendors.

MORE FUN WITH COOKING

There are daily quests available only to characters with Cooking. Visit Shattrath City in Outland, Dalaran in Northrend, and Orgrimmar (for Horde) or Stormwind (for Alliance) to obtain these quests. There are Achievements tied to these daily quests as well as unique recipes which can't be obtained in any other way.

On a final note, you can't go wrong learning Cooking if you plan on raiding or running heroic dungeons. Cooked meals provide a variety of statistical bonuses (although only one type of statistical boost from cooking can be active at a time), and there are even feasts you can set out for anyone in your party to eat and reap their benefits. While not everyone needs to be a cook, someone needs to create and distribute the food to your group and only you know what type of food buff is best for your character.

FIRST AID

BASICS OF FIRST AID

First Aid enables you to create bandages which are used to restore health, and antidotes to remove poisons. Bandages are created from cloth drops in the game, and they can be used outside of combat or even while in the middle of it. Bandages can be used on yourself, other players, or pets.

Characters that are damage dealers should use First Aid even more aggressively than most. In really big team fights, the tanks and healers get the most attention when it comes to healing. Damage dealers are last on the list, and if there isn't enough mana to go around they are the ones that come up short. Being able to restore some health during these fights is a godsend.

You shouldn't try to use a bandage when an enemy is in the middle of attacking you. This disrupts the process, ending your health restoration. Bandages have a cooldown period, so you can't continually apply them. Stun an enemy or otherwise get away from them for a few moments and use your First Aid.

FIRST AID PROGRESSION

Proficiency Level name	Character Level minimum	Skill Level minimum	Skill level maximum
Apprentice	1	0	75
Journeyman	1	50	150
Expert	1	125	225
Artisan	35	200	300
Master	50	275	375
Grand Master	65	350	450
Illustrious Grand Master	75	425	525

CLOTH

Cloth	Where Found
Linen	Level 1-15 enemies
Wool	Level 14-26 enemies
Silk	Level 25-41 enemies
Mageweave	Level 40-51 enemies
Runecloth	Level 50-60 enemies
Felcloth	Level 48-60 Demons

FROM NORTHREND

Cloth	Where Found
Frostweave	Any Humanoid enemy in Northrend

FROM CATACLYSM'S NEW ZONES

Cloth	Where Found
Embersilk	Any Humanoid enemy in Cataclysm's high-level zones

FROM OUTLAND

Cloth	Where Found
Netherweave	Any Humanoid enemy in Outland

PRACTICING FIRST AID

Clicking on the First Aid icon opens a window which shows all the bandages you can create. Creating bandages can be done anywhere, and all you need are the cloth pieces required for the specific bandages, or spider venom glands to create anti-venoms.

Until you reach Embersilk, bandages come in two varieties per type of cloth: regular and heavy. Each regular bandage requires one piece of cloth while you need two pieces of cloth to create a heavy bandage. There are three types of Embersilk bandage: regulary, heavy, and dense. Dense requires three Embersilk cloths but restores a considerable amount of health. You also learn how to combine two Heavy Embersilk bandages into a Dense Embersilk bandage.

FISHING

BASICS OF FISHING

Fishing allows you to cast your line into any body of water deep enough and see what you bring up. You can catch fish, of course, but you may also catch other marine life, junk, or treasure. A fishing pole is required but, unlike the other Professions, you must equip it (fishing poles are considered two-hand weapons) in order to do some fishing.

Fish have many uses, including Alchemy, but they are mainly used for food. Most types of fish can be eaten raw by your character or Hunter pets, but it's better to cook the fish first if you have the appropriate Cooking recipe.

The types of fish available from a body of water are not determined by your Fishing skill. Instead, the types of fish are determined by the area. However, if your skill isn't considered high enough for the area, you only catch random trash items.

There are also schools of fish in the waters around the world. These schools enable you to catch specific fish, if your casting is accurate. When you gain the ability to track fish, these schools of fish appear on your mini-map making it easy to find them.

FISHING PROGRESSION

Proficiency Level name	Character Level minimum	Skill Level minimum	Skill level maximum
Apprentice	5	0	75
Journeyman	5	50	150
Expert	5	125	225
Artisan	5	200	300
Master	5	275	375
Grand Master	5	350	450
Illustrious Grand Master	5	425	525

PRACTICING FISHING

Purchase a fishing pole (there's often a vendor near the fishing trainers) and put Fishing on one of your Action Bars. Click on Fishing and watch your character cast a line. A bobber appears on the water's surface; move your mouse cursor over the bobber until it turns into the gear icon. Watch that carefully until the bobber moves, and then quickly right-click the bobber. If successful, you receive a loot window that includes a fish or another item of some value.

There are many unique Fishing Poles in the game, some with improved Fishing skills or other buffs, such as underwater breathing. You can also use a variety of baits, lures and enchanted fishing lines to improve your odds of catching a fish.

Combat Caution

If you are attacked while fishing, your weapon is your Fishing Pole. Fishing Poles are not really designed to be combat weapons, so switch back to your normal weapon if something's gnawing on your back.

MORE FUN WITH FISHING

There are daily quests available only to characters with Fishing. Visit Shattrath City in Outland and Dalaran in Northrend to obtain these quests. There are Achievements tied to these daily quests as well as unique pets that can't be obtained in any other way.

There are also weekly fishing contests on two continents. The goblins of Booty Bay host an event, and the Kalu'ak of Northrend host another in the city of Dalaran. There are some great rewards for the players who manage to win these contests.

On a final note, Fishing is essentially a necessity if you want to create the best food available via the Cooking Profession. Cooked fish provide a variety of statistical boosts, and there are even fish feasts you can set out for anyone in your party to eat and reap benefits.

 BESTIARY

Whether you're discovering new zones or revisiting older parts of the world to observe the changes wrought by Deathwing's return, you're sure to encounter creatures with revised appearances and completely new types of humans, beasts, and other creatures.

New Mounts: Camel and Seahorse

Some of the creatures introduced in Cataclysm function as mounts. To obtain a Seahorse mount, you must spend some time completing quests in Vashj'ir.

Look for Camel mounts in the sands of Uldum. The locals there offer to sell one to you if you improve your Reputation with them enough.

DEEP MURLOC

These distant cousins of the amphibious murlocs found throughout Azeroth are completely aquatic. They inhabit the deepest reaches of the zones found within Vashj'ir: Abyssal Depths, Kelp'thar Forest, and Shimmering Expanse.

DJINN

There are few known Djinn to date. You encounter one throughout Uldum, but you must wait for a trip to the Lost City of Tol'vir to actually battle against one.

ELEMENTALS

Elementals aren't new, but the events of the Cataclysm opened the way for more of them to appear. These Elementals have an entirely new look and are found throughout the world. Some of these Elementals are aggresive, but others act as allies. If you wish to learn more about what drives these Elementals, spend time in Deepholm.

GILBLINS

Gilblins are relatives of Goblins who have adapted to life underwater. The adaptations that allow Gilblins to survive aquatic life has apparently drained some of their higher brain functions. Their actions are guided almost entirely by greed. They lack any of the intelligence and guile displayed (at times) by the Goblins found on land.

HOBGOBLIN

These brutish humanoids often appear in the company of Goblins around Kezan. You can feel reasonably confident that any actions taken by Hobgoblins are on the orders of another Goblin. They just aren't that bright of creatures!

ETTIN

You won't find many of these two-headed creatures around the world. A Small number infest Redridge Mountains, and a larger clan has taken up residence amongst ogres in Twilight Highlands.

PYGMY

The Pygmys which appear on Kezan are much less dangerous versions of what you encounter in Uldum and the Lost City of Tol'vir, but they're just as wild and untamed. There's a good chance they'll be the first creatures you encounter in Uldum, but they don't exactly roll out the welcome wagon for you. Most Pygmys stick to crude weapons, but a handful have picked up tribal magic and assume the role of Witchdoctor.

TOL'VIR

The land of Uldum is covered with a desert and populated by a centaur-like people known as the Tol'vir. The tribes of Tol'vir are often at war with each other, presenting you with an opportunity to curry the favor of the Ramkahen at the expesne of their enemies, the Neferset. You won't need to look hard in Uldum to find Tol'vir, and you should also expect to find them throughout the Lost City of Tol'vir.

STONE TROGG

Troggs are an ancient foe of the Dwarves as the groups often compete over areas since they have similar tastes in environments for their homes. As their rock-like appearance suggests, Stone Troggs are much tougher than the Troggs encountered around Dun Morogh and Loch Modan. They continue to use primitive weapons such as clubs but their warriors are augmented by a handful of spellcasters who call upon the elements in various ways. Stone Troggs appear throughout Deepholm and the Halls of Origination.

TWILIGHT HAMMER CULT

The Twilight Hammer Cult's influence has spread from its original locations in and around Blackfathom Deeps and Blackrock Mountain. You can find nearly every humanoid race from Azeroth among their ranks. Their members are well-versed in various forms of combat, both melee and magical. Their initiates have spread into Azshara, while their highest level members infest Mount Hyjal and Deepholm.

NEW BEASTS

While the following information should be of interest to everyone exploring the world, Hunters should really pay attention here. The Beasts are broken down by new family type, meaning there are tamable examples of each!

BEETLES

While flying silithids have been tamable for some time, their ground-bound compatriots eluded Hunters attempts to tame them. Look for Beetles anywhere you find silithid hives, such as Tanaris, Thousand Needles, and Uldum.

FOXES

Foxes appear in many places, and with many different coat colors. Redridge Mountains and Loch Modan are great places to start, but there are a few in Western Plaguelands as well.

BIRDS

There are a handful of additions to the Birds of Prey familly for Hunters to consider. Look in the Deadmines and around Thousand Needles for Parrots, and Macaws in many colors. However, if you're looking for something really different visit Thousand Needles and tame a Saltspray Gull!

MONKEYS

If you're looking to add a smaller simian to your stable than a gorilla, look throughout Stranglethorn Vale for a few different types of Monkey. They are native to both halves of Stranglethorn Vale, but some of the new inhabitants of Westfall pilfered some from their homes and now put them to work in the Deadmines.

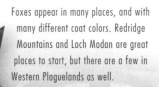

DOGS

Dogs are new for Cataclysm and are common around Gilneas, but there are many familiar places where you might find them. Almost anywhere you remember encountering a tamed hyena (such as under the care of Scarlet Crusaders, or in Dire Maul) that beast has been replaced by a mastiff.

SHALE SPIDER

While they bear striking similarities to the spiders found elsewhere in Azeroth and Draenor, the Shale Spides from Deepholm are a class of their own. They're considered as Exotic pets, so not every Hunter is able to tame them!

ACHIEVEMENTS

Achievements are a different way to show what you have accomplished in World of Warcraft. To see a full list of achievements, click on the icon in the interface bar, or press the letter "y". This area lists thousands of in-game achievements. You get them for almost anything you can imagine. They are awarded in PvP, seasonal activities, dungeons, while soloing, etc. The list is mind blowing.

While Achievements won't lead to improved weapons, or armor, they do provide special titles, companion pets, and mounts. Sometimes you get a reward for getting a certain achievement, while others require you to unlock a set of Achievements that take an entire year to earn! Achievements are in the game purely for fun. Love them or leave them, but these achievements are not supposed to make or break your day. They give you an awesome way to smell the roses while exploring the world.

TYPES OF ACHIEVEMENTS

Click on individual achievements to learn more about them. Most of these are quite specific, so it isn't hard to understand what is required to grab them. Indeed, making the events happen is the trickier part.

Achievements are broken down into different categories to make it easier to find which Achievements are available to you depending on where your interests lie. The Achievement categories are General, Quests, Exploration, Player vs. Player, Dungeons & Raids, Professions, Reputation, World Events, Guilds, and Feats of Strength.

GENERAL

Some Achievements don't fall easily into other categories, so General is a catchall category. There are many extra tabards available from these Achievements, but many players focus more on the companion pets and a bonus mount.

Collecting 50 and 75 companion pets unlock both an Achievement and award you with bonus Companions. At 50 pets, you get a skunk with an odd attraction to cats, while the 75-pet Achievement, Lil' Game Hunter, awards you a Little Fawn Salt Lick. To get started on your companion pet collection, visit all the major cities in your faction and seek out the pet vendors. Beyond that, you may need to get creative (such as using the neutral Auction House to obtain the companion pets from the other faction) to build your collection. If you're really serious about pets, visit the Blizzard store as they have a handful of companion pets available for purchase.

Mount collectors are also addressed in the General Achievements. Should you get 50 mounts, you are awarded a bonus mount! Mounts are trickier to obtain than companion pets since you must achieve certain reputation levels with various factions if you wish to purchase their mounts. There are special mounts that drop from certain bosses (such as the Bronze Drake in heroic Culling of Stratholme or Baron Rivendare's mount in Stratholme) and some that are specific to Professions.

QUESTS

Quest Achievements involve completing a specific number of quests. Some Achievements here are tied solely to the overall number of quests you have completed, while others narrow their focus to how many quests you have completed in a certain zone, or on a certain continent.

There are two Achievements that award extras in the Quest category. When you complete enough quests, you earn the title "The Seeker." When you earn the Loremaster Achievement, you get the title, "Loremaster" and a bonus tabard.

EXPLORATION

Almost every Exploration Achievement is tied to uncovering hidden nooks and disovering the out of the way places found in every zone. When you're still leveling up your characters and visiting new zones, it's a good idea to keep searching until you get the Achievements for exploring it since you're earning experience points the whole time! The other type of Exploration Achievement is tied to finding and killing one of the rare enemies which spawn in Outland or Northrend.

Exploring the known world provides you with the title "Explorer" while Brann Bronzebeard awards the characters who explore all of Northrend with a special tabard.

PLAYER VS. PLAYER

Player vs. Player Achievements are almost all tied to battlegrounds and arenas. Many of these Achievements call for meeting incredibly specific conditions in a single battleground, or for long-term accomplishments such as being on the winning side in a battleground 100 times!

Most of the rewards for Player vs. Player Achievements are titles, but there are a handful of tabards and mounts as well. In particular, any character who participates in the slaying of the opposing faction's leaders eventually earns a Black War Bear.

DUNGEONS & RAIDS

Many Dungeons & Raids Achievements are given for defeating the bosses which appear in the world dungeons and raids of World of Warcraft. When you start running heroic versions of dungeons, there are additional Achievements tied to meeting specific conditions while facing the bosses in the dungeons. There are even more Achievements tied to the raid bosses, some requiring heroic attemtps while others can be done to the regular version of the boss encounter. The rewards for Achievements in Dungeons & Raids include titles and bonus mounts.

PROFESSIONS

Profession Achievements are more focused on the Secondary Professions (Archaeology, Cooking, First Aid, and Fishing) since each character is limited to only two Primary Professions. There are Achievements for reaching the maximum skill level in your Primary Professions, but that's it. Archaeology Achievements reward you many titles, and you can become a "Chef" with enough patience with Cooking. A Fishing-exclusive reward, a Titanium Seal of Dalaran, calls for a little luck and a great deal of patience, as does the "Salty" title.

REPUTATION

Improving your Reputation with the many factions found in World of Warcraft has become an increasingly important facet of the game to every type of player, and for many reasons. Many factions are the source of improved equipment, mounts, companion pets, and special enchantments for your armor. The Achievements tied to these improved Reputations are mainly new titles, but the Achievement tied to the Sunreavers (the faction who holds the Argent Tournament) unlocks additional daily quests.

WORLD EVENTS

World Events are special dates (typically marked on the in-game calendar) that include holidays and celebrations. There are Achievements tied to each date, and these Achievements take on many forms. While many are tied to completing quest lines, some holiday Achievements require trips to dungeons to face bosses that appear only during the holiday or visiting battlegrounds.

There are many titles to earn from World Event Achievements, but if you complete the Achievement "What A Long, Strange Trip It's Been" you earn a Violet Proto-Drake, which is an incredibly fast mount.

GUILD

Guild Achievements can be unlocked only while you are in a guild, and most of these achievements require groups made up mainly of characters from the same guild to work together in various ways. Many of these Achievements mirror those found in other categories (mainly Dungeons & Raids and Player vs. Player) so you should earn an individual Achievement at the same time as the Guild Achievement.

FEATS OF STRENGTH

Feats of Strength Achievements are generally awarded from one-time occurences, such as logging in during an Anniversary celebration, obtaining a Collector Edition pet, or being part of a leading Arena Team for a specific season. Other Feats of Strength are the result of changes to the game which remove the ability to earn some Achievements. Recent examples are the changes to the way characters obtain weapon skills. Before Cataclysm, there were Achievements for raising your Unarmed, or raising your skills in four different weapon types, to their maximum levels. However, the system changed in Cataclysm, and characters no longer level up weapon skills.

Quara the Explorer

OFFICIAL STRATEGY GUIDE

Contributors: Joe Branger, Michael Lummis, Jennifer Sims, Kenny Sims, Andrew Vassallo

© 2010 DK/BradyGAMES, a division of Penguin Group (USA) Inc. BradyGAMES® is a registered trademark of Penguin Group (USA) Inc. All rights reserved, including the right of reproduction in whole or in part in any form.

DK/BradyGames, a division of Penguin Group (USA) Inc.
800 East 96th Street, 3rd Floor
Indianapolis, IN 46240

©2010 Blizzard Entertainment, Inc. All rights reserved. Cataclysm is a trademark, and World of Warcraft and Blizzard Entertainment are trademarks or registered trademarks of Blizzard Entertainment, Inc., in the U.S. and/or other countries.

The ratings icon is a registered trademark of the Entertainment Software Association. All other trademarks and trade names are properties of their respective owners.

Please be advised that the ESRB ratings icons, "EC", "E", "E10+", "T", "M", "AO", and "RP" are trademarks owned by the Entertainment Software Association, and may only be used with their permission and authority. For information regarding whether a product has been rated by the ESRB, please visit www.esrb.org. For permission to use the ratings icons, please contact the ESA at esrblicenseinfo@theesa.com.

ISBN: 978-0-7440-1241-5

Printing Code: The rightmost double-digit number is the year of the book's printing; the rightmost single-digit number is the number of the book's printing. For example, 10-1 shows that the first printing of the book occurred in 2010.

13 12 11 10   4 3 2 1

Printed in the USA.

BradyGAMES Staff

Publisher
Mike Degler

Editor-In-Chief
H. Leigh Davis

Digital & Trade Category Publisher
Brian Saliba

Credits

Senior Development Editor
Ken Schmidt

Book Designers
Dan Caparo
Brent Gann

Production Designers
Wil Cruz
Bob Klunder

Blizzard Staff

Licensing
Matt Beecher
Gina Pippin
George Hsieh
Jon Bias

Cdev
Skye Chandler
Vanessa Lopez
Zachariah T. Owens
Glenn Rane
Doug A. Gregory
Kyle Williams
Jeremy Cranford

QA
Nathan LaMusga
Kelly Chun
Danny Flannagan
Michael Thompson

Platform Services
Paul Sardis
Clayton Dubin
Jason Lescalleet
Andrea Opimitti
Hansa Wahla
Pietro Gobbato
Jonathan Hankey
John Pombo
Ashok Viswanathan

Marketing
Kevin Carter
Marc Hutcheson
Erik Jensen
Carolin Wu
Dave Amason

World of Warcraft Team
Ray Cobo
Lee Sparks

Special thanks to the Blizzard European team for their hard work and commitment!

WORLD OF WARCRAFT
THE OFFICIAL MAGAZINE

EVERY ISSUE FEATURES:

- Interviews • Community
- Strategy • Lore and More!
- Deluxe, high quality, collectible
- MASSIVE! 148 pages— NO ADS!
- Specially commissioned artwork available nowhere else

SUBSCRIBE NOW!

www.worldofwarcraftthemagazine.com

© 2010 Blizzard Entertainment, Inc. All rights reserved. Warcraft, World of Warcraft and Blizzard Entertainment are trademarks and/or registered trademarks of Blizzard Entertainment, Inc. in the U.S. and/or other countries. All other trademarks referenced herein are the properties of their respective owners. © 2010 Future US, Inc. All Rights Reserved.

New York Times Bestseller

READ THE PREQUEL NOVEL TO

Thrall, wise shaman and the warchief of the Horde, has sensed a disturbing change…

The fate of Azeroth's great races is shrouded in a fog of uncertainty. The elemental spirits have become erratic and no longer heed the shaman's call. Troubling as this may be, it is only the first ominous warning sign of the Cataclysm to come….

Available wherever books are sold.

Also available as an eBook.

www.blizzard.com

GALLERY BOOKS
A Division of Simon & Schuster
A CBS COMPANY

www.simonandschuster.com

© 2010 Blizzard Entertainment, Inc. All Rights Reserved. Warcraft, World of Warcraft and Blizzard Entertainment are trademarks and/or registered trademarks of Blizzard Entertainment, Inc., in the U.S. And/or other countries. All other trademarks referenced herein are the properties of their respective owners.